Handbook of Behavioral Assessment *edited by Anthony R. Ciminero, Karen S. Calhoun, and Henry E. Adams*

Counseling and Psychotherapy: A Behavioral Approach *by E. Lakin Phillips*

Dimensions of Personality *edited by Harvey London and John E. Exner, Jr.*

The Mental Health Industry: A Cultural Phenomenon *by Peter A. Magaro, Robert Gripp, David McDowell, and Ivan W. Miller III*

Nonverbal Communication: The State of the Art *by Robert G. Harper, Arthur N. Wiens, and Joseph D. Matarazzo*

Alcoholism and Treatment *by David J. Armor, J. Michael Polich, and Harriet B. Stambul*

A Biodevelopmental Approach to Clinical Child Psychology: Cognitive Controls and Cognitive Control Theory *by Sebastiano Santostefano*

Handbook of Infant Development *edited by Joy D. Osofsky*

Understanding the Rape Victim: A Synthesis of Research Findings *by Sedelle Katz and Mary Ann Mazur*

Childhood Pathology and Later Adjustment: The Question of Prediction *by Loretta K. Cass and Carolyn B. Thomas*

Intelligent Testing with the WISC-R *by Alan S. Kaufman*

Adaptation in Schizophrenia: The Theory of Segmental Set *by David Shakow*

Psychotherapy: An Eclectic Approach *by Sol L. Garfield*

Handbook of Minimal Brain Dysfunctions *edited by Herbert E. Rie and Ellen D. Rie*

Handbook of Behavioral Interventions: A Clinical Guide *edited by Alan Goldstein and Edna B. Foa*

Art Psychotherapy *by Harriet Wadeson*

Handbook of Adolescent Psychology *edited by Joseph Adelson*

Psychotherapy Supervision: Theory, Research and Practice *edited by Allen K. Hess*

Psychology and Psychiatry in Courts and Corrections: Controversy and Change *by Ellsworth A. Fersch, Jr.*

Restricted Environmental Stimulation: Research and Clinical Applications *by Peter Suedfeld*

Personal Construct Psychology: Psychotherapy and Personality *edited by Alvin W. Landfield and Larry M. Leitner*

Mothers, Grandmothers, and Daughters: Personality and Child Care in Three-Generation Families *by Bertram J. Cohler and Henry U. Grunebaum*

Further Explorations in Personality *edited by A.I. Rabin, Joel Aronoff, Andrew M. Barclay, and Robert A. Zucker*

Hypnosis and Relaxation: Modern Verification of an Old Equation *by William E. Edmonston, Jr.*

Handbook of Clinical Behavior Therapy *edited by Samuel M. Turner, Karen S. Calhoun, and Henry E. Adams*

Handbook of Clinical Neuropsychology *edited by Susan B. Filskov and Thomas J. Boll*

The Course of Alcoholism: Four Years After Treatment *by J. Michael Polich, David J. Armor, and Harriet B. Braiker*

Handbook of Innovative Psychotherapies *edited by Raymond J. Corsini*

The Role of the Father in Child Development (Second Edition) *edited by Michael E. Lamb*

Behavioral Medicine: Clinical Applications *by Susan S. Pinkerton, Howard Hughes, and W.W. Wenrich*

Handbook for the Practice of Pediatric Psychology *edited by June M. Tuma*

Change Through Interaction: Social Psychological Processes of Counseling and Psychotherapy *by Stanley R. Strong and Charles D. Claiborn*

Drugs and Behavior (Second Edition) *by Fred Leavitt*

(*continued on back*)

Psychological Perspectives on Childhood Exceptionality

A HANDBOOK

Edited by

Robert T. Brown
University of North Carolina-Wilmington

Cecil R. Reynolds
Texas A&M University

A WILEY–INTERSCIENCE PUBLICATION

JOHN WILEY & SONS

New York • Chichester • Brisbane • Toronto • Singapore

Library of Congress Cataloging-in-Publication Data:
Main entry under title:

Psychological perspectives on childhood exceptionality.

  (Wiley series on personality processes)
  "A Wiley-Interscience publication."
  Includes indexes.
  1. Exceptional children—Psychology. I. Brown,
Robert T. II. Reynolds, Cecil R., 1952–
III. Series. [DNLM: 1. Child, Exceptional. 2. Handi-
capped. WS 105.5.H2 P9739]
BF723.E9P78 1986   155.4'5   85-17967
ISBN 0-471-08589-8

Printed in the United States of America

10 9 8 7 6 5 4 3 2 1

Contributors

Robert T. Brown, Ph.D.
Professor
Department of Psychology
University of North Carolina-
    Wilmington
Wilmington, North Carolina

Craig Edelbrock, Ph.D.
Associate Professor and Research
    Director
Department of Psychiatry
University of Massachusetts
    Medical School
Worcester, Massachusetts

Stephen N. Elliott, Ph.D.
Associate Professor
Department of Psychology
Louisiana State University
Baton Rouge, Louisiana

Charles J. Golden, Ph.D.
Professor of Medical Psychology
Department of Psychiatry
The University of Nebraska Medical
    Center
Omaha, Nebraska

Terry B. Gutkin, Ph.D.
Associate Professor
Department of Educational
    Psychology and Measurement
University of Nebraska-Lincoln
Lincoln, Nebraska

Patricia L. Hartlage, M.D.
Professor of Pediatrics
    and Neurology
Medical College of Georgia
Augusta, Georgia

Lawrence C. Hartlage, Ph.D.
Professor of Neurology
    and Pediatrics
Medical College of Georgia
Augusta, Georgia

George W. Hynd, Ed.D.
Research Professor and Chair
School Psychology Program
Department of Educational
    Psychology
University of Georgia
Athens, Georgia

Susan M. Jay, Ph.D.
Director of Research and Education
Psychosocial Program,
    Children's Hospital
    and
Assistant Professor of Pediatrics
University of Southern California
    School of Medicine
Los Angeles, California

Paul A. McDermott, Ph.D.
Director of Psychological
    Measurement

The Psychological Corporation
San Antonio, Texas
and
Professor
Graduate School of Education
University of Pennsylvania
Philadelphia, Pennsylvania

Barclay Martin, Ph.D.
Professor
Department of Psychology
University of North Carolina
Chapel Hill, North Carolina

T. Ernest Newland, Ph.D.
Professor Emeritus
Department of Educational
    Psychology
University of Illinois-Urbana
Urbana, Illinois

John E. Obrzut, Ph.D.
Professor
Department of Educational
    Psychology
University of Arizona
Tucson, Arizona

Daniel J. Reschly, Ph.D.
Professor and Director
School Psychology Program
Department of Psychology
Iowa State University
Ames, Iowa

Cecil R. Reynolds, Ph.D.
Professor and Director of Doctoral
    Training in School Psychology
Department of Educational
    Psychology
Texas A&M University
College Station, TX

Donald K. Routh, Ph.D.
Professor
Department of Psychology

University of Miami
Coral Gables, Florida

Linda J. Stevens
Doctoral Candidate
Department of Educational
    Psychology
University of Minnesota
Minneapolis, Minnesota

Jack Tureen, Ph.D.
Professor of Speech Pathology
Hofstra University
Hempstead, New York

Phyllis Tureen, Ph.D.
Program Director of Speech
    Pathology and Audiology
Department of Communication Arts
    and Sciences
New York University
New York, New York

Diana Brown Waters, Ph.D.
Clinical Director
Family Life Center
Oklahoma City, Oklahoma

Bahr Weiss
Doctoral Candidate
Department of Psychology
University of North Carolina
Chapel Hill, North Carolina

John R. Weisz, Ph.D.
Associate Professor
Department of Psychology
University of North Carolina
Chapel Hill, North Carolina

George S. Welsh, Ph.D.
Professor Emeritus
Department of Psychology
University of North Carolina
Chapel Hill, North Carolina

Greta N. Wilkening, Psy.D.
Assistant Professor of Pediatrics
  and Neurology
The Children's Hospital
University of Colorado Health
  Sciences Center
Denver, Colorado

Diane J. Willis, Ph.D.
Professor of Medical Psychology
Department of Pediatrics
  and

Director of Psychological Services
Child Study Center
University of Oklahoma Health
  Sciences Center
Oklahoma City, Oklahoma

James E. Ysseldyke, Ph.D.
Professor
Department of Psychoeducational
  Studies
University of Minnesota
Minneapolis, Minnesota

Series Preface

This series of books is addressed to behavioral scientists interested in the nature of human personality. Its scope should prove pertinent to personality theorists and researchers as well as to clinicians concerned with applying an understanding of personality processes to the amelioration of emotional difficulties in living. To this end, the series provides a scholarly integration of theoretical formulations, empirical data, and practical recommendations.

Six major aspects of studying and learning about human personality can be designated; personality theory, personality structure and dynamics, personality development, personality assessment, personality change, and personality adjustment. In exploring these aspects of personality, the books in the series discuss a number of distinct but related subject areas: the nature and implications of various theories of personality; personality characteristics that account for consistencies and variations in human behavior; the emergence of personality processes in children and adolescents; the use of interviewing and testing procedures to evaluate individual differences in personality; efforts to modify personality styles through psychotherapy, counseling, behavior therapy, and other methods of influence; and patterns of abnormal personality functioning that impair individual competence.

IRVING B. WEINER

University of Denver
Denver, Colorado

Preface

Interest in exceptional children, from the most gifted at one extreme to the most handicapped at the other, is burgeoning among both professionals and the public. Interest by the public in educational opportunities is reflected in the passage of acts such as Public Law 94–142, The Education for All Handicapped Children Act, enacted in 1975. Interest among professionals is seen in the recent publication of numerous books and journals concerned with exceptional children. Many of the concerns about these children involve psychological perspectives. The movement of exceptional children out of institutions and segregated classrooms into mainstream participation reflects a significant shift away from perception of the handicapped as dangerous deviates who should be housed in institutions for their good and ours toward perception of them as, for the most part, people who share our needs and emotions although they are limited in some way. Concerns about preventing handicaps and fostering giftedness have important psychological aspects as do, of course, remediation programs. Issues that only a few years ago were of interest largely to psychologists have burst upon the public scene. Recent court cases over possible bias in standardized intelligence tests used for assignment of minority group children to special education classes, the many suits over denial of services, and litigation concerning criteria for special education placement are all clear examples.

Questions about diagnosis and classification, family interactions, etiology, and intervention all require psychological information for a satisfactory answer. In fact, much research and theorizing about exceptional children has been by educational, differential, neuro-, and developmental psychologists. Additionally, these issues call for information from other disciplines. Advances in medical and genetic diagnosis have led to significant shifts in our basic conceptualization of some conditions, particularly disorders such as schizophrenia and infantile autism. Interdisciplinary approaches are necessary for a satisfactory understanding of many aspects of exceptionality.

Other considerations are also influencing our views of exceptional children. Traditionally, the study of exceptional children has been strongly bound to individual categories, such as mental retardation, learning disabilities, and sensory impairments. But issues such as assessment, etiology, family interactions, and remediation cut across these boundaries, making the division into categories sometimes inappropriate. The noncategorical approach for educationally handicapped children, particularly mildly handicapped ones, is becoming increasingly accepted. On the other hand, there are important differences among individuals with different conditions, and the traditional categories still have value.

This book presents current psychological perspectives on exceptional children. It is an attempt not only to organize and to summarize current knowledge but to help direct future research, theory, and practice. The organization of the book is designed to meet both cross- and within-category interests. Part One, Orientations Toward Psychological Aspects of Exceptionality, contains chapters on background and current concerns and on reading and understanding research on exceptionality. Part Two, Perspectives on General Issues Regarding Exceptional Children, contains chapters on topics that are cross-categorical in interest, and Part Three, Perspectives on Specific Areas of Exceptionality: Characteristics, Etiologies, and Treatments, consists of detailed, state-of-the-art discussions of individual categories of exceptional children. Most chapters contain a personal perspective in which the chapter authors express their views on some aspect of the topic. Authors are researchers and/or practitioners who have integrated material from their own disciplines with that from related areas to provide integrated coverage of their topics. Thus environmental, biological, and medical aspects of exceptionality are viewed from a psychological perspective. Further, the authors' strong empirical orientations have resulted in chapters where theoretical and conceptual issues are clearly tied to data.

This book is intended to serve two related purposes: (1) as a short handbook for professional researchers, educators, and practitioners in psychology, education, and related disciplines, and (2) as a sound textbook for graduate and advanced undergraduate courses in Psychology of Exceptional Children, Developmental Disabilities, and Childhood Psychopathology. At this time, most books that discuss exceptional children have a clear educational emphasis. Although a large number of books of different levels deal with childhood psychopathology, there is a surprising dearth of psychological material dealing with the broad range of exceptionalities from the gifted to the sensorily and motorically handicapped. Interest in children is increasingly spreading across and breaking down traditional disciplinary boundaries such as those between "childhood psychopathology" and "childhood exceptionality." We hope this book will further increase interest in and concern about all exceptional children. Its broad and current coverage and consistent psychological orientation should enable it to be used as both a handbook and a textbook.

We wish specifically to acknowledge the contributions of several people. First we thank the authors for their efforts, cooperation, and patience. Herb Reich and his associates at Wiley-Interscience have been notably supportive as they helped nurture this book to fruition through a variety of problems and delays, none of which was their responsibility. Of those associates, Diana Cisek was consistently of great help in the production of this book. Elaine Fletcher and Mary Leon Peery produced the excellent indexes. The secretaries in the Psychology Department at UNC-Wilmington went beyond reasonable expectations in helping prepare materials. Of those, we especially want to acknowledge Martha Jo Clemmons, Eleanor Martin, whose death saddened us greatly, and Lydia Woodward. Finally, we thank our families for their support and encouragement.

ROBERT T. BROWN
CECIL R. REYNOLDS

Wilmington, North Carolina
College Station, Texas
January 1986

Contents

PART THREE   PERSPECTIVES ON SPECIFIC AREAS
OF EXCEPTIONALITY: CHARACTERISTICS,
ETIOLOGIES, AND TREATMENTS

PSYCHOLOGICAL PERSPECTIVES
ON CHILDHOOD EXCEPTIONALITY

PART ONE

Orientations Toward Psychological Aspects of Exceptionality

CHAPTER 1

Exceptionality:
Historical Antecedents
and Present Positions

GEORGE W. HYND AND JOHN E. OBRZUT

The population of the United States is now well in excess of 220 million and of that number approximately 20 million make up at one level or another our population of exceptional children. Comprised of the gifted, mentally retarded, hard of hearing, deaf, speech impaired, visually impaired, emotionally disturbed, orthopedically handicapped, health handicapped, multihandicapped, and learning disabled, these children remain a significant minority in our school population (Kirk, 1973). This minority requires services that are inordinate in relation to their percentage of the school population. In fact, it is largely to this population of pupils that school psychologists, audiologists, speech therapists, counselors, and, of course, special education teachers owe their professions.

It was not always the case that these special children were afforded the educational opportunities available to them today. As recently as 1971 volumes in school law had no sections even mentioning this population, although all states had enacted laws directly addressing the needs of these children (Bolick, 1974). Clearly much has happened since then, and this book represents well the enormously complex range of topics and issues prevalent within the field of childhood exceptionality.

In the United States more than anywhere else in the world education stands out as being reflective of contemporary society's values. Each era in our brief history has been reflected in educational development (Sarason & Doris, 1979). For example, after World War I many were concerned about the health of our high school graduates. As a result, healthful living was stressed in the schools and physical education courses proliferated (Stone & Schneider, 1965). Fol-

This chapter was prepared while the senior author was a Post Doctoral Fellow in Neuropsychology at the GRECC, VA Medical Center, Minneapolis, Minnesota. Appreciation is expressed to Marlys Anderson and Karen Malikowski for their assistance in typing the manuscript.

lowing the launching of Sputnick by the Russians in 1957, the National Defense Education Act (1958) was passed; its avowed purpose was the promotion of scientific inquiry among our high school and college students.

The purpose of education in the United States has been under continuous screening. One of the earlier and best known formulations of a revised purpose of education in the United States was published in 1918 by the Commission on the Reorganization of Secondary Education. The Seven Cardinal Objectives outlined included health, command of fundamental processes, worthy home membership, vocational competence, effective citizenship, worthy use of leisure time, and ethical character (Stone & Schneider, 1965). These objectives, as will be seen in following sections, led eventually to an increased concern and sensitivity to the needs of the individual. Coupled with the increased sensitivity, classes for special children began to proliferate and the right for free and appropriate public education was upheld in the courts. Consequently, today we have perhaps the best, most comprehensive, and undoubtedly the most controversal system of education for exceptional children.

As an introduction to the contents of this book, this chapter outlines a basic framework for comprehending the many complex issues in the psychology and education of exceptional children. To accomplish this objective, the historical antecedents to our present dilemma are presented with a focus on the social and legislative developments as well as court decisions which have shaped our path. Then the present positions, which may well mark the "winter" of childhood exceptionality, are briefly addressed as they relate to some important emerging directions.

First, however, the reader should realize that at the basis of the entire field of exceptionality lie two fundamental assumptions: first, individual differences exist and second, they can be reliably and accurately assessed. For this reason, the initial part of this chapter focuses on historical developments related to the appraisal of individual differences. The historical perspective which follows should not be perceived by the readers as a parade of individual contributions but as a line of critical psychological inquiry encouraged and nurtured by researchers pursuing a common goal.

APPRAISAL OF INDIVIDUAL DIFFERENCES: EARLY DEVELOPMENTS

While we may take it for granted that testing or some form of individual assessment is an integral part of our lives, it is very likely that our great-grandparents never once took a standardized examination. Certainly the use of tests to measure individual differences and capabilities is not new. In fact, there exists good evidence that the Chinese administered a standardized civil service examination to potential employees as early as 2200 *B.C.* (DuBois, 1970).

The proliferation of standardized examinations in the United States in the twentieth century is nothing short of phenomenal. It has been estimated that in 1929 approximately 5 million tests were administered annually (Houts, 1975) but by 1969 that figure had increased to approximately 250 million—a quarter billion tests (Brim, Glass, Neulinger, Firestone, & Lerner, 1969)! To what purpose are we, as psychologists and educators, putting the information gained from these administrations?

Prior to answering this question it may be beneficial to understand that there are some inherent assumptions regarding the use of tests. Long a critic of standardized examinations, Wolfensburger (1965) outlined what he saw as essential assumptions regarding the use of clinical tests. These include: (1) diagnosis is better than no diagnosis; (2) early diagnosis is better than late diagnosis; (3) diagnosis is essential to successful treatment or case management; (4) differential diagnosis is important for differential treatment; (5) extensive evaluation is better than limited evaluation; and (6) team diagnosis is better than individual diagnosis. With these assumptions well in mind, it may now be appropriate to respond to the question posed.

Within the public schools, we are interested in fostering individual growth. Within the general area of special education, we are interested in identifying areas of exceptionality so that individual growth can be achieved within the limitations of the exceptionality. Wolfensburger's (1965) assumptions seem most appropriate within this framework. Consequently, it might be said that in education we appraise individual differences for the following reasons:

To group children for classroom instruction

To evaluate their achievement

To identify those in need of remediation

To identify those in need of other special services

To evaluate the effectiveness of teaching

To certify students accomplishments

To conduct educational and psychological research

The comparatively recent focus on the needs of the exceptional child has contributed greatly to the increase in the efforts to assess individual differences so that these purposes could be served with this population. Undoubtedly the controversy over how best to achieve the educational needs of these children will continue. If one is to understand the arguments and issues current today, some understanding of the historical events that have led us to our current situation is needed.

Historical Antecedents

It is of interest to note that the development of our modern tests is due in large part to certain international events, which, over several centuries, shaped our perception of what we should examine. As Linden and Linden (1968) note, contributors to the testing movement came from Spain, Germany, England, and France as well as America.

Encouraged by the work of Fitzherbort (1470–1538), who proposed that an idiot could be tested using such items as counting 20 pence, telling his size, identifying his parents, and so on, Juan Huarte (1530–1589), in Spain, published what developed into a best seller of sorts on testing. In *The tryal of wits, discovering the great differences of wits among men and what sorts of learning suits best with each genius*, Huarte set forth his views on intelligence. He proposed that intelligence was revealed in docility in learning from a master, understanding and independence in judgment, and inspiration without extravagence. His book was widely circulated and helped shape the thoughts of those interested individual differences.

German investigators were interested not so much in intelligence as in perception. Bessel (1784–1846), an astronomer at Königsberg, was fascinated with the differences he observed in the reports of two astronomers who tracked the path of a star. Ernst Weber (1795–1878) followed upon this "personal equation" and studied what are now termed "just noticeable differences" (JND) in perception. Wilhelm Wundt (1832–1920), often referred to as the Father of Psychology, established the first course in psychology at the University of Heidelberg and later founded the first psychological laboratory to study similarities in perception at the University of Leipzig. It is important to note that the significance of the German investigators was that they applied the scientific method to the appraisal of the individual. Their objective measurements greatly influenced the English, who, following Darwin's lead, were very interested in heredity (Boring, 1950; Linden & Linden, 1968).

Galton (1822–1911), the founder of Individual Psychology, established the first Anthropometric Laboratory at the South Kensington Museum in London in 1884. He suggested:

> There is a continuity of natural ability reaching from one knows not what height, and descending to one can hardly say what depth. I propose . . . to range men according to their natural abilities, putting them into classes represented by equal degrees of merit, and to show the relative number of individuals included in the several classes . . . the method I shall employ for discovering all this is an application of the very curious theoretical law of "deviation from an average." (Galton, 1892)

Although Galton invested a great deal of time in examining differences, the results of his investigations were not really important as his tests were too brief, samples too small, and his subjects were not representative of the population at large (Linden & Linden, 1968). What was important, however, was that he had developed the statistical means to establish relationships between variables. Furthermore, Galton represents the beginning of an era in terms of scientific inquiry. His research methods, influenced in great part by the Germans, became the hallmark for further research.

Such was the cumulative influences of the work of Wundt and Galton. While the American psychological community pursued the study of individual differences through the work of Cattell at Columbia University, it was the French who would ultimately provide us with the model upon which later assessment instruments were developed. The work of Alfred Binet deserves special consideration.

Alfred Binet—The French Contribution

It is with the French that concern over services to exceptional individuals was manifested, which in turn led to attempts to appraise formally individual mental differences.

Today we are aware of those factors that contribute to mental deficiency and they can generally be differentiated as those of genetic origin (e.g., neurofibromatosis, phenylketonuria, Down's syndrome, cri du chat syndrome) or of environmental causation (e.g., rubella, congenital syphilis, head injury, head encephalopathy). These factors have been delineated elsewhere and need not be reviewed here (Berg, 1974; Kirman, 1974). However, it is important to realize that at one point in time mental retardation was not differentiated from mental illness. A French physician, Jean Esquirol (1772–1840), was one of the first to consider the two as different ailments. In fact, Esquirol was convinced that the two could be clinically differentiated on the basis of skull size! Unfortunately, Esquirol concluded (based on the work of Jean Itard, a student of his, who worked with the "Wild Boy of Aveyron") that mentally retarded individuals could not be trained. Disagreeing with Esquirol, Edouard Séguin (1812–1880) became an ardent protagonist of teaching the retarded. He proposed that the success of any educator could be directly measured by or correlated with the progress in learning among the retarded. At the age of 25 Séguin developed his first school for the retarded at the Hospice des Incurables in Paris. Because of political difficulties Séguin took his "physiological method" of teaching to the United States and established a school for the retarded in Vineland, New Jersey (Nazzaro, 1977). Esquirol, Itard, and Séguin all recognized the need for some objective measure of ability to accurately identify the retarded. It was to this need that Alfred Binet devoted his expertise.

Binet (1857–1911) received his degree in law from the Lycée Saint-Louis in 1878 and over a period of time became enamored with research in the sciences. This interest eventually resulted in the receipt of a doctorate from the Sorbonne where his work on the nervous system of insects was highly regarded. This interest in research led to a study of intelligence, palmistry, and phrenology. Like Galton, Binet believed that study of individual differences should focus on deviations from a population mean. Very concerned with the identification of the retarded pupil, the Minister of Public Instruction appointed a commission to recommend identification procedures. Along with Theophile Simon (1873–1961), Binet was invited to submit recommendations. The result of Binet and Simon's work was the *Measuring Scale of Intelligence,* which was composed of 30 items arranged in order of difficulty. The score obtained was simply the number of items passed. In 1908 the test was expanded to include 59 items grouped at age levels from 3 to 13. The resulting score was the percentage of items passed at each age level and the administration was relatively simple—starting at an age level where all items were passed and continuing upward until all items at a given age level were failed (Boring, 1950; Linden & Linden, 1968; Sattler, 1974).

As with most significant contributions, controversy immediately followed Binet and Simon's efforts. It is critical to note that the two issues which confronted Binet are *still* areas of considerably varied opinion as will be seen in later contributions in this book. Since these issues are of such importance they will be briefly addressed.

The first issue confronting Binet was that regarding the constancy of mental ability. While Esquirol and Itard's work suggested that beyond a certain young age ability was immutable, Séguin's efforts clearly demonstrated that the retarded could in fact be trained. The motivating factor behind the Minister of Public Instruction's directive was to identify such children and provide special classes. Spearman (1904) probably best represented the views of those who believed ability could not be altered when he wrote, "From this moment, there normally occurs no further change even into extreme old age. The function almost entirely controls the relative position of children at school, and is nine parts out of ten responsible for success in such simple acts as discrimination of pitch" (quoted by Clarke & Clarke, 1974). Disturbed by those perceptions, Binet eloquently responded to these notions:

> Some recent philosophers appear to have given their moral support to the deplorable verdict that the intelligence of the individual is a fixed quantity, a quantity which cannot be augmented. We must protest and act against this brutal pessimism . . . A child's mind is like a field for which an expert farmer has advised a change in the method of cultivating, with the result that in place of desert land we now have a harvest. It is in this particular sense, the only one that is significant, that we say that the intelligence of children may be increased . . . namely the capacity to learn, to improve with instruction. (Quoted by Skeels & Dye, 1939)

Paradoxically, many of the critics of the modern assessment practices (e.g., Gross, 1962; Hoffman, 1961; Holtzman, 1971; Laosa, 1973; Newland, 1973; Wallace & Larsen, 1978) would probably agree strongly with Binet's statement. Indeed it is most significant that one of the most controversial issues in education today addresses this notion—that IQ is fixed and not amenable to compensatory education (Hunt, 1961; Jensen, 1969). It is indeed unfortunate that Binet died relatively young, for he might have dramatically altered the assessment practices he helped to develop.

The second important controversy Binet found himself mired in dealt with test results of children examined with the Binet scales. Decroly in Belgium had examined a number of children who, although assumed to be of normal ability, were actually found to be performing substantially above their expected levels of ability. The implications to Decroly and Binet were as obvious as they were profound. Did the results imply that the children in Belgium were different or that the Binet scale was invalid as an age scale? In examining the results, Binet found that the pupils who took the test "belong to a social class in easy circumstance; they have parents who are particularly gifted and understand education in the broad sense."

The notion of cultural bias disturbed Binet but he found that these Belgian children did especially well on verbal tasks. Addressing this he concluded:

> Does our scale fail to do justice to a child of uncommon intelligence without culture or with scholastic culture much inferior to his intelligence? We do not think so. Such a child will show his superiority in the repetition of figures, in the repetition of sentences, paper cutting, the arrangement of weights, the interpretation of pictures, etc. And it is an especially interesting feature of these tests that they permit us, when necessary, to free a beautiful native intelligence from the trammels of the school. (1916)

Clearly Binet understood the many complex issues related to the appraisal of individual differences and attempted to address them. While Binet's scale has been modified many times since its conceptualization, the test itself is not as important as the fact that his scales demonstrated conclusively that individual differences existed and mental measurements were indeed possible (Sattler, 1974). It is with this foundation that the psychological inquiry of childhood exceptionality could proceed.

The academic freedom allowed Itard, Galton, Wundt, Binet, and others, fostered the rapid exchange of ideas, prejudices, and innovative approaches. However, such developments do not occur in a vacuum as history is continuous and interactive. To comprehend fully present positions and emerging trends the reader should have an appreciation of the cultural and social developments which have shaped the field of childhood exceptionality.

CULTURAL, SOCIAL, AND HISTORICAL INTERACTIONS

Before the beginning of the twentieth century the general state of affairs for the handicapped was not good. Just prior to Lincoln's election as President in 1860, it was estimated that 60% of the inmates of poor houses were deaf, blind, insane, or idiots (Nazzaro, 1977). Following the efforts of reformers like Dorothea Dix (1802–1887) some progress was made in providing services to the nation's handicapped. In a series of landmark legislation, The U.S. Congress passed Public laws 33-4, 34-46, and 45-186, which established a government hospital for the insane and an institution for the education of the deaf, mute, and blind, and provided funds for the production of braille material respectively.

The late 1800s to early 1900s was a period of phenomenal growth in the United States, encouraged and nurtured through countless inventions, imaginative leadership, and increased social awareness of the plight of the less fortunate. By the time Binet and Simon submitted their final version of the *Measuring Scale* to the Minister of Education, a number of significant private developments had occurred in the United States with regard to the handicapped. The most notable included the founding of a school for the deaf by Amos Kendall and Edward Gallaudet, the development of a program for the gifted in St. Louis, the invention of the audiophone bone conduction amplifier by Rhodes, international recognition and graduation from Radcliffe for Helen Keller and the establishment by Lightner Witmer of the first psychological clinic at the University of Pennsylvania. Encouraged by the rapid developments in both the public and private sector, state governments took the lead in educating handicapped children. By the year 1899, 14 state institutions for the mentally retarded existed and a number of states required health and medical examinations which resulted in the early identification of many handicapped children and adults (Nazzaro, 1977; Sarason & Doris, 1979).

World War I and Increased Concern

Between 1909 and the beginning of World War I the United States grappled with issues related to its place in the world community. The accomplishments of individuals like Peary and Amundsen, the reality of transoceanic travel, the potential for air travel, continued inflow of immigrants, and the ever increasing involvement in international events led conclusively to U.S. involvement in the war. With the advent of war it was recognized that thousands of recruits had to be assessed. Arthur Otis (1886–1964) and a committee of experts in measurement developed the *Group Examination A* and later the *Group Examination B* to test these draftees. In reacting to the fact that many of these draftees were so impoverished intellectually (the mean mental age of the American soldier was reported to be 13 years, 5 months), H. L. Mencken suggested "A new breed of man was being spawned in the western hemisphere—'Boobus Americanus'"(quoted by Reisman, 1966).

Increased concern over the education of normal as well as handicapped children developed and, as a result, special interest groups and professional associations were organized. Between 1919 and 1939 the American Society for the Hard of Hearing, the National Society for Crippled Children, the American Foundation for the Blind, and the International Council for the Education of Exceptional Children were founded. Also, within this period of time, standards for training teachers of the handicapped were developed and enacted.

Although the rights of the handicapped were still largely ignored (in 1929, 23 states legally sterilized the retarded and it was estimated that 7,000 sterilizations occurred), some progress in this direction was accomplished. For instance, the first attempt at providing a handicapped child with a least restrictive environment was made at Battle Creek, Michigan's private Kellogg School in 1930. Generally, however, little progress occurred until change was mandated through legislation and litigation.

Affirmation of Individual Rights

Probably no court case has ever had the impact of the Brown decision in 1954. The United States Supreme Court ruled that segregation in the public schools was a violation of the 14th Amendment. With the courts upholding the rights of racial and ethnic minorities it seemed only reasonable that a similar line of attack would prove to be fruitful in ensuring the rights of handicapped persons. The recognition of this fact and an increased commitment to social justice led eventually to the passage of a series of laws (e.g., amendments to NDEA of 1958; ESEA, Title I) which provided funding for the handicapped based on the premise that they had a right to free and appropriate educational opportunity.

It was not until the 93rd Congress, however, that PL 93-380 was enacted, guaranteeing due process in placement of the handicapped, nondiscriminatory testing, and confidentiality of records. PL 94-142, the Education for All Handicapped Children Act, required that all handicapped children be identified and be provided free and appropriate public education. The enactment of these two laws in addition to a number of landmark court cases (e.g., *Diana v. The State Board of Education in California; Pennsylvania Association for Retarded Citizens v. The Commonwealth of Pennsylvania; Larry P. v. Riles*) made profound changes in our perceptions regarding what constitutes relevant and appropriate educational and psychological services for exceptional children. Furthermore, attempts at meeting the intent of various laws has often proved to be inadequate or at best inappropriate.

For instance, contemporary critics of appraisal procedures employed in the school setting often suggest that rather than liberating children's abilities through their identification and treatment with testing procedures, we are contributing to society's ills through the use of tests (Laosa, 1973, 1977; Laosa & Oakland, 1974; Lesser, Fiffer, & Clark, 1965; Mercer, 1973; Newland, 1973; Wallace & Larsen, 1978; Wolfensburger, 1965). A variety of alternatives to standardized assessment procedures have been proposed, including Prescriptive Teaching (Peter, 1965); Ability and Process Training (Ysseldyke & Salvia, 1974); Task Analysis (D. Johnson, 1967); and, of course, Pluralistic Assessment Procedures (Mercer & Ysseldyke, 1977). The point to be made is that as educational policy and public concern continue to change with regard to the exceptional child, conflict is likely to increase rather than decrease. Certainly the increased propensity to confront relevant issues in the courts documents this fact (Abeson & Bolick, 1974; Knitzer, 1976; Sarason & Doris, 1979; Zedler, 1953). Those trends and practices which are apparent in the education of exceptional children today reflect this rapidly changing environment of public policy, and the potential fragmentation of public education by diverse forces is a very real concern. As will be seen in the following section the issues and relevant emerging trends are more complex and fraught with potential controversy than at any time in the brief written history of the exceptional child.

EMERGING DIRECTIONS

Trends in exceptionality may be more difficult to discern today than ever before. So many political, social, economic, and psychological factors need to be considered in the treatment of the exceptional child that clearly identifiable trends may be masked. However, there are those areas of concentration which can be discussed where the interaction of political, social, and psychological efforts have become manifest.

It has been recognized that over 50% of all handicapped children come from impoverished environments. Thus it seems reasonable that the desired psychological perspective is to eliminate conditions that lead to such an effect. Conditions such as urban decay, poverty, insensitive public education, and prejudice are thought of as root causes for much of special education (Dunn, 1973). It seems obvious that an ecological approach is needed to deal adequately with exceptional populations. In essence, a coordinated effort among special programs and social services working to improve the home, school, and community environment of children is sorely needed.

It is believed that through the passage of PL 94–142 many noticeable changes are taking place in the field of childhood exceptionality. One such change is related to the diagnostic and placement processes. The prime responsibility for educational/psychological diagnosis, placement, and treatment is being accomplished by educators and not members of other professions or by the multidisciplinary team as in the past. For example, there is a growing involvement by parents of exceptional children where decisions regarding placement are concerned. The diagnostic process is particularly geared toward determining the level at which the child is functioning. Interventions by perspective-clinical teachers are considered temporary until effective ones are found. This is made possible through the process of continuous evaluation. This assumes a positive match between instructional program, pupil learning style, and teacher teaching style.

Another change taking place in the field relates to the categorization of exceptional children. Conventional labels that served to stigmatize and stereo type children are being replaced by designations of different types of special educational treatments such as those in the visual, auditory, language, cognitive, and affective domains. Since wide individual differences exist among children in each area of exceptionality, the learning requirements of exceptional pupils should determine the organization and administration of special education services (Reynolds, 1971).

As the twenty-first century approaches, segregated special education is likely to be reduced even more than is currently in vogue. It is apparent that exceptonal children need individualized instruction to develop their personal academic skills and knowledge but need group instruction with their own agemates to develop social effectiveness (Reynolds, 1971).

Other emerging directions directly related to implementation of PL 94–142 are found in the areas of training and research. Major changes in teacher-preparation programs have begun by training special educators to act as consultants, team teachers, diagnostic-prescription specialists, and tutors for complex cases to regular educators (Dunn, 1973). Since the number of children with multiple disabilities continues to increase, more and more special educators will be required to work in integrated situations.

To date the most successful techniques for effectively teaching children formerly considered uneducable and/or untrainable have been derived from behavioral research (e.g., see Reynolds, 1969). Legislation now requires that classroom practices be based on sound experimentation. It is strongly suggested that research emphasis should be placed on developing and evaluating specialized instructional approaches. However, the ultimate goal is to develop a balance between the psychological and educational knowledge states of the child. In this regard the behavioral-instructional objective approach to education has been far more successful than most other movements in the field.

Finally, the trend toward early education will remain a top priority but will likely be paralleled by pre- and post-high school programs. However, not all of these programs will be designed for the handicapped student. Priorities will also be given to those exceptional students who are creative, innovative, and more intellectually able.

As the field of exceptionality progresses through the decade of the 1980s, major changes will be made in such areas as nondiscriminatory assessment, labeling techniques, and individualized instruction. In addition, research will attempt to identify the relation between child abuse and neglect and educational problems. A better understanding of primary and secondary effects of retardation will be elucidated. In effect, much discussion will ensue surrounding the organic versus the functional bases of exceptionality. These are all considered critical issues that must be addressed in the coming years if advances are to be forthcoming in dealing with exceptional behavior.

Nondiscriminatory Intervention

Nondiscriminatory assessment is explicitly required by PL 94–142 with the intent that tests measure in a meaningful manner and not prejudice the placement decisions of individuals who use test results in program planning (Public Law 94–142, 1977). Some procedures have been advocated to eliminate discrimination in test bias. Alley and Foster (1978) suggested four common procedures used to negate discrimination: (1) translating traditional tests into the minority language, (2) norming existing tests on specific minority groups, (3) using an examiner of the same minority group as the children being tested, and (4) evaluating competencies which are underattained by minority children and directly teaching these competencies. However, it should be recognized that all of our procedures have serious flaws inherent in their rationale and/or use. As Ysseldyke (1978) points out, bias occurs in relation to such factors as parent's occupation (i.e., socio-economic level), physical attractiveness of children, and self-fulfilling prophecies.

Several factors have been outlined by Ysseldyke (1978) if progress toward nondiscriminatory assessment is to be made. First, differentiation of assessment devices and procedures must be obtained depending on the kinds of decisions one makes. For example, measures of intelligence are useful in making classification and placement decisions but provide little information for planning instructional programs for children. Second, norm-referenced interpretation of performance will be biased for those children whose background experiences and opportunities differ from those of the group on whom the test was standardized. Third, data for use in making decisions about children should be technically adequate, that is, instruments used should have adequate reliability and validity. Too often many of the tests used in educational settings have reliabilities far below .90 or have little or no data regarding validity in the technical manual. Fourth, naturally occurring pupil characteristics bias assessment and placement decisions. These include pupil characteristics such as race, sex, physical attractiveness, socio-economic status, and parental attitude. Some or all of these factors influence who is referred, the settings to which pupils are assigned, and the particular kinds of instructional programs that children receive. Fifth, bias following assessment is as prevalent as bias during assessment. The goal is to treat child behavior objectively rather than relying on the use of labels to describe the behavior of exceptional children.

It seems obvious then that adherence to some of the preceding recommendations should eliminate the disproportionately large number of children from minority groups in programs for exceptional children. Clearly educators should be familiar with and sensitive to the special needs of children from different cultures. Extra caution is needed in interpreting test data on children not represented in the norm group on which the test was standardized. When criterion-referenced tests are used, assessment should not be biased by conflicts between the criterion established and the culture of the child being tested.

Recent litigation and legislation directing psychologists to use measures which are free of cultural bias may provide the impetus for change to nondiscriminatory assessment in the schools (Oakland, 1977). This movement may force schools to view individual children and their needs more carefully as arbitrarily set standardized test scores will not be the final basis for deciding an educational plan. However, by indiscriminately generalizing from the *Diana* v. *State Board of Education* (1970) and *Larry P.* v. *Riles* (1979) court cases many school children may be ill-served. The fact is that given the severe drop in educable mentally retarded enrollments and that each placement may not be consonant with the severity of academic failure, one has to believe that there is a host of children without adequate help. Thus nondiscriminatory assessment should not consist of tests with heavy subcultural content which predict success in a subcultural educational program but are less valid than present broadly based tests for predicting success in the regular program (MacMillan & Meyers, 1980). The psychologist as well as the educator would do well to review basic issues related to test construction, validity, and reliability since debate in the area of nondiscriminatory assessment will undoubtedly become more sophisticated and complicated by judicial mandates. Certainly the judicial process has provided the impetus for two other emerging areas of research inquiry.

The Effects of Categorical Labeling

The issue of labeling has been one of the central questions of recent court actions and is far from being resolved (e.g., *Larry P.* v. *Riles,* 1979). The major focus of these court actons is whether the many psychological characteristics used in classifying exceptional pupils can be reliably and validly measured. It is clearly not enough to argue advantages and disadvantages of using labels to categorize exceptional children. The need is to show some evidence between the label provided and the attitudes and resultant actions of others primarily in the educational system. Some data has been generated along these lines.

An early study by Johnson (1950) found that retarded students were isolated and rejected (according to sociometric data in the regular classroom) even when they were not identified and labeled. More recently, Goodman, Gottlieb, and Harmon (1972) found similar results when retarded children were identified, labeled, and placed in a regular class under a mainstream program.

Following the early studies by Rosenthal and Jacobson (1968) regarding the effects of teacher expectancy on behavior, Smith and Greenberg (1975) found that teachers tended to accept a diagnosis of mental retardation in hypothetical cases if the child was from a low-income family. Also, Gillung and Rucker (1977) found that regular educators and some special education teachers had lower expectations for children who were labeled than for children with identical behaviors who were not labeled. However, critiques of Rosenthal and Jacobson's efforts have raised doubts about the generalizability of the expectancy phenomenon (e.g., Elashoff & Snow, 1971). Gottlieb (1974) studied the attitude of peers in a fourth grade toward children labeled retarded. He was convinced that the judgment of peers about a retarded child was based on their academic achievement and not on the label. Kirk (1974), in an experimental study of the impact of labeling on the rejection of the mentally ill, found that there is little evidence that labeling makes a significant difference in how people react to them.

It may be, as Smith and Neisworth (1975) have indicated, that the results of psychological tests, prior grades, and so on may serve as cues which influence the behaviors of teachers and evaluators toward the student. In turn, the teacher's behavior may alter the student's behavior so that it "drifts in the predicted or expected direction.'' The altered behavior of the student then confirms and reinforces the teacher's behavior. It is the result of this dynamic interaction that causes the expectancy effect.

Some would argue that current labels reflect a preoccupation with medical, psychiatric, legal, and sociological perspectives that are remotely related to educational decision making (Smith & Neisworth, 1975). These dispositional labels isolate children with assumed conditions that do not identify relevant and specific educational characteristics that make instructional intervention feasible. As Stuart (1970) suggested earlier, a behavioral or "phenotypic" approach focuses on identifying the problems of children, measuring them, and relating them to actual (rather than hypothetical) variables subject to manipulation for purposes of positive intervention. Classifying children with "genotypes" or dispositional labels diverts the attention of educators from implementing a direct intervention.

Controversy about labeling reached such proportions in the 1970s that a task force was established by the Secretary of Health, Education and Welfare to study its effects. Basically, the final report (Hobbs, 1975) recommended (1) improvements in the classification system, (2) some constraints on the use of psychological tests, (3) improvements in procedures for early identification of children at developmental risk, (4) some safeguards in the use of records, and (5) attention to due process of law in classifying and placing exceptional children.'' (pp. 232–233).

Based on this brief review a distinct trend within the field of exceptionality is emerging. It appears that traditional categorical schemes will be replaced with systems synonymous with the scientific purposes of classification. Systems that seek order, enhance communication, identify relationships, and promote research will be used. For example, a recent study by Pfeiffer (1980) has investigated the influence of diagnostic labeling on special education placement decisions. Two experimental groups of school personnel, including school psychologists, were administered different versions of the Rucher-Gable Educational Programming Scale: one version required selection of appropriate placement only, and the other version required diagnostic labeling and selection of appropriate educational placement. No differences between the two experimental groups were found in their selection of special education placements. Although the research did not answer the question of whether labeling is justifiable, it suggests that labeling does not, in itself, adversely affect special education decisions by child study team members. This is essentially the type of research approach needed to avoid litigation related to labeling in the future.

Least Restrictive Environment and Mainstreaming

One of the most significant movements during the decade of the 1970s and trends in the 1980s is provision of special services to handicapped children in the least restrictive environment. The factors that provided the impetus for the original efforts to promote the concept of mainstreaming were related to (1) testing and placement procedures being biased racially and ethnically, (2) a tendency to place students in special classes as a substitute for developing other programs, (3) increased recognition of the value of interaction with normal peers, and (4) special classes showing few beneficial results (Kirk & Gallagher, 1979).

All the forces mentioned have come together to create a powerful movement within the public schools toward abandoning special class programs for exceptional children and replacing them with regular class programs, which would be supplemented by special educational services (Reynolds & Birch, 1977).

From a psychological point of view, as program objectives are broadened from the cognitive to other dimensions, such as social and emotional development, the need for mainstreaming becomes even more important. The fact is that children learn much of their patterns of behavior from observation and imitation. Thus there is little advantage in placing emotionally disturbed children in a special class with other emotionally disturbed children, all of whom are reinforcing one another for behaving inappropriately. It is of significant importance for children to model appropriate social interactional patterns. This can be accomplished only by providing these children in question some time to be in the presence of other children whose behavior is deemed socially acceptable.

Studies in child development indicate that peer interaction contains numerous factors through which it contributes to the socialization of the child (Hartup, 1978). "Such contributions are unique in that aggressive socialization, sex-role learning, and moral development would be seriously impeded if children did not have contact with other children in their formative years" (pp. 47–48). However, merely placing exceptional children with normal peers can hardly be expected to produce educational and social development for the child or transform the attitudes of his or her normal peers. There is some research evidence on the effects of special classes and the effects of mainstreaming.

Studies on the value of special EMR classes have been analyzed for a number of years (Corman & Gottlieb, 1978; Guskin & Spicker, 1968; MacMillan & Meyers, 1979; Semmel, Gottlieb, & Robinson, 1979). However, because of the basic sampling bias inherent in all but one study, no definitive conclusions can be drawn. The one study that used random assignment (Goldstein, Moss, & Jordan, 1965) found significant differences in achievement between the two groups at the end of the first year: regular class children were scoring higher. By the end of the third year there were no differences in achievement. This finding fails to support the superiority of special classes and tends to argue against the conclusion reached by the court that children are worse off in special classes (MacMillan & Meyers, 1980).

Research on the psychological adjustment of children placed in special classes indicates that when mildly handicapped learners are mainstreamed, regular class peers are less accepting of them than when they are enrolled in special classes (Gottlieb, 1975; Corman & Gottlieb, 1978). Thus the assumption that mainstreaming will increase normal children's acceptance of those handicapped has not been supported. Rather, the more the normal children get to know the handicapped learners, the less they like them. Schurr, Towne, and Joiner (1972) investigated the self-concepts of children prior to placement into EMR classes and then monitored self concept after placement. The results indicated that the self-concepts were more favorable in special class children and the self-concept increased after special class placement.

The effects of mainstreaming have been reported by a number of investigators. Positive results have been found in studies of preschool and primary-age mildly handicapped children, those with mild orthopedic, visual, and auditory impairments, and with the gifted (Cantrell & Cantrell, 1976; Fredericks, Baldwin, Grove, Moore, Riggs, & Lyons, 1978; Gottlieb & Baker, 1975; Kaufman, Agard, & Semmel, 1978; Shotel, Iano, & McGettigan, 1972). The questionable group is that of the intermediate-age mentally retarded, the seriously emotionally disturbed, and the severely handicapped. In general, sufficient evidence has now been accumulated which consistently shows that the social adjustment of these children is not improved by putting them into regular classrooms (see Corman & Gottlieb, 1978, and Semmel et al., 1979, for reviews). With reference to achievement, Semmel et al. (1979) stated that "there is no indication of differential achievement gains among EMR pupils as a function of regular or special class placement" (p. 247). General conclusions warranted by the mainstreaming evidence are that mildly handicapped children are not achieving very well or being very well accepted socially, regardless of the label given to them and regardless of the educational placement into which they are programmed. The fact is that these children need special services, and mainstreaming as presently defined is not an adequate resolution of educational problems at all levels.

Logically the trend in special programming for exceptional children in the 1980s will be to incorporate a selective pattern of mainstreaming along with individualized instruction. Exceptional children who are of preschool and early primary grade level would be mainstreamed while children in the intermediate grade levels would attend special classes and receive individualized instruction. The issue in the future is not whether to accept or reject the provision of mainstreaming but when and with whom will it be used.

Child Abuse and Neglect

A basic issue that will be a source of study and debate for many years to come is that of child abuse and neglect. The Child Abuse Prevention and Treatment Act (PL 93–247) defines child abuse and neglect as the "physical or mental injury, sexual abuse, negligent treatment, or maltreatment of a child under the age of eighteen by a person who is responsible for the child's welfare under circumstances which indicate that the child's health or welfare is harmed or threatened thereby."

Early studies described it as the "battered child syndrome." The problem of physical abuse of children was identified as a medical syndrome, a childhood disease with a set of symptoms and named by its cause (Kempe, Silverman, Steele, Droegemuller, & Silver, 1962). During the 1970s attention turned to the consequences of the disease other than the physical effects on severely battered children. The focus was directed to the educational community where symptoms of abuse, neglect, or sexual molestation or exploitation were seen as possible causes of handicapping conditions. In particular, low achievement in school or behavioral problems in the school and community environments have been suggested as consequences of such abuse (Kline, Cole, & Fox, 1981).

Approximately 1 million children are abused, neglected, or sexually molested each year, according to the National Center for Child Abuse and Neglect. Approximately one-half (49%) of the reported abuse and neglect involves school age children (Sears, 1980). The causes are difficult to isolate. Child abusers come from all income levels, geographic locations, family settings, religious backgrounds, and ethnic backgrounds. One factor that seems to be related to child abuse is that many child abusers were themselves abused as children.

Relatively few data are available on the relationship that exists between child abuse and neglect and developmental disabilities (e.g., emotional problems, speech, language development, physical disabilities). Although a cause–effect sequence has not been determined, Kline (1977) reported a clear relationship between child abuse and handicapping conditions. For example, Kline and Christiansen (1975) investigated the relationship between abuse/neglect and placement in special education classes. These authors studied 138 abused children on such variables as the frequency of special placement; the need for specialized services; the frequency of institutional placement; the type and frequency of traits and behaviors indicative of psychological problems; and achievement levels in mathematics, spelling, and reading. Results indicated that children who were abused were placed more frequently than nonabused children in classes for the educable mentally retarded, learning disabled, and emotionally disturbed. Also, children who were sexually abused were placed in these classes more frequently than those who had been physically abused. In his own research, Kline (1977) found that of children judged to be abused or neglected, 27% were subsequently enrolled in special education classes. Many of these children had symptoms resembling those of behavior disorders. Wilkinson and Donaruma (1979) matched 1228 subjects enrolled in special education classes with students in regular education programs and found a significantly higher incidence of abuse, neglect, and sexual exploitation in the experimental group.

It appears that there is a significant relationship between child abuse and educational problems. However, it is not clear whether developmental delays encourage abuse and neglect or whether abuse and neglect cause educational liabilities. The emerging trend will be early identification and reporting of child abuse cases in an effort to avoid academic and emotional problems. Although primary prevention through education and counseling may aid in the reduction of abusive behavior, research such as that being conducted by Egeland and his colleagues (Egeland & Brunnquell, 1979; Vaughn, Egeland, Stroufe, & Waters, 1979; Vaughn, Gove, & Egeland, 1980; Waters, Vaughn, & Egeland, 1980) will provide the most insight into the psychological and physiological factors of abuse. Preliminary findings of 275 high-risk mothers and infants showed that adequate mothers could better understand the psychological complexity of their infants than mothers who were at risk. In addition, adequate mothers displayed a better relationship with their infants as based on observations of caretaking skills, positive affect used, and their infant's social responsiveness (Egeland & Brunnquell, 1979). The implication stated by these authors is clearly that a major focus of intervention must be the mother's awareness of the psychology of the child. Conversely, the mother must be helped to realize and accept her own psychological complexity in order to accept that of the child.

While this type of study will not end abuse, neglect, or exploitation, research aimed at understanding the complex etiologies of child abuse is sorely needed in the 1980s.

Differentiation of Primary and Secondary Dysfunction

On a more theoretical level, one of the most promising directions and important challenges for the future will be to differentiate between primary and secondary dysfunction. Psychologists and educators are beginning to acknowledge that all behavior is mediated by the brain and central nervous system. The basic assumption is that to understand fully exceptional (i.e., disturbed) behavior, knowledge regarding neuropsychological functioning of the child is imperative. As Hebb (1949) stated earlier, a neuropsychological theory of behavior can aid in understanding not only deficit behavior but also normal behavior. More recently the view in education (Pollack, 1976) has been to acknowledge the role of brain structure and function as fundamental to learning theory. It is not just the recognition of neurological data that is useful but its application in deciding on an appropriate treatment program for exceptional children.

All human subjects possess varying degrees of cerebral dysfunction that ranges from normal to severely impaired. Some children presumably possess nervous systems that are healthy and function in an optimal manner. However, others, such as many exceptional children, inherit imperfect brains with genetic defects, or they may have been exposed to traumatic injury either prior postnatally. Because the neural system is so complex, the nature of cognitive impairment resulting from central nervous system dysfunction is incalculable. This means that any group research with exceptional children suspected of having some form of brain damage includes a heterogeneous population. For this reason it is necessary to identify different groups of exceptional children with basic similarities.

The types of exceptional behavior, considered deficit behavior, that result from central nervous system damage can be thought of as primary dysfunction. The primary dysfunction may stem from congential deficits, that is, may be developmental, or it may result from postnatal traumatic brain damage. Secondary dysfunction then stems from cultural and educational causes. These may include hostile family climate, parental rejection or neglect (as described earlier in this chapter), and social or educational deprivation. Labeling exceptional behavior "primary" when it results from organic dysfunction does not imply a greater importance than "secondary" cultural or emotional ones, but they are less responsive to conventional teaching methods because of central processing dysfunctions (Gaddes, 1980).

In one academic area numerous studies have appeared since the early 1900s relating perinatal events as precursors of learning and reading disabilities. Balow, Rubin, and Rosen (1976) reviewed more than 30 studies and point out that abnormal perinatal conditions likely have a long-term impairing effect only to the extent that they have permanently damaged neurological functioning. If the perinatal disturbance was temporary enough, no neurological insult will result.

When injuries are severe, academic retardation is permanent and only partially responsive to therapeutic teaching. Probably most children with chronically severe educational or physical difficulties have had early brain injury or some obscure genetic anomaly that interferes with normal learning. At this time, the best diagnostic and remedial approach to the treatment of exceptional children is to discover as much as possible about the child's perceptual, intellectual, motor, cross-modal, sequential, and sensorimotor skills. This information should be provided to the teacher, who, together with the psychologist, can develop a useful remedial program.

When the possibility of any seriously impeding organic cause of exceptional behavior has been ruled out, then the logical causes of etiology would seem to be of a psychological or social nature. Successful intervention would rely on skilled methods of behavior management coupled with proven methods of teaching to the academically deficient area.

Childhood exceptionalities result from both primary and secondary dysfunctions. Future work should consider these two etiologies as distinct from one another. By doing so, one recognizes the involvement of the central nervous system in certain disorders while attributing other factors such as emotional disturbance, environmental disadvantage, inadequate teaching, and sensory impairment as causal agents.

Deficit or Delay

One of the major issues that arise from the preceding discussion is whether childhood exceptionalities are the result of deficit or delay. The brain-deficit model proposes that there is a cerebral dysfunction underlying the inability to acquire appropriate learning skills. Descriptions on the nature of this deficit have ranged from brain damage to more subtle chemical or electrical imbalances. The maturational-lag or delay model, in contrast, adopts a developmental persepective and suggests cerebral maturation to be less rapid in educationally deficient children. These two models represent general theories from which more elaborate and specific hypotheses have emerged.

The deficit model implies that aberrations in position, form, or pattern of connectivity of neural cells make cognitive processing in a normal fashion impossible. Continued effort to assess the functional cortical organization of these children is necessary.

The delay model of exceptionality implies an atypical developmental pattern of growth which tends to interfere with cognitive processing. This model predicts that individuals developing more slowly would be less prepared to achieve successfully at the expected level on academic tasks.

Some current research investigating the theoretical constructs underlying the delay model has rejected the maturational-lag hypothesis in favor of a deficit explanation because of the faulty notion that delay necessarily implies "catch-up." For example, many researchers still advocate Orton's (1937) idea that learning disorders are the result of developmental delays in cerebral lateralization. Our own investigations have shown, in contrast, that hemispheric functions do not develop from a diffuse state but are, at the least, predisposed for specialization (Hynd & Obrzut, 1977; Hynd & Obrzut, 1981; Hynd, Obrzut, Weed, & Hynd, 1979; Obrzut & Hynd, 1981; Obrzut, Hynd, Obrzut, & Leitgeb, 1980; Obrzut, Hynd, Obrzut, & Pirozzolo, 1981). These studies have suggested that learning disabled children are susceptible to attentional biases, and their inability to process simultaneous information is probably related to a *deficit* in collosal functioning. The result of this deficit is that the two cerebral hemispheres in these exceptional children may function somewhat independently and without the contralateral interaction found in normal children (Obrzut et al., 1981).

The debate over whether exceptional behavior is the result of a brain deficit or a developmental delay will undoubtedly continue. The primary question to address is whether we can reliably group individuals under these two etiologies. It appears that one problem in subdividing groups on the basis of these etiologies is that the criteria used may be interpreted as evidence of both neurological dysfunction and maturational delay. However, this may be due to the many methodological problems in the literature. Continued research should explore whether certain types of exceptionality relate more closely with a particular etiology.

The practical value of a neuropsychological approach is to attempt to explain the basis of some exceptionality. Adequate explanations may give direction for interventions, whether educational, medical, or psychological. Also, the possibility exists that such research may provide means for preventing developmental problems. For progress to be made in this area, attention must be directed on theory articulation in addition to methodological advances in neuropsychology. As Gaddes (1980) points out, all behavior is mediated by the brain. Consequently, it seems imperative that researchers and educators consider a neuropsychological perspective for a better understanding of human behavior, especially disturbed behavior as it affects perception, cognition, and learning in general.

REFERENCES

Abeson, A., & Bolick, N. (Eds.), *A Continuing Summary of Pending and Completed Litigation Regarding the Education of Handicapped Children* (No. 8). Reston, Va.: Council for Exceptional Children, 1974.

Alley, G., & Foster, C. Non-discriminatory testing of minority and exceptional children. *Focus on Exceptional Children,* 1978, *9,* 1–13.

Balow, B., Rubin, R., & Rosen, J. J. Perinatal events as precursors of reading disability. *Reading Research Quarterly,* 1976, *11,* 36–71.

Berg, F. M. Aetiological aspects of mental subnormality: Pathological factors. In A. M. Clarke & A. D. B. Clarke (Eds.), *Mental deficiency: The changing outlook.* New York: Free Press, 1974.

Binet, A. *The development of intelligence in children* (Trans. E. S. Kite). Baltimore: Williams and Wilkins, 1916.

Bolick, N. (Ed.), *Digest of state and federal laws: Education of handicapped children.* Reston, Va. Council for Exceptional Children, 1974.

Boring, E. G. *A history of experimental psychology* (2nd ed.). New York: Appleton-Century-Crofts, 1950.

Brim, O. G., Jr., Glass, P. C., Neulinger, S., Firestone, I. J., & Lerner, S. C. *American beliefs and attitudes about intelligence.* New York: Russell Sage Foundation, 1969.

Cantrell, R. P., & Cantrell, M. L. Preventive mainstreaming: Impact of a supportive service program on pupils. *Exceptional Children,* 1976, *42,* 381–386.

Clarke, A. D. B., & Clarke, A. M. The changing concept of intelligence: A selective historical review. In A. M. Clarke & A. D. B. Clarke (Eds.), *Mental deficiency: The changing outlook* (3rd ed.). New York: Free Press, 1974.

Corman, L., & Gottlieb, J. Mainstreaming mentally retarded children: A review of research. In N. R. Ellis (Ed.), *International review of research in mental retardation* (Vol. 9). New York: Academic, 1978.

Diana v. State Board of Education No. C-70 37 RFP United States District Court for the Northern District of California, San Francisco, 1970.

DuBois, P. H. *A history of psychological testing.* Boston: Allyn & Bacon, 1970.

Dunn, L. M. (Ed.). *Exceptional children in the schools.* New York: Holt, Rinehart & Winston, 1973.

Egeland, B., & Brunnquell, D. An at-risk approach to the study of child abuse: Some preliminary findings. *Journal of the American Academy of Child Psychiatry,* 1979, *18,* 219–235.

Elashoff, J. D., & Snow, R. E. *A case study in statistical inference: Reconsideration of the Rosenthal-Jacobson data on teacher expectancy* (SCRDT Tech. Rep. 15). Stanford, Calif.: Stanford University, School of Education, 1971.

Fredericks, H., Baldwin, V., Grove, D., Moore, W., Riggs, C., & Lyons, B. Integrating the moderately and severely handicapped preschool child into a normal day care setting. In M. Guralnick (Ed.), *Early intervention and the integration of handicapped and nonhandicapped children.* Baltimore, University Park Press, 1978.

Gaddes, W. H. *Learning disabilities and brain function: A neuropsychological approach.* New York: Springer-Verlag, 1980.

Galton, F. *Hereditary geniuses* (2nd ed.). London: Macmillan, 1892.

Gillung, T. B., & Rucker, C. H. Labels and teacher expectations. *Exceptional Children,* 1977, *43,* 464–465.

Goldstein, H. J., Moss, J. W., & Jordan, L. J. *The efficacy of special class training on the development of mentally retarded children* (U.S. Office of Education Cooperative Project No. 619). Urbana: University of Illinois, 1965.

Goodman, H., Gottlieb, J., & Harmon, R. Social acceptance of EMP's integrated into a nongraded elementary school. *American Journal of Mental Deficiency,* 1972, *76,* 412–417.

Gottlieb, J. Attitudes toward retarded children: Effects of labeling and academic performance. *American Journal of Mental Deficiency,* 1974, *79,* 268–273.

Gottlieb, J. Public, peer, and professional attitudes toward mentally retarded persons. In M. Begab & S. Richardson (Eds.), *The mentally retarded and society: A social science perspective.* Baltimore: University Park Press, 1975.

Gottlieb, J., & Baker, J. Socio-emotional characteristics of mainstreamed children (*Report at CEC*). 1975.

Gross, M. J. *The brain-watchers.* New York: Random House, 1962.

Guskin, S. L., & Spicker, H. H. Educational research in mental retardation. In N. R. Ellis (Ed.), *International review of research in mental retardation* (Vol. 3). New York: Academic, 1968.

Hartup, W. Peer interaction and the process of integration. In M. Guralnick (Ed.), *Early intervention and the integration of handicapped and non-handicapped children.* Baltimore: University Park Press, 1978.

Hebb, D. O. *Organization of behavior.* New York: Wiley, 1949.

Hobbs, N. *The futures of children: Categories, labels, and their consequences.* San Francisco: Jossey-Bass, 1975.

Hoffman, B. *Tyranny of testing.* New York: Crowell-Collier, 1961.

Holtzman, W. H. The changing world of mental measurement and its social significance. *American Psychologist,* 1971, *26.*

Houts, P. L. Standardized testing in America. *The National Elementary Principal,* 1975, *54,* 2–3.

Hunt, J. McV. *Intelligence and experience.* New York: Ronald Press, 1961.

Hynd, G. W., & Obrzut, J. E. Effects of grade level and sex on the magnitude of the dichotic ear advantage. *Neuropsychologia,* 1977, *15,* 689–692.

Hynd, G. W., & Obrzut, J. E. Reconceptualizing cerebral dominance: Implications for reading and learning disabled children. *Journal of Special Education,* 1981, *15,* 447–457.

Hynd, G. W., Obrzut, J. E., Weed, W., & Hynd, C. R. Development of cerebral dominance: Dichotic listening asymmetry in normal and learning disabled children. *Journal of Experimental Child Psychology,* 1979, *28,* 445–454.

Jensen, A. R. How much can we boost IQ and scholastic achievement? *Harvard Educational Review,* 1969, *39,* 1–123.

Johnson, D. Educational principles for children with learning disabilities. *Rehabilitation Literature,* 1967, *28,* 317–322.

Johnson, G. O. A study of the social position of mentally handicapped children in the regular grades. *American Journal of Mental Deficiency,* 1950, *55,* 60–89.

Kaufman, M., Agard, J., & Semmel, M. *Mainstreaming: Learners and their environment.* Baltimore: University Park Press, 1978.

Kempe, C., Silverman, F., Steele, B., Droegemuller, W., & Silver, H. The battered child syndrome. *Journal of the American Medical Association,* 1962, *181,* 17–24.

Kirk, S. A. *Educating exceptional children.* Boston: Houghton Mifflin, 1973.

Kirk, S. A. The impact of labelling or rejection of the mentally ill. *Journal of Health and Social Behavior,* 1974, *15,* 108–117.

Kirk, S. A., & Gallagher, J. J. *Educating exceptional children.* Boston: Houghton Mifflin, 1979.

Kirman, B. H. Individual differences in the mentally subnormal. In A. M. Clarke & A. D. B. Clarke (Eds.), *Mental deficiency: The changing outlook.* New York: Free Press, 1974.

Kline, D. F. *Child abuse and neglect: A primer for school personnel.* Reston, Va.: Council for Exceptional Children, 1977.

Kline, D. F., & Christiansen, J. *Educational and psychological problems of abused children* (Final Report: Contract No. G00 75–00352). Washington, D.C., U.S. Office of Education, DHEW, 1975.

Kline, D. F., Cole, P., & Fox, P. Child abuse and neglect: The school psychologist's role. *School Psychology Review,* 1981, *10,* 65–71.

Knitzer, J. E. Child advocacy. *American Journal of Orthopsychiatry,* 1976, *46,* 200–216.

Laosa, L. M. Reform in educational and psychological assessment: Cultural and Linguistic issues. *Journal of the Association of Mexican-American Educators,* 1973, *1,* 19–24.

Laosa, L. M. Non-biased assessment of children's abilities: Historical anticedents and current issues. In T. Oakland (Ed.), *Psychological and educational assessment of minority children.* New York: Brunner/Mazel, 1977.

Laosa, L. M., & Oakland, T. *Social control in mental health: Psychological assessment and the schools. Paper presented at the 51st annual meeting of the American Orthopsychiatric Association,* San Francisco, April 1974.

Larry P. Riles, (No. C-71 2279 RFP). United States District Court for the Northern District of California, San Francisco, October 1979 (slip opinion).

Lesser, G. S., Fiffer, G., & Clark, D. H. Mental abilities of children from different social class and cultural groups. *Monographs of The Society for Research in Child Development,* 1965, *30.*

Linden, K. W., & Linden, J. D. *Modern mental measurement: A historical perspective.* Boston: Houghton Mifflin, 1968.

MacMillan, D. L., & Meyers, C. E. Educational labeling of handicapped learners. In D. C. Berliner (Ed.), *Review of research in education* (Vol. 7). Washington, D.C.: American Educational Research Association, 1979.

MacMillan, D. L., & Meyers, C. E. Larry P.: An educational interpretation. *School Psychology Review,* 1980, *9,* 136–148.

Mercer, J. R. *Labeling the mentally retarded.* Berkeley: University of California Press, 1973.

Mercer, J. R., & Ysseldyke, J. E., Designing diagnostic-intervention programs. In T. Oakland (Ed.), *Psychological and educational assessment of minority children.* New York: Brunner/Mazel, 1977.

Nazzaro, J. N. *Exceptional time tables: Historical events affecting the handicapped and gifted.* Reston, Va.: Council for Exceptional Children, 1977.

Newland, T. E. Assumptions underlying psychological testing. In T. D. Oakland & B. N. Phillips (Eds.), *Assessing minority group children: A special issue of the journal of school psychology.* New York: Behavioral Publications, 1973, 315–322.

Oakland, T. *Psychological and educational assessment of minority children.* New York: Brunner/Mazel, 1977.

Obrzut, J. E., & Hynd, G. W. Cognitive development and cerebral lateralization in learning disabled children. *International Journal of Neuroscience,* 1981, *14,* 139–145.

Obrzut, J. E., Hynd, G. W., Obrzut, A., & Leitgeb, J. L. Time sharing and dichotic listening in normal and learning disabled children. *Brain and language,* 1980, *11,* 181–194.

Obrzut, J. E., Hynd, G. W., Obrzut, A., & Pirozzolo, F. J. Effect of directed attention on cerebral asymmetries in normal and learning disabled children. *Developmental Psychology,* 1981, *17,* 118–125.

Orton, S. T. *Reading, writing, and speech problems in children.* New York: Norton, 1937.

Peter, L. J. *Perscriptive teaching.* New York: McGraw-Hill, 1965.

Pfeiffer, S. The influence of diagnostic labeling on special education placement decisions. *Psychology in the Schools,* 1980, *17,* 346–350.

Pollack, C. Neuropsychological aspects of reading and writing. *Bulletin of the Orton Society,* 1976, *26,* 19–33.

Public Law 94–142, The Education of All Handicapped Children Act of 1975. *Federal Register,* 1977, 42496–49497.

Reisman, J. *The development of clinical psychology.* New York: Appleton-Century-Crofts, 1966.

Reynolds, M. C. The education of exceptional children. *Review of Educational Research,* 1969, *39.*

Reynolds, M. C. Policy statements: Call for response. *Exceptional Children,* 1971, *37,* 421–433.

Reynolds, M. C. & Birch, J. W. *Teaching exceptional children in all America's schools.* Reston, Va.: Council for Exceptional Children, 1977.

Rosenthal, R., & Jacobson, L. *Pygmalion in the classroom.* New York: Holt, Rhinehart & Winston, 1968.

Sarason, S. B., & Doris, J. *Educational handicap, public policy, and social history.* New York: Free Press, 1979.

Sattler, J. M. *Assessment of children's intelligence.* (Rev. rep.). Philadelphia: Saunders, 1974.

Schurr, K. T., Towne, R. C., & Joiner, L. M. Trends in self concept of ability over 2 years of special placement. *Journal of Special Education,* 1972, *6,* 161–166.

Sears, D. W. Incidence of child abuse and neglect. *Region VIII News,* 1980, *2,* (2).

Semmel, M. I., Gottlieb, J., & Robinson, N. M. Mainstreaming: Perspectives on educating handicapped children in the public schools. In D.C. Berliner (Ed.), *Review of research in education* (Vol. 7). Washington, D.C.): American Educational Research Association, 1979.

Shotel, J., Iano, R., & McGettigan, J. Teacher attitudes associated with the integration of handicapped children. *Exceptional Children,* 1972, *38,* 677–683.

Skeels, H. M., & Dye, H. G. A study of the effects of differentiated stimulation on mentally retarded children. *Proceedings of the American Association of Mental Deficiency,* 1939, *44,* 114–136.

Smith, I. & Greenberg, S. Teacher attitudes and the labelling process. *Exceptional Children,* 1975, *41,* 319–324.

Smith, R. M., & Neisworth, J. T. *The exceptional child: A functional approach.* New York: McGraw-Hill, 1975.

Spearman, C. "General intelligence: Objectively determined and measured. *American Journal of Psychology,* 1904, *115,* 201–292.

Stone, J. C., & Schneider, F. W. *Foundations of Education.* New York: Thomas Y. Crowell Company, 1965.

Stuart, R. B. *Trick or treatment: How and when psychotherapy fails.* Champaign, Ill.: Research Press, 1970.

Vaughn, B. E., Egeland, B., Stroufe, L. A., & Waters, E. Individual differences in infant-mother attachment at 12 and 18 months: Stability and change in families under stress. *Child Development,* 1979, *50,* 971–975.

Wallace, G., & Larsen, S. C. *Educational assessment of learning problems: Testing for teaching.* Boston: Allyn & Bacon, 1978.

Waters, E., Vaughn, B., & Egeland, B. Individual differences in infant-mother attachment relationships at age one: Antecedents in neonatal behavior in an urban, economically disadvantaged sample. *Child Development,* 1980, *51,* 208–216.

Wilkinson, J. K., & Donaruma, P. L. *The incidence of abuse and neglect among children in special education vs. regular education.* Boulder, Colo.: Family Resources Center, 1979.

Wolfensburger, W. Diagnosis is diagnosed. *Journal of Mental Subnormality,* 1965, *11,* 62–70.

Ysseldyke, J. E. Nondiscriminatory assessment: Is it achievable? *Centerfold,* 1978, 3.

Ysseldyke, J. E., & Salvia, J. A. A critical analysis of the assumptions underlying diagnostic-prescriptive teaching. *Exceptional Children,* 1974, *41,* 181–195.

Zedler, E. Y. *Public opinion and public education for the exceptional childcourt decisions 1873–1950.* Reston: *Council For Exceptional Children,* 1953.

CHAPTER 2

Reading and
Evaluating Research
on Exceptional Children

CRAIG EDELBROCK

Research on exceptional children is extremely diverse—just as the term "exceptional children" encompasses a vast array of individuals who deviate from normal in some respect. The causes and implications of such deviations are innumerable and are subject to inquiry by professionals from many disciplines. Even within scientific subspecialties, research encompasses a wide range of procedures, perspectives, and theoretical persuasions. A sample of articles regarding exceptional children may have no common methodological or theoretical thread. Thus there are no simple formulas for reading and evaluating research on exceptionality. Only general guidelines can be offered and they must be applied in a flexible manner. Occasionally even general guidelines must be bent or discarded to accommodate a particular study.

The purpose of this chapter is to provide such guidelines for appraising research on exceptional children. Emphasis will be placed on problems and issues that are common or particularly crucial to research in this area. Whenever possible, examples will be drawn from research regarding mentally retarded, behaviorally disordered, blind, hearing-impaired, learning disabled, gifted, handicapped, or otherwise exceptional children. My goal is not to reiterate introductory statistics and research methods but rather to outline a general strategy for reading research reports. Readers who are not familiar with basic statistics and research methods are referred to the many excellent introductory texts on these topics (e.g., Achenbach, 1978; Kerlinger, 1973; McCall, 1980; Weinberg & Schumaker, 1969).

Getting Oriented

Research is rarely understood on first reading. Before launching into a detailed analysis, it is often useful to gain a general orientation to the study. The title and abstract of a report can provide clues as to the purpose, procedures, and findings of the study. The article can also be read over lightly to set the stage for a more thoughtful dissection. Some general questions should be kept in mind when scanning a research report: What was the nature and purpose of this study? What theoretical paradigm was employed? How does this research relate to other work on the same topic?

Nature and Purpose

Most research on exceptional children can be categorized according to general purpose. It may be useful, for example, to categorize a study as being *basic* or *applied*. It is difficult to say exactly what makes basic research basic. Some define basic research as when "you don't know what you are doing." A more adequate definition of basic research is *"the study of the fundamental laws of nature for their own sake"* (Selye, 1959). Immediate applications of basic research findings may not be obvious. Basic research involves discovery: it is creative and abstract. Applied research, on the other hand, involves the application of natural laws to specific problems and is more practical and useful. The benefits of applied research are more immediately recognized and obtained than those of basic research.

It may be difficult to categorize some studies of exceptional children as being either basic or applied. The "either/or" distinction is not necessary. Studies may fall between the two extremes. Some examples can be drawn from research regarding children's memory. Several studies fall toward the basic end of the continuum (Kelly, Scholnick, Travers, & Johnson, 1976; Salatas & Flavell, 1976). The goals of these studies were to describe fundamental memory processes in children and to determine how memory processes interrelate and change developmentally. Other studies have focused upon how normal and mentally retarded children differ in their memory skills and processes (Ashcraft & Kellas, 1974; Milgram, 1967). The practical applications of such studies are more obvious, since differences may suggest strategies for improving the memory skills of mentally retarded children. Such research is not directly applied, however, and falls in the middle of the basic–applied continuum. Other studies are clearly applied, such as those with goals of training mentally retarded children to use specific mnemonic strategies (Reichart, Cody, & Borkowski, 1975; Turnbull, 1974; Winschel, Ensher, & Blatt, 1977). The benefits of such studies are practical and immediate. Retarded children can be trained to remember more information and recall information more accurately. The implications for educational practice are obvious.

Research can also be categorized as being *exploratory, descriptive,* or *casual* (cf. Selltiz, Jahoda, Deutsch, & Cook, 1959). Exploratory studies are less structured and more flexible than other types of research. The goal may be to clarify a problem or formulate hypotheses for further investigation. Such "pilot" studies may be based on an informal hunch or clinical insight. Pilot studies often represent an initial foray into an area about which little is known.

The goal of descriptive studies is to describe individuals or phenomena. Such studies are built on a broader basis of knowledge and a premium is placed on the *accuracy* and *reliability* of the data obtained. In causal research, the goal is to establish a causal relationship between variables. Such research, as we shall see, requires more stringent rules of evidence and more complex designs than either exploratory or descriptive studies.

In addition to determining the general nature and purpose of the study, it is valuable to ascertain the specific hypotheses that guide the research. Hypotheses are propositions about facts which have yet to be proven. In other words, they are questions the researcher wishes to answer or expectations the researcher holds regarding the study's findings. Hypotheses are of the utmost importance because they provide a basis for the subsequent explanation of the findings and they should not be thought of as restricting the scope of research but should be seen as being absolutely essential to the value of the findings. Hypotheses should be explicitly stated, particularly in causal research.

Theoretical Paradigms

Theories are heuristic tools which provide a framework for empirical inquiry. They provide a basis for organizing our knowledge, explaining phenomena, and making predictions. There is no single *correct* theoretical paradigm for studying exceptionality. On the contrary, a variety of theoretical paradigms are used in behavioral research (e.g., behaviorist, psychodynamic, organismic-developmental). They differ in their assumptions regarding the nature and causes of behavior and development and comprise different concepts, constructs, and explanatory mechanisms.

Theoretical paradigms influence how we see the world, as well as how we interpret what we see. Thus the same empirical findings are subject to diverse interpretations. In reviewing research on early childhood autism, for example, Ward (1970) employed a psychodynamic theoretical framework invoking terms such as "body ego" and "protective ego barrier." After weighing the evidence, he attributed autism to the "lack of a varying, patterned stimulation in the child's developmental history." Both L'Abate (1972) and Rimland (1972) commented on Ward's review from a very different theoretical viewpoint. Both commentators employed terms such as "biological cause," "biochemical defect," "constitutional factors," "information processing," and "visual and auditory input." As these terms suggest, both L'Abate and Rimland favor a biological or transactional explanation for autism involving an interplay between the child's constitutional factors and the environment. The goal here is not to debate psychogenic versus biological theories of autism. The point is simply that different theoretical paradigms may be brought to bear on the same empirical evidence—with quite different results.

A Broader Context

Research articles should include discussions of previous research and theory on the same topic and researchers should point out how their study builds upon previous findings or relates to important theoretical issues. It is also valuable to discern whether a study fits into an on-going program of research. Too often studies of exceptional children represent one-shot efforts employing idiosyncratic subject samples, procedures, and measures. Such studies make little contribution to our knowledge of exceptionality, in that they cannot be related to previous research. Such one-shot studies are rarely replicated and generalization of the findings of such studies is tenuous.

Summary

To get oriented to a research report, read the title and abstract, then scan the entire report. Determine the nature and purpose of the study. Was it basic or applied? Exploratory, descriptive, or causal? Were specific hypotheses stated? What theoretical paradigm was employed? How did this influence the ways in which the research was formulated? Finally, how does this research relate to previous research and theory on the same topic? Was it a one-shot study or does it fit into a broader program of research?

ASSESSMENT AND CLASSIFICATION ISSUES

After obtaining a general orientation to a study, research reports can be read from an evaluative point of view. Several important considerations involve the definition and assessment of variables and the type of exceptional children under study. Problems and issues involving the assessment and classification of exceptional children are discussed elsewhere in this book (see McDermott, Chapter 5 and Reynolds, Chapter 4). A few key considerations are outlined here.

Defining and Measuring Variables

Operational Definitions

As previously mentioned, one's theoretical paradigm will dictate, to a large extent, the concepts and constructs one employs in research. However, researchers may employ the same theoretical construct (e.g., intelligence) but measure it in different ways. Thus it is important to note how constructs are operationally defined in a study. An operational definition is simply a description of how a construct or variable was measured. They are particularly important because a single measure is rarely equivalent to a theoretical variable. Researchers may refer to the same theoretical construct but measure it in vastly different ways. Failure to replicate findings may be caused in part by differing operational definitions of the constructs being investigated.

Validity and Reliability

The validity and reliability of measures used in reasearch should also be carefully evaluated. There are various definitions of validity and reliability and they suit different situations and purposes. In general, validity involves *what* is being measured, whereas reliability involves the *accuracy* and *stability* of measures. These concepts are presented from a psychometric perspective by Reynolds (Chapter 4) but are reviewed here with an eye toward their impact on reading and evaluating research.

Researchers may report different types of evidence to support the validity of their measures. Three types of validity are commonly discussed. *Content* validity involves judgments of the adequacy of the content of a measure. One may ask, for example, if items on an intelligence test reflect intelligence the way the researcher has defined it. *Criterion* or *predictive* validity involves the ability of a measure to predict an external criterion. At third type of validity, *construct validity,* is extremely important in behavioral research and deserves further discussion.

Construct Validity

As Kerlinger has pointed out (1973 pp. 461–473), construct validity is important because it combines both empirical evidence and theoretical conceptions. From a purely empirical viewpoint, a researcher may claim a measure is valid because it yields accurate predictions. The more important question in psychological research, however, is *why* it is predictive. Thus construct validity involves explanation as well as prediction. In seeking to establish construct validity of a measure, the researcher is asking: What psychological constructs account for variance in scores?

Two lines of evidence can be used to establish construct validity: *convergence* and *discriminability*. Convergence involves a degree to which different measures of the same construct agree. Different IQ measures, for example, should be highly correlated because they tap the same underlying construct—intelligence. The validity of a measure can also be established by demonstrating what it is *not* related to. That is, it should be possible to discriminate one construct from another. A particular theory may state that X and Y are separate, unrelated constructs. Thus valid measures of X should not correlate with valid measures of Y.

To carry this example further, suppose we wish to establish both the convergent and discriminant validity of X and Y. We would try to show that different measures of X correlate with each other and different measures of Y correlate with each other. At the same time, measures of X and Y should not be correlated. A study could be designed to establish the convergent and discriminant validity of X and Y simultaneously. One simultaneous validation procedure is called the "multitrait-multimethod matrix" (Campbell & Fiske, 1959) and is a landmark contribution to measurement theory and procedure. As the term multitrait-multimethod implies, more than one trait or attribute is measured according to more than one method of measurement. In the subsequent correlation matrix, we would expect *similar* traits measured by *different* methods to be highly correlated and *different* traits to be uncorrelated, whether they were measured by the same or different methods.

An example of the multitrait-multimethod matrix can be drawn from a study of the validity of project PRIME's *Guess Who?*, an assessment instrument that has been used in the evaluation of mainstreaming (MacMillan, Morrison, & Silverstein, 1980). Using *Guess Who?*, children are nominated who fit various items (e.g., Who breaks the rules? Who is the best in math?). Versions of *Guess Who?* have been developed for children and teachers and both measures yield three factors labeled *Disruptive, Bright* and *Dull*.

To validate this measure, *Guess Who?* was administered to the children and teachers in 143 self-contained classrooms for mildly handicapped children. A total of 1095 children were assessed by their teachers and peers. The resulting multitrait-multimethod matrix is shown in Table 2.1, where the three factors represent different traits and students' versus teachers' reports represent different methods. This correlation matrix supports both the convergent and discriminant validity of *Guess Who?* Convergent validity is supported by the relatively high correlations between student and teacher ratings of the same factors. Discriminant validity is supported by the finding of low or negative correlations among dissimilar factors and dissimilar factors were found to be uncorrelated both within and across methods.

Reliability

Reliability refers to the *accuracy* and *consistency* of the scores obtained by measurement procedure. A perfectly reliable measure would yield the same score upon repeated administration, assuming that what is being measured is uniform across time. Of course, the assumption of stability over time is not always tenable. Some behaviors, traits, and abilities are stable, whereas others are not. Longitudinal studies of mental ability, for example, have obtained stability coefficients of .85 to .95 for IQs (Hindley & Owen, 1978; McCall, Appelbaum, & Hogarty, 1973). Some individuals changed dramatically in their IQs as they grew from infancy to adulthood, but on the average, IQs were stable over time (cf. McCall, 1981). This can be contrasted with measures of problem behavior. Edelbrock and Reed (1981), for example, obtained observational ratings of problem behavior on a sample of emotionally disturbed

Table 2.1. Multitrait-Multimethod Matrix for Guess Who?

	Student Ratings			Teacher Ratings		
	Disruptive	Bright	Dull	Disruptive	Bright	Dull
Student ratings						
Disruptive	—					
Bright	− .17	—				
Dull	.12	− .29	—			
Teacher ratings						
Disruptive	.65			—		
Bright	− .17	.50		− .04	—	
Dull	.03	− .26	.44	.25	− .09	—

Source: Adapted with permission from MacMillan, Morrison, & Silverstein, 1980, p. 80.

boys in a school setting. Each boy was rated by two independent observers on six separate occasions spread out over two weeks. For global ratings of problem behavior, interrater correlations were high (.85 to .95), but intersession correlations—reflecting stability over time—were low (.20 to .30). In other words, the observers agreed highly on their ratings of problem behavior, but the behaviors varied markedly from session to session.

Even if behaviors and abilities were stable across time, we would find that our measures are less than perfectly reliable. To some extent, scores embody error variance. In fact, the reliability of a measure can be defined in terms of proportion of "true" score versus "error" (cf. Kerlinger, 1973, pp. 442–455). Reliable scores reflect mainly "true" differences, with little "error." Scores reflecting a high proportion of error, on the other hand, are not dependable indices of true differences and are therefore unreliable. A complete discussion of theory and methods of reliability is beyond the scope of this chapter. For an introduction to the concepts of reliability, readers are referred to Kerlinger. A more advanced discussion of reliability has been offered by Cronbach, Gleser, Nanda, and Rajaratnam (1972).

One important form of reliability in behavioral research not previously discussed is interrater reliability. Interrater reliability refers to the degree to which two raters or judges agree on assigning values to a variable. Interrater reliability is often reported in observational studies where two or more observers are used to assess behavior. See Berk (1979) and Kazdin (1977) for a more detailed discussion of the issues surrounding interrater reliability.

Other Assessment Issues

Few measures for children have been adequately developed and standardized and fewer still have designed for children who are exceptional. As Achenbach (1977) pointed out, this situation often forces researchers to use inadequate instruments of their own device or to employ a measure on a population for which it was not intended. Both alternatives are less than desirable. First, the use of ad hoc instruments results in the proliferation of measures having unknown properties—most of which are only used once. Second, we cannot assume that a measure is appropriate for exceptional children simply because its reliability and validity have been established for children in general.

Suppose, for example, we wished to assess the Performance IQ of deaf children, using the Wechsler Intelligence Scale for Children (WISC). The standard verbal instructions are clearly inappropriate—alternative administration procedures must be used. Written instructions can be used with deaf children who can read. In addition, detailed pantomime instructions for the Performance Scale subtests of the WISC have been given by Sattler (1974, pp. 170–172). However, little is known about these modifications affect the reliability and validity of the subsequent scores.

Pilot testing may also be necessary to adapt measures for use with special populations. Careful analysis of pilot cases may reveal ways in which the content, administration, or scoring of a measure should be modified. Modifications should be described in sufficient detail to permit replication by other researchers. Restandardization may also be necessary to accommodate such modifications. Graham and Shapiro (1953), for example, found that for *normal* children pantomime instructions led to significantly *lower* scores on the WISC Performance Scale than the standard instructions. This suggests that separate norms are necessary for children who require the pantomime instructions—or, at least the resulting IQs should be interpreted as conservative estimates of the children's true levels of ability.

Classification of Exceptional Children

Classification is fundamental to scientific progress. Without classificatory systems, we could not make accurate generalizations regarding similar individuals or phenomena. Taxonomies of exceptional children provide frameworks for organizing our knowledge, professional training, communication, service delivery, and research. Unfortunately, such taxonomies are often inadequate and occasionally even controversial.

Many professionals believe that current labels used for exceptional children do more harm than good, in that they do not facilitate appropriate treatment and they stigmatize children. Foster and Salvia (1977), for example, showed elementary teachers a videotape of a normal fourth grade boy engaged in various activities. Half of the teachers were told that the boy was "learning disabled," while the other half were told that the boy was "normal." The teachers were then asked to rate the child's grade level on eight academic skills and to rate 24 behavioral problems. Teachers who were told the boy was learning disabled produced lower ratings of academic grade levels and higher ratings of problem behavior than those who were told the boy was normal. Thus it appears that a negative label may affect the ways in which adults perceive and rate normal childhood behavior. Similar labeling effects have been documented in other research (e.g., Foster, Ysseldyke, & Reese, 1975; Salvia, Clark, & Ysseldyke, 1973). Despite these problems of labeling, most professionals who work with exceptional children agree that classification is necessary, although there is little agreement regarding what form of classification is appropriate (cf. Hobbs, 1975).

Whatever their form, taxonomies of exceptional children should be carefully evaluated. Blashfield and Draguns (1976) proposed four evaluative criteria: reliability, coverage, descriptive validity, and predictive validity. Reliability of classification is similar to the notion of measurement reliability discussed previously. It refers to the consistency of the classification across time or between raters. One may ask, for example, whether a child labeled "learning disabled" by one school psychologist would necessarily receive the same label if diagnosed by another school psychologist. Several factors contribute to disagreements among diagnosticians. For one, they may employ different definitions of a category. There is considerable controversy, for example, regarding the definition and diagnosis of "learning disability" (Keogh, Major, Omori, Gandara, & Reid, 1980; Sabatino, 1979; Schere, Richardson, & Bialer, 1980). Diagnoses also vary according to professional training, the amount and type of information obtained on a child, and the ways in which information is used to formulate a diagnosis.

The *coverage* of a classification refers to the proportion of individuals that are classified. Using current taxonomic systems, it may not be possible or even desirable to categorize all individuals. Blashfield (1973), for example, has demonstrated that coverage and reliability are inversely related. That is, the use of narrow well-defined diagnostic categories results in reliable classification of individuals but reduces the proportion of individuals who can be classified. The use of broader, less rigorously defined categories increases the proportion of individuals who can be classified but decreases the reliability of classification.

The *descriptive validity* of a classificatory system refers to the degree to which individuals assigned to the same category are homogeneous with respect to specific criteria. In general, diagnostic groups used in research on exceptional children do not encompass homogeneous sets of individuals. Children labeled "learning disabled" or "mentally retarded" may manifest a wide range of behaviors, abilities, traits, and cognitive skills.

Predictive validity refers to the degree to which categorization is predictive of external criteria. Thus labels used for exceptional children would be expected to relate to such factors as success in school, peer relations, appropriate school placement, and so on. As previously noted, however, such labels may encompass very heterogeneous groups. In general, there is a direct relationship between descriptive validity and predictive validity. The more homogeneous diagnostic groups are, the more predictive such diagnoses are likely to be.

Summary

An operational definition refers to how a theoretical construct or variable is measured. Remember that researchers may refer to the same construct but measure it in different ways. This can contribute to differences among studies. Validity of a measure refers to *what* is being assessed, whereas reliability refers to the *accuracy* or *stability* of the measure. Construct validity is important because it involves *why* a measure is predictive. Campbell and Fiske's (1959) multitrait-multimethod matrix provides strong evidence of construct validity and should be used. Of the various types of reliability, internal consistency is easy to calculate but is weak evidence because it does not account for variability across time, raters, and so on. Pilot testing may also be necessary to adapt a measure for use with exceptional children.

Classification of exceptional children is essential but also controversial. Labeling effects may constitute a bias in research on special children. Whatever type of classification scheme is used, it should be evaluated in terms of its *reliability, coverage, descriptive validity,* and *predictive validity.*

SAMPLING AND DESIGN

Complete coverage of sampling methods and research design is not possible here, so the discussion will be limited to a few important considerations. In general, the goal of sampling is to reduce potential biases and increase the degree to which research results can be generalized to larger populations of individuals as well as to other times and places. The basics of research design will be covered, with emphasis on designs common in research on exceptional children. The goal of research design is to permit unambiguous interpretation of results, particularly regarding causal relations among variables. Designs will be evaluated from the point of view of reducing potential threats to the validity of the findings and providing evidence of causal relations.

Sampling

A perfect sample is one that is free from biases and representative of larger populations of individuals. Two studies involving nearly perfect samples are the Kauai Longitudinal Study (Werner, Bierman, & French, 1971; Werner & Smith, 1977), which focused on the entire population of children born on Kauai, Hawaii in 1955; and the Isle of Wight Study (Rutter, Tizard, & Whitmore, 1970), which dealt with the entire school-age population of the Isle of Wight, England in June 1964. Both of these studies involved comprehensive sampling of an entire target population of children. Of course, these are very exceptional research efforts. Most studies of children involve haphazard sampling methods that introduce many uncontolled variables that influence the findings. Thus the degree to which the results can be generalized to any larger population is often open to debate.

Unfortunately, it is difficult to account for all variables that influence behavior, particularly when dealing with exceptional children. Source of subjects alone may represent a substantial bias. For example, hearing impaired children drawn from different sources (e.g., regular classes, special classes, schools for the deaf) may differ widely on behavioral and psychological indices, despite their equivalence on other variables such as degree of hearing loss, age, sex, and race. A selective bias may be operating whereby children manifesting different characteristics, competencies, or motives are over- or underrepresented in different settings. Settings also provide different experiences for children which may shape their behavior, expectancies, attitudes, and abilities in different ways. Experiences provided by different settings may also influence how children respond to adults, including research personnel.

It is not feasible to draw samples of exceptional children from all possible settings and sources. Thus it is essential that researchers specify the sources from which their sample were drawn. If findings replicate across settings, we may have confidence in their applicability. Alternatively, if findings do not replicate across settings we will have gained valuable information regarding the degree to which source of subjects limits the generalizability of research results.

Subject Characteristics

In addition to source of subjects, it is essential for researchers to describe subject characteristics such as sex, age, race, socioeconomic status, IQ, and developmental level. These characteristics are crucial because they powerfully influence the experience, learning, and behavior of children. Developmental level is particularly important to note when dealing with exceptional children, since they often deviate from normal. For many types of exceptional children (e.g., mentally retarded, hearing impaired, learning disabled) chronological age is not a good index of developmental level. Comparisons among groups of children matched for chronological age, therefore, are likely to be confounded with inherent differences in developmental level. A measure of cognitive level, such as *mental age*, would be a more appropriate index of the abilities of such children. In comparing mentally retarded and normal children, for example, matching on mental age rather than on chronological age will be more revealing of differences in traits and abilities of such groups. It is also important to remember that IQ is an index of cognitive *skill*, not cognitive *level*. Thus IQ indexes developmental level only if all subjects are the same chronological age.

It is also valuable to ascertain *how* subjects were obtained for research. Too often research on exceptional children is based on haphazard samples of convenience (e.g., a single class) which are likely to embody many uncontrolled biases. It is much more desirable for researchers to specify the source, size, and characteristics of the sample they desire, then seek such a sample. Such purposive samples have a greater chance of being representative of larger populations because important variables can be controlled.

Researchers may also construct stratified samples comprised of particular numbers or proportions of children manifesting specific characteristics. In comparing the behavioral problems of normal and clinically referred children aged 4 to 16, for example, Achenbach and Edelbrock (1981) constructed a sample stratified according to age, sex, race, and socioeconomic status. This permitted the simultaneous analysis of the influence of these characteristics on problem behaviors reported by parents. A probability sample of clinically referred children, on the other hand, would have been substantially overrepresented by boys aged 6 to 11, who dominate mental health referrals. Such a sample would have been more representative of the actual clinical population, but the precise assessment of the contribution of other important characteristics to the behavioral ratings would have been more difficult.

Sampling Unit

The *sampling unit* is also important to consider when reading a research report. It involves the level (school, class, individual subject) at which units are selected for the study or assigned to different treatments. There is no absolute rule for determining the best sampling unit for a study, but sampling unit can be an important consideration. Suppose, for example, that a researcher wants to evaluate a new educational curriculum for retarded children. Half of the children in a class are randomly assigned to receive the new curriculum, while the other half received the regular curriculum. In this case, the sampling unit is individual children who are asigned to different curricula.

A possible risk in this study is that the control group children will become aware of the special curriculum, or will be aware at least that others in the classroom are receiving something special. This may bias the performance of the untreated group. Alternately, there may be some "spillover" of the treatment from the special group to the control group. Children may, for example, talk about the content of the special curriculum to other children. In this situation, it would be an advantage if the sampling unit were *classes*, rather than *individual pupils* within one class. If the researcher had the resources, it would be desirable to select a representative number of classes from a school district and randomly assign entire classes to the experimental versus control curricula.

Sample Size

Sample size should also be noted when reading and evaluating a research report. There is no correct or minimum sample size for behavioral research. Valid research can be done on a single subject. However, sample size is still an issue in most behavioral research because it affects statistical power. Statistical power is the probability of rejecting the null hypothesis when it is in fact false. In other words, statistical power is the probability of detecting a real difference. Low statistical power implies a high probability of making a Type II Error—overlooking a real difference.

Many studies in the behavioral sciences have low statistical power: there is little chance of detecting real differences. There are many reasons for low statistical power, including the lack of control over the many extraneous sources of variance that impinge upon behavior and the less than perfect reliability of measures used in the behavioral sciences. The size of the effects under study also affects statistical power. Large differences are easy to detect, whereas small differences are easily missed. Many of the effects we seek to document in behavioral sciences are small and can be detected only by powerful research designs.

Cohen (1977) has shown how sample size affects statistical power for a wide variety of statistical procedures used in the behavioral sciences. To illustrate the importance of sample size, suppose a researcher wished to test the significance of a correlation between two variables (X and Y) at the $p < .05$ level of significance. Suppose further that the "true" correlation between X and Y is fairly small, in that they share $< 10\%$ common variance. In other words, the "true" correlation between X and Y is approximately .30—not a large correlation but typical of many relations between behavioral measures.

Figure 2.1 illustrates the relationship between sample size and statistical

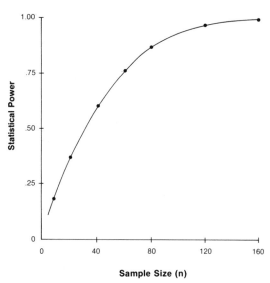

Figure 2.1.   The relationship between sample size and statistical power for detecting a correlation of ~ .30 at $p < .05$.

power for this example. As sample size increases, statistical power increases asymptotically toward 1. For small sample sizes (i.e., $n = 10$), statistical power is low. There is little chance of detecting a significant correlation, even though one exists. Adding a few more subjects will substantially increase statistical power. Large sample sizes, on the other hand, afford high statistical power. Adding more subjects will only slightly increase power.

Statistical power provides a basis for evaluating sample size. Too often, behavioral research is conducted on inadequate samples which afford low statistical power. Researchers could make more efficient use of their resources if they considered statistical power in obtaining their samples. In the previous example, it would be possible to determine in advance the statistical power one sought (say .90), then seek a sample large enough to afford such power. A comprehensive discussion of these issues is beyond the scope of this chapter. Readers are referred to Cohen (1977) for a comprehensive treatise. It is important to realize, however, that although valid research can be done on a single subject, sample size is often crucial in psychological research.

Design Considerations

In this chapter, discussion of design characteristics is limited to causal research. This is because the issues and problems surrounding research design often are encountered in causal rather than exploratory or descriptive research. Research design will be defined as *the arrangement of conditions for the collection and analysis of data in order to permit causal inferences.* A broader definition would be required to discuss design of exploratory and descriptive studies, but this narrow definition will have heuristic value in this discussion.

Concepts of Causality

In order to evaluate research designs, it is necessary to review briefly the concept of causality. There is considerable debate among philosophers and practitioners of science regarding the notion of causality, particularly as it applies to the behavioral sciences (Brand, 1976; Cook & Campbell, 1979). There is consensus, however, regarding some of the basic requirements for causal inference. Simply put, there are three requirements establishing a causal relationship between an independent variable X and a dependent variable Y. First, *concomitant variation* must be established. That is, X and Y must covary—which is to say that X and Y are correlated or, in frequency terms, when X is present Y is also present (and when X is absent Y is absent). Second, it is necessary to establish the *time order of occurrence* between X and Y. If X is the cause of Y, X must precede Y in time. Third, *alternative causes of Y must be held constant or ruled out*. This *ceteris paribus* (Latin for "other things being equal") requirement is exceedingly important for establishing causality and is particularly problematic in the behavioral sciences. More often than not, other things are *not* equal when we seek to establish a causal relationship.

This situation is complicated by the fact that behavior is multiply determined. Rarely does Y have only one cause or X have only one effect. Thus much of the "arrangement of conditions" in research design is aimed at reducing alternative explanations for the occurrence of Y. A good research design will reduce uncertainty regarding causes and effects, but uncertainty is never reduced to zero. There are no perfect research designs in the sense of producing absolute certainty regarding causal relationships. However, some designs support causal inferences, whereas others do not.

Ex Post Facto Designs

Ex post facto or "after the fact" designs fall into the category of designs that do not support causal inferences. An example of such a design is the measurement of a single group after an event has occurred. A researcher, for example, may wish to show that a certain type of brain damage among children causes a specific learning deficit. Using an *ex post facto* design, the researcher may test a group of brain damaged children.

This type of single group–posttest design does not meet any of the requirements for causal inference. Concomitant variation is not established, in that *all* children of comparable age and developmental level may score equivalently on the learning test, whether they are brain damaged or not. A comparison or "control" group is obviously required to establish that the learning deficit varies as a function of the brain damage. Even if a comparison group were used, the requirement regarding time order would not be satisfied, in that there is no evidence that the learning deficit occurred only after the brain damage.

Testing one group before and after brain damage would also constitute an inadequate design for causal inference. Suppose, for example, a researcher had data on a large sample of school children and followed-up and retested only those who had brain damage resulting from accidents or other traumata. Evidence regarding concomitant variation and time order of effects could be obtained through this design, but alternative explanations of the learning deficit could not be ruled out (initial differences between normal children and those prone to accidents, experiences following the brain damage, etc.).

To satisfy the requirements for causal inference, research designs commonly involve two groups: the "experimental group" experiences X while the "control group" does not. Furthermore, both groups are tested at two points in time (before and after X has occurred). In a "true experiment," the researcher would randomly assign sampling units to experimental and control conditions. Randomization is an important principle of research design because it results in groups which are likely to be comparable in terms of Y (at Time 1) and reduces biasing effects of other uncontrolled variables. Randomization does not guarantee equivalence between groups but is probabilistic in nature. Randomly constructed groups may still differ in important ways.

Quasiexperiments

Randomization is often not feasible. Many causal variables researchers wish to study (brain damage, age, sex, race, socioeconomic status, etc.) are not under experimental control. In other situations, randomization is not ethical. For example, it is often not possible to withhold treatment from certain groups in order to make comparisons. Moreover, even when randomization is feasible and ethically justified, it is occasionally not effective in equating the groups and controlling for extraneous variables. Children may be randomly assigned to treatment and control groups, for instance, but the groups may differ at Time 2 as a result of attrition from one group over the course of the study or differential refusal to participate.

Since randomization is often not feasible, many research studies in the social and behavioral sciences are not "true experiments" but are "quasiexperiments." The goal of both types of experiments is to make causal inferences, but in quasiexperiments the groups are not based on random assignment. The three types of quasiexperimental approaches are (1) nonequivalent control group designs, (2) time series designs, and (3) correlational designs.

NONEQUIVALENT CONTROL GROUP DESIGNS.   As previously mentioned, a common design for causal inference involves two groups measured at two points in time. In the absence of random assignment, such designs are called "nonequivalent control group designs." The term "nonequivalent" arises from the fact that the comparison groups are not based on random assignment and hence may differ in important respects. A simple nonequivalent control group design is outlined in Table 2.2. Y represents the dependent variable assessed at Time 1 (Y_1) and Time 2 (Y_2). X denotes the independent variable or "treat-

Table 2.2.   Examples of Various Research Designs[a]

	Simple Nonequivalent Control Group Design			
	Time 1			Time 2
(Experimental group)	Y_1	X		Y_2
(Control group)	Y_1			Y_2

	Design with Two Control Groups			
	Time 1			Time 2
(Experimental group)	Y_1	X		Y_2
(Control group 1)	Y_1			Y_2
(Control group 2)				Y_2

	Time Series Design								
(Experimental group)	Y_1	Y_2	Y_3	Y_4	X	Y_5	Y_6	Y_7	Y_8	Y_9
(Control group)	Y_1	Y_2	Y_3	Y_4		Y_5	Y_6	Y_7	Y_8	Y_9

	Time Series Design with Switching Replications								
	Y_1	Y_2	X	Y_3	Y_4	Y_5	Y_6	Y_7	Y_8	Y_9
	Y_1	Y_2		Y_3	Y_4 X Y_5		Y_6	Y_7	Y_8	Y_9

[a] Y indicates assessment of the dependent variable; X indicates occurrence of the experimental manipulation.

ment.'' In this simple design, two groups are measured at Time 1 and Time 2. One group is exposed to X, while the other is not. For convenience the group exposed to X is called the ''experimental group,'' whereas the group that does not experience X is called the ''control group.''

Such designs are commonly used in the behavioral and social sciences and are called ''natural experiments.'' They are not true experiments because subjects were not assigned to conditions randomly. Nevertheless, such designs often permit causal inferences. Evidence regarding concomitant variation and time order of effects can be obtained in such designs, but since the groups were not necessarily equivalent at time one, it is necessary to go to greater lengths to rule out alternative explanations for changes in Y. Inferring causality from such designs, however, also depends partly upon the nature of the initial differences between groups as well as the pattern of results that are obtained.

A number of variations in the basic two group nonequivalent control group design have been described by Cook and Campbell (1979) and are worth careful study. Design variations are necessary to counteract or control for various biases which may threaten the validity of the findings. The effects of initial testing, for example, constitute one source of potential bias. For many psychological measures there is a ''practice effect'' whereby scores are enhanced by having taken the test previously. One way to avoid pretesting biases is to employ alternative forms of the test—that is, forms comprised of different items but presumed to measure the same construct.

The design can also be altered to control for pretesting effects. One alteration involves using separate samples for the pretest and posttest. For example, only half of the children in classes A and B may be pretested. Class A then receives the experimental curriculum while class B receives the standard curriculum. At Time 2 the other half of the children in each class are retested (i.e., those children who were not previously tested). Changes caused by the curriculum would be reflected in differences between scores obtained by half samples within each class. Obviously, the validity of such comparisons depends on the comparability of the half samples at Time 1. Comparability may be increased by randomly determining which children are tested at Time 1 and Time 2.

A research design may also be modified to estimate pretesting effects. Table 2.2 illustrates a nonequivalent control group design with two control groups. The Experimental Group receives the pretest and posttest and is exposed to the treatment. Control Group 1 receives the pretest and posttest but not the experimental treatment. Control Group 2 receives the posttest only and no treatment and is used to estimate the magnitude of pretesting effects. If no pretesting effect is expected, the posttest scores for the control groups would be similar (if we assume they were comparable at Time 1). If large pretesting advantage exists, Control Group 1 should obtain higher scores than Control Group 2. Using such a design, it is possible to estimate the effects of the pretest alone. Improvements resulting from experimental treatment may then be calculated as those which are "over and above" improvement attributed to pretesting.

TIME SERIES DESIGNS.   Time series designs involve multiple observations or measurements over time, often on the same unit (individuals or groups). This makes it possible to chart changes in the dependent variable over time and, if it is know when X is introduced, it may be possible to attribute changes in Y to the occurrence of X. A simple time series design is shown in Table 2.2. It is an extension of the basic nonequivalent control group design involving multiple measures over time instead of measures at two points in time.

Time series designs have many advantages. Consider a situation where the effects of X are delayed rather than immediate. Using the simple nonequivalent control group design with one posttest, the effects of X may not be detected. Alternatively, suppose the effects of X are immediate but deteriorate over time. Using a simple nonequivalent control group design, an immediate effect might be documented, but this would lead to an erroneous conclusion regarding the persistence of such effects.

Time series designs have an additional advantage in that experimental control over Y can be demonstrated. One way to demonstrate experimental control is to introduce and remove treatments at various points in time. In a simple ABA design, for example, a treatment may be first introduced (condition A), then withdrawn (condition B), then reintroduced (condition A). Changes in Y

may be shown to be contingent upon the presence of the treatment. Cook and Campbell (1979) described yet another way of demonstrating experimental control over *Y*. One design, the "interrupted time series with switching replications," involves two groups which receive the experimental treatment at different points in time, each group serving as the other's control (see Table 2.2). Thus treatment effects can be documented on two samples at different points in time. For further discussion of statistical and design issued in time series research, readers are referred to Cook and Campbell (1979) and Hersen and Barlow (1976).

Correlational Designs

The goal of some studies is to infer causality from patterns of correlations among variables assessed in naturalistic settings. Such correlational designs are employed, for example, when one cannot control the independent variables under investigation. Two types of correlational methods used in research on exceptional children are outlined briefly here: cross-lagged correlations and structural equation models.

CROSS—LAGGED CORRELATIONS.   Using the cross-lagged correlational method, two variables are assessed at two points in time. Evidence regarding causal relations is derived from two "cross-lagged" correlations. One correlation is between Variable 1 assessed at Time 1 and Variable 2 assessed at Time 2. The other is the reverse—the correlation between Variable 2 assessed at Time 1 and Variable 1 assessed at Time 2. Under certain circumstances, the relative magnitude of such cross-lagged correlations may support a causal argument. If one cross-lagged correlation is significantly higher than the other, a causal priority is established and one may assert that one variable causes the other but not vice versa.

Although the cross-lagged correlational method has been widely endorsed (Crano, 1974, 1977; Humphreys & Stubbs, 1977; Kenny, 1975), it has serious deficiencies. Rogosa (1980), for example, recently demonstrated that for many types of causal effects, cross-lagged correlations yield erroneous conclusions regarding causal structure. Logically, it is easy to see how cross-lagged correlations meet two requirements for causal inference, concomitant variation and time order of occurrence. However, effects of other variables are not ruled out. Extraneous variables may explain the difference between the cross-lagged correlations, and this difference is the sole basis of the causal inference. The potential effects of extraneous variables are particularly problematic in research on exceptional children, because we may not know which variables are crucial when attempting to unravel complex causal relations. Causal inferences drawn from cross-lagged correlations may therefore be misleading.

STRUCTURAL EQUATION MODELS.   Structural equation modeling (also called "path analysis" or "causal modeling") involves the construction of a model which is believed to portray causal relations among selected variables. Unlike the cross-lagged correlational method, relations among many variables may be considered simultaneously and there may be complex causal relations among variables. A causal model may embody reciprocal relations, for instance, wherein two or more variables mutually influence one another. The relative influence of several variables on one or more dependent variables may also be assessed.

Structural equation modeling can be illustrated by a recent study, Olweus' (1980) model of aggressive behavior among adolescent boys. The model, shown in Figure 2.2, is comprised of one dependent variable (boys' aggression as rated by peers) and four independent variables: (1) mothers' negativism early in her son's life, (2) boys' temperament in early life, (3) mothers' permissiveness for aggression, and (4) parents' use of power assertive methods with their sons. Several assumptions were made regarding the causal relations within this model. For example, mother's negativism and boy's temperament in early years are assumed to influence each other mutually. This is indicated by a curved bidirectional arrow in Figure 2.2.

The degree of casual influence between variables is reflected by path coefficients which are determined by multiple regression methods. A path coefficient is a standardized partial regression coefficient and it represents the proportion of variance in one variable that is uniquely explained by another variable. Mothers' permissiveness for aggression, for example, was found to have a large direct effect on boys' aggression (the path coefficient = .321). This means that a change of one standard deviation in mothers' permissiveness scores resulted in a change of .321 standard deviations in boys' aggression scores. Some variables in the model have indirect as well as direct effects on

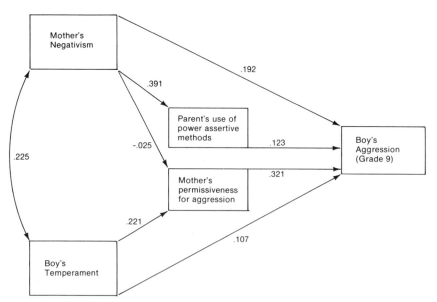

Figure 2.2. Olweus' casual model of aggressive behavior among adolescent boys. (Adapted from Olweus, © 1980 by the American Psychological Association. Reprinted by permission.)

aggression. Boys' temperament, for instance, has a direct effect on aggression. It also has a direct effect on mothers' permissiveness for aggression, which in turn influences boys' aggression. The total causal effect of a variable is the sum of its direct and indirect effects.

Structual equation models can provide *evidence* regarding causal relations but not *proof*. Nevertheless, such models have several advantages. For one, they force investigators to make their assumptions regarding causal structure explicit and to submit their assumptions to statistical tests. Such models can also portray complex causal relations among many variables simultaneously. Structural equation modeling is not an infallible method. Including additional variables in the model, for example, may substantially alter the causal picture. Structural equation models represent a very promising methodology for the behavioral sciences. For a more complete discussion of these methods, readers are referred to treatises by Alwin and Hauser (1975), Bielby and Hauser (1977), Duncan (1975), Heise (1975) and Kenny (1975).

Summary

Proper sampling can reduce biases of uncontrolled variables and increase the generalizability of research findings. Source of subjects, as well as subject characteristics such as sex, age, IQ, developmental level, race, and socioeconomic status should be described in the research report. Sample size and the sampling unit should also be evaluated.

Research designs can be evaluated in terms of three criteria for causal inference: concomitant variation, time order of occurrence, and the elimination of alternative explanations. Several designs, such as the *ex post facto* design, do not permit causal inferences. Because randomization is often not feasible, most research on exceptional children is quasiexperimental. In the nonequivalent control group design, there are treatments, outcomes, and comparison groups, but not random assignment. Time series designs involve multiple measures over time. They have the advantages that experimental control over the dependent variable may be demonstrated and that either delayed or temporary changes may be detected. Correlational designs do not involve direct manipulation of the independent variable. Causal inferences are based on patterns of correlations among variables observed in naturalistic settings. The cross-lagged correlation method has serious weaknesses. Structural equation modeling, on the other hand, appears to be a promising methodology for the behavioral sciences.

Statistical Problems and Issues

Several considerations must be brought to bear on the validity of statistical conclusions in research. The most basic considerations, such as the appropriateness of the statistical analysis for the data at hand, the level of statistical significance, and level of measurement, are covered in introductory statistics texts. This discussion is limited to a few selected problems and issues which arise frequently in research on exceptional children.

Analyzing Change

Although the assessment of changes in behavior over time is a frequent research goal, the analysis of change is a methodologically perilous enterprise. At first glance, analysis of change seems simple enough. One can simply calculate the difference between scores obtained at Time 1 and Time 2 and obtain a measure of the degree to which an individual or group has changed over the course of the study. Several authors have pointed out methodological problems in using such difference scores as an index of change (Harris, 1963; Cronbach & Furby, 1970. Two problems should be noted. First, difference scores are notoriously unreliable. Scores obtained at both Time 1 and Time 2 are likely to be fallible estimates of true scores and, since errors of measurement are additive, the differences between such scores will be even more fallible estimates of true change. There has been considerable discussion regarding the problems and paradoxes which surround the unreliability of change scores (see Cronbach & Gleser, 1972).

The second problem is that difference scores are negatively correlated with initial standing. Individuals who obtained high scores at Time 1 are likely to obtain somewhat lower scores at Time 2. Conversely, those who obtain low scores at Time 1 are likely to obtain higher scores at Time 2. This phenomenon of "regression toward the mean" has been recognized for many years and can seriously bias research designed to detect change.

Regression effects are particularly problematic in research on exceptional children because groups are often defined on the basis of extreme scores, and the more extreme scores are the larger the regression effect. Figure 2.3 illustrates potential regression effects for three groups of children defined by their IQs: gifted (IQ > 130), average (90 < IQ < 110), and retarded (IQ < 70). Even if true scores do not change from Time 1 to Time 2, the mean IQs of the extreme groups would regress toward the mean. Gifted students would decline in their IQs while retarded children would increase. These effects are caused partly by measurement error. At Time 1, an extremely high IQ is comprised of two components: a high true score and some *positive* measurement error which made the obtained IQ even higher. Suppose true scores remain stable. Given the chance of fluctuations of measurement error, the IQ obtained at Time 2 is not likely to be as high as it was at Time 1. A decline in IQ may be obtained, even though the "true" IQ had not changed.

Various solutions have been proposed for dealing with regression effects. Many involve correcting scores to account for the degree of expected regression. Such statistical adjustments are often less than perfect, however, and may result in over- or undercorrection of change scores. Final solutions regarding the analysis of change are not available. Cronbach and Furby (1970) have argued that the problems of analyzing change are so intractable that researchers should seek alternative strategies that avoid analyzing change alto-

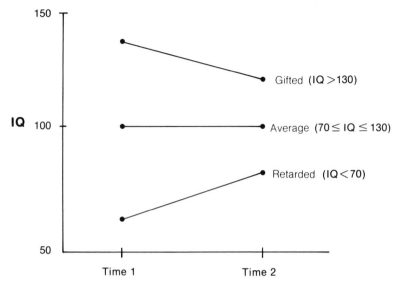

Figure 2.3. Examples of hypothetical regression effects for IQs of gifted, average, and retarded children assessed at two points in time.

gether. Nesselroade, Stigler, and Baltes (1980), however, recently argued that problems created by regression effects can be overcome by obtaining measures at multiple points in time, rather than at two points in time.

Regression effects should be kept in mind when reading and interpreting research reports, particularly since they can contribute to misleading results. Figure 2.3 illustrates hypothetical regression effects in the evaluation of a special curriculum. Suppose children were selected for a special program for the gifted on the basis of having IQs > 130. Due to regression effects, they may obtain lower IQs at Time 2, although their true IQs had not changed. This may lead one to mistakenly conclude that the special program was harmful (cf. Campbell & Erlebacher, 1970)!

Multivariate Statistics

For many years studies of exceptional children dealt with only one variable or characteristic at a time. The goal was to unravel cause and effect relations "one thread at a time." In recent years, however, the trend has been away from such limited "univariate" studies, towards "multivariate" investigations wherein many variables are analyzed at once. This change has occurred partly because of the growing recognition that behavior is complex, multidimensional, and determined by many interrelated factors. Studies concerned with a single variable are now viewed as too narrowly focused and unrepresentative of the "whole child." Moreover, we now know that causal variables interact in complex ways and their net effect upon target variables is not simply the sum of their individual effects.

Sophisticated statistical procedures are required to unravel the interrelations among many variables. Examples of two multivariate statistical procedures—cross-lagged correlations and structural equation modeling—were discussed previously. Other multivariate methods, such as *factor analysis, discriminant analysis,* and *cluster analysis* are becoming more widely used in research on exceptional children and deserve mention here. Readers are also referred to more comprehensive treatises by Harris (1975) and Tatsuoka (1971).

Factor analysis is a statistical procedure for summarizing correlations among many variables in terms of a few "factors" or dimensions. Each factor is comprised of loadings, which reflect the proportion of variance in each variable that is accounted for by the factor. Variables that correlate highly with one another will have high loadings on the same factor and thus comprise an empirical grouping that is often interpretable in terms of an underlying dimension or construct. Peterson (1961), for example, obtained teacher ratings of the behavior problems of school children using a 58 item checklist. He was interested in which behavior problems co-occur to form syndromes of psychopathology. Examining the relations between each item and every other item would obviously be very time consuming (and confusing) since it would involve the consideration of more than 1600 separate correlations. Peterson therefore used factor analysis to summarize these correlations in terms of a parsimonious set of factors.

The factor analysis of teacher ratings revealed two groupings of items that accounted for a large proportion of variance in the correlation matrix. One factor, which Peterson labeled "Conduct Problem," was comprised of outwardly directed, disruptive behaviors such as fighting, arguing, and disobedience. The second factor, labeled "Personality Problem," included inwardly directed behaviors such as feelings of inferiority, social withdrawal, and anxiety. This global distinction between Personality Problems and Conduct Problems has been replicated in many other studies—although the factors have not always been given the same labels (see Achenbach & Edelbrock, 1978; Edelbrock, 1979; Quay, 1979).

Peterson's classic study illustrates how factor analysis can be used as heuristic tool for summarizing complex relations among many variables. Groupings of variables identified by factor analysis often have theoretical meaning and predictive value. The distinction between Personality Problems and Conduct Problems, for example, has been useful in the assessment and classification of child psychopathology.

Discriminant analysis is a multivariate statistical procedure designed to determine the optimal linear combination of variables that best discriminates between predetermined groups of individuals. This procedure is well suited to the task of determiming group membership and is obviously relevant to the diagnosis and classification of exceptional children. Achenbach and Edelbrock (1981), for example, used discriminant analysis to determine the optimal combination of parent-reported behavior problems to distinguish between clinically referred and nonreferred children. In other words, the goal was to find the best weighted combination of behavior problem items to predict whether a child was referred for services or not. The results bear on the problems of screening and identification of children who may warrant referral for mental health services.

Achenbach and Edelbrock used a step-wise discriminant analysis procedure. First, the item that best discriminates between the two criterion groups is added to the discriminant equation. Next, the item that best improves the discrimination between groups is added to the equation. This is repeated until no more items yield significant improvement in discriminative power (i.e., adding more items does not result in more accurate classification of individuals). As is common in discriminant analysis, only a few items (i.e., 3 to 7) were required to maximize predictive power. This is partly because many items are positively correlated with one another, so they make little *unique* contribution to the discriminant equation.

After deriving the discriminant equation, Achenbach and Edelbrock determined how accurately children could be classified according to clinical status. This was determined on a separate sample of children, not the original sample upon which the discriminant equation was derived. Testing the discriminant equation on the original sample would result in spuriously high predictive accuracy, since this would capitalize on chance to some degree. In the cross-validation sample, the discriminant equation resulted in 82.6% correct classifications. This suggests that a small subset of behavior problem items may be used to screen children for mental health services, although this may not be the best methodological alternative (see Achenbach & Edelbrock, 1981, p. 62).

Finally, the term "cluster analysis" encompasses a large, heterogeneous family of statistical procedures designed to identify groups of individuals for purposes of developing a classification. Cluster analysis is a relatively new statistical procedure for the behavioral sciences and is becoming more widely used, particularly in the areas of psychopathology and deviant behavior (see Blashfield, 1976, for a review). Unlike factor analysis, which is typically used to identify groups of correlated items, cluster analysis is typically used to identify homogeneous groups of *individuals*—that is, individuals who share similar characteristics or have similar patterns of scores on selected variables.

There are numerous clustering methods and they differ in the ways in which they construct groups (see Anderberg, 1973 for a review of clustering methods). Hierarchical methods construct groups by stepwise amalgamations of individuals into larger and larger clusters, or by splitting the entire sample into successively smaller and smaller clusters. Many nonhierarchical methods, by contrast, begin with a random grouping then rearrange individuals so as to optimize some statistical criterion. For instance, individuals may be rearranged to maximize the within-group homogeneity of the resulting clusters.

Cluster analysis has not been used widely in research on exceptional children, but we may expect more clustering studies in the future. In one of the first applications of cluster analysis in this area, Spivack, Swift, and Prewitt

(1971) used a hierarchical clustering method to identify subgroups of school children manifesting similar patterns of scores on the Devereux Elementary School Behavior Rating Scales. Six clusters were obtained in separate analyses of children in grades K through 6. Children in these clusters were found to differ significantly in IQ, school achievement, parents' education, race, and gender. More recent applications of cluster analysis in research on exceptional children have been reported by Edelbrock and Achenbach (1980) and by Eisenberg, Gersten, Langner, McCarthy, and Simcha-Fagan (1976).

Multiple Comparisons

Many studies of exceptional children represent "fishing expeditions" wherein researchers assess numerous characteristics of one or more groups then analyze all possible relationships and differences. Findings that are statistically significant can then be presented as if they pertained to the original hypotheses of the study, which were in fact nonexistent. More often than not, such nominally "significant" findings do not replicate in subsequent studies. Why?

Significant results obtained in fishing expeditions are often statistical artifacts, not genuine findings. Statistical significance, of course, is not a guarantee that findings are real. Level of significance simply represents the chance of being wrong when the null hypothesis is rejected. In other words, significance level represents the probability of making a Type 1 error. The "problem of multiple comparisons" arises when numerous statistical tests are made. Specifically, the probability of making Type I errors increases rapidly as the number of statistical tests increase. In running 100 correlations, for example, we would expect five significant correlations ($p < .05$), even with *perfectly random data*. Sometimes we would find less than five significant correlations and other times we would find more, but on the average we would find five "significant" correlations that were artifacts.

In making several statistical tests, therefore, it is necessary to make adjustments to control for Type I errors. Several adjustments have been proposed (cf. Larzelere & Mulaik, 1977). One involves simply raising the significance level, from $p < .05$ to $p < .01$, for example. This reduces the risk of making Type I errors but does not completely eliminate the problem, particularly when numerous statistical tests are run. An alternative procedure involves replicating findings across samples. Replication is a general principle for reducing artifactual findings and it is easy to show how this would help solve the problems of multiple comparisons. In the previous example involving random data, for instance, suppose we replicated the 100 correlations on two independent samples. We would expect five correlations to be significant ($p < .05$) in each sample. However, it would be extremely unlikely that the *same two variables* would be significantly correlated in both samples. In fact, assuming independence among variables and samples, the chance of the same two variables being significantly correlated in both samples is less than .0025— a fairly remote possibility.

Raising significance criteria and replicating findings are two simple procedures for reducing Type I errors. More sophisticated procedures have been proposed that are appropriate for various statistical methods and research situations (cf. Larzelere & Mulaik, 1977). Researchers may or may not follow such procedures, however, so it is important to remember that multiple comparisons can yield misleading statistical conclusions.

Developmental versus Trait Variance

Many behavioral measures are highly correlated with developmental level. This creates problems in research aimed at determining relationships among various behavioral traits and abilities. Specifically, correlations among behavioral indices may be artifacts of their common correlation with developmental level, rather than revealing relations among underlying traits. This is a serious problem in research on exceptional children where developmental differences among subjects may be large. In determining relations among various behavioral measures, therefore, it is necessary to control for developmental differences.

This can be done by matching subjects on developmental indices such as chronological or mental age. Taylor and Achenbach (1975) explored the relationships between moral and cognitive development among normal and retarded children. Since cognitive tasks and moral judgment scores were correlated with mental age, the relations between such measures may have been due to their mutual association with developmental level. In determining the relations between cognitive and moral measures, therefore, the overall effect of mental age was removed by matching normal and retarded children on mental age.

The confounding effects of developmental level can also be controlled by statistical adjustments. Achenbach and Weisz (1975), for instance, sought to determine the relationship between Impulsivity/Reflectivity and hypothesis behavior. In a preliminary analysis, reflective children were found to employ significantly more hypotheses than impulsive children. However, both Impulsivity/Reflectivity scores and hypothesis behavior were strongly related to mental age. Using analysis of covariance to control for differences in mental age, Achenbach and Weisz found that Impulsivity/Reflectivity accounted for *no unique variance* in hypothesis behavior.

Personal Perspective

The goal of this chapter has been to outline a strategy for reading research on exceptional children. Selected problems and issues regarding sampling, design, and statistical analysis have also been discussed. It is hoped that this chapter will be helpful in reading and evaluating research, although it represents a cursory treatment of an almost limitless topic. Potential researchers, as well as consumers of research, are encouraged to delve further into the complexities of research methods. Increased expertise regarding research will be rewarded by an increased understanding of our collective knowledge regarding exceptional children. It will also prevent misinterpretation and misapplication of research findings. Some words of caution are also necessary. The more one learns about research methods and statistics, the less adequate *all* studies appear. Although researchers aspire to do competent work, no research study is perfect. Every study has flaws and limitations. At the same time, almost all studies make some contribution to our knowledge. While research articles should be critically evaluated, they should also be read with an eye for what new and useful information such studies can reveal.

Of course it is not advisable to take the results of any study at face value. A study may report findngs of dramatic importance—but they may be wrong. If we simply took research results at their face value, we might base policy and practice on erroneous conclusions. Fortunately, the scientific enterprise has self-corrective mechanisms. Science is a joint effort of many investigators uncovering a network of interrelated findings—replicating, extending, and refining our collective knowledge. A dramatic finding, for example, may not replicate in subsequent studies or additional work may uncover a crucial flaw or methodological artifact unseen in the original investigation. This should be kept in mind when reading a research report.

Research results must also be interpreted in a broad context. Progress can rarely be attributed to a single study. Even studies that report impressive "breakthroughs" are subject to independent corroboration and refinement. Studies that appear to "single-handedly" advance our understanding are doubtlessly based on previous research and theory. Despite the appearance of being isolated contributions, such studies are intimately linked to previous work. No study stands alone and the contribution each study makes does not represent a definitive achievement. The findings of any one study must be interpreted with respect to a broader network of research results and theoretical formulations—*past, present,* and *future.*

The future of research on exceptional children looks promising and exciting. We may expect research in this area to incorporate better assessment instruments, more elaborate research designs, and more sophisticated multivariate statistical procedures to unravel the mysteries of exceptional children. I believe that studies of exceptional children will also begin to bridge the gap between *research* and *practice.* The gap between these "two worlds" is wide, but it is beginning to narrow. Many research efforts are undertaken with some hope of relevance to education, remediation, or clinical practice. Unfortunately, few research results are translated into practice. Researchers are becoming more aware of the practical applications of their findings, however, and in a larger sense, society is demanding more accountability regarding their investment in research. Thus we may expect research to address more socially relevant problems in the future—problems such as the prevention of disabling conditions in children, remediation of childhood deficits, and specialized education and training for exceptional children. This does not mean that research will become more "applied" and less "basic." The need for basic research on exceptional children has never been greater. This does mean, however, that the translation of research findings into action on behalf of exceptional children will increase.

Finally, we may expect increasing collaboration between researchers and practitioners and between professionals in different disciplines in research on exceptionality. Progress on behalf of exceptional children is not solely in the hands of researchers. Practitioners, teachers, administrators, clinicians, pediatricians, and others concerned with children are becoming more attuned to the contributions that research can make to their activities and programs. Such consumers of research are also becoming more intelligent in their appraisal and use of research findings. It is hoped that this chapter will make some small contribution to such future collaborative efforts.

REFERENCES

Achenbach, T. M. *Research in developmental psychology: Concepts, strategies, methods.* New York: Free Press, 1978.

Achenbach, T. M. Psychopathology of childhood: Research problems and issues. *Journal of Consulting and Clinical Psychology,* 1977, *46,* 759–776.

Achenbach, T. M., & Edelbrock, C. The classification of child psychopathology: A review and analysis of empirical efforts. *Psychological Bulletin,* 1978, *85,* 1275–1301.

Achenbach, T. M., & Edelbrock, C. Behavioral problems and competencies reported by parents of normal and disturbed children aged 4 through 16. *Monographs of the Society for Research in Child Development,* 1981, *46*(Serial No. 188).

Achenbach, T. M., & Weisz, J. R. Impulsivity-reflectivity and cognitive development in preschoolers: A longitudinal analysis of developmental and trait variance. *Developmental Psychology,* 1975, *11,* 413–414.

Alwin, D. F., & Hauser, R. M. The decomposition of effects in path analysis. *American Sociological Review,* 1975, *40,* 37–47.

Anderberg, M. R. *Cluster analysis for applications.* New York: Academic, 1973.

Ashcraft, M. H., & Kellas, G. Organization in normal and retarded children: Temporal aspects of storage and retrieval. *Journal of Experimental Psychology,* 1974, *103,* 502–508.

Berk, R. A. Generalizability of behavioral observations: A clarification of interobserver agreement and interobserver reliability. *American Journal of Mental Deficiency,* 1979, *83,* 460–472.

Bielby, W. T., & Hauser, R. M. Structural equation models. *Annual Review of Sociology,* 1977, *3,* 137–161.

Blashfield, R. K. Evaluation of the DSM-II classification of schizophrenia as a nomenclature. *Journal of Abnormal Psychology,* 1973, *82,* 382–389.

Blashfield, R. K., & Draguns, J. G. Evaluative criteria for psychiatric classification. *Journal of Abnormal Psychology,* 1976, *85,* 140–150.

Brand, M. *The nature of causation.* Urbana: University of Illinois Press, 1976.

Campbell, D. T., & Erlebacher, A. E. How regression artifacts in quasi-experimental evaluations can mistakenly make compensatory education look harmful. In J. Hellmuth (Ed.), *Compensatory education: A national debate* (Vol. 3). New York: Brunner/Mazel, 1970.

Campbell, D. T., & Fiske, D. W. Convergent and discriminant validation by the multitrait-multimethod matrix. *Psychological Bulletin,* 1959, *56,* 89–105.

Cohen, J. *Statistical power analysis for the behavioral sciences* (rev. ed.). New York: Academic, 1977.

Cook, T. D., & Campbell, D. T. *Quasi-experimentation: Design and analysis issues for field settings.* Chicago: Rand McNally, 1979.

Crano, W. D. Casual analysis of the effects of socioeconomic status and initial intellectual development on patterns of cognitive development and academic achievement. In D. Green (Ed.), *The aptitude-achievement distinction.* New York: McGraw-Hill, 1974.

Crano, W.D. What do infant mental tests test? A cross-lagged panel analysis of selected data from the Berkeley Growth Study. *Child Development,* 1977, *48,* 144–151.

Cronbach, L. J., & Furby, L. How should we measure "change" —or should we? *Psychological Bulletin,* 1970, *74,* 68–80.

Cronbach, L. J., Gleser, G. C., Nanda, H., & Rajaratnam, N. *The dependability of behavioral measures.* New York: Wiley, 1972.

Duncan, O. D. *Introduction to structural equation models.* New York: Academic, 1975.

Edelbrock, C. Empirical classification of children's behavioral disorders: Progress based on parent and teacher ratings. *School Psychology Digest,* 1979, *8,* 355–369.

Edelbrock, C., Achenbach, T. M. A typology of Child Behavior Profile paterns: Distribution and correlates for disturbed children aged 6–16. *Journal of Abnormal Child Psychology,* 1980, *8,* 441–470.

Edelbrock, C. S., & Reed, M. Temporal stability of children's problem behavior in classroom settings. Manuscript in preparation, 1981.

Eisenberg, J. G., Gertsen, J. C., Langner, T. S., McCarthy, E. D., & Simcha-Fagan, O. A behavioral classification of welfare children from survey data. *American Journal of Orthopsychiatry,* 1976, *46,* 447–463.

Foster, G. G., & Salvia, J. Teacher response to label of learning disabled as a function of demand characteristics. *Exceptional Children,* 1977, *43,* 533–534.

Foster, G. G., Ysseldyke, J. E., & Reese, J. H. I wouldn't have seen it if I hadn't believed it. *Exceptional Children,* 1975, *41,* 469–473.

Graham, E. E., & Shapiro, E. Use of the performance scale of the Wechsler Intelligence Scale for children with the deaf child. *Journal of Consulting Psychology,* 1953, *17,* 396–398.

Harris, C. W. (Ed.). *Problems in measuring change.* Madison: University of Wisconsin Press, 1963.

Harris, R. J. *A primer of multivariate statistics.* New York: Academic, 1975.

Heise, D. R. *Causal analysis.* New York: Wiley, 1975.

Hersen, M., & Barlow, D. H. *Single case exerimental designs.* New York: Pergamon, 1976.

Hindley, C. B., & Owen, C. F. The extent of individual changes in IQ for ages between

6 months and 17 years, in a British longitudinal sample. *Journal of Child Psychology and Psychiatry,* 1978, *19,* 329–350.

Hobbs, N. *Issues in the classification of children.* San Francisco: Jossey-Bass, 1975.

Humphreys, L. G., & Stubbs, J. A longitudinal analysis of teacher expectation, student expectation, and student achievement. *Journal of Educational Measurement,* 1977, *14,* 261–270.

Kazdin, A. E. Artifact, bias, and complexity of assessment: The ABC's of reliability. *Journal of Applied Behavioral Analysis,* 1977, *10,* 141–150.

Kelly, M., Scholnick, E. F., Travers, S. H., & Johnson, J. W. Relations among memory, memory appraisal, and memory strategies. *Child Development,* 1976, *47,* 648–659.

Kenny, D. A. Cross-lagged panel correlation: A test for spuriousness. *Psychological Bulletin,* 1975, *82,* 887–903.

Keogh, B. K., Major, S. M., Omori, H., Gandara, P., & Reid, H. P. Proposed markers in learning disabilities research. *Journal of Abnormal Child Psychology,* 1980, *8,* 21–31.

Kerlinger, F. N. *Foundations of behavioral research* (2nd ed.). New York: Holt, Rinehart & Winston, 1973.

L'Abate, L. Early infantile autism: A reply to Ward. *Psychological Bulletin,* 1972, *77,* 49–51.

Larzelere, R. E. & Mulaik, S. A. Single sample tests for many correlations. *Psychological Bulletin,* 1977, *84,* 557–569.

MacMillan, D. L., Morrison, G. M., & Silverstein, A. B. Convergent and discriminant validity of Project PRIME's Guess Who? *American Journal of Mental Deficiency,* 1980, *85,* 78–81.

McCall, R. B. *Fundamental statistics for psychology* (3rd ed.). New York: Harcourt Brace Jovanovich, 1980.

McCall, R. B. Nature-nurture and the two realms of development: A proposed integration with respect to mental development. *Child Development,* 1981, *52,* 1–12.

McCall, R. B., Appelbaum, M. I., & Hogarty, P. S. Developmental changes in mental performance. *Monographs of the Society for Research in Child Development,* 1973, *38,* (3, Serial No. 150).

Milgram, N. A. Retention of mediation set in paired associate learning of normal and retarded children. *Journal of Experimental Child Psychology,* 1967, *5,* 341–349.

Nesselroade, J. R., Stigler, S. M., & Baltes, P. B. Regression toward the mean and the study of change. *Psychological Bulletin,* 1980, *88,* 622–637.

Olweus, D. Familial and tempermental determinants of aggressive behavior in adolescent boys: A causal analysis. *Developmental Psychology,* 1980, *16,* 644–660.

Peterson, D. R. Behavior problems of middle childhood. *Journal of Consulting Psychololgy,* 1961, *25,* 205–209.

Quay, H. C. Classification. In H. C. Quay, & J. S. Werry (Eds.), *Psychopathological Disorders of childhood* (2nd ed.). New York: Wiley, 1979.

Reichart, G. J., Cody, W. J., & Borkowski, J. G. Training and transfer of clustering and cumulative rehearsal strategies in retarded individuals. *American Journal of Mental Deficiency,* 1975, *79,* 648–658.

Rimland, B. Comment on Ward's "early infantile autism." *Psychological Bulletin,* 1972, *77,* 52–53.

Rogosa, D. A. critique of cross-lagged correlation. *Psychological Bulletin,* 1980, *88,* 245–258.

Rutter, M., Tizard, J., & Whitmore, K. *Education, health, and behavior.* London: Longman, 1970.

Sabatino, D. A. When a definition is in trouble, there may be trouble with the definition. *Journal of Pediatric Psychology,* 1979, *4,* 221–228.

Salatas, H., & Flavell, J. H. Behavioral and meta-mnemonic indicators of strategic behavior under remember instructions in first grade. *Child Development,* 1976, *47,* 80–89.

Salvia, J., Clark, G. M., & Ysseldyke, J. E. Teacher retention of stereotypes of exceptionality. *Exceptional Children,* 1973, *39,* 651–652.

Sattler, J. M. *Assessment of children's intelligence.* Philadelphia: W. B. Saunders, 1974.

Schere, R. A., Richardson, E., & Bialer, I. Toward operationalizing a psychoeducational definition of learning disabilities. *Journal of Abnormal Child Psychology,* 1980, *8,* 5–20.

Selltiz, C., Jahoda, M., Deutsch, M., & Cook, S. W. Research methods in social relations (rev. ed.). New York: Holt, Rinehart & Winston, 1959.

Selye, H. What makes basic research basic? *Saturday Evening Post,* 1959, *231,* 30–31.

Spivack, G., Swift, M., & Prewitt, J. Syndromes of disturbed classroom behavior: A behavioral diagnostic system for elementary school. *Journal of Special Education,* 1971, *5,* 269–292.

Tatsuoka, M. M. *Multivariate analysis.* New York: Wiley, 1971.

Taylor, J., & Achenbach, T. M. Moral and cognitive development in normal and retarded children. *American Journal of Mental Deficiency,* 1975, *80,* 43–50.

Turnbull, A. P. Teaching retarded persons to rehearse through cumulative overt labeling. *American Journal of Mental Deficiency,* 1974, *79,* 331–337.

Ward, A. J. Early infantile autism: Diagnosis, etiology, and treatment. *Psychological Bulletin,* 1970, *73,* 350–362.

Weinberg, G. H., & Schumaker, J. A. *Statistics: An intuitive approach* (2nd ed.). Belmont, Calif.: Brooks-Cole, 1969.

Werner, E. E., Bierman, J. M., & French, F. E. *The children of Kauai.* Honolulu: University of Hawaii Press, 1971.

Werner, E. E., & Smith R. S. *Kauai's children come of age.* Honolulu: University of Hawaii Press, 1977.

Winschel, J. F., Ensher, G. L., & Blatt, B. Curriculum strategies for the mentally retarded: An argument in three parts. *Education and Training of the Mentally Retarded,* 1977, 26–31.

PART TWO

Perspectives on General Issues Regarding Exceptional Children

CHAPTER 3

Neuropsychological Bases of Exceptionality

CHARLES J. GOLDEN AND GRETA N. WILKENING

Attitudes toward the brain, as held by psychologists and educators, have varied greatly over the years. We have recently gone through a period in which the brain was seen as significantly irrelevant when compared to such factors as environment, learning, and proper developmental experiences (e.g., Ross, 1976), but this state of affairs has begun to change. We have again come to recognize what should be a simple fact; almost all behavior, and certainly all behavior we consider as important to being human, is mediated through the brain. While this does not suggest that all behavioral dysfunction is caused by brain dysfunction or abnormality, it does force us to take a closer look at the important interaction between individuals' environments and their processing of the information gathered from that environment in the central nervous system.

It is important to recognize that there is no single "organic brain syndrome"; virtually any symptom of abnormal behavior that one can name can arise, under the proper circumstances and with the proper injury, from a dysfunction of the brain. Thus our focus changes from looking at the occasional brain-injured child with "classic" symptoms to an attempt to understand the way in which the brain works, the ways in which it may become dysfunctional, and the ways in which many forms of abnormal behavior in the child, adolescent, and adult arise from brain damage.

We must develop an understanding of how the brain works. This is an area of many myths which have usually been the result of people theorizing from inadequate data. Only in the relatively recent past have we begun to understand brain function better through the use of noninvasive techniques which actually allow us to see the brain as it exists in the living individual. Although such procedures are new, we are collecting valuable and objective knowledge about brain function at a rate faster than at any time in the history of this field. One realization that has become clear is that the brain is an incredibly complex organ for which the simplistic theories of the past are simply not adequate. We need to review briefly the historical antecedents to modern theories of brain function.

HISTORICAL DEVELOPMENT OF THE BRAIN

It is traditional in reviews such as this to attempt to trace the roots of neuropsychology back as far as possible. The present authors are not aware of any earlier beginning for neuropsychology than the era of the cavemen. Early cave drawings show a crude but nonetheless accurate awareness of brain–behavior relationships (i.e., people without heads do not perform as well as people with heads—it is actually not clear if the brain was recognized as being in the head; Chapman & Wolff, 1959). From this point, there was little progress for several thousands of years until the time of the Greeks who became interested in the ventricles, fluid-filled spaces in the brain. (Readers who are not familiar with brain anatomy are referred to Golden, 1981a, for a short discussion of relevant terms.) The Greeks argued that since intelligence and thought were "fluid," they must be represented by a fluid medium.

The Romans, in the early centuries of the Christian era, began to develop remarkably modern ideas about the roles of the more solid structures of the brain. However, such ideas were eventually rejected as being inconsistent with the classic Greek views that had become accepted as the only rational way to explain behavior. This state of affairs lasted through the dark ages and into the early Renaissance period. As civilization emerged from the dark ages, scientists concerned themselves with developing more accurate maps of the ventricular system. However, as increased attention was focused on the brain, interest also began to develop in examining cortical structures (Golden, 1981a).

It was not until the 1800s, and the work of Gall, that modern neuropsychological theory began to develop (Krech, 1962). Gall postulated that the brain consisted of numerous individual organs, referring to what are today viewed simply as specific cortical areas. Each organ, he stated, has a specific psychological function such as reading, writing, arithmetic, walking, talking, and friendliness. Furthermore, the size of a given organ determined the amount of skill a person had in a given area. For instance, a person who was good at reading was assumed to have a large reading organ. Brain injury caused deficits in specific skills by interfering with those organs which controlled a given function. If an organ was intact, the skill was intact. This belief about the significance of organ size led to the study of skull configuration, because it was postulated that if an underlying organ was large, the skull in that area would be pushed out forming a "bump" and if an organ was small, there would be a valley in the skull. These postulates led to the study of the skull and the clinical diagnosis of personality and intellectual skill on the basis of skull configuration, the field of phrenology (Luria, 1980).

Gall's theories, of course, served as the forerunner of the localizationist doctrine, suggesting that each area of the brain has a specific function which is exercised in isolation from skills in the rest of the brain. This assumption met great resistance in many scientific circles of the time. Of Gall's opponents, one of the most influential and persuasive was Flourens (Luria, 1980). Flourens did not believe localizationist doctrine, and set out to do a series of experiments disproving such theories. Using pigeons and chickens, Flourens selectively removed parts of their brains. On the basis of these experiments, Flourens found little support for Gall's localizationist doctrine. He found that the area of the chicken or animal brain that was removed made little difference in the nature of the symptoms shown by the chicken or hen. The only thing that seemed to make a difference was a mass of the lesion; large lesions seemed to cause much more impairment than small lesions.

Based on these results, Flourens postulated the assumptions that underlie the equipotential theory of brain function. He stated that all areas of the brain are equipotential; there is no differentiation of brain tissue for psychological behavior as suggested by the localizationists. It is from this assumption that the name equipotentialism comes, with the name indicating that all brain tissue is equivalent in terms of what it does or can do. A second, related assumption is the postulate of mass action. Since all brain tissue is equal, the effects of brain injury are determined by the size of the injury rather than its location. Another well-known proponent of the equipotential approach to the understanding of brain behavior relationships was Lashley (1929).

These two theories, with minor changes, have essentially remained the same since the time of the first studies. Localizationists have become more precise in defining specific skills and have rejected the assumptions underlying phrenology. However, they continue to publish maps of the skulls showing the function associated with each area of the brain. Equipotentialists have limited their theories to higher cortical functions, generally acknowledging the localization of basic skills such as motor functions, auditory reception, and visual reception.

These two approaches have generally dominated American psychology and education. Most theories of brain function, rehabilitation, and assessment utilize the assumptions of one of these approaches in their formulations, though these underlying theoretical beliefs have not always been recognized or stated by the individuals formulating these theories. For example, the classic descriptions of "the brain-damaged child" include attentional deficits, emotional lability, coordination difficulties, and poor academic functioning as being characteristic of such children. Though never stated, such a description implies that all brain-damaged children are alike, regardless of the localization of their injury, and that the brain is homogeneous in terms of function; for example, reflects equipotential thinking.

Despite this, neither the equipotentiality nor the localizationist approach has enjoyed universal acceptance. Many modern theorists have begun to question the assumptions underlying both of them. For example, localizationist theory has been criticized since many clinical and experimental cases have been observed with lesions in a specific area which are not accompanied by the symptoms predicted by localizationist theory. In other cases, a specific area may be intact but the patient still shows symptoms associated with that area. Equipotentiality theory has similar problems. Some small lesions result in extensive deficits, whereas some large lesions produce relatively few problems in comparison. For example, Halstead (1947) was unable to find any support for the doctrine of mass action in his extensive studies of brain injured patients.

Luria's Alternative

The evidence in regard to the inadequacies of both the localizationist and equipotential approach to brain–behavior relationships has resulted in a growing exploration of alternatives to these basic theories. Probably the most comprehensive and well-known alternative was postulated by the Soviet neuropsychologist A. R. Luria. Luria, in his extensive publications, noted that any alternative theory must do three things: (1) explain the data that fit the localizationist hypothesis; (2) explain the data that support the equipotential hypothesis; and (3) explain the data inconsistent with one or both theories. (See Luria, 1973, for the most basic introduction to his theory, or Golden, 1981a, or Reynolds, 1981, for an introduction to Luria's thinking.)

Luria developed a set of alternative hypotheses to describe brain function. The most basic and important concept in this theory is that of the *functional system*. A functional system is probably best explained by first looking to the operation of the rest of the human body (Mecacci, 1979). Mecacci suggests that the function of a brain system is similar to the function of other systems, such as the digestive system. For example, if we were to remove the stomach from a person, we would find that digestion had stopped in that person. Using the same techniques as employed by localizationist research, we would then conclude that the stomach is the digestion center of the body. (Indeed, the same methodology was used to identify the function of various areas of the brain.)

It is clear that the assignment of digestion to the stomach alone is a fallacious assumption. Although the stomach plays a specific role in digestion, it is not solely responsible for that process. If the rest of the digestive system were removed, the stomach would not be able to carry on digestion by itself. The brain, Luria (1973, 1980) suggests, operates in a similar manner. Each area of the brain can operate only in conjunction with other areas of the brain to produce a behavior. No area of the brain is singly responsible for any voluntary human behavior. However, just as the stomach plays a specific role in the digestive system, each area of the brain plays a specific role in given behaviors. The assumption that functional systems produce behavior is consistent, to some degree, with both the equipotential and localization theories. Like the equipotential theory, Luria regards behavior as the result of an interaction of many areas of the brain. Like the localizationist theory, Luria assigns a specific role to each area of the brain.

However, Luria's theory has clear disagreements with both the localization and the equipotentiality approaches. Luria assumed that only specific parts, not all parts of the brain, combine to form a behavior. Furthermore, there is no equipotentiality of brain tissue. Brain tissue is conceptualized as being specialized both psychologically and physiologically. Localizationist assumptions of centers for specific observable behaviors are in contradiction to this theory. Behavior is conceived of as being a function of systems of brain areas rather than unitary specific areas. A given behavior will be impaired when any part of the functional system responsible for the behavior is impaired. Thus, for example, some individuals without injury to the "reading center" still are unable to learn to read if there is damage to any of the number of parts of the functional system for reading.

Some additional assumptions need to be made to account for all observations. The most important of these is the concept of *alternative* functional systems. This concept suggests that a given behavior may be produced by more than one functional system. In more colloquial terms, there is more than one way to skin a cat—and more than one way to engage in most behaviors. This principle both accounts for the lack of expected deficits in some patients and explains many cases of spontaneous recovery of behavior despite permanent damage to the brain. (Cases of recovery after temporary damage need not be explained by this assumption.) This recovery can take place in several ways. In some cases, higher level brain skills can compensate for lower level skills. For example, an adult with a partial deficit in auditory discrimination may compensate by using lip reading to supplement his or her ability to decode spoken language and use the context of the talk to decipher further words or phrases which were not understood. Under informal conditions, it may be impossible to notice any deficit in such individuals.

Recovery can be enhanced by using lower skills for higher level skills. For example, a person may lose the ability to generate problem-solving strategies after certain injuries. By teaching this person a concrete approach to problems that requires no independent generation of a problem-solving strategy this deficit can be minimized. Finally, the role of the injured area may be assumed by other areas of the brain. The brain, under the right conditions, is indeed plastic and the normal organization of skills is not absolute. In addition, by changing the nature of the task (e.g., by changing the composition of the functional system used to complete a task), we can change where in the brain the information is processed. This might involve using another input or output modality, or changing the verbal or nonverbal emphasis of the information transmitted to the patient.

Luria's theory, based on these assumptions, is attractive in that it can explain nearly all the observations which have been made of brain injured patients, regardless of the approach used to generate that information. However, we should recognize that it remains a theoretical structure and that while consistent with current data, it is not necessarily more correct than were the former models. There still remains much we do not understand about the operation of the brain. Indeed, despite our growing sophistication, we remain relatively primitive in our analysis of brain–behavior relationships. This theory does, however, fit the data currently available (see Golden, 1981a) and provides, as we shall see, a strong theoretical basis for understanding the neuropsychology of exceptionality.

STRUCTURE OF FUNCTIONAL SYSTEMS

To understand fully the applications of Luria's theories, we need to understand how functional systems work. As noted previously, Luria assigns specific functions to each of the areas of the brain, with this assignment based on both physiological data and psychological observations. Each area in turn participates in functional systems. An area can be involved in any number of functional systems, depending on the importance to the person's behavior of the discrete skill mediated by that area. The multiple functional role of each area of the brain is referred to as *pluripotentiality*. This distinguishes it from equipotentiality (or the localizationist theory). An area can then be involved in relatively few or many behaviors.

The specific areas involved in a behavior depend upon how the behavior has been taught (Luria, 1980). The person taught a phonetic approach to reading does not use the same functional systems for reading as the sight reader. As a consequence, we can never assume that because overt behaviors are similar the underlying functional systems are the same. Indeed, such assumptions about equivalence of underlying functional systems are a major error even in many theories that outwardly agree with Luria's basic conceptions. Thus a test administered to a child as a measure of specific neuropsychological skills may not, in fact, measure what we assume it does. This can lead to significant misunderstandings about the neuropsychological basis of a behavior and to inappropriate treatment or rehabilitative programs.

To understand further functional systems, we must have some recognition of the basic skills which go into any given functional system. It is not within the scope of this chapter to describe Luria's entire theory, so an attempt will be made only to give a general description of these skills. The reader is referred to Golden (1981a) for a more structured introduction and to Luria (1973, 1980) for a more intensive explanation of the basic theory.

Luria divides the brain into three basic units. In addition, two of these units are further subdivided into more distinctive areas. Each of these units is involved in *all* behavior without exception, although the relative contribution of each unit will vary with the behavior. Similarly, the role of specific areas within each unit will vary with every behavior. The three units can be described as Arousal and Attention Processes (Unit I), Sensory Reception and Integration, (Unit II) and Motor Execution, Planning, and Evaluation, (Unit III). The location of these units of the brain is depicted schematically in Figure 3.1.

First Unit

The Arousal Unit (Unit I) consists of those parts of the brain identified as the Reticular Activating System (RAS). This system is a collection of diffuse intertwined structures which act to raise or lower cortical arousal. The structure itself extends from the pons and medulla through the thalamus to the cortex. The system is absolutely necessary for survival and behavior, since without

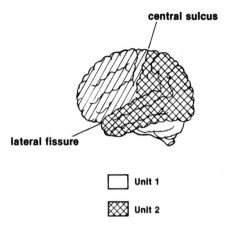

central sulcus

lateral fissure

☐ Unit 1

▨ Unit 2

▨ Unit 3

Figure 3.1. Lateral surface of left cerebral hemisphere indicating the general location of the three functional units. Unit 1 is largely represented in the medial (internal) aspect of the brain, which is not pictured here.

arousal the cortex is unable to respond to incoming stimuli. Disorders of the RAS can vary in the extreme, from narcolepsy (chronic, pathological sleep) to insomnia.

In addition to its role in arousal, the RAS is also responsible for the filtering of input, especially from those senses which are always "on" (tactile/kinesthetic, auditory). This prevents the cortex from being flooded with constant, irrelevant stimuli which can interfere with cognitive processing. Thus this system plays an important role in focusing attention, concentration, and similar tasks.

Second Unit

The second unit is the sensory reception and integration unit. This unit is responsible for most early life learning skills, as well as for many of the abilities tapped by tests of intelligence for young children.

The second unit can be subdivided into three types of areas: primary, secondary, and tertiary. The primary areas act as sensory reception areas. Of all of the areas of the cortex, this area is the most "hard wired," meaning that the functions of the primary areas and the connections within the area are largely predetermined by genetics. In the primary areas, input is received on a general "point-to point" basis from the appropriate sensory organs. It is at this stage as well that initial cortical integration of the material occurs. In the second unit, there are three primary areas, each devoted to a specific sense. The auditory primary area is in the temporal lobe; the visual primary area is in the occipital lobe; and the tactile/kinesthetic primary area is in the parietal lobe. There is little difference in the primary areas of the two hemispheres. One can be injured very early in life with only minor effects (Dennis & Whitaker, 1977; Golden, 1981b; Lewin, 1980). Destruction of both primary areas for a given modality results in such conditions as cortical blindness or cortical deafness.

There is a secondary area corresponding to each of the primary areas of the second unit. It is the role of the secondary area to analyze and integrate the information received at the primary areas. Thus the acoustic secondary area (in the temporal lobe) is responsible for analyzing sounds, organizing them into phonemes, pitch, tone, rhythm, and so on. The secondary visual area (in the occipital lobe) does the analogous task for vision, differentiating foreground from background, detecting movement, analyzing color, shape, and form, and so on. The secondary tactile area (in the parietal lobe) will analyze direction, strength, localization of touch, movement of muscles and joints, and so on.

The secondary areas of the second unit process information sequentially. This allows us to be aware of stimulus changes (e.g., detect movement) and to link events temporally. This is an important function. For example, in the case of speech, phonemes must be sequentially linked in order to form words and sentences. Injuries to the secondary area generally will first affect the sequential nature of the analysis. For example, a person may be able to understand two but not three phonemes in a row, after a partial injury to the auditory secondary area. An individual may only be able to examine one object at a time, or one word (or letter) at a time in injuries to the secondary visual area. Injuries to the secondary parietal area will not impair sensation, but may inhibit two point discrimination, detection of direction of movement, or recognition of shapes or letters traced on the skin.

At the secondary level there is a greater differentiation of function between the parts of the second unit in the left and right hemispheres. The left hemisphere (in most individuals) predominates in the analysis of verbal, overlearned material while the right hemisphere predominates in the analysis of nonverbal material, especially spatial relationships and musical skills. However, it should be recognized that both hemispheres play a role in most behaviors. Thus there are linguistic skills mediated by the right hemisphere [as in the recognition of long, complex words (McKay & Golden, 1981), and the perception and retention of consonant sounds (Luria, 1980)] and the left hemisphere is capable of some spatial analysis (as in recognition of familiar figures). Indeed for many behaviors there is an interaction between the hemispheres that is necessary for efficient behavior. Physiologically, there are large tracts in the brain (chiefly the corpus callosum) the purpose of which is the integration and coordination of behavior between the hemispheres.

Another way of looking at the right–left hemisphere differences is in terms of how overlearned material may be. In the case of music, for example, primary musical interpretation is usually localized in the right hemisphere. However, in accomplished musicians such skills may be localized more in the left hemisphere. Similarly, verbal skills, when not overlearned, require extensive right hemisphere input to analyze unfamiliar sounds (when first learning speech or in learning a foreign language later in life), to analyze squiggles which eventually become overlearned letters and numbers, and to analyze the spatial movements necessary to write, which begins as a simple right hemisphere copying task. Thus the stage at which one is in learning a given type of material may strongly influence the brain areas across the hemispheres that are primarily involved in those behaviors.

This differentiation of hemispheric function is also similar to the concept of specific analysis of more familiar material, whereas more overall, integrated analysis occurs in the right hemisphere. Indeed there are physiological differences between the hemispheres that promote this differentiation. The left hemisphere functions as a discrete analyzer and is more attuned to material in which there is a standard method of analysis. The right hemisphere is more diffusely organized, with structures emphasizing interconnections between areas and deemphasizing localization of function. This allows the right hemisphere to function in a more holistic or gestalt manner, a skill necessary when facing new material (Luria, 1980). All of these approaches to functions of the hemispheres are obviously similar and represent different attempts to describe roughly the same observations. It should be noted, however, that as a result of these considerations, the specific localization where a behavior is processed will differ depending upon level of experience, method of attacking the task, and general environmental feedback, as well as the intactness of each of these areas. In most cases behaviors involve both hemispheres rather than being processed by only one. These differences between hemispheres extend to the other areas of the second and third units of the brain that will be discussed below.

The tertiary level of the second unit, located primarily in the parietal lobe of the two hemispheres, is responsible for cross-modal integration and simultaneous (as opposed to sequential) analysis of input from the sensory modalities. This simultaneous integration across sense modalities complements the sequential analysis of the secondary units. However, these areas are also capable of sequential analysis of material that is initially integrated.

The tertiary parietal areas play a primary role in many of the tasks commonly subsumed under "intelligence." Auditory–visual integration is necessary for reading, whereas auditory–tactile integration is necessary for writing. Arithmetic, as well as body location in space and visual–spatial skills, depends upon visual–tactile integration. Grammatical skills, syntax, abstractions, logical analysis, understanding of prepositions, spatial rotation, angle determination, and stereognosis are just a few of the skills mediated by the tertiary parietal area (Luria, 1980). Indeed with only a few exceptions, all of the skills measured on the WISC-R are mediated by the tertiary area of the second unit.

There is increasing hemispheric differentiation of tasks at the tertiary level of the second unit. The left hemisphere is largely responsible for reading, writing, and the understanding of arithmetic symbols and processes. Grammar, syntax, and other language related skills are generally left hemisphere. The left tertiary area also is involved in the reproduction of complex figures, especially in the reproduction of details (rather than major outlines). The right hemisphere is responsible for visual–spatial relationship of parts, the spatial nature of arithmetic (such as borrowing or carrying over), verbal–spatial skills, facial recognition, recognition of emotional (nonverbal) facial and postural reactions, and the analysis of unusual or unknown pictures.

Third Unit

The primary area of the third unit is the motor output area of the brain. Commands are sent from this area (through the motor tracts of the brain) to the specific muscles needed to perform any given behavioral act (including speech functions). The secondary area of the third unit is responsible for organizing the sequence of motor acts. Whereas the primary areas send individual commands, the secondary areas must organize and sequence the temporal pattern of movement.

These two areas do not function independently. For motor movements to take place, there must be adequate information available on muscle and joint status (kinesthetic and proprioceptive feedback). To allow for this, there are multiple connections between the motor and tactile primary areas and between the motor and tactile secondary areas. In addition, 20% of the cells in the primary motor area are tactile cells and 20% of the cells in the primary tactile area are motor cells (Luria, 1980). Thus these areas interact on a behavioral level. Developmentally, these areas also tend to develop in tandem (i.e., the two primary areas and the two secondary areas develop in about the same time, in the absence of injury). Coordination with both the visual and auditory-sensory areas is also necessary for accurate motor movement (Luria, 1980).

The functions of the tertiary area of the third unit, most commonly called the prefrontal lobes, are in many ways dramatically different from the functions of the primary and secondary areas. The tertiary area of the third unit of the brain represents the highest level of development of the mammalian brain. The major tasks of this area can be described as follows: planning (decision making), evaluation, temporal continuity, impulse and emotional control (delay of gratification), focusing of attention, and flexibility (creativity).

The planning function is unquestionably central to human behavior. The prefrontal lobes receive information from the tertiary area of the second (sensory) unit, as well as from the emotional (limbic) system and the first unit. They proceed to analyze this information, and then plan behavioral reactions. This function allows one to respond rationally to environmental changes and demands according to sensory input and past experience. This function is especially important for long range planning, rather than the short term "reactions" which dominate behavior in most animals as well as children. This ability is closely related to the skill of delaying gratification (without external reward or restraint) and impulse control (again, without external restraint or reward), two more important functions of the prefrontal lobes (Golden, 1981a).

As the prefrontal lobes develop, they assume dominance over the first unit of the brain (RAS). The prefrontal tertiary areas thereafter direct attentional focus and have direct connections with the subcortical areas, so that the level of arousal may be consciously modulated.

Another major function of the frontal lobes is evaluative skills. The frontal lobes must evaluate whether a person's behavior is consistent with long term goals and plans, much as the secondary (premotor) area monitors behavior to ensure that short term motor goals are accomplished (e.g., walking across a room or communicating specific information). Evaluative skills, when intact in injured people, can be a source of depression. These individuals continue to exercise the capacity to recognize when they are unable to formulate or put long term plans into action.

Since many of the skills mediated by the tertiary frontal lobe area can be subsumed under the word "maturity," it is difficult to be sure if one is seeing a frontal lobe deficit or immaturity due to environmental training in children and adolescents. Thus it may be late adolescence or young adulthood before the behavioral pattern of such a deficit is clearly discriminable from childishness, juvenile delinquency, or psychiatric disorders common to the adolescent period.

DEVELOPMENTAL SEQUENCING

In adult neuropsychology, all the units of the brain are theoretically fully functioning before the onset of a given disorder. Thus all one has to do is identify deficits in order to identify brain injury (assuming a normal environment). However, child neuropsychology presents a unique difficulty because the child is developing and changing. All skills do not exist at any given age. Thus it is of no concern to anyone that a 6-month-old does not speak. Such an infant is not expected to talk. The major problem that developmental change causes in neuropsychological evaluation is the need to be able to identify, for a given child, what skills should exist. This is further complicated by the fact that children develop neurologically at different rates, making dubious any set list of expected skills. At any given age, lack of some skills might be considered sure signs of brain damage and lack of other skills might be considered normal, whereas still others may be seen as indicating dysfunction. To complicate matters even further, this neurological growth must interact with an appropriate environment: if one is raised only by monks who never speak, one will never learn to speak.

Given this situation, it is absolutely critical for anyone wishing to understand child neuropsychology to be aware of the developmental sequences likely to be reflected in children. In general, there are two major types of theories to describe neurodevelopmental processes (Golden, 1981b). The first assumes that the child's brain is the equal of the adult's brain—it is capable of all skills and skill levels but must develop sequentially, with quantitative gains being made as the child grows older. Thus at 3 years a child can fingertap 12 times, at 4 years 16 times, and so on, until one reaches adult speeds. Similarly, the young child is viewed as having all essential problem-solving skills: only the complexity, speed, and other related dimensions with which the child can successfully cope change with age.

Other theories assume that there are distinct neurodevelopmental periods in which *qualitative* rather than just quantitative changes in skills occur (Piaget & Inhelder, 1969; Teuber & Rudel, 1962). Thus one is not able to use certain problem strategies appropriately until a certain stage is reached. This type of theory is very similar to developmental theories advocated by Piaget, Vygotsky (Luria, 1980), and others.

It is this latter type of theory on which the following discussion is based. It is assumed that certain skills are more developmentally advanced than others and that the child cannot learn them until that neurological stage is reached. Thus if frontal lobe skills do not develop until age 12, it is senseless to include a test of frontal lobe abilities in a battery designed for the 8-year-old. Although the child may give an answer, its correctness or incorrectness will not measure frontal lobe activity because that area is not contributing to the child's behavioral processing at that age.

In the present context, neurological development is seen as the end product of several factors: myelinization, dendritic growth, growth of cell bodies, establishment of pathways among neurons, and other related physical and biochemical events. All of these processes are necessary for complete neurological development but none alone is sufficient. Thus there is at present no known one-to-one relationship between periods of physical growth in the brain (such as myelinization) and psychological maturation. Any such relationship that exists remains poorly understood. As a result, times for various developmental periods given here are based on behavioral rather than physiological observations. As such, they are subject to change as our understanding increases and are not to be seen as rigid or essential to the basic theory.

In addition to the necessary physiological substrate, there is also an environmental requirement before behavior emerges. Thus at any level above the basic primary sensory and motor skills, physiological maturation serves only as a potential basis for the emergence of skills mediated by that area. Without the appropriate experience, the abilities will not develop. Thus although the secondary visual area (and the eye itself) can differentiate red from blue, one will not give import to these differences unless one is taught to see them. This is true of all the skills that are mediated by secondary or tertiary levels of the brain. In the following discussion, for the sake of simplicity, normal environmental experience will be assumed.

Finally, it needs to be recognized that as a child passes through developmental stages, the nature of functional systems underlying a behavior changes. Even though the child may have the same behavior at 5 that the adolescent has at 19, the way in which the brain processes the information for that behavior and executes the behavior is quite likely to be different. If we were to give the same test to both the 5- and the 19-year-old, we cannot assume that we are measuring the same skills or the same underlying processes. Nor can we test the child at age 5 to predict a skill that does not develop until age 8 or 13. Since the child has not passed through the developmental stage required for the emergence of the more sophisticated behavior, our "information" on the skill at age 5 is essentially meaningless. This phenomenon particularly explains why IQs for adolescents cannot be predicted reliably at early ages (Anastasi, 1976): the areas necessary for that later "IQ" are not yet developed in the young child. Teuber and Rudel (1962) noted that the predictive potential of any task is dependent upon the developmental pattern normally associated with that task. We must be careful at each stage to be aware of the limitations on the child's ability that are defined by the developmental stage the child has reached, and the constraints this places on our possible conclusions.

Five Stages of Development

For our purposes, we can divide brain development into five stages: (1) development of Unit 1; (2) development of the primary motor and sensory areas; (3) development of secondary motor and sensory areas; (4) development of the tertiary areas of the Second Unit (parietal lobe); and (5) development of the tertiary areas of the Third Unit (prefrontal lobes). Each of these stages is discussed individually.

Stage 1

The most basic part of the brain clearly lies in the RAS and related structures. This system is in general developed by birth and certainly fully operational by 12 months after conception. The neuropsychologist, in working with infants, should be clearly aware that the development of this unit depends upon time since conception, not since birth. We cannot expect a premature infant born at 6 months after conception to show behavior that we see in a full term baby. Before development of this system, we would expect the child to show disorders of arousal and attention relative to the full term baby, although such deficits need not be permanent if the problem is developmental and not related to brain dysfunction.

The RAS is particularly sensitive to damage during the time it is being formed. While we need not concern ourselves with more severe disorders (which often lead to death or severe retardation), disorders of attention/filtering appear to be much more likely in injuries prior to 12 months after conception. Indeed Rutter and his associates found that head injuries in childhood after this period produce no unusual attention deficits (Rutter, 1980). His data suggest that the only true physiological hyperactivity is caused by these early injuries. Later hyperactivity may then be related to emotional/environmental factors rather than to brain damage. This idea would suggest that children with acquired brain damage, contrary to clinical lore, should not necessarily be more active, or have greater difficulty with concentration than their normal peers.

After this initial period, injuries to the RAS appear to result more often in disorders of consciousness (coma, stupor, etc.) rather than disorders of attention (the direction of conscious activity toward specific and appropriate stimuli). Injuries to the nearby limbic system may cause emotional disorders which simulate hyperactivity to some degree. These disturbances are qualitatively different from true attention disorders and are more stress and anxiety related. (Later, similar behavior can be created by frontal lobe dysfunction, but not until Stage 5.)

Stage 2

State 2 of neurological development proceeds concurrently with Stage 1 development. Stage 2 involves the primary areas of the brain in the second unit and the third unit. Unlike the secondary and tertiary areas, the "wiring" of the primary areas is built in, not the result of environmental interaction. Generally, this area is fully operational by 12 months after conception similar to the timing in Unit 1.

During the early part of life, cortical response to the outside world is "dominated" by these primary areas. Built into these areas are basic motor behaviors—for example, crying, grasping,—and basic sensory behaviors—depth discrimination, recognition of high pitched voices, and so on. All of these behaviors are genetically "built-in," and all appear to have (or have had—such as the Moro response) some definite survival function. In general these behaviors last only as long as the primary areas dominate cortical functioning. As secondary areas take over, these more primitive behaviors become quiescent. For example, a baby may be able to make a differential response to certain sounds as an infant but, if not taught the differential response on a secondary level, will be unable to make the discrimination at age 3.

Depending upon the age and extent of injury children respond differently to damage to the primary areas of the cortex. If the injury occurs early—before birth or shortly thereafter—the complete destruction of sensory primary area can be compensated for by the primary area in the opposite hemisphere (Rudel, Teuber, & Twitchell, 1974). This, of course, applies only to unilateral injuries. For example, a child might be born partially paralyzed on one side of the body because of primary level injuries. But if the child is seen at age 5, there may be no residual behavioral sequelae—the child has apparently normal motor and sensory function. If the injury occurs early enough, no deficit may be seen even at birth. One child seen by this author was born without a right hemisphere, yet showed no motor, tactile, visual, or auditory deficits of any kind. Caution should be taken in applying these results, however. Injuries must be of a certain size (severity) and must include certain areas for this takeover to occur (Milner, 1974). Moreover, many motor deficits and sensory deficits arise from injuries to places other than the four primary areas.

Injuries after this period are more serious, but many can be compensated for by the brain (Netley, 1972). Thus loss of a primary auditory area on one side will result in a higher threshold of hearing but otherwise not interfere with day to day life. Loss of the primary visual areas will cause the loss of half the eye fields, which can be compensated partially by eye movement. Motor loss can cause hemiplegia, but with proper therapy and exercise some control can be regained. Bilateral injuries are much more serious. These can cause deafness, blindness, or paralysis. Partial injuries produce some fraction of the above results depending upon their seriousness.

Stage 3

This stage begins concommittent with the first two stages but extends through about age 5. Secondary level discriminations begin to develop as soon as the adequate attentional focus of Stage 1 and the capacity to relay information from the primary areas to secondary levels are adequate. Such behaviors as fear of strangers mark the emergence of significant secondary visual discriminations, whereas such behaviors as differential responses to a particular woman's voice as opposed to other female voices mark auditory development. Eye–hand coordination, crawling, early walking, and so on, mark secondary motor milestones.

The secondary areas are highly related to the concept of dominance. It is at this level of the brain that we see the first significant differentiation of the brain into "verbal" and "nonverbal" hemispheres. However, the brain is not committed to the left hemisphere as verbal (as it is in 93% of the population according to Milner, 1975) until the development of the secondary areas is markedly advanced. This occurs at about age 2, or, more precisely, when the child develops consistent verbal skills. Injuries prior to this time to the left hemisphere will result in much less deficit than injuries after this time (Dennis & Whitaker, 1977, Woods, 1980). In general, injuries prior to 2 years will result in switch of dominance for verbal skills to the right hemisphere. The earlier this occurs the better and more complete the transfer. After age 2 some transfer may occur, but this is usually minimal. The results of injuries incurred subsequent to 2 years of age begin to resemble the results of adult injuries more and more (Alajouanine & Lhermitte, 1965). Thus there appears to be a critical period in which these unilateral injuries are minimized; thereafter, they are much more serious. Such "plasticity" mechanisms do not apply when the injury is diffuse.

This plasticity of the brain also does not occur with small injuries—only when there is significant injury to these secondary areas (Milner, 1975). As a consequence, we have the paradox that a small injury at birth may produce no less deficit than larger injuries and in some cases have greater effects on later behavior.

During the first five years of life, the secondary areas are the primary sites of learning in the human cortex. This age limit, like others in this chapter, is only approximate. There are extensive individual differences. During this period, the child's primary and most important learning occurs within single modalities rather than between them. Cross-modality learning at this stage does not represent integrative learning but rather rote memory. The child learning to read at this level must memorize the letter or word–sound combinations. The visual symbol for a word lacks meaning for the young child except through its association with the spoken word. Thus the child must say the word to understand it, or repeat the phonemes in an attempt to integrate the sounds and recognize the word. It is not surprising that countries such as the Soviet Union, which emphasize early reading, teach by rote repetition until the lesson is learned. It is not until Stage 4 that the child is capable of true, integrative cross-modality learning.

State 4

Stage 4 is concerned primarily with the tertiary area of the second unit, located primarily in the parietal lobe. This area, along with the prefrontal lobes of Stage 5, represents the most advanced parts of the human brain. More of the human brain is devoted to tertiary, integrative areas than is the brain of any other animal (Luria, 1980).

The parietal tertiary area is responsible for efficient performance in most major educational skills: reading, writing, arithmetic, grammar, syntax, drawing, logic, analogies, naming, categorizing, dimensionality, and other similar skills. Nor surprisingly, most major IQ tests tap skills related to this tertiary unit.

The tertiary parietal area is not psychologically active until about age 5 to 8. As a result the effect of earlier injuries to the tertiary area may not be observable until ages 8 to 12. Therefore, if a child has an injury limited to this area at age 2, one might conclude that at age 3 the child is normal and unharmed, only to discover that at age 10 the child has serious learning impairments. This consideration is extremely important in legal cases or situations in which one is asked to predict future behavior. It is essentially impossible to do better than actuarial data in predicting whether a 4-year-old will later have tertiary level problems (except, of course, in cases where brain damage in other areas is already obvious). Neither a young normal child nor a young child with a discrete tertiary parietal injury will be able to complete tasks requiring development of this area. Failure to perform such tasks successfully subsequent to brain damage is meaningless, for the normal child will fail as well. In cases where the injury is limited to the tertiary injuries, real prediction is impossible at the earlier ages.

Stage 5

During this final stage of brain development, the prefrontal (tertiary) areas of the third unit develop. In general this development does not begin until the 10 to 12-year age range, and may continue into the earlier twenties. The age of onset of development in this period varies significantly across children. Initiation of development is often related to the onset of puberty but may precede or lag behind this event.

During this stage, many of the behaviors we associate with maturity begin to develop. As Smith (1965) pointed out, individuals with injuries to these areas do not necessarily show any decrease on intelligence tests, which focus on skills in the second unit and the primary and secondary areas of the third unit. During this stage such skills as inhibition of impulses, inhibition of response to outside distractors, inhibition of emotional impulses, and organization and planning for the future take place. The ability to evaluate one's behavior fully is developed, as is the ability to develop higher levels of moral and ethical control. Sophistication in the interpretation of complex and abstract events is increased, especially in the areas of analyzing emotional cues and interpersonal interactions. Without these areas, as we shall see, severe behavioral disorders may develop.

ETIOLOGY OF EXCEPTIONALITY

Neuropsychologically it is assumed that injury to one or more of the units of the brain is responsible for the development of various psychiatric and learning disorders in children. However, it is also recognized that these disorders may have other etiologies as well. Consequently, nothing written here should be construed to suggest that all exceptional children have a dysfunction of the brain, or that other etiologies discussed elsewhere in this book may not be equally valid in a given child.

Before turning to the specific disorders arising out of injuries to each area of the brain, a comment should be made about the etiology of neuropsychological disorders. Neuropsychological etiologies cover a wide range of disorders. The more obvious are the acquired brain injuries which happen to a child who is otherwise developing normally; this may include automobile accident or other forms of trauma, cerebral anoxia, metabolic disorders of the major organ systems of the body, tumors, hydrocephalus, cerebral vascular disorders, poisoning, and similar etiologies. However, a host of other potential defects in brain development also fall within the category of neuropsychological disorders: birth trauma, intrauterine disorders resulting from injuries to the mother or ingested substances such as alcohol or drugs, genetic defects which interfere with the development of brain areas, malnutrition to a degree which impairs brain development or function, disorders of development during growth periods, and many other potential defects. Thus when we speak of brain disorders we refer to this whole range of problems, whether acquired at conception or before or after birth.

Disorders of the Reticular System

Disorders of the RAS are of particular interest in the etiology of childhood disturbances. In extreme forms, disorders of this system may lead to death or complete lack of conscious awareness of the world. Injuries of this type are rarely of concern to educators since these children most often die young, since the areas in which the RAS resides are responsible for basic motor processes such as heart rate and breathing, as well as elementary sensory processing. Less severe injuries may result in disorders of the motor or sensory tracts which lead from the cerebral hemispheres to the various parts of the body. Injuries to these tracts account for most instances of cerebral palsy, and can lead to most of the syndromes associated with cerebral palsy.

It should be emphasized that these injuries to the brain stem and other subcortical areas do not lead to a direct impairment of cognitive skills, as the cortical areas may remain intact. However, it is easy to mistake the deficits for cognitive disturbances because of impairment in the motor system which may make communication or contact with the individual difficult or impossible without highly specialized equipment. Further, these injuries can result in a lessening of adequate sensory input, making it difficult for the person to perceive reality and thus to develop normally even in the presence of a normal cortical potential.

Although the injuries discussed here are rather clear cut, of more interest are injuries which theoretically disrupt attention and arousal processes but do not cause motor or sensory impairment of a clear nature. These types of disorders have been associated potentially with a wide variety of deficits, possibly including hyperactivity, autism, and childhood schizophrenia.

Hyperactivity

Diverse theories exist on the etiology of hyperactivity (see Golden & Anderson, 1979). The two major theories involve the arousal/attention functions of the RAS. Basically, one theory argues that hyperactivity is the result of overarousal caused by a dysfunction in this area of the brain. The overarousal makes the child hyperresponsive and unable to control attentional processes, just as an infant is in the early months of life. In the case of the hyperactive child, a decrease in this stimulus-bound behavior, which usually accompanies maturation of the brain, never takes place. The alternate theory argues just the opposite: the hyperactive child is underaroused. This results in a state of stimulus deprivation which the child finds unpleasant. As a consequence the child attempts to increase stimulation of the brain in the only way he or she knows how; by increased motor behavior and attention to high level stimuli, thereby increasing motor sensory feedback.

Both theories have strong adherents and both can be justified on the basis of some available evidence (Golden & Anderson, 1979). It is possible that both are correct, and some children may show different types of hyperactivity, despite the fact that the overt behavior is similar. One hypothesized difference between these children would exist, however, in the first two years of life. We would expect the overaroused child to be fussy, difficult to put to sleep, find difficulty in establishing long sleep periods, and generally overreactive. On the other hand, the underaroused child might resist going to sleep, but would sleep well after falling asleep. Indeed, the child might even seem somewhat lethargic, and may be referred to as a "good" (meaning quiet) baby. In general, children wtih both types of history may be found in the hyperactive population.

Another discriminator may be response to medication. The overaroused child—exposed to a stimulant—might get much worse, while the underaroused child might be expected to get better (although dosage may play an important role in each case). Since there are hyperactive children who respond in both ways (as well as not at all), this evidence suggests the possibility of two forms of neuropsychological hyperactivity.

In general, a review of the literature is of little help in deciding which theory is correct (Golden & Anderson, 1979). One problem is that if there are two or more forms of hyperactivity, these forms have been mixed in most research, causing contradictory results and inadequate conclusions. Until this issue is addressed more directly, it is unlikely that any substantive progress in this area will be made.

Another important issue in the development of childhood hyperactivity is the question of time of injury. Rutter (1980) presented evidence that children with injuries after age 2 or 3 do not develop hyperactivity at a rate higher than that of a normal control population. His studies indicated that a separate form of hyperactivity did exist, however, that appeared to result from injuries before birth or very early in life which might have an organic basis. Thus the type of hyperactivity discussed here may occur only in very early injuries, whereas later forms are caused by emotional or other neuropsychological problems.

Autism and Childhood Schizophrenia

Both of these disorders are, of course, very controversial, with the main distinction between them being time of onset. Autism is assumed to start before 30 months of age, childhood schizophrenia after 30 months of age. It is unquestionable that many of the children with these disorders show signs of mental retardation and other severe cognitive deficits (when they are testable). However, these are not necessary symptoms and probably reflect involvement of the second unit of the brain (as discussed later). Since many children with learning problems or mental retardation do not have these disorders, it is clear that the association is simply a chance one in which the child has suffered multiple injuries of the brain.

Therefore, it has been hypothesized that these disorders may also reflect injury to the subcortical reticular areas of the brain. These disorders may be the extreme ends of the continuum of the arousal disorders seen in hyperactivity. Arousal may be at such a high level as to make it impossible for the child to make sense of reality. Such a problem may also cause stimulation to actually be painful or unpleasant to the child, resulting in withdrawal and isolative behavior. On the other hand, arousal may be so low that even hyperactive behavior is insufficient to allow the child any normal contact with the world. The child may produce behavior designed to intensify stimulus input even more (such as head banging) or withdraw into an inner world cut off from the reality of the situation. Either of these mechanisms can be invoked to explain the symptoms of some children.

Such a theoretical explanation does not satisfactorily explain the child with relatively late onset schizophrenia (after age 3) who was previously normal. In some cases there is etiology involving a clear precipitating event (e. g., meningitis), while in other cases there is no clear cut cause. In the latter case, there may of course be a precipitant that was simply not recognized because of inadequate history or evaluation, or because it is so subtle that current evaluation techniques cannot detect the problems. Alternately, later onset cases may have no neurological cause but may result from functional factors alone, or some interaction between early mild brain dysfunction and functional factors. Much more research is necessary before we can answer these questions.

Learning Problems

As noted previously, learning problems are not directly associated with injuries to the first unit of the brain, although such disorders as hyperactivity, autism, and childhood schizophrenia may make learning difficult or impossible. True childhood cognitive learning deficits are usually associated with disorders of the second and third units of the brain. These deficits may of course be present in a child with Unit I dysfunction, since a brain injury is not necessarily limited to only one unit of the brain.

Mental Retardation

It is not a surprise to observe that mental retardation may be the function of many different injuries to the brain. Mental retardation may arise from severe dysfunction of Unit I, by inhibiting input to the cortex. This, of course, is not a true cortical disability but can result in the severest forms of retardation as such children may have little or no contact with objective reality and are probably represented in populations with Binet IQs below 40.

Retardation can result from injury to most or all of the primary areas of the brain, again inhibiting the ability of the cortex to process sensory input. Similarly, diffuse injury to the secondary areas of the brain bilaterally may also result in a similar syndrome. Injuries to only one hemisphere may, as noted earlier, be much more benign. Children with unilateral injuries may average IQs in the 80's (e.g., Milner, 1974; Woods, 1980) even when the language dominant hemisphere is involved. This effect, however, is highly age dependent. Injuries before age 2 result in relatively milder deficits which may be evident only on specialized tasks (Dennis & Whitaker, 1977). Injuries of the same magnitude later in life may result in mental retardation. Thus a child with an early injury can do remarkably well with very little remaining brain, while the same injury at age 5 may cause severe lifelong learning and behavioral problems. After the first few years of life, the effects of the injury will generally be less severe with increasing age, as the older child or adult has some backlog of skills to draw upon, whereas the child with an injury in the 3 to 5 age range has few skills to fall back on. However, with diffuse injuries, the later the injury, the fewer the effects (e.g., Boll, 1976).

Injuries limited to the tertiary areas of the second unit produce the "mildest form" of retardation in the very young child. Since this area has only a minor role in the development of skills through age 5, such children may be "slow" but may be found on testing to be "within normal limits." However, as tertiary level skills become more important, the child's IQ declines (because of increasing normative standards, not actual decline of absolute level of skill) into the low normal or mild range of mental retardation. In adults and older children, injuries to the tertiary areas are most likely to cause massive drops in IQ, with left hemisphere injuries impairing function more seriously than right hemisphere injuries (Golden, 1981a). These deficits, of course, may simply result from the failure of these areas to devleop rather than any insult or trauma.

Learning Disabilities

This area has received the attention of numerous brain researchers (see Golden & Anderson, 1979, for a review of some of this literature). Despite this, there is much that we do not know. This is related primarily to the problems with the techniques that have been used in the research (see last section of this chapter) and in the very definition of what a learning disability is. For our purposes, we will look at three forms of learning disabilities: (1) disorders in specific sensory modalities; (2) disorders in cross-modality integration; and (3) disorders of motor functions.

Specific modality disorders, in which the child is unable to process information from one sensory modality, are the easiest of these disorders to deal with. In general, they are theoretically caused by specific injuries to the primary or secondary levels of the second unit associated with a specific sensory modality as described earlier. Injuries to the primary areas are probably a rare cause of disability, as their injuries, if unilateral, can be compensated for by the child. Compensation is possible because of the presence of connections from both sides of the body to both sides of the brain in auditory and tactile modalities and the use of eye movements as compensation in the visual modality. In addition, serious deficits of this type are obvious on a thorough physical examination and have rarely been noted. Secondary level disorders, however, are much more subtle. The child may possess basic processing skills but be unable to process sequential stimuli quickly, causing slowness in functioning within that modality and impairment in day-to-day life. Such a secondary area deficit has been posited by some to be the etiology of developmental aphasia (Eisenson, 1968, 1969). In these cases the automaticity of processing, so important to verbal skills, never develops.

The effects of injuries to the secondary areas, as noted earlier, depend on the size and time of the lesion. Learning disabilities may result from any injury to single secondary area after age 3, but larger injuries before age 2 will be compensated for in some cases by the intact hemisphere (Hécaen, 1976; Rudel, Teuber, & Twitchell, 1974; Woods, 1980; Woods & Teuber, 1973). However, small injuries at an early age may not be compensated for by the brain resulting in later specific learning disabilities (DeRenzi & Piercy, 1969).

Disorders of cross-modality integration, when individual modality processing is intact, arise from injuries to the tertiary area of the second unit or from injuries to the connections between the tertiary and secondary areas of the second unit. Depending on exact location and extent of the lesion, integration among all modalities may be affected or just between any given combination of modalities. In general, these injuries are limited in extent (otherwise more far-reaching deficits would be seen, including mild retardation). In these cases, the child can process the information adequately but is unable to do the simultaneous integration required of skills like reading and writing at higher levels of complexity and speed. The learning styles of these children are much like the learning styles of a 3- or 4-year-old who has not yet developed tertiary level skills. These children are able to do elementary processing and school skills but seem to get "stuck" at about fourth grade level and are unable to make progress beyond this point. However, they are able to learn in the modality combinations which are left intact. Under proper conditions this allows them to continue to show stable IQs, although neuropsychological analysis will continue to show clear deficits.

The last form of learning disabilities—motor disabilities—may be caused by a number of specific injuries. Assuming that there is no paralysis, as might be seen in a primary level injury to the third unit of the brain, the most common site of injury is the secondary area of the third unit. Since this unit is charged with the coordination of motor activity, such deficits can cause clumsiness, writing disorders, and disorders of eye movements which may result in reading difficulties, especially when fine print or closely spaced lines are involved. However, these deficits may arise from other sources as well. Since motor skills are highly dependent on adequate feedback in all three major sensory modalities (kinesthetic/proprioceptive/tactile feedback for movement in general, visual feedback to coordinate with the environment and to check eye movements, and auditory feedback for motor-speech development), injuries in any of the sensory areas or their connections to the third unit can mimic pure motor symptoms, when only observation of deficits is used as a diagnostic technique. Finally, spatial difficulties arising from some right hemisphere deficits may make it difficult for the child to initially complete copying, form letters, or to establish eye–hand coordination in sports. This latter deficit can be corrected most easily through intensive practice and repetition to switch the major site of processing to the left hemisphere.

Of course, in addition to these common syndromes and their various subtypes, further problems can be caused by injuries which overlap with these areas. Thus it is very important to analyze the full constellation of a child's problems, since they rarely fall totally into any single categories.

Disorders of Adolescence

Two classes of disorders of adolescence can be recognized. The first is those disorders which are simply an extension of injuries that produced, or would have produced had they been present, problems seen in younger children that have already been discussed. The second class is those disorders related to prefrontal area functioning.

Before turning to disorders of the frontal lobes, however, it is appropriate to look at the effects of an intact prefrontal lobe on children with previous disorders. It has long been recognized that in some children with apparent or known brain injury there is recovery at about the time of adolescence or shortly thereafter. In these cases it is hypothesized that the development of an intact prefrontal area serves to compensate for previously existing deficits. Thus the hyperactive child, as he or she matures, may demonstrate greater cortical activity in general and of the prefrontal area in particular. In the case of the learning-disabled child, the higher levels of brain function allow the child to substitute alternate functional systems for the more basic skills which are impaired. In other cases, of course, the prefrontal lobes are not able to do this because of insufficient development or the seriousness of the deficit. In some cases a dysfunctional prefrontal area can actually intensify the seriousness of the deficits, in addition to ameliorating problems.

As noted earlier, one of the primary functions of the prefrontal lobe is inhibition over the lower emotional and arousal centers of the brain, as well as the ability to inhibit one's response to impulses. Failure of adequate prefrontal development results in the failure to establish these skills. In essence, the child fails to show normal maturational growth and the failure to develop autonomous self-control. This does not result in behavioral regression, but the child reaches a plateau in development at the level of maturity characteristic of the 8- or 9-year-old. This becomes especially serious as the child matures physically. Behavior that can be controlled or tolerated in a younger child is neither tolerable, since the adolescent is more dangerous, nor as controllable. Deficits of this kind are not unusual to see in the impulsive child who may be disruptive in school and eventually classified as "unsocialized aggressive reaction of adolescence" or as a "juvenile delinquent," depending on whether the criminal justice, psychiatric, or both systems get hold of the child. These children will also show disorders in their ability to appreciate consequences, to plan for the future, and to evaluate their own behavior effectively. Drug use and alcohol use may be common because of lack of judgment and impulsivity and the ease in which their behavior can be modified by strong outside influence (e.g., peer pressure) whether good or bad. Early drug or alcohol use can lead to greater impairment as these substances further interfere with brain function (see Golden, Graber, Blose, Berg, Coffman, & Bloch,

1981). These deficits can lead to later adult disorders, such as schizophrenia or manic depressive disease. (The reader is referred to Newlin, Carpenter, & Golden, 1981, and Newlin & Golden, 1980, for a review of this research, as it is not directly germane to our current topic.)

Developmental Lag

Up until now we have discussed most of these disorders as if the impairment to the brain were permanent. This, of course, is not always the case. Development of a brain area in a given child may simply be slower than in other children. Indeed, statistically speaking half of all children must develop slower than the other half, while 10% of *normal* children will develop slower than the other 90%. In other words, whatever criteria we set for development, there will always be slow children. In these children, deficits similar to the ones we have described will develop but eventually disappear as the child matures. It is impossible to predict which child will eventually spontaneously develop normal behavior, and which child needs special intervention. This produces a strong tendency to overdiagnose serious problems when, in fact, the child in question is demonstrating a transient developmental lag that will remit with further development. Indeed over the past century and especially the past three decades we have steadily increased out expectations of what a child should do at a given age. Concomitant with this has been an increase in the number of "exceptional" children. It is likely that this increase in expectation has been partially responsible for the increasing number of children who apparently need special help. This trend of increased expectation is unfortunately not at all in tune with the rate of brain development, which has probably not noticeably changed over the past several thousand years.

INTERACTING VARIABLES

In applying these considerations several important interacting variables must be considered by the clinician. These include the influence of environment, multidetermination of behavior, and functional autonomy of behavior.

Although we are born with a general brain organization, the specifics of that organization depend on interaction with the environment, especially in the tertiary and secondary areas, which are responsible for most voluntary, intelligent behavior. As a result, deficits may exist simply because one has never been taught the skill. While this is generally recognized for more complex behaviors like reading, Luria's work stresses that this is true for such simple secondary discriminations as distinguishing one phoneme from another, or perceiving the curvature of a line. As a result, there is no such thing as a culture-free test within this system. There are no experiences which are common to all people, no matter how "basic" they may be within a given culture. As a result, neuropsychological tests may yield either grossly or subtly different results in different populations, both within and between major cultural groups. This is especially serious in children, and such factors must be taken into account before one infers brain dysfunction.

The second important variable is the multidetermination of behavior. Behavior occurs as it does for a wide variety of reasons in addition to brain function: experience (as described above), emotional factors, reinforcement history, motivation, cooperation, biological status, sleep status, strength, peripheral sensory and motor factors, presence of drugs or medicines in the body, nutrition, blood oxygen levels, and so on. Rarely is there a behavior whose etiology lies solely on the realm of a neuropsychological deficit. In some cases, these other factors may exaggerate the severity of the deficit, in others it may attenuate the severity of the deficit. In either case, these factors must be considered in studying the individual.

Finally, we must recognize the role of functional autonomy. Basically, as used here, this concept recognizes that while a behavior may initially have been engaged in because of a physiological dysfunction of some kind, the behavior may continue long after the physiological reason for the behavior has disappeared. In these cases the behavior is said to have become functionally autonomous of its original cause. For example, the hyperactive child may indeed mature to a stage where hyperactivity is no longer necessary, but the behavior continues since it is the only way the child knows to get attention, to control his or her teachers, and to dominate matters at home. Another child may neurologically improve to the point of now being able to read at age 10 or 12, but be so convinced that this is impossible that the child engages in behavior that makes learning impossible. (One such child told me he didn't have time to study the "kid's stuff" that 6-year-olds studied.) This is of course related to the concept of the self-fulfilling prophecy; once we have decided we are unable to learn something, it is quite unlikely that the material will be learned. As a consequence, a continuing apparent deficit may not necessarily be an indication of a brain injury that is permanent, especially when, for example, the "reading deficit" is not accompanied by other basic skill deficits which one would expect if a part of the functional system for reading had been injured.

PERSONAL PERSPECTIVE: RESEARCH STATUS PAST AND FUTURE

Although theoretical approaches abound in this area, there is little "hard" or indisputable evidence to back them up in the area of child neuropsychology. While Luria's theory is impressively consistent with psychological and neurological research on the whole (see Golden, 1981a; Luria, 1973, 1980), little research has been completed with children. Some of the major problems, given this state of affairs, are outlined below.

First, there is the problem of adequate validating data. While Luria could work with adult patients with war wounds and tumors, lesions that can be highly specific and localized, such lesions are rare and more the exception in children. Most childhood disorders are diffuse or indeterminate, making it difficult to state with any scientific certainty that something is wrong in any particular area of the brain. Indeed in many of the populations studied (such as the learning disabled) there is rarely any neurological evidence for a lesion that can be considered confirmatory, and that evidence which exists across children can at best be described as contradictory (see Golden & Anderson, 1979). As a result, it is difficult to prove a point in this area. Usually one can speak only of whether the theory is consistent or inconsistent with the data.

Another major problem is the inability to establish firmly a premorbid baseline for most children. An adult with an injury was known to function at some level in terms of work, home, and other activities. In the case of many children who are born with their disorders we have no such baseline. We are forced to assume that the child would have been "normal," even though this assumption may not be correct. If the 3-year-old with IQ 75 has an accident and subsequently does poorly in school, does the child do poorly because of the preexisting IQ or because of the accident? Since the adult has already had the opportunity to learn a variety of skills we are in a much stronger position to answer that question.

An additional problem is that many of the major studies in child neuropsychology have used only psychological tests as the criterion for brain damage. Since we are aware from previous sections (as are most from clinical experience as well) that deficits may exist independent of brain dysfunction, such studies are limited in the extent we can rely on their conclusions. While such data are indeed suggestive (e.g., a recent study by Sherrets, 1980, found a high incidence of brain dysfunction-like behavior in juvenile delinquents) and in our opinion consistent with the theory presented here, it is not proof that the theory is correct. Indeed, other theorists may construe the data to support their opinion as well. Only as we expand our study of children who acquire localized lesions will some of this confusion be cleared up.

Another serious problem is the very diagnosis of the conditions we are supposed to be studying. There is extensive disagreement in the literature over who is retarded, who is learning disabled, who is autistic, and who is emotionally disturbed. These differences stem both from theoretical differences in basic orientation, to practical problems in analyzing the effects of such complicating variables as culture, motivation, peripheral disorders, social class, experience, environment, and other similar variables. Thus what one person regards as "mildly retarded' another regards as "culturally deprived." Some studies have set up elaborate, replicable criteria for defining a learning disabled child, while another study assumes all children referred from the school system who are not retarded are learning disabled. Reasonable clinicians will differ on whether a disorder has a "functional" or "organic" etiology. In the real world things are rarely that clear cut. The child with functional problems may indeed also have an organic dysfunction, while the brain-injured child is at considerable risk to develop emotional problems. The questions of how we manage to make these distinctions in our subject populations, and how we know if we are truly identifying what we should be looking at presents serious methodological problems. (For example, Golden and Anderson, 1979, in a review of the literature, cited one study that eliminated all children with signs of "organicity" from a study on learning disabilities. They then concluded that no learning disabled child was "organic.")

The effects of all these problems are clearly to make us tentative about our conclusions and knowledge. While we must theorize and attempt to organize an incredibly complex literature for clinical use, we must also recognize what we see as answers today may not be what we believe 15 years from now. There has been some excellent research, but it all suffers from some of the limitations discussed above as well as numerous other serious problems. For the future, we must turn toward increasing our knowledge with more solid research.

This is not going to be an easy task. Such research must recognize that all conditions we are examining in this chapter may have multiple etiologies. Any project that assumes only a single cause for these complex conditions is likely to only add to our long-term confusion. Projects need to be aimed not so much at identifying *the* cause of a condition, but to separate the children within a heterogeneous condition out so that we can develop homogeneous subgroups in which all the members may indeed have a common etiology. At present, while attempts have been made in this direction (such as regarding learning disabled children in such groups as math or reading disabled), these attempts have been inadequate and have failed to recognize the true diversity of these conditions.

In addition to taking these factors into account, we must also develop strong theoretical positions with which we can make predictions as to outcome of an injury in a child and to predict such factors as response to rehabilitation. Without such specific predictions, we will continue to be in a position to see all evidence as "supporting" our positions. Only when there are hypotheses to be refuted that are fairly specific and mutually exclusive will we be able to make advances in our understanding. In many cases we now have data which have little theoretical basis and little integration into a comprehensive theory of brain function in the child. This makes the data we do have seem much more chaotic than they need to be. Luria's original theory grew out of the efforts of the localizationist and equipotential theorists to gather evidence to support themselves, and a clear recognition that they had failed to do so. While Luria's theory seems to account for the data generated, new evidence may lead us to reject or modify this theory. Thus not only do we need theory but also the willingness and capacity to reject that theory when empirical data contradict it.

Finally, as indicated above, we need to extend and solidify our diagnostic criteria. In studies of brain-injured children with known injuries (where we must begin before working with children with unknown injuries) we need to look at finer variables than "left hemisphere" and "right hemisphere" injuries, or where a child was hit on the head (which, because of the mechanisms of head trauma, is not where the injury may be; see Golden, 1981a). Only when we begin to look at these variables, along with such variables as age of onset, current age, cause, and the other factors suggested by Reitan (1966) will we begin to understand their interactions. Coupled with this is the need for improved external neurological criteria. This does not, however, mean blind belief in any single criteria. As Filskov and Goldstein (1974) pointed out (see also Golden, 1981a) each neurological technique is limited in the kinds of disorders it will find. For example, the EEG might miss as many as 50% of known lesions (Golden & Anderson, 1979). In a child population where many lesions are subtle at best, one is quite likely to miss an even greater percentage. Such techniques as computer tomography (CT), positron emission tomography (PET), and regional cerebral blood flow (rCBF) have the potential to improve our sophistication if used in an appropriate and empirical manner.

CONCLUSIONS

Working with Luria's comprehensive theory as a model, we have attempted to explain the working of the brain and the application of this model to the development of exceptional children. While we freely admit that the model is indeed only tentative, we believe that it provides a useful framework for clinical assessment and intervention with the disordered child. Indications of the need for the future research and suggestions for research directions have been made, as well as a discussion of the complicating factors to which one must be sensitive in understanding these disorders.

REFERENCES

Alajouanine, T., & Lhermitte, F. Acquired aphasia in children. *Brain,* 1965, *88,* 653–662.

Anastasi, A. *Psychological Testing* (4th ed.). New York: Macmillan, 1976.

Boll, T. J. The effect of age at onset of brain damage on adaptive abilities in children. *Proceedings of the American Psychological Association,* 1976.

Chapman, L. F., & Wolff, H. The cerebral hemispheres and the highest integrative functions of man. *Archives of Neurology,* 1959, *1,* 357–424.

Dennis, M., & Whitaker, H. A. Hemispheric equipotentiality and language acquisition. In S. S. Segalowitz & F. Gruber (Eds.), *Language development and neurological theory.* New York: Academic, 1977.

DeRenzi, E., & Piercy, M. The fourteenth international symposium of neuropsychology. *Neuropsychologia,* 1969, *7,* 383–386.

Eisenson, J. Developmental aphasia: A speculative view with therapeutic implications. *Journal of Speech and Hearing Disorders,* 1968, *33,* 3–13.

Eisenson, J. Developmental aphasia (Dyslogia): A postulation of a unitary concept of the disorder. *Cortex,* 1969, *4,* 184–200.

Filskov, S. A., & Goldstein, S. G. Diagnostic validity of the Halstead-Reitan Neuropsychological Battery. *Journal of Consulting and Clinical Psychology,* 1974, *42,* 382–388.

Golden, C. J. *Diagnosis and rehabilitation in clinical neuropsychology,* (2nd ed.). Springfield, Ill.: Charles C. Thomas, 1981(a).

Golden, C. J. The Luria-Nebraska Children's Battery: Theory and initial formulation. In G. Hynd & J. Obrzut (Eds.), *Neuropsychological assessment and the school-aged child: Issues and procedures.* New York: Grune & Stratton, 1981(b).

Golden, C. J., & Anderson, S. *Learning disabilities and brain dysfunction.* Springfield, Ill.: Charles C. Thomas, 1979.

Golden, C. J. Graber, B., Blose, I., Berg, R., Coffman, J., & Bloch, S. Difference in brain densities between chronic alcoholic and normal control patients. *Science,* 1981, *211,* 508–511.

Halstead, W. C. *Brain and intelligence.* Chicago: University of Chicago Press, 1947.

Hécaen, H. Acquired aphasia in children and the ontogenesis of hemispheric functional representation. *Brain and Language,* 1976, *3,* 114–134.

Krech, D. Cortical localization of function. In L. Postman (Ed.), *Psychology in the making.* New York: Knopf, 1962.

Lashley, K. S. *Brain mechanisms and intelligence.* Chicago: University of Chicago Press, 1929.

Lewin, R. Is your brain really necessary? *Science,* 1980, *210,* 1232–1234.

Luria, A. R. *The working brain.* New York: Basic Books, 1973.

Luria, A. R. *Higher cortical functions in man* (2nd ed.). New York: Basic Books, 1980.

McKay, S. E., & Golden, C. J. The assessment of specific neuropsychological skills using scales derived from factor analysis of the Luria-Nebraska Neuropsychological Battery. *International Journal of Neuroscience,* 1981, *14,* 189–204.

Mecacci, L. *Brain and History: The Relationship between neuropsychology and psychology in Soviet research.* New York: Brunner/Mazel, 1979.

Milner, B. Hemispheric specialization: Scope and limits. In F. O. Schmitt & F. G. Worden (Eds.), *The neurosciences, third study program.* Cambridge: M.I.T. Press, 1974.

Milner, B. Psychological aspects of focal epilepsy and its neurosurgical management. *Advances in Neurology,* 1975, *8,* 299–321.

Netley, C. Dichotic listening performance of hemispherectomized patients. *Neuropsychologia,* 1972, *10,* 233–240.

Newlin, D., Carpenter, B., & Golden, C. J. Hemispheric asymmetries in schizophrenia. *Biological Psychiatry,* 1981, *16,* 561–582.

Newlin, D. B., & Golden, C. J. Hemispheric asymmetries in manic-depressive patients: Relationship to hemispheric processing of affect. *Clinical Neuropsychology,* 1980, *2,* 163–169.

Piaget, J., & Inhelder, B. *The psychology of the child.* New York: Basic Books, 1969.

Reitan, R. M. Problems and prospects in studying the psychological correlates of brain lesions. *Cortex,* 1966, *2,* 127–154.

Reynolds, C. R. The neuropsychological basis of intelligence. In G. W. Hynd & J. E. Obrzut (Eds.), *Neuropsychological assessment of the school-aged child :Issues and Procedures.* New York: Grune & Stratton, 1981.

Ross, A. O. *Psychological aspects of learning disabilities and reading disorders.* New York: McGraw-Hill, 1976.

Rudel, R. G., Teuber, H. L., & Twitchell, T. E. Levels of impairment of sensori-motor functions in children with early brain-damage. *Neuropsychologia,* 1974, *12,* 95–108.

Rutter, M. *Childhood disorders.* Speech given to the Conference on the Hyperactive Child, Omaha, Nebraska, April 1980.

Sherrets, S.D. *Behavior disorders in adolescents: Neuropsychological and behavioral correlates.* Unpublished dissertation, University of Nebraska, Lincoln, 1980.

Smith, A. Verbal and nonverbal test performances of patients with "acute" lateralized brain injuries (tumors). *Journal of Nervous and Mental Disorders,* 1965, *141,* 517–523.

Teuber, H. L., & Rudel, R. G. Behavior after cerebral lesions in children and adults. *Developmental Medicine and Child Neurology, 1962, 4,* 3–20.

Woods, B. T. The restricted effects of right hemisphere lesions after age one: Wechsler test data. *Neuropsychologia,* 1980, *18,* 65–70.

Woods, B. T., & Teuber, H. L. Early onset of complementary specialization of cerebral hemispheres in man. *Transactions of the American Neurological Association,* 1973, *98,* 113–117.

CHAPTER 4

Measurement and Assessment of Exceptional Children

CECIL R. REYNOLDS

Measurement is a set of rules for assigning numbers to objects or entities. A psychological measuring device (typically a test), then, is a set of rules (the test questions, directions for administration, scoring criteria, etc.) for assigning numbers to an individual that are believed to represent a level of some particular psychological trait, attribute, or behavior of the individual. Assessment is a more comprehensive process of deriving meaning from test scores and clinical information in order to describe the individual both broadly and in depth. Psychological tests are the nonexclusive tools of assessment. A proper assessment must also consider the background and current cultural milieu of the individual and actual observed behavior. This chapter does not attempt to deal with all aspects of assessment but rather focuses on the use of measurement techniques in the assessment process. An introduction to basic measurement technology and theory will be provided along with material concerning different methods of measurement necessary to the understanding of other chapters in this work.

There are many problems and controversial issues in psychological and educational assessment and, obviously, all cannot be treated in this work. As one example, assessment and the testing that accompanies it occur within a particular situational context. The results that are obtained may thus be strongly influenced by situational factors in the case of some individuals but less so or not at all for others. The question of the generalizability of test results obtained under a specified set of conditions takes on major importance in interpreting the test scores. Not all variables that influence generalizability are known and few that are have been well researched. Test anxiety is one factor thought to influence strongly the generalizability of results across settings and has been researched extensively, yet the complete articulation of the relationship among test anxiety, test performance, and the validity of test score interpretations across settings is far from complete. The assessment of children in particular poses special problems because of their rapid growth and development as well as their susceptibility to external environmental factors. Many of these factors are treated at length in Anastasi (1981), Cronbach (1983), Kaufman (1979), and Reynolds and Willson (in press), and the interested reader is referred to these sources for further reading on the problems, issues, and limitations of educational and psychological testing.

NORMS AND SCALES OF MEASUREMENT

Many pieces of information are necessary before one can attach the proper meaning to a test score. Among the basic are knowledge of what scale of measurement has been employed and with what sort of reference group the individual is being compared. Different scales have different properties and convey different levels of information. The four basic scales of measurement are nominal, ordinal, interval, and ratio scales. As one moves from nominal scales toward ratio scales, increasingly sophisticated levels of measurement are possible.

Scales of Measurement

Nominal Scales

A nominal scale is a qualitative system of categorizing people (or objects, traits, or other variables) or individual observations regarding people into mutually exclusive classes or sets. Sex is an example of a nominal scale; one is either male or female. Diagnostic categories such as hyperactive behavior syndrome, learning disabled, aphasia, severely emotionally disturbed, or anxiety neurosis represent nominal scaling categories. Nominal scales provide so little quantitative information about members of categories that some writers prefer to exclude nominal scales from the general rubric of measurement. As Hays (1973) points out, the term measurement typically is reserved for a situation where each individual is assigned a relational number. Because the quantitative relationship among nominal categories is unknown, many common statistical tests cannot be employed with nominal scale data. However, since nominal scales do allow for the classification of an event into a discrete category, many writers (e.g., Nunnally, 1978) do include them as one type of measurement.

Ordinal Scales

Ordinal scales provide considerably more quantitative information regarding an observation than do nominal scales. Ordinal scales allow one to rank objects or people according to the amount of a particular attribute they display. Ordering usually takes the form of the "most" to the "least" amount of the attribute in question. If children in a classroom were weighed and then ranked from heaviest to lightest with the heaviest child assigned rank of 1, the next heaviest a 2, and so on, until all children had been assigned a number, the resulting measurement would be on an ordinal scale. Although an ordinal scale provides certain quantitative information about each individual, it does not tell how far apart each observation is from the next one. Between adjacent pairs of ranks there may be a different degree of difference. Ordinal scales thus designate relative positions among individuals, an advance over nominal scaling, but are still crude with regard both to describing individuals and to the possible statistical treatments that can be meaningfully applied. Means and standard deviations are usually without meaning when applied to ordinal scales, although the median and mode can be determined.

Interval Scales

Interval scales afford far more information about observations and can be mathematically manipulated with far greater confidence and precision than nominal or ordinal scales. To have an interval scale of measurement, one must have an ordinal scale on which the difference between any two adjacent points on the scale is equal. Most of the measurement scales and tests used in psychology and education assume an interval scale. Intelligence tests are one good example of an interval scale and can also illustrate the distinction between interval and the highest level of measurement, ratio scales. Although nearly all statistical methods can be applied to measurements on an interval scale, the interval scale has no true zero point, where zero designates total absence of an attribute. If one were to earn an IQ of zero on an intelligence test (by failing to answer a single question correctly) this would not indicate the *absence* of intelligence, for without intelligence no human could remain alive. (It is not possible on most tests of intelligence to earn an IQ of zero even if all test questions are responded to incorrectly).

Ratio Scales

Ratio scales possess the attributes of ordinal and interval scales but also have a true zero point—a score of zero indicates the complete absence of the attribute under consideration. Length and weight are ratio scales. There are few instances of ratio scales in psychology outside of measurement of simple sensory and motor functions. Ratio scales have useful quantitative features, in particular, as indicated by the name: ratios are meaningful—six feet is twice three feet. Ratios are not meaningful with interval scales. A person with an IQ of 100 cannot be said to be twice as intelligent as a person with an IQ of 50. Fortunately, it is not necessary to have ratio scales to attack the vast majority of problems in the psychology of exceptional children.

This discussion of scales of measurement has necessarily been limited to the most basic elements and distinctions among scales. The reader who desires to explore this topic will find an extensive mathematical presentation of scales of measurement in Hays (1973).

Norms and Reference Groups

To understand the individual's performance or score on a psychological measurement device, it is necessary, except with certain very specific tests, to evaluate the individual's performance relative to the performance of some preselected group. To know simply that an individual answers 60 out of 100 questions correctly on a history test and 75 out of 100 questions correctly on a biology test conveys very little information. On which test did this individual earn the better score? Without knowledge of how a comparable or other relevant group of persons would perform on these tests, the question of which score is better cannot be answered.

Raw scores on a test, such as the number or percentage of correct responses, take on meaning only when evaluated against the performance of a normative or reference group of individuals. For convenience, raw scores are typically converted to a standard or scaled score and then compared against a set of norms. The reference group from which the norms are derived is defined prior to the standardization of the test. Once the appropriate reference population has been defined, a random sample is tested, with each individual tested under as nearly identical procedures as possible. Many factors must be considered when developing norms for test interpretation. Ebel (1972) and Angoff (1971) have discussed a number of necessary conditions for appropriate development and use of normative reference data. The following points are taken principally from these two sources, especially the latter, with some elaboration by the present author. Some of these conditions place requirements on the test being normed, some on the psychological trait being measured, and others on the test user.

1.   The psychological trait being assessed must allow the ranking of individuals along a continuum from high to low, that is, it must be amenable to at least ordinal scaling. If a nominal scale was employed, only the presence or absence of the trait would be of interest and relative amounts of the trait could not be determined; norms, under this unusual condition, would be superfluous if not distracting or misleading.

2.   The content of the test must provide an adequate operational definition of the psychological trait under consideration. With a proper operational definition, other tests can be constructed to measure the same trait and should yield comparable scores for individuals taking both tests.

3.   The test should assess the same psychological construct throughout the entire range of performance.

4.   The normative reference group should consist of a large random sample representative of the population on whom the test is to be administered later.

5.   The normative sample of examinees from the population should "have been tested under standard conditions, and . . . take the test as seriously, but no more so, than other students to be tested later for whom the norms are needed" (Ebel, 1972, p. 488).

6.   The population sampled to provide normative data must be appropriate to the test and *to the purpose for which the test is to be employed*. The latter point is often misinterpreted, especially with regard to evaluation of exceptional children. Many adequately normed psychological tests are inappropriately maligned for failure to include significant numbers of handicapped children in their normative sample. The major intelligence scales designed for use with children (i.e., the various Wechsler scales and the McCarthy Scales of Children's Abilities) have been normed on stratified random samples of children representative of children in the United States at large. Thus scores from these scales may be correctly interpreted as indicating a child's current intellectual standing *relative to other children in the United States*.

Some authors (e.g., Salvia & Ysseldyke, 1981) criticize tests such as the McCarthy Scales as inappropriate for measuring the intellectual level of various categories of exceptional children because large numbers of these children were not included in the test's standardization sample. Whether this is a valid criticism depends on the purpose to which the test is applied. If knowledge of an emotionally disturbed child's level of intellectual functioning relative to age mates in the United States is desired, comparing the child's performance to that of other emotionally disturbed children would be inappropriate. However, if we were interested in learning how the child compared intellectually to other similarly emotionally disturbed children, then a reference group of emotionally disturbed children would be appropriate. The latter information is not frequently sought nor has it been shown to be more useful in developing appropriate intervention strategies.

Salvia and Ysseldyke (1981) would likely agree with the basic premise of this argument; however, they contend that it would be inappropriate to base predictions of future intellectual or academic performance on test scores for an exceptional child that have been derived through comparison with the larger, normal population's performance. To make predictions, they would first require that the reference group from which scores are derived be a group of similar sociocultural background, experience, and handicapping condition. Although this may be an appropriate, if not noble, hypothesis for research, implementation must await empirical verification, especially since it runs counter to traditional psychological practice. Indeed, all interpretations of test scores should be principally guided by empirical evidence. Once norms have been established for a specific reference group, the generalizability of the norms becomes a matter of actuarial research; just as norms based on one group may be inappropriate for use with another group, the norms may also be appropriate and *a priori* acceptance of either hypothesis would be incorrect (Reynolds & Brown, 1984). Current evidence demonstrates clearly that test scores predict most accurately (and equally well for a variety of subgroups) when based on a large, representative random sample of the population, rather than on highly specific subgroups within a population (e.g., Hunter, Schmidt, & Rauschenberger, 1984; Jensen, 1980a; Reynolds, 1982).

7. Normative data should be provided for as many different groups as it may be useful for an individual to be compared against. Although this may at first glance seem contradictory to the foregoing conclusions, there are instances when it is useful to know how a child compares to members of other specific subgroups. The more good reference groups available for evaluating a child's performance on a test, the potentially more useful the test may become.

Once the normative reference group has been obtained and tested, tables of standardized or scaled scores are developed. These tables are based on the response of the standardization sample and are frequently referred to as norms tables. There are many types of scaled scores or other units of measurement that may be reported in the "norms tables" and just which unit of measurement has been chosen may greatly influence score interpretation.

UNITS OF MEASUREMENT

Raw scores are tedious to work with and to interpret properly. Raw scores are thus typically transformed to another unit of measurement. Scaled scores are preferred but other units such as age and grade equivalents are common. Making raw scores into scaled scores involves creating a set of scores with a predetermined mean and standard deviation that remain constant across some preselected variable such as age.

The mean is simply the sum of the scores obtained by individuals in the standardization sample divided by the number of people in the sample ($\Sigma X_i/N$). In a normal distribution of scores (to be described in the next paragraph) the mean breaks performance on the test into two equal halves, with half of those taking the test scoring above the mean and half scoring below the mean, though the *median* is formally defined as the score point which breaks a distribution into two equal halves; in a normal distribution, the mean and median are the same score.

The standard deviation (SD) is an extremely useful statistic in describing and interpreting a test score. The SD is a measure of the dispersion of scores about the mean. If a test has a mean of 100 and an individual earns a score of 110 on the test, we still have very little information except that the individual performed above average. Once the standard deviation is known one can determine how far from the mean the score of 110 falls. A score of 110 takes on far different meaning depending on whether the SD of the scores is 5, 15, or 30. The standard deviation is relatively easy to calculate once the mean is known; it is determined by first subtracting each score from the mean, squaring the result, and summing across individuals. This sum of squared deviations from the mean is then divided by the number of persons in the standardization sample. The result is the variance of the test scores; the square root of the variance is the standard deviation.

Once the mean and standard deviation of test scores are known, an individual's standing relative to others on the attribute in question can be determined. The normal distribution or normal curve is most helpful in making these interpretations. Figure 4.1 shows the normal curve and its relationship to various standard score systems. A person whose score falls 1 SD above the mean performs at a level exceeding about 84% of the population of test takers. Two SDs will be above 98% of the group. The relationship is the same in the inverse below the mean. A score of 1 SD below the mean indicates that the individual exceeds only about 16% of the population on the attribute in question. Approximately two-thirds (68%) of the population will score within 1 SD of the mean on any psychological test.

Standard scores such as those shown in Figure 4.1 (z-scores, T-scores, etc.) are developed for ease of interpretation. Though standard scores are typically linear transformations of raw scores to a desired scale with a predetermined mean and SD, normalized scaled scores can also be developed. In a linear transformation of test scores to a predetermined mean and SD, Equation 4.1

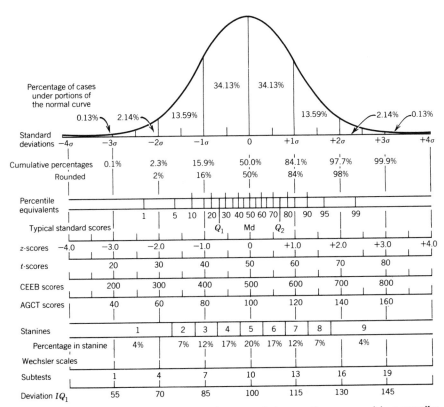

Figure 4.1. Relationships among the normal curve, relative standing expressed in percentiles, and various systems of derived scores. (Reprinted from Test Service Bulletin No. 50, courtesy of The Psychological Corporation.)

must be applied to each score:

$$\text{scaled score} = \overline{X}_{ss} + SD_{ss} \left(\frac{X_i - \overline{X}}{SD_x} \right) \tag{4.1}$$

where X_i = raw score of any individual i
$\overline{X}$ = mean of the raw scores
SD_x = standard deviation of the raw scores
SD_{ss} = standard deviation scaled scores are to have
$\overline{X}_{ss}$ = mean scaled scores are to have

Most tests designed for use with children along with some adult tests standardize scores within age groups so that a scaled score at one age has the same meaning at all other ages. Thus a person age 10 who earns a scaled score of 105 on the test has the same percentile rank within his or her age group as a 12-year-old with the same score has in his or her age group. That is, the score of 105 will fall at the same point on the normal curve in each case.

Not all scores have this property. The grade equivalent is one very popular type of score that is much abused because it is assumed to have scaled score properties when in fact it represents only an ordinal scale. Grade equivalents ignore the dispersion of scores about the mean although the dispersion changes from grade to grade. Under no circumstances do grade equivalents qualify as standard scores. The calculation of a grade equivalent is simple. When a test is administered to a group of children, the mean raw score is calculated at each grade level and this mean raw score then is called the "grade equivalent" score for a raw score of that magnitude. If the mean raw score for beginning fourth graders (grade 4.0) on a reading test is 37, then any person earning a score of 37 on the test is assigned a grade equivalent score of 4.0. If the mean raw score of fifth graders (grade 5.0) is 38, then a score of 38 would receive a grade equivalent of 5.0. A raw score of 37 could represent a grade equivalent of 4.0, 38 could be 5.0, 39 could be 5.1, 40 be 5.3, and 41, 6.0. Thus differences of one raw score point can cause dramatic differences in the grade equivalent received, and the differences will be inconsistent across grades with regard to magnitude of the difference in grade equivalents produced by constant changes in raw scores.

Table 4.1 illustrates the problems of using grade equivalents to evaluate a child's academic standing relative to his or her peers. Frequently in both research and clinical practice, children of normal intellectual capacity are diagnosed as learning disabled through the use of grade equivalents such as "two years below grade level for age" on a test of academic attainment. The use of this criterion for diagnosing learning disabilities or other academic disorders is clearly inappropriate (Reynolds, 1981a). As seen in Table 4.1, a child with a grade equivalent score in reading two years below the appropriate grade placement for age may or may not have a reading problem. At some ages this is within the average range, whereas at others a severe reading problem may be indicated.

Table 4.1. **Standard Scores and Percentile Ranks Corresponding to Performance "Two years Below Grade Level for Age" on Three Major Reading Tests**

Grade Placement	Two Years Below Placement	Wide Range Achievement Test		Woodcock Reading Mastery Test[a]		Stanford Diagnostic Reading Test[a]	
		SS[b]	%R[c]	SS	%R	SS	%R
2.5	K.5	72	1	—		—	
3.5	1.5	69	2	64	1	64	1
4.5	2.5	73	4	77	6	64	1
5.5	3.5	84	14	85	16	77	6
6.5	4.5	88	21	91	27	91	27
7.5	5.5	86	18	94	34	92	30
8.5	6.5	87	19	94	34	93	32
9.5	7.5	90	25	96	39	95	37
10.5	8.5	85	16	95	37	95	37
11.5	9.5	85	16	95	37	92	30

Source: Adapted from Reynolds (1981a).

[a]Total test.

[b]All standard scores in this table have been converted for ease of comparison to a common scale having a mean of 100 and an SD of 15.

[c]Percentile rank.

Grade equivalents tend to become standards of performance as well, which they clearly are not. Contrary to popular belief, grade equivalent scores on a test do not indicate what level of reading text a child should be using. Grade equivalent scores on tests simply do not have a one-to-one correspondence with reading series placement or the various formulas for determining readability levels.

Grade equivalents are also inappropriate for use in any sort of discrepancy analysis of an individual's test performance and for use in many statistical procedures for the following reasons (Reynolds, 1981a):

1. The growth curve between age and achievement in basic academic subjects flattens out at upper grade levels. This can be seen in Table 4.1 where there is very little change in standard score values corresponding to two years below grade level for age after about grade 7 or 8. In fact, grade equivalents have almost no meaning at this level since reading instruction typically stops by high school. An example of the difficulty in interpreting grade equivalents beyond about grade 10 and 11 has been provided by Thorndike and Hagen (1977) using an analogy with age equivalents. Height can be expressed in age equivalents just as reading can be expressed as grade equivalents. It might be helpful to describe a tall first grader as having the height of an 8½-year-old, but what happens to the 5 foot, 10 inch 14-year-old female since at no age does the mean height of females equal 5 feet, 10 inches? Since the average reading level in the population changes very little after junior high school, grade equivalents at these ages become virtually nonsensical with large fluc-

tuations resulting from a raw score difference of two or three points on a 100 item test.

2.   Grade equivalents assume that the rate of learning is constant throughout the school year and that there is no gain or loss during summer vacation.

3.   Grade equivalents involve an excess of extrapolation, especially at the upper and lower ends of the scale. However, since tests are not administered during every month of the school year, scores between the testing intervals (often a full year) must be interpolated on the assumption of constant growth rates. Interpolations between sometimes extrapolated values on an assumption of constant growth rates is a somewhat ludicrous activity.

4.   Different academic subjects are acquired at different rates and the variation in performance varies across content areas so that "two years below grade level for age" may be a much more serious deficiency in math than in reading comprehension.

5.   Grade equivalents exaggerate small differences in performance between individuals and for a single individual across tests. Some test authors even provide a caution on record forms that standard scores only, and not grade equivalents, should be used for comparisons.

The principal advantage of standardized or scaled scores with children lies in the comparability of score interpretation across age. By standard scores of course, I refer to scores scaled to a constant mean and SD such as the Wechsler Deviation IQ and not to ratio IQ types of scales employed by the early Binet and Slosson Intelligence Test, which give the false appearance of being scaled scores. Ratio IQs or other types of *quotients* have many of the same problems as grade equivalents and should be avoided for many of these same reasons. Standard scores of the deviation IQ type have the same percentile rank across age since they are based not only on the mean but the variability in scores about the mean at each age level. For example, a score that falls two-thirds of a standard deviation below the mean has a percentile rank of 25 at every age. A score falling two-thirds of a grade level below the average grade level has a different percentile rank at every age.

Standard scores are more accurate and precise. When constructing tables for the conversion of raw scores into standard scores, interpolation of scores to arrive at an exact score point is typically not necessary, whereas the opposite is true of grade equivalents. Extrapolation is also typically not necessary for scores within 3 SDs of the mean, which accounts for more than 99% of all scores encountered.

Scaled scores can be set to any desired mean and standard deviation, with the fancy of the test author frequently the sole determining factor. Fortunately a few scales can account for the vast majority of standardized tests in psychology and education. Table 4.2 illustrates the relationship between various scaled score systems. If reference groups are comparable, Table 4.2 can also be used to equate scores across tests to aid in the comparison of a child's performance on tests of different attributes.

Table 4.2. Conversion of Standard Scores Based on Several Scales to a Commonly Expressed Metric

Scales

$\bar{X}=0$ SD $=1$	$\bar{X}=10$ SD $=3$	$\bar{X}=36$ SD $=6$	$\bar{X}=50$ SD $=10$	$\bar{X}=50$ SD $=15$	$\bar{X}=100$ SD $=15$	$\bar{X}=100$ SD $=16$	$\bar{X}=100$ SD $=20$	$\bar{X}=500$ SD $=100$	Percentile Rank
2.6	18	52	76	89	139	142	152	760	>99
2.4	17	51	74	86	136	138	148	740	99
2.2	17	49	72	83	133	135	144	720	99
2.0	16	48	70	80	130	132	140	700	98
1.8	15	47	68	77	127	129	136	680	96
1.6	15	46	66	74	124	126	132	660	95
1.4	14	44	64	71	121	122	128	640	92
1.2	14	43	62	68	118	119	124	620	88
1.0	13	42	60	65	115	116	120	600	84
.8	12	41	58	62	112	113	116	580	79
.6	12	40	56	59	109	110	112	560	73
.4	11	38	54	56	106	106	108	540	66
.2	11	37	52	53	103	103	104	520	58
0.0	10	36	50	50	100	100	100	500	50
−.2	9	35	48	47	97	97	96	480	42
−.4	9	34	46	44	94	94	92	460	34
−.6	8	33	44	41	91	90	88	440	27
−.8	8	31	42	38	88	87	84	420	21
−1.0	7	30	40	35	85	84	80	400	16
−1.2	6	29	38	32	82	81	76	380	12
−1.4	6	28	36	29	79	78	72	360	8
−1.6	5	26	34	26	76	74	68	340	5
−1.8	5	25	32	23	73	71	64	320	4
−2.0	4	24	30	20	70	68	60	300	2
−2.2	3	23	28	17	67	65	56	280	1
−2.4	3	21	26	14	64	62	52	260	1
−2.6	2	20	24	13	61	58	48	240	1

ACCURACY OF TEST SCORES

When evaluating test scores, it is also necessary to know just how accurately the score reflects the individual's true score on the test. Tests typically do not ask every possible question that could be asked or evaluate every possible relevant behavior. Rather a domain of possible questions or test items is defined and a sample taken to form the test. Whenever less than the total number of possible behaviors within a domain is sampled, sampling error occurs. Psychological and educational tests are thus destined to be less than perfect in their accuracy. Certainly, psychological tests contain error produced from a variety of other sources as well, most of which are situational. Error resulting from domain sampling is the largest contributor to the degree of error in a test score, however (Nunnally, 1978), and is the type of error about which measurement theory has the greatest concern. Fortunately, this type of error is also the easiest and most accurately estimated.

Error caused by domain sampling is determined from an analysis of the degree of homogeneity of the items in the test, that is, how well the various items correlate with one another and with an individual's true standing on the trait being assessed. The relative accuracy of a test is represented by a reliability coefficient symbolized as r_{xx}. Since it is based on the homogeneity or consistency of the individual items of a test and no outside criteria or information are necessary for its calculation, r_{xx} is frequently referred to as internal consistency reliability or as an estimate of item homogeneity. Error caused by domain sampling is also sometimes estimated by determining the correlation between two parallel forms of a test (forms of a test that are designed to measure the same variable with items sampled from the same item domain and believed to be equivalent). The correlation between the two equivalent or alternate forms is then taken as the reliability estimate and is usually symbolized as r_{xx}, r_{ab}, or r_{xy} (although r_{xy} is generally used to represent a validity coefficient).

Split-half reliability estimates can also be determined on any specific test as a measure of internal consistency. Split-half reliability is typically determined by correlating each person's score on the first half of the items with his or her score on the latter half of the test with a correction for the original length of the test, since length will affect reliability. Predetermined or planned split-half comparisons such as correlating scores on odd numbered items with scores on the even numbered items may take advantage of chance or other factors resulting in spuriously high estimates of reliability. A reliability coefficient called alpha is a better method for estimating reliability since it is the mean of all possible split-half correlations, thus expunging any sampling error resulting from the method of dividing the test for purposes of calculating a correlation between each half.

As noted earlier, a number of techniques exist for estimating reliability. Throughout this chapter, reliability has been referred to as estimated. This is because the absolute or "true" reliability of a psychological test can never be

determined. Alpha and all other methods of determining reliability are, however, considered to be lower bound estimates of the true reliability of the test.
One can be certain that the reliability of a test is at least as high as the calculated estimate and possibly even higher.

Once the reliability of a test has been estimated, it is possible to calculate
a sometimes more useful statistic known as the standard error of measurement. Since there is always some error involved in the score a person obtains
on a psychological test, the obtained score (X_i) does not truly represent the
individual's standing with regard to the trait in question. Obtained scores estimate an individual's true score on the test (the score that would be obtained
if there was no error involved in the measurement). Since this is not possible,
the true score (X_∞) is defined as the mean score of an individual if administered
an infinite number of equivalent forms of a test and there were no practice
effects or other intervening factors. The standard error of measurement (S_{em})
is the SD of the individual's distribution of scores about his or her true score.
To determine the S_{em} it is necessary to know only the SD and the reliability
(preferably an internal consistency estimate) of the test in question. The calculation of X_∞ and S_{em} are only estimates, however, since the conditions for
determining a true score never actually exist.

Since the distribution of obtained scores about the true score is considered
to be normal, one can establish a degree of confidence in test results by band-
ing the estimated true score by a specified number of S_{em}'s. A table of values
associated with the normal curve (pictured in Figure 4.1) quickly tells us how
many S_{em}'s are necessary for a given level of confidence. In a normal distribution, about 68% of all scores fall within 1 SD of the mean, and about 95%
of all scores fall within 2 SDs of the mean. Therefore, if one wanted to be
68% certain that a range of scores contained a person's true score, X_∞ would
be banded by ± 1 S_{em}. To be 95% certain that a range of scores contained the
true score, a range of $X_\infty \pm 2$ S_{em}'s would be necessary.

When evaluating a test or performance on a test, it is important to ascertain
just what type of reliability estimate is being reported. S_{em}'s should typically
be calculated from an internal consistency estimate. Comparisons of reliability
estimates across tests should be based on the same type of estimate. For example, one should not compare the reliability of two tests based on an alternate forms correlation for one test and estimation by coefficient alpha for the
other. Test–retest correlations, also frequently referred to as reliability coefficients, should not be confused with measures of the accuracy or precision
of a test at a given point in time.

Test–retest "reliability" is one of the most often confused concepts of psychometric theory. Even Anastasi (1976), in introducing reliability, refers to
reliability as a measure of the degree to which a person would obtain the same
score if tested again at a later time. In the earlier stages of development of
psychology when traits were considered unchanging, test–retest reliability was
properly considered to be a characteristic of the test and indeed was believed
to be an indication of the degree to which a person would obtain the same

score if tested again. Test–retest reliability speaks principally to the stability of the trait being measured and has little to do with the accuracy or precision of measurement unless the psychological construct in question is considered to be totally unchangeable. Given that traits such as anxiety and even intelligence do in fact change over time and that testing from one time to the next is positively correlated, it is still possible to use the test–retest correlation to determine estimates of what score a person would obtain upon retesting. Internal consistency estimates, however, should not be interpreted in such a manner. When psychological constructs are not highly labile and believed to change only over long periods of time, test–retest correlations may be considered to reflect the accuracy of a test if the two testings occur at close points in time during which the trait under consideration is believed to be stable.

VALIDITY OF TEST SCORES

Reliability refers to the degree of precision or accuracy of a test score, the degree to which the true score is reflected in the obtained score. Validity refers to what the test measures and not specifically to how well the test measures a particular trait, although this is certainly a consideration when evaluating validity. The question of validity for a test is whether the test measures what it is purported to measure. For a test such as the Wechsler Intelligence Scale for Children-Revised (WISC-R) (Wechsler, 1974) to be considered valid it must be demonstrated to measure intelligence. Reliability of a measure enters into the evaluation and determination of validity but only indirectly; reliability is a necessary but insufficient condition for validity. A test without reliability cannot be valid but a reliable test may or may not be a valid measure of the claimed trait; this becomes a problem for empirical investigation at both the pre- and postpublication stages of a test. Validation is not static and is more than the corroboration of a particular meaning of a test score, it is a *process* for developing better and sounder interpretations of observations that are expressed as scores on a psychological test (Cronbach, 1971).

Just as reliability may take on a number of variations, so may validity. Quite a bit of divergent nomenclature has been applied to test validity— Messick (1980) recently listed 17 "different" types of validity that are referred to in the technical literature! Traditionally, validity has been broken into three major categories: content, construct, and predictive or criterion-related validity. These are the three types of validity distinguished and discussed in the joint *Standards for Educational and Psychological Tests* (American Psychological Association, 1985). Content validity is most clearly related to the internal properties of a test; construct validity cuts across all categories, and criterion-related validity is definitely a question of the relationship of test performance to other methods of evaluating behavior.

The content validity of a test is determined by how well the test items and their specific content sample the set of behaviors or subject matter area about which inferences are to be drawn on the basis of the test scores. Criterion-related or predictive validity refers to either comparisons of test scores with performance on accepted criteria of the construct in question taken in close temporal relationship to the test or the level of prediction of performance at some future time. Criterion-related validity is determined by the degree of correspondence between the test score and the individual's performance on the criterion. If the correlation between these two variables is high, no further evidence may be considered necessary (Nunnally, 1978).

Construct validity of psychological tests is one of the most complex issues facing the psychometrician and permeates all aspects of test development and test use. Psychology for the most part deals with intangible constructs. Intelligence is one of the most intensely studied constructs in the field of psychology, yet it cannot be directly observed or evaluated. Intelligence can only be inferred from the observation and quantification of what has been agreed upon as "intelligent" behavior. Personality variables such as dependence, anxiety, need achievement, mania, and on through the seemingly endless list of personality traits that psychologists have "identified" also can not be directly observed. Their existence is only inferred from the observation of behavior. Construct validity thus involves considerable inference on the part of the test developer and the researcher; construct validity is evaluated by investigating just what psychological properties a test measures.

Prior to being used for other than research purposes, a test must be clearly shown to demonstrate an acceptable level of validity. For use with various categories of exceptional children, validation with normally functioning individuals should be considered insufficient. A test's validity needs to be demonstrated for each category of exceptional children with whom it is used. This can be a long and laborious process but is nevertheless a necessary one. There are many subtle characteristics of various classes of exceptional children that may cause an otherwise appropriate test to lack validity with special groups (e.g., see Newland, 1980).

As has been noted by Cronbach (1971) and others, the term "test validation" can cause some confusion. In thinking about and evaluating validity, we must always keep in mind that one does not ever actually validate a test but only the interpretation that is given to the score on the test. Any test may have many applications and a test with originally a singular purpose may prove promising for other applications. Each application of a test or interpretation of a test score must undergo validation. Whenever hearing or reading that a test has been validated, we need to know for what purpose it has been validated, and what interpretations of scores from the instrument in question have been empirically shown to be justifiable and accurate.

THE ASSESSMENT PROCESS

As noted at the opening of this chapter, assessment is an involved, comprehensive process of deriving meaning from test scores to achieve a broad but detailed description and understanding of the individual. The description here of assessment as a process is important. Assessment, properly carried out, is not a static collection of information, but an ongoing dynamic synthesis and evaluation of data, reliably obtained, from multiple sources relevant to the current, and possibly future, status of the individual. Assessment is open ended—new information can occur daily that can properly alter one's perception of the ecological validity of prior impressions and recommendations.

Crucial to the assessment process, and far too frequently neglected or overlooked, is follow-up evaluation that should occur after more formal diagnostic assessments have been made and habilitative recommendations implemented. There are no absolutes in psychological and educational testing; no profile of assessment information is inexorably linked with a single method of remediation or intervention that will always be successful. Currently, the opposite is the case; the search for the aptitude × treatment interaction is nearly as elusive as that for the neural engram. The follow-up component of the assessment process is crucial to the fine tuning of existing intervention procedures and in many cases more massive overhauling of an intervention.

Psychoeducational testing and assessment are far from exact, just as are the clinical assessment procedures of medicine and related specialties. When used in diagnosis, assessment allows one simply to narrow the number of disorders under serious consideration. Similarly, when used in the search for an appropriate method of habilitation for a handicapped youngster, the assessment process allows the psychologist to narrow the number of strategies (i.e., hypotheses) from which to choose one that is believed to be most effective. There are no guarantees that the first strategy adopted will be the most effective program (or be effective at all for that matter). Kaufman (1979) described the proper attitude of the psychologist involved in assessment to be that of a "detective" who evaluates, synthesizes, and integrates data gleaned from the assessment process with knowledge of psychological theories of development and the psychology of individual differences (Reynolds, 1981b; Reynolds & Clark, 1982). As described here, the assessment process is a major component in psychological problem solving. Individuals are not randomly selected for an expensive, time consuming psychological evaluation. They are referred to a psychologist for some more or less specific reason; a problem of some kind exists. The assessment process then plays a major role in accurately identifying and describing the problem, suggesting solutions, and, properly carried through, provides ideas in modifying the initially proposed interventions.

It is necessary in the assessment process to entertain and evaluate information from a variety of sources if the assessment is to be ecologically valid. Each situation will dictate the relevance and appropriate weighting of each piece of information. Age and physical condition are two obvious factors that influence the gathering of information regarding exceptional children. Palmer (1980), Newland (1980), Salvia and Ysseldyke (1981), and Sattler (1982) have discussed factors to be included in the assessment process when evaluating exceptional children in the schools. The following are generally accepted to be important aspects of assessment: medical condition, sensory and motor skills, school performance and behavior (e.g., group achievement tests, grades, teacher checklists), individual intelligence test scores, special aptitude and achievement test performance, affective characteristics (e.g., personality tests), teacher reports on behavior and peer interaction, the child–school interaction, characteristics of the classroom, parent reports on behavior, the social and cultural milieu of the home, and the child's developmental history. Each of these factors takes on more or less importance for individual children, and more specialized types of knowledge may be required for any given case. For example, in certain genetically based disorders of learning, a complete family history may be necessary to achieve a good understanding of the nature of the child's difficulty.

Numerous methods of psychological testing can be used in the assessment process. Each will have its own strengths and weaknesses. There are frequent debates in the psychological literature over the relative merits of one category of assessment over another, with some respondents carrying on with nearly religious fervor. However, these arguments can be quickly resolved by recalling that tests are tools of assessment and most certainly not an end in themselves. Different methods and techniques of testing are best seen and used as complementary in assessment, which is a problem-solving process requiring much information. With these admonitions in mind, it is time to turn to a discussion of various methods of testing and their role in the assessment process.

MODELS AND METHODS OF ASSESSMENT

A variety of assessment methods are available for evaluating exceptional children. Some of these methods grew directly from specific schools of psychological thought, such as the psychoanalytic view of Freud (projective assessment techniques) or the behavioral schools of Watson, Skinner, and more recently Bandura (applied behavior analysis). Other methods have grown out of controversies in and between existing academic disciplines such as personality theory and social psychology. New and refined methods have come about with new developments in medicine and related fields, whereas other new testing methods stem from advances in the theory and technology of the science of psychological measurement. Unfortunately, still other new techniques stem from psychological and educational faddism with little basis in psychological theory and little if any empirical basis. Any attempt to group tests by characteristics such as norm-referenced versus criterion-referenced, traditional versus behavioral, maximum versus typical performance, and so on, is doomed to criticism. As will be seen in the pages that follow, the demarcations between assessment methods and models are not so clear as many would contend. In many cases, the greatest distinctions lie in the philosophical orientation and intent of the user. As one prominent example, many "behavioral" assessment techniques are as bound by norms and other traditional psychometric concepts as are traditional intelligence tests. Even trait measures of personality end up being labeled by some as behavioral assessment devices (e.g., Barrios, Hartmann, & Shigetomi, 1981). The division of models and methods of assessment to follow is based in some part on convenience and clarity of discussions but also with an eye toward maintaining the most important conceptual distinctions between these assessment methods.

Traditional Norm-Referenced Assessment

Intelligence, Achievement, and Special Abilities

These assessment techniques have been grouped together primarily because of their similarity of content and, in some cases, their similarity of purpose. There are, however, some basic distinctions between these measures. Intelligence tests tend to be broad in terms of content; items sample a variety of behaviors that are considered to be intellectual in nature. Intelligence tests are used both to evaluate the current intellectual status of the individual and to predict future behavior on intellectually demanding tasks and to help achieve a better understanding of past behavior and performance in an intellectual setting. Achievement tests measure relatively narrowly defined *content,* sampled from a specific subject matter domain that typically has been the focus of purposeful study and learning by the population for whom the test is intended. Intelligence tests by contrast are oriented more toward testing intellectual *processes* and use items that are more related to incidental learning and not as likely to have been specifically studied as are achievement test items. Tests of special abilities, such as mechanical aptitude and auditory perception, are narrow in scope as are achievement tests but focus on process rather than content. The same test question may appear on an intelligence, achievement, or special ability test, however, and closely related questions frequently do. Tests of intelligence and special abilities also focus more on the application of previously acquired knowledge, whereas achievement tests focus on testing just what knowledge has been acquired. One should not focus on single items; it is the collection of items and the use and evaluation of the individual's score on the test that are the differentiating factors.

INTELLIGENCE TESTS. These are among the oldest devices in the psychometric arsenal of the psychologist and are likely the most frequently used category of tests in evaluation of exceptional children, especially in the cases of mental retardation, learning disabilities, and intellectual giftedness. Until rather recently, mental retardation was defined almost exclusively on the basis of intelligence test performance; intellectual giftedness still is so defined in many school districts throughout the country. Since the translation and modification of Alfred Binet's intelligence test for French schoolchildren was introduced in the United States by Lewis Terman (of Stanford University, hence the Stanford-Binet Intelligence Scale), a substantial proliferation of such tests has occurred. Many of these tests measure very limited aspects of intelligence (e.g., Peabody Picture Vocabulary Test, Columbia Mental Maturity Scale, Ammons and Ammons Quick Test), whereas others give a much broader view of a person's intellectual skills, measuring general intelligence as well as more specific cognitive skills (e.g., the various Wechsler scales). Unfortunately, while intelligence is a hypothetical psychological construct, most intelligence tests were developed from a primarily empirical basis, with little if any attention given to theories of the human intellect. Empiricism is of major importance in all aspects of psychology, especially psychological testing, but is insufficient in itself. It is important to have a good theory underlying the assessment of any theoretical construct such as intelligence.

Intelligence tests in use today are for the most part individually administered (i.e., a psychologist administers the test to an individual in a closed setting with no other individual present). For a long time, group intelligence tests were used throughout the public schools and in the military. Group tests of intelligence are used quite sparingly today because of their many abuses in the past and the limited amount of information they offer about the individual. There is little of utility to the schools, for example, that can be gleaned from a group intelligence test that cannot be better obtained from group achievement tests. Individual intelligence tests are far more expensive to use but offer considerably more and better information. Much of the additional information, however, comes from having a highly trained observer (the psychologist) interacting with the person for more than an hour in a quite structured setting, with a variety of tasks of varying levels of difficulty.

The most widely used individually administered intelligence scales with children today are the Wechsler scales, the McCarthy Scales of Children's Abilities, and the Stanford-Binet Intelligence Scale (Form L-M). Though the oldest and best known of intelligence tests, the Binet has lost much of its popularity in recent years. The Stanford-Binet offers only a single summary score of an individual's performance, has been modified only slightly in more than 40 years, and does not lend itself to ipsative interpretation (i.e., evaluating intraindividual differences in an individual's various mental abilities). The most recent norming of the Stanford-Binet (1972) also leaves much to be desired; very little is known or has been made public about this sample. The Stanford-Binet has long been known to be a poor measure of intelligence for adults with its limited ceiling and rather narrow sampling of abilities at upper ages. Until recently, the Stanford-Binet had maintained its popularity in the assessment of young children from about 2½ to 6½ years. With the introduction of the McCarthy Scales in 1972 and its increasing acceptance by users in the field, use of the Stanford-Binet even at these younger age levels has significantly declined. The Stanford-Binet has problems in addition to its antiquated nature and the lack of precise information regarding the 1972 normative sample. There is a tendency toward racial and sexual stereotyping of behavior in the test items, and the Mental Age scores yielded by the scale are misleading (Shorr, McClelland, & Robinson, 1977). Although a revision of the Stanford-Binet is underway, it does not appear that it will represent major changes in the items or the test structure. Thus, for now, it is perhaps best to relegate this venerable scale to the history of psychological assessment, as Friedes (1972) has offered, *requiescat in pace.* Yet the legacy of the Binet tradition will be felt whenever an intelligence test is administered.

The McCarthy Scales (McCarthy, 1972) was designed as a measure of intellectual skill for children between the ages of 2½ and 8½ years. It consists of 18 subtests divided into 5 subscales: verbal, perceptual-performance, quantitative, memory, and motor. All but the gross motor tasks are collapsed into a global intelligence scale called the General Cognitive Scale. Dorothea McCarthy was a developmental psycholinguist who worked with children for many years, and the McCarthy Scales reflects her clinical acumen and extensive experience with this age group. In addition, considerable psychometric sophistication was provided by Alan S. Kaufman (then project director for development of the McCarthy Scales) and his staff at the Psychological Corporation. Kaufman has provided an excellent volume on the use and interpretation of the McCarthy Scales (Kaufman & Kaufman, 1977) that should be consulted by users of the test. A more recent, extensive review of research on the McCarthy Scales is also available (Kaufman, in press). The McCarthy Scales is a comprehensive measure of intelligence for the young child, designed with the young child in mind, and is making significant contributions to our understanding of disturbances of cognitive functioning in this age group.

The Wechsler scales, referring to the Wechsler Adult Intelligence Scale-Revised (WAIS-R; Wechsler, 1981), Wechsler Intelligence Scale for Children-Revised (WISC-R; Wechsler, 1974), and the Wechsler Preschool and Primary Scale of Intelligence (WPPSI; Wechsler, 1967), have enjoyed immense popularity with psychologists since their inception (the original WISC in 1949, and the WAIS in 1955). The WISC-R and WAIS-R are by far the instruments of choice by most psychologists for evaluating the intellectual functioning of school aged children and adults respectively. The WPPSI, designed only for use with children between the ages of 4 and 6½ years, has not obtained the popularity of use of the WISC-R and WAIS-R even though it is a comparable tool from a purely psychometric perspective. The WPPSI is a downward extension of the 1949 WISC, which was itself a downward extension of the earliest of the adult Wechsler Scales (the Wechsler-Bellevue; Wechsler was chief psychologist at Bellevue Hospital, thus the name Wechsler-Bellevue for his early work in developing an intelligence test). The WPPSI is thus not as directly relevant to a child's normal activities as scales designed specifically for this younger group. The WPPSI is also somewhat long for the young child; without frequent changes in activities, the preschooler's attention rapidly wanes. The WPPSI is nevertheless used with some frequency with this age group and can provide considerable information in the quest to understand the intellectual functioning of the young child.

For the school aged child between the ages of 6 and 16½ years, the WISC-R is by far the instrument of choice in the assessment of intellectual functioning. It provides a relatively broad sampling of cognitive skills, calling upon a variety of verbal and nonverbal skills, involving several levels of abstraction. The test is quite reliable and has accumulated a hulking mass of empirical investigation over the past 30 plus years. The WISC-R, as other Wechsler scales, is divided into a verbal, a performance (or nonverbal), and a summary full scale. The verbal and performance scales are each composed of five subtests, with an alternate available in case the psychologist makes an error in administering one of the subtests or simply desires the added information regarding this other area of cognitive functioning.

Intelligence testing, which can be very useful with exceptional children, is also a controversial activity, especially with regard to the diagnosis of mild mental retardation among minority cultures in the United States. Used with care and compassion, as a tool toward understanding, such tests can prove invaluable. Used recklessly and with rigidity, they can cause irreparable harm. Extensive technical training is required to properly master the administration of an individual intelligence test (or any individual test for that matter). Even greater sensitivity and training are required to interpret these powerful and controversial devices. Extensive knowledge of statistics, measurement theory, and the existing research literature concerning testing is a prerequisite to using intelligence tests. To use them well requires mastery of the broader field of psychology, especially differential psychology, the psychological science that focuses on the psychological study and analysis of human individual differences, and theories of early cognitive development. An extensive discussion of the clinical evaluation of intelligence can be found in Kaufman and Reynolds (1983).

ACHIEVEMENT TESTS. Various types of achievement tests are used throughout the public schools with regular classroom and exceptional children. Most achievement tests are group tests administered with some regularity to all students in a school or system. Some of the more prominent group tests include the Iowa Test of Basic Skills, the Metropolitan Achievement Test, the Stanford Achievement Test, and the California Achievement Test. These batteries of achievement tests typically do not report an overall index of achievement but rather report separately on achievement in such academic areas as English grammar and punctuation, spelling, map reading, mathematical calculations, reading comprehension, social studies, and general science. The tests change every few grade levels to accommodate changes in curriculum emphasis. Group achievement tests provide schools with information concerning how their children are achieving in these various subject areas relative to other school systems throughout the country and relative to other schools in the same district. They also provide information about the progress of individual children and can serve as good screening measures in attempting to identify children at the upper and lower ends of the achievement continuum. Group administered achievement tests help in achieving a good understanding of the academic performance of these individuals but do not provide sufficiently detailed or sensitive information on which to base major decisions. When decision making is called for or an in-depth understanding of a child's academic needs is required, individual testing is needed.

There is a growing number of individually administered achievement tests. Some are broad measures of academic attainment that attempt to assess many areas of academic skill such as the Peabody Individual Achievement Test (PIAT). The PIAT provides scores in the areas of mathematics, spelling, reading recognition, reading comprehension, and general information. Although the PIAT is frequently used for differential diagnosis of academic disorders, this use is probably inappropriate due to the large general achievement factor inherent in such a scale and the relatively low reliability of the individual subtests of the PIAT (Reynolds, 1979a).

Typically, one administers an individual test of achievement to obtain an in-depth understanding of a child's academic skill in a single area of achievement. In this regard, the Woodcock Reading Mastery Tests (WRMT; Woodcock, 1973) is a more typical entry. The WRMT provides five scores, all in areas of reading, dealing with word attack skills, word recognition, word comprehension, passage comprehension, and letter recognition. An overall summary score of the child's reading ability is also provided. By observing how the child with a reading difficulty responds to different skill areas, all within the more global aspect of reading, considerably greater insight is possible than with a general measure of reading achievement. Tests are available conceptually similar to the WRMT for math, spelling, and writing skills as well. In fact, a host of such tests is currently available. These tests are reviewed and discussed at some length in Buros' *Mental Measurement Yearbooks* series.

TESTS OF SPECIAL ABILITIES.   These are specialized methods for assessing thin slices of the spectrum of abilities for any single individual. These measures can be helpful in further narrowing the field of hypotheses about an individual's learning or behavior difficulties when used in conjunction with intelligence, achievement, and personality measures. The number of special abilities that can be assessed is quite large. Some examples of these abilities include visual–motor integration skill, auditory perception, visual closure, figure-ground distinction, oral expression, tactile form recognition, and psychomotor speed. While these measures can be useful, depending on the questions to be answered, one must be particularly careful in choosing an appropriate, valid, and reliable measure of a special ability. The use and demand for these tests are significantly less than that for the more popular individual intelligence tests and widely used achievement tests. This in turn places some economic constraints on development and standardization procedures, which are very costly enterprises when properly conducted. One should always be wary of the "quick and dirty" entry into the ability testing market. There are some very good tests of special abilities available, although special caution is needed. For example, simply because an ability is named in the test title is no guarantee that the test measures that particular ability. As with all tests, what is actually measured by any collection of test items is a matter for empirical investigation and is subject to the process of validation.

To summarize, norm-referenced tests of intelligence, achievement, and special abilities provide potentially important information in the assessment process. Yet each supplies only a piece of the needed data. Equally important are observations of how the child behaves during testing and in other settings, and performance on other measures.

Norm-Referenced, Objective Personality Measures

Whereas tests of aptitude and achievement can be described as maximum performance measures, tests of personality can be described as typical performance measures. When taking a personality test, one is normally asked to respond according to one's typical actions and attitudes and not in a manner that would present the "best" possible performance (i.e., most socially desirable). The "faking" or deliberate distortion of responses is certainly possible, to a greater extent on some scales than others (e.g., Jean & Reynolds, 1982), and is a more significant problem with personality scales than cognitive scales. Papers have even been published providing details on how to distort responses on personality tests in the desired direction (e.g., Whyte, 1967). Although there is no direct solution to this problem, many personality measures have built "lie" scales or social desirability scales to help detect deliberate faking to make one look as good as possible.

The use and interpretation of scores from objective personality scales also has implications for this problem. Properly assessed and evaluated from an empirical basis, response to the personality scale is treated as the behavior of immediate interest and the actual content conveyed by the item becomes nearly irrelevant. As one example, there is an item on the Revised-Children's Manifest Anxiety Scale (RCMAS; Reynolds & Richmond, 1978, 1985), a test designed to measure chronic anxiety levels in children, that states "My hands feel sweaty." Whether the child's hands actually do feel sweaty is irrelevant. The salient question is whether children who respond "true" to this question are in reality more anxious than children who respond "false" to such a query. Children who respond more often in the keyed direction on the RCMAS display greater general anxiety and exhibit more observed behavior problems than do children who respond in the opposite manner. Although face validity of a personality or other test is a desirable quality, it is not always a necessary one. It is the actuarial implications of the behavioral response of choosing to respond in a certain manner which holds the greatest interest for the practitioner who is assessing the exceptional child. Personality scales are frequently used when assessing children referred because of behavior problems (Ysseldyke, Algozzine, Regan, & McGue, 1981), although they can also be useful in evaluating academic disorders and helping design appropriate therapeutic and curricula programs for such children. (Anderson, 1981).

The emphasis on inner psychological constructs typical of personality scales poses special problems for their development and validation. A reasonable treatment of these issues can be found in most basic psychological measurement texts (e.g., Anastasi, 1976; Cronbach, 1970). The state of the art in objective personality testing is that the majority of these scales are appropriate only for research or purely clinical purposes, even though the area of personality tests is the most rapidly proliferating of all areas of commercially published psychological tests (Reynolds & Elliott, 1982). Several examples of personality scales that are being used currently in the evaluation of children's personalities follow.

Anxiety has been shown to be related to a number of behavioral and some cognitive disturbances. These are a number of scales available for the measurement of children's anxiety levels; two of the most widely used and researched scales are the Revised Children's Manifest Anxiety Scale (RCMAS; Reynolds & Richmond, 1978, 1985) and the State-Trait Anxiety Inventory for Children (STAIC; Spielberger, 1973). The RCMAS contains 29 anxiety and 9 lie (or social desirability) scale items. It is primarily a measure of generalized trait anxiety (A_g) but can be broken in to three subscales of anxiety that have been designated physiological anxiety, worry and oversensitivity, and concentration anxiety. These names correspond to the content of the items defining these factors. The STAIC consists of two 20 item scales, one designed to measure state anxiety, a transient mental climate, and the other trait anxiety, essentially the same factor measured by the general score of the RCMAS (Reynolds, 1980).

Although brief scales such as these are helpful in evaluating and assessing children's mental status, a number of broader, and hence much longer, personality scales for children may be used to measure multiple personality traits. The Personality Inventory for Children (PIC) by Wirt, Lachar, Kleindinst, and Seat (1977; also see Lachar & Gdowski, 1979), has gained rather quick acceptance in this field, given its recent publication. The PIC has been under development since the 1950s, however, and has been used in numerous dissertations at the University of Minnesota over the last several decades. The PIC has 12 content scales designated as achievement, intellectual screening, development, somatic concern, depression, family relations, delinquency, withdrawal, anxiety, psychosis, hyperactivity, and social skills. The PIC was designed to mimic the Minnesota Multiphasic Personality Inventory (MMPI) as much as possible but differs from this widely used adult scale in two important ways (Achenbach, 1981). Information is taken on the scale as reported by the mother or some significant other person reports the information rather than having the child complete the scale, and the items could not be developed through the use of preexisting criterion groups. As should be obvious, this means that it is primarily the mother's personality as it interacts with the child's behavior that is being assessed. Evaluation of the PIC will rest on actuarial studies of its utility in predicting children's actual behavior and its ability to allow accurate grouping and classification of child behavior problems. The PIC can provide a good point of demarcation in family therapy and in counseling parents since it primarily yields information of the interaction described above. A computerized scoring and interpretive service has been developed by the publisher much like computerized MMPI services but tends only to cluster and print in paragraph form items checked by the respondent.

Scales designed as broad measures of the child's personality that are completed by the child include such tests as the California Test of Personality (CTP), the Children's Personality Questionnaire (CPQ), and the Early School Personality Questionnaire (ESPQ). Scales have also been developed that are specific to certain contexts or situations (e.g., Bradfield Classroom Interaction Analysis and the Classroom Environment Scale). The Mental Measurements Yearbooks prepared by the Buros Institute of Mental Measurement are a good source of information about the substantial (and growing) number of personality scales for children.

Projective Assessment

Projective assessment of personality has a long, rich, but very controversial history in the evaluation of clinical disorders and the description of normal personality. This controversy stems largely from the subjective nature of the tests used and the lack of good evidence of predictive validity coupled with sometimes fierce testimonial and anecdotal evidence of their utility in individual cases by devoted clinicians.

The subjectiveness of projective testing necessarily results in disagreement concerning the scoring and interpretation of responses to the test materials. For any given response by any given individual, competent professionals would each be likely to interpret differently the meaning and significance of the response. Projective tests are sets of ambiguous stimuli, such as ink blots or incomplete sentences, and the individual responds with the first thought or series of thoughts that come to mind or tells a story about each stimulus. Typically no restrictions are placed on individual's response options. They may choose to respond with anything desired; in contrast, on an objective scale, individuals must choose between a set of answers provided by the test. The major hypothesis underlying projective testing is taken from Freud (Exner, 1976). When responding to an ambiguous stimulus, individuals are influenced by their needs, interests, and psychological organization and tend to respond in ways that reveal, to the trained observer, their motivations and true emotions, with little interference from the conscious control of the ego. Various psychodynamic theories are applied to evaluating test responses, however, and herein too lie problems of subjectivity. Depending on the theoretical orientation of the psychologist administering the test, very different interpretations may be given. Despite the controversy surrounding these tests, they remain very popular; as reported as late as 1971, 5 of the 10 most frequently used tests in psychology were projective techniques (Lubin, Wallis, & Paine, 1971).

Projective methods can be roughly divided into three categories according to the type of stimulus presented and the method of response called for by the examiner. The first category calls for the interpretation of ambiguous visual stimuli by the child with an oral response. Tests in this category include such well known techniques as the Rorschach and the Thematic Apperception Test (TAT). The second category includes completion methods, whereby the child is asked to finish a sentence when given an ambiguous stem or to complete a story begun by the examiner. This includes the Despert Fables and a number of sentence completion tests. The third category includes projective art, primarily drawing techniques, although sculpture and related art forms have been used. In these tasks, the child is provided with materials to complete an artwork (or simple drawing) and given instructions for a topic, some more specific than others. Techniques such as the Kinetic-Family-Drawing, the Draw-A-Person, and the Bender-Gestalt Test fall in this category. The use of these methods with children has been described by Koppitz (1982) and several of the examples are described further below.

The set of 10 inkblots known as the "Rorschach" is perhaps the most famous of all psychological tests throughout the world. First published by Hermann Rorschach in 1921, perhaps prompted by work originated by Binet in the use of inkblots to test imagination in children, the inkblot technique for the projective study of personality was further developed and popularized in the United States following Rorschach's untimely death in 1922 at the age of only 38 (Exner, 1976). The term Rorschach now refers only to the set of 10 plates published by Rorschach himself. A variety of schools of interpretation and scoring of the Rorschach developed in the United States. Exner (1976) notes at least five major schools, and the specific methods of Rorschach interpretation employed appear largely to be based on to which school one's mentor may trace his or her Rorschachian roots. Rather heated exchanges between these various devotees have taken place over the last 50 years.

The Rorschach takes nearly an hour to administer and requires more extensive training than most tests. The child views the inkblots and tells what each blot resembles. Responses are recorded verbatim and typically analyzed according to three very broad categories: the location of the area of the blot used by the child, the specific features of the blot that caused the child to interpret the blot in the specified manner, and the actual content of the response. Interpretation of the Rorschach is a complex process that requires a human of considerable expertise with people as well as the method. Elaborate computer attempted Rorschach interpretations have not been successful (Exner, 1976).

The TAT is a projective storytelling technique which presents individuals with an ambiguous picture and asks them to tell a story about what is happening in the picture, what happened just before the picture, what is going to happen next, and an explanation or description of how the people in the story feel. Binet had also been a pioneer in the use of pictures to measure ideation but the technique was not adequately formalized or popularized until the publication of the TAT by Murray in the 1930s. There has developed even greater diversification of scoring systems for the TAT than the Rorschach. A form of the TAT using animal figures has been developed for use with children (the CAT) as well as a children's set with human figures in much the same poses as the animal form. Stories derived from the TAT and its derivatives reflect a variety of need states in the child but can be difficult to score accurately. Frequently examiners are aided in understanding the individual child best by examining recurrent themes and symbolic figures in the stories.

Incomplete sentence methods have been quite popular, especially in the evaluation of children and adolescents. Standard forms are available (e.g., Rotter Incomplete Sentences Blank) with elaborate scoring systems. However, part of the popularity of these methods with children is being able to develop incomplete sentence stems for the specific child and his or her referral problem. Traditional work in validation of projective methods has proven most promising with incomplete sentence methods. Indeed children can be surprisingly candid and informative in their response to the direct nature of this method.

Projective drawing techniques are another area of great controversy, with the Draw-A-Person (DAP) leading the way. Frequently with children, drawing tests double as measures of cognitive skill, through the clear developmental sequence of children's drawing. IQ and emotional status are thus hopelessly confounded in such methods, along with age and sex, all producing a complex interaction with the child's visual–motor integration skills. The hypothesis underlying the use of projective drawing techniques is the same as for other methods; the unique contribution of projective drawings lies in their nonverbal nature. They require a minimal mastery of language as the child need not verbalize any response although some questioning typically occurs to clarify aspects of the drawing. Following the DAP, the Kinetic-Family-Drawing (KFD), wherein a child is asked to produce a picture of all the members of his or her family all doing something, is probably the most popular human figure drawing technique. In spite of the confounding with age, sex, IQ, and visual–motor skill, projective drawing techniques appear to be able to contribute to the understanding of a child's current status but do not stand up well against traditional psychometric standards.

Criterion-related and predictive validity have proven especially tricky for advocates of projective testing. Although techniques such as the Rorschach are not amenable to study and validation through the application of traditional statistical and psychometric methods, many clinical researchers have made such attempts with less than heartening results. None of the so-called objective scoring systems for projective devices has proved to be very valuable in predicting behavior, nor has the use of normative standards been fruitful. This should not be considered so surprising; however, it is indeed the nearly complete idiographic nature of projective techniques that can make them useful in the evaluation of a specific child. It allows for any possible response to occur, without restriction, and can reveal many of a child's *current* reasons for behaving in a specific manner. When used as part of a complete assessment, as defined in this chapter, projective techniques can be quite valuable.

When applied rigidly and without proper knowledge and consideration of the child's ecology, they can, as with other tests, be detrimental to our understanding of the child. For a more extensive review of the debates over projective testing, the reader is referred to Exner (1976), Jackson and Messick (1967, Part 6), and O'Leary and Johnson (1979).

Behavioral Assessment

The rapid growth of behavior therapy and applied behavior analysis has led to the need for tests that are consistent with the theoretical and practical requirements of these approaches to the modification of human behavior. Thus the field of behavioral assessment has developed and grown at an intense pace. Book length treatments of the topic have now become commonplace (e.g., Haynes & Wilson, 1979; Hersen & Bellack, 1976; Mash & Terdal, 1981) and entire journals are now devoted to research regarding behavioral assessment (e.g., *Behavioral Assessment*). The general term "behavioral assessment" has come to be used to describe a broad set of methods including some traditional objective personality scales, certain methods of interviewing, physiological response measures, naturalistic observation, norm-referenced behavior checklists, frequency counts of behavior, and a host of informal techniques requiring the observation of a child's behavior with recording of specific responses. Behavioral assessment will be discussed here in its more restricted sense to include the rating (by self or others) of observable behavioral events, primarily taking the form of behavior checklists and rating forms that may or may not be normed. Although I would certainly include psychophysiological assessment within this category, the scope of the work simply will not allow us to address this aspect of behavioral assessment except to say that it is indeed a most useful one in the treatment of a variety of clinical disorders.

The impetus for behavioral assessment comes not only from the field of behavior therapy but also from a general revolt against the high level of inference involved in such methods of assessing behavior as the Rorschach and the TAT. The greatest distinguishing characteristic between the behavioral assessment of childhood disorders and most other techniques is the *level of inference* involved in moving from the data provided by the assessment instrument to an accurate description of the child and the development of an appropriate intervention strategy. This is a most useful strength for behavioral assessment strategies but is their greatest weakness when it is necessary to understand what underlies the observed behaviors. Traditional and behavioral approaches to assessment can certainly be contrasted on other dimensions as well (Goldfried, 1976; Goldfried & Kent, 1972; Kratochwill, 1982).

There are still many conceptual and methodological issues to be resolved in this area of assessment. The importance of norms and other traditional psychometric concepts such as reliability and validity has yet to be resolved (e.g., Cone, 1977; Nelson, Hay, & Hay, 1977). Problems of interobserver reliability and observer drift remain but are well on their way to being resolved.

Unquestionably, behavioral assessment is an exciting and valuable part of the assessment process. Behavioral assessment grew from a need to quantify observations of a child's current behavior and its immediate antecedents and consequences, and this is the context within which it remains most useful today.

There are numbers of formal behavior rating scales or behavior checklists now available. These instruments typically list behaviors of interest in clearly specified terms and have a trained observer or an informant indicate the frequency of occurrence of these behaviors. Interpretation can then take on a normative or a criterion-reference nature depending on the purpose of the assessment and the availability of norms. Clusters of behaviors may be of interest that define certain clinical syndromes such as attention deficit disorder. On the other hand, individual behaviors may be the focus (e.g., hitting other children). More frequently, behavioral assessment occurs as an "informal" method of collecting data on specific behaviors being exhibited by a child and is dictated by the existing situation into which the psychologist is invited. An informal nature is dictated by the nature of behavioral assessment in many instances. Part of the low level of inference in behavioral assessment lies in not generalizing observations of behavior across settings without first collecting data in multiple settings. In this regard, behavioral assessment may for the most part be said to be psychosituational. Behavior is observed and evaluated under existing circumstances, and no attempt is made to infer that the observed behaviors will occur under other circumstances.

Another area of assessment that stems from behavioral psychology and is considered by many to be a subset of behavioral assessment is *task analysis*. Whereas behavioral assessment typically finds its greatest applicability in dealing with emotional and behavioral difficulties, task analysis is most useful in evaluating and correcting learning problems. In task analysis, the task to be learned (e.g., brushing one's teeth or multiplying two-digit numbers) is broken down into its most basic component parts. The child's skill at each component is observed and those skills specifically lacking are targeted for teaching to the child. In some cases, hierarchies of subskills can be developed, but these have not held up well under cross-validation. Task analysis can thus be a powerful tool in specifying a child's existing (and needed) skills for a given learning problem. Task analysis should form an integral part of any behavioral intervention for a child with specific learning problems. The proper use of these procedures requires a creative and well-trained individual conversant with both assessment technology and behavioral theories of learning, since there are no standardized task analysis procedures. Those involved in task analysis need to be sensitive to the reliability and validity of their methods. As with other behavioral assessment techniques, some contend that behavioral assessment techniques need only demonstrate that multiple observers can agree on a description of the behavior and when it has been observed. Though not having to demonstrate a relationship with a hypothetical construct, behavioral techniques must demonstrate that the behavior observed is consistent and relevant to the learning problems. For behavior checklists and more formal behavioral assessment techniques, most traditional psychometric concepts apply and must be evaluated with regard to the behavioral scale in question. A more complete discussion of task analysis model may be found in Salvia and Ysseldyke (1981).

Neuropsychological Assessment

Along with behavioral assessment, perhaps the most rapidly growing area in the evaluation of exceptional children is neuropsychological assessment, despite it being one of the most controversial areas of assessment in the schools. As with behavioral assessment, neuropsychological testing has been the subject of many recent books (e.g., Hynd & Obrzut, 1981), new journals (e.g., *Clinical Neuropsychology*), special issues of journals (e.g., Hynd, 1981), and even a debate at the annual meeting of the American Psychological Association in 1981. The debate was chaired by Lawrence Hartlage and titled "Can Neuropsychology Contribute to Rehabilitation in Educational Settings?," with several well-known and respected scholars taking opposing sides of the issue. Neuropsychological assessment is focused on the evaluation of brain–behavior relationships and invokes a high level of inference in many cases; high inference activities are destined to evoke controversy.

Much of the controversy stems from three factors: (1) a simplistic view of neuropsychological assessment as merely a set of tests, (2) rejection by many of a nomothetic approach to the amelioration of childhood disorders, and (3) a naive belief that neuropsychological techniques always result in a vague and useless designation of a child as having minimal brain damage or minimal brain dysfunction (MBD). Far from being a set of techniques, the major contribution of neuropsychology to the assessment process is the provision of a strong paradigm from which to view assessment data (Reynolds, 1981a). Without a strong theoretical guide to test score interpretation, one quickly comes to rely upon past experience and illusory relationships and trial and error procedures when encountering a child with unique test performance. As with most areas of psychology, there are competing neuropsychological models of cognitive functioning, any one of which may be most appropriate for a given child. Thus considerable knowledge of neuropsychological theory is required to evaluate properly the results of neuropsychological testing.

Since the 1950s, clinical testing in neuropsychology has been dominated by the Halstead-Reitan Neuropsychological Test Battery (HRNTB), although the Luria-Nebraska Neuropsychological Battery is now making substantial inroads. The prevalence of use of the HRNTB is partly responsible for perceptions of clinical neuropsychology as primarily a set of testing techniques. However, a brief examination of the HRNTB should quickly dispell such ideas. The HRNTB consists of a large battery of tests taking a full day to administer. There is little that can be said to be psychologically or psychometrically unique about any of these tests. They are all more or less similar to tests that psychologists have been using for the past 50 years. The HRNTB also typically includes a traditional intelligence test such as one of the Wechsler Scales or the Henmon-Nelson Test of Mental Ability. The HRNTB is unique in the particular collection of tests involved and the method of evaluating and interpreting performance. While supported by actuarial studies, HRNTB performance is evaluated by the clinician in light of existing neuropsychological theories of cognitive function, giving the battery considerable explanatory and predictive power.

Current neuropsychological models of cognitive function have been extensively discussed and debated (e.g., Das, Kirby, & Jarman, 1979; Reynolds, 1981b) and the design of educational strategies based on neuropsychological test results presented in some detail (e.g., Hartlage & Reynolds, 1981). Neuropsychological testing techniques have been demonstrated to be useful in planning instructional programs for children with learning disorders (Hynd & Obrzut, 1981; Reynolds, 1981a) and can be very helpful in the evaluation of exceptional children. With more serious disorders, when there are clear implications of central nervous system involvement, neuropsychological assessment should be considered a nearly routine procedure. Neuropsychological approaches can be most helpful in defining areas of cognitive-neuropsychological integrity and not just in evaluating deficits in neurological function. Neuropsychological techniques can also make an important contribution by ruling out specific neurological problems and pointing toward environmental determinants of behavior. The well-trained neuropsychologist is aware that the brain does not operate in a vacuum but is an integral part of the ecosystem of the child. As with other methods of assessment, neuropsychological assessment has much to offer the assessment process when used wisely; poorly or carelessly implemented, it can create seriously false impressions, lessen expectations, and precipitate a disastrous state of affairs for the child it is designed to serve.

Learning Potential Assessment

Learning potential assessment makes generic reference to techniques that rely on a test-teach-test model of evaluation of children's ability to profit from instruction. A child is tested with regard to skill in a specific area and then taught, through a variety of methods, and the amount of learning that has occurred under each condition is then evaluated to determine the process by which the child should be taught future skills. While this approach to assessing learning potential has been around for some time, it has received a great deal of attention lately as a function of the research and writing of Reuven Feuerstein (1979) and the availability of his *Learning Potential Assessment Device* (LPAD). Discussion of this area of assessment will center around Feuerstein's work.

Feuerstein developed the LPAD and the process of what he calls dynamic assessment from what he perceived as the severe cultural bias of traditional norm-referenced tests and their ineffectiveness in providing useful information for facilitating children's development. This basis for the development of Feuerstein's methods underlies their greatest fault. As has been presented throughout this chapter, assessment is anything but static and thus has many of the qualities desired by Feuerstein. Traditional and other methods of assessment (e.g., behavioral, neuropsychological) have much to offer in the design of habilitative methods for exceptional children. Feuerstein's arguments concerning the perceived ineffectiveness of traditional methods focuses heavily on traditional tests having a *product* orientation while the LPAD has a *process* orientation. In fact, traditional tests have both, and can be chosen for evaluating either the process by which the child thinks, reasons, and develops new skills or for evaluating the product the child is capable of producing at the time of the evaluation. Kaufman (1979) has eloquently described the process of "intelligent testing" that allows/demands the psychologist to derive, in a sophisticated fashion, from traditional norm-referenced tests just the information Feuerstein seeks from his methods in addition to the information regarding the product the child is able to produce at the present time. Additionally, as will be seen later in this chapter, empirical evaluation of cultural bias in psychological tests has not supported the cultural test bias hypothesis. Another principal fault of Feuerstein's model is his assertion that the LPAD model "permits an assessment of the child's capacity to learn" (Feuerstein, 1979, p. 99). This is a rather dramatic claim, especially given that there is little consensus regarding just what the "capacity to learn" actually is and it conveys the impression that the LPAD is able to determine the biological potential of the organism for performing intelligent functions.

The LPAD and related techniques nevertheless have a place in the assessment process. They can provide a more formalized approach to following up on hypotheses regarding the methods by which a child will best acquire new skills. The test-teach-test model affords some efficiency in this regard as well as a set of organized materials. The LPAD can also become an intervention technique in itself. Feuerstein has developed a set of teaching materials for intervention based on LPAD outcomes that look very promising. Thus far, however, many of the claims for the validity of the LPAD and its accompanying materials are anecdotal or without sufficient documentation and, though promising, must be viewed with appropriate skepticism. Education is certainly prone to fads, and valuable techniques may be lost if adopted too quickly, before they are fully elaborated and validated.

EARLY SCREENING FOR EXCEPTIONALITY

It is generally not economically feasible or physically likely that a comprehensive evaluation of every child be periodically undertaken. Yet it is generally accepted that the earlier a problem is detected, the greater is the likelihood that it can be corrected or at least held to its minimum impact. For these reasons, the development and application of effective screening procedures has occupied considerable energy. The direct goal of screening is to identify children who have or are most likely to develop learning, behavior, or other problems that interfere with appropriate social, emotional, or academic development. Screening measures are designed to be administered to large numbers of children and are typically quick and easy to administer. At school age levels most screening tests are group administered.

Screening is conducted on a probability basis and reduces the cost of identifying exceptional children by specifying those children most likely to have problems. However, a screening test is not a criterion measure and no matter how badly a child performs on a screening test, it does not necessarily mean that the child is handicapped. Instead, test results indicating that a child may be handicapped can serve as the basis of referral for a comprehensive psychological assessment. Properly employed, screening tests have a built-in pathological bias, that is, the screening test should identify more children as potentially handicapped than would be expected on the basis of prevalence estimates. Whenever a screening test is "in doubt" regarding a child's performance, the child should be declared at risk and referred for an individual evaluation. The purpose of the individual evaluation is either to determine that the child was incorrectly identified and is not handicapped or in need of special services or to confirm and more accurately appraise the specific problem(s) the child is experiencing and to provide appropriate classification and delineation of a suitable intervention program.

Many screening procedures provide limited, restricted samples of behavior and are of limited utility in diagnostic decision making and instructional planning. Screening tests are usually less accurate measures of skills, and since they are designed to detect areas of deficiency or handicap, do not typically allow for the identification of a child's strengths. Thus the results of a screening test, while useful in the context of the assessment process, cannot substitute for a comprehensive individual assessment and cannot be allowed to override the outcome of an individual evaluation. Even though many screening tests are individually administered, individual administration per se does not elevate the status of the test.

Depending on the age at which screening is being conducted and whether one is looking for a specific problem or more generalized difficulties, the nature of the screening test will change dramatically. Screening for developmental disabilities generally begins at birth when a child's Apgar score is determined. The Apgar determines a grossly defined level of general physiological well-being in the newborn by assessing such general characteristics as color, muscle tonus, and some reflexes. Children with very low Apgar scores at birth generally will continue to have problems, but a moderate or high score tends not to be predictive. At this time certain other specific medical screening tests are conducted to detect such disorders as galactosemia and phenylketonuria, which may result in severe handicapping conditions if not detected early. Tests for Down's syndrome and a host of other genetic disturbances may also be required if suspicions of abnormality arise or are in the family history. In many cases the evaluation of genetic abnormalities occurs prior to birth.

Once the child is a few days old, more meaningful psychological assessment becomes possible. The Neonatal Behavioral Assessment Scales (NBAS) are becoming popular in the evaluation of the infant's response to the environment and interaction with adults. Recent work on the NBAS suggests that it may be useful in identifying children who, without intervention, will exhibit a myriad of behavioral problems later in life. Although not specifically a screening technique, the Bayley Scales of Infant Development are also quite useful in evaluating the current mental and psychomotor development of infants up to 36 months, aiding primarily in the detection of less obvious delays in the development of cognitive and motor skills.

As children become older, screening on the basis of cognitive skill becomes more important and more feasible in the detection of potential psychological or educational handicaps. Screening for specific disturbances continues, however, and virtually every child in the United States undergoes screening for sensory defects early in life. At the preschool level, most screening tests must be individually administered, due to the nature of young children (behaviorally labile, distractible, and unaccustomed to the disciplined nature of group testing). A host of such tests are available, yet it seems that the most efficacious approach is to employ short forms of the major individually administered scales for this age group (Reynolds & Clark, 1982). These short forms (such as those derived from the McCarthy Scales) are typically at least as reliable as other brief tests, have more validity information available, are almost without exception better normed and more well-standardized than other tests for the preschooler, and take no more time to administer (though more highly trained personnel are usually required). Short forms of the major scales have an added advantage in that if a child is noted to be at risk on the screening measure, the remainder of the scale can be administered without duplication of effort.

As children begin kindergarten, group tests become more prevalent as screening techniques. Although called group tests, at this age a teacher and an aide are typically necessary for testing groups of kindergarten children ranging in size from 4 to 10. Larger groups can quickly become unmanageable at this age. Screening tests at this age focus heavily on visual-motor skill and such preacademic skills as color naming, letter naming, and determining similarities and differences between objects or pictures. Some, such as the Boehm Test of Basic Concepts, directly assess the child's knowledge of basic language concepts of other narrowly defined skills.

Once children reach school age, nearly all screening occurs as a function of group administered standardized tests. At one time, group intelligence tests were widely used for group screening. However, these tests were subject to such abuse and ill-informed interpretation that they have all but been banned in most public school systems. Screening tests now used in the schools focus largely on academic skill development, particularly in the areas of reading and arithmetic. Some screening occurs for emotional and behavioral problems through the use of brief personality scales or teacher completed problem behavior checklists but this practice is not widespread. For school age children, much screening occurs through informal evaluation of academic performance and behavior by the child's teacher, who, upon noticing aberrant performance, typically initiates referral for an individual evaluation.

A number of objections to formal screening of children have been raised, especially at the preschool level. One major objection to the early identification of handicapped children is the assumed negative impact of attaching a formal label to a child at such an early age. Even without the application of a formal, codified label by a professional diagnostician, teachers, parents, and peers engage in a constant form of informal labeling that is almost certainly more harmful than the administrative labeling by a recognized professional. Indeed research shows that young children with certain types of learning problems are likely to be perceived as emotionally disturbed by school personnel rather than being seen as slow learners or as having a specific learning problem. Contrary to the popular press view, the issue of whether formal labels have any net detrimental effects on children is still under debate in the scholarly literature and is far from being settled. Other writers have objected to early screening and identification of handicapped children on the basis of potential deleterious effects on the mother–child attachment relationship and the parents' feelings of responsibility in child-rearing, still others object to the identification and diagnosis of disorders that we do not yet know how to treat. These criticisms and others have been reviewed by Reynolds (1979b) and do not seem to hold as cogent arguments against early screening and identification of handicapping conditions. Properly carried out and followed through, screening is one of the most important aspects of the assessment process.

THE PROBLEM OF CULTURAL BIAS
IN PSYCHOLOGICAL ASSESSMENT

The issue of potential cultural bias in educational and psychological tests has been with psychology since at least the 1920s. The past two decades with their surge of support and concern for individual liberties, civil rights, and social justice have seen the issues involved in test bias become a substantial focus of concern by psychologists, educators, and the lay public alike. Lawmakers and the courts have begun to show increasing concern as well, as witnessed by the passage of so-called truth-in-testing legislation in New York State and the contemplation of similar bills at the federal level. Two major federal district courts of equivalent rank recently handed down legal decisions on whether tests are biased against black children—decided in exactly opposite directions (*Larry P. v. Riles,* 1979; *PASE v. Hannon,* 1980).

Much of the furor over bias in testing has centered around the use of intelligence tests to evaluate minority children suspected of mental retardation. Even though definitions and conceptualizations of mental retardation have been modified over the last decade to add emphasis to a child's adaptive behavior (ability to function independently within his or her own culture and within the larger society) and social maturity, level of intellectual functioning remains an important consideration in the diagnosis of mental retardation. Since black children as a group earn a lower mean score on intelligence tests (e.g., Reynolds & Gutkin, 1981), a significantly larger proportion of black than white children are diagnosed as mildly mentally retarded. Although the cause of the mean difference in performance of blacks and whites on intelligence tests is not yet known, one (among many) proposed explanation is that the tests are faulty. This explanation has become known as the cultural test bias hypothesis and, briefly, contends that minority children earn lower scores on intelligence tests not because they have less ability but rather because the inherent cultural bias of the tests causes the tests to be artificially more difficult for minority children. These biases are generally stated to stem from the white middle-class orientation of test authors and publishers and the lack of relevant experience for taking such tests among black and other minority children. Although psychologists have been aware of the potential for such problems since the early days of testing (Reynolds & Brown, 1984), most significant research on bias in testing is relatively recent.

The Association of Black Psychologists' early efforts to raise the consciousness of the psychological community were successful in spurring much empirical research on the various issues involved and also resulted in the appointment of an American Psychological Association committee to study the issues (Cleary, Humphreys, Kendrick, & Wesman, 1975). At its 1969 annual meeting, the Association of Black Psychologists adopted an official policy statement on educational and psychological testing stating strong support for parents who wish to deny the use of tests with their children and calling for an end to testing black children.

Many potentially legitimate objections to the use of educational and psychological tests with minorities have been raised by black and other minority psychologists. Too frequently the objections of these groups are viewed as fact without a review of any empirical evidence (e.g., CEC, 1978; Hilliard, 1979). The problem most often cited in the use of tests with minorities fall into the following categories as described by Reynolds (1982).

1. *Inappropriate content.* Black or other minority children have not been exposed to the material involved in the test questions or other stimulus materials.

2. *Inappropriate standardization samples.* Ethnic minorities are underrepresented in the collection of normative reference group data. R. L. Williams (Wright & Isenstein, 1977) has criticized the WISC-R standardization sample for including blacks only in proportion to the United States total population. Williams contends that such small actual representation has no impact on the test.

3. *Examiner and language bias.* Since most psychologists are white and primarily speak only standard English, they intimidate black and other ethnic

minorities. They also are unable to communicate accurately with minority children.

4. *Inequitable social consequences.*   As a result of bias in educational and psychological tests, minority group members are disproportionately relegated to dead end educational tracks and thought unable to learn. Labeling effects also fall under this category.

5. *Measurement of different constructs.*   This position asserts that the tests are measuring significantly different attributes when used with children from other than the white middle-class culture. Mercer (1979), for example, contends that when IQ tests are used with minorities, they are measuring only the degree of Anglo-centrism of the home.

6. *Differential predictive validity.*   While tests may accurately predict a variety of outcomes for white middle-class children, they fail to predict at an acceptable level any relevant criteria for minority group members.

Contrary to the position of a decade ago, a considerable body of research now exists in each of the foregoing areas of potential bias in assessment. To the extent that the cultural test bias hypothesis is a scientific question, as it must be to receive rational consideration, it must be evaluated via a thorough consideration of carefully conceived research. As with other scientific questions, one must be guided by the data. Recently the evidence regarding the cultural test bias hypothesis has been reviewed extensively (Jensen, 1980a; Reynolds, 1981c, 1982) and debated (Reynolds & Brown, 1984). Empirical research into the question of bias has failed to substantiate the existence of cultural bias in well-constructed, well-standardized educational and psychological tests when used with native-born American ethnic minorities. The internal psychometric characteristics of intelligence and other aptitude tests behave in essentially the same manner across ethnic groupings, and the tests predict later and concurrent academic performance equivalently for all groups. Although most of this research has focused on adults and school age children, recent studies have also dealt with preschool tests. Across the age span, with a variety of tests and criteria, the results have been consistent. Whatever intelligence tests measure for white middle-class children, be it scholastic aptitude, learning potential, or intelligence, they appear to measure the same construct in native-born ethnic minorities.

Other areas of bias remain to be extensively investigated. The potential for bias in personality scales is surely greater than that for cognitive scales, yet this area has been relatively meagerly researched compared to the cognitive area. Several interesting studies of bias in the evaluation of personality and behavior disorders have recently appeared that well illustrate some of the problems as well as the importance of this area of study. Lewis, Balla, and Shanok (1979) reported that black adolescents seen in community mental health settings and displaying behaviors symptomatic of schizophrenia, psychoneurosis, paranoia, and other disorders are frequently considered to be merely displaying normal "cultural aberrations" appropriate to coping with the antagonistic white culture. White adolescents exhibiting similar behaviors are given psychiatric diagnoses and referred to residential treatment facilities. Lewis and colleagues contend that the failure to diagnose mental problems in the black population results in an inappropriate, discriminatory denial of services. Another study (Lewis, Shanok, Cohen, Kligfield, & Frisone, 1980) found that, among court ordered referrals, many seriously emotionally disturbed and highly aggressive black adolescents are being sent to correctional facilities while equally disturbed white adolescents are assigned to residential treatment facilities. Such differences in test interpretation can be attributed directly to critics of testing who contend that behaviors unacceptable in society-at-large are not only acceptable in the black culture but adaptive and in some cases necessary. Through such criticisms psychologists are led to believe that aggression and violence are not pathological among certain groups and to interpret behavioral and personality scales differently. As with intelligence tests, personality scale interpretations should not be modified on the basis of unsubstantiated opinion.

There is relatively little study of the issue of bias in the evaluation of behavior and personality thus far and, again, conflicting opinions abound. While some minority spokespersons (e.g., R. L. Williams) claim that entirely distinct tests are needed to assess the black personality, Lewis and her colleagues believe it is discriminatory to interpret these tests and the behaviors they represent any differently for black children. The research that has been done in this area has focused on objective personality measures and has been reviewed by Reynolds (1981c). Thus far research with personality scales parallels findings with cognitive measures but work with regard to bias in personality assessment must be considered preliminary at present. Much remains to be done.

The issues regarding cultural bias in psychological and educational assessment are complex and not given to simple resolution. The strong emotions from otherwise competent, objective professionals is a further indication of the level of complexity involved in the issues of bias. The controversy over bias will likely remain with psychology and education for at least as long as the nature/nurture controversy even in the face of a convincing body of evidence failing to support cultural test bias hypotheses. Bias in intelligence testing will remain in the spotlight for some time to come as well, especiallly now that the *Larry P.* v. *Riles* (1979) and *PASE* v. *Hannon* (1980) decisions have been appealed, and given their propensity to elicit polemic emotional arguments.

The empirical evidence regarding test bias does not support the contentions of minority spokespersons; only scattered, inconsistent evidence for bias exists. The few findings of bias do suggest guidelines to follow in order to ensure nonbiased assessment: (1) assessment should be conducted with the most reliable instrumentation available, and (2) multiple abilities should be assessed. In other words, psychologists need to view multiple sources of accurately derived data prior to making decisions concerning all children. This probably is not too far afield from what has actually been occurring in the practice of psychological assessment, though one continues to hear isolated stories of grossly incompetent placement decisions. This is not to say that psychologists should be blind to a child's environmental background. Information concerning the home, community, and school environment must all be evaluated in the individualized decision-making process. Some would deny services to minority children, claiming that they are not handicapped but only artificially appear so on culturally biased tests. However, the psychologist cannot ignore the data demonstrating that *low IQ, ethnic disadvantaged children are just as likely to fail academically as are white middle-class low IQ children, provided that their environmental circumstances remain constant.* Indeed recall that it is the purpose of the assessment *process* to beat the prediction, to provide insight into hypotheses for environmental interventions that prevent the predicted failure. Low IQ minority children have the same entitlements to remedial, compensatory, and preventive programs as the white middle-class low IQ child, and ethnic minorities should not be denied services on unfounded assumptions that the test caused the low score and not a deficiency or dysfunction on the part of the child or the child's environment. These issues and the empirical research to date with children are reviewed in detail in Reynolds (1981c, 1982) and Reynolds and Brown (1984).

NEW DIRECTIONS IN PSYCHOLOGICAL ASSESSMENT: PERSONAL PERSPECTIVE

Psychology and education are readily influenced by fads and political pressure. For these reasons, as well as others, psychologists must view "advances" or "new" techniques in assessment with a healthy dose of scientific and professional skepticism. The rapid and immense impact of PL 94–142 (Education for All Handicapped Children Act of 1975) and its heavy demands for assessment and documentation prompted a flurry of publication of tests with poor norms and little if any research base that promised to provide the necessary answers to the problems being experienced by handicapped children. Many of these tests are colorfully and attractively packaged, very well marketed, and have titles that promise much more than they can deliver. They are, for the most part, a repackaging of old materials (and sometimes stale ideas) or the publication of someone's informal testing techniques accompanied by limited normative data. The unwary can quickly be led astray by such materials and the promise of new techniques that will yield great insights.

Rather than a repackaging of old ideas, renorming and updating of old instruments, or the development of new tests around old, tired themes and concepts, rather than from the advent of new statistical modeling of test scores, new directions and advances in psychological assessment must come from advances in basic psychological theorizing. All work in psychology, regardless of how applied it may seem, is guided by psychological theory and its empirical basis; each guides the other in a reciprocal relationship. Data shape theories and theories shape the type of data being generated. As new theories are developed and existing theories modified, new tests will be developed and new paradigms for viewing test data will occur that will represent the greatest new directions in assessment.

One area of new direction in assessment stems from the earliest of work in psychological testing. Galton was interested in reaction time and measures of sensory skill as measures of mental capacity. When these measures did not turn out to be directly related to more directly observed criteria of intelligence, such seeming simplistic notions of measurement were abandoned by the psychometric community. Jensen (1979, 1980b) has rekindled interest in this area through a thorough analysis of past efforts and a new approach to the measurement and interpretation of reaction time data. By evaluating information that had previously been considered a nuisance or byproduct of such studies (primarily intraindividual variation in response times to a constant level of stimulus complexity), Jensen developed multiple regression models of the relationship between reaction time and traditional measures of intelligence (e.g., WISC-R) that produce correlations nearly as large as the correlations between intelligence tests. Through such work Jensen is significantly affecting our understanding of the nature of intelligence and the interpretations that can be given to traditional measures of intelligence. As these methods become more refined and the theory underlying these relationships more sophisticated, major new techniques for the practical assessment of children's intellectual power may result.

Research by Eysenck (1980) and his colleagues on the physiological basis of intelligence also has considerable promise to deliver ultimately new methods for the evaluation of intelligence. In work evaluating intraindividual variation in the electrophysiological response of the brain to repeated stimulation with the same stimulus, Eysenck reports substantial correlations with psychometric measures of intelligence. Although at first seeming unrelated, Eysenck's and Jensen's work appear to have highly similar theoretical underpinnings and are leading us, perhaps, to a new conceptualization of the nature of intelligence and human information processes. Such advances in theory must precede any new techniques and methods in psychometric assessment.

The Kaufman Assessment Battery for Children (K-ABC; Kaufman & Kaufman, 1983) is a good example of a new direction in psychological assessment. The K-ABC is based primarily on Luria's theory of the neuropsychological functioning of the brain as modified and researched over the last three or four decades. While the K-ABC has some interesting and innovative features in the various tasks that the child is required to perform, there are few truly "new" or totally unique tasks that have not been used by other tests or are at least in the experimental psychology literature. Yet the K-ABC represents a significant advance as well as a new direction in assessment because of the paradigm it offers for interpreting the data about a given child. K-ABC data, cast into a sound neuropsychological paradigm, have far more practical and heuristic value than traditional views of a child's performance on such tasks. The K-ABC was a long time coming. Psychological tests soundly based in psychological theory (with the exception of the personality field) are unfortunately the exception rather than the rule but will perhaps be on the increase following the impetus of the K-ABC.

The strict empiricism of behavioral observation scales and behavior checklist that was perhaps necessary in the early stages of development of this field of assessment is showing signs of developing instruments based on carefully defined and empirically articulated dimensions of children's behavior. This effort, when in full swing, will be a welcome advance in our understanding of behavioral disorders of children, will allow us to assess these problems in a much more refined manner, and ultimately lead to better treatment plans, the ultimate goal of the assessment process.

It is from basic psychological research into the nature of human information processing and behavior that advances in psychological assessment must come. While some of these advances will be technological, the more fruitful area for movement is in the development of new paradigms of test interpretations. With each advance, with each "new" test that appears, we must proceed with caution and guard against jumping on an insufficiently researched bandwagon. Fruitful techniques may be lost if implemented too soon to be fully understood and appreciated; children may also be harmed by the careless or impulsive use of assessment materials that are poorly designed (but attractively packaged) or without the necessary theoretical and empirical grounding. When evaluating new psychological assessment methods, surely *caveat emptor* must serve as the guard over our enthusiasm and our eagerness to provide helpful information about children in the design of successful intervention programs.

REFERENCES

Achenbach, T. M. A junior MMPI? *Journal of Personality Assessment,* 1981, *45,* 332–333.

Anastasi, A. *Psychological testing* (4th ed.). New York: Macmillan, 1976.

Anastasi, A. *Psychological testing* (5th ed.). New York: Macmillan, 1981.

Anderson, L. W. *Assessing affective characteristics in the schools.* Boston: Allyn & Bacon, 1981.

Angoff, W. H. Scales, norms, and equivalent scores. In R. L. Thorndike (Ed.), *Educational measurement* (2nd ed.). Washington, D.C.: American Council on Education, 1985.

American Psychological Association. *Standards for educational and psychological tests.* Washington, D. C.: Author, 1985.

Barrios, B. A., Hartmann, D. P., & Shigetomi, C. Fears and anxieties in children. In E. J. Marsh & L. G. Terdal (Eds.), *Behavioral assessment of childhood disorders.* New York: Guilford, 1981.

Cleary, T. A., Humphreys, L. A., Kendrick, S. A., & Wesman, A. Educational uses of tests with disadvantaged students. *American Psychologist,* 1975, *30,* 15–41.

Cone, J. D. The relevance of reliability and validity for behavioral assessment. *Behavior Therapy,* 1977, *8,* 411–426.

Council for Exceptional Children. Minorities position policy statements. *Exceptional Children,* 1978, *45,* 57–64.

Cronbach, L. J. *Essentials of psychological testing* (3rd ed.). New York: Harper & Row, 1970.

Cronbach, L. J. Test validation. In R. L. Thorndike (Ed.), *Educational measurement* (2nd ed.). Washington, D.C.: American Council on Education, 1971.

Cronbach, L. J. *Essentials of psychological testing* (4th ed.). Harper & Row, 1983.

Das, J. P., Kirby, J. R., & Jarman, R. F. *Simultaneous and successive cognitive processes.* New York: Academic, 1979.

Ebel, R. L. *Essentials of educational measurement.* Englewood Cliffs, N.J.: Prentice-Hall, 1972.

Exner, J. E. Projective techniques. In I. B. Weiner (Ed.), *Clinical methods in psychology.* New York: Wiley-Interscience, 1976.

Eysenck, H. J. *The psychophysiology of intelligence.* Invited address to the annual meeting of the American Psychological Association, Montreal, August 1980.

Feuerstein, R. *The dynamic assessment of retarded performers: The learning potential assessment device, theory, instruments, and techniques.* Baltimore: University Park Press, 1979.

Friedes, D. Review of the Stanford-Binet Intelligence Scale, 3rd rev. In O. K. Buros (Ed.), *The seventh mental measurements yearbook.* Highland Park, N.J.: Gryphon, 1972.

Goldfried, M. R. Behavioral assessment. In I. Weiner (Ed.), *Clinical methods in psychology.* New York: Wiley-Interscience, 1976.

Goldfried, M. R., & Kent, R. N. Traditional versus behavioral assessment: A comparison of methodological and theoretical assumptions. *Psychological Bulletin,* 1972, *77,* 409–420.

Hartlage, L. C., & Reynolds, C. R. Neuropsychological assessment and the individualization of instruction. In G. Hynd & J. Obrzut (Eds.), *Neuropsychological assessment and the school-age child: Issues and procedures.* New York: Grune & Stratton, 1981.

Haynes, S. N., & Wilson, C. C. *Behavioral assessment.* San Francisco: Jossey-Bass, 1979.

Hays, W. L. *Statistics for the social sciences.* New York: Holt, Rinehart & Winston, 1973.

Hersen, M., & Bellack, A. S. *Behavioral assessment: A practical handbook.* New York: Pergamon, 1976.

Hilliard, A. G. Standardization and cultural bias as impediments to the scientific study and validation of "intelligence." *Journal of Research and Development in Education,* 1979, *12,* 47–58.

Hunter, J. E., Schmidt, F. L., & Rauschenberger, J. Methodological and statistical issues in the study of bias in mental testing. In C. R. Reynolds & R. T. Brown (Eds.), *Perspectives on bias in mental testing.* New York: Plenum, 1984.

Hynd, G. (Ed.), Neuropsychology in the schools. *School Psychology Review, 1981, 10*(3).

Hynd, G., & Obrzut, J. E. *Neuropsychological assessment and the school-age child: Issues and procedures.* New York: Grune & Stratton, 1981.

Jackson, D. N., & Messick, S. (Eds.). *Problems in human assessment.* New York: McGraw-Hill, 1967.

Jean, P. J., & Reynolds, C. R. *Sex and attitude distortions: The faking of liberal and traditional attitudes about changing sex roles.* Paper presented to the annual meeting of the American Educational Research Association, New York, March 1982.

Jensen, A. R. *g:* Outmoded theory or unconquered frontier? *Creative Science and Technology.* 1979, *2,* 16–29.

Jensen, A. R. *Bias in mental testing.* New York: Free Press, 1980.(a)

Jensen, A. R. Chronometric analysis of intelligence. *Journal of Social and Biological Structures, 1980, 3,* 103–122.(b)

Kaufman, A. S. *Intelligent testing with the WISC-R.* New York: Wiley-Interscience, 1979.

Kaufman, A. S. A review of almost a decade of research on the McCarthy Scales in T. R. Kratochwill (Ed.), *Advances in school psychology* (Vol. 2), Hillsdale, N.J.: Erlbaum Associates, in press.

Kaufman, A. S., & Kaufman, N. L. *Clinical evaluation of young children with the McCarthy Scales.* New York: Grune & Stratton. 1977.

Kaufman, A. S., & Kaufman, N. L. *Kaufman Assessment Battery for Children.* Circle Pines, Minn.: American Guidance Service, in press.

Kaufman, A. S., & Reynolds, C. R. Clinical evaluation of intellectual function. In I. Weiner (Ed.), *Clinical methods in psychology* (2nd ed.). New York: Wiley-Intersciences, 1983.

Koppitz, E. M. Personality assessment in the schools. In C. R. Reynolds & T. B. Gutkin (Eds.), *The handbook of school psychology.* New York: Wiley, 1982.

Kratochwill, T. R. Advances in behavioral assessment. In C. R. Reynolds & T. B. Gutkin (Eds.), *The handbook of school psychology.* New York: Wiley, 1982.

Lachar, D., & Gdowski, C. L. *Actuarial assessment of child and adolescent personality: An interpretive guide for the Personality Inventory for Children.* Los Angeles: Western Psychological Services. 1979.

Larry P. v. Riles (No. C 7122 70RFP). United States District Court for the Northern District of California, San Francisco, October 1979 (slip opinion).

Lewis, D. O., Balla, D. A., & Shanok, S. S. Some evidence of race bias in the diagnosis and treatment of the juvenile offender. *American Journal of Orthopsychiatry, 1979, 49,* 53–61.

Lewis, D. O., Shanok, S. S., Cohen, R. J., Kligfeld, M., & Frisone, G. Race bias in the diagnosis and disposition of violent adolescents. *American Journal of Psychiatry, 1980, 137,* 1211–1216.

Lubin, B., Wallis, R. R., & Paine, C. Patterns of psychological test usage in the United States: 1935–1969. *Professional Psychology, 1971, 2,* 70–74.

Mash, E. J., & Terdal, L. G. *Behavioral assessment of childhood disorders.* New York: Guilford, 1981.

McCarthy, D. *McCarthy scales of Children's Abilities*. New York: The Psychological Corporation, 1972.

Mercer, J. R. In defense of racially and culturally nondiscriminatory assessment. *School Psychology Digest*, 1979, *8*, 89-105.

Messick, S. Test validity and the ethics of assessment. *American Psychologist*, 1980, *35*, 1012-1027.

Nelson, R. O., Hay, L. R., & Hay, W. M. Comments on Cone's "The relevance of reliability and validity for behavioral assessment." *Behavior Therapy*, 1977, *8*, 427-430.

Newland, T. E. Psychological assessment of exceptional children and youth. In W. M. Cruickshank (Ed.), *Psychology of exceptional children and youth* (4th ed.). Englewood Cliffs, N.J.: Prentice-Hall, 1980.

Nunnally, J. *Psychometric theory*. New York: McGraw-Hill, 1978.

O'Leary, K. D., & Johnson, S. B. Psychological assessment. In H. C. Quay & J. S. Werry (Eds.), *Psychopathological disorders of childhood*. New York: Wiley, 1979.

Palmer, D. J. Factors to be considered in placing handicapped children in regular classes. *Journal of School Psychology*, 1980, *18*, 163-171.

PASE: Parents in action on special education v. Hannon (No. C 74 3586RFP). United States District Court for the Northern District of Illinois, Eastern Division, July 1980 (slip opinion).

Reynolds, C. R. Factor structure of the Peabody Individual Achievement Test at five grade levels between grades one and twelve. *Journal of School Psychology*, 1979, *17*, 270-274.(a)

Reynolds, C. R. Should we screen preschoolers? *Contemporary Educational Psychology*, 1979, *4*, 175-181.(b)

Reynolds, C. R. Concurrent validity of what I think and feel: The revised children's manifest anxiety scale. *Journal of Consulting and Clinical Psychology*, 1980, *48*, 774-775.

Reynolds, C. R. The neuropsychological assessment and the habilitation of learning: Consideration in the search for the aptitude × treatment interaction. *School Psychology Review*, 1981, *10*, 343-349.(a).

Reynolds, C. R. The neuropsychological basis of intelligence. In G. Hynd & J. Obrzut (Eds.), *Neuropsychological assessment and the school-age child: Issues and procedures*. New York: Grune & Stratton, 1981.(b)

Reynolds, C. R. The fallacy of "two years below grade level for age" as a diagnostic criterion for reading disorders. *Journal of School Psychology*, 1981, *19*, 350-358.(c)

Reynolds, C. R. *Test bias: In God we trust, all others must have data*. Invited address to the annual meeting of the American Psychological Association, Los Angeles, August 1981.(d)

Reynolds, C. R. The problem of bias in psychological assessment. In C. R. Reynolds & T. B. Gutkin (Eds.), *The handbook of school psychology*. New York: Wiley, 1982.

Reynolds, C. R., & Brown, R. T. Bias in mental testing: An introduction to the issues. In C. R. Reynolds & R. T. Brown (Eds.), *Perspective on bias in mental testing*. New York: Plenum, 1984.

Reynolds, C. R., & Clark, J. Cognitive assessment of the preschool child. In K. D. Paget & B. Bracken (Eds.), *Psychoeducational assessment of the preschool and primary aged child.* New York: Grune & Stratton, 1982.

Reynolds, C. R., & Elliott, S. N. *Trends in test publishing.* Paper presented to the annual meeting of the National Council on Measurement in Education, New York, April 1982.

Reynolds, C. R., & Gutkin, T. B. A multivariate comparison of the intellectual performance of blacks and whites matched on four demographic variables. *Personality and Individual Differences,* 1981, *2,* 175–181.

Reynolds, C. R., & Richmond, B. O. What I think and feel: A revised measure of children's manifest anxiety. *Journal of Abnormal Child Psychology,* 1978, *6,* 271–280.

Reynolds, C. R., & Richmond, B. O. *Revised children's manifest anxiety scale.* Los Angeles: Western Psychological Services, 1985.

Reynolds, C. R., & Willson, V. *Application of measurement in the classroom.* New York: Wiley, in press.

Salvia, J., & Ysseldyke, J. E. *Assessment in special and remedial education* (2nd ed.). Boston: Houghton Mifflin, 1981.

Sattler, J. M. *Assessment of children's intelligence and special abilities* (2nd ed.). Boston: Allyn & Bacon, 1982.

Shorr, D. N., McClelland, S. E., & Robinson, H. B. Corrected mental age scores for the Stanford-Binet Intelligence Scale. *Measurement and Evaluation in Guidance,* 1977, *10,* 144–147.

Spielberger, C. D. *Manual for the state-trait anxiety inventory for children.* Palo Alto, Calif.: Consulting Psychologists Press, 1973.

Thorndike, R. L., & Hagen, E. P. *Measurement and evaluation in psychology and education* (4th ed.), New York: Wiley, 1977.

Wechsler, D. *Wechsler Preschool and Primary Scale of Intelligence.* New York: Psychological Corporation, 1967.

Wechsler, D. *Wechsler Intelligence Scale for Children—Revised.* New York: Psychological Corporation, 1974.

Wechsler, D. *Wechsler Adult Intelligence Scale—Revised.* New York: Psychological Corporation, 1981.

Whyte, W. H. How to cheat on personality tests. In D. Jackson & S. Messick (Eds.), *Problems in Human Assessment.* New York: McGraw-Hill, 1967.

Wirt, R. D., Lachar, D., Kleindinst, J. K., & Seat, P. D. *Multidimensional description of child personality. A manual for the Personality Inventory for Children.* Los Angeles: Western Psychological Services, 1977.

Woodcock, R. W. *Woodcock Reading Mastery Tests.* Circle Pines, Minn.: American Guidance Service, 1973.

Wright, B. J., & Isenstein, V. R. *Psychological tests and minorities.* Rockville, MD: NIMH, DHEW Publication # ADM 78–482, 1977.

Yssseldyke, J. E., Algozzine, B., Regan, R., & McGue, M. The influence of test scores and naturally-occurring pupil characteristics on psychoeducational decision making with children. *Journal of School Psychology,* 1981, *19,* 167–177.

CHAPTER 5

The Observation and Classification of Exceptional Child Behavior

PAUL A. MCDERMOTT

The study of children's extraordinary behavior has concerned behavioral scientists and educators for more than 150 years. Our understanding has benefited greatly by the continuous and systematic observation of children in the natural social environs of their learning and development. Frequently, however, scientific advancement is impeded by preoccupation with certain theoreocentric notions about children's intrapsychic emotions and thought processes and by an overemphasis on the value of professional prerogative and clinical intuition.

We now face the harsh reality that conventional methods of child diagnosis and classification are woefully inadequate. Evaluation research shows that child specialists are simply unable to render consistent (and therefore valid) diagnoses in child clinical psychiatry and psychology (Beitchman, Dielman, Landis, Benson, & Kemp, 1978; Freeman, 1971), school psychology (McDermott, 1980a), or special education (Flor, 1978; Petersen & Hart, 1978; Thurlow, Ysseldyke, & Casey, 1984). The advent of newly revised and expanded clinical classification systems by the World Health Organization (1978) and American Psychiatric Association (1980) brought little improvement, with child clinicians being unable to demonstrate levels of diagnostic agreement significantly beyond what might be expected of untrained individuals (Rutter & Shaffer, 1980; Spitzer, Forman, & Nee, 1979). More critically, the typologies of major clinical classification systems lack the fundamental empirical bases upon which all valid scientific classification rests (see Achenbach & Edelbrock, 1978, for a comprehensive review).

I wish to express deep appreciation to my wife, Andrea, and children, Mac and Megan, for their valuable assistance throughout the preparation of this chapter. Gratitude is extended further to the many developers of behavior rating instruments who provided materials for analysis and to the Graduate School of Education of the University of Pennsylvania for its partial support of this work.

Problems with clinical classification systems have been attributed to a variety of factors. Garfield (1978) noted the absence of true reference standards against which clinical classifications may be evaluated. Spitzer, Endicott, and Robins (1975) point to the inevitable irregularities in diagnostic practice caused by contradictory diagnostic criteria, and McDermott (1981c) detailed specific sources of diagnostic error linked to clinicians' theoretical inconsistency, vulnerability to biasing cues, and adoption of idiosyncratic decision-making styles. Each of these concerns accents the need for sound, empirically derived, and reliable systems for the classification of childhood exceptionality.

This chapter is devoted to the foundation and application of empirical systems of child classification. As an alternative to the more traditional clinical or *categorical* approaches, the chapter presents primary criteria for the development of empirical classification schemes and then assesses existing empirical or *dimensional* classification schemes in the light of such criteria. Focus turns next to the application of emergent and advanced *multidimensional* classification systems and to their still unexplored relationships with clinical systems of child psychopathology.

REQUIREMENTS FOR EMPIRICAL SYSTEMS OF BEHAVIOR CLASSIFICATION

Sound empirical approaches to classification of childhood exceptionality are formed upon twelve primary principles. These are as follows:

1.   Phenomenological measures. The system must be based on phenomenological versus inferential measures of exceptionality; that is, children's problems and aberrant characteristics must be directly observable, behaviorally defined, and verifiable, and not inferred merely through subjective reasoning. Hence whereas this strategy does not reject the potential importance of hypothetical constructs (such as anxiety) or internal psychological processes (such as thoughts or desires), it does not rest necessarily upon the verity of such concepts. Moreover, by eliminating the need for subjective interpretation of the significance of abnormal child behaviors, the phenomenological measures may be applied readily by persons not trained in clinical decision making.

The ideal tool for gathering phenomenological measures is a behavior rating scale, checklist, or questionnaire. Such instruments provide respondent observers with clear behavioral descriptions that can be used to describe children's different styles of coping with self and others in naturalistic, rather than contrived, social settings. These standardized behavioral observations further make it possible to draw comparisons across children, age groups, cultures, and social contexts.

2.   Competent observers. Phenomenological measures of child behavior should be obtained through observations by those most familiar with children and contextually knowledgeable of the social situations in which they function. Ordinarily this means parents and other responsible adults who spend large amounts of time with children, such as nurses, day care workers, and teachers. It is a mistake to assume that clinical specialists can better ascertain the nature of exceptional child behavior. Indeed compelling evidence demonstrates that clinical "experts" have no advantage over the untrained in accurately assessing problem behavior (Sarbin, Taft, & Bailey, 1960; Weintraub, Meale, & Liebert, 1975) with agreement among behavioral observations by parents and teachers exceeding that found among observations by clinicians (Miller, 1964).

For school age children, observations by teachers afford a special perspective inasmuch as teachers see large numbers of children interacting in a variety of social, competitive, and learning situations. This makes possible the nomothetic comparison of children with agemates. Parents, on the other hand, have unique knowledge of children's eating and sleeping habits, free-time activities, physical vulnerabilities, and the like.

3. Summative evaluations. Reliable and externally relevant assessments of child behavior should be concluded on the basis of a continuous series of observations. For classroom behavior this means summative evaluations gathered after 50 or more school days. Sufficient time is required to observe children's recurrent behavior patterns, subtle reactions, and methods of coping under a variety of circumstances. Assessments drawn from continuous observation in common social settings are more directly and immediately generalizable than assessments drawn from observations in brief and isolated clinical examination sessions with children.

4. Unobtrusive observations. Objective measurement of children's behavior should not change discernibly the behavior being measured. Traditional diagnostic procedures, including testing, interviews, and home or classroom observation by outside persons, have a profound impact upon child behavior (Hunter, 1977; Webb, Campbell, Schwartz, & Secrest, 1981) to the extent that the results obtained are more or less a function of children's knowledge that they are being observed. The reactive effects of obtrusive measurement upon natural child behavior cannot be overemphasized. It seems far more reasonable to base measurement upon observations by persons intrinsically natural to specific social environments, such as the parent at home or teacher in the classroom.

5. Dimensional typologies. An empirically based classification system must result in a dimensional rather than categorical typology. Clinical or *categorical typologies* are formed when children are grouped into presumably homogeneous types sharing discrete traits; hence, for example, children with rather low IQs are separated by that characteristic into the categorical typology known as "mentally retarded" and children displaying deviant behaviors are relegated to the "behaviorally" or "emotionally disturbed" category. The intended purpose of a category is to bring together children requiring a similar treatment course. However, unintended and undesirable consequences frequently result.

In the first place, it is assumed that category members are more similar to one another than to nonmembers. This notion makes little sense inasmuch as categorical membership is typically determined on the basis of a few arbitrarily selected traits attributed to children without regard for the greater variety of qualities children manifest (e.g., motivation levels, opportunity, differential learning styles, cultural orientation). Second, children grouped into discrete categories are soon viewed as inherently and permanently possessing the traits for which the category is named (e.g., "retarded"). In addition, members of categories, in an effort to cope with perceived social expectations, often accommodate to the group norm by assimilating more of the nominal trait quality; that is, children may adjust by behaving more and diversely "mentally retarded" or "emotionally disturbed."

In contrast, *dimensional typologies* are built upon one or more continuous qualities which all children manifest to some extent. For example, every child may be seen as sharing the dimensional quality referred to as "assertiveness." However, whereas the quality assertiveness is universal among children, its manifest intensity will vary depending upon social climate, development, remedial education, and a host of other factors.

6. *Appropriate norm base.* Observational measures must be standardized in a manner compatible with whatever differential comparisons are to be made among children or across types of exceptionality. This means that any behavioral dimension to be applied in determining the degree of children's normal versus deviant behavior must have been developed from a representative normative group composed of relatively normal *and* deviant children. Such general norm bases are obtained by either of two methods, that is, random aggregation or selected cohort aggregation.

In random aggregation a large target population (e.g., all elementary school children in a geographical area) is identified first. A random (and manageably smaller) sample of the population is chosen and behavioral observations are compiled. Since the sample is a random portion of the larger population, it will be maximally representative of that population in terms of frequency, prevalence, and patterns of behaviors observed. Comparisons of behaviors of newly observed children with those of children in the randomly aggregated norm base will reveal the rarity of the behavior, as well as its similarity to behaviors observed in normal and deviant segments of the population. Thus differential classification is carried out easily.

In *selected cohort aggregation* predetermined subgroups within the general population constitute the sample. Selected numbers of children from specific segments of the population (normals, behaviorally disturbed, behaviorally talented, etc.) are combined to form a single cohort of children. Whereas the selected cohort approach does not enable one to learn much about the prevalence or rarity of exceptional behavior, it does permit the comparisons necessary to discern children's probable membership in specific subgroups of the population. One limitation of selected cohorts is that one cannot know the probability of children's membership in subgroups not included in the aggregation process.

Both randomly and arbitrarily constructed norm groups are, in one way or another, representative of some general population of children; therefore, the resultant measures are deemed *general norms*. This suggests that for every pertinent behavioral dimension, there must be a normative distribution of scores, usually with normal and deviant children having scores at opposite extremes of the dimension. Occasionally, however, one finds behavior rating devices that provide no general norms for the entire collection of children but, instead, *furcated norms* with different continua and different distributions of scores, for each specific subgroup. Thus a set of norms may exist for normal children and others for different types of exceptional children. A furcated norm base has no use in making differential classifications of children into subgroups of the general population. They are applied only when one already knows the subgroup membership of a given child and is interested merely in knowing how that child compares to other members of the subgroup.

7.   *Healthy behavior variants.* An objective classification scheme must provide "healthy," positive, or benign variations of child behavior that observers may choose alternatively in describing a child's behavior patterns. Even though the principal focus of study is children's exceptional behavior, it is inappropriate to ask observers to select phenomenological indicators from collections composed exclusively of exceptional (usually negative) behaviors. Measurement specialists warn of the potential biasing effects wrought by unidirectional polarity or valence in scale development. Respondents seeing only negative behavior items may assume they are expected to find something wrong with the child. Other respondents, particularly parents, may become concerned or annoyed about being asked to describe the nature and frequency of their child's "bad" behaviors only, and some observers react by refusing to complete rating devices or by compensating through response biases in an erroneously positive direction.

Healthy behavioral variants can be included in observation instruments in a variety of ways. One technique is to develop bipolar behavioral items (see Herbert, 1974). Thus, for example, a child's behavior in competitive school games may be rated on a continuum ranging from "always assertive" to "always unassertive." Nunnally (1978), however, noted that the design of seemingly appropriate bipolar continua is a very difficult task. Another way is to balance the number of healthy behavior variants by altering the valence of items. For instance, Figure 5.1 shows a behavior rating instrument designed to measure children's differential styles of learning (Stott, McDermott, Green, & Francis, 1985). The first eight behavioral descriptions are positive (healthy) in valence, whereas descriptions in the latter half of the scale are negative in valence. Actually, there are few behavioral phenomena that cannot be described from either a positive or negative perspective. One other useful method, demonstrated by Stott (1985), presents an environmental context and a variety of behaviors that might occur therein, including a number of ordinary or unexceptional behaviors. In most cases, the availability of healthy item variants reduces biasing effects by breaking down a respondent's tendency to adopt response sets in rating behavior.

Child's Name _____ Male _____ Female _____

Teacher Completing Scale _____ Date Scale Completed _____

Mark the appropriate space against each of the following statements, *taking into consideration the child's age.*

	Usually applies	Sometimes applies	Doesn't apply
Shows by his answers that he is giving attention.	——	——	——
Settles down well at an activity that needs some concentration.	——	——	——
Copes with something new without getting nervous or upset.	——	——	——
Is willing to fall in with the general activities of the class.	——	——	——
Is willing to try on his own.	——	——	——
Accepts help when he cannot manage a task.	——	——	——
Is an alert child who enters into activities with interest.	——	——	——
Moves on easily from one task to another.	——	——	——
Prefers his own way of doing things, which often doesn't work out.	——	——	——
Dull or bright as it pleases him to be.	——	——	——
Acts without taking time to look or to think things out.	——	——	——
Shows a limited range of interests.	——	——	——
Looks for ways of evading learning tasks.	——	——	——
Quits tasks before they are completed.	——	——	——
Makes mistakes without learning from them.	——	——	——
Seems unaware of what tasks call for.	——	——	——

Figure 5.1. The Study of Children's Learning Styles. (Copyright © 1985 by Denis H. Stott, Paul A. McDermott, Leonard F. Green, and Jean M. Francis. Reproduced with permission.).

8. *Behavioral specificity.* Observers' descriptions of child behavior must be exact enough to indicate the specific phenomenologic nature of behavior and to distinguish contextual conditions under which the behavior occurs. To isolate the specific phenomenologic nature of behavior is to go beyond vague global descriptive terms such as "aggressive," "withdrawn," or "impulsive." Such indistinct rubrics have no place as behavioral indicators in an objective system of measurement. If it is important to learn whether a child is "impulsive" or not, it is necessary to present a set of specific behaviors that cumulatively combine to indicate impulsivity. Simply requesting a respondent to rate a child's overall impulsivity compels the respondent to draw an inference about the meaning of a child's behavior.

Table 5.1 presents examples of behavioral items taken from dimensions (referred to as syndromes) on the Bristol Social Adjustment Guides (BSAG; Stott, 1985). Looking, for example, at the selected items under the dimension called "withdrawal," one discovers that the dimension is defined by a variety of specific behaviors occurring in different situations. A youngster could be considered "withdrawn" only when a sufficient quantity and variety of withdrawn behaviors are observed. This suggests also that behavior rating instruments must be comprehensive in that each behavioral dimension will necessitate a suitably representative set of items. Including a multiplicity of items under each dimension further enhances the reliability of resulting measures.

Observation instruments also must tap behaviors that are situationally spe-

Table 5.1.   Representative Behavior Items and Contextual References for Syndromes and Associated Groupings on the Bristol Social Adjustment Guides[a]

| | Underreactive Syndromes | |
Unforthcomingness [13 items]	Withdrawal [9 items]	Depression [10 items]
Chats only when alone with teacher (talking with teacher)	Never makes any sort of social relationship good or bad (liking for sympathy)	Too lacking in energy to bother (asking teacher's help)
Wants adult interest but can't put himself forward (desire for approval or attention)	Quite cut off from people, you can't get near him as a person (general manner with teacher)	Couldn't care whether teacher sees his work or not (general manner with teacher)
Too timid to be any trouble (classroom behavior)	Distant, never wants to talk (talking with teacher)	Too lethargic to be troublesome (classroom behavior)
So quiet you don't really know if he is following or not (paying attention in class)	Never appeals to adult even when hurt or wronged (liking for sympathy)	Shows complete indifference (facing new learning tasks)
Too timid to stand up for himself or even to get involved in an argument (physical courage)	Distant, ignores all others (companionship)	Sits lifelessly most of the time (sitting in desk)

Table 5.1.   *(continued)*

Overreactive Syndromes		
Inconsequence [22 items]	Hostility [17 items]	Peer Maladaptiveness [12 items]
Attends to anything but his work (paying attention in class)	Inclined to be moody (talking with teacher)	Starts off others in scrapping and rough play, disturbs others' game (informal play)
Shouts out or waves arms before he has had time to think (answering questions)	Seems to go out of his way to earn disapproval (desire for approval or attention)	Attacks other children viciously (physical courage)
Has a hit and miss approach to every problem (facing new learning tasks)	Openly does things he knows are wrong in front of teacher (classroom behavior)	Tries to dominate and won't cooperate when he can't get his own way (informal play)
Borrows books from desk without permission (other people's belongings)	May spoil his work purposely (manual tasks or free activity)	Snatches things from other children (other people's belongings)
Twists about in his seat, slips onto floor, climbs about on desk (sitting in desk)	Tries to argue against teacher (asking teacher's help)	Tells on others to try to gain teacher's favor (ways with other children)

Associated Groupings		
Non-Syndromic Underreaction [9 items]	Non-Syndromic Overreaction [12 items]	Neurological [6 items]
Is too unaware of people to greet (greeting teacher)	Has stolen within the school in a cunning underhand way (other people's belongings)	Gets confused and tongue tied (answering questions)
Has not the confidence to try anything difficult (facing new learning tasks)	Mixes mostly with unsettled types (companionship)	Too restless and overactive to heed even for a moment (effect of correction)
Shrinks from active play (informal play)	Foolish or dangerous pranks with a gang (physical courage)	Makes aimless movements with hands (nervous habits, fidgets, etc.)
Lets the more forward push ahead of him (standing in line)	Has truanted once or twice, often suspected of truancy (attendance)	Very jumpy and easily scared (physical courage)
Has his own solitary activity to which he reverts (informal play)	Destructive, defaces with scribbling (belongings)	Has unwilled twitches, jerks (nervous habits, fidgets, etc.)

[a]Entries in brackets are the total number of available behavior items for each syndrome or grouping, with the BSAG having a total of 110 items. Parenthetical entries are situational or social contexts within which behavioral items are presented on the BSAG. BSAG items are reprinted with permission of the author (Copyright © 1970 by Denis H. Stott).

cific. It is worth little to know that a child is perceived as "aggressive" unless it is clear "when," "how," and "with whom." Is the aggression physical? Is it more provocative and intrusive in nature? Is it a competitive sort? Is it related to peer pressure? Is it directed primarily toward authorities or toward agemates? Such questions can be answered only when behavioral items are presented with *contextual references,* that is, when the sociosituational context of observed behavior is explicit. The component behaviors of the BSAG (shown in Table 5.1) illustrate how items can be set within particular contexts. For example, in comparing the sample items for the dimension called "hostility" with those for the "peer maladaptiveness" dimension, it will be noticed that the contextual references (parenthetically enclosed following each item in Table 5.1) for the first dimension indicate overreactive behavior directed toward the teacher while those for the latter dimension indicate overreactive behavior directed toward classmates. These contextual distinctions permit one to isolate important differences in children's behavior problems.

Observation instruments devoid of item specificity or contextual references may pose serious threats to measurement validity. Herbert (1974) cautioned against use of scales amounting to undifferentiated lists of symptoms or malbehaviors. Dimensions measured by sets of specific items within situational contexts help "disguise the factorial hypothesis" (Herbert, 1974, p. 236) of the measurement process; that is, they serve to obscure the underlying behavioral dimension (e.g., aggression or withdrawal) so that respondents having presentiments or prejudices about a child are forced to substantiate their opinions through observation of specific behaviors rather than being allowed to make global trait attributions.

9. Instrument brevity. Behavior rating scales and questionnaires must be sufficiently brief to facilitate convenient application and avoid threats to validity. Whereas the behavioral specificity criterion requires instruments to be sufficiently comprehensive, instruments cannot be so lengthy as to "exhaust" respondents with seemingly endless queries about child behavior. The more popular observation devices contain as few as 11 and as many as 164 behavior items. The briefest of these are considered quick-screening devices or are focused on one type of child behavior to the exclusion of others (e.g., the scale shown in Figure 5.1 is designed to study styles of learning in preschool and primary school children). These scales are brief enough to be applied for observation of entire classrooms of children without imposing greatly on teacher time. The more comprehensive instruments (containing 90 or more items) are intended for differential classification across a variety of behavioral dimensions, for example, depression, somatic complaints, delinquency, or peer maladaptation.

There is little justification for employing instruments that require observers to respond to more than 200 or so behaviors. Some scales go so far as to expect respondents to rate over 500 items. Such devices attempt to give maximum coverage of child behavior but are more likely to cause serious *observer-instrument interaction effects* wherewith respondents become fatigued and bored and begin to adopt patterned response sets (such as rating everything in a neutral, "can't say," or "good behavior" direction) just to terminate the rating process quickly. A similar problem arises when teachers are asked to evaluate whole classes with the more extensive 100–item instruments over a short time period. Response sets emerge such as carefully rating problem children first and thereafter quickly rating everyone else in a positive or neutral direction. If teachers are willing to assist in the measurement process, it makes more sense for the order of children rated to be randomly determined and for the period of rating to be extended over a more reasonable schedule.

10.   Appropriate scaling. The basic unit of measurement used for behavioral observation rating should be compatible with the type of behavioral items employed. Item scaling can range anywhere from 2–point scales (indicating that a particular behavior is or is not observed) to 12–point Likert-type scales. A behavioral checklist usually includes only 2- or 3–point scales corresponding to the behaviors' being "never," "sometimes," or "often" observed. A bipolar continuum spanning between extremes of positive and negative behavior might require a 5- or 7–point scale. Too often, however, scale builders attempt to give instruments an air of precision by supplying scales far too exacting. Sometimes the larger 5- or 7–point scale is employed in the hope that the ratings will yield parametric versus nonparametric score values.

It is usually unreasonable to expect observers to *objectively* discern fine measurement gradations unless items are full bipolar continua. Bipolar behavioral continua are rare. Most behavior rating scales are constructed to indicate problem behavior; that is, the items depict a single extreme pole of a theoretical continuum. The consequent skew in the distribution of ratings (since most children do not exhibit malbehaviors and some few do) makes superfluous the use of scales beyond 2 or 3 points.

11.   Reliability. Behavior observation scales must maintain consistency in their measurement values and produce congruent evaluations across observers. These instruments are subject to the same reliability constraints as conventional psychometric instrumentation. Basically, the *internal consistency* of measured dimensions of child behavior must be substantiated: this means that each dimension must consistently reflect the same behavioral phenomena. Second, the *stability* of behavior measures should be ascertained through test-retest analysis. Behavior measures must be assessed also for *congruence,* that is, interobserver reliability inasmuch as two or more observers evaluating the same children under identical circumstances (e.g., two parents or a teacher and teacher's aide) render similar assessments.

All of the major child rating scales address these issues by providing correlational indices of scale reliability (e.g., see Behar & Stringfield, 1974; Edelbrock, 1979; Isett & Spreat, 1979; Kohn & Rosman, 1972b; Miller, Hampe, Barrett, & Noble, 1972; Quay, 1979; Stott, 1985). (For techniques to assess reliability of behavioral observations in lieu of repeated observations, *see* Rowley, 1976.)

One additional matter deserves consideration at this point. Too frequently scale developers assume that the behavior classifications by two or more observers significantly "agree' because they correlate with one another. However correlation statistics indicate the *relationship between* measures, not the *agreement of* measures (for detailed discussion, see Hopkins & Hermann, 1977). Consider, for example, the case of a group of parents and teachers who independently observe and rate the behaviors of the same children. One might note that, for more problematic children, teachers regularly rate high frequencies of problem behavior. Parents, too, would probably see these children as relatively problematic and would rate them as having more problem behavior. A correlation coefficient is calculated between teacher and parent ratings and it is found positive and significant. Does this mean that teachers' and parents' ratings agree? The answer is no because teachers might rate problem children as significantly more problematic than do parents. To support the agreement hypothesis, it would be necessary initially to demonstrate that the mean levels of problem behavior observed by teachers and parents were not significantly different. Thereafter, the correlation coefficient can be used to confirm interobserver agreement. When item scales are nominal in nature (e.g., the child is "too tired" versus "shy" versus "indifferent"), it is appropriate to employ reliability and agreement statistics designed specially for qualitative data (see Light, 1973).

12. *Validity.* Validity is the single most important requirement of any classification system, empirical or otherwise (see Cromwell, Blashfield, & Strauss, 1975, for further discussion). A classification system must adequately serve the purpose for which it was intended. It is not surprising, therefore, to discover that this requirement is satisfied in one fashion or another by each of the more prominent observation scales. Foremost examples include uses of scale dimensions to predict *retrospectively* to perinatal events (Stott, 1978), to predict *concurrently* to existing criterion groups of exceptional children (Cajar, 1980; Gully & Hosch, 1979) and to discern externally verified incidence of exceptional behavior (Cullinan, Epstein, & Dembinski, 1979; Marston & Stott, 1970; Stott, Marston, & Neill, 1975; Wilson, 1974), and to predict *prognostically* to confirmed future events such as academic success or failure (Kohn & Rosman, 1972a) and criminal involvement (Stott & Wilson, 1977).

EMPIRICAL DIMENSIONS OF EXCEPTIONAL CHILD BEHAVIOR

Derivation of Behavior Dimensions

All quantitative techniques for identifying principal dimensions of behavior derive from the fact that behaviors which are strongly correlated with (related to) one another reflect some of the same phenomena, referred to as common variance. When two or more behaviors are so closely related that common variance is substantial (e.g., when behaviors ordinarily occur simultaneously or consecutively), it is said that a common entity or *dimension* permeates the behaviors. Should the dimension account for much of the variance within a set of behaviors, that dimension may stand as a substitute, thereby reducing a larger collection of individual behaviors to a lesser number of more stable dimensions.

Analytic methods for extracting dimensions from sets of behavior vary according to the type and quantity of behavior, item scaling, and preference of the investigator. Most researchers use factor analytic techniques, but some use cluster or pattern analysis or variance specificity analysis. Each approach is designed to identify integral dimensions within a data set. Factor analysis is more appropriate for large sets of intercorrelated behaviors. Pattern analysis is employed usually when observed behavior is rated on nominal or qualitative scales. Sometimes behaviors are grouped into mutually exclusive dimensions by a cluster analytic process: afterwards, variance specificity tests are applied to determine whether dimensions retain sufficient amounts of reliable and unique variance (i.e., variance not shared with other dimensions).

Behaviors most strongly associated with a dimension define that dimension. In fact, the robust nature of quantitative dimensions is such that only those more strongly related behaviors need be considered thereafter (for empirical proofs of this premise, see Wainer, 1976), with each child obtaining a score equaling the cumulative sum of observed behaviors on that dimension. Thus, on every dimension, a child receives a score representing the degree to which the dimensional quality (called a "trait" by Tryon, 1979) is manifested in typical behavior.

Comparability and Generality of Behavior Dimensions

Over 30 years of factor, cluster, and pattern analytic work have produced a remarkably parsimonious and orderly collection of behavior dimensions across different populations of children and at different points in time (e.g., Achenbach, 1980; Lessing & Zagorin, 1971; Lorr & Jenkins, 1953). This comparability will be illustrated in a later section of the chapter. On the other hand, whereas *comparability across populations* seems evident, behavior *generality within the same population* does not.

Behavioral dimensions may be inconstant across segments of a given population. Recent studies (Campbell & Steinert, 1978; Lobitz & Johnson, 1975) suggest that the nature of what constitutes exceptional behavior may differ qualitatively across normal and deviant subpopulations of children. More precisely, McDermott (1982b) demonstrated that dimensions of disturbed child behavior vary across adjusted and maladjusted children and adolescents. The variation is related to the fact that most behavior rating instruments provide observers with descriptions of problem or symptomatic behaviors and require the presence or intensity of the behaviors to be specified. Consequently, relatively normal children obtain very low scores and deviant children high scores. Since the preponderance of children in the general population are normal (hence, low- or nonscorers), the result is a positively skewed distribution of behaviors, with marked constriction of scores among normals and spread of scores among deviant children. In turn, the strengths and patterns of behavioral intercorrelations within each subpopulation will vary, producing some unique behavior dimensions for each. Indeed at the intuitive level, one might surmise that the component behaviors comprising a dimension (such as "aggression") would differ qualitatively (as well as quantitatively) between adjusted and maladjusted children. This suggests that researchers and practitioners must proceed cautiously before assuming that quantitative dimensions have generality beyond more homogeneous segments of a population, such as disturbed children.

Coverage of Behavior Dimensions

One notable opinion by certain developers of empirical classification systems (e.g., Kohn, 1977; Peterson, 1961; Rutter, 1967) holds that all child psychopathology can be relegated to two or more *broad-band* behavioral dimensions resembling Eysenck's (1953) "extraversion–introversion" versus "neuroticism" dichotomy. An alternative position (whose advocates include Achenback & Edelbrock, 1978, Cattell, 1963, and Stott et al., 1975) contends that the broad-band division is rather simplistic and fails to recognize the great diversity of exceptional behavior observed by clinicians and laypersons. The latter position postulates the existence of a greater number of *narrow-band* dimensions defining specific types of exceptional behaviors beyond the omnidimensional dichotomy.

The coverage controversy basically asks how many behavioral dimensions there are and how many there should be to accurately explain human differences. However, the distinction between broad- and narrow-band dimensions is dubious at best since not all essential factors are held constant when comparisons are made. For example, comparisons of so-called broad- versus narrow-band dimensions are made too often across instruments containing markedly different numbers of component behaviors. Yet the number of behavioral items considered can have an effect on the number of dimensions extracted (Cattell, 1966). Comparisons are sometimes made across sets of dimensions derived through different analytic techniques; it is clear, for instance, that orthogonal versus oblique, principal components versus centroid, and first- versus second-order factoring solutions, and cluster versus factor analytic processes are inclined to yield different numbers of dimensions. The criterion used for deciding upon the number of factors considered significant produces varying numbers of factors (see Harman, 1976, pp. 161ff.). Moreover, assertions regarding the broad- versus narrow-band distinction are often made without considering the specificity of behavioral components across instruments. Some instruments attempt to tap a behavioral concept through one or two representative items, whereas others provide large selections of relevant behaviors. It is likely that items in the former case will be swallowed up by larger dimensions (resembling broad bands) while items in the latter case will form their own integral (narrow-bandlike) dimensions.

Rather than continue this line of controversy, it seems more reasonable to understand that all emergent dimensions of child exceptionality are more or less associated with a limited number of general behavioral *domains*. I include among these a domain of *underreactive-internalized adjustment* dimensions, a domain of *overreactive-externalized adjustment* dimensions, one of *learning effectiveness* dimensions, and one of *social effectiveness* dimensions. The relationship of various empirical dimensions of exceptionality to the overall behavioral domains is illustrated below.

Major Instruments for Assessing Dimensions of Exceptionality

Information pertaining to 20 leading behavior rating scales and checklists is presented in Table 5.2. (In order to conserve space, references for the rating scales are omitted from the chapter's text. References for each scale are cited in Table 5.2, with mailing addresses for obtaining further information listed in the chapter appendix.) Since all of the more popular instruments provide reasonably good data to substantiate basic claims for psychometric reliability and validity, Table 5.2 posts distinguishing properties of each scale. In addition, each scale is evaluated against the requirements earlier introduced for development of empirical classification systems, including methods of sample aggregation, brevity, appropriate scaling, percentage of behavioral indicators found to be phenomenological versus inferential, behavioral specificity, and provision of healthy behavior variants. The statistical procedures for deriving behavioral dimensions are indicated and the resultant dimensions are listed under appropriate domain areas. (Table entries in the column labeled Typological Dimensionality will be discussed later.)

Eighteen of the instruments are designed to measure disturbed behavior, six measure learning problems, and two measure social competence, whereas the AAMD Adaptive Behavior Scale-School Edition (ABS-SE) and The Study of Children's Learning Styles (SCLS) uniquely measure respective adaptive behavior and learning style traits. Most scales require teacher respondents. Children's age levels span from 2 to 18 years with devices such as the Kohn Social Competence Scale (KSC) and Problem Checklist (KPC) and the Preschool Behavior Questionnaire (PBQ) tailored for preschoolers, The AML and Teacher Referral Form (TRF) reserved for elementary school children, and other scales, such as the Louisville Behavior Checklist (LBC) and Conners Parent Rating Scale (CPRS), covering preschool through late adolescent children.

The most striking problem found among some of the evaluated scales is the use of inferential item content. This is confounded whenever contextual references and healthy item variants are absent. Examples include items requiring parents or teachers to evaluate global characteristics such as a youngster's achievement in mathematics or language, items requiring parents to rate children on hypothetical constructs such as anxiety or guilt, items requiring respondents to understand clinical terms such as hyperactivity or depression, items expecting residential care workers to assess observations against what is "normal" or "average," and items compelling observers to determine the nature of children's feeling states and thoughts. One worthwhile method for avoiding many of these difficulties was demonstrated by the BSAG. The item

Table 5.2. Characteristics of 20 Major Child Behavior Rating Scales, Checklists, and Questionnaires

Instrument[a]	Primary Behavioral Focus[b]	Observer[c]	Children's Age Level[d]	Sample Size[e]	Population Type[f]	Aggregation Method[g]	Number of Items	Item Scaling	% Phenomenological Items[h]
AAMD Adaptive Behavior Scale-School Edition (ABS-SE)[1] (Lambert & Nicoll, 1976; Lambert, 1981)	ab, bd	tr	3–17	6523	nm, mr	Sa	570[m]	2-pt, 3-pt	97
The AML (AML)[2] (Cowen et al., 1973)	bd, lp	tr	5–8	2629	gn	Sa	11	5-pt	64
Bristol Social Adjustment Guides (BSAG)[3] and Profile (BSAP)[4] (McDermott, 1980c, 1981a, 1981b, 1982c, 1984; McDermott & Watkins, 1981)	bd	tr	5–15	2527	gn	Ra	110	2-pt	93
Child Behavior Checklist (CBCL)[5] and Profile (CBP)[5] (Achenbach, 1978; Achenbach & Edelbrock, 1979)	bd	pt	6–16	1800	cl	Sa	114	3-pt	71
Children's Behaviour Questionnaire (CBQ)[6] (Rutter, 1967)	bd	tr	7–13	479	nm, cl	Sa	26	3-pt	88
Conners Parent Rating Scale (CPRS)[7] (Goyette, Conners, & Ulrich, 1978)	bd, lp	pt	3–17	891	gn	Sa	48	4-pt	77
Conners Teacher Rating Scale (CTRS)[8] (Trites, Blouin, & Laprade, 1982)	bd	tr	4–12	9585	gn	Ra	39	4-pt	77

				Behavioral Dimension			
Healthy Item Variants[i]	Contextual References[j]	Method of Deriving Dimensions[k]	Typological Dimensionality[l]	Under-reactive-Internalized Adjustment Domain	Over-reactive-Externalized Adjustment Domain	Learning Effectiveness Domain	Social Effectiveness Domain
−	+	ca	Uni	Personal adjustment	Social adjustment	Personal self-sufficiency Community self-sufficiency	Personal-social responsibility
−	−	fa	Uni	Moody-internalized	Aggressive-acting out	Learning disability	
+	+	ca, fa, va	Multi	Underreaction[n] Unforthcomingness Withdrawal Depression	Overreaction[n] Inconsequence Hostility Peer maladaptiveness		
−[o]	−	fa, so	Multi	Internalizing[n] Schizoid Depressed Obsessive-compulsive Social withdrawal Somatic complaints Uncommunicative (boys) Immature (older boys) Anxious obsessive (girls)	Externalizing[m] Hyperactive Aggressive Delinquent Cruel (girls) Sex problems (girls)		
−	−	fa	Uni	Neurotic	Antisocial		
−	−	fa	Uni	Anxiety Psychosomatic	Conduct problem Impulsive-hyperactive	Learning problem	
−	−	fa	Uni	Anxious-passive	Hyperactivity Conduct problem		

(continued)

Table 5.2. (*continued*)

Instrument[a]	Primary Behavioral Focus[b]	Observer[c]	Children's Age Level[d]	Sample Size[e]	Population Type[f]	Aggregation Method[g]	Number of Items	Item Scaling	% Phenomenological Items[h]
Devereux Child Behavior Rating Scale (DCB)[9] (Spivack & Spotts, 1965)	bd	cw	6–12	252	rd	Sa	97	5-pt to 9-pt	90[p]
Devereux Elementary School Behavior Rating Scale (DESB)[9] (Spivack & Swift, 1966)	bd, lp	tr	5–11	579	nm, mr, ed, rd	Sa	111	3-pt to 7-pt	93[p]
Kohn Social Competence Scale (KSC)[10] (Kohn & Rosman, 1972b; Kohn, Parnes, & Rosman, 1979)	sc	tr	3–5 pre-school	1232	dc	Sa	73	7-pt	92
Kohn Problem Checklist (KPC)[10] (Kohn & Rosman, 1972b; Kohn et al., 1979)	bd	tr	3–5 pre-school	1232	dc	Sa	49	3-pt	90
Louisville Behavior Checklist (LBC)[11] (Miller, 1967a,	bd, lp	pt	3–17	1293	nm, cl, jd	Sa	164	2-pt	86

Healthy Item Variants[i]	Contextual References[j]	Method of Deriving Dimensions[k]	Typological Dimensionality[l]	Behavioral Dimension			
				Under-reactive-Internalized Adjustment Domain	Over-reactive-Externalized Adjustment Domain	Learning Effectiveness Domain	Social Effectiveness Domain
−	+	fa	Uni	Social need-dependence Autistic withdrawal Anxious-fearful ideation Timidity with peers Unresponsiveness to stimulation Eating disturbance	Social aggression Emotional overresponsiveness Inability to delay Unethical behavior Impulse ideation Distractability Inadequate need for independence Messiness-sloppiness	Poor memory and awareness Pronoun confusion Incontinence Poor coordination	Poor self care
−	+	fa	Multi	Achievement anxiety External reliance Inattentive-withdrawn Need for closeness to teacher	Classroom disturbance Impatience Disrespect External blame Irrelevant responsiveness	Creative initiative Comprehension	
+	+	fa	Uni				Interest-participation versus Apathy-withdrawal Cooperation-compliance versus Anger-defiance
−	+	fa	Uni	Apathy-withdrawal versus Interest-participation	Anger-defiance versus Cooperation-compliance		
−	+	fa, so	Uni	Inhibition (internalizing)[n]	Aggression (externalizing)[n]	Learning disability (younger)	

(continued)

Table 5.2. (*continued*)

Instrument[a]	Primary Behavioral Focus[b]	Observer[c]	Children's Age Level[d]	Sample Size[e]	Population Type[f]	Aggregation Method[g]	Number of Items	Item Scaling	% Phenomenological Items[h]
1967b, 1980; Miller, Barrett, Hampe, & Noble, 1971)									
Ohio State Behavior Questionnaire (OSBQ)[12] (Arnold & Smeltzer, 1974)	bd	pt	2–18	351	cl	Sa	74	4-pt	88
Preschool Behavior Questionnaire (PBQ)[13] (Behar, 1977)	bd	tr	3–6	598	nm, cl	Sa	30	3-pt	83
Pupil Behavior Rating Scale (PBRS)[14] (Lambert & Nicoll, 1977)	bd, lp	tr	6	193	gn	Sa	11	3-pt	54
Referral Form Checklist (RFCL)[15] (Kaufman, Swan, & Wood, 1979)	bd	tr, pt	3–13	194	ed	Sa	38	5-pt	74

| Healthy Item Variants[i] | Contextual References[j] | Method of Deriving Dimensions[k] | Typological Dimensionality[l] | Behavioral Dimension | | | |
				Under-reactive-Internalized Adjustment Domain	Over-reactive-Externalized Adjustment Domain	Learning Effectiveness Domain	Social Effectiveness Domain
				Social withdrawal (younger) Anxiety (younger) Sleep disturbance (younger) Immaturity (younger) Apathetic isolation (older) Neuroticism (older) Dependent-inhibited (older) Fear Sensitivity	Infantile aggression (younger) Hyperactivity (younger) Anti-social (younger) Egocentric-exploitive (older) Distructive-assaultive (older) Social delinquency (older) Adolescent turmoil (older)	Academic difficulty (younger)	
−	−	fa	Uni	Withdrawal-depression Inattentive unproductive Somatic complaint (younger) Somatocism (older) Sleep disturbance (older)	Unsocialized aggression Sociopathy Hyperactivity		
−	−	fa	Uni	Anxious-fearful	Hostility-aggressive Hyperactive-distractible		
−	+	ca	Uni	Intrapersonal behavior	Interpersonal behavior	Adaptation (to learning)	
−	−	fa	Uni	Personality problem Inadequacy-immaturity	Conduct problem		

(continued)

Table 5.2. (*continued*)

Instrument[a]	Primary Behavioral Focus[b]	Observer[c]	Children's Age Level[d]	Sample Size[e]	Population Type[f]	Aggregation Method[g]	Number of Items	Item Scaling	% Phenomenological Items[h]
Revised Behavior Problem Checklist (RBPC)[16] (Quay & Peterson, 1983)	bd	tr, pt, cw	5–17 K–12th grd.	1125	nm, gf, ed, cl, rd	Sa	77	3-pt	88
Social Behaviour Rating Scale (SBRS)[17] (Herbert, 1974)	bd, sc	tr	10–11	141	gn (boys)	Sa	49	5-pt[q]	90
The Study of Children's Learning Styles (SCLS)[10] (McDermott & Beitman, 1984)	ls	tr	4–10	2350	nm, se, gf	Sa	16	3-pt	94
Teacher Referral Form (TRF)[18] (Clarfield, 1974)	bd, lp	tr	5–11	373	sr	Sa	49	3-pt	33

[a]References are for cluster and factor dimension studies only: numerical superscripts indicate sources for obtaining additional information on each instrument as listed in the chapter's appendix.

[b]ab = adaptive behavior, bd = behavior disturbance, lp = learning problem, sc = social competence, and ls = learning style.

[c]tr = teacher, pt = parent, and cw = child care worker.

[d]Age in years is based on samples drawn for cluster and factor analytic studies; age range for studies reporting grade levels only, are based on the assumption that most first graders are 6 years old, second graders are 7, and so on.

[e]N = cumulative sample size across available cluster and factor analyses.

[f]nm = normal, mr = mentally retarded, gn = general sample including exceptional children, ed = emotionally disturbed, jd = juvenile delinquent, cl = psychiatric clinic clients, rd = disturbed children in residential care, dc = day care, se = mixed special education, gf = gifted, and sr = school referrals.

[g]Ra = random aggregation and Sa = selected aggregation.

[h]% is not based on scale items omitted from cluster or factor analyses.

[i]A + indicates that positive items are, and a − that they are not, provided regularly.

Healthy Item Variants[i]	Contextual References[j]	Method of Deriving Dimensions[k]	Typological Dimensionality[l]	Behavioral Dimension			
				Under-reactive-Internalized Adjustment Domain	Over-reactive-Externalized Adjustment Domain	Learning Effectiveness Domain	Social Effectiveness Domain
−	+	fa	Uni	Anxiety-withdrawal	Conduct disorder Socialized aggression Attention problem-immaturity Psychotic behavior Motor excess		
+	+	fa	Uni	Personality problem	Conduct problem	Competence	Social extraversion toward children Social extraversion toward adults
+	+	ca, fa	Uni			Overall learning style[n] Avoidant Inattentive Overly independent	
−	−	fa	Uni	Shy-anxious	Acting out Emotional overindulgent Asocial Daydreams/attendance problem	Learning	Social class

[i]A + indicates sufficient, and a − indicates insufficient, behavioral specificity or contextual references for most scale items.

[k]ca = cluster analysis, fa = factor analysis, va = variance specificity analysis, and sc = second-order factor analysis.

[l]Uni = unidimensional and Multi = multidimensional.

[m]The ABS-SE contains 96 behavioral topics, each consisting of several items combining to form 2- to 12-point scales.

[n]A dimension based on second-order factor analysis.

[o]Although the CBCL does not offer healthy behavior variants, it is usually administered subsequent to a social competence questionnaire inquiring about many positive child characteristics.

[p]The DCB and DESB frequently require respondents to assess child behaviors against an undefined standard of "average" or "normal" behavior.

[q]The SBRS provides full bipolar item continua rather than Likert scales applied to unipolar behavioral anchors.

pool for this instrument was compiled over a 30–year period, with the verbal terminology for depicting behaviors being drawn from the parlance of prospective observers, that is, school teachers.

To summarize the evaluations in Table 5.2, nearly all of the instruments fared adequately to exceptionally well. The BSAG and Conners Teacher Rating Scale (CTRS) are the only scales normed on randomly aggregated samples—a most desirable feature. Consistently positive ratings are found also for the KSC, the Social Behaviour Rating Scale (which is the only scale employing true bipolar item continua), and the SCLS. Most of the remaining scales, although showing some problem features, offer advantages in terms of utility for special populations (clinical, residential, juvenile delinquent, etc.) or special respondents (parents, day care workers, etc.), and a wealth of published research work.

MULTIDIMENSIONAL SYSTEMS OF BEHAVIOR CLASSIFICATION

Unidimensional, Multidimensional, and Multiaxial Concepts

The behavior classification systems reviewed thus far are essentially *unidimensional* ones. This means that the behavioral typologies, that is, the distinctly unique types of exceptionality, are based solely on single dimensions. Turning to the lists of dimensions shown in Table 5.2, one might expect then to find among children exceptionality of the "conduct problem" type, or of the "anxiety" type, or "neurotic" type. Whereas unidimensional classifications are certainly more objective than traditional category types, they are, nevertheless, limited in their scope of the distinct patterns of exceptional behavior because they fail to recognize that if every child retains a score on every dimension, some children will have exceptional scores on more than one dimension. Recent analyses of the prevalence of behavior disturbance in a large random population of school children (McDermott, 1980b) demonstrated that 60% of significantly maladjusted children exhibit problems on more than one behavioral dimension. In other words, *multidimensional* typologies better represent the different kinds of exceptionality manifest in the general population of children.

In systems of clinical categorical classification, the notion of multidimensional classification was earliest appreciated by Rutter and his associates (Rutter, Shaffer, & Shepherd, 1973, 1975) who proposed the development of *multiaxial* classifications of child and adult psychiatric disorders, that is, classification grounded upon clinical evaluations of patterns on each of several *axes*. Rutter suggested, for example, an axis of intellectual functioning upon which cognitive deviations such as mental retardation could be classified and an axis of psychiatric functioning on which states of emotional disturbance could be indicated. Multiaxial classification is the clinical counterpart to multidimensional classification in the quantitative sphere.

The multiaxial premise has influenced profoundly the development of the newly revised *Diagnostic and Statistical Manual of Mental Disorders* (DSM-III) (APA, 1980), which sets out rules for psychiatrically assessing children and adults along several axes of functioning. However, the DSM-III version of multiaxial clinical classification diverges appreciably from Rutter's original conceptions: many of the alterations are viewed as obscuring the purposes of multiaxial diagnosis (for comprehensive reviews, see Helmchen, 1980; Meehl, 1979; Rutter & Shaffer, 1980).

Multidimensional Assessment

One unique approach to multidimensional classification emerges from Mc-Dermott's (1982a) development of "actuarial assessment" systems for the grouping and classification of preschool and school age children. The technique, known as McDermott Multidimensional Assessment of Children (M-MAC), employs the usual sort of psychometric and observational tests used by psychologists but applies these data as input for a decision-making process based on statistical probability. The process follows one of many prescribed pathways through a hierarchical logic system, at each step along the way testing the relationships among information gathered from the clinician, the child, teacher, and parents.

The M-MAC classification technique requires information about each child along four integrated dimensions: (1) level of general *intellectual functioning* (based on IQs obtained from one of six individually administered tests); (2) levels of *academic achievement* in reading, mathematics, and other subject areas deemed important (based on one of six popular achievement tests that are administered individually); (3) levels of *adaptive behavior* derived through teacher observations using the ABS-SE, through parent interviews using the Adaptive Behavior Inventory for Children (Mercer & Lewis, 1982), the Vineland Adaptive Behavior Scale (Sparrow, Balla, & Cicchetti, 1983), or Vineland Social Maturity Scale—Revised (Doll, 1965), or based on clinical judgments in accordance with guidelines of the American Association on Mental Deficiency (Grossman, 1983); and (4) levels of *social-emotional adjustment* based on standardized observations through the BSAG, CTRS, KPC, LBC, or RBPC, or on clinical judgments according to DSM-III criteria for child and adolescent disorders.

To facilitate the process, M-MAC is available from The Psychological Corporation for use with Apple microcomputers (McDermott & Watkins, 1985). The microcomputer system retains a variety of distributional and relational statistics for each measuring device and permits the storage and alteration of certain diagnostic criteria, including cutting scores for giftedness, retardation and social-emotional maladjustment, population parameters unique to special subgroups (by race, sex, clinical type, etc.), and population prevalence rates for disorders.

When decisions across the four dimensions are combined, multidimensional classifications result. Each classification is commensurate with national or local special education guidelines and with international standards under the DSM-III and World Health Organization. Moreover, the process is sensitive to clinically derived information such as major sensory handicaps, medical status, unusual talents, linguistic features, environmental conditions, educational background, and cultural differences. M-MAC also provides individual educational plans stated as specific behavioral objectives as developed through criterion-referenced tests of reading, mathematics, and learning styles.

Multidimensional Cluster Analysis

Cluster analytic strategies for empirical classification are distinctly *multivariate* in their ability to consider the simultaneous variation, interdependence, and homogeneity of behavioral data. When used for classification purposes, most clustering methods proceed to "break down" and "divide" large samples of children into groups (clusters). Children in each cluster are maximally similar in terms of the *profile patterns* they have across a number of behavioral dimensions (ergo, multidimensional classifications). This idea of clustering children to draw out characteristic patterns of multiple behavior is consistent with the position that the study of the complex configurations and interactions of behavioral exceptionality is fundamental to the full understanding of human behavior. Application of multidimensional clustering techniques to child classification has been endorsed by leaders in the taxonomy field such as Cromwell et al. (1975) and Achenbach (1980).

Although application of cluster analysis to identify empirical typologies of children is a rather new venture, some worthwhile examples exist (note the designation "Multi" posted in Table 5.2 for Typological Dimensionality of several scales). The McDermott (1980b) study affords some advantages in that it was conducted on the 2527 *randomly* drawn children for the BSAG standardization, thus allowing a unique perspective on the prevalence of exceptional behavior in the general population. Moreover, the BSAG is recognized as a leading international rating scale, having been applied in clinical and research investigations involving over 20,000 American, Canadian, and British children (Davis, Butler, & Goldstein, 1972; Hale & McDermott, 1984; Stott, 1979).

The BSAG cluster study employed six core syndrome (dimension) scores for each child. The six dimensions included: (1) unforthcomingness (U); (2) withdrawal (W); (3) depression (D); (4) inconsequence (Q); (5) hostility (H); and (6) peer maladaptiveness (PM). Sample items from each of these syndromes were presented in Table 5.1. A sequential hierarchical clustering strategy with multiple replications identified 16 homogeneous clusters or patterns of syndromes among the 2527 children. Each cluster constituted a *multidimensional typology* founded upon observed behavior.

To interpret the composition of each typology, mean syndrome values were calculated for each group of children. Additionally, the degree of adjustment versus maladjustment of group members was ascertained through the BSAG's two overall adjustment scales, the underreaction scale (Unract) and the over-reaction scale (Ovract). Table 5.3 displays mean overall adjustment scale and individual syndrome scores in standardized T-score form for each typology. Analysis of the levels and patterns of T scores, as well as group constituency in terms of sex, age prevalence, and component behavior of each typology, produced a brief description of each typology. These descriptions are presented in Table 5.4.

To classify a newly observed child according to this multidimensional system, the child's raw syndrome scores are converted to T scores through the standardized Bristol Social Adjustment Profile (BSAP; McDermott, 1983) shown in Figure 5.2. The youngster is classified to whichever typology in Tables 5.3 and 5.4 the child's profile most closely approximates.

Table 5.3.   Mean Adjustment Scale and Syndrome Scores, Prevalence, and Severity for 16 Typological Clusters of Child Behavior Disturbance on the Bristol Social Adjustment Profile[a]

Cluster Type	% Prevalence in General Population	Overall Adjustment Scale		Core Syndrome					
				Underreaction			Overreaction		
		Unract	Ovract	U	W	D	Q	H	PM
1.	57.0	47	44	48	50	50	45	47	49
2.	8.3	46	56	45	50	50	*61*	52	49
3.	6.0	46	56	48	50	50	54	52	*64*
4.[b]	5.6	*69*	45	*79*	50	57	45	47	49
5.	3.8	47	56	48	50	50	50	*67*	49
6.[c]	3.6	46	*70*	45	50	50	*79*	56	58
7.[b]	3.3	*67*	49	*60*	*78*	57	48	48	49
8.	2.7	56	56	48	56	*71*	59	52	58
9.[c]	2.7	50	*70*	48	50	57	*64*	*67*	*80*
10.[c]	2.0	53	*71*	48	56	57	59	*84*	*64*
11.[c]	1.4	*71*	52	57	*67*	*88*	54	52	49
12.[d]	1.0	50	*91*	48	56	57	*74*	*99*	*89*
13.[c]	1.0	*78*	52	57	*92*	*80*	50	52	49
14.[c]	0.7	*74*	46	57	*99*	*63*	48	47	49
15.[e]	0.5	*67*	*66*	48	50	*96*	*61*	*63*	*64*
16.[d]	0.4	47	*87*	48	50	57	*79*	*78*	*99*

[a]Overall adjustment scale and syndrome scores are mean T scores ($M = 50$, $SD = 10$) for each cluster. Significant T scores, that is, those ≥ 60, are italicized. Names of scales and syndromes corresponding to symbolic abbreviations are found in Table 5.4. $N = 2527$.
[b]Mildly maladjusted where adjustment scale score ≥ 60 and < 70.
[c]Moderately maladjusted where adjustment scale score ≥ 70 and < 80.
[d]Severely maladjusted where adjustment scale score ≥ 80.
[e]Moderately maladjusted where composite of Unract and Ovract scale scores ≥ 70.

Table 5.4. Synopsis of Cluster Types and Component Behaviors for Children's Social Disturbance on the Bristol Social Adjustment Profile[a]

Type 1. Well Adjusted

A group composed of the majority of children in the regular school population in whom teachers observe few, if any, behaviors considered maladaptive; the well-adjusted school child, somewhat more often an early elementary school girl than either a boy or an early adolescent girl.

Type 2. Adjusted with Mild Impulsivity (Q)

A detectable, yet mild, tendency to engage in impulse-ridden behavior carried out in the absence of preplanning or consideration of possible adverse consequences; a style attributed to boys versus girls two out of three times; a sociosyntonic behavior pattern to the extent that it is tolerated by peers and adults and does not elicit social disdain.

Type 3. Adjusted with Mild Peer Conflict (PM)

A noticeable, but mild, degree of difficulty in getting along with some peers although relationships with adults probably remain quite positive; more often seen among preadolescents than adolescents of either sex, and may be associated with typical preadolescent academic and social competition in the school environs.

Type 4. Maladjusted with Moderate Unassertiveness and Avoidance (U)

A moderate and significant unwillingness or inability to assertively express and extend oneself in social and learning situations; found among girls versus boys about two-thirds of the time, somewhat more frequently among early elementary and early adolescent girls and among kindergarten level children of both sexes, and may reflect efforts to cope with the demands of new and changing social roles.

Type 5. Adjusted with Moderate Emancipatory Traits (H)

A complex of attacking and avoiding behaviors which operate to sever unrewarding affiliative relationships through provocative and unfriendly postures and actions; these behaviors almost always are directed toward adults and authorities rather than age mates; most often observed among early and middle adolescent youngsters and is thus considered adaptive to the extent that it reflects common emancipatory reactions.

Type 6. Maladjusted with Moderate Impulsivity and Immaturity (Q)

A behavioral style characterized by successions of erratic, unplanned, physical interventions such as aggressiveness, disruptiveness, attention-seeking, and domineering behaviors; associated with boys versus girls at all age levels about three-quarters of the time; although this pattern is sociosyntonic inasmuch as such children are tolerated by most peers and adults, and are frequently thought to be displaying "boyish" qualities, these youngsters are significantly maladjusted and do not seem to benefit from the conventional social conditioning within the school experience; differential diagnosis should be made between simple overactivity and a hyperactive syndrome (e.g., refer to the Neurological scale [N] on the BSAG).

Type 7. Maladjusted Moderate Withdrawal (W) with Unassertiveness and Shyness (U)

A marked indifference toward or aversion for association with other persons, demonstrated through a general unwillingness to enter into social contexts that might require interpersonal exchanges, such as in cooperative academic performance, games, recreation, and so on; a defensive isolationism.

Type 8. Adjusted with Moderate Motivational Deficit (D)

An observable, yet relatively adaptive, motivational deficit manifesting itself in a failure to respond to, or to seek out, stimulation in the school environment; associated primarily with boys versus girls; sometimes seen as lethargy or laziness, but not considered significantly maladaptive.

Type 9. Maladjusted with Moderate General Overreaction (Ovract)

A general pattern of significant acting-out behavior distinguished by particularly poor relations with age and classmates; may be associated with corresponding behavior modeled by parents or guardians outside of the school.

Type 10. Maladjusted Moderate Hostility Towards Adults (*H*) with Mild Peer Conflict (*PM*)

A collection of instigative and provocative behavioral reactions directed to test the expectations and limitations imposed by authorities; sometimes viewed as predelinquent behavior, but it is more defiant than antisocial; the incidence increases from early childhood through middle adolescence.

Type 11. Severe Depression (*D*) with Mild Withdrawal (*W*)

A relatively serious lack of motivation and/or ability to cope with work and social requirements of common schooling, with an inclination to shun other people, especially adults who would impose performance demands; found predominantly among young adolescent boys and for that reason may be transient; not deemed "clinical depression" inasmuch as affiliative relationships with unimposing persons are maintained.

Type 12. Severe Hostility Towards Others (*H* & *PM*) with Moderate Impulsivity and Immaturity (*Q*)

A class of severe general overreactive behaviors marked by thoughtless aggressions and intrusions upon others' rights; a vicious cycle may be evident involving the child's initial lack of forethought, consequent rejection by peers and adults and, in turn, induced hostility on the child's part; delinquentlike behavior, at least partly reactive; seen in boys versus girls three-fourths of the time.

Type 13. Severe Withdrawal (*W*) and Depression (*D*)

Most profoundly serious of all underreactive types of maladjustment, distinguished by overall socioemotional constriction involving loss of initiative and affiliative needs, and manifesting behaviors usually thought of as "clinical depression"; may be more pronounced among groups of adolescents who have become academic or social failures, or whom perceive themselves as such.

Type 14. Severe Withdrawal (*W*)

A rather outstanding indifference toward human attachments, or perhaps, an active defensiveness against them; when observed, it occurs about four out of five times among early and middle elementary school children; in many cases it may reflect a conditioned defense related to repeated affectional disappointments, such as seen in abandoned or abused children, while in other cases, it may reflect a home-spawned resistance to involvement with the regular school social norm, as sometimes seen among children from subcultural groups.

Type 15. Severe Motivational Deficit (*D*) with Mild General Overreaction (Ovract)

A combination of reaction patterns keyed to a markedly profound and sustained inattentiveness and resistance to the formal educational process, frequently accompanied by relatively obscure aggressive behaviors such as obstructionism, argumentativeness, or uncooperativeness, sometimes directed toward peers, sometimes toward teachers, but usually toward whomever applies pressure for the child's enthusiastic participation in the school milieu; found in boys versus girls two out of three times.

Type 16. Maladjusted Moderate General Overreaction (Ovract) with Severe Peer Conflict (*PM*)

A particularly severe form of general conduct disorder involving much insightless provocation, manifest contempt for authority, aggression and other types of acting-out, with an unusually high level of defiance for peer norms and affiliation; more antisocial than group delinquent oriented; discovered among boys versus girls about three-quarters of the time.

*a*Parenthetical symbols represent BSAG syndrome and scales as noted in the chapter's text.

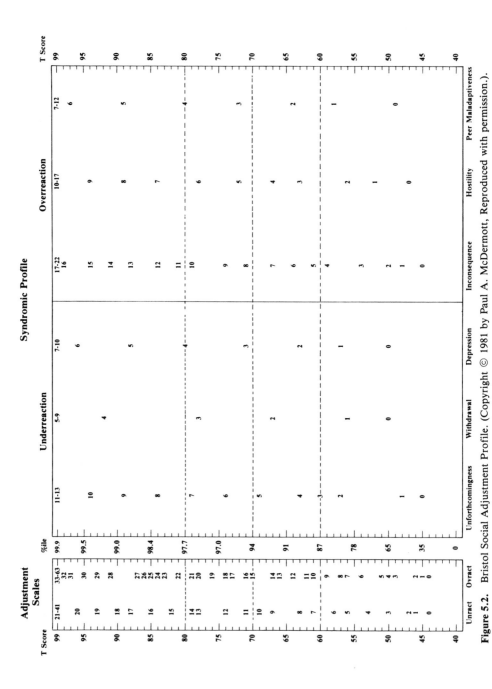

Figure 5.2. Bristol Social Adjustment Profile. (Copyright © 1981 by Paul A. McDermott, Reproduced with permission.).

164

PERSONAL PERSPECTIVE

The principal schools of study in childhood exceptionality, that is, the clinical and what I refer to as the empirical, are progressing at an ever-quickening pace. The clinical school is no longer the "traditional" clinical school, for it is undergoing remarkable transformations in the wake of new classification schemes (viz., ICD-9 and DSM-III) which begin to appreciate the value of behavioral definitions of childhood exceptionality. Empiricists, too, are beginning to wonder whether their quantitative inductions have any counterparts in the clinical systems. Attempts have been made to find some compatibility, some reciprocal confirmation, between major clinical and empirical typologies (e.g., Achenbach, 1980; Lahey, Green, & Forehand, 1980; Miller, 1980). But these cross-system comparisons give a bleak picture, with most clinically deduced child typologies having no empirical counterpart and many empirically based typologies having no match in clinical experience.

However, all efforts thus far to compare clinical and empirical systems have assessed clinical types against *unidimensional* empirical types, that is, empirical systems studied at more formative stages of refinement. Yet the position developed in this chapter holds that advanced *multidimensional* systems produce classifications more reflective of the complex behavioral variations one might expect to discover in children. What would result from a comparison of multidimensional quantitative and clinical disorders? Would we begin to see convergence of these major perspectives? I believe so!

To help our thinking on this, Table 5.5 presents all of the pertinent clinical types found in the DSM-III and the *International Classification of Diseases* (ICD-9) and empirical types identified via multidimensional clustering and actuarial classification analyses. The Devereux Elementary School Behavior Rating Scale (DESB) typologies were extracted from a general sample of 809 kindergarten through sixth-grade children; the BSAP typologies are those described above, identified amid the 2527 randomly drawn 5- to 15-year-old school children from the BSAG; and the Child Behavior Profile (CBP) types are from a cohort of 2553 children aged 6 to 16 referred to guidance clinics for psychological services. The M-MAC typologies are those resulting from computer-assisted statistical analysis of integrated data representing dimensions of intellectual functioning, academic achievement, adaptive behavior, and social-emotional adjustment among 2- to 18-year-old children.

Cross-system counterparts of typologies are approximated by comparing and matching component behaviors and descriptions for each type. Inasmuch as the ICD-9 provides no specific behavioral criteria for classification, specifications from the American clinical modification of ICD-9 (Commission on Professional and Hospital Activities, 1979) were adopted. Each individual typology, whether found to have an approximate counterpart or not, is assigned a type designation (e.g., Tp 1, Tp 2, etc.) in Table 5.5.

Whereas the DSM-III was formed in the image of the ICD-9 and is thereby congruent with it, the various multidimensional systems originated indepen-

Table 5.5. Summary of Approximate Counterparts Among Typologies of Exceptional Child Behavior for Major Clinical and Empirical Classification Systems

	Clinical Classification System		Multidimensional Quantitative Classification System			
Type Code	DSM-III (American Psychiatric Association, 1980)	ICD-9[a] (World Health Organization, 1978)	DESB[b] (Spivack, Swift, & Prewitt, 1971)	BSAP (McDermott, 1980b, 1983)	CBP[c] (Edelbrock & Achenbach, 1980)	M-MAC (McDermott & Watkins, 1985)
	No Psychiatric Condition		*Normal*	*Adjusted*		*No Disorder*
Tp 1/	V71.09. No diagnosis or condition.		Type A. High comprehension-creative initiative [57% girls from 5-9].	Type 1. Well adjusted [57% girls; slightly fewer from 11-13].		1AJ. Good social-emotional adjustment.
Tp 2/	V71.09. No diagnosis or condition.		Type B. Comprehension-initiative [6-10].	Type 1. Well adjusted [57% girls; slightly fewer from 11-13].		1AJ. Good social-emotional adjustment.
Tp 3ᵍ				Type 2. With mild impulsivity (Q) [69% boys].[d]		2AJ. Adequate social-emotional adjustment.
Tp 4ᵍ				Type 3. With mild peer conflict (PM) [slightly more from 8-10][d]		2AJ. Adequate social-emotional adjustment.
Tp 5ᵍ				Type 5. With moderate emancipatory traits (H) [68% from 11-15].[d]		
Tp 6ᵍ				Type 8. With moderate motivational deficit (D) [69% boys].[d]		
Tp 7ᵍ			Type C. Achievement anxiety-compliant [62% girls; 5-7].			
	Adjustment Disorder	*Adjustment Reaction*		*Maladjusted*		
Tp 8/	309.00. With depressed mood.	309.0. Brief depressive reaction.		Type 11. Severe depression (D) with mild withdrawal (W) [85% boys; 44% from 11-13].		
Tp 9/	309.30. With disturbance of conduct.	309.3. With predominant disturbance of conduct.		Type 9. Moderate general overreaction (Ovract).		

(continued)

Tp				*Clinical*	*Disorder*
Tp 10'	309.83. With withdrawal.	309.2. With predominant disturbance of emotions.	Type 7. Moderate withdrawal (W) with unassertiveness and shyness (U).		
	Attention Deficit Disorder	*Hyperkinetic Syndrome of Childhood*	*Aberrant*		
Tp 11'	314.00. Without hyperactivity [90% boys].	314.0. Simple disturbance of activity and attention.	Type E. Classroom disturbance-irrelevance [64% boys]. Type 6. Moderate impulsivity and immaturity (Q) [73% boys].[d]		XAD1. Attention deficit disorder without hyperactivity (X = level).
Tp 12'	314.01. With hyperactivity [90% boys].	314.2. Hyperkinetic conduct disorder.	Type 6. Moderate impulsivity and immaturity (Q) with neurological signs (N) [boys].	YBG-E, OB-D. Hyperactive[d] or OG-D. Immature-Hyperactive.[d]	XAD2. Attention deficit disorder with hyperactivity (X = level).
	Conduct Disorder of Childhood or Adolescence	*Disturbance of Conduct Specific to Childhood or Adolescence*			
Tp 13'	312.XX. Nonspecific conduct disorder [boys].	312.X. Nonspecific	Type F. Disturbance-defiance with impulsivity [71% boys from 5-7].		XCD. Conduct disorder (X = level).
Tp 14'	312.00. Undersocialized, aggressive, with 314.00. Attention deficit disorder [boys].	312.0. Unsocialized aggressive disorder with 314.0. Disturbance of activity and attention.	Type 12. Severe hostility towards others (H and PM) with moderate impulsivity and immaturity (Q) [76% boys; fewer from 5-7].	OB-C. Immature-Aggressive [boys 12-16, slightly more 12-13].	
Tp 15'	312.00. Undersocialized, aggressive, or 301.70. Antisocial personality disorder [boys].	312.0. Unsocialized aggressive disorder or 301.7. Antisocial personality disorder.	Type 16. Moderate general overreaction (Ovract) with severe peer conflict (PM).	YOG-G. Aggressive-cruel [girls].	
Tp 16	312.10. Undersocialized, nonaggressive.				
Tp 17'	312.21. Socialized, nonaggressive [boys].	312.1. Socialized disturbance of conduct.	Type 10. Moderate hostility towards adults (H) with mild peer conflict (PM) [44% from 14-15].	YG-F, OG-E. Delinquent.[d]	
Tp 18'	312.23. Socialized, aggressive [boys].			YOB-F. Delinquent[d] or OB-E. Uncommunicative-delinquent [boys from 12-16, mostly 13-14].	

Table 5.5. (*continued*)

Type Code	Clinical Classification System		Multidimensional Quantitative Classification System			
	DSM-III (American Psychiatric Association, 1980)	ICD-9[a] (World Health Organization, 1978)	DESB[b] (Spivack, Swift, & Prewitt, 1971)	BSAP (McDermott, 1980b, 1983)	CBP[c] (Edelbrock & Achenbach, 1980)	M-MAC (McDermott & Watkins, 1985)
	Anxiety Disorder of Childhood or Adolescence	*Disturbance of Emotions Specific to Childhood or Adolescence*				
Tp 19[f]	313.XX. Nonspecific anxiety disorder.	313.X. Nonspecific.				XAW. Anxiety-withdrawal disorder (X=level).
Tp 20[f]	313.00. Overanxious disorder [apparently boys].				OG-A. Anxious obsessive [girls from 12–16, more at 13].[d]	
Tp 21[f]	313.00. Overanxious disorder with 312.23. Socialized, aggressive, conduct disorder [boys].	313.3. With mixed disturbance of conduct and emotions.			OG-C. Anxious obsessive-aggressive [girls from 12–16].	
Tp 22[f]	313.21. Avoidant behavior.	313.2. With sensitivity, shyness, and social withdrawal.		Type 4. Moderate unassertiveness and avoidance (U) [68% girls; 68% from 5–7 and 11–13].[d]		
Tp 23	309.21. Separation anxiety disorder.	309.2. With predominant disturbance of other emotions.				
	Other Disorders of Childhood and Adolescence					
Tp 24[f]	313.23. Elective mutism [slightly more girls].	313.2. Elective mutism.[e]			OB-B. Uncommunicative [boys from 12–16].	CM(P). Possible communication disorde..
Tp 25	313.82. Identity disorder.	313.8. Other or mixed disturbance of emotions.				

(continued)

		Personality Disorder	Type 15. Severe motivational deficit (*D*) with general overreaction (Ovract) [67% boys].	YB-B. Depressed-social withdrawal-aggressive [boys from 6-11].
Tp 26[f]	313.81. Oppositional disorder or 301.84. Passive-aggressive personality disorder.	301.8. Passive-aggressive personality disorder.		
		Neurotic Disorder	Type 14. Severe withdrawal (*W*) [80% from 5-10].[d]	YB-C, OB-A. Schizoid[d] or YB-A. Schizoid-social withdrawal or YG-C. Schizoid obsessive[d] [both sexes 6-16, but mostly 6-11]. OG-F. Depressed withdrawal-delinquent [girls from 12-16, mostly 14-15].
Tp 27[f]	313.22. Schizoid disorder [mostly boys].	301.2. Schizoid personality disorder.		
Tp 28[f]	313.22. Schizoid disorder with 310.21. Socialized, aggressive, conduct disorder [boys].	301.2. Schizoid personality disorder with 312.1. Socialized disturbance of conduct.		
		Other Specific Disorders	Type 13. Severe withdrawal (*W*) and depression (*D*) [60% 14-15].	YG-A. Depressed-Social withdrawal [girls from 6-11].
Tp 29[f]	300.40. Dysthymic disorder [equal cross-sex frequency among children].	300.4. Neurotic depression.		
Tp 30[f]	300.81. Somatization disorder.	300.8. Somatization disorder.[e]		YB-D, YOG-B. Somatic complaints[d] [both sexes from 6-11, girls from 12-16].
Tp 31[g]				YG-D. Sex problems [girls from 6-11].
	Pervasive Developmental Disorder	*Psychosis with Origin Specific to Childhood*		
Tp 32	299.0X. Infantile autism.	299.0. Infantile autism.		
Tp 33	299.9X. Childhood onset, pervasive developmental disorder.	299.9. Schizophrenic syndrome of childhood.		

Table 5.5. *(continued)*

	Clinical Classification System		Multidimensional Quantitative Classification System			
Type Code	DSM-III (American Psychiatric Association, 1980)	ICD-9[a] (World Health Organization, 1978)	DESB[b] (Spivack, Swift, & Prewitt, 1971)	BSAP (McDermott, 1980b, 1983)	CBP[c] (Edelbrock & Achenbach, 1980)	M-MAC (McDermott & Watkins, 1985)
	Disorder with Physical Manifestation	*Syndromes Not Elsewhere Classified*	*Aberrant (contd.)*	*Maladjusted (contd.)*	*Clinical (contd.)*	*Disorder (contd.)*
Tp 34	307.XX. Other disorders (eating, stereotyped movements, sleep).	307. Special syndromes.				
	Specific Developmental Disorder	*Specific Delay in Development*				
Tp 35*f*	315.00. Developmental reading disorder [68% boys].	315.0. Specific reading retardation.	Type D. Underachievement [69% boys from 5–6].			DV1. Developmental reading disorder (learning disability).
Tp 36*f*	315.10. Developmental arithmetic disorder [68% boys].	315.1. Specific arithmetic retardation.	Type D. Underachievement [69% boys from 5–6].			DV2. Developmental arithmetic disorder (learning disability).
Tp 37*f*	315.31. Developmental language disorder [68% boys].	315.3. Developmental speech or language disorder.				CM(P). Possible communication disorder.
	Mental Retardation	*Mental Retardation*				
Tp 38*f*	317.OX. Mild mental retardation or 318.XX. Moderate, severe, or profound mental retardation [68% boys].	317. Mild mental retardation or 318. Other specific mental retardation.				1MR. Mild mental retardation or XMR. Moderate, severe, or profound mental retardation (X=level).

	Conditions Not Attributable to a Mental Disorder	
Tp 39[f]	V62.20. Academic problem.	AOX(P). Possible academic overcompensation (X = subject area) or XER. Educational retardation (X = level).
Tp 40[f]	V62.89. Borderline intellectual functioning.	BD. Borderline intellectual functioning.

Note: Typological entries represent the full complement of disorders and conditions pertinent to children and adolescents as posted in the major clinical classification systems and includes all of the typologies derived through the various empirical clustering procedures. The determination of whether typologies across the systems were reasonably equivalent was based upon comparisons of component behaviors, severity, cross-sex and age prevalence, evidence of external correlates such as physical anomalies and school performance, and constituency of the norm base, for example, random samples from regular schools versus clinic referrals versus school referrals. Since comparisons of typologies are a matter of judgment, the decision to consider typologies as similar or different is subject to error.

[a] the ICD-9 classification system provides no estimates of age or cross-sex prevalence for child or adult typologies.

[b] Inasmuch as cluster typologies for the Devereux scale were based upon children from 5 to 11 years of age only, age prevalence is designated only when it is evident for restricted age groups within the 5 to 11 age range.

[c] Child Behavior Profile clusters are identified according to sex, general age group, and type; for example. OB-C specifies a cluster common to older (O) boys (B) referred to as type C (C) and YBG-E specifies one common to young (Y) boys (B) and girls (G) and designated type E (E).

[d] A typology characterized by a pattern with one significantly elevated dimension amidst several nonelevated dimensions emergent through multidimensional cluster analysis; not to be confused with a unidimensional typology based upon a single syndrome or factor.

[e] The ICD-9 system maintains no exact counterpart to the DSM-III typology provided for this disorder. The typology displayed here is that appearing in the American clinical modification to the ICD-9, known as the ICD-9-CM (Commission on Professional and Hospital Activities, 1979).

[f] Clinical typologies apparently confirmed by a counterpart quantitative typology.

[g] Quantitative typologies with no approximate clinical counterpart.

dently. Despite this and the use of different child populations and, no doubt, the tendency of different clustering strategies to yield somewhat different results (Blashfield, 1980; Everitt, 1979), there is a great deal of congruence among the multidimensional systems. Far more intriguing, however, is the apparent agreement across the clinical and empirical classification systems.

Clinical matches were not found for empirically derived Tp 3 through Tp 7. This is to be expected inasmuch as these types represent different patterns of *normal* child behavior, whereas the DSM-III and ICD-9 clearly focus upon *abnormal* behavior. Tp 31 "sex problems" has no approximate clinical counterpart. On the other hand, clinically based Tp 16, "undersocialized, nonaggressive," is without an empirical counterpart. However, the clinical ICD-9 also fails to recognize such a nosology. Empirical counterparts are absent for Tp 23 "separation anxiety" and Tp 25 "identity disorder," and for the two clinical variations of child psychosis, Tp 32 and 33. Finally, clinical Tp 34, concerning disorders with "physical manifestations," is without an empirical counterpart. The overall rate of congruence across systems (excluding the several empirical typologies of normal behavior) approaches 83% — a rather encouraging figure, notwithstanding the fact that the comparisons are more a matter of judgment than a more fully objective assessment.

I believe there is much to gain in the study of cross-system mismatches. For example, Tp 23 "separation anxiety" may well be the sort of pathology that conventional observation scales cannot readily detect because the respondents either have little opportunity (teachers) or are themselves principals in the syndrome (parents). Presumed pathologies such as Tp 25 "identity disorder" are keyed to theoretical propositions regarding certain intrapsychic processes that would be impossible to confirm or disconfirm. Although difficult to speculate, disorders such as Tp 32's "autism" and Tp 33's "schizophrenia" may be so *rare,* their empirical verification might necessitate observation of large groups of more severely disturbed children. Finally, clinical disorders such as Tp 34's eating, stereotyped movements, and sleep problems are the kinds of conditions manifested through single, but acutely debilitating symptoms. Current dimensional typologies will not reflect conditions based on independent, isolated behaviors: instead they tend to define disorders manifesting a multiplicity of malbehavior. Nonetheless, as Kessler notes (1966, p. 71), a solitary symptomatic behavior, if potent enough, can be devastating in the life of a child.

Comparative analysis of clinical and multidimensional empirical classification systems, such as introduced here, should stimulate much thought and research. The refinement and utility of empirically based classification systems will depend ultimately on how they can provide answers to questions about the genesis and treatment of exceptional child behavior. Our clinical heritage has much to offer in suggesting where to find the answers. Our newly acquired quantitative skills provide much insight into where we have erred in the past and they provide a means for establishing a truly reliable, efficient, and objective approach to observing and classifying exceptional behavior in children.

REFERENCES

Achenbach, T. M. The Child Behavior Profile, 1. Boys aged 6–11. *Journal of Consulting and Clinical Psychology,* 1978, *46,* 478–488.

Achenbach, T. M. DSM-III in light of empirical research on the classification of child psychopathology. *Journal of the American Academy of Child Psychiatry,* 1980, *19,* 395–412.

Achenbach, T. M., & Edelbrock, C. S. The classification of child psychopathology: A review and analysis of research efforts. *Psychological Bulletin,* 1978, *85,* 1275–1301.

Achenbach, T. M., & Edelbrock, C. S. The Child Behavior Profile, 2. Boys aged 12–16 and girls aged 6–11 and 12–16. *Journal of Consulting and Clinical Psychology,* 1979, *47,* 223–233.

American Psychiatric Association. *Diagnostic and statistical manual of mental disorders* (3rd ed.). Washington, D. C.: Author, 1980.

Arnold, L. E., & Smeltzer, D. J. Behavior checklist factor analysis for children and adolescents. *Archives of General Psychiatry,* 1974, *30,* 798–804.

Behar, L. B. The Preschool Behavior Questionnaire. *Journal of Abnormal Child Psychology,* 1977, *5,* 265–275.

Behar, L. B., & Stringfield, S. A. A behavior rating scale for the preschool child. *Developmental Psychology,* 1974, *10,* 601–610.

Beitchman, J. H., Dielman, T. E., Landis, J. R., Benson, R. M., & Kemp, P. L. Reliability of the Group for the Advancement of Psychiatry diagnostic categories in child psychiatry. *Archives of General Psychiatry,* 1978, *35,* 1461–1468.

Blashfield, R. K. Propositions regarding the use of cluster analysis in clinical research. *Journal of Consulting and Clinical Psychology,* 1980, *48,* 456–459.

Cajar, A. H. Characteristics across exceptional categories: EMR, LD, and ED. *Journal of Special Education,* 1980, *14,* 165–173.

Campbell, S. B., & Steinert, Y. Comparison of rating scales of child psychopathology in clinic and nonclinic samples. *Journal of Consulting and Clinical Psychology,* 1978, *46,* 358–359.

Cattell, R. B. Teachers' description of 6-year-olds' personality: A check on structure. *British Journal of Educational Psychology,* 1963, *33,* 210–235.

Cattell, R. B. The scree test for the number of factors. *Multivariate Behavioral Research,* 1966, *1,* 245–276.

Clarfield, S. P. The development of a teacher referral form for identifying early school maladaptation. *American Journal of Community Psychology,* 1974, *2,* 199–210.

Cromwell, R. L., Blashfield, R. K., & Strauss, J. S. Criteria for classification systems. In N. Hobbs (Ed.). *Issues in the classification of children* (Vol. 1). San Francisco: Jossey-Bass, 1975.

Cullinan, D., Epstein, M. H., & Dembinski, R. J. Behavior problems of educationally handicapped and normal pupils. *Journal of Abnormal Child Psychology,* 1979, *7,* 495–502.

Commission on Professional and Hospital Activities. *International classification of* diseases, clinical modification (ICD-9-CM) (9th rev.). Ann Arbor, Mich.: Edwards Bros., 1979.

Cowen, E. L., Dorr, D., Clarfield, S., Kreling, B., McWilliams, S., Pokracki, F., Pratt, D., Terrell, D., & Wilson, A. The AML: A quick-screening device for early identification of school maladaptation. *American Journal of Community Psychology,* 1973, *1,* 12–35.

Davis, R., Butler, N. R., & Goldstein, N. *From birth to seven: Second report of the National Child Development Study.* London: Longman and National Children's Bureau, 1972.

Doll, E. A. *Vineland Social Maturity Scale.* Circle Pines, Minn.: American Guidance Services, 1965.

Edelbrock, C. Empirical classification of children's behavior disorders: Progress based on parent and teacher ratings. *School Psychology Digest,* 1979, *8,* 355–369.

Edelbrock, C., & Achenbach, T. M. A typology of Child Behavior Profile patterns: Distribution and correlates for disturbed children aged 6–16. *Journal of Abnormal Child Psychology,* 1980, *8,* 444–470.

Everitt, B. S. Unresolved problems in cluster analysis. *Biometrics,* 1979, *35,* 169–181.

Eysenck, H. J. *The structure of human personality* (1st ed.). London: Methuen, 1953.

Flor, J. E. Service provider agreement and special education reform. *Dissertation Abstracts International,* 1978, *39,* 10A (University Microfilms No. 79-8734).

Freeman, M. A reliability study of psychiatric diagnosis in childhood and adolescence. *Journal of Child Psychology and Psychiatry,* 1971, *12,* 43–54.

Garfield, S. L. Research problems in clinical diagnosis. *Journal of Consulting and Clinical Psychology,* 1978, *46,* 596–601.

Goyette, C. H., Conners, C. K., & Ulrich, R. F. Normative data on revised Conners' Parent and Teacher Rating Scales. *Journal of Abnormal Child Psychology,* 1978, *6,* 221–236.

Grossman, H. J. (Ed.). *Classification in mental retardation.* Washington, D. C.: American Association on Mental Deficiency, 1983.

Gully, K. J., & Hosch, H. M. Adaptive Behavior Scale: Development as a diagnostic tool with discriminant analysis. *American Journal of Mental Deficiency,* 1979, *83,* 518–523.

Hale, R. L., & McDermott, P. A. Pattern analysis of an actuarial strategy for computerized diagnosis of childhood exceptionality. *Journal of Learning Disabilities,* 1984, *17,* 30–37.

Harman, H. H. *Modern factor analysis* (3rd ed.). Chicago: University of Chicago Press, 1976.

Helmchen, H. Multiaxial systems of classification: Types of axes. *Acta Psychiatrika Scandinavia,* 1980, *61,* 43–51.

Herbert, G. W. Teachers' ratings of classroom behaviour: Factorial structure. *British Journal of Educational Psychology,* 1974, *44,* 233–240.

Hopkins, B. L., & Hermann, J. A. Evaluating interobserver reliability of interval data. *Journal of Applied Behavior Analysis,* 1977, *10,* 121–126.

Hunter, C. P. Classroom observation instruments and teacher inservice training by school psychologists. *School Psychology Monograph,* 1977, *3*(2), 45–88.

Isett, R. D., & Spreat, S. Test-retest and interrater reliability of the AAMD Adaptive Behavior Scale. *American Journal of Mental Deficiency,* 1979, *84,* 93–95.

Kaufman, A. S., Swan, W. W., & Wood, M. M. Dimensions of problem behaviors of emotionally disturbed children as seen by their parents and teachers. *Psychology in the Schools,* 1979, *16,* 207–217.

Kessler, J. W. *Psychopathology of childhood.* Englewood Cliffs, N.J.: Prentice-Hall, 1966.

Kohn, M. *Social competence, symptoms and underachievement in childhood: A longitudinal perspective.* Washington, D. C.: Winston-Wiley, 1977.

Kohn, M., & Rosman, B. L. Relationship of preschool socio-emotional functioning to later intellectual achievement. *Developmental Psychology,* 1972, *6,* 445–452. (a)

Kohn, M., & Rosman, B. L. A social competence scale and symptom checklist for the preschool child: Factor dimensions, their cross-instrument generality, and longitudinal persistence. *Developmental Psychology,* 1972, *6,* 430–444. (b)

Kohn, M., Parnes, B., & Rosman, B. L. *A rating & scoring manual for the Kohn Problem Checklist & Kohn Social Competence Scale.* New York: Authors, 1979.

Lahey, B. B., Green, K. D., & Forehand, R. On the independence of ratings of hyperactivity, conduct problems, and attention deficits in children: A multiple regression analysis. *Journal of Consulting and Clinical Psychology,* 1980, *48,* 566–574.

Lambert, N. M. *AAMD Adaptive Behavior Scale-School Edition: Diagnostic and technical manual.* Monterey, Calif.: Publishers Test Service, 1981.

Lambert, N. M., & Nicoll, R. C. Dimensions of adaptive behavior of retarded and nonretarded public school children. *American Journal of Mental Deficiency,* 1976, *81,* 135–146.

Lambert, N. M., & Nicoll, R. C. Conceptual model for nonintellectual behavior and its relationship to early reading achievement. *Journal of Educational Psychology,* 1977, *69,* 481–490.

Lessing, E., & Zagorin, S. Dimensions of psychopathology in middle childhood as evaluated by three symptom checklists. *Educational and Psychological Measurement,* 1971, *31,* 175–198.

Light, R. J. Issues in the analysis of qualitative data. In R. M. Travers (Ed.), *Second handbook of research on teaching.* Chicago: Rand McNally, 1973.

Lobitz, G. K., & Johnson, S. M. Normal vs. deviant children: A multimethod comparison. *Journal of Abnormal Child Psychology,* 1975, *3,* 353–374.

Lorr, M., & Jenkins, R. L. Patterns of maladjustment in children. *Journal of Clinical Psychology,* 1953, *9,* 16–19.

Marston, N., & Stott, D. H. Inconsequence as a primary type of behaviour disturbance in young children. *British Journal of Educational Psychology,* 1970, *40,* 15–20.

McDermott, P. A. Congruence and typology of diagnoses in school psychology: An empirical study. *Psychology in the Schools,* 1980 *17,* 12–24. (a)

McDermott, P. A. Prevalence and constituency of behavioral disturbance taxonomies in the regular school population. *Journal of Abnormal Child Psychology,* 1980, *8,* 523–536. (b)

McDermott, P. A. Principal components analysis of the revised Bristol Social Adjustment Guides. *British Journal of Educational Psychology, 1980, 50,* 223–228. (c)

McDermott, P. A. The manifestation of problem behaviour in ten age groups of Canadian school children. *Canadial Journal of Behavioural Science,* 1981, *13,* 310–319. (a)

McDermott, P. A. Patterns of disturbance in behaviorally maladjusted children and adolescents. *Journal of Clinical Psychology,* 1981, *37,* 867–874. (b)

McDermott, P. A. Sources of error in the psychoeducational diagnosis of children. *Journal of School Psychology,* 1981, *19,* 31–44. (c)

McDermott, P. A. Actuarial assessment systems for the grouping and classification of schoolchildren. In C. R. Reynolds & T. B. Gutkin (Eds.), *The handbook of school psychology.* New York: Wiley, 1982. (a)

McDermott, P. A. Generality of disordered behavior across populations of normal and deviant school children: Factorial relations analyses. *Multivariate Behavioral Research,* 1982, *17,* 69–85. (b)

McDermott, P. A. Syndromes of social maladaptation among elementary school boys and girls. *Psychology in the Schools,* 1982, *19,* 281–286. (c)

McDermott, P. A. A syndromic typology for analyzing school children's disturbed social behavior. *School Psychology Review,* 1983, *12,* 250–259.

McDermott, P. A. Child behavior disorders by age and sex based on item factoring of the revised Bristol Guides. *Journal of Abnormal Child Psychology,* 1984, *12,* 15–35.

McDermott, P. A., & Beitman, B. S. Standardization of a scale for The Study of Children's Learning Styles: Structure, stability, and criterion validity. *Psychology in the Schools,* 1984, *21,* 5–14.

McDermott, P. A., & Watkins, M. W. Dimensions of maladaptive behavior among kindergarten level children. *Behavioral Disorders,* 1981, *7,* 11–17.

McDermott, P. A., & Watkins, M. W. *Microcomputer systems manual for McDermott MultiDimensional Assessment of Children.* New York: The Psychological Corporation, 1985.

Meehl, P. E. A funny thing happened to me on the way to the latent entries. *Journal of Personality Assessment,* 1979, *43,* 564–577.

Mercer, J. R., & Lewis, J. F. *Adaptive Behavior Inventory for Children.* New York: The Psychological Corporation, 1982.

Miller, L. C. Q—sort agreement among observers of children. *American Journal of Orthopsychiatry,* 1964, *34,* 71–75.

Miller, L. C. Dimensions of psychopathology in middle childhood. *Psychological Reports,* 1967, *21,* 897–903. (a)

Miller, L. C. Louisville Behavior Checklist for males, 6–12 years of age. *Psychological Reports,* 1967, *21,* 885–896 (b)

Miller, L. C. Dimensions of adolescent psychopathology. *Journal of Abnormal Child Psychology,* 1980, *8,* 161–173.

Miller, L. C., Barrett, C. L., Hampe, E., & Noble, H. Revised anxiety scales for the Louisville Behavior Checklist. *Psychological Reports,* 1971, *29,* 503–511.

Miller, L. C., Hampe, E., Barrett, C. L., & Noble, H. Test-retest reliability of parent ratings of children's deviant behavior. *Psychological Reports,* 1972, *31,* 241–250.

Nunnally, J. D. *Psychometric theory* (2nd ed.). New York: McGraw-Hill, 1978.

Petersen, C. R., & Hart, D. H. Use of multiple discriminant function analysis in evaluation of state-wide system for identification of educationally handicapped children. *Psychological Reports,* 1978, *43,* 743–755.

Peterson, D. R. Behavior problems of middle childhood. *Journal of Consulting Psychology,* 1961, *25,* 205–209.

Quay, H. C. Classification. In H. C. Quay & J. S. Werry (Eds.), *Psychopathological disorders of childhood* (2nd ed.). New York: Wiley, 1979.

Quay, H. C., & Peterson, D. R. *Interim manual for the Revised Behavior Problem Checklist.* Coral Gables, Fla.: Authors, 1983.

Rowley, G. L. The reliability of observational measures. *American Educational Research Journal,* 1976, *13,* 51–59.

Rutter, M. A children's behaviour questionnaire for completion by teachers: Preliminary findings. *Journal of Child Psychology and Psychiatry,* 1967, *8,* 1–11.

Rutter, M., & Shaffer, D. DSM-III: A step forward or back in terms of the classification of child psychiatric disorders? *Journal of the American Academy of Child Psychiatry,* 1980, *19,* 371–394.

Rutter, M., Shaffer, D., & Shepherd, M. An evaluation of a proposal for a multiaxial classification of child psychiatric disorders. *Psychological Medicine,* 1973, *3,* 244–250.

Rutter, M., Shaffer, D., & Shepherd, M. *A multi-axial classification of child psychiatric disorders.* Geneva: World Health Organization, 1975.

Sarbin, T. R., Taft, R., & Bailey, D. E. *Clinical inference and cognitive theory.* New York: Holt, Rinehart & Winston, 1960.

Sparrow, S. S., Balla, D. A., & Cicchetti, D. V. *Vineland Adaptive Behavior Scales.* Circle Pines, Minn.: American Guidance Service, 1983.

Spitzer, R. L., Endicott, J. F., & Robins, E. Clinical criteria for psychiatric diagnosis and DSM-III. *American Journal of Psychiatry,* 1975, *132,* 1187–1192.

Spitzer, R. L., Forman, J. B. W., & Nee, J. DSM-III field trials, 1. Initial interrater diagnostic reliability. *American Journal of Psychiatry,* 1979, *136,* 815–817.

Spivack, G., & Spotts, J. The Devereux Child Behavior Scale: Symptom behaviors in latency age children. *American Journal of Mental Deficiency,* 1965, *69,* 839–853.

Spivack, G., & Swift, M. The Devereux Elementary School Behavior Rating Scale: A study of the nature and organization of achievement related classroom behavior. *Journal of Special Education,* 1966, *1,* 71–91.

Spivack, G., Swift, M., & Prewitt, J. Syndromes of disturbed classroom behavior: A behavioral diagnostic system for elementary school. *Journal of Special Education,* 1971, *5,* 269–292.

Stott, D. H. Epidemiological indicators of the origin of behavior disturbance as measured by the Bristol Social Adjustment Guides. *Genetic Psychology Monographs,* 1978, *97,* 127–159.

Stott, D. H. The Bristol Social Adjustment Guides. *Therapeutic Education,* 1979, *7,* 34–44.

Stott, D. H. *Manual to the Bristol Social Adjustment Guides.* San Diego: Educational and Industrial Testing, 1985.

Stott, D. H., Marston, N. C., & Neill, S. J. *Taxonomy of behaviour disturbance.* Guelph, Ontario: Brook Educational, 1975.

Stott, D. H., McDermott, P. A., Green, L. F., & Francis, J. M. *The Study of Children's Learning Styles.* New York: The Psychological Corporation, 1985.

Stott, D. H., & Wilson, D. M. The adult criminal as juvenile. *British Journal of Criminology,* 1977, *17,* 47–57.

Thurlow, M. L., Ysseldyke, J. E., & Casey, A. Teachers' perceptions of criteria for identifying learning disabled students. *Psychology in the Schools,* 1984, *21,* 349–355.

Trites, R. L., Blouin, A. G. A., & Laprade, K. Factor analysis of the Conners Teacher Rating Scale based on a large normative sample. *Journal of Consulting and Clinical Psychology,* 1982, *50,* 615–623.

Tryon, W. W. The test-trait fallacy. *American Psychologist,* 1979, *34,* 402–406.

Wainer, H. Estimating coefficients in linear models: It doesn't make no never-mind. *Psychological Bulletin,* 1976, *83,* 213–217.

Webb, E. J., Campbell, D. T., Schwartz, R. D., & Secrest, L. *Unobtrusive measures: Nonreactive research in the social sciences* (2nd ed.). Boston: Houghton Mifflin, 1981.

Weintraub, S., Meale, J. M., & Liebert, D. E. Teacher ratings of children vulnerable to psychopathology. *American Journal of Orthopsychiatry,* 1975, *45,* 838–845.

Wilson, J. A. Adjustment in the classroom, 2. Patterns of adaptation. *Research in Education,* 1974, *11,* 18–29.

World Health Organization. *Mental disorders: Glossary and guide to their classification in accordance with the ninth revision of the International Classification of Diseases.* Geneva: Author, 1978.

APPENDIX: SOURCES FOR OBTAINING MORE INFORMATION ON CHILD BEHAVIOR OBSERVATION INSTRUMENTS*

1. AAMD ADAPTIVE BEHAVIOR SCALE-SCHOOL EDITION

    Publishers Test Service
    Del Monte Research Park
    Monterey, CA 93940

    Nadine M. Lambert, Ph.D.
    School of Education,
    4507 Tolman Hall
    University of California
    Berkeley, CA 94720

2. THE AML

    Emory L. Cowen, Ph.D.
    Department of Psychology
    University of Rochester
    Rochester, NY 14627

3. BRISTOL SOCIAL ADJUSTMENT GUIDES

    Educational and Industrial
    Testing Service
    Test Department
    P.O. Box 7234
    San Diego, CA 92107

    Denis H. Stott, Ph.D.
    30 Colborn Street
    Guelph, OT N1G 2M5
    Canada

4. BRISTOL SOCIAL ADJUSTMENT PROFILE

    Paul A. McDermott, Ph.D.
    Graduate School of Education

University of Pennsylvania
3700 Walnut Street
Philadelphia, PA 19104

5. CHILD BEHAVIOR CHECKLIST
    AND PROFILE

    Thomas M. Achenbach, Ph.D.
    %Laboratory of
    Developmental Psychology
    Building 15K
    National Institute of Mental
    Health
    9000 Rockville Pike
    Bethesda, MD 20014

6. CHILDREN'S BEHAVIOUR
    QUESTIONNAIRE

    Michael Rutter, M.D.
    Department of Child
    and Adolescent Psychiatry
    Institute of Psychiatry
    De Crespigny Park,
    Denmark Hall
    London SE5 8AF
    England

7. CONNERS PARENT RATING
    SCALE

    C. Keith Conners, Ph.D.
    Department of Behavioral
    Medicine
    Children's Hospital
    111 Michigan Avenue, N.W.
    Washington, DC 20010

8. CONNERS TEACHER RATING
    SCALE

    R. L. Trites, Ph.D.
    Neuropsychology Laboratory
    Royal Ottawa Hospital
    1145 Garling Avenue
    Ottawa, OT K1Z 7K4
    Canada

    C. Keith Conners, Ph.D.
    Department of Behavioral
    Medicine
    Children's Hospital

111 Michigan Avenue, N.W.
Washington, DC 20010

9. DEVEREUX CHILD BEHAVIOR
    RATING SCALE;
    DEVEREUX ELEMENTARY
    SCHOOL BEHAVIOR RATING
    SCALE

    The Devereux School
    Devereux Foundation Press
    Devon, PA 19333

10. KOHN SOCIAL COMPETENCE
    SCALE;
    KOHN PROBLEM CHECKLIST;
    THE STUDY OF CHILDREN'S
    LEARNING STYLES;
    MCDERMOTT
    MULTIDIMENSIONAL
    ASSESSMENT OF CHILDREN

    The Psychological Corporation
    555 Academic Court
    San Antonio, TX 78204

11. LOUISVILLE BEHAVIOR
    CHECKLIST

    Western Psychological Services
    12031 Wilshire Boulevard
    Los Angeles, CA 90025

    Lovick C. Miller, Ph.D.
    Keller Child Psychiatry
    Research Center
    University of Louisville
    Louisville, KY 40292

12. OHIO STATE BEHAVIOR
    QUESTIONNAIRE

    L. Eugene Arnold, M.D.
    Ohio State University
    473 West 12th Avenue
    Columbus, OH 43310

13. PRESCHOOL BEHAVIOR
    QUESTIONNAIRE

    Lenore Behar, Ph.D.
    Division of Mental Health,
    Mental Retardation, and
    Substance Abuse Services

325 North Salisbury Street
Raleigh, NC 27611

14. PUPIL BEHAVIOR RATING SCALE

Process for the Assessment of
Effective School Functioning
Publishers Test Service
2500 Garden Road
Monterey, CA 93940

Nadine M. Lambert, Ph.D.
School of Education,
4507 Tolman Hall
University of California
Berkeley, CA 94720

15. REFERRAL FORM CECKLIST

Mary M. Wood, Ed.D.
Developmental Therapy
Institute
Aderhold Hall
University of Georgia
Athens, GA 30602

16. REVISED BEHAVIOR PROBLEM CHECKLIST

Herbert C. Quay, Ph.D.
Box 248074
University of Miami
Coral Gables, FL 33124

17. SOCIAL BEHAVIOUR RATING SCALE

Geoffrey W. Herbert, Ph.D.
The Queen's College
Somerset Road, Edgbaston
Birmingham B15 2Q4
England

18. TEACHER REFERRAL FORM

Steven P. Clarfield, Ph.D.
Children's Psychiatric Center,
Inc.
59 Broad Street
Eatontown, NJ 07724

CHAPTER 6

Etiology and Development
of Exceptionality

ROBERT T. BROWN

The deformity which I am now exhibiting was caused by my mother being frightened by an elephant; my mother was going along the street when a procession of animals were passing by, there was a terrible crush of people to see them, and unfortunately she was pushed under the Elephant's feet, which frightened her very much; this occurring during a time of pregnancy was the cause of my deformity.
JOSEPH CAREY MERRICK (reprinted in Howell & Ford, 1980, p. 182)

Thus did Merrick—"The Elephant Man"—"The Ugliest Man in the World"— explain the cause of his massive deformities. His belief in what amounts to a form of prenatal imprinting was a widely accepted "fact" in the nineteenth century. More than an "old wives' tale," it also had some degree of scientific acceptability. In an early book on retardation in children, Ireland (1898, p. 24) discusses the effects of fright on pregnant women:

> In all ages women have believed that fright or extreme distress is dangerous to their offspring, causing weakness, deformities, or deafness . . . Mr. Paget gave a case where a girl bore a great resemblance to a monkey, and had a crop of brown, harsh, lank hair on the back and arms. The mother had in early period of pregnancy been terrified by a monkey jumping on her back from a street organ.

But Merrick was wrong in particular and Ireland in general about this particular type of prenatal influence. Merrick had an extremely severe case of neurofibromatosis or von Recklinghausen's syndrome. Von Recklinghausen had described the neurofibromas and fleshy tumors associated with the disease in 1882, during Merrick's lifetime. But only decades later did scientists recognize the link between the syndrome as originally described and Merrick's extreme condition. Further, the condition is now known to be a dominant single-gene

I thank Carol McLean for assistance with the library research for this chapter.

disorder genetically transmitted or arising through spontaneous mutation. Although the genetic basis is known, little can be done short of surgery to treat neurofibromatosis.

Not even surgery can help Mary R., who lives in a rural county in North Carolina. At age five, her IQ is so low as to be unmeasurable—she functions at the level of 3-6 months, appears to have severe visual and auditory disabilities, is subject to generalized (grand mal) seizures, and even shows the rooting reflex. Her functioning is so limited that the exact nature of her disabilities cannot be determined, and lifelong institutionalization is likely. But Mary's Apgar score at birth was 9 (out of a possible 10), and her medical record was normal up to about four years of age.

What happened to Mary? Through a freak and devastating environmental accident, Mary received such an overexposure to lead that when admitted to hospital because of seizures she had a blood-lead level several times that sufficient for a diagnosis of lead poisoning. In some areas of North Carolina, elevated blood-lead levels are common, frequently from eating dirt ("pica") containing flakes of lead-based paint. But Mary's case was different—her parents, poor and uneducated, burned automobile batteries in their house stove for heat. The heated batteries released enough lead into the air to contaminate the whole house and produce severe brain damage in Mary.

The cases of Joseph Merrick and Mary illustrate just two of the ways in which exceptional conditions can arise and some of the ignorance which has— and too often still does—surround them.

PLAN OF THE CHAPTER

Initially some background historical information and important issues are described. Some concepts related to genetic-environment interactions are then presented. The bulk of the chapter catalogs and describes specific genetic and environmental bases of exceptionality and some factors that influence their development. Learning factors will not be specifically considered both because most readers are well aware of their general influences and because authors of other chapters in this volume will be describing the role of learning in various types of exceptional behavior. Learning obviously plays a crucial role in the development of normal and exceptional behavior, and that role will be apparent throughout this chapter and book. Absence of specific coverage does not imply absence of importance. In addition, the influence of family interactions, also of clear importance in development of exceptional behavior, will only be touched on in this chapter; they are discussed in detail in a separate chapter (Martin, Chapter 8, this volume). Where possible, references are made to recent literature reviews rather than to primary sources because the research on many areas is too voluminous to be cited in this overview. In addition, readers may have greater access to the reviews. Throughout, I emphasize that the development of the exceptional is, like that of the normal, a dynamic and interactive process that belies simple statements about static relationships in which initial causes determine final outcomes.

Because of the organization of the book, some overlap between this chapter and others is inevitable. Because of the interactive nature of the development of exceptional children, some of the same processes mentioned in this chapter are discussed by Martin (Chapter 8, this volume). In particular, because so many specific factors associated with handicaps affect overall cognitive development, this chapter and that on mental retardation (Weiss & Weisz, Chapter 10, this volume) cover some of the same topics. As will be seen, however, the two chapters emphasize different information.

SOME IMPORTANT ISSUES

Several issues, which can be framed in the form of questions, are of basic concern in understanding etiology of exceptionality. They appear in one form or another in many chapters on individual exceptionalities in Part 3. They are not independent; a position on one leads to a position on several others.

Are Exceptionalities Caused by Heredity or Environment?

Mark Twain said, "I can stop smoking anytime; I've done it a hundred times." The nature-nurture issue has been routinely "solved" by philosophers and scientists for thousands of years. A new or resurrected solution appears every few years, depending as much on dominant social and political opinions as on new research data or refined theories. After all, Hunt's *Intelligence and Experience* (1961), which emphasized the role of environmental factors on intelligence and which was influential in the development of Head Start, and Jensen's "How Much Can We Boost IQ and Scholastic Achievement?" (1969), which argued that the preschool programs had failed and that IQ was largely genetically based, were separated by only eight years.

The current position, of course, is that normal and exceptional behavior develops through the interaction of heredity and environment. Anastasi's (1958) admonition is generally accepted—we cannot legitimately ask in individual development whether a behavior has occurred by heredity or environment or even how much of a behavior is caused by one or another. We need to study *how* development occurs.

But, understandably, the search for initial causative agents goes on, and with the discovery of such agents advances in treatment and prevention occur.

Are Exceptional Children Continuous or Discontinuous with Normal Children?

Exceptionalities may be viewed as stemming from basically the same causes as normal behavior or from different ones. Similarly, exceptionalities themselves may be viewed as continuous or discontinuous with normal behavior.

The continuity position views exceptionalities as being at the extremes of the distribution of a particular trait, as in, for example, variations in intelligence, selective attention, or coordination. They arise from the same complex of causes as do normal levels. The discontinuity position views exceptionalities as on a distribution separate from normality and arising from different causes. These different causes generally involve a real or putative genetic or environmental cause which produces a defect. In reference to mental retardation, Zigler (1967) has described these as developmental and defect models, respectively.

This issue is similar to what Telford and Sawrey (1981) refer to as quantitative versus qualitative conceptions of exceptionalities. They suggest that a qualitative, discontinuous approach puts the exceptional into separate categories that call for fundamentally different explanations than does normal behavior.

Labels tend to foster qualitative views. Thus the terms "autistic" and "epileptic" imply that there is something distinctively different about the person. Different all too often implies less desirable. Characteristics can be attributed to a label that have little basis in reality. North Carolina uses a label, "Willie M.," after a court case, to describe children and adolescents who have shown violent or aggressive behavior. "Willie M." has come popularly to imply that such children are always violent, whereas for the most part they are basically normal but subject to brief periods of aggressive behavior.

Arguments still rage over whether the continuous or discontinuous approach is more valid. Telford and Sawrey (1981) argue that the quantitative view is becoming more prevalent and in sociopolitical terms that appears to be true. On the other hand, both positions may apply to certain groups. Zigler (1967) has argued for a "two-group" approach to mental retardation. The distribution of mental retardation is bimodal, with one distribution having a mean of 100 and a second, much smaller, one having a mean of about 40. Thus there are far more moderately, severely, and profoundly retarded children than would be expected on the basis of a normal distribution, although the number of mild retardates is about what would be expected. Bimodal distributions frequently reflect two separate distributions plotted together. Zigler suggests that most seriously retarded children have an organic defect of some kind, whereas milder retardates have nothing specifically wrong with them but are less intelligent than normal for the same complex of genetic and environmental factors that makes other people average or above average. Thus, in his terminology, "organic" retardates are discontinuous with normal whereas "familial" are continuous.

Are Handicapping Conditions Organic or Functional?

Handicapping conditions can be viewed as having some particular physiological (organic) basis, which may or may not be continous with normality, or as having been acquired through learning. This question clearly overlaps with the first two. It should be noted, however, that although functional bases are environmental, organic ones may be either genetic or environmental.

Stuttering, schizophrenia, and autism are all conditions about which controversy over organic versus functional basis has raged. As will be seen below, some of the controversy stems from the particular model of exceptionality one adopts.

Which Effects of Exceptionalities Are Direct and Which Are Indirect?

When a particular condition is identified, there is a tendency to attribute all differences affected individuals show to that condition. But except for the most profoundly handicapped, exceptional children, like normal ones, learn from and adapt to their environment and form concepts of their own competence. Behavior of exceptional individuals reflects both the direct effects of the conditions and the indirect effects that occur through learning. Thus although the direct effect of epilepsy is a tendency toward seizures, epileptics are so frequently discriminated against and have such feelings of helplessness that Thompson and O'Quinn (1979) describe them as susceptible to a complex of negative personality factors—fear, anger, sadness, and guilt—that arises indirectly from their experience with their condition and interactions with others.

Occasionally direct and indirect effects become so linked that it is difficult to separate them, and a condition can gain excess characteristics. There is, for example, the notion that truly blind individuals have hyperacuity in other senses that compensates for their lack of vision (see Lowenfeld, 1980, for a review of the literature). Further, according to Zigler (1967), indirect personality-emotional characteristics of mentally retarded children affect them to such an extent that theorists mistake them for direct effects of the retardation. Research by Zigler and his colleagues has demonstrated that the persistence shown by institutionalized retardates apparently results from social deprivation and not from the retardation itself. Zigler suggests that retardates develop other indirect characteristics—fear of failure, outerdirectedness (a tendency to look to others for solutions to problems), and anxiety—that magnify the direct effects of the retardation itself.

Is Early Experience Different from Prior Experience in the Development of Exceptionality?

Implicitly in some philosophers' writings about children (see Kessen, 1965, for examples) and explicitly in clinical, experimental, and developmental psychological literature, early experience has been viewed as crucial for later behavior. Freud (e.g., 1938) viewed traumatic infantile sexual experiences as the inevitable underpinnings of adult neuroses, Hebb (1949) theorized that early complex experience was necessary for the formation of certain brain processes, and Hunt (1961) proposed that early experience was important in the development of human intelligence. Spitz (1945), Bowlby (1951), and many others reported supposedly devastating effects of early maternal deprivation on later social adjustment. Evidence for apparently permanent effects of various early experiences appeared in animal research on, for example, imprinting (e.g., Hess, 1959), effects of early environment on learning and brain structure (e.g., Krech, Rosenzweig, & Bennett, 1962), and effects of early social experience on social behavior in monkeys (e.g., Harlow, 1966).

Along with the research on early experience came behavioral theories of critical periods, some of them patterned after the biological concept (e.g., Scott, 1962). These theories proposed that not only was early experience more important than prior experience but that early experience had permanent effects, with appropriate experience being crucial for normal development and inappropriate experience leading to lasting deleterious effects. Thus, for example, on the basis of studies of recovery from brain damage, Lenneberg (1967) proposed a critical period for language acquisition. Indeed Wachs and Gruen (1982) proposed an enrichment "curriculum" for infants and young children based on early experience research. On the other hand, considerable evidence now indicates that many early experiences do not have long-term effects (e.g., Kagan, Kearsley, & Zelazo, 1978) and that considerable recovery from early deleterious social and physical experience can occur in both nonhumans (e.g., Suomi & Harlow, 1972) and humans (e.g., Clarke & Clarke, 1976). The relatively rapid development during intensive therapy of significant social and other adaptive behaviors, including some language, in a severely isolated child, "Genie," has drawn particular attention (Curtiss, Fromkin, Rigler, Rigler, & Krashen, 1975).

Is Early Behavior Continuous or Discontinuous with Later Behavior?

This issue may be viewed as a variation on the previous one and is one of the most basic issues in developmental psychology. According to the continuity position, which has been dominant in development psychology, later behavior is a predictable outcome of early behavior. Behavior or behavioral dimensions should be stable over time, and the effects of early experience should persist over time. The discontinuity position is a more dynamic one, holding that shifts in development are common and that early behavior does not necessarily lead into later behavior. Recent evidence (e.g., Kagan, Kearsley, & Zelazo, 1978) suggests that noncontinuity may be the general rule of development. Much current research and theorizing are directed toward the description and explanations of trends in development with age. We shall return to the issues of early experience and continuity–noncontinuity at the end of the chapter.

HISTORICAL BACKGROUND

Recency of Knowledge about Causes of Exceptional Behavior

The renaissance in the arts and natural sicences that arose in the fourteenth to the sixteenth centuries did not extend to behavior until the seventeenth and eighteenth centuries. Superstitions about people and their behavior persisted into the nineteenth and even twentieth centuries (Alexander & Selesnick, 1966). For much of history exceptional behavior has been attributed to gods or devils, putative but unobservable organic defects, or extraordinary events. When observable causes were suggested, they were often the result of illogical *post hoc ergo propter hoc* (after this, therefore because of this) reasoning. As with many illnesses, only in the nineteenth century did scientifically based explanations of exceptional behavior emerge.

Examples of misattribution of abnormal behavior are common. Masturbation became linked with mental illness through an eighteenth-century observation that inmates of an asylum masturbated frequently. The correlational observation became a causal interpretation—masturbation caused the mental illness—that had remarkable staying power. Tissot, a Swiss physician, gave masturbation as a cause of epilepsy in 1770. Even Samuel Howe (1848, reprinted in Rosen, Clark, & Kivitz, 1976, p. 54), whose views about mental retardation were generally enlightened, gave it as one cause of idiocy: "Self-abuse, vampyre-like, sucks the very life-blood from its victims by night . . . There are some who not long ago were considered young gentlemen and ladies, but who are now moping idiots." The belief persisted into the twentieth century. Melendy (1917, p. 261), warned against masturbation in the most lurid terms: "It lays the foundation for consumption, paralysis and heart disease. It weakens the memory . . . and even causes many to lose their minds, and others when grown, to commit suicide."

Lest we feel smug about our current scientific integrity, we should keep in mind that recent suggestions that hyperactivity and learning disabilities always stem from minimal brain damage or dysfunction (MBD) and that XYY males are hyperaggressive rested on similar data and reasoning.

Thus most scientific knowledge about both normal and abnormal behavior is both relatively recent and subject to change. A variety of explanations of Down's syndrome have been offered in the twentieth century. (See Weiss & Weisz, Chapter 10, this volume, for Down's original explanation.) Gesell (1928) presciently suggested a "germinal defect," on the basis of virtually complete concordance in identical twins and discordance in dizygotic twins. But most explanations focused on the well-known correlation with mother's age. Down's syndrome was attributed, for example, to fertilization of a subnormal ovum which had been weakened through disease or exhaustion (Lande-Champain, 1954) or to excess oxygen in early pregnancy. Only the development of accurate methods for identifying chromosomes enabled Le Jeune and his co-workers to identify the chromosomal basis (trisomy 21) for Down's syndrome in 1959 (LeJeune, Gautier, & Turpin).

Until relatively recently, the prenatal environment has been viewed as well isolated from the mother, with the "placental barrier" acting to filter out noxious influences. The effect of maternal rubella on congenital cataracts was reported only in 1941, and much of our current knowledge is a result of the rubella epidemic in the United States in 1964 (Cooper, 1977). The fetal alcohol syndrome was described only in 1973 (Jones, Smith, Ulleland & Streissguth).

Not many years earlier, experts denied that ingestion of alcohol by pregnant women had any adverse effects on the offspring (e.g., Montagu, 1965).

Interpretation of the etiology of whole classes of severe behavior disorders has shifted since the early 1960s. At that time, when psychodynamic approaches were dominant, theorists and practitioners attributed most psychopathology, even extreme forms such as infantile autism, to disturbed parent–child relations. Parents, particularly mothers, were blamed for inducing children's disturbed behavior (e.g., Bettelheim, 1967). This orientation led to terms such as "refrigerator mother" or "schizophrenogenic mother" (one who induces schizophrenia in her child). At present the basis for autism and schizophrenia is attributed largely to biological factors. The replacement of the psychological model with a medical one occurred long after convincing empirical evidence supported the medical model, indicating the powerful effects that models or paradigms (Kuhn, 1962) can have on scientific thought and medical and psychological practice.

Recency of Concern about Childhood Exceptionality

For most of the history of study of handicapped people, no distinction has been made between children and adults or childhood and adulthood disorders. Thus no separate consideration of causes of handicaps in children was made, and there was little consideration of developmental influences. Aries (1962) provided considerable evidence to suggest that the concept of childhood is a relatively recent development of Western civilization, arising in the seventeenth or eighteenth century. Before that time, Aries suggests, children were simply viewed as little adults. Indeed scientists who first looked at sperm through a microscope saw and drew a miniature human, a "homunculus," inside the sperm. This clear preformationist view denied an important role to childhood developmental factors.

In the early nineteenth century, attempts were made to classify some childhood conditions separately from those of adults. Among the first to distinguish between mental retardation in children and severe behavior disorders in children was Esquirol in 1838 (Alexander & Selesnick, 1966). By the middle of the nineteenth century, interest in specifying the causes of retardation and other handicaps had increased. By the end of that century, handicaps in children were more clearly identified and etiology of each was considered separately (e.g., Ireland, 1898).

Models of Etiology of Exceptionality

Models or paradigms (Kuhn, 1962) provide frameworks within which researchers and practitioners organize phenomena and explanations. Models determine the way questions are asked and how answers are framed. In relation to exceptionalities, different models not only suggest different potential causes but different diagnostic techniques, treatments, and evaluation of outcomes.

Three basic models of handicaps and pathologies have competed for thousands of years: the magical or demonic, the medical or organic, and the psychological (Alexander & Selesnick, 1966). However, the psychological model has been of serious importance only since the nineteenth century. Its late arrival may reflect a reluctance among people to assume responsibility for their own problems (Alexander & Selesnick, 1966).

The *magical model,* the oldest and most persistent, arose prehistorically and is still seen occasionally today. Ignorant of principles governing the world and the functioning of the human body, primitive people turned to supernatural explanations of the unexpected. Disordered behavior was generally attributed to demonic possession, with treatment consisting or exorcism or even trephining (boring a hole in the skull) to allow the evil spirits to escape from the afflicted body. In ancient Greece the "divine disease," epilepsy, was attributed to habitation by the gods, whereas in other cultures seizures were attributed to habitation by evil spirits.

The *medical model,* or organic model, is the most consistent, having survived virtually unchanged since Hippocrates. Pathological behavior, like a pathological physical condition, is viewed as symptomatic of some underlying organic disorder. The approach is epitomized by Hippocrates (460–377 B.C.E.), who argued that abnormal behavior had its origins in the body. The "divine disease" was not divine at all but based on brain disturbance, stemming, perhaps, from perinatal damage. This modern sounding explanation was part of a larger system that included the theory of the "four humours" that explained a variety of physical and mental disorders in terms of an imbalance among blood, phlegm, yellow bile, and black bile. The humours were linked with particular personality types, the "four temperaments." For example, melancholia resulted from an excess of black bile.

The Roman physician Galen (131–200 C.E.) integrated much of the Hippocratic corpus with his own and others' observations into a mixed bag of fact and fancy, including the theory of the four humours. Since Galen's medical theory was linked to a monotheistic religious philosophy, it appealed to early Christians and dominated Western medicine for over 1500 years, surviving intact into the sixteenth century (see Hunter & Macalpine, 1963, for examples). The humoral theory of mental illness—black bile and all—continued into the eighteenth and nineteenth centuries (Alexander & Selesnick, 1966). Even when the humours were discarded, some authorities tied the accompanying theory of the four temperaments to phrenology and physiognomy (e.g., Powell, 1856).

Until the seventeenth century the only serious competitor with Galen's medical model was the magical model. With the dominance of Galen and the ascendance of Christianity, magical beliefs receded. However, in medieval times there was a resurgence of demonic belief. Thousands who would now be classified as psychotic were burned at the stake or hanged as witches. In the United States, some 20 accused witches were executed in Salem, Massachusetts, in 1682. It is worth noting that a medical model may account for the "bewitched'' girls' affliction: they may have had convulsive ergotism, a type of food poisoning arising from consumption of ergot-tainted rye (Caporael, 1976; Matossian, 1982). During the Reformation, Luther and Calvin both suggested that the retarded were inhabited by the devil (Rosen, Clark, & Kivitz, 1976). Medievel texts debated whether mental illness resulted from an imbalance of humours or habitation by the devil (Hunter & Macalpine, 1963).

The eighteenth century marked the beginning of a more rational and scientific approach in both Europe and the United States. Witch hunts stopped, concerns about treatment of the handicapped increased, and more careful case histories were taken. Pinel's famous release of the insane from their chains at Bicetre, the Paris insane asylum, in 1792 was an outgrowth of his belief that the insanes' disorders were from natural, not sinful, causes. By the mid-nineteenth century, Mackay (1852) attributed the witch hunts to mass hysteria and ignorance:

> There are so many wondrous appearances in nature for which science and philosophy cannot even now account, that it is not surprising that, when natural laws were still less understood, men should have attributed to supernatural agency every appearance which they could not otherwise explain. The merest tyro now understands various phenomena which the wisest of old could not fathom.

In the eighteenth and nineteenth centuries, the medical model made great advances: more careful description of disease forms and syndromes, application of scientific methods to study of diseases, the development of the germ theory of disease, and the development of more sophisticated diagnostic devices. These advances also bore fruition in the study of etiology of abnormal and retarded behavior. The descriptions of "mongolism," cretinism, and cerebral palsy are but three examples of the isolation of homogeneous groups that is a necessary precursor to the discovery of causes. Broca and Wernicke's discoveries that lesions in specific areas of the left hemisphere were associated with forms of aphasia provided evidence that disturbance in behavior may be linked to specific brain damage. The discovery of the germ basis of syphilis, the *spirochete pallida,* in 1913, marked another important advance.

Currently the medical model involves searches for genetic, biochemical, and neuroanatomical bases of exceptional behavior.

The *psychological model* emphasizes the role of past and present environmental factors, the processes through which behavior is acquired, and their interaction with our basic characteristics as humans (or, rather, the characteristics each particular theorist viewed humans as having). It has a quantitative orientation toward exceptionalities in that basically the same influences operate on all people. This model is the most varied and difficult to trace. Obviously, by its name, it has Greek origins: psychology meaning the study of spirit or mind. But more than a name is due to Greek influence—Plato blamed the family for the development of much abnormal behavior (Simon, 1978). Important glimmerings of psychological approaches can be seen in the writings of Cicero and particularly St. Augustine, who can be seen as the "earliest forerunner of psychoanalysis" (Alexander & Selesnick, 1966, p. 59). But until the Renaissance, most "psychological" intervention was done by clerics in the form of exorcism.

In the Renaissance and thereafter, psychological interpretations of the basis of mental illness increased. One famous example, *The Anatomy of Melancholy*, published in 1621, chronicled the experiences of its author, Robert Burton, with depression. Of particular interest is his report of an unhappy and affectionless childhood which left him unable as an adult to find satisfaction with either others or himself.

Although it is not possible to chronicle in detail the gradual awareness that childhood is a time of construction (Kessen, 1965), psychologically and educationally oriented philosophers had important influence on eighteenth and nineteenth century thought about both normal and exceptional behavior. John Locke's (1632–1704) empiricist and constructionist view of development, with the infant as a *tabula rasa* and knowledge arising through association, and Jean-Jacques Rousseau's (1712–1778) emphasis on the importance of self-directed education both had great impact. The acceptance of a role of experience in the development of disordered behavior led to new optimism about the potential reversibility of mental illness and retardation. Jean Marc Itard's attempt to educate Victor, the "Wild Boy of Aveyron," reflected this optimism. Itard, in turn, influenced Edouard Séguin, who proposed in 1846 that retarded people had prolonged infancies and could be educated into normality, a view which was both highly psychological and highly optimistic.

In the twentieth century, psychological models of abnormal behavior and other exceptional conditions became more common and varied. In Sigmund Freud's psychodynamic theory of personality development, early psychosexual experiences, largely mediated by the parents, were held responsible for adult neuroses. The approach adopts aspects of a medical model, in that abnormal behavior is seen as symptomatic of underlying disturbance, but the disturbance itself is a psychological one. Freud's emphasis on early experience, psychological determinism, and parental influences on children's behavior had revolutionary impact on the study of both normal and abnormal behavior. As indicated earlier, the influence of the psychodynamic approach has waned since the 1950s.

The learning version of the psychological model emphasizes the role of operant and respondent conditioning and observational learning as either primary or contributory factors in the development of exceptional behavior. Thus the pairing of a neutral stimulus with an aversive one may, through classical conditioning, result in a phobia. The cognitive version emphasizes the role of learning factors on the child's cognitive processes, both those involved with problem solving and with self-appraisal.

Although competition between organic and psychological explanations of some handicapping conditions has been long bitter, some resolution seems to be occurring. As in so many "either–or" disputes, the resolution is that both models have their place. As will be seen throughout this chapter and book, organic and psychological approaches are frequently intertwined in the form of interactions: a particular condition is manifested only if both an organic predisposing factor and particular environmental condition are present.

DIAGNOSIS AND ETIOLOGY

Accurate diagnosis is as important for understanding etiology as it is for prescribing effective treatment. From the Greek, it literally means thorough (dia) knowledge (gnosis) but essentially refers to the identification of a common set of symptoms that enables one condition to be accurately distinguished from others. Thus diagnosis should lead to categories whose members are homogeneous in their characteristics and different from members of other categories. Once such a homogeneous group has been identified, a possible cause may be found through common factors in such indicators as case histories, biochemical assays, or genetic karyotypes. Once the mechanism of development is understood, treatment or prevention becomes more feasible. Of course, accurate diagnosis is no guarantee of either determination of etiology or development of effective treatment. Further, it should be clear that diagnosis can occur only when the condition is distinctive enough for a clear set of symptoms to exist.

Two examples will serve to show the relationship between diagnosis and etiology. When Fölling noted that the urine of some institutionalized retardates had a distinctive "mousy" odor, he described the symptom that led to the discovery of phenylketonuria. Family history information showed it to be a single-gene recessive disorder, and the affected individuals were found to be unable to metabolize the essential amino acid phenylalanine. That discovery in turn led to development of a diagnostic test for newborn infants and special low phenylalanine diet that prevents the brain damage caused by the condition.

The second case points to the importance of simultaneously identifying common symptoms and of obtaining good case history information. The director of a clinic told the author that diagnosticians would occasionally write on children's folders "syndromish in appearance" or even FLK, "funny looking kid"—something looked different about these children, but no available classification fit. In 1973 the first papers appeared that described and named the fetal alcohol syndrome (Jones & Smith, 1973; Jones et al., 1973). The characteristic facial patterns and other anomalies fit some of the "syndromish" children, who are now classified as having fetal alcohol syndrome.

AN EXAMPLE OF GENETIC-ENVIRONMENT INTERACTION: PKU

Phenylketonuria (PKU) will be used to illustrate several conceptualizations of genetic–environment interactions. PKU is the most common of an increasingly long list of inborn errors of metabolism (McKusick, 1978). No damage occurs prenatally because the embryo and fetus receive nutrients, digested by the mother, through the umbilical cord.

Incomplete metabolism begins when the infant self-feeds after birth. In PKU the homozygotic recessive genotype results in a deficiency in the liver enzyme phenylalanine hydroxylase that normally converts phenylalanine, an essential amino acid common in most foods, to tyrosine. The deficit blocks normal metabolism, leading to high levels of phenylalanine in the blood and excretion of phenylpyruvic acid in the urine. High levels of phenylalanine in the blood produce biochemical and physiological effects which, in an as yet unknown way, damage developing brain tissue. Since damage of brain cells is irreversible, permanent and severe mental retardation and other pathologies are predictable outcomes. Damage is progressive and, until the 1950s, prognosis was poor; most affected individuals were institutionalized.

Prognosis changed dramatically, however, with the development of screening tests that reliably identified affected newborns and a synthetic diet containing very low levels of phenylalanine. This diet, Lofenalac, removes the metabolite ahead of the enzyme block, therefore preventing most brain damage (Vogel & Motulsky, 1979). Effectiveness of the diet varies with the age of the child when treatment begins. Individuals put on the diet shortly after birth and who consume virtually only the diet have average IQs in the low normal range of 90, whereas treatment beginning only at three years of age or so is ineffective (Figure 6.1). The impact of the diet is hard to exaggerate—individuals who would previously have been severely retarded now can lead virtually normal lives. Of course the diet has not "cured" PKU; the affected individual still cannot metabolize phenylalanine. The diet also presents serious management problems. The taste is aversive, and maintaining the affected child on the diet while the rest of the family eats normal food is a problem that gets increasingly serious as the child grows and is able to get into food storage areas. Although there is still some controversy as to how long PKU children should stay on the diet, evidence now suggests that little harm occurs if they begin eating regular food at about eight years of age. By that time, brain development is largely completed, and phenylalanine damages only developing brain tissue.

The effectiveness of the diet has had one perverse and tragic effect. Women with PKU who have been raised on the diet are able to lead normal lives and have children. In the late 1960s, it became clear that children born to PKU women who had eaten normal food during pregnancy suffered prenatal growth retardation, microcephaly, and brain damage even though they did not themselves have PKU. Although the effects were variable, many offspring died early or became severely retarded. Indeed the problems appear more severe than in untreated PKU itself. (See Lenke & Levy, 1980, for a review.) The pregnant woman transmitted unmetabolized phenylalanine to the the embryo and fetus at the most critical period for adverse influences on brain development. Thus the offspring had been exposed to a prenatal environmental biochemical insult that resulted from the mother's genetically based error of metabolism. The initially plausible solution of putting affected women back on the diet when

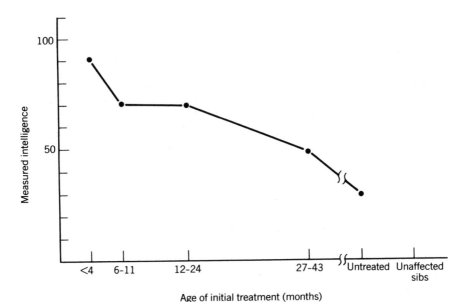

Figure 6.1.   Intelligence of PKU children as a function of age when dietary treatment was begun. (Data from Berman, Waisman, & Graham, 1966.)

they become pregnant is not effective; pregnancy is generally not determined until a time when much damage has already occurred. A common recommendation now is for treated PKU women to return to a low phenylalanine diet throughout the time they may become pregnant. Unfortunately, because phenylalanine is an essential amino acid and because regulation of phenylalanine levels is very complicated, no completely effective dietary program is available. The only wholly safe procedure is for PKU women not to have children. It should be noted that this problem is not limited to PKU, and will apply to all inborn errors of metabolism that can be treated with a special diet. As previously indicated, the diet is not a cure; affected individuals are still unable to metabolize the relevent substance. Thus treated women have an additional responsibility through childbearing years. Because some will be at a marginal level of functioning, social service agencies may need to provide assistance.

CONCEPTS OF GENETIC–ENVIRONMENT INTERACTIONS

This section briefly discusses some ways of describing the dynamic relationships between genetic and environmental factors in development. It should be understood that these are concepts, not mechanisms, and they portray the increasing extent to which the epigenetic relationship between genotype and phenotype is seen as probabilistic and interactive instead of predetermined (Gottlieb, 1983).

Epigenetic Landscape, Canalization, and Critical Periods

Waddington (1962) suggested that the organism can be pictured prenatally as proceeding down an epigenetic landscape largely comprised of "creodes," genetic pathways that are highly buffered against environmental factors. If development tends to go outside the designated pathway, canalizing factors operate to bring the organism back on track. Thus some development should be stable across a variety of environmental factors. Gottlieb (1983) has cogently criticized the concept of canalization as being little more than a new term for innate, and the term does not reflect what is now known about developmental plasticity.

On the other hand, the epigenetic landscape makes clear both the importance of critical periods in development and the facts that similar genotypes can result in different phenotypes and different genotypes result in similar phenotypes via environmental influence. Indicated by forks in the epigenetic landscape, critical periods occur during differentiation of particular organ systems and may shunt the organism irreversibly down a different pathway. As the case of thalidomide clearly indicated, development of even such highly canalized structure as limbs and digits can be adversely affected by teratogens, substances likely to cause development defects.

PKU can be seen as a normally highly canalized system associated with brain damage. But implementation of the special diet during postnatal brain development shunts the organism off of its genetically oriented pathway toward severe mental retardation onto a more normal one leading to phenotypic near normality. Once the critical period has ended, the diet is no longer needed. On the other hand, the genetically normal embryo of a PKU mother eating normal food is shunted off of its pathway oriented toward normality down one that leads to brain damage. Because the teratogen is present during the prenatal critical period for brain differentiation, massive damage occurs.

Continuum of Indirectedness

In a classical article, Anastasi (1958) suggested that genetic effects on behavior be viewed as occurring on a "continuum of indirectedness." Since we inherit genes, not behavior, and since all genetic influences on behavior occur through intermediate steps, all genetic effects on behavior are more or less indirect. They fall on a continuum from "least indirect," such as untreatable genetic syndromes and color blindness, to "most indirect," where a genetically based effect operates through its impact on other people. Social stereotypes are an example of the latter, where individual's behavior is affected by others' behavior toward them on the basis of genetically determined factors such as skin color. The more indirect the genetic effect, the more the environment can influence development. In PKU what is inherited are two recessive genes, not mental retardation. Only through a long and not understood sequence does the genetically determined lack of an enzyme produce brain damage. Further, with new knowledge, a particular effect may shift on the continuum. At the time of Anastasi's paper, dietary treatment was not available and PKU was at the "least indirect" end of the continuum. With the development of the diet, the effects of PKU became more indirect and probabilistic.

Range of Reaction

Genetic background does not predetermine development but establishes a range of quantitatively different phenotypes that may develop under normal variations in the environment (Gottesman, 1963). The word "normal" is used advisedly because under totally adverse conditions, no development will occur and because novel changes in the environment can shift the range of reaction. The three upper lines in Figure 6.2a are typical examples of range of reaction for intelligence across a normal range of environments. The different genotypes are associated with ranges that differ both in degree of range and hypothetical upper limit. The basic point is clear—different genotypes may react differently in different environments. The lowest line indicates that for a PKU genotype across normal variations in the environment, range of reaction is virtually zero. Figure 6.2b shows a very different pattern of range of reaction of two genotypes, one normal and one PKU, to environments that differ in levels of dietary phenylalanine. As we have seen, phenotypic IQ of an individual with PKU will be markedly increased on a low phenylalanine diet. The effects of highly restricted phenylalanine would be expected to interfere with the intelligence of a non-PKU individual. Thus ranges of reaction can show interactional patterns and can change with changes in the environment.

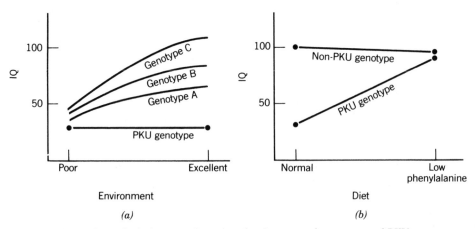

Figure 6.2. (a) Hypothetical ranges of reactions for three normal genotypes and PKU genotype in a normal range of environments. (b) Hypothetical ranges of reaction for a non-PKU and PKU genotype on normal or low phenylalanine diets.

GENETIC INFLUENCES

A variety of handicapping conditions can be traced either to specific genetic defects or to genetic predispositions. Rarely, however, is there a one-to-one correspondence between genotype, an individual's particular genetic endowment, and phenotype, its actual physical characteristics and behavior. This lack of correspondence follows from both the basic principles of genetic influences and the complexity of the interaction between genetic and environmental factors in development. Further, in a few cases, interventions can now successfully prevent or ameliorate the deleterious effects predicted by the genotype from being manifested in the phenotype.

Chromosomal Abnormalities

Chromosomal abnormalities are common in humans, occurring in perhaps half of all fertilizations. Although most lead to spontaneous abortion early in pregnancy, frequently before the woman had any indications of being pregnant, about 1 in 200 survive until birth. Many die shortly after birth and others have shortened life expectancies (Plomin, DeFries, & McClearn, 1980). These abnormalities occur on both autosomes and sex chromosomes and can involve the addition or deletion of whole chromosomes or addition or deletion of parts of chromosomes. As would be expected from the number of genes involved, chromosomal abnormalities tend to have broad physical and behavioral effects. By definition, each syndrome has specific characteristics. Most chromosomal abnormalities lead to general intellective deficiencies, minor in some types but severe in others. Combined, they may account for as many as 25% of institutionalized retardates (Shields, 1977).

In this section we describe the basic types of abnormalities with some examples of each. Incidence figures will be given for some conditions, but such figures vary from study to study and should be treated as approximations. A summary of the major effects of each is in Table 6.1. More detailed descriptions may be found in Vogel and Motulsky (1979), Thompson and Thompson (1980), Kopp (1983), or Pueschel and Thuline (1983).

Syndromes Caused by Abnormal Number of Chromosomes

Two mechanisms, nondisjunction and translocation, are largely responsible for abnormal numbers of individual chromosomes. In nondisjunction a chromosome pair which normally would separate (disjoin) during meiosis instead remains together and migrates to one pole. One resulting gamete will have a "double dose" of that chromosome and the other will have none. If fertilization with a normal gamete occurs, the resulting zygote will be trisomic or monosomic, respectively, at that locus. Nondisjunction can also occur mitotically. If it occurs early in development, the individual will be a "mosaic," who has bodily cells with normal, monosomic, and trisomic composition of

Table 6.1. Characteristics of Chromosomal Abnormalities

Genotype	Incidence	Major Phenotypic Characteristics
		Autosomal Abnormalities
Trisomy 8	Very rare	About 75% male, growth failure, mental retardation, muscle hypotonus, clumsy gait, slender hands and feet, prominent forehead
Trisomy 9	Very rare	Growth failure, mental retardation, microcephaly, malformation of cerebellum, congenital heart disease
Trisomy 13	1 per 10,000	Growth failure, severe mental retardation, microcephaly, cardiac defects, malformations of eyes and ears, polydactyly, cleft lip and palate, early death
Trisomy 18 (Edwards's syndrome)	1 per 8000	About 80% female, growth failure, mental retardation, hypertonia, prominent occiput, malformed ears, congenital heart disease, early death
Trisomy 21 (Down's syndrome)		Growth failure, broad flat face, epicanthus, small palate, congenital heart disease, malformations of ears, greater than normal variability in age of attaining developmental milestones, mental retardation generally but IQ may be 70 or even higher
		Partial Addition and Deletion
9 p+	Rare	More frequent in females, mental retardation, brachycephaly, facial deformities
4 p−	Rare	Severe or profound mental retardation, generalized seizures, microcephaly, facial deformities
5 p−	1 per 50,000	Growth failure, severe mental retardation, microcephaly, epicanthus, hypotonia, crying sounds like meowing of a cat
18 p−	Rare	Highly variable IQ (profound to low normal), variable facial and bodily abnormalities
		Sex Chromosome Aneuploidies
XXY (Klinefelter's syndrome)	2 per 1000 m	Subnormal intelligence ($\overline{X}_{IQ} \approx 90$) after puberty, tall stature, testicular atrophy, poorly developed secondary sexual characteristics, tendency toward breast enlargement
XXXY, XXYY, XXXXY (Klinefelter's variants)	1 per 2500	More extreme version of XXY; tendency toward mild mental retardation, greater dysmorphism, severe sexual underdevelopment
XYY	1 per 8000 m	Subnormal intelligence ($\overline{X}_{IQ} \approx 90$), tall stature, impulsivity, some personality problems
XXX	1 per 1000 f	Physically normal, some tendency toward gonadal malfunction and subnormal intelligence
XO (Turner's syndrome)	1 per 1000 f	Subnormal intelligence ($\overline{X}_{IQ} \approx 90$), broad flat chest, webbed neck, short stature, failure to go through puberty, specific deficits in spatial relations

the affected chromosome. The severity of a condition is generally less in mosaics than in individuals in whom the nondisjunction occurred during meiosis. Mosaicism particularly affects sex chromosomes (Thompson & Thompson, 1980). Because nondisjunction anomalies occur during formation of germ cells or early in the germinal stage of prenatal development, they are not familial in the sense of being passed from generation to generation. As such they are frequently described as being genetic but not inherited.

Translocation occurs during meiosis when two nonhomologous chromosomes break and part of one is transferred to the other. In Robertsonian translocation whole chromosome arms are exchanged. Because of the nature of the process, individuals can have 45 chromosomes but an extra chromosome arm. They will be phenotypically normal but carriers of extra chromosomal information such that a percentage of their offspring will be affected. Other mechanisms that result in chromosomal abnormalities are described in Vogel and Motulsky (1979) and Thompson and Thompson (1980).

Autosomal Trisomies

The first described, most common autosomal trisomy, and among the most common genetic anomalies is Down's syndrome, Trisomy 21. About 95% of Down's syndrome cases result from nondisjunction and most of the rest from Robertsonian translocation. A small percentage are mosaics. As has been long known, rate increases dramatically with mother's age, particularly after age 30. As seen in Figure 6.3 the rate is about 1 per 1200 births to mothers under

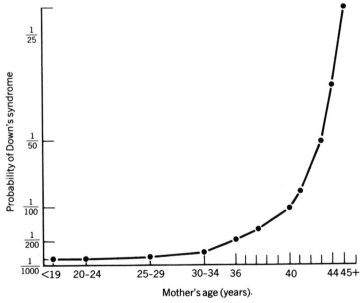

Figure 6.3. Incidence of Down's syndrome as a function of mother's age. Similar age relationships hold for other chromosomal trisomies. (Data from Thompson & Thompson, 1980.)

30 but rises rapidly to 1 per 25 to mothers over 45 (Thompson & Thompson, 1980). The relationship between rate and mother's age is also seen in virtually all autosomal and sex-chromosome trisomies and some other chromosomal anomalies as well (Vogel & Motulsky, 1979). Down's syndrome, and some other anomalies, also appear now to increase with paternal age independently of maternal age (e.g., Mikkelson, Hallberg, & Poulsen, 1976; Erickson, 1979).

For many decades, long before the chromosomal basis was discovered, Down's syndrome was viewed as virtually immutable to environmental influence. The distinctive physical appearance of affected children and general decline in development lent credence to the notion that severe retardation was predetermined. Indeed most Down's syndrome children who had been routinely institutionalized at early ages showed very low levels of cognitive functioning. But then Stedman and Eichorn (1964) provided evidence suggesting that supportive environments markedly benefit the intellectual functioning of Down's syndrome children. A variety of programs designed to provide extra stimulation (see Kopp & Parmelee, 1979, for a summary) reported significant impact on Down's syndrome children. It appears that Down's syndrome children may have an unusually wide range of reaction to variations in the environment. With appropriate early stimulation and enrichment and follow through support, most Down's syndrome children will function in the mild to moderate range of retardation, with some in the low normal range. Here again the eventual outcome is clearly a developmental one, very much a function of interaction with the environment rather than a simple one-to-one cause–effect relationship.

Several other rarer autosomal trisomies have been discovered. As shown in Table 6.1, each is associated with a set of particular physical characteristics but all result in brain damage, which leads to generally at least a moderate degree of mental retardation. In addition, virtually all autosomal trisomies are associated with low birth weight, short stature, anomalies of the head, face, hands, and feet, and congenital heart defects. Other conditions, such as trisomy 16, are almost always lethal prenatally.

Sex-Chromosome Aneuploidies

An aneuploidy is an abnormal number of chromosomes in a cell (Vogel & Motulsky, 1979). Sex-chromosome aneuploidies involve either one or more additional, or one missing, sex chromosome. They differ markedly from autosomal trisomies in several ways. First, intelligence is much less affected, in many syndromes averaging in the low normal level of about 90. Thus although more affected than normal individuals will be mentally retarded, most will be at least close to average intelligence, and some will be above average. It is unfortunate, therefore, that these syndromes have traditionally been described along with autosomal trisomies in chapters on mental retardation. Second, physical anomalies are less severe than in autosomal trisomies and, except for Turner's syndrome, generally involve development of the sex organs and sex hormone–based changes such as secondary sexual characteristics. Where the syndrome involves additional sex chromosomes, the degree of intellective impairment and physical anomalies increases with additional chromosomes beyond a trisomy condition. Because of the relationship of these syndromes to sexual characteristics, many are not routinely identified until the age of normal puberty. Sex-chromosome syndromes involving added chromosomes are similar to autosomal trisomies in one respect. Resulting frequently from nondisjunction, many increase in rate with parental age. The relationship is strongest with maternal age but in some syndromes is significant with father's age as well. Major characteristics of sex-chromosome aneuploidies are shown in Table 6.1.

KLINEFELTER'S SYNDROME. This occurs only in males and was first described in 1942. Its basic chromosomal composition is XXY resulting from nondisjunction. Rate increases with mother's age but about 40% of cases appear to result from nondisjunction during paternal spermatogenesis (Thompson & Thompson, 1980).

XYY MALES. This results from paternal nondisjunction during spermatogenesis. They have been a very controversial group because of claims that they are hyperaggressive and tend toward violent, criminal acts due to a putative "criminal chromosome," the extra Y. At times the discussion has been reminiscent of that surrounding Lombroso's nineteenth century concept of innate criminality. For Lombroso anatomy was indeed destiny (Gould, 1981), and criminals could be identified on the basis of certain atavistic physical features. Although Lombroso's theories were eventually shown to be baseless, much damage was done through their implementation into social policy. The XYY controversy is similar enough to Lombroso's "criminal mind" to warrant a summary, although it is too complex to be described in detail (see Vogel & Motulsky, 1979).

In 1965 Jacobs and a number of co-workers reported that the percentage of XYY males institutionalized for violent behavior was far above what would be expected on the basis of their incidence in the population. When other studies appeared to confirm the relationship, particularly for tall men, Lombrosoism was resurrected in the form of a "criminal chromosome." Some suggested that all newborn males be karyotyped and parents of XYYs be warned about possible hyperaggressive tendencies; others proposed putting XYY males under restriction as a precaution before they did anything wrong!

Fortunately it became clear both that most XYY males led normal, socially acceptable lives and that what criminal acts they did commit were similar to those of other criminals, involving mainly nonviolent property crimes. In a now classic study, Witkin and colleagues (1976) obtained the karyotypes of over 4000 tall men in an unbiased sample in Denmark and found 12 XYY males and 16 XXY males. Five (42%) of the XYYs and three (19%) of the XXYs had criminal records, as opposed to about 9% of normal males. Both groups with abnormal karyotypes were below average in intelligence. Their crimes were largely nonviolent, and in fact some of the XYYs had committed crimes in a way that virtually guaranteed their capture. Witkin et al. suggested that the higher percentage of criminal records among the XYYs was related to their lower intelligence and might reflect a greater likelihood of getting caught rather than of actually committing crimes.

Thus little evidence supports the notion that XYY men are hyperaggressive. However, some research (see Vogel & Motulsky, 1979) suggests that XYY men do have some personality characteristics, including impulsivity, which may partly underlie the tendency toward criminal behavior.

The case of the XYY "criminal chromosome" illustrates the tendency, even in the age of science, to infer causality and general relationships from correlational data based on small and biased samples.

TURNER'S SYNDROME.   This was first described in 1938 and affects only females. It has a number of distinctive physical features so that it can occasionally be identified at birth. It becomes particularly apparent at adolescence when puberty does not occur. Although Turner's syndrome is associated with sterility, estrogen therapy facilitates development of secondary sexual characteristics. About 60% show the standard karyotype, 45, XO; the other 40% show mosaicism and deletion of part of one X-chromosome.

Contrary to earlier beliefs that they are generally mentally retarded, Turner's syndrome individuals show little deficit in overall intelligence. However, some affected individuals have specific deficits in mathematics, spatial relations, and perceptual organization (Vogel & Motulsky, 1979).

XXX FEMALES (AND VARIANTS).   These are the equivalents of Klinefelter's syndrome in men (Thompson & Thompson, 1980); they show no distinctive physical features and may have children. There is, however, a tendency toward retardation and predisposition toward epilepsy. The rarer variants (XXXX and XXXXX) have skeletal defects and mental retardation (Plomin et al., 1980).

Partial Autosomal Additions and Deletions

Several low frequency syndromes are associated with the addition or deletion of part of one autosome. The best known is *cri du chat,* or cat's cry, in which part of chromosome 5 is deleted (5 *p* del or 5 *p-*). The cries of affected infants sound like a cat meowing, thus the name. Characteristics of some syndromes are in Table 6.1. The conditions generally arise in meiosis through chromosome breakage and loss in the case of partial deletions and translocation in the case of partial additions. For a more detailed discussion, see Pueschel and Thuline (1983).

Single-Gene Effects

Single-gene effects follow Mendelian principles of inheritance. That is, a dominant effect will be expressed phenotypically if the individual has at least one dominant gene for the trait. The genotype can be either homozygotic or heterozygotic. Genotype refers to the individual's genetic makeup, whereas phenotype refers to actual physical appearance and behavior at any point in time. A recessive trait will be expressed only if the individual is homozygotic for the trait, having inherited the recessive gene from each parent. Other patterns including codominance and partial dominance are also possible. Matters are further complicated by the phenomena of penetrance, an all-or-none phenomenon which describes the percentage of individuals with a given genotype who actually show the trait, and expressivity, the extent to which the genotype is expressed in a given individual. When dealing with abnormal conditions, expressivity is roughly equivalent to clinical severity (Thompson & Thompson, 1980).

A different pattern of expression can occur for traits carried on the sex chromosome. Females have two long X chromosomes, whereas males have one long X and one shorter Y. In part because the shorter Y chromosome carries fewer genes to suppress or interact with genes on the X chromosome, some traits carried on the X chromosome will be expressed in males much more frequently than in females. Some such X-linked recessive traits occur solely in males. They are transmitted from mothers, when they are heterozygous carriers, to sons.

The number of well-identified autosomal and X-linked single-gene disorders has increased threefold in the last two decades (see Table 6.2). McKusick (1978) lists 124 dominant, recessive, or X-linked genetic conditions leading to hearing impairment, some with no other effects and others associated with visual, motor, or other affects; 15 conditions leading to spinocerebellar ataxia; and over 200 protein defects, 170 of which involve altered activity of enzymes. Many demonstrate pleiotropy, multiple phenotypic effects of a single gene or gene pair. Because of the number of such traits, only a few can be discussed.

Dominant Single-Gene Traits

There is a 50% chance of an offspring having a dominant trait manifested by one parent. Such traits may also arise through spontaneous mutation, which accounts for a significant percentage of the dominant-gene syndromes (Abuelo, 1983). Once the gene appears, it will be transmitted to approximately 50% of the offspring of the affected individual. If the effects are severe, affected individuals may not reproduce, leading the genes to disappear from the gene

Table 6.2. Increase in Single-Gene Conditions: 1958–1978

Type of Condition	1958	1978
Autosomal dominant	285	736
Autosomal recessive	89	521
X-linked	38	107
Total	412	1364

Source: Condensed from McKusick, 1978.

pool. Variable expressivity is a general characteristic of dominant gene syndromes; the effects on individuals with the genotype range from severe to virtually nonobservable. Indeed some syndromes may appear to skip generations in affected families when the effects in one generation are minimal (Thompson & Thompson, 1980). Pleiotropy in dominant-gene defects commonly involves characteristic skeletal, neuromuscular, cranial, and ocular deformities. Intelligence is frequently, but not always, impaired. A summary of several syndromes is in Table 6.3.

Neurofibromatosis is a fairly common disorder that frequently results in skeletal deformities as well as the characteristic neurofibromatomas and cafe-au-lait spots on the skin. As mentioned in the introduction, Joseph Merrick was a case of particularly severe neurofibromatomas and skeletal defects with apparently no intellectual impairments. Although about 10% show mild mental retardation, the intelligence of most is in the normal range.

The combination of severe physical, particularly facial, deformities with normal intelligence in many affected individuals would be expected to lead to a variety of indirect effects. Given our stereotypes concerning physical appearance, many normal people react negatively to those with severe physical deformities. These reactions, in turn, may produce anxiety, particularly over social interactions, negative self-concepts, sadness, and other emotional ef-

Table 6.3. Examples of Dominant Single-Gene Traits

Disorder	Incidence	Major Phenotypic Characteristics
Neurofibromatosis (von Recklinghausen's disease)	1 per 3000	Cafe-au-lait spots, scoliosis, multiple subcutaneous tumors, multiple neurofibromas, seizures (12%), mental retardation (10%), variable expressivity
Achondroplasis	—	Homozygote—lethal; heterozygote—short-limbed dwarfism, large head with bulging forehead, normal intelligence
Tuberous sclerosis	1 per 30,000	Mental retardation, seizures, sebaceous adenomata of skin, "butterfly rash" on face, variable expressivity
Myotonic dystrophy	—	Myotonia (difficulty in relaxing contracted muscles), weakness of extremities, "expressionless" face, mental retardation, progressive disorder, variable expressivity
Craniosynotosis syndromes (includes Apert's syndrome)	—	Premature closure of cranial sutures, syndactyly, facial abnormalities, mental retardation
Marfan's syndrome	Rare	Elongated extremities, ocular and cardiovascular defects, tendency toward mental retardation, specific learning disabilities, arachnodactyly (long "spiderlike" fingers), variable expressivity

fects in affected individuals. The equation of beautiful with good and ugliness with bad in our society, notably in children's stories, helps produce unwarranted stereotypes. A thoughtful discussion of this issue is in Telford and Sawrey (1981).

Recessive Single-Gene Traits

INBORN ERRORS OF METABOLISM. As indicated earlier, a large number of syndromes results from an inherited defect that interferes with normal metabolism. Metabolism refers to a sequence of biochemical reactions, each involving a particular enzyme, that normally results in usable nutrients. Inborn errors of metabolism are genetically determined biochemical disorders in which a defective or absent enzyme leads to a block in normal metabolism. As a result, substances that are normally metabolized accumulate in the body and interfere with or damage developing central nervous system tissue, resulting in mental retardation and/or motor and sensory impairments. Because the metabolic defect generally does not manifest itself until the infant begins feeding after birth, most affected individuals appear normal at birth but show progressive deterioration within days or weeks. Blocks at different points in the metabolism of a particular substance may lead to different syndromes. Thus an early block of metabolism of phenylalanine leads to phenylketonuria; later blocks lead to several types of hereditary cretinism (Vogel & Motulsky, 1979). As shown in Table 6.4, blocks in metabolism of many types are known; those of amino acids are the most frequent.

Of the amino acid disorders, phenylketonuria is the best known and most common. As described earlier in this chapter, it involves the absence of the enzyme that converts the essential amino acid, phenylalanine, into tyrosine. Phenylpyruvic acid is secreted into the urine. Untreated individuals virtually always develop severe mental retardation and other effects as a result of progressive brain damage. PKU can be reliably detected by a blood test, mandated by law in most states, within a few days of birth. If dietary treatment begins shortly after birth, most adverse effects are eliminated, but terminal intelligence generally is slightly below average.

In maple syrup urine disease, a key symptom is the distinctive odor of the urine that is the basis for the name. Symptoms, including feeding problems and loss of the Moro reflex, appear within the first week of life; deterioration is frequently rapid with death occurring within a few weeks. Surviving individuals show symptoms similar to PKU (Nyhan, 1977). Blood and urine contain increased amounts of the three branched-chain amino acids, valine, leucine, and isoleucine, and a diet low in those amino acids may block the progression of the disease.

Galactosemia results from an absent enzyme that interferes with carbohydrate metabolism and leads to accumulations of galoctose. Symptoms, including failure to thrive, jaundice, and susceptibility to fatal infections, appear in early infancy. Untreated infants who survive develop cataracts, mental retardation, and cirrhosis of the liver. Once diagnosed, galactosemia can be

Table 6.4. Examples of Inborn Errors of Metabolism

Disorder	Incidence	Major Phenotypic Characteristics
Cerebral lipidoses Tay-Sachs disease	1 per 3600 in Ashkenazic Jews	Normal at birth, rapid deterioration in infancy, death in early childhood
Mucopolysaccharidoses Hurler's syndrome	1 per 100,000	"Gargoylelike" face, hydrocephaly, growth retardation, mental retarda- tion, early death.
Scheie's syndrome	1 per 500,000	Stiff joints, corneal opacity, normal in- telligence, facial abnormalities
Hunter's syndrome (X- linked) Carbohydrate	1 per 150,000	Stiff joints, dwarfing, facial abnormali- ties, progressive mental retardation
Galactosemia	1 per 50,000	Untreated: growth retardation, jaundice, cataracts, severe mental retardation, early death Treated: elimination of most adverse ef- fects, IQ ≈ 90
Amino acid Phenylketonuria	1 per 14,000	Untreated: severe mental retardation, seizures, behavior disorders. Treated early: elimination of most ad- verse effects, IQ ≈ 90
Maple syrup urine disease	1 per 175,000	Urine smells like maple syrup, progres- sive neurological and mental deterio- ration, early death.

Purine
  Lesch-Nyhan syndrome
  (HGPRT deficiency) (X-
linked)
	Rare, male only	Moderate to severe mental retardation,
		spasticity, self-mutilation, normal at
		birth

treated by excluding galactose from the diet through omission of milk and milk products. As with PKU, the earlier treatment is begun, the more effective it is, such that initiation before one month results in a near-average IQ (e.g., Fishler, Koch, Donnell, & Wenz, 1980). Unfortunately, positive test results frequently are not obtained until the infant is some weeks of age, by which time serious irreversible damage may already have occurred. For this reason, if a sick newborn has a family history of early death or severe mental retardation galactosemia and other metabolic disorders should be tested for immediately (Abuelo, 1983).

Tay-Sachs is the best known of the cerebral liposodal disorders but other rarer ones (e.g., infantile Gaucher's disease) are also associated with mental retardation and various neurological abnormalities. No treatment is currently available. Tay-Sachs infants are generally normal at birth and for some time after. But then deterioration replaces development, total blindness, spasticity, and severe mental retardation occur, and death follows in early childhood.

Tay-Sachs is relatively common among Ashkenazic Jews, with about one in 60 being a heterozygous carrier, but it is rare otherwise. It can be detected prenatally by assaying amniotic cell cultures after amniocentesis. Of value in reducing prevalence, carriers have about half the normal level of the relevant enzyme and can be identified through screening programs. These programs and genetic counseling have led to a significant reduction in Tay-Sachs in the United States (Abuelo, 1983).

The X-linked Lesch-Nyhan syndrome, expressed only in males, results from the absence of the enzyme hypoxanthine-guanine phosphorbosyltransferase (HGPRT). Affected individuals develop normally for some time after birth, but then control over motor behavior deteriorates and symptoms of cerebral palsy, including hypertonia and athetosis, appear. Very high levels of uric acid are secreted, and there are urinary tract and renal complications. Mental retardation of at least moderate level is typical. The most striking behavioral manifestation is self-mutilation, typically involving biting of lips and fingers that is so severe that permanent tissue damage and loss of fingers frequently result. Aggression against others is common. Although behavior modification is sometimes effective, physical restraint is usually required to prevent self-mutilation. Affected fetuses can be identified through amniocentesis (Abuelo, 1983).

X-LINKED MENTAL RETARDATION.   As is well known, mental retardation is more prevalent among males than females. Further, mentally retarded males are more likely to have affected male relatives than mentally retarded females have affected female relatives. These relationships suggest that many cases of nonspecific mental retardation in males may be X-linked (Abuelo, 1983). Some of those cases may result from "fragile-X syndrome," in which a portion of the X chromosome in males is constricted and broken off. There are no clear physical signs except for enlarged testicles. Incidence is not known but, according to reports summarized by Abuelo (1983), it may turn out to be second only to Down's syndrome as a specific cause of mental retardation. Further, some female carriers are mildly affected which may further its association with lowered intelligence.

Polygenic Influences

Although the chromosomal and single-gene disorders discussed previously and the environmentally based syndromes to be discussed account for a significant percentage of more severely handicapped children, other severe conditions and many milder ones have no known specific genetic or environmental basis. A variety of these conditions, however, have genetic predispositions that result from an interaction among many genes. "By predisposition" simply means that a particular complex of genes makes it more likely that certain behaviors will be exhibited under certain environmental conditions. The links between genes and behavior are more indirect, complex, and uncertain than in the case of specific genetically based syndromes. Indeed, some individuals may qualify as exceptional because they fall at the extreme end(s) of the distribution of a trait which has polygenic influences. Thus mild retardates are at the lower end of the normal distribution of intelligence, quantitatively lower but not qualitatively different from normal. Giftedness in the form of high IQ can also be presumed to have genetic predisposition on the basis that similarity in intelligence varies with similarity in genetic background (see Table 6.5 for references).

Polygenic influences are inferred from twin studies (which yield concordance rates), studies that compare adopted children to their adoptive and biological parents, and studies that look at the degree to which a trait varies as a function of genetic similarity. Because alternative interpretations can be offered for many of the studies, inference of genetic influences may be controversial (see Shields, 1977 or Vogel & Motulsky, 1979, for a discussion of the issues).

Various conditions appear to have polygenic influences, as indicated in Table 6.5. Also given are some of the types of evidence supporting such influences and representative references. Reviews are cited where possible because of the large number of individual studies that have been conducted. Some of that evidence is described briefly. Across three studies concordance rate for mild mental retardation averages about 85% for monozygotic (MZ) twins and 40% for dizygotic (DZ) twins. For dyslexia, a specific learning disability involving severe reading and other perceptual problems, concordance for MZ twins may be as high as 90% and for MZ twins about 40%. Stuttering occurs three to seven times often in close relatives of stutterers than in the population at large.

Table 6.5. Polygenic Factors

Condition	Evidence	Reference
Mild mental retardation	Concordance rates	Vogel & Motulsky, 1979[a]
High intelligence (gifted)	Twin studies; family patterns	Vogel & Motulsky, 1979[a]
Learning disabilities	Family patterns	Shields, 1977[a]
Stuttering	Family patterns	Shields, 1977[a]
Epilepsy (idiopathic)	Concordance rates; family patterns	Lennox, 1954
Schizophrenia	Adoption studies; concordance rates	Heston, 1966; Gottesman & Shields, 1972[a]; Plomin et al., 1980[a]
Infantile autism	Concordance rates; family patterns	Folstein & Rutter, 1978[a]
Affective disorders	Concordance rates	Vogel & Motulsky, 1979[a]
Neural tube defects	Family patterns	Thompson & Thompson, 1980[a]
Criminality	Concordance rates	Vogel & Motulsky, 1979[a]

[a] Literature reviews.

In addition to the severe behavior disorders listed in Table 6.5, concordance studies suggest a genetic predisposition to a variety of milder behavior disorders. For example, in a study of twins in London schools, Shields (1977) found that both members of MZ twins pairs were more likely to have a behavior disorder than were both members of DZ twin pairs. Further, considering only those pairs in which both members did show a disorder, MZ twins were more likely than DZ twins to have similar types of disorder.

Evidence for genetic predispositions toward particular behavior disorders now appears very strong. Both concordance and adoption studies indicate such influences on schizophrenia. However, concordance rates vary considerably across studies. Concordance among MZ twins, considered across several recent studies, ranges from about 15 to 60%, whereas for DZ twins it is only about 5 to 25%. In each study, however, concordance is higher in MZ than DZ twins (Plomin et al., 1980; Vogel & Motulsky, 1979). In a particularly interesting adoption study, Heston (1966) compared the offspring of a group of schizophrenic mothers with those of a group of normal mothers, all of whom had been separated from their mothers at birth. As adults, 5 of 47 offspring of schizophrenic mothers but none of 50 offspring of normal mothers had been diagnosed as schizophrenic.

Neural tube defects are congenital malformations of the spinal cord and brain which originate during organogenesis in the early weeks of embryonic development. They include anencephaly and spina bifida. In anencephaly major parts of the skull and brain are missing, and affected infants die within a few hours after birth. Spina bifida is a general term for a number of conditions in which the arches of the vertebra, frequently in the lumbar section, fail to fuse. The severity ranges from relatively mild, in the case of spina bifida occulta where the bony arch only is defective, to meningomyelocele, in which pouches of neural elements and meninges protrude through the spinal cord. The most severe cases are lethal, but some cases of spina bifida occulta will show almost no defects. Intermediate cases involve hydrocephaly, mental retardation, paralysis, and lack of bladder and motor control. Problems vary with the location as well as the degree of the defect. Spina bifida and anencephaly can be diagnosed prenatally through amniocentesis. They are reflected in elevated levels of alpha fetoprotein in amniotic fluid (Thompson & Thompson, 1980).

Search for a teratogen associated with neural tube defects has been notably unsuccessful. Overall incidence is fairly common, about 1 per 1000 births, but varies greatly with geographic area, socioeconomic status of parents, and even season of conception. But incidence in siblings of a child with a neural tube defect is approximately 1 in 20–40. Occurrence appears to rest on some polygenic predisposition interacting with undetermined environmental influences. Neural tube defects occur more frequently in females than males.

As might be expected in a condition that is both rare and heterogeneous, controversy exists over etiological factors in infantile autism. Given heterogeneity of the condition, heterogeneity in etiology may also be expected. Indeed that appears to be the case (see Rutter & Schopler, 1978, for discussions). Genetic factors are involved in some cases. For example, although only 2% of siblings of autistics are autistic, that is 50 times the incidence in the population at large (Folstein & Rutter, 1978). Further, Folstein and Rutter reported a twin study in which 4 of 11 (36%) MZ twin pairs showed concordance for autism, whereas none of 10 DZ twin pairs did. Further, with a broader designation of cognitive disorders including autism, concordance for MZ twins rose to 82% and DZ to only 10%. In all cases the deficit was speech or language related. The fact that the pairs were generally disconcordant for perinatal biological hazards increases confidence that genetic factors were involved. However, the importance of environmentally based brain damage was seen in the case of the disconcordant MZ twins. Of those seven pairs, four of the autistics, but none of the nonautistic co-twins, had experienced a hazard likely to cause brain damage. That three of the four nonautistics had some cognitive deficit suggests that autism in the other twins resulted from an interaction between the genetically based deficit and an environmental trauma.

Perhaps the most controversial area is criminality. In part because of Lombroso and other hypotheses about criminal minds or genes, reaction against suggested genetic bases is strong. But all nine studies reviewed by Vogel and Motulsky (1979) show higher concordance for court convictions in MZ than DZ twins. Some of the studies are quite old and perhaps unreliable, but others (e.g., Hutchings & Mednick, 1975) are more recent. It is important to remember that there is no suggestion that criminality as such is inherited, but that personality and intellective factors that are involved in criminal behavior have some genetic influence.

Not indicated in any of these studies is the physiological pathway by which genetic background affects behavior. In all cases, as might be expected, the issue is complex and most evidence is indirect. For schizophrenia, the dominant theories involve neurotransmitter abnormalities, in particular excessive transmission in dopaminergic neuronal pathways. The enzyme monoamine oxidase (MAO) may be one factor involved in dopamine metabolism (for an extended discussion, see Strauss & Carpenter, 1981). For infantile autism, disturbed serotonin metabolism may be one underlying factor (e.g., Ritvo, Rabin, Yuwiler, Freeman & Geller, 1978; Also see Jay, Waters, & Willis, Chapter 14 of this volume).

A Note About Heritability

Few concepts concerning influences on development have led to such confusion and controversy as has heritability. Heritability is a quantitative genetics statistic that is the proportion of phenotypic variance on a trait that can be attributed to genotypic variance. There are different ways of calculating heritability but, typically, heritability as used to study human traits is defined as $h^2 = Vg/Vp$, where Vg and Vp are overall genotypic and phenotypic variance, respectively. Heritability ranges from 0 to 1.00, or from none to all of the phenotypic variance being due to genotypic variance.

The concept of heritability was relatively obscure to psychologists until 1969 when Jensen, in his classic paper "How Much Can We Boost IQ and Scholastic Achievement?", estimated that for IQ, $h^2 = .80$, and thus 80% of the variance in human intelligence is due to genetic variance. Because of the implications that relatively little could be done to change intelligence through environmental manipulation and that race differences in intelligence were caused mainly by genetic differences, Jensen's position became very controversial. Heritability of intelligence remains debatable.

Some of the controversy appears to stem from misunderstandings about heritability. It is important to understand what heritability is and is not and what affects it.

1.   Heritability is a statistic that, strictly speaking, applies only to the population from which the actual sample of scores was drawn. Until recently, virtually all estimates of heritability were based on whites and could not legitimately be generalized to other groups. Further, most estimates are based on twin studies. The uniqueness of twins and their upbringing has led to reservations about the extent to which the estimates can be generalized to the population even of whites.

2.   Thus heritability estimates are estimates of a population value based on a sample. They may vary depending on the sample and the environments from which the sample is taken and may change if the population or environment changes. Heritability estimates, then, apply to particular phenotypes that arise from a particular set of genetic and environmental factors at a particular time. As Plomin, et al., (1980, p. 225) state: "Heritability is neither constant nor immutable." If a new environmental factor is introduced into a population, then considerable phenotypic changes may result even if heritability had been high.

3.   Different techniques for computing heritability of intelligence yield widely varying estimates, no one of which is either unbiased or clearly more accurate than the others.

4.   Heritability does not apply to individuals. If heritability of intelligence happens to be 0.60, it does not mean that 60% of an individual's intelligence is due to genetic factors. Individual development results from an interaction between genetic and environmental factors and the relative contribution of each cannot be assessed. Statements can be made about the population but not about individuals within it.

Estimates of heritability do, however, provide information on the extent to which individual differences in a trait are influenced by differences in genetic and environmental factors. Consideration of the various estimates suggests that heritability of intelligence is about .60 for whites in industrialized countries (Vogel & Motulsky, 1979). If correct, this indicates that variability in both genetic and environmental factors is in fact, as well as in theory, important in determining variability in intelligence. Apparent lower heritability in blacks (Scarr-Salapatek, 1971) suggests further that poorer environmental conditions are at least partly responsible for blacks' overall lower measured intelligence than whites.

CHEMICAL AND TRAUMATIC ENVIRONMENTAL INFLUENCES

Chemical and physical insult can produce major organic defects in the developing human. A variety of pre-, peri-, and postnatal chemical factors and peri- and postnatal traumatic factors have been identified. This section summarizes the major types, their time of influence, and their major effects.

Prenatal Influences

Although the human embryo/fetus is generally well protected from environmental insult in the uterus, a number of chemical agents, called teratogens, can cross the placenta and cause congenital malformations either by interfering with normal organogenesis or by destroying incompletely developed systems. Early in development, during the germinal period (weeks 0–2 of gestation), teratogens generally either have no effect or are lethal, although some can also cause major malformations by affecting the primitive streak, the source of much connective tissue. By inducing mitotoc nondisjunction during cleavage, teratogens may also produce mosaics, chromosomal abnormalities discussed earlier.

Teratogens generally have their greatest impact during the embryonic period (weeks 2–8 of gestation), when the most rapid differentiation of organ systems is occurring. Major morphological abnormalities result. During the fetal period (weeks 9 to birth), teratogens produce minor morphological abnormalities and physiological defects. Some teratogens will affect facial structure during the fetal period. Because some differentiation of the nervous system, eyes, and external genitalia continues even after birth, they are unusually sensitive to later teratogenic influences (Moore, 1977).

Times when tissue differentiation is most rapid and teratogens have major morphological impact are called critical periods. The embryonic period is occasionally called *the* critical period, but this is an oversimplification. Each organ system has its own critical and sensitive period. Further, Stockard, the developer of the critical period concept, held the position that all teratogens have the same effect at the same period, which is incorrect. As Moore (1977) describes, different teratogens have specific effects when present at the same time: radiation produces brain and eye damage, rubella produces mainly cataracts and deafness, and thalidomide produces skeletal deformities. As might be expected, given their intended action of inhibition of cellular proliferations, antitumor drugs used in chemotherapy for cancer are among the most potent teratogens. Even so they affect less than 50% of exposed infants (Moore, 1977). The difficulty of isolating the effects of a specific agent from those of others when all have variable impact makes definite identification of teratogens difficult.

Several general statements describe the basic ways in which teratogens act (see Wilson, 1973; Moore, 1977; and Fanaroff & Martin, 1983 for fuller discussions):

1. No agent is 100% teratogenic.
2. Teratogens act in specific ways and have specific effects, but individual teratogens may have multiple effects and different teratogens may have similar effects.
3. The embryo's genotype and its interaction with the prenatal environment affect susceptibility to teratogens.
4. Maternal factors, including nutritional and uterine condition, affect the extent to which teratogens are transmitted to the embryo. Some factors may be genotype based.
5. Organ systems have individual, but largely overlapping, critical and sensitive periods of susceptibility to teratogens.
6. Teratogens generally have four effects: death, malformation, growth retardation, and functional deficits.
7. Adverse effects increase in frequency and severity with increase in severity and duration of teratogenic influence.
8. Agents which have teratogenic effects on the embryo, producing major morphological defects, may have little or no effect, or even positive effect, on the mother.

Known teratogens that lead to behavioral abnormalities and their major effects are summarized in Table 6.6. Detailed presentations may be found in Lott (1983) and Fanaroff and Martin (1983). The effects listed are severe manifestations. It is important to keep in mind that effects are highly variable and that many cases, except where noted, are asymptomatic.

Maternal Infections

The clinical manifestations of maternal infections are so similar, including visual and auditory defects and brain damage, that differentiation among them on the basis of those symptoms alone may not be possible. Indeed some researchers (Nahmias & Tomeh, 1977; Thompson & O'Quinn, 1979) group them as the "TORCH complex" (**TO**xoplasmosis, **R**ubella, **C**ytomegalovirus, and **H**erpes). However, the symptoms in detail, the mechanism of action, and the time of major impact differ among them. Generally speaking the infections have only mild effects on the mother, but those on the offspring can be severe. The infections generally destroy already formed tissue rather than interfere with development. Unfortunately, no effective therapy is available for most viral maternal infections. Toxoplasmosis has its major effects following ma-

Table 6.6. Known Teratogenic Agents

Teratogen	Major Effects of Severe Impact
Radiation	Microcephaly, skeletal malformation, growth retardation
Maternal infection	
Toxoplasmosis	Microcephaly, hydrocephaly, seizures, mental retardation, visual defects
Rubella	Deafness and visual defects, especially cataracts, congenital heart defects, severe mental retardation, growth retardation, seizures
Cytomegalovirus (CMV)	Growth retardation, microcephaly, mental retardation, seizures, visual defects
Herpes simplex	Multiple defects, microcephaly, visual defects, mental retardation
Syphilis	Menigitis, hydrocephaly, mental retardation.
Thalidomide	Limb and digit malformation (phocomelia, meromelia), malformed external ear
Alcohol	Fetal alcohol syndrome (FAS), microcephaly, facial abnormalities, short stature, mental retardation, prematurity
Androgens	Varying degrees of masculinization of females, enlarged clitoris
Antitumor agents	Effects vary with particular drug but generally involve skeletal defects; also CNS defects, growth retardation
Anticonvulsants	Growth retardation, limb and facial anomalies, mental retardation
Anticoagulants	Growth retardation, eye and ear abnormalities

ternal infection in the first trimester, although less severe manifestations may occur through later pregnancy. Most infants are born without clinical signs; seizures and symptoms of hydrocephaly or microcephaly appear after one month of age. Most infected infants, perhaps 90%, develop symptoms.

Rubella is the classic paradigm for maternal infections. Major effects occur through maternal infection in the first trimester, but deafness may result from maternal rubella well into the fetal period. Again many affected infants are asymptomatic at birth, although lethargy may be apparent. But hearing loss, severe mental retardation, and cataracts may develop even years later. Autism and other behavior disorders have also been associated with maternal rubella.

Cytomegalovirus (CMV) may be the most common maternal infection (Lott, 1983), affecting 1 in 1000 births. Infection apparently has its effects in the first and second trimester. Most infants are asymptomatic at birth but may later develop hearing loss and intellectual deficits.

Herpes simplex differs from the other maternal infections in that it is generally a perinatal infection transmitted as the infant passes through the birth canal or contacts the virus following rupture of fetal-maternal membranes. Symptoms rarely appear for several days after birth. Known infected mothers generally deliver via caesarean section to bypass infant contact with the virus. More rarely herpes can affect the neonate prenatally, with more severe sequelae. Also, herpes can be acquired postnatally by contact with an infected mother or others. Although syphilis has been well controlled by antibiotics, recent upsurges indicate that increasing numbers of infants may be affected.

Drugs

Thalidomide is a classic example of a substance which had positive effect on mothers but devastating consequences on over 30% of their infants. Now withdrawn from the market, thalidomide produced major limb defects when taken by the mother in about the third to fifth week of pregnancy. Effects varied directly with the time the drug was present, from absence of thumbs to megomelia (shortened limbs) and phocomelia (absence of limbs). Although other systems were affected, apparently the central nervous system was not.

Alcohol is now estimated to be one of the major teratogenic substances in Western countries, affecting perhaps 3–6 per 1000 live births. It readily crosses the placenta and produces a variety of malformations, collectively termed the fetal alcohol syndrome (FAS). As would be expected, incidence and severity of effects varies with the level of maternal alcohol consumption. Estimates of incidence of FAS range from 10% if mothers regularly consume 1–2 ounces of pure alcohol per day to 40% when consumption reaches 5 ounces. Major effects occur when alcohol is present during the embryonic period, but the fetus is also at serious risk. Initially it was thought that alcohol might produce its effects indirectly through maternal malnutrition, but it is now clear that it has a direct effect. FAS is associated with microcephaly, facial abnormalities, and low birth weight, but it may be difficult to identify reliably at birth. Affected infants do not show postnatal "catch-up" growth as do normally small infants and become increasingly small for their age. Mental retardation, generally in the mild to moderate range, is a common outcome. Less severe manifestations are now being termed "fetal alcohol effects" (Abel, 1984).

Although reports of its teratogenic influence are conflicting, maternal smoking is a major correlate of prematurity and low birth weight (Abel, 1983).

Perinatal Influences

The perinatal (around the time of birth) period is from the seventh month of pregnancy to shortly after birth. Perinatal influences can be either chemically or physically mediated. The upper part of Table 6.7 summarizes major examples. As indicated in the previous section, most transmission of herpes simplex is during birth, making it a perinatal teratogenic influence.

Asphyxia of some duration is an inevitable consequence of the birth process. Normally the duration is short and of little consequence. But as long ago as 1861 Little suggested that prolonged labor and attendant asphyxia were associated with mental retardation and severe deficits in muscle coordination. "Little's disease" is now recognized as cerebral palsy and confirmed as a consequence of extended perinatal asphyxia or physical trauma to the brain. Brain tissue is particularly sensitive to oxygen deprivation and suffers first and most

Table 6.7.   Perinatal and Postnatal Influences

Influence	Major Effects
Perinatal	
Herpes simplex	Multiple defects, mental retardation, visual defects
Asphyxia	Hypoxic ischemic encephalopathy (HIE): cerebral palsy, seizures, disorders in neonatal reflexes, mental retardation
Prematurity, low birth weight	Disorders in neonatal reflexes, mental retardation
Intracranial hemorrhage	Variety of neurological problems
Postnatal	
Infections	Febrile seizures, mental retardation, cerebral palsy
Toxins	
Lead	Seizures, mental retardation, cerebral palsy, sensory impairments
Food additives(?)	Learning disabilities, attentional deficit disorder
Malnutrition	Kwashiorkor, lethargy, mental retardation
Accidents	Any disorder involving damage to brain, spinal cord, or sensory systems; varies with location, extent of damage, and age of insult
Child abuse	Same as accidents

severely from such deprivation. As many as 20% of newborns suffer oxygen deprivation significant enough potentially to have eventual adverse consequences. Signs of brain damage at birth or neonatal seizures predict serious later complications (e.g., Stewart, 1983). But outcome when no signs other than low Apgar scores are present is variable and depends to some extent on subsequent environmental factors.

A similar situation exists with prematurity and low birth weight (low weight for date). Severe prematurity (birth at <32 weeks gestational age) and very low birth weight (<1500 grams) are associated with later general and specific cognitive deficits and impairments of motor coordination and a variety of other neural problems. Study of these groups is complicated by heterogeneity of causes of prematurity and low birth weight, variation in condition at birth, and variations in the degreee of prematurity and low weight. Both conditions may be associated with factors such as maternal smoking, undernutrition, illness, and drug use, as well as factors within the fetus itself associated with nervous system or other organic dysfunction. Although they strictly represent separate conditions (e.g., Kopp & Parmalee, 1979) they are discussed together here because of their similar causes, treatments, and outcomes. They, along with infants who have had to be resuscitated following perinatal asphyxia, may be described as at "high-risk" for development of physical and cognitive deficits (Klaus & Fanaroff, 1979).

Until recently as many as 40% of preterm and low birth weight infants developed intellectual and neurological deficits. The prognosis for highly premature and low weight infants is still that they will show at least some degree of later deficits; some 5–15% will show severe deficits (Kopp & Parmelee, 1979). As would be expected, prognosis is worse where signs of congenital pathology accompany prematurity and low birth weight.

Inadequate physical care and stimulation in incubators have been responsible for some of the later deficits shown by premature and low birth weight infants. Until relatively recently, diet has been inadequate and ambient temperature too low (Kopp & Parmalee, 1979), putting additional stress on an organism not yet fully able to maintain bodily temperature. Further, only minimal handling and movement of the infant has been—and in many cases still is—typical, which may lead to reduced infant production of growth regulators, resulting in slow growth (Schanberg, Evoniuk, & Kuhn, 1984). Improvements in feeding, monitoring of bodily fluids and oxygen levels, and in some cases provision of physical stimulation have markedly improved the prognosis for high-risk infants (e.g., Klaus & Fanaroff, 1979).

Improvement in monitoring of high-risk infants has largely eliminated one common and tragic effect of traditional incubators. In the 1950s the toxic effects of oxygen therapy on the visual system became apparent. The high level of oxygen routinely supplied to infants in incubators caused a particular vascular disorder in the retina, retrolental fibroplasia. A true iatrogenic disorder, it caused virtually complete blindness in thousands of premature infants. Through accurate monitoring of blood-oxygen levels and direct presentation of oxygen, retrolental fibroplasia now occurs almost solely in children with severe pulmonary complications.

More recently psychologists and physicians have become concerned over the stimulus deprivation conditions that operate in typical neonatal care units. Levels of tactile, vestibular, and gross bodily stimulation are typically far below those for either fetuses in utero or full-term newborns in interaction with their caregivers and physical environment. Indeed the level of stimulus deprivation in traditional incubators is similar to experimental deprivation conditions which produce prolonged perceptual and motor deficits in nonhumans. Further, experience of a variety of kinds evokes neural development under a variety of conditions, particularly in young organisms whose central nervous systems are relatively plastic (see e.g., Walsh & Greenough, 1975, and Gollin, 1981, for reviews).

Indeed extra stimulation of premature newborns in hospital isolettes does increase growth and responsiveness. Extra handling or cuddling or placement on a gently rocking waterbed produces higher weight gain, neurological scores, mental and motor scores, and fewer apneic episodes relative to unstimulated controls (e.g., Korner, Kraemer, Hoffner, & Cosper, 1975; Neal, 1968; Solkoff, Yaffe, Weintraub, & Blase, 1969). As Schanberg et al. (1984) suggested, the extra stimulation may have its effect in part by inducing infant production of growth hormone. As a result of studies such as these, neonatology units are increasingly providing extra stimulation to newborns in isolettes.

The "continuum of reproductive casualty" (e.g., Pasamanick & Knoblock, 1966) suggested that degree of neonatal impairment resulting from reproductive difficulties, including perinatal birth complications, directly predicted degree of later impairment. Mild complications with no observable effect on the newborn should lead to no or minimal later problems, moderate complications to moderate problems, and severe complications to severe deficits. As we have seen, however, such a linear or main-effects model (Sameroff, 1976) does not adequately account for the complexity of development patterns. In the present case, severe perinatal complications are predictive of later difficulties. But the extent to which mild or moderate complications have effects is partly a function of the adequacy of the infant's environment. Thus the interaction between infants' initial condition and their environment determines outcome.

Outcome is additionally determined by the way in which caregivers react to infants who have suffered from pre- or perinatal complications. Sameroff and Chandler (1975) use the term "continuum of caretaking casualty" to describe the interactional nature of the relationship between infant and caretaker. This concept is discussed in greater detail in a subsequent section. Briefly, the continuum posits that both infants and their caretakers differ in their behaviors. Of importance, caretakers differ in the way in which they respond to "difficult infants," ones who are irritable, difficult to sooth, lethargic, or have other negative characteristics. Pre- and perinatal complications frequently lead infants to have these characteristics and some caretakers will have difficulty coping with them, creating or exacerbating difficulties (see Martin, Chapter 8 of this volume for details).

Postnatal Chemical and Physical Effects

Although birth obviously exposes the newborn directly to an external environment and leads to self-breathing and feeding, ongoing development processes continue. There is, therefore, no clear break in pre- and postnatal influence. As an example, occasionally early postnatal rubella produces brain damage that results in mental retardation. In addition, physical insults can directly produce damage. A few postnatal determinants of brain damage are in the bottom part of Table 6.7.

Infants are at particular risk for infection (e.g., Thompson & O'Quinn, 1979). Diseases such as meningitis may result in seizures and brain damage that later are manifested as mental retardation, cerebral palsy, epilepsy, or specific learning disabilities. Additionally, any infection in young children which results in very high fever may evoke febrile seizures which, in turn, increase the child's likelihood of developing epilepsy (Thompson & O'Quinn, 1979).

The major toxin of concern with children is lead. As seen in the case of Mary R. at the outset of the chapter, severe lead poisoning can have devastating effects. Lead may be ingested by eating lead-based paint or dirt (pica) into which lead paint has flaked, by eating vegetables on which atmospheric lead has settled, or by inhaling lead-contaminated air. A major source of atmospheric lead is automobile emissions and, as would be expected, children's blood-lead levels are relatively high in urban areas where such emissions are dense. Levels are also high in lower socioeconomic areas where lead-based paint is prevalent. The effects of lead poisoning recently were summarized by Graham (1983). Severe lead poisoning causes brain damage and is associated with the full range of adverse consequences of such damage. At mild or moderate levels of blood lead, effects are more inconsistent but generally involve loss of about 2–5 points in IQ and an increase in behavioral and specific learning problems. There does appear to be a dose–response effect, but separation of the effects of blood lead from other factors that might have adverse effects is difficult. The effects of exposure to lead are complicated by interaction with nutritional variables, many of which are associated with low socioeconomic status. Thus low levels of both iron and calcium exacerbate the effects of lead itself. Lactose intolerance, particularly prevalent among Blacks, leads to low intake of milk. Resulting calcium deficits may increase these children's susceptibility to adverse effects of lead (Huber, 1983).

Accidents are a common cause of brain damage (e.g., Rutter, Chadwick, & Shaffer, 1983), and child abuse is increasingly seen as another factor (Appelbaum, 1977). A major controversy of current research and practice is over the effect of age at the time of brain damage on subsequent recovery. Based on research with monkeys (Kennard, 1942), the Kennard principle—early brain damage has less effect than later brain damage—has long been accepted. Indeed the famous neuropsychologist Hans Lukas Teuber is reported to have said, "If I'm going to have brain damage, I'd best have it early rather than later in life" (Finger & Stein, 1982, p. 135). Indeed greater effect of left hemispheric lesions on language loss in older children was one factor that led Lenneberg (1967) to propose his theory of a critical period for language acquisition.

However, the Kennard principle has been subjected to such severe criticism (e.g., Isaacson, 1975) that it is no longer accepted in any simple form. As recently stated (e.g., Rutter, Chadwick, & Shaffer, 1983; Rutter & Garmezy, 1983), however, it would be a mistake to induce what might be called an anti-Kennard principle that age has no effect on recovery from brain damage. But the relationships are very complex. Three statements that can be made now are that (1) early diffuse damage to the entire brain is more harmful than later diffuse damage, as would be expected on the basis of biological critical periods; (2) recovery of language and related skills is better after early brain damage; and (3) degree of recovery from focal lesions is the result of the interaction among a number of factors including location and severity of injury, age at injury, and the individual's environment both before and after injury. Reviews of this complex and confusing area are in Finger (1978); Finger and Stein (1982), and Walsh and Greenough (1976). See also Golden and Wilkening, Chapter 3 of this volume, for detailed discussion.

THE ROLE OF TEMPERAMENT

It has already been suggested in this chapter that children's own characteristics influence their development through the ways in which they react to the environment and their behavior influences others' behavior toward them. A series of studies (e.g., Thomas, Chess, & Birch, 1968; Thomas & Chess, 1977, 1981) arising from the seminal New York Longitudinal Study (NYLS) documents the important role of temperament as an individual difference factor contributing to normal or disordered development. Temperament is a personality variable that "comprises those behavioral attributes that show some overall degree of consistency at any one time over various, although not necessarily all, life situations, and that do not reflect motivation or ability" (Thomas & Chess, 1981, p. 231). It involves differences in such things as adaptation to new situations, persistence in response to frustration, and emotional reactivity. Although temperament probably has a genetic loading, no specific etiology is implied. Indeed shifts in individual children's temperament over time suggest that environmental factors are influential. Empirically based, this concept of temperament should not be confused with that of Hippocrates mentioned earlier in this chapter!

The method of the NYLS can be described briefly. The main study group was a sample of 133 children of white middle to upper class parents in New York City. Four other samples, consisting of children of Puerto Rican parents, mildly retarded children, premature children, and children whose mothers had had rubella during pregnancy, were also studied for comparison. Data have been collected from the time the children were 2–3 months of age into adulthood. Initial data came from parental interviews and later from direct observation of and interviews with children. The researchers rated the children on nine scales: activity level, rhythmicity, approach to or withdrawal from new stimuli or situations, adaptability to new situations, threshold of responsiveness (the intensity of a stimulus needed to evoke a response), intensity of reaction, quality of mood (amount of happy versus unhappy behavior), distractability, and attention span and persistence.

Analysis of the ratings indicated that about 65% of the children could be described as having one of three temperamental styles. The *easy child* (40%) showed regularity in biologically based behaviors such as eating and sleeping, approach to and interaction with new stimuli and people, rapid adaptability to change, and positive mood. The *difficult child* (10%) showed opposite tendencies, toward irregularity, withdrawal from and slow adaptability to new stimuli or change, and frequent negative moods. The *slow-to-warm-up child* (15%) had many of the characteristics of the difficult child but less intense mood expression and negative mood. As the name implies, the child's initial reaction to new situations was negative, but he or she eventually adapted more readily than the difficult child. Temperament begins to stabilize in infancy and is generally stable in childhood but, as would be expected, is lower across longer time periods. It is not an immutable trait and may shift for a variety of reasons (Thomas & Chess, 1981).

Of particular importance here is the relation of temperament to behavior disorders. Of the main sample, the 10% who were difficult children comprised 23% of the children who had some kind of behavior disturbance in childhood;

10 of 14 difficult children were referred for clinical intervention. This relationship also held for the children with specified handicaps: in both the retarded and congenital rubella groups, children identified as having several signs of the difficult child were much more likely to show behavior disorders than were children who had few such signs. Incidence of behavior disorders in the retarded and congenital rubella group was higher overall than in the main sample. Thomas and Chess (1981) suggest that difficult temperament is an additional vulnerability that increases likelihood of a behavior disorder.

Quantification of temperament has made scientifically respectable what parents, particularly those of more than one child, have long known—children differ from an early age, react differently to parental and other influences, and interact differently with situations and other people. Children bring these characteristics with them and cannot be viewed as totally plastic. Again the outcome of temperament is interactive, depending on the characteristics of the child and its physical and social environments and the transactions among them. Others, including Buss and Plomin (1975) and Rutter (1977), have studied the effects of temperament on children's development. The roles of children's temperament and others' reactions to it as an ameliorating or exacerbating factor on children's behavior are discussed in detail by Martin in Chapter 8 of this volume.

INTERACTIONS IN EXCEPTIONALITIES

Development of normal or exceptional behavior cannot accurately be conceptualized in linear "if A, then B" terms, as indicated throughout this chapter. Development of the organism at any point in time reflects the trace effects of its genotype and structure and their continuous interaction or transaction with the sequence of physical and social environments to which it has been exposed (Gottlieb, 1983; Sameroff, 1976; Schneirla, 1966). The traditional concept of genetic-environment interaction, though still important, is yielding to one that emphasizes the dynamic interplay between individuals and environment that might better be termed organism–environment interaction. Part of this shift occurred because of the increasing evidence, since Bell's (1968) landmark reinterpretation of the direction of causality in parent–offspring relations, of the effects children have on their caregivers (e.g., Bell & Harper, 1978). In other cases, interactions between organisms and their physical environment have been demonstrated. For example, the extent to which the effects of infant malnutrition are expressed in later cognitive functioning depends on the physical environment. An enriched environment may overcome the effects of malnutrition which would be expressed in an impoverished environment (e.g., Levitsky, 1979).

Infants differ as a result of genetic, congenital, and peri- and postnatal factors in a number of ways. In extreme, as indicated in this chapter, they show clear clinical signs of brain damage. At lower levels variations in clinical signs and Apgar scores reflect varying degrees of impairment. This dimension, as indicated earlier, has been described as the continuum of reproductive casualty (Pasamanick & Knoblock, 1966). More affected infants may show increased levels of crying, irritability, and lethargy, decreased alertness and cuddliness, and may be more difficult to sooth.

Caretakers and their environments also differ, in factors such as socioeconomic status, personality, and availability of support from others. The role of parental characteristics is apparent even on a clinical level. A neonatalogist told the author that she can predict which infants who have required support in her neonatal intensive care unit will have later problems on the basis of the parents' behavior. Martin discusses parent–child interactions in detail in Chapter 8 of this book.

PERSONAL PERSPECTIVE

At the outset of this chapter, several important questions regarding exceptional children were raised, many in dichotomous terms. However helpful such framing may be in addressing issues, it should be clear now that answers rarely come in "either–or" terms. Although increasing numbers of specific genetic and environmental bases for handicaps are being discovered, the cause for most is still unknown. Indeed in many cases the notion of *a* cause may be misguided when both organisms and environmental factors are intertwined.

The issues of early experience as a determinant of later behavior and continuity–noncontinuity are particularly complex. In cases of clinically identifiable organic damage there is, as would be expected, some continuity of deficits. As indicated in this chapter, however, there is evidence of substantial recovery under appropriate conditions from complications apparent at birth, postnatal chemical and physical influences, and extreme psychosocial deprivation. Under other conditions, however, early behavioral deficits persist and may become magnified through development of indirect effects such as learned helplessness and fear of failure.

Prenatal and some postnatal experiences may have significant adverse effects on physical development that result in continuity from early to later development. There are true critical periods when teratogenic agents disrupt normal tissue differentiation or destroy recently differentiated tissue. However canalized certain systems are, development may be dramatically and permanently altered. The systems, once developed, are resistant to change, but attempts to apply strict biological notions of critical periods to behavior have been notably unsuccessful. Behavioral critical periods are a linear, main-effects model in an increasingly interactive world.

How then to account for continuity and noncontinuity in the development of exceptional behavior? The continua of reproductive and caretaker casualty and the interaction between them are important concepts but many other factors are clearly involved. The role of the physical environment before and after brain damage on recovery from such damage and the effects of diet on children's reaction to lead ingestion are just two of those factors. The author here proposes two additional concepts, "behavioral canalization" and "continuum of therapeutic intervention," that may play a role in the extent to which adverse influences whether genetic or environmental in origin may affect later behavior. No claim for great originality is made; the notion of behavioral canalization is similar to ideas of Hebb (1949) and those of several learning theorists, and the continuum of therapeutic intervention is a more general version of the continuum of caretaker casualty.

Behavioral canalization simply suggests that once a behavior or behavioral tendency has become incorporated into an individual's repertory, it will tend to persist even if it is clearly maladaptive if no other behavior is readily available. The phenomenon of learned helplessness may be seen as an extreme example of behavioral canalization: punishment of virtually all responses in the organism's repertory leaves it virtually—and apparently permanently—immobilized. Thus continuity is apparent. Only highly unusual intervention breaks down the learned helplessness and introduces new, more adaptive behaviors. On the other hand, initially teaching the organism how to cope with the environment enables it to resist the effects of subsequent uncontrollable aversive events (e.g., Seligman, 1975). Similarly, monkeys reared in isolation for 12 months adapt to that isolation and develop a repertory of responses limited to it. Sudden placement with a like-aged socially reared monkey results in interactions between animals with two wholly incompatible response repertories. The isolate animal vacillates between withdrawal and hyperaggression, which evokes aggressive behavior from the other monkey. The isolate monkey's maladaptive behavior normally persists and continuity is apparent. With the behavioral repertory it has and the environment it is in, there is no opportunity for adaptive social behavior to develop. In considering exceptional children, then, their initial maladaptive behaviors may channel them in such a way that development of more adaptive behaviors is unlikely in a normal environment. Indeed as Sameroff and Chandler (1975) indicated, initial behavior may have an avalanche effect resulting in abuse.

The continuum of therapeutic environment simply suggests that the greater the degree of impairment, the more unusual may be the required therapy. The effects of learned helplessness and isolation-rearing are overcome only by exposure to situations that are outside those which normally reared animals experience. Suomi and Harlow (1972), for example, instituted a unique and creative therapeutic environment for isolate-reared monkeys—they placed individual isolate-reared juveniles with infant monkeys. The infant's persistent attempts at contact and absence of aggressive behavior helped the juvenile acquire social behaviors that enabled it then to interact better with socially reared peers. Although these examples from animal research are extreme, they illustrate the extent to which novel therapeutic interventions can influence apparently rigid behavior. Treatment of PKU is an example of the need in some cases for extreme deviation from normal environments to effect remediation—

the artificial diet is never found in nature. Similarly, Genie, the isolate-reared child described at the beginning of the chapter, would have been expected, even if placed in a normal environment, to remain mute and to have severe motor handicaps, showing continuity of early experience. Her remediation is testimony not only to human plasticity and potential for recovery from adverse early experience but also to the ingenious treatments applied by the multidisciplinary group of therapists who worked with her. Thus some of the noncontinuity in development of some exceptional children results from the provision of extreme interventions that enable these children to acquire adaptive behavior that would not otherwise develop.

The author has one final comment. Regardless of how much we do not know about development of exceptionalities, application of our present knowledge would significantly reduce the incidence and degree of impairments and handicaps. Many influences on handicaps are associated with the cycle of poverty and are self-perpetuating (see Reschly, Chapter 12 of this volume). Some effective preventive measures can be briefly listed: (1) more thorough genetic screening and counseling; (2) adequate prenatal care that ensures that pregnant women are aware of the dangers of alcohol, smoking, and other adverse chemical agents and have adequate nutrition; (3) readily available information and training on family planning and birth control to help reduce family size in at-risk groups and early pregnancy among adolescents; (4) training in parenting skills and routine therapy for parents on the low end of the continuum of caretaker casualty; and (5) provision of adequate postnatal nutrition and stimulation for at-risk infants. There are others equally obvious. Indeed most of us know already what could be done. That we choose to remediate or to ignore rather than to prevent is a tragedy. As Walt Kelly said, through the mouth of Pogo Possum, "We have met the enemy, and he is us."

REFERENCES

Abel, E. L. *Marihuana, tobacco, alcohol and reproduction.* Boca Raton, Fla.: CRC Press, 1983.

Abel, E. L. *Fetal alcohol syndrome and fetal alcohol effects.* New York: Plenum, 1984.

Abuelo, D. N. Genetic disorders. In J. L. Matson & J. A. Mulick (Eds.), *Handbook of mental retardation.* New York: Pergamon, 1983.

Alexander, F. G., & Selesnick, S. T. *The history of psychiatry.* New York: Harper & Row, 1966.

Anastasi, A. Heredity, environment, and the question "how?" *Psychological Review,* 1958, *65,* 197–208.

Appelbaum, A. S. Developmental retardation in infants as a concomitant of physical child abuse. *Journal of Abnormal Child Psychology,* 1977, *5,* 417–422.

Aries, P. *Centuries of childhood* (R. Baldick, trans.). New York: Knopf, 1962.

Bell, R. Q. A reinterpretation of the direction of effects in studies of socialization. *Psychological Review,* 1968, *75,* 81–95.

Bell, R. Q., & Harper, L. V. (Eds.). *Child effects on adults.* New York: Wiley, 1978.

Berman, P. W., Waisman, H. A., & Graham, F. K. Intelligence in treated phenylketonuric children: A developmental study. *Child Development,* 1966, *37,* 731-747.

Bettelheim, B. *The empty fortress.* New York: Free Press, 1967.

Bowlby, J. *Maternal care and child health. Bulletin of the World Health Organization,* 1951, *3,* 355-534.

Buss, A. H., & Plomin, R. P. *A temperament theory of personality.* New York: Wiley, 1975.

Caporael, L. R. Ergotism: The satan loosed in Salem? *Science,* 1976, *192,* 21-26.

Clarke, A. M., & Clarke, A. D. B. (Eds.) *Early experience: Myth and evidence.* New York: Free Press, 1976.

Cooper, L. Z. Rubella. In A. M. Rudolph (Ed.), *Pediatrics* (16th ed.). New York: Appleton-Century-Crofts, 1977.

Curtiss, S., Fromkin, V. Rigler, D., Rigler, M., & Krashen, S. An update on the linguistic development of Genie. In D. P. Data (Ed.), *Georgetown University round table on language and linguistics.* Washington, D.C.: Georgetown University Press, 1975.

Erickson, J. D. Paternal age and Down's syndrome. *American Journal of Human Genetics,* 1979, *31,* 489-497.

Fanaroff, A. A., & Martin, R. J. (Eds.). *Behrman's neonatal-perinatal medicine* (3rd ed.). St. Louis: Mosby, 1983.

Finger, S. (Ed.). *Recovery from brain damage.* New York: Plenum, 1978.

Finger, S., & Stein, D. G. *Brain damage and recovery: Research and clinical perspectives.* New York: Academic, 1982.

Fishler, K., Koch, R., Donnell, G. N., & Wenz, E. Developmental aspects of galactosemia from infancy to childhood. *Metabolism,* 1980, *19,* 38-44.

Folstein, S., & Rutter, M. A twin study of individuals with infantile autism. In M. Rutter & E. Schopler (Eds.), *Autism, a reappraisal of concepts and treatment.* New York: Plenum, 1978.

Freud, S. *A general introduction to psychoanalysis.* New York: Garden City, 1938.

Gesell, A. *Infancy and human growth.* New York: Macmillan, 1928.

Gollin, E. S. (Ed.). *Developmental plasticity.* New York: Academic, 1981.

Gottesman, I. I. Genetic aspects of intelligent behavior. In N. Ellis (Ed.), *Handbook of mental deficiency.* New York: McGraw-Hill, 1963.

Gottesman, I. I., & Shields, J. *Schizophrenia and genetics.* New York: Academic, 1972.

Gottlieb, G. The psychobiological approach to developmental issues. In P. H. Mussen, M. M. Haith, & J. J. Campos (Eds.), *Handbook of child psychology* (4th ed., Vol. 2). New York: Wiley, 1983.

Gould, S. J. *The mismeasure of man.* New York: W. W. Norton, 1981.

Graham, P. J. Poisoning in childhood. In M. Rutter (Ed.), *Developmental neuropsychiatry.* New York: Guilford, 1983.

Harlow, H. F. The heterosexual affectional system in monkeys. *American Psychologist,* 1966, *17,* 1-9.

Hebb, D. O. *Organization of behavior.* New York: Wiley, 1949.

Hess, E. H. Imprinting. *Science,* 1959, *130,* 133–141.

Heston, L. L. Psychiatric disorders in foster home reared children of schizophrenic mothers. *British Journal of Psychiatry,* 1966, *112,* 819–325.

Howe, S. G. *Report of commission to inquire into the conditions of idiots of the commonwealth of Massachusetts* (Senate Document 51). Boston, 1848.[Reprinted in Rosen, M. Clark, G. R. & Kivitz, M. S., (Eds.). *The history of mental retardation* (Vol. 1). Baltimore: University Park Press, 1976.]

Howell, M., & Ford, P. *The true history of the elephant man.* New York: Penguin, 1980.

Huber, A. M. Nutrition and mental retardation. In J. L. Matson & J. A. Mulick (Eds.), *Handbook of mental retardation.* New York: Pergamon, 1983.

Hunt, J. McV. *Intelligence and experience.* New York: Ronald, 1961.

Hunter, R., & Macalpine, I. (Eds.). *Three hundred years of psychiatry, 1535–1860.* London: Oxford University Press, 1963.

Hutchings, B., & Mednick, S. A. Registered criminality in the adoptive and biological parents of registered male criminal adaptees. In R. R. Fieve, D. Rosenthal, & H. Brill (Eds.), *Genetic research in psychiatry.* Baltimore: Johns Hopkins University Press, 1975.

Ireland, W. W. *Mental affections of children, idiocy, imbecility, and insanity.* London: J. & A. Churchill, 1898.

Isaacson, R. L. The myth of recovery from early brain damage. In N. R. Ellis (Ed.), *Aberrant development in infancy.* Potomac, Md,: Erlbaum, 1975.

Jensen, A. R. How much can we boost IQ and scholastic achievement? *Harvard Educational Review,* 1969, *39,* 1–123.

Jones, K. L., & Smith, D. W. Recognition of the fetal alcohol syndrome in early infancy. *Lancet,* 1973, *2,* 999–1001.

Jones, K. L., Smith, D. W., Ulleland, C. N., & Streissguth, A. P. Pattern of malformation in offsprings of chronic alcoholic mothers. *Lancet,* 1973, *1,* 1267–1271.

Kagan, J., Kearsley, R. B., & Zelazo, P. R. *Infancy: Its place in human development.* Cambridge, Mass.: Harvard University Press, 1978.

Kennard, M. A. Cortical reorganization of motor function. *Archives of Neurology and Psychiatry,* 1942, *48,* 227–240.

Kessen, W. *The child.* New York: Wiley, 1965.

Klaus, M. H., & Fanaroff, A. A. *Care of the high-risk neonate* (2nd ed.). Philadelphia: W. B. Saunders, 1979.

Kopp, C. B. Risk factors in development. In P. H. Mussen, M. M. Haith, & J. J. Campos (Eds.), *Handbook of child psychology* (4th ed., Vol. 2). New York: Wiley, 1983.

Kopp, C. B., & Parmelee, A. H. Prenatal and perinatal influences on infant behavior. In J. D. Osofsky (Ed.), *Handbook of infant development.* New York: Wiley.

Korner, A. F., Kraemer, H. C., Hoffner, E., & Cosper, L. M. Effects of waterbed flotation on premature infants: A pilot study. *Pediatrics,* 1975, *56,* 361–367.

Krech, D., Rosenzweig, M. R., & Bennett, E. L. Relations between brain chemistry and problem-solving among rats raised in enriched and impoverished environments. *Journal of Comparative and Physiological Psychology,* 1962, *55,* 801–807.

Kuhn, T. S. *The structure of scientific revolutions.* Chicago: University of Chicago Press, 1962.

Lande-Champain, L. The etiology of mongolism. *Journal of Child Psychiatry,* 1954, *3,* 53–69.

LeJeune, J., Gautier, M., & Turpin, R. Etude des chromosomes somatiques de neuf enfants mongoliens. *Comptes Rendus de l' Academic des Sciences,* 1959, *248,* 1721–1722.

Lenke, R. R., & Levy, H. Maternal phenylketonuria and hyperphenylalanemia: An international survey of the outcome of untreated and treated pregnancies. *New England Journal of Medicine,* 1980, *303,* 1202–1208.

Lenneberg, E. H. *Biological foundations of language.* New York: Wiley, 1967.

Lennox, W. G. The social and emotional problems of the epileptic child and his family. *Journal of Pediatrics,* 1954, *44,* 591–601.

Levitsky, D. A. (Ed.). *Malnutrition, environment, and behavior.* Ithaca, N.Y.: Cornell University Press, 1979.

Lott, I. T. Perinatal factors in mental retardation. In J. L. Matson & J. A. Mulick (Eds.), *Handbook of mental retardation.* New York: Pergamon, 1983.

Lowenfeld, B. L. Psychological problems of children with severely impaired vision. In W. M. Cruickshank (Ed.), *Psychology of exceptional children and youth* (4th ed.). Englewood Cliffs, N. J.: Prentice-Hall, 1980.

Mackay, C. *Memoirs of extraordinary popular delusions and the madness of crowds.* London: R. Bentley, 1852. (Reprinted as *Extraordinary popular delusions and the madness of crowds.* New York: Bonanza Books, 1981.)

Matossian, M. K. Ergot and the Salem witchcraft affair. *American Scientist,* 1982, *70,* 355–357.

McKusick, V. A. *Mendelian inheritance in man* (5th ed.). Baltimore: Johns Hopkins University Press, 1978.

Melendy, M. R. *Sex-life, love, marriage, maternity.* W. R. Vansant, 1917. (Published with Hadden, W. J. *The science of eugenics.*

Mikkelson, M., Hallberg, A., & Poulsen, H. Maternal and paternal origin of extra chromosome in trisomy 21. *Human Genetics,* 1976, *32,* 17–21.

Montagu, A. *Life before birth.* New York: Signet, 1965.

Moore, K. L. *The developing human.* Philadelphia: W. B. Saunders, 1977.

Nahmias, A. J., & Tomeh, M. O. Herpes simplex virus infections. In A. M. Rudolph (Ed.), *Pediatrics* (16th ed.). Englewood Cliffs, N.J.: Prentice-Hall, 1977.

Neal, M. V. Vestibular stimulation and developmental behavior of the small premature infant. *Nursing Research Report,* 1968, *3,* 2–5.

Nyhan, W. L. Disorders of amino acid metabolism. In A. M. Rudolph (Ed.), *Pediatrics* (16th ed.). New York: Appleton-Century-Crofts, 1977.

Pasamanick, B., & Knoblock, H. Retrospective studies on the epidemiology of reproductive casuality: Old and new. *Merrill-Palmer Quarterly,* 1966, *12,* 7–26.

Plomin, R., DeFries, J. C., & McClearn, G. E. *Behavioral genetics.* San Francisco: Freeman, 1980.

Powell, W. B. *The natural history of the human temperaments.* Cincinnati: H. W. Derby, 1856.

Pueschel, S. M., & Thuline, H. C. Chromosome disorders. In J. L. Matson & J. A. Mulick (Eds.), *Handbook of mental retardation.* New York: Pergamon, 1983.

Ritvo, E. R., Rabin, K., Yuwiler, A., Freeman, B. J., & Geller, E. Biochemical and hematologic studies: A critical review. In M. Rutter & E. Schopler, (Eds.), *Autism, a reappraisal of concepts and treatment.* New York: Plenum, 1978.

Rosen, M., Clark, G. R., & Kivitz, M. S. (Eds.). *The history of mental retardation.* Baltimore University Park Press, 1976.

Rutter, M. Individual differences. In M. Rutter & L. Hersov (Eds.), *Child psychiatry: Modern approaches.* Oxford: Blackwell Scientific, 1977.

Rutter, M., Chadwick, O., & Shaffer, D. Head injury. In M. Rutter (Ed.), *Developmental neuropsychiatry.* New York: Guilford, 1983.

Rutter, M., & Garmezy, N. Developmental psychopathology. In P. H. Mussen & E. M. Hetherington (Eds.), *Handbook of child psychology* (4th ed., Vol. 4). New York: Wiley, 1983.

Rutter, M., & Schopler, E. (Eds.). *Autism, a reappraisal of concepts and treatment.* New York: Plenum, 1978.

Sameroff, A. J. Early influences on development: Fact or fancy? *Merrill-Palmer Quarterly,* 1976, *21,* 267–294.

Sameroff, A. J., & Chandler, M. J. Reproductive risk and the continuum of caretaking casualty. In F. D. Horowitz, M. Hetherington, S. Scarr-Salapatek, & G. Siegel (Eds.), *Review of child development research* (Vol. 4). Chicago: University of Chicago Press, 1975.

Scarr-Salapatek, S. Race, social class, and IQ. *Science,* 1971, *174,* 1285–1295.

Schanberg, S. M., Evoniuk, G., & Kuhn, C. M. Tactile and nutritional aspects of maternal care: Specific regulators of neuroendocrine function and cellular development. *Proceedings of the Society for Experimental Biology and medicine,* 1984, *175,* 135–146.

Schneirla, T. C. Behavioral development and comparative psychology. *Quarterly Review of Biology,* 1966, *41,* 283–302.

Scott, J. P. Critical periods in behavioral development. *Science,* 1962, *138,* 949–958.

Seligman, M. E. P. *Learned helplessness.* San Francisco: Freeman, 1975.

Shields, J. Polygenic influences. In M. Rutter & L. Hershov (Eds.) *Child psychiatry: Modern approaches.* Oxford: Blackwell Scientific, 1977.

Simon, B. *Mind and madness in ancient Greece.* Ithaca, N.Y.: Cornell University Press, 1978.

Solkoff, N., Yaffe, S., Weintraub, D., & Blase, B. Effects of handling on the subsequent developments of premature infants. *Developmental Psychology,* 1969, *1,* 765–768.

Spitz, R. Hospitalism: An inquiry into the genesis of psychiatric conditions in early childhood. *The psychoanalytic study of the child,* 1945, *1,* 53–74.

Stedman, D. J., & Eichorn, D. H. A comparison of the growth and development of infants and young children with Down's syndrome (mongolism). *American Journal of Mental Deficiency,* 1964, *69,* 391–401.

Stewart, A. Severe perinatal hazards. In M. Rutter (Ed.), *Developmental neuropsychiatry.* New York: Guilford, 1983.

Strauss, J. S., & Carpenter, W. J., Jr. *Schizophrenia.* New York: Plenum Medical, 1981.

Suomi, S. J., & Harlow, H. F. Social rehabilitation of isolate reared monkeys. *Developmental Psychology,* 1972, *6,* 487–496.

Telford, C. W., & Sawrey, J. M. *The exceptional individual* (4th ed.). Englewood Cliffs, N.J.: Prentice-Hall, 1981.

Thomas, A., & Chess, S. *Temperament and development.* New York: Brunner/Mazel, 1977.

Thomas, A., & Chess, S. The role of temperament in the contributions of individuals to their development. In R. M. Lerner & N. A. Busch-Rossnagel (Eds.), *Individuals as producers of their development.* New York: Academic, 1981.

Thomas, A., Chess, S., & Birch, H. G. *Temperament and behavior disorders in children.* New York: New York University Press, 1968.

Thompson, J. S., & Thompson, M. W. *Genetics in medicine* (3rd ed.). Philadelphia: W. B. Saunders, 1980.

Thompson, R. J., & O'Quinn, A. N. *Developmental disabilities.* New York: Oxford University Press, 1979.

Vogel, F., & Motulsky, A. G. *Human genetics.* Berlin: Springer-Verlag, 1979.

Wachs, T. D., & Gruen, G. E. *Early experience and human development.* New York: Plenum, 1982.

Waddington, C.H. *New patterns in genetics and development.* New York: Columbia University Press, 1962.

Walsh, R. N., & Greenough, W. T. (Eds.). *Environments as therapy for brain dysfunction.* New York: Plenum, 1976.

Wilson, J. G. *Environment and birth defects.* New York: Academic, 1973.

Witkin, H., Mednick, S. A., Schulsinger, F., Bakestrom, E., Christiansen, K. O., Goodenough, D. R., Hirschhorn, K., Lundsteen, C., Owen, D. R., Philip, J., Rubin, D. B., & Stocking, M. Criminality in XYY and XXY men. *Science,* 1976, *193,* 547–555.

Zigler, E. Familial mental retardation: A continuing dilemma. *Science,* 1967, *155,* 292–298.

CHAPTER 7

Interface Between
Psychology and Education:
Services and Treatments
for Exceptional Children

STEPHEN N. ELLIOTT AND TERRY B. GUTKIN

The relationship between psychology and education is pervasive if one considers the development of intellectual and social-emotional independence an important goal for children in our society. Although pervasive, the relationship between the domains of education and psychology is primarily indirect in nature. There is not a linear progression from the discovery of knowledge in one field to a technology in the other field. Unfortunately, happenings in one discipline often are not directly communicated to the other discipline, for the intercommunication system is in general diffuse, while the knowledge domains of psychology and education are vast.

Interrelationships between education and psychology were inevitable since a central concern of both disciplines has always been the cognitive and affective growth of humans. Many persons can be credited with fostering relationships between the disciplines; however, the work of five men deserves special attention: William James, John Dewey, Alfred Binet, Jean Piaget, and Edward L. Thorndike.

HISTORICAL ANTECEDENTS TO THE
PSYCHOLOGY-EDUCATION RELATIONSHIP

In 1892 William James was invited to Harvard University to give a series of lectures on psychology to teachers of the Cambridge, Massachusetts schools. The lectures were later published as *Talks to Teachers on Psychology: And to Students on Some of Life's Ideals* (James, 1899/1922). James' lectures served to highlight educators' keen interest in the application of psychological knowledge, as well as the reality that psychologists had little of immediate substance to offer educators. Quoting James:

> I say moreover that you make a great, a very great mistake, if you think that psychology, being the science of the mind's laws, is something from which you can deduce definite programmes and schemes and methods of instruction for immediate school room use. Psychology is a science, and teaching is an art; and sciences never generate arts directly out of themselves. (p. 7)

James, however, did provide teachers with some basic principles of psychology that were relevant to teaching, such as encouraging students to actively respond and to practice correct responses. Although his optimism about psychologists' offerings to educators was guarded, his talks to the Cambridge teachers initiated an important dialogue between psychologists and educators in the United States.

John Dewey, although a philosopher by training, played a central role in developing a relationship between psychology and education. In fact, as President of the American Psychological Association, his major address to the membership focused on the desirability of interrelations between psychology and education (Dewey, 1900). Dewey was also a founding father of functionalism, a precursor to behaviorism (Boring, 1950). He understood the relevance of psychology to teaching and learning, and thus established an experimental elementary school at the University of Chicago (Hilgard & Bower, 1975). Dewey's "progressive education," as practiced at the school, emphasized the role of children's interests and motivation in solving their own problems. Another interest of Dewey's was individual differences in mental abilities. Functional psychology as a whole became interested in differential mental abilities and how to measure such abilities with mental tests. Although practitioners concerned with the measurement of cognitive functioning gradually drifted away from functionalism, the influence of Dewey and other functionalists had been instrumental in the development of mental testing, an area of immense interest to present-day psychologists and educators.

Alfred Binet's impact on education and psychology, in many respects, was similar to that of Dewey, for Binet was also concerned with the testing of mental abilities. In 1904 administrators in the overcrowded Paris school system commissioned Binet and his associate, Theophile Simon, to devise a means of distinguishing between children who were retarded or unable to benefit from traditional classes and those who had the capacity to learn and could benefit from education (Binet & Simon, 1905). Binet and Simon questioned teachers about the various learning difficulties children experienced and the kinds of tasks most children were capable of mastering at particular ages. As a result they developed 30 problems based on academic skills and arranged them in ascending order of difficulty. Performance on the problems was used to predict future academic achievement. Binet and Simon were remarkably successful in developing an academic screeening device. In fact their work provided the foundation for much of the current testing of intellectual abilities, a practice that has played a central role in providing services to exceptional children.

Another figure who played a significant role in fostering relations between psychology and education was Jean Piaget, the Swiss genetic epistemologist. Piaget's contributions to knowledge concerning children's intellectual development are singularly unsurpassed. His investigation of children's intellect started in 1920 when he accepted a position with Theophile Simon in the Binet Laboratory in Paris (Ginsburg & Opper, 1969). Piaget's task was to develop a standardized French version of some English reasoning tests. Initially it was reported that he was not enthusiastic about the tedious standardization work; however, he soon became fascinated by the patterns of incorrect answers given by children of approximately the same ages. Piaget concluded that older children were not just "brighter" than younger ones, instead the thought of younger children was qualitatively different from that of older ones. The real problem of intelligence, according to Piaget, was to discover different methods of thinking used by children of different ages. Thus he rejected a purely quantitative definition of intelligence.

Concurrent with his work in the Binet Laboratory, Piaget was also studying abnormal children at the Salpetriere hospital in Paris. He believed, as did Freud, that knowledge of abnormal functioning might provide insight into the normal working of the human mind (Ginsburg & Opper, 1969). Hence the years Piaget spent working and studying in Paris were very fruitful.

Piaget's seminal work (1950, 1952) in characterizing children's intellectual development captured the interest of modern psychologists and educators for many reasons. A primary reason is that Piaget's work is more securely based on the direct study of children than all other theories of child development. He spent over 50 years observing, interviewing, and testing children of all ages. The implications of his work for education are promising but like most offerings from psychology there is not a simple linear progression from psychological research to educational technology.

A final figure who played a significant role in both psychology and education was Edward L. Thorndike. Thorndike's contributions to knowledge range from experimental animal psychology to the psychology of arithmetic (Thorndike, 1911, 1922, 1931). For many years he served on the faculty at Teachers College, Columbia University where he undertook studies on the applied psychology of education (Hill, 1971). Thorndike was a prolific writer and may be best known for his works on fundamentals of learning (1932) and educational psychology (1913).

Thorndike's theory of learning, referred to as connectionism, dominated all others in America for nearly half a century. The basis of learning, according to Thorndike, were associations between sense impressions and impulses to action. These associations were called connections and were believed to be strengthened or weakened as a result of consequences. As such Thorndike's connectionism was the original stimulus–response psychology of learning. A similar, yet more recent, view of learning can be found in the works of B. F. Skinner (1957, 1968, 1969).

The work of James, Dewey, Binet, Piaget, and Thorndike has been examined briefly to illustrate the developmental roots of the current relations between psychology and education. Clearly education and psychology share a prestigious history in the persons of these five men.

PRESENT RELATIONSHIPS BETWEEN PSYCHOLOGY AND EDUCATION

We conceptualize the relationship between the disciplines of psychology and education as operating through the actions of three groups of individuals: psychologists, educators, and children. The ways in which these groups interact and influence each other vary.

Psychologists have the potential to influence children and educators both directly and indirectly. For example, psychologists frequently interact with children on a one-to-one basis to assess an ability or skill, or to modify problem behaviors. Psychologists also function as consultants where they directly affect teachers and administrators' behavior, who in turn affect the behavior of children. Educators, on the other hand, directly influence children's thinking and behavior but seem to be in a position where they can only indirectly influence psychologists. That is, through the delivery of special services to children in schools, educators can influence psychologists' thinking and subsequent practice.

The present-day relations between psychology and education are explicated by numerous individuals (e.g., Ausubel or Gagne) and several areas of specialized human inquiry, such as educational psychology, instructional psychology, developmental psychology, educational measurement and evaluation, school psychology, and special education. Investigators in each of these specialized areas are involved in theoretical and empirical research that has the potential to positively influence the education of children. School psychology and special education, however, are the areas where applied, as well as basic psychology and education truly interface. This interface is best exemplified by services and treatment for exceptional children.

School psychology can be defined simply as the practice of psychology in the schools. It shares much with other applied areas of psychology (i.e., clinical, community, counseling, and industrial), and yet it is different. School psychologists are primarily concerned with the assessment of children's learning and behavior problems and the development of interventions to modify such problems. School psychologists are also typically involved in research and problem-solving consultation with parents and educators. A definition of special education could also include many of the school psychologist's tasks; however, the role of special education is a more focused one. Specifically, special education is concerned primarily with instruction for handicapped children (visually impaired, hearing impaired, physically handicapped, mentally retarded, learning disabled, emotionally disturbed, etc.).

The developmental histories of psychology, in particular school psychology, and special education are both rich and interrelated, sharing many persons and issues (Frampton & Rowell, 1938; Hewett & Forness, 1974). A significant landmark in the development of both psychology and special education occurred in 1896 when Lightner Witmer established a laboratory clinic for children at the University of Pennsylvania (Levine & Levine, 1970). This clinic is considered the first child guidance clinic in America and was from its inception closely tied to education, for Witmer's major goal was to train psychologists to help teachers remediate children's problems (Bardon & Bennett, 1974). Following Witmer's lead, many public school districts formed special classes for children with learning or behavior problems. Many other examples of psychology and special education's common history could be discussed, but an overriding concern is that one understands that the relationship between psychology and special education has been inextricably bound to society's perspectives on the treatment of exceptional children. These perspectives have changed radically over the past 50 years and are still evolving, hence the relationship between special education and school psychology will continue to be a dynamic one. Frampton and Gall (1955) characterized the development of attitudes toward handicapped children into three historical stages. They described the first stage as occurring during the pre-Christian era when the handicapped were persecuted and neglected. The second stage followed the spread of Christianity and was characterized by protection and pity for the handicapped. The third stage, which followed the advent of the mental testing movement in the early 1900s, was characterized by an attitude of acceptance for handicapped persons and the gradual integration of such persons into society to the fullest possible extent. According to Kirk (1972), educational programs for exceptional children were made possible only after the advent of mental abilities tests. With the diagnostic methods of psychometrists came concepts of inter- and intra-individual differences which are central to special education. Based on Frampton and Gall's work, we believe the movement to place exceptional children in the least restrictive environment (i.e., mainstreaming), which was stimulated by PL 94–142 (Education for All Handicapped Children Act of 1975), represents the beginning of a fourth attitudinal stage toward handicapped persons. This fourth stage appears to be characterized by concern for individuality and normalization.

Today the relationship between education and psychology and, in particular, special education and school psychology is much more than mental abilities testing. Testing was only the beginning. Services for the educational benefit of children now include parent and teacher consultation, behavior management techniques, personalized instruction with specialized curriculum materials, modified classrooms, and direct therapy when necessary.

Buktenica (1980) suggested that school psychology and special education currently "exist in a relatively cooperative, congenial, coterminous relationship of tension within the schools" (p. 228). He sees both disciplines working toward the same ends but through separate efforts:

That pattern of functioning [testing, labeling, and placing children in special classes] is passing from the scene and the roles are being renegotiated . . . Special education services to children are moving more toward resource/consulting teacher and diagnostic-prescriptive roles, i.e., moving away from categorization. Although the testing function is paramount, school psychologists talk about moving toward a consultation model in its broadest sense. (Buktenica, 1980, p. 228)

The relationship between school psychologists and special educators can be conceptualized as consisting of three levels of varying degrees of interaction: self-actional, interactional, or transactional (Buktenica, 1980). At the self-actional level people act under their own power. At the interactional level one person is balanced against another person in a causal interconnection. Finally, at the transactional level persons function in a mutually determined and interdependent relationship (Dewey & Bentley, 1949). Although these three levels of relating are not clearly discriminated, they seem to serve a useful analytic function in distinguishing the nature of relationships.

Using the three-level framework, Buktenica posited that most relationships between school psychologists and special educators currently occur at the self-actional level while some relations are at the interactional level. He characterized those at the interactional level as being similar to a "billiard ball" phenomenon, where each action resulted in an opposite and equal reaction. Very few relationships have reportedly been achieved at the transactional level. Currently, however, external forces are pressuring both disciplines toward a transactional working relation.

Other authors have also discussed the school psychology–special education relationship from slightly different perspectives than Buktenica. Gallagher (1969) characterized the relationship as symbiotic since the psychologist is a necessary first step in any special education program. Lambert (1973) concluded that school psychologists' traditional sources of influence were the result of special education activities. Catterall (1972), following a similar line of logic, pointed out that over half of the finances for school psychology resulted from service relationships with special education. Finally, Miller and Dyer (1980) suggested that educational accountability and legal mandates (e.g., PL 94-142) have resulted in the further entwining of school psychology and special education. Together these perspectives on the relationship between school psychology and special education result in a scenario whereby the direct reactions of psychologists and educators to individual children ultimately have an impact upon social, economic and political systems.

Factors that are influencing the relationship between psychologists and educators include parents, organized groups interested in the welfare of children with various problems, legal cases, and professional training programs in school psychology and special education. The combined impact of these factors may necessitate more collaborative or transactional relations on the part of psychologists and educators. If such a relationship is achieved, exceptional children as well as the professions of school psychology and special education will benefit. If, however, the professions ignore each others' strengths, services to exceptional children are likely to suffer and neither profession will flourish.

In the remainder of this chapter we will focus on and critically examine some services or techniques from each discipline that can possibly help exceptional children. Specifically we believe that three of psychology's major contributions to education include models of human behavior, consultative services, and practical approaches to changing children's behavior. Education's major contributions to psychology are less direct but nevertheless very important. Education's contributions include the provision of a setting and a mode for providing psychological services to children and families. Thus we will examine the utility of behavioral analysis techniques, school-based consultation, preventive educational programs, and special classrooms. Assessment is also a psychological service that plays a major role in special education decision making; however, we will not be discussing it in detail because other authors in this text (McDermott, Chapter 5; Reynolds, Chapter 4) have already done so. Three questions that we hope to answer are: What does psychology have to contribute to education? What does education have to contribute to psychology? What do psychology and education have to offer exceptional children? The chapter will conclude with a look into the future at issues critical to the well-being of the psychology–education relationship.

CONTRIBUTIONS FROM PSYCHOLOGY TO THE THEORY AND PRACTICE OF EDUCATION

Models of Human Behavior

There are many ways to view differences in children's behavior, some of which psychologists have developed into models of human behavior. Models can provide a theoretical framework for understanding past behavior and predicting future behavior. Thus models of human behavior have influenced how psychologists and educators think about and interact with children, especially exceptional children. The models that have had the greatest impact on education are the medical and the behavioral models, and to a lesser extent the ecological model.

The medical model in psychology emerged from psychoanalytic theory and postulates that psychological disturbances are best understood and modified through the intensive study of intrapsychic life (Stuart, 1970). Two basic assumptions inherent to the medical model are (1) behavior that deviates in negative direction from normative standards is a reflection of a personal disease (or disturbance, disorder, or dysfunction), and (2) behavior that has been classified as deviant must be changed within the individual by a curative process (Reger, 1972). The first assumption implies that children who cannot be maintained or accommodated in a regular educational program are suffering from an internal psychoeducational disorder. In other words, the problem is believed to be *in the child*. Subsequently they may be diagnosed, labeled, and placed in a special program by a team composed of a psychologist and educators. The second assumption also has practical implications that influence educational programs. Once children are classified as deviant or "diseased," the educational system must respond to cure them. Educational "cures" seem to come most frequently in the form of special classes which tend to isolate the "diseased" child from normal or healthy children.

The medical model of psychological and educational services for children experiencing learning and behavior problems has been critically challenged on conceptual, empirical, and practical grounds (Reger, 1972; Szasz, 1960; Zubin, 1967). Szasz (1960) argued that many of the basic assumptions underlying the medical model were untenable. The assumption with which he took the greatest issue was that psychopathology was best conceptualized as "mental illness." He believed that psychotherapists dealt with problems in living, rather than with mental illness. Therefore, psychological disturbance was better understood in the context of human value systems than in mental symptoms. This conceptualization of psychological problems was influential for it removed the locus of psychopathology from the human psyche and focused on the relationship between individuals and society. Traditional psychotherapies which were rooted in the "mental illness" notion were subsequently scrutinized. For example, Zubin's (1967) review of empirical research pointed out that degree of diagnostic agreement among medical model practitioners was poor. McDermott (1980), like Zubin, observed in an empirical study a similar trend of low diagnostic congruence among school psychologists with various levels of training and experience. Zubin concluded that medical model diagnosis was questionable if individuals with the same diagnostic label did not respond similarly to given therapies. Reger (1972) also questioned the utility of the medical model, particularly when used in special education:

> When a child is seen as a "patient" in school, when he is looked at as carrier of a medical-model illness (or deviation, etc.) then the teacher and the school are relieved of much of the responsibility for the child. If he makes little or no progress, it is because of him and his condition rather than the school teacher. (pp. 11–12)

Alternative models of human behavior that acknowledge the role that other people and environmental factors have in shaping a child's behavior are currently prominent in the eyes of many educators and psychologists. Chief among these are the behavioral and the ecological models. The major postulate of these espousing the behavioral model is that human behavior is primarily a function of environmental events (Skinner, 1953). The ecological model is built on a similar supposition that human behavior results from a complex interaction between environmental factors and the individual characteristics of people (Barker, 1965, 1968; Hunt, 1967; Lewin, 1951; Reilly, 1974).

Both the behavioral and ecological models provide an alternative approach to understanding human behavior that is responsive to the criticisms directed at the medical model. For example, pathology is viewed as behavior which is deemed inappropriate (generally excessive or deficient) when compared to subjective norms and values, rather than as an "illness" in any absolute sense (Ullmann & Krasner, 1969). Advocates of both approaches reject a "mental illness" or intrapsychic causal explanation of psychopathology and instead are oriented toward the belief that human problems are primarily the result of interactions between people and their environments. Consequently, many psychologists and educators are once again optimistic about the possibilities of positively affecting the development of exceptional children. This optimism stems from the belief that it is easier to modify a person's environment rather than some unobservable, intrapsychic phenomenon.

With the development of behaviorally oriented models of human behavior, psychologists had finally provided educators with a pragmatic approach/process (i.e., functional analysis of behavior) to understand abnormal, as well as normal, behavior of children. The theoretical assumptions underlying behavioral models of human functioning directly influenced the development of behavior modification, a technology used widely by educators and psychologists alike. Although behavior modification techniques are by no means a panacea for all psychopathologies or educational difficulties, they have provided professionals with a multitude of strategies for helping exceptional children.

Functional Analysis of Behavior

In 1970 Bijou published an article entitled *What Psychology Has to Offer Education—Now.* In this article Bijou argued that psychologists ascribing to the behavioral model, although in the minority, had something to offer teachers and school psychologists:

> We behavioral psychologists can offer a set of concepts and principles derived exclusively from experimental research; we can offer a methodology for applying these concepts and principles directly to teaching practices; we can offer a research design which deals with changes in the individual child (rather than inferring them from group averages); and we can offer a philosophy of science which insists on observable accounts of the relationships between individual behavior and determining conditions. (Bijou, 1970, p. 66)

The offers were made and accepted by many psychologists and educators. The functional analysis of behavior gave educators a systematic means for analyzing the learning skills and social tasks required of children. The concepts and principles of behavior analysis were applied directly to a variety of classroom and teaching situations: the observable behavior of a student responding to a teacher's instructional techniques, the interaction between a student and printed material, and the interactions among students. The analysis of teaching and the application methodology for behavior analysis were clearly set forth by Skinner in *The Technology of Teaching* (1968). Most educators' and many psychologists' knowledge of functional behavior analysis is, however, based on popularized approaches that have incorporated Skinner's basic ideas. These various approaches are referred to as applied behavior analysis (Sulzer-Azaroff & Mayer, 1977), task analysis (Ysseldyke & Salvia, 1974), and behavioral assessment (Ciminero, 1977). Each of these approaches varies somewhat in its stated purpose, but all three offer educators a procedure for studying and characterizing the observable behavior of children. Thus one comes to understand what children can and cannot do and how they learn or interact. This *what* and *how* information is valuable prerequisite information to the development of successful interventions.

A number of factors have contributed to the large-scale adoption of behavioral techniques by school psychologists and educators. A major factor is communication. That is, communications between psychologists and educators tend to contain less jargon, be more understandable, and be more specific when human behaviors and environmental events, rather than intrapsychic dynamics, are the focus of change. Hence the chances for working together to modify or remediate children's problems are enhanced. Communication with parents of exceptional children is also a very important step toward a successful intervention. The nature of a child's problem is relatively easy to communicate in behavioral terms which helps to demystify the problem and encourage parental involvement.

Another major factor that has contributed to educators' interest in behavioral psychology concerns the need for classroom management skills. Many techniques for managing students' classroom behavior have been designed recently that employ behavioral principles (Krumboltz & Krumboltz, 1972). In general these behavior management techniques can be easily integrated into the organizational systems that exist in most classrooms, for teachers can usually manipulate the existing reinforcement contingencies once they recognize their relationship to students' behavior. With the advent of the legal and philosophical efforts to mainstream exceptional students, teachers may more than ever rely on behavior management systems.

A final factor contributing significantly to educators' affinity for behavioral psychology concerns its utility in the evaluation of individualized instructional programs. The strategy of teaching-oriented, applied research consists of searching for ways to engineer an educational environment so that a child can learn a specified task and then, when the task is successfully achieved, compare that achievement with achievement in other learning situations. With a functional analysis of behavior approach, educators no longer have to design impractical, large scale studies that compare teaching methods across children. Single-subject or small *N* research techniques (Hersen & Barlow, 1976; Kazdin, 1975; Kratochwill, 1977a) offer a practical and equally valid alternative that can be used to document a child's learning successes or failures under various schooling conditions.

The intervention methodology which follows from a functional analysis of an individual's behavior is commonly referred to as behavior modification or b-mod. One should understand that behavior analysis represents a procedure or process for understanding human behavior, while behavior modification represents the content or techniques for changing human behavior. A multitude of behavioral techniques have been designed to change (increase or decrease) behaviors; in fact, dozens of books (e.g., Bandura, 1969; Sulzer-Azaroff & Mayer, 1977) and several scholarly journals (e.g., *Behavior Modification, Behavior Therapy, Journal of Applied Behavior Analysis*) are concerned entirely with behavior change techniques and issues.

Common principles that underlie most behavior techniques include either reinforcement or punishment. Reinforcement is defined solely by an increasing or maintaining effect upon behavior. Two basic reinforcement procedures include positive reinforcement and negative reinforcement. When a stimulus, such as an object or event, follows or is presented as a consequence of a response and the rate of that response increases or maintains as a result, the stimulus is said to be a positive reinforcer. Praise, attention, food, and money are positive reinforcers for many people. Negative reinforcement involves the removal of an aversive stimulus as a consequence of a person's response and results in the maintenance or an increased rate of behavior. Negative reinforcement is often exhibited in interactions between parents and children. For example, John is nagged by his mother until he does his homework. Punishment is characterized as the presentation of an aversive stimulus or the removal of a positive stimulus immediately following a response that results in a reduction of the rate of the response. Punishment, like reinforcement, is defined solely by its effect upon behavior.

Numerous strategies for managing human behavior have been designed based on either one or both of the two basic principles of reinforcement and punishment. Once a person can identify and control objects or events that a child desires or avoids, he or she is in a position to modify that child's behavior.

Although we feel confident in our assessment of educators and school psychologists' interest in behavioral psychology, we cannot conclude that all or even most persons accurately interpret behavioral principles (e.g., negative reinforcement) or employ behavior techniques appropriately. As Bijou (1970) warned, "A thorough grounding [in the basic principles] is necessary because behavioral analysis does not offer a touchstone." The approach has an apparent simplicity that can be deceptive, consequently more than a definitional understanding of reinforcement and punishment is necessary for effective application.

School-Based Consultation

According to surveys and position papers, school psychologists view consultation as one of their most preferred job functions (Barbanel & Hoffenburg-Rutman, 1974; Giebink & Ringness, 1970; Manley & Manley, 1978; Meacham

& Peckham, 1978). Fortunately, school personnel including teachers and superintendents also believe that consultation is a valuable psychoeducational service (Bardon, 1976; Cowen & Lorion, 1976; Fairchild, 1976; Gutkin, 1980; Gutkin, Singer, & Brown, 1980; Lambert, Sandoval, & Corder, 1975; Lolli, 1980; Martin, Duffey, & Fischman, 1973; Waters, 1973). Consultation thus appears to be a major contribution to the psychology–education interface.

Consultation has no single definition. In fact several writers (Gallessich, 1973; Gibbins, 1978; Reschly, 1976) believe the term consultation is practically devoid of meaning because it is used in a plethora of contexts and to describe a variety of service relationships. We believe, however, that Medway's (1979) definition of consultation best describes the process as typically employed when servicing children with learning or behavior problems. He defined consultation as a process of "collaborative problem-solving between a mental health specialist (the consultant) and one or more persons (the consultees) who are responsible for providing some form of psychological assistance to another (the client)" (p. 276). Based on this definition, consultation is a service that not only illustrates an interaction between education and psychology but demands an interaction between psychologists and educators in an effort to influence children positively.

Major Characteristics

The most definitive characteristic of consultation is the concept of indirect service to a client. Psychologists have worked traditionally in direct modes of service, that is, their primary interactions have been with clients. In school-based consultation, however, the psychologist works primarily through a consultee, which is usually a teacher. For example, suppose that Barry, a third grader, is referred to the psychologist by Ms. Cline, his teacher, because of aggressive behavior toward his peers. When functioning within a direct service approach, the psychologist would treat Barry directly, probably relying primarily on individual psychotherapy sessions. Within an indirect service or consultation model, however, the psychologist (the consultant) would spend the bulk of his or her time interacting with Ms. Cline (the consultee) rather than with Barry (the client). The analysis of Barry's problem and the design of a treatment program would be jointly devised by the psychologist and Ms. Cline. Above and beyond this, the remedial intervention plan derived through this process would be implemented by the consultee rather than by the consultant. The psychologist's impact on Barry is thus indirect as his or her contact with this child is very minimal. A schematic illustration of the conceptual differences between direct and indirect service models can be seen in Figure 7.1.

Theoretically, indirect models of psychoeducational services have several major advantages over direct models. For example, it is assumed that through consultative interactions, consultees (e.g., teachers, parents) will gain expertise with intervention techniques for changing human behavior and may also become more organized and resourceful problem solvers. Consultees' new knowledge of problem-solving and intervention techniques can be used to re-

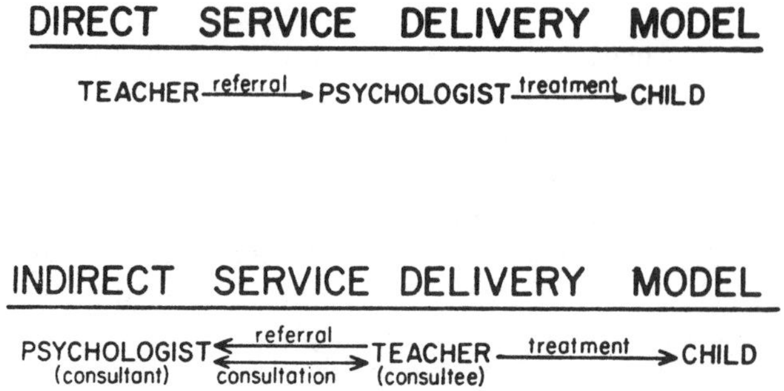

DIRECT   SERVICE   DELIVERY   MODEL

TEACHER —referral→ PSYCHOLOGIST —treatment→ CHILD

INDIRECT   SERVICE   DELIVERY   MODEL

PSYCHOLOGIST ⇄ referral / consultation → TEACHER —treatment→ CHILD
(consultant)   (consultee)

Figure 7.1.   Direct and indirect service delivery models. (Reprinted with permission from Gutkin & Curtis, 1982.)

mediate problems of immediate concern and should also result in preventing future problems. Thus consultation has the potential to function as a time efficient and effective mode of service for exceptional children. Paraphrasing Miller (1969), psychological consultants in the schools "give psychology away" to teachers as a means of promoting children's welfare.

A second important characteristic of most forms of consultation concerns the relationship between consultants and consultees. Bergan (1977) refers to the need for a collaborative relationship in which both the consultant and consultee are considered professionals with expertise to offer one another. Thus the psychologist is viewed as an expert in human behavior, whereas the teacher is an expert in the area of instruction and classroom operation. A number of writers (Alpert, 1977; Kramer & Nagle, 1980; Tageson & Corazzini, 1974) have expressed the belief that consultations characterized by hierarchical power relationships might restrict the free flow of communication and hinder rapport. A study by Wenger (1979) indirectly supports this assumption. He found that consultees were more satisfied with collaborative than noncollaborative consultation contacts. The consultant–consultee relationship should also be characterized by the active and voluntary participation of the consultee, the consultee's right to reject consultant suggestions, and confidentiality. Each of these parameters is consistent with treating the consultee as a knowledgeable professional rather than as a subordinate.

Process, Content, and Stages

Several investigators (Broskowski, 1973; Schein, 1969; Williams, 1972) have assumed that consultants can be effective problem solvers even in substantive areas in which they have little knowledge. We cannot strongly support this assumption, for we believe content expertise is critical to a psychologist's credibility with teachers and parents. However, there is consensus that the major responsibility of a consultant is to maintain and direct the problem-solving process. In a truly collaborative form of school-based consultation, the consultant would be responsible for outlining and controlling the procedures/process of problem solving, while both the consultant and the consultee would be responsible for contributing content expertise toward solving a client's problem.

Psychologists have designed and implemented numerous models of consultation (Dworkin & Dworkin, 1975; Reschly, 1976), all of which can be conceptualized as systems of problem solving. Inherent to most of these models are procedural steps designed to provide for a comprehensive and logical problem-solving interaction (D'Zurilla & Goldfried, 1971; Osborn, 1963). Although terminology varies among authors, there has been good agreement concerning the steps perceived to be necessary for successful problem solving. According to Gutkin and Curtis (1982), there are seven major procedural steps that can be differentially discerned from the variety of models germane to consultation in the schools. These steps are illustrated in Table 7.1. Variations of these seven steps have been presented by several other authors (Bergan, 1977; Brown & Kelly, 1976; Hollister & Miller, 1977; Schmuck, Runkel, Arends, & Arends, 1977). Bergan, for example, consolidated similar steps into a four-stage model of behavioral consultation that consisted of problem identification, problem analysis, plan implementation, and problem evaluation.

Actual problem solving rarely proceeds in the exact sequence as depicted in Table 7.1. According to Gutkin and Curtis (1982), movement back and forth between steps is quite frequent. They attribute this movement to two factors: imprecision in controlling communication and the need to reinterpret parts of a problem when new information is provided. Although a problem-solving sequence like that in Table 7.1 cannot ensure a successful intervention outcome, it would seem to enhance the *probability* that communication is well established and a viable intervention is designed. For a detailed discussion of the various steps in consultative problem solving, readers are referred to Gutkin and Curtis (1982) and Bergan (1977).

Research Outcomes

There is a significant gap between theories of consultation and the practice of consultation resulting from the relative lack of good research. Meyers, Parsons, and Martin (1979) acknowledged this research gap and believed it could be attributed primarily to the fact that most practitioners with consultative

---

Table 7.1. Problem Solving Sequence

   I. Define and clarify the problem
  II. Analyze the forces impinging on the problem
 III. Brainstorm alternative strategies
  IV. Evaluate and choose among alternatives
   V. Specify consultee and consultant responsibilities
  VI. Implement the chosen strategy
 VII. Evaluate the effectiveness of the action and recycle if necessary

Source: Reprinted with permission from Gutkin and Curtis, 1982.

skills do not possess research skills and vice versa. However, recent research efforts have provided some empirical support for the effectiveness of consultation. We will briefly discuss some of these investigations. For a more detailed examination the reader is referred to Mannino and Shore (1975) and Medway (1979).

Investigators have provided a variety of evidence that supports problem-solving models of consultation. For example, Curtis and Watson (1980) found that teachers demonstrated significant improvements in their perceptions and understanding of children's problems after working with consultants rated as effective. Similarly, Gutkin, Singer, and Brown (1980) reported that when presented with an identical list of children's problems, teachers in schools using consultants found problems to be less serious than teachers in matched schools without consultants. A study by Jackson, Cleveland, and Merenda (1975) demonstrated that consultation is effective with parents as well as with teachers. When teachers and parents of underachieving children received consultation services while their children were in fourth, fifth, and sixth grades, the children scored significantly higher than a control group on several academic measures at the time of high school graduation.

Less empirical evidence is available concerning the direct preventive impact of consultation. Two investigations (Jason & Ferone, 1978; Meyers, 1975), however, have reported that client gains following consultation generalized to other children as a result of increased teacher effectiveness. A group of investigators headed by Cowen (Cowen, Trost, Lorion, Dorr, Izzo, & Isaacson, 1975) found that psychological consultation could be combined with early screening and the use of paraprofessionals to effect secondary prevention in a school setting.

The Relationship between Consultation and Assessment

Assessment has long been viewed as a valuable psychological service for exceptional children. Generally assessment is construed as a direct service by a psychologist, who employs standardized tests to determine a child's strengths and weaknesses in areas of academic achievement and intellectual abilities. On the other hand, as we have discussed, consultation is an indirect service by a psychologist working through a communication process with a teacher or parent to help effectively solve a problem observed in a child. Consultation may seem only tangentially related to assessment; however, we believe they are highly interrelated means of providing service to exceptional children.

Several factors, most of which were stimulated by the passage of PL 94-142, essentially necessitate the interrelation of assessment and consultation services. These factors include service goals such as mainstreaming (placement of exceptional persons in the least restrictive environment), nondiscriminatory assessment, and individualized educational programming. The trend within psychology and special education toward informal modes of assessment (Dickinson, 1978; Kratochwill, 1977b; Smith, 1980; Tidwell, 1980) has also strongly influenced thinking about the merging of assessment and consultation services.

The composite impact of all the above factors seems to have resulted in the need for (1) more direct interactions among psychologists, special educators, and regular educators and (2) more direct links between psychologists' assessment outcomes and their recommended classroom interventions. Consultation, communication, information sharing, or whatever else you want to call it, has the potential to serve as a medium whereby assessment data and intervention strategies from an array of sources (e.g., teachers, parents, principals, peers, psychologists) can be collected and integrated into a plan for educators and the exceptional child. Thus we conceptualize consultation as the desired model for providing psychoeducational services; assessment and intervention are substages within the model.

CONTRIBUTIONS FROM EDUCATION: THE PROVISION OF SETTINGS AND SERVICES FOR PSYCHOLOGY

Primary Prevention of Problem Behavior

The "school" has access to a large number of children over long periods of time during formative years. Thus educators have significant opportunities to influence children's social and emotional development. In fact many persons believe the "school" has become the primary socializing agent for children.

The role that educators play in shaping children's social-emotional development can range from preventive to corrective interventions. Preventive intervention, although not unique to an educational setting, is a service psychologists rarely have an opportunity to provide for children. Thus educators may assume the function of "front line" prevention specialists for children. The term primary prevention means different things to different people, but according to Clarizio (1979a, p. 434) "there is basic agreement that it refers to lowering the rate of emotional disorders in a population and to building psychological health and resources in people." In other words, it is assumed that emotional problems can be avoided by managing one's life in a defined, appropriate manner.

In 1977 Cowen examined various preventive mental health efforts and concluded that such efforts could be divided into two categories, those aimed at changing high-impact environments (e.g., schools) and those aimed at competence building. Educators have the potential to affect children with preventive interventions characteristic of either of Cowen's two categories, but those in the competence building category are most direct and will be examined further.

Competence Building Strategies

The thrust of the competency building approach is educational and involves explicitly teaching children mental health concepts. This teaching can occur as a result of a planned curriculum or during teachable moments where instruction deals with real human problems. For example, teachers and their classes might discuss the significance of lying to a friend or the death of a parent.

The work of Ojemann and his associates (1961, 1967) is the most well developed example of an educational approach to competence building. Ojemann refers to his preventive program as causal education. Causal education focuses on human problems and examines causes, understandings, and analytic processes necessary for coping with and overcoming personal and interpersonal problems. Ojemann believes that causal education helps children to acquire analytic skills and competencies needed to cope effectively with later adaptive demands.

Ojemann (1967) contends that educational curricula, starting with kindergarten, should lay a foundation in the causal approach to understanding children's behavior. Then as children grow into adults they can add to this foundation and apply their knowledge in marriage and family relationships and in employer–employee interaction. Thus, in theory, this causal educational approach enables a child to surmount current crises, as well as establish strategies for solving crises later in life.

The content of causal education entails reading or discussing realistic stories about how individuals solve daily problems. The intended focus of these stories is on the behaviors and attitudes of individuals involved in a problem situation. A common teaching strategy used during primary grades consists of presenting students with narratives in which a surface or superficial approach to problem solving is contrasted with a causal or introspective approach. Teacher-guided discussions follow the narratives focusing on the meaning and causes of the behaviors of characters in a story.

Evaluation of outcomes from Ojemann's causal education approach has been promising. According to Cowen and Gesten's (1978) review of the literature, children exposed to the approach clearly acquired the causal mode of thinking, were better able to generalize knowledge and weigh alternatives, became more sensitive to the factors underlying human behavior, and had lower scores on measures of arbitrary punitiveness and authoritarianism.

Several studies over the past 20 years have examined the personal adjustment consequences of children exposed to causal teaching. Muuss (1960) found that groups of fifth and sixth graders who participated in a causal education program had healthier adjustment profiles and significantly lower anxiety and insecurity scores than a matched control group. Similarly, Griggs and Bonney (1970) found that a group of fourth- and fifth-grade students in a causal education program performed better than matched controls on sociometric measures, self-ideal congruence measures, and on an overall adjustment index. Hence some reviewers have described Ojemann's approach as the best example of a genuine preventive program (Allen, Chinsky, Larcen, Lochman, & Selinger, 1976).

Spivack and Shure (1974) developed another approach which stresses the acquisition of problem-solving skills by children. On the basis of research, these investigators argue that children's interpersonal cognitive problem-solving skills (ICPS) are critical mediators of adjustment. They reasoned that if young children could acquire social problem-solving skills in school such knowledge should generalize to other interpersonal situations and result in "appropriate" behavior. Thus Spivack and Shure developed a two-stage curriculum for directly teaching social problem-solving skills to young children. The curriculum was built on games and dialogues designed to teach word concepts and cognitive skills. The first stage of the ICPS program involves teaching pre–problem-solving thinking skills such as basic word concepts like "same" or "different." The second stage of the program focuses on the development of four major ICPS components: sensitivity to interpersonal problems, generation of alternative solutions to problems, understanding means–end relationships, and awareness of the social consequences of one's behavior.

Spivack and Shure's (1971) initial test of the ICPS program was undertaken with over 200 four-year-old inner-city children attending a Head Start program in Philadelphia. Half of the children received the ICPS curriculum, while the other half of the children participated only in the regular Head Start program. Children in the ICPS groups were exposed over a three month period to 46 lessons which required approximately 15 minutes each. Teachers taught the lessons to groups of six to eight children.

The results of this initial study indicated that children in the ICPS program (1) had acquired social problem-solving skills which were superior to those of children in the control group and (2) were less likely to suggest irrelevant or forceful-aggressive problem solutions. Based on a six-month follow-up study of the children, Shure and Spivack (1975) reported stable gains in social problem solving.

Various other versions of the ICPS curricula have been used successfully in class settings with preschoolers, kindergartners, adolescents, and adults (Platt & Spivack, 1976; Platt, Spivack, & Swift, 1974) as well as with emotionally disturbed and mentally retarded children (Spivack, Platt, & Shure, 1976). Recently Shure (1979) demonstrated that ICPS skills could be successfully taught to inner-city children by their mothers who had received ICPS training.

In summary, Spivack and Shure's work with the ICPS program has demonstrated that behavioral adjustments to interpersonal problems can be modified. Children exposed to the ICPS curriculum have improved (relative to matched peers) on dimensions such as concern for others, the ability to take initiative, and autonomy. In addition, increases in social problem-solving skills have been correlated significantly with decreases in teachers' ratings of maladjusted behaviors. This approach of primary prevention, like that offered by Ojemann, merits extensive future investigation.

Educational Treatments for Exceptional Children

In education, as in psychology, there are some generally accepted procedures for treating children's problems. Central to most educational treatment regimes are special classes where reduced teacher-student ratios allow for more individualized instruction. Psychology's impact on those who administer and actually teach in special education programs is evidenced by the frequent use of behavioral technology and concern for the psychological well-being of children. However, in most cases, educators' approaches to the treatment of children extend and complement those offered by psychologists. Educators are generally better prepared to remediate learning problems and have control of a number of important treatment variables, such as secondary reinforcements and the amount of classroom time devoted to treatment. Thus psychologists can learn some valuable information about treatment of exceptional children from educators' interventions.

Special Services

At least four aspects are "special" about special education: specialized educators, special curricular content, special instructional methodologies, and special instructional materials. Prior to the mainstreaming trend that resulted from the implementation of PL 94-142, these four services were usually provided to children within the context of special classes or schools. These classes and schools are commonly categorized along a continuum reflecting their degree of separation from the mainstream. Resource rooms, self-contained classes, special day schools, and residential treatment centers reflect this continuum with the former being the least restrictive.

The current educational *Zeitgeist* in services and treatments for exceptional children is mainstreaming. In its most basic form, "mainstreaming means moving handicapped children from their segregated status in special education classes and integrating them with 'normal' children in regular classrooms" (Brenton, 1974, p. 23). A central thrust of mainstreaming is the establishment of an educational environment that is as near normal as possible. Thus for many exceptional children full-time placement in a regular classroom may be considered mainstreaming, whereas for other children placement in a special education resource or self-contained class may be viewed as mainstreaming. The goal is to place a child in the least restrictive environment relative to the severity of his or her handicapping condition(s). Even with the current trend toward mainstream programs, many exceptional children will receive some, if not all, of their education in one or more of the special environments enumerated above. Thus we will briefly describe the various gradations of classes and then discuss research concerning their efficacy. (More detailed evaluation of education of the retarded is in Weiss & Weisz, Chapter 10 of this volume.)

Amount of special attention is a critical variable that influences the particular class environment in which a child is placed. In a typical resource room arrangement the exceptional child is enrolled in a regular program but is provided with additional educational and emotional support in one or maybe two areas of weakenss (e.g., mathematics and/or social skills). The resource class would most likely be organized in a small group or tutorial fashion. In the self-contained special class arrangement, exceptional children are usually physically segregated from other groups of children and recieve all academic instruction from special educators but on a limited basis throughout the day share in other activities such as sports, dining, and assemblies with "normal" peers. Some school systems have organized special day-schools for different groups of exceptional children, especially emotionally disturbed, physically handicapped, trainable mentally retarded, and multiply handicapped. In general, these special schools are located some distance from the regular schools, which segregates children and staff such that infrequent and limited interaction with "normal" peers takes place. Finally, there are residential schools or institutions for children with various severe handicapping conditions. Children live at the school and can receive intensive educational, psychological, and medical services on a daily basis.

Research on the Efficacy of Special Programs

Given the range of various treatment programs, one can ask how effective they are with various groups of exceptional children. Recently there have been several critical examinations of the efficacy of resource and self-contained special education programs (Carlberg & Kavale, 1980; O'Connor, Stuck, & Wyne, 1979; Sindelar & Deno, 1978). We next examine the results of two of these reviews.

Sindelar and Deno reviewed the results of 17 studies of resource programs and their effects on the academic achievement and personal-social development of exceptional children. The summary tables that they developed to compare the results and critical variables in each of these studies are presented as Tables 7.2, 7.3, and 7.4. We will only summarize Sindelar and Deno's major conclusions because much information from their review is presented in these tables.

Concerning academic achievement, Sindelar and Deno concluded "it has not been clearly established that resource programs in general will be effective in improving the academic performance of all populations" (p. 24). In general, programs for learning disabled and mildly disturbed children (Glavin, Quay, Annesley, & Werry, 1971; Quay, Glavin, Annesley, & Werry, 1972; Sabatino, 1971) proved to influence academic achievement more effectively than did programs for retarded children (Budoff & Gottlieb, 1976; Carroll, 1967; Smith & Kennedy, 1967; Walker, 1974).

Sindelar and Deno were less optimistic about the efficacy of programs for improving personal and social adjustment. After reviewing correlational studies (Bruininks, Rynders, & Gross, 1974; Flynn, 1974; Flynn & Flynn, 1970; Guerin & Szatlocky, 1974; Lapp, 1957; Sheare, 1974) and experimental studies (Budoff & Gottlieb, 1976; Carroll, 1967; Glavin, 1973, 1974; Glavin et al., 1971; Quay et al., 1972; Smith & Kennedy, 1967; Walker, 1974) they concluded neither static assessment nor experimentation had established the efficacy of resource programming in improving children's personal or social adjustment.

Carlberg and Kavale (1980) reviewed over 800 research investigations from which they selected 50 data-based articles for inclusion in a meta-analysis con-

Table 7.2. Studies of Academic Achievement

Reference	Population/N/ Assignment	Comparisons	Duration	Measures	Results
Carroll, 1967	Mildly retarded $N = 39$ Naturally existing groups	Resource program with special class	One school year	Wide Range Achievement Test (WRAT)	1. Children in both treatments realized significant gains 2. Special class group made greater gains on reading subtest than resource group
Smith & Kennedy, 1967	Mildly retarded $N = 96$ Randomly assigned	Resource program (45 min/day) with control activity (45 min/day) with regular class placement	Unclear (authors cite "short period of time" as major limitation—pretests 9/61; posttests 4/63)	California Achievement Test (CAT) Wechsler Intelligence Scale for Children (WISC)	1. No significant differences among groups on either measure
Walker, 1974	Mildly retarded $N = 58$ Matched on CA, IQ, and reading level	Resource program with special class placement	Two-year program, first and second evaluations	Word reading, vocabulary, and arithmetic subtests of Stanford Achievement Test (SAT)	1. Resource program group scored significantly higher in word reading and vocabulary than special class group 2. No difference in arithmetic

Budoff & Gottlieb, 1976	Educable mentally retarded $N = 31$ Randomly assigned	Resource program (45 min/day minimum) with special class placement	Three evaluations (1) pretest (2) two months after assignment (3) nine months after assignment	Metropolitan Achievement Test	1. At time two and time three, no significant differences attributable to placement
Glavin et al., 1971	Behaviorally, disruptive, or overly withdrawn Experimental, $N = 27$ Control, $N = 34$ Random assignment of teacher identifications	Resource program with regular class placement	Two-year program, first year evaluation	CAT	1. Resource program group scored significantly higher on reading comprehension and arithmetic fundamentals than regular class group
Quay et al., 1972	(Same as above)	Evaluation following second year of the program described	Two-year program, second year evaluation	CAT	1. Resource program group scored significantly higher than regular class group on: reading vocabulary, total reading; arithmetic fundamentals, total arithmetic
Glavin, 1973	(Same as above)	First year evaluation following termination of program	Two-year program, first year post-check	CAT	1. Resource program group scored significantly higher than regular class group on arithmetic fundamentals only

(continued)

Table 7.2 *(continued)*

Reference	Population/N/ Assignment	Comparisons	Duration	Measures	Results
Glavin, 1974	(Same as above)	Second year evaluation following termination of program	Two-year program second year post-check	CAT	1. No significant differences between groups
Sabatino, 1971	Learning disabled $N = 114$ Matched on CA, sex, IQ, and perceptual impairment	Special class with resource program: A (1 hr/daily); resource program B (1/2 hr/twice weekly); regular class placement	One school year	14 selected subtests of WRAT, WISC, and Illinois Test of Psycholinguistic Abilities (ITPA)	1. All three "special" groups gained significantly more than regular class group 2. Resource program A group superior to both resource program B and special class groups, which did not differ
Affleck, Lehning, & Brow, 1973	Learning disabled $N = 29$ Within-subject comparisons	Interpolated historical rates of improvement with rate of improvement in resource program	One school year	Spache Diagnostic Reading Scales	1. Ss made significant pre- to post-test gains 2. Ss rates of progress significantly improved during resource program placement

Jenkins & Mayhall, 1974	A. Educable mentally retarded and learning disabled $N = 6$ and $N = 24$ Random assignment	Special class versus special class and resource program for EMRs; resource program versus regular class	A. Three and a half months	WRAT	1. Resource program group improved at significantly faster rate than either special or regular class group
	B. Learning disabled, $N = 28$ Half randomly assigned; lowest seven of remaining half	For learning disabled; resource program (for reading only) versus regular class placement	B. One school year	WRAT	1. Resource program group significantly outgained regular group on reading subtest 2. No difference on arithmetic subtest

Source: Sindelar and Deno, 1978. Reprinted with permission.

Table 7.3. Correlational Studies of Personal/Social Adjustment

Reference	Population/N/ Assignment	Comparisons	Duration	Measures	Results
Lapp, 1957	Slow learners N = 16 Naturally existing groups Regular class children N = 32 Random selection	Resource program with regular class normals	Unclear. At least one school year. Subjects evaluated two consecutive springs	Sociometric questionnaire. Vineland Social Maturity Scale (VSMS)	1. Both acceptance and rejection scores lower for resource program group
A. Flynn, 1974	Mildly retarded in resource program N = 61; mildly retarded awaiting placement. N = 61; normal controls, N = 61	Resource program with regular class referrals with regular class normals	No information regarding length of treatment before subjects evaluated	Social Adjustment Scale	1. Normal controls scored significantly higher than either resource program group or referral group
B. Flynn & Flynn, 1970	(Assignment as above)	(Same as above)	(Same as above)	Teacher ratings; student satisfaction interviews	1. Teachers approve of resource program 2. Resource program group satisfied with school placement
Bruininks, Rynders, & Gross, 1974	Mildly retarded N = 65 Nonretarded classmates N = 1234	Resource program with nonretarded classmates (with urban versus suburban and same versus opposite sex analyses)	In resource program for minimum of 18 months before evaluation	Peer Acceptance Scale (PAS)	1. No significant differences in social acceptance between resource program group and nonretarded classmates for either urban or suburban groups

Author/Date	Subjects	Treatment	Duration	Measure	Results
					2. Urban same sex ratings were significantly higher for resource program group; suburban, same sex ratings were significantly lower for resource program group
Guerin & Szatlocky, 1974	Mildly retarded $N = 27$ Natural groups Regular class normals $N = 54$ Random selection	Special class, partial integration; special class, full-time; resource program and regular class normals	No information regarding length of treatment before evaluated	Coping Analysis	1. Retarded girls more (positively) manipulative in peer interactions than nonretarded peers 2. Resource program and special class (full-time) groups showed significantly more self-directed behavior than special class (P. I.) group
Sheare, 1974	Nonretarded ninth graders $N = 400$ Random assignment	Two or more classes with educable mentally retardates (integrated normals) and none (segregated normals)	Three and a half months	PAS	1. Integrated normals more accepting of educable mentally retardates than segregated normals 2. Females more accepting than males

Source: Sindelar and Deno, 1978. Reprinted with permission.

Table 7.4. Experimental Studies of Personal/Social Adjustment

Reference	Population/N/ Assignment	Comparisons	Duration	Measures	Results
Carroll, 1967	Previously described (see Table 7.2)	Previously described	Same	Illinois Index of Self-Derogation (IISD)	1. Significant decreases in self-derogation for resource program group; significant increases for special class group 2. Special class group made significantly more self-derogating remarks than resource placement group
Walker, 1974	Previously described (see Table 7.2)	Previously described	Same	Bristol Social Adjustment Scale and IISD	1. No significant differences between resource program and special class groups in self concept 2. Resource program group showed significantly better social adjustment than special class group

Study				Measures	Results
Smith & Kennedy, 1967	Previously described (see Table 7.2)	Previously described	Same	VSMS Sociometric questionnaire	1. No significant differences between groups
Budoff & Gottlieb, 1976	Previously described (see Table 7.2)	Previously described	Same	1. Seven measures of Motivation 2. Two measures of Cognitive Style 3. Teacher's Behavior Rating form (not all administered at each testing session)	1. At time two, no significant differences attributable to placement 2. At time three resource program students scored significantly greater than special class students on measures of motivation and on measure of cognitive style
A. Glavin et al., 1971	Previously described (see Table 7.2)	Previously described	Same	Behavior Problem Checklist	A.1. Improved behavior for both groups in regular class 2. Behavior of resource program groups significantly better in resource room
B. Quay et al., 1972			Same		B.1. No significant differences between groups in regular class in attending behavior

(continued)

Table 7.3 *(continued)*

Reference	Population/N/ Assignment	Comparisons	Duration	Measures	Results
					2. Resource pro- gram group at- tended more in resource room than regular class
C. Glavin, 1973			Same		C. No significant differences be- tween groups
D. Glavin, 1974			Same		D. No significant differences be- tween groups

Source: Sindelar and Deno, 1978. Reprinted by permission.

cerning the efficacy of special versus regular class placement for exceptional children. Meta-analysis (Glass, 1976, 1978) is a recently developed analytic procedure that allows one to integrate large amounts of data from a variety of research efforts in order to reach global conclusions regarding treatment effects. Meta-analysis would be unnecessary if every investigator of the effect of special versus regular class placement had measured outcomes in the same way; however, investigators have used an array of tests and measures to evaluate the academic and social consequences of each type of placement. Thus, according to Carlberg and Kavale, meta-analysis provides a statistical method for analyzing such "apples and oranges" comparisons. The goal of this massive analysis of previous research was to determine if there was an empirical foundation for mainstreaming exceptional children. Discussing this prior research, Carlberg and Kavale stated:

> The question remains, however, of whether this movement was justified. The most vocal advocates of mainstreaming have built their arguments on a philosophical rather than an empirical foundation. But the philosophical commitment to mainstreaming appears to be firmer than the empirical evidence warrants. (pp. 295–296)

Carlberg and Kavale's review and analysis included children from regular classes, as well as exceptional children categorized three ways: educable mentally retarded (IQ 50–75), slow learner (IQ 75–90), and learning disabled and behavior disordered/emotionally disturbed. These investigators reported that no differential placement effects emerged across studies regardless of whether achievement or personality/social variables were analyzed. Similarly, it was reported that the variables of IQ, age, percentage of male subjects, duration of treatment, and sample size had little effect on the relative superiority of regular class placement or special class placement. The only factor that revealed a significant effect for differential placement was category of expectionality. The results of the meta-analysis indicated the problems of learning disabled and behaviorally disordered/emotionally disturbed children were apparently more appropriately handled in a special class environment than the problems of children categorized as slow learners or educable mentally retarded. Thus the investigators concluded the present trend toward mainstreaming by regular class placement may not be appropriate for certain groups of exceptional children and encouraged special educators to look at the issue of mainstreaming as a continuum rather than as a dichotomy between special versus regular class placement.

Another body of research also concerns the effectiveness of special classes for exceptional children. This research involves the proactive design and experimental manipulation of classroom settings and management systems. Seminal thinking and research on such "engineered" classrooms was done by Hewett (1967, 1968). The best example of this type of research, however, has been conducted by researchers at the Center at Oregon for Research in Behavioral Education of the Handicapped (CORBEH). CORBEH was a research and development center funded by the Bureau of the Handicapped, U.S. Office of Education from 1971 to 1979. The educational researchers at CORBEH developed four behavior management educational packages for children with behavior disorders. Briefly, packages were developed and tested for the following disorders: acting out behaviors, low academic survival skills, social withdrawal, and socially negative/aggressive behavior. The packages designed for each of these behavior disorders are referred to as CLASS, PASS, PEERS, and RECESS respectively. According to Walker and Hops (1979), the packages were developed for use with children in kindergarten through third grades who are demonstrating behavior disorders in mainstream settings.

To illustrate further the nature of these CORBEH programs, the CLASS (Contingencies for Learning Academic and Social Skills) program is described briefly. CLASS consists of a structured set of procedures designed to remediate the disruptive behavior of acting out children enrolled in grades K to 3. CLASS is based on social learning theory and primarily consists of behavioral interventions. The intervention components include: (1) a point system with positive token reinforcement and response cost components; (2) contracting procedures; (3) adult praise; (4) school and home rewards; and (5) systematic suspension for specific disruptive or destructive school behavior. This program requires a minimum of 30 school days for implementation and the services of a consultant and a teacher (Walker & Hops, 1979).

To date, several field tests of the CORBEH programs have indicated that they are effective (Hops, Walker, Fleischman, Nagoshi, Omura, Skinrud, & Taylor, 1978; O'Connor et al., 1979; Walker & Hops, 1979). For example, O'Connor et al. employed the CORBEH package for students with low academic survival skills (i.e., PASS) with elementary students identified as being a year or more behind in reading and/or math achievement and who were also frequently off-task. These researchers had a comparison group who did not receive the instructional treatment. The results indicated that those students who were taught using the CORBEH package spent significantly more time-on-task and achieved at significantly higher levels in reading and math than did their counterparts who did not participate in the 10-week resource room intervention.

It should be noted that all the CORBEH instructional packages for exceptional children integrate behavior management techniques, psychological and educational consultants, and specialized instructional methodologies. Thus they illustrate that the interface between psychology and education can be a positive and two-way interaction which helps exceptional children.

A PERSPECTIVE ON FUTURE INTERACTIONS

Past Behavior Predicts Future Interactions

The behavioral premise that past behavior is the best predictor of future behavior serves as an appropriate advanced organizer to this section for we will be discussing possible future psychology–education relationships from the perspective of past services and treatments for exceptional children. However, before we speculate about the future, let us briefly review our conceptualization of the past by answering the questions that motivated the writing of this chapter.

First we asked, "What does psychology have to contribute to education?" Our answer was threefold. We believe that psychology has directly influenced educators' conceptions of normal and abnormal human behavior and has resulted in the prevalence of a model in which behavior is viewed as an interaction between a person and an environment. We also believe that the technology of behavioral psychology, applied behavioral analysis/behavior modification, has provided educators with techniques that can be employed effectively to improve children's learning and behavior problems. Finally, we stressed how psychological consultants can function as a valuable resource to educators and parents who are directly involved in solving children's problems.

In a reciprocal fashion we asked, "What does education have to contribute to psychology?" Here our answer was twofold. We believe that educators have a unique opportunity to provide children with direct instruction and experiences which may function to prevent psychological problems in adolescence and adulthood and thus reduce the number or severity of human problems psychologists might face at a later age. We also discussed how effective special education classes have been in remediating learning and behavior problems and concluded that such classes may be an appropriate intervention for some but not all exceptional children.

The final and summative question we asked was, "What do psychology and education have to offer exceptional children?" This question was based on the supposition that the interface between psychology and education was best exemplified by the services for and the treatment of exceptional children. Hence a composite of the various offerings from psychology and education which were discussed influences services and treatments that are typically offered to exceptional children.

At this point there is a temptation to conclude this discussion of the relationship between education and psychology on an optimistic note; however, too many factors mitigate against it. Four factors which may have important future consequences for the psychology–education relationship and subsequent services for children include the implementation of consultative services, the implementation of preventive services, the mainstreaming movement, and the development of assessment–intervention links.

Consultative Services

Consultation was presented as an indirect service in which a psychologist and educator collaboratively attempt to analyze client (e.g., child) problems and subsequently design an appropriate intervention plan. Such consultative methods have come to be seen as one of the most important job functions for psychologists in the schools according to psychologists and educators alike.

However, problems in implementing such services exist and must be addressed in the future.

First and foremost, consultative approaches will need to be integrated with other school psychology functions, particularly with that of assessment. Gutkin and Curtis (1982) hypothesized that a successful integration of consultative and assessment services would result in lowering the resistance to consultation services by (1) educators who may be unfamiliar with an indirect model of service, (2) psychologists adhering to a psychometric approach, and (3) funding agencies of the state and federal government. As was discussed earlier, the relationship between consultation and assessment is quite natural; testing should never take place without some initial consultation with the referral source (e.g., teacher) to determine the nature of a child's "problem." Recommendations resulting from testing should likewise never be made without some follow-up consultation to determine if they were properly understood by the consultee and to determine their effectiveness.

More refined research on consultation is needed. Consulting psychologists need to employ rigorous evaluation methods and follow up on the quality of services that consultees ultimately provide to children. Many methods used to assess effects of consultation have been inadequate. For example, most researchers have used questionnaires or self-reports as outcome measures of consultation, both of which are difficult to interpret objectively. In addition, most researchers have focused on consultees' responses to consultation rather than consultees' interventions with the target child or client. The evidence for or against consultative services, however, should lie in the quality of the resulting services children receive.

Another concern is the need for effective preservice and inservice programs for psychologists and educators who have had little or no training in consultation techniques. Meyers (1978) reported, after a comprehensive survey, that only 38% of the school psychology training programs surveyed offered courses designed solely for training in consultation and still fewer (30%) offered an experiential component in this training. Sandoval, Lambert, and Davis (1977) discussed the importance of training educators to be skillful consultees, an outcome many have naively assumed would occur without the aid of preservice and inservice experiences. If consultative services are ever to be as valuable to educators, parents, and children as we think they can be, this paucity in training will have to be alleviated.

Preventive Services

We believe educators and psychologists can and should work together to initiate and develop curriculum-based programs that focus on the development of positive mental health. However, there are several deterrents which need to be overcome. The foremost problem is one of perception. Psychologists and educators are generally overwhelmed by the complexities involved in designing and establishing preventive programs. Thus a lack of know-how coupled with the relative paucity of prepackaged programs seems to be a significant limiting factor. If, however, we were to take the advice of some community psychologists (e.g., Allen et al., 1976), we would not hesitate to develop experimental problem-solving programs at all elementary grade levels, similar to the programs developed by Ojemann (1967).

Another major deterrent to the development of prevention programs resides within the ranks of psychologists. Apparently a majority of psychologists and associated mental health specialists view assessment and treatment as their primary function. According to Cruickshank (1963), preventive work is regarded as less concrete, less exciting, and less urgent than treatment which is geared toward the immediate, the tangible, and the already overt disturbance.

Other deterrents to prevention that require some thought have been outlined by Clarizio (1979b). They include invasion of privacy and the difficulty of specifying and evaluating the goals of prevention. To prevent maladjustment is to intrude to some degree into the private affairs of other persons. Thus the crux of the invasion of privacy issue is to develop interventions acceptable to the public. If prevention programs are implemented, there will be a need to evaluate their effectiveness so improvements can be made. According to Clarizio (1979b), it will be essential to "establish both operational definitions of objectives and evaluative baselines . . . The day of the 'soft sell' may well be on the way out for the mental health fields" (p. 323).

The future of preventive programs does not appear to fall squarely on the shoulders of any single profession. Both educators and psychologists have a stake in prevention and will need to work together to successfully implement and maintain such programs. One means by which preventive practices should continue to develop within schools is via consultation. Specifically, the problem-solving skills and subsequent interventions that result from any one consultation should continue to be employed by a consultee with children to prevent future problems.

Mainstreaming

The implementation of mainstreaming presents a major challenge to all educators, special and regular, and requires a coordinated effort from psychologists. Many practical as well as philosophical issues have to be resolved before the promise of mainstreaming can be fulfilled. In fact, several writers believe that many special educators have failed to differentiate between mainstreaming as a principle and mainstreaming as a practice (Keogh & Levitt, 1976; MacMillan, Jones, & Meyers, 1976). Thus one must wonder whether special educators have oversold their ability to remediate problems exceptional children experience!

Although interest in mainstreaming has increased (Meisgeier, 1976), there has been no commensurate increase in research concerning the efficacy of mainstreaming (Gickling & Theobald, 1975; MacMillan & Semmel, 1979). Instead, comparative reviews investigating the relative effectiveness of special versus regular class placements for children with a variety of handicaps have been done (Carlberg & Kavale, 1980; Sindelar & Deno, 1978). The results of these two major reviews were discussed. Future investigators need to test directly basic assumptions underlying the principle of mainstreaming. Specifically, educators and psychologists need to know whether mainstreaming (1) functions to reduce the stigma and increase the social acceptability of mainstreamed exceptional children, (2) elicits helping or hostile reactions from regular educators, and (3) increases or decreases the academic achievement of exceptional children (Abramson, 1980).

Psychologists' roles in the mainstreaming of exceptional children, although secondary to that of special educators, may be critical to the success or failure of any given program. Psychologists will be needed for inservice, consultation, and program evaluation. These needs are based on the belief that many regular educators do not possess the refined behavioral management and instructional programming skills required of special educators. In addition, there is evidence to indicate that many regular educators feel impotent in the special education decision-making processes concerning programmming and placement (Yoshida, Fenton, Maxwell, & Kaufman, 1978). Hence psychologists and special educators wiil need to continue collaborative efforts to ensure appropriate services and treatments are provided for exceptional children.

Assessment-Intervention Links

The direct assessment of children who are experiencing learning or behavioral problems in school has been almost exclusively a task for school psychologists, whereas the development of individual educational plans has been almost exclusively a task for educators. In theory such a division of labor seems appropriate and efficient, but in practice problems have arisen. Consequently, many educational programs for exceptional children have been developed that are not based on assessment information, may not be individualized, and may in fact hinder a child's educational progress.

Traditionally, psychological assessments have served a screening or a placement function, rather than a programming function. Psychologists have not typically been trained as teachers and have not employed assessment techniques that provide specific information directly pertinent to instructional planning. Yet according to Ysseldyke (1978), the consumers of psychological reports (e.g., teachers and parents) want to know specifically what to do for and with children both academically and behaviorally.

Psychologists and educators sensitive to the shortcomings of traditional assessment practices (i.e., standardized, norm-referenced testing) have advocated the use of new approaches and techniques. Such techniques as behavioral observations, task analysis, and diagnostic teaching have increasingly become part of the assessment process. In most cases these informal techniques are a means of providing teachers specific information about what a child knows and how he or she learns. Thus we believe informal techniques are valuable supplements to the standardized assessment instruments used in a traditional assessment paradigm and will be increasingly employed by psychologists. Several of our colleagues (e.g., Smith, 1980; Tidwell, 1980) have stated similar beliefs and have provided persuasive rationales for the inclusion of informal or nonstandardized testing, teaching, and observational techniques in the typical evaluations of children. Recently several psychologists and special educators have outlined approaches to assessment which include gathering information about children's learning and behavior skills with curriculum-related materials and behavioral observations. These approaches have been termed Process Assessment (Kratochwill & Severson, 1977), Differentiated Assessment (Ysseldyke, 1979), Learning Potential Assessment (Feuerstein, 1979), and the Systems Approach of Assessment (Eaves & McLaughlin, 1977).

Given that primary goals of psychoeducational assessment are to determine *what* a child does and does not know or do and *how* the child learns best, a move toward an informal model of assessment should be welcome. However, like many other services for exceptional children, informal assessment techniques almost necessitate a coordinated interaction between psychologists and educators in order to assess a child with tasks that he or she typically encounters in class. The benefit of an assessment approach that combines standardized tests and informal techniques is that educational interventions can be designed directly from the successes and failures with curriculum-based tasks which were observed during assessment.

CONCLUSIONS

We have selectively discussed a number of ways in which education and psychology interact. Had other persons written this chapter we are quite confident that you would have been exposed to some different issues and different perspectives, for the interaction between education and psychology is multifaceted and complex.

We chose to focus on the relationship between school psychology and special education because it is in these two fields that the interface between psychology and education directly affects exceptional children. We believe this relationship has been difficult at times. Professionals in both fields have had high expectations for each other and subsequently have been disappointed. Even though both professions have complementary knowledge and skills to offer each other, without strong economic ties and a common interest in and desire to help children the relationship would have been terminated long ago.

Society expects so much from both psychology and education and wants so much for its children that we are left to conclude that future interactions between psychology and education will need to be even more extensive than those of the past. All children, not just exceptional children, stand to benefit should a majority of educators and psychologists work together to improve the social and educational experiences provided in schools.

REFERENCES

Abramson, M. Implications of mainstreaming: a challenge for special education. In L. Mann & D. A. Sabatino (Eds.), *The fourth review of special education.* New York: Grune & Stratton, 1980.

Affleck, J. Q., Lehning, T. W., & Brow, K. Expanding the resource concept: The resource school. *Exceptional Children,* 1973, *39,* 446–453.

Allen, G. J., Chinsky, J. M., Larcen, S. W., Lochman, J. E., & Selinger, H. V. *Community psychology and the schools: A behaviorally oriented multi-level preventive approach.* Hillsdale, N.J.: Erlbaum, 1976.

Alpert, J. Some guidelines for school consultants. *Journal of School Psychology,* 1977, *15,* 308–319.

Bandura, A. *Principles of behavior modification.* New York: Holt, Rinehart & Winston, 1969.

Barbanel, L., & Hoffenberg-Rutman, J. Attitudes toward job responsibilities and training satisfaction of school psychologists: A comparative study. *Psychology in the Schools,* 1974, *11,* 425–429.

Bardon, J. I. The state of the art (and science) of school psychology. *American Psychologist,* 1976, *31,* 785–791.

Bardon, J. I., & Bennett, V. C. *School psychology.* Englewood Cliffs, N.J.: Prentice-Hall, 1974.

Barker, R. G. Explorations in ecological psychology. *American Psychologist,* 1965, *20,* 1–14.

Barker, R. G. *Ecological psychology.* Stanford, Calif.: Stanford University Press, 1968.

Bergan, J. R. *Behavioral consultation.* Columbus, Ohio: Charles E. Merrill, 1977.

Bijou, S. W. What psychology has to offer education—now. *Journal of Applied Behavior Analysis,* 1970, *3,* 65–71.

Binet, A., & Simon, T. Methodes nouvelles pour le diagnostic du niveau intellectural des anormanux. *Année Psychologie,* 1905, *11,* 191–244.

Boring, E. G. *A history of experimental psychology* (2nd ed.). New York: Appleton-Century-Crofts, 1950.

Brenton, M. Mainstreaming the handicapped. *Today's Education,* 1974, *63,* 20–24.

Broskowski, A. Concepts of teacher-centered consultation. *Professional Psychology,* 1973, *4,* 50–58.

Brown, J. H., & Kelly, W. F. A conceptual model for home-school consultation. *Corrective and Social Psychiatry and Journal of Behavior Technology Methods and Therapy,* 1976, *22,* 15–20.

Bruininks, R. H., Rynders, J. E., & Gross, J. C. Social acceptance of mildly retarded pupils in resource rooms and regular classes. *American Journal of Mental Deficiency,* 1974, *78,* 377–383.

Budoff, M., & Gottlieb, J. Spcial-class EMR children mainstreamed: A study of an aptitude (learning potential) × treatment interaction. *American Journal of Mental Deficiency,* 1976, *81,* 1–11.

Buktenica, N. A. Special education and school psychology: Whither the relationship? *School Psychology Review,* 1980, *9,* 228–233.

Carlberg, C., & Kavale, K. The efficacy of special versus regular class placement for exceptional children: A meta-analysis. *Journal of Special Education*, 1980, *14*, 295–309.

Carroll, A. W. The effects of segregated and partially integrated school programs on self-concept and academic achievement of educable mental retardates. *Exceptional Children*, 1967, *34*, 93–99.

Catterall, C. D. Special education in transition: Implications for school psychology. *Journal of School Psychology*, 1972, *10*, 91–98.

Ciminero, A. R. Behavioral assessment: An overview. In A. R. Ciminero, K. S. Calhoun, & H. E. Adams (Eds.), *Handbook of behavioral assessment*. New York: Wiley, 1977.

Clarizio, H. F. Primary prevention of behavioral disorders in the schools. *School Psychology Digest*, 1979, *8*, 434–445. (a)

Clarizio, H. F. School psychologists and the mental health needs of students. In G. D. Phye & D. J. Reschley (Eds.), *School psychology: Perspectives and issues*. New York: Academic, 1979. (b)

Cowen, E. L. Baby-steps toward primary prevention. *American Journal of Community Psychology*, 1977, *5*, 1–22.

Cowen, E. L., & Gesten, E. L. Community approaches to intervention. In B. B. Wolman, J. Egan, & A. O. Ross (Eds.), *Handbook of treatment of mental disorders in childhood and adolescence*. Englewood Cliffs, N.J.: Prentice Hall, 1978.

Cowen, E. L., & Lorion, R. P. Changing roles for the school mental health professional. *Journal of School Psychology*, 1976, *14*, 131–138.

Cowen, E. L., Trost, M. A., Lorion, R. P., Dorr, D., Izzo, L. D., & Isaacson, R. V. *New ways in school mental health: Early detection and prevention of school maladaptation*. New York: Human Sciences Press, 1975.

Cruickshank, W. *Psychology of exceptional children and youth* (2nd ed.). Englewood Cliffs, N.J.: Prentice-Hall, 1963.

Curtis, M., & Watson, K. Changes in consultee problem clarification skills following consultation. *Journal of School Psychology*, 1980, *18*, 210–221.

Dewey, J. Psychology and social practice. *Psychological Review*, 1900, *7*, 105–124.

Dewey, J., & Bentley, A. F. *Knowing and the known*. Boston: Beacon, 1949.

Dickinson, D. J. Direct assessment of behavioral and emotional problems. *Psychology in the Schools*, 1978, *15*, 472–477.

Dworkin, A. L., & Dworkin, E. P. A conceptual overview of selected consultation models. *American Journal of Community Psychology*, 1975, *3*, 151–160.

D'Zurilla, T. J., & Goldfried, M. R. Problem solving and behavior modification. *Journal of Abnormal Psychology*, 1971, *78*, 107–126.

Eaves, R. C., & McLaughlin, P. A systems approach for the assessment of the child and his environment: Getting back to basics. *Journal of Special Education*, 1977, *11*, 99–111.

Fairchild, T. N. School psychological services: An empirical comparison of two models. *Psychology in the Schools*, 1976, *13*, 156–162.

Feuerstein, R. *The dynamic assessment of retarded performers*. Baltimore: University Park Press, 1979.

Flynn, T. M. Regular class adjustment of EMR students attending a part-time special education program. *Journal of Special Education,* 1974, *8,* 167–173.

Flynn, T. M., & Flynn, L. A. The effect of a part-time special education program on the adjustment of EMR students. *Exceptional Children,* 1970, *36,* 680–681.

Frampton, M. E., & Gall, E. D. *Special education for the exceptional.* Boston: Porter Sargent, 1955.

Frampton, M. E., & Rowell, H. G. *Education of the handicapped.* New York: Harcourt Brace Jovanovich, 1938.

Gallagher, J. J. Psychology and special education—The future: Where the action is. *Psychology in the Schools,* 1969, *6,* 219–226.

Gallessich, J. Organizational factors influencing consultation in schools. *Journal of School Psychology,* 1973, *11,* 57–65.

Gibbins, S. Public Law 94-142: An impetus for consultation. *School Psychology Digest,* 1978, *7,* 205–210.

Gickling, E. E., & Theobald, J. T. Mainstreaming: Affect or effect. *Journal of Special Education,* 1975, *9,* 317–328.

Giebink, J. W., & Ringness, T. A. On the relevancy of training in school psychology. *Journal of School Psychology,* 1970, *8,* 43–47.

Ginsburg, H., & Opper, S. *Piaget's theory of intellectual development.* Englewood Cliffs, N.J.: Prentice-Hall, 1969.

Glass, G. V. Primary, secondary, and meta-analysis of research. *Educational Researcher,* 1976, *5,* 3–8.

Glass, G. V. Integrating findings: The meta-analysis of research. *Review of Research in Education,* 1978, *5,* 351–379.

Glavin, J. P. Follow-up behavioral research in resource rooms. *Exceptional Children,* 1973, *40,* 211–213.

Glavin, J. P. Behaviorally oriented resource rooms: A follow-up. *Journal of Special Education,* 1974, *8,* 337–347.

Glavin, J. P., Quay, H. C., Annesley, F. R., & Werry, J. S. An experimental resource room for behavior problem children. *Exceptional Children,* 1971, *38,* 131–137.

Griggs, J. W., & Bonney, M. E. Relationship between "causal" orientation and acceptance of others, "self-ideal self" congruency and mental health changes of fourth and fifth grade children. *Journal of Educational Research,* 1970, *63,* 471–477.

Guerin, G. R., & Szatlocky, K. Integration programs for the mildly retarded. *Exceptional Children,* 1974, *41,* 173–179.

Gutkin, T. B. Teacher perception of consultative services provided by school psychologists. *Professional Psychology,* 1980, *11,* 637–642.

Gutkin, T. B., & Curtis, M. J. School-based consultation: Theory and techniques. In C. R. Reynolds & T. B. Gutkin (Eds.), *The handbook of school psychology.* New York: Wiley, 1982.

Gutkin, T. B., Singer, J. H., & Brown, R. Teacher reactions to school based consultation services: A multivariate analysis. *Journal of School Psychology,* 1980, *18,* 126–134.

Hersen, M. H., & Barlow, P. H. *Single case experimental designs.* New York: Pergamon, 1976.

Hewett, F. M. Educational engineering with emotionally disturbed children. *Exceptional Children,* 1967, *33,* 459–470.

Hewett, F. M. *The emotionally disturbed child in the classroom.* Boston: Allyn and Bacon, 1968.

Hewett, F. M., & Forness, S. R. *Education of exceptional learners.* Boston: Allyn and Bacon, 1974.

Hilgard, E. R., & Bower, G. H. *Theories of learning* (4th ed.). Englewood Cliffs, N. J.: Prentice-Hall, 1975.

Hill, W. F. *Learning: A survey of psychological interpretations* (rev. ed.). London: Chandler, 1971.

Hollister, W. G., & Miller, F. T. Problem-solving strategies in consultation. *American Journal of Orthopsychiatry,* 1977, *47,* 445–450.

Hops, H., Walker, H. M., Fleischman, D. H., Nagoshi, J., Omura, R., Skinrud, K., & Taylor, J. CLASS: A standardized in-class program for acting out children. 2. Field test evaluations. *Journal of Educational Psychology,* 1978, 70(4), 444–636.

Hunt, J. M. Traditional personality theory in the light of recent evidence. In E. P. Hollander & R. G. Hunt (Eds.), *Current perspectives in social psychology* (2nd ed.). New York: Oxford Univeristy Press, 1967.

Jackson, R. M., Cleveland, J. C., & Merenda, P. F. The longitudinal effects of early identification and counseling of underachievers. *Journal of School Psychology,* 1975, *13,* 119–128.

James, W. *Talks to teachers on psychology: And to students on some of life's ideals.* New York: Holt, 1922 (originally published, 1899).

Jason, L. A., & Ferone, L. Behavioral versus process consultation interventions in school settings. *American Journal of Community Psychology,* 1978, *6,* 531–543.

Jenkins, J. R., & Mayhall, W. F. *Development and evaluation of a resource program: The resource specialist model.* Unpublished manuscript, University of Illinois, 1974.

Kazdin, A. E. The impact of applied behavior analysis on diverse areas of research. *Journal of Applied Behavior Analysis,* 1975, *8,* 213–229.

Keogh, B. K., & Levitt, M. L. Special education in the mainstream: A confrontation of limitations. *Focus on Exceptional Children,* 1976, *8,* 8–11.

Kirk, S. A. *Educating exceptional children* (2nd ed.). Boston: Houghton Mifflin, 1972.

Kramer, J. J., & Nagle, R. J. Suggestions for the delivery of psychological services in secondary schools. *Psychology in the Schools,* 1980, *17,* 53–59.

Kratochwill, T. R. $N = 1$: An alternative research strategy for school psychologists. *Journal of School Psychology,* 1977, *15,* 239–249. (a)

Kratochwill, T. R. The movement of psychological extras onto ability assessment. *Journal of Special Education,* 1977, *11,* 299–311. (b)

Kratochwill, T. R., & Severson, R. A. Process assessment: An examination on reinforcer effectiveness and predictive validity. *Journal of School Psychology,* 1977, *15,* 293–300.

Krumboltz, J. D., & Krumboltz, H. B. *Changing children's behavior*. Englewood Cliffs, N. J.: Prentice-Hall, 1972.

Lambert, N. M. The school psychologists as a source of power and influence. *Journal of School Psychology*, 1973, *11*, 245-250.

Lambert, N., Sandoval, J., & Corder, R. Teacher perceptions of school-based consultants. *Professional Psychology*, 1975, *6*, 204-216.

Lapp, E. R. A study of the social adjustment of slow learning children who were assigned part-time to regular classes. *American Journal of Mental Deficiency*, 1957, *62*, 254-262.

Levine, M., & Levine, A. *A social history of helping services: Clinic, court, school, and community*. New York: Appleton-Century-Crofts, 1970.

Lewin, K. *Field theory in the social sciences*. New York: Harper & Row, 1951.

Lolli, A. Jr. Implementing the role of the school psychologist. *Psychology in the Schools*, 1980, *17*, 70-75.

MacMillan, D. L., Jones, R. L., & Meyers, C. E. Mainstreaming the mildly retarded: Some questions, cautions, and guidelines. *Mental Retardation*, 1976, *14*, 3-10.

MacMillan, D. L., & Semmel, M. I. Evaluations of mainstreaming programs. In E. L. Meyen, G. A. Vergason, & R. J. Whelan (Eds.), *Instructional planning for exceptional children*. Denver: Love, 1979.

Manley, T. R., & Manley, E. T. A comparison of the personal values and operative goals of school psychologists and school superintendents. *Journal of School Psychology*, 1978, *16*, 99-109.

Mannino, F. V., & Shore, M. F. Effecting change through consultation. In F. V. Mannino, B. W. MacLennan, & M. F. Shore (Eds.), *The practice of mental health consultation*. New York: Gardner Press, 1975.

Martin, R. P., Duffey, J., & Fischman, R. A time analysis and evaluation of an experimental internship program in school psychology. *Journal of School Psychology*, 1973, *11*, 263-268.

McDermott, P. A. Congruence and typology of diagnosis in school psychology: An empirical study. *Psychology in the Schools*, 1980, *17*, 12-24.

Meacham, M., & Peckham, P. D. School psychologists at three-quarters century: Congruence between training, practice, preferred role and competence. *Journal of School Psychology*, 1978, *16*, 195-206.

Medway, F. J. How effective is school consultation: A review of recent research. *Journal of School Psychology*, 1979, *17*, 275-282.

Meisgeier, C. A review of critical issues underlying mainstreaming. In L. Mann & D. A. Sabatino (Eds.), *The third review of special education*. New York: Grune & Stratton, 1976.

Meyers, J. Consultee-centered consultation with a teacher as a technique in behavioral management. *American Journal of Community Psychology*, 1975, *3*, 111-121.

Meyers, J. Training school psychologists for a consultation role. *School Psychology Digest*, 1978, *7*, 26-32.

Meyers, J., Parsons, R. D., & Martin, R. *Mental health consultation in the schools*. San Francisco: Jossey-Bass, 1979.

Miller, G. A. Psychology as a means of promoting human welfare. *American Psychologist,* 1969, *24,* 1063–1075.

Miller, T. L., & Dyer, C. O. Role-model complements of school psychology with special education. In L. Mann & D. A. Sabatino (Eds.), *The fourth review of special education.* New York: Grune & Stratton, 1980.

Muuss, R. E. The effects of a one- and two-year causal learning program. *Journal of Personality,* 1960, *28,* 479–491.

O'Connor, P. D., Stuck, G. B., & Wyne, M. D. Effects of a short-term intervention resource-room program on task orientation and achievement. *Journal of Special Education,* 1979, *13,* 375–385.

Ojemann, R. H. Investigations on the effects of teacher understanding and appreciation of behavioral dynamics. In G. Caplan (Ed.), *Prevention of mental disorders in children.* New York: Basic Books, 1961.

Ojemann, R. H. Incorporating psychological concepts in the school curriculum. *Journal of School Psychology,* 1967, *5,* 195–204.

Osborn, A. *Applied imagination* (3rd ed.). New York: Scribners, 1963.

Piaget, J. *The psychology of intelligence* (M. Percy & D. E. Berlyne trans.). London: Routledge and Kegan Paul, 1950.

Piaget, J. *The origins of intelligence in children* (M. Cook trans.). New York: International Universities Press, 1952.

Platt, J., & Spivack, G. *Workbook for training in interpersonal problem-solving thinking.* Philadelphia: Department of Mental Health Sciences, Hahnemann Community Mental Health/Mental Retardation Center, 1976.

Platt, J., Spivack, G., & Swift, M. *Problem-solving therapy with maladjusted groups* (Research and Evaluation Report No. 28). Philadelphia: Department of Mental Health Sciences, Hahnemann Medical College and Hospital, 1974.

Quay, H. C., Glavin, J. P., Annesley, F. R., & Werry, J. S. The modification of problem behavior and academic achievement in a resource room. *Journal of School Psychology,* 1972, *10,* 187–198.

Reger, R. The medical model in special education. *Psychology in the Schools,* 1972, *9,* 8–12.

Reilly, D. H. A conceptual model for school psychology. *Psychology in the Schools,* 1974, *11,* 165–170.

Reschly, D. J. School psychology consultation: "Frenzied, faddish, or fundamental?" *Journal of School Psychology,* 1976, *14,* 105–113.

Sabatino, D. An evaluation of resource rooms for children with learning disabilities. *Journal of Learning Disabilities,* 1971, *4,* 84–93.

Sandoval, J., Lambert, N., & Davis, J. M. Consultation from the consultee's perspective. *Journal of School Psychology,* 1977, *2,* 303–310.

Schein, E. H. *Process consultation.* Reading, Mass.: Addison-Wesley, 1969.

Schmuck, R. A., Runkel, P. J., Arends, J. H., & Arends, R. I. *The second handbook of organization developing in schools.* Palo Alto, Calif.: Mayfield, 1977.

Sheare, J. B. Social acceptance of EMR adolescents in integrated programs. *American Journal of Mental Deficiency,* 1974, *78,* 678–682.

Shure, J. Real life problem solving with parents and children: An approach to social competence. In M. Kent & J. Rolf (Eds.), *The primary prevention of psychopathology,* 3. *Promoting social competence and coping in children.* Hanover, N.H.: University Press of New England, 1979.

Sindelar, P. T., & Deno, S. L. The effectiveness of resource programming. *Journal of Special Education,* 1978, *12,* 17–28.

Skinner, B. F. *Science and human behavior.* New York: Free Press, 1953.

Skinner, B. F. *Verbal behavior.* New York: Appleton-Century-Crofts, 1957.

Skinner, B. F. *The technology of teaching.* New York: Appleton-Century-Crofts, 1968.

Skinner, B. F. *Contingencies of reinforcement: A theoretical analysis.* New York: Appleton-Century-Crofts, 1969.

Smith, C. R. Assessment alternatives: Non-standardized procedures. *School Psychology Review,* 1980, *9,* 46–57.

Smith, H. W., & Kennedy, W. A. Effects of three educational programs on mentally retarded children. *Perceptual and Motor Skills,* 1967, *24,* 174.

Spivack, G., Platt, J., & Shure, M. *The problem solving approach to adjustment.* San Francisco: Jossey-Bass, 1976.

Spivack, G., & Shure, M. *Social adjustment in young children.* San Francisco: Jossey-Bass, 1974.

Stuart, R. B. *Trick or treatment: How and when psychotherapy fails.* Champaign, Ill.: Research Press, 1970.

Sulzer-Azaroff, B., & Mayer, G. R. *Applying behavior-analysis procedures with children and youth.* New York: Holt, Rinehart & Winston, 1977.

Szasz, T. S. The myth of mental illness. *American Psychologist,* 1960, *15,* 113–118.

Tageson, C. W., & Corazzini, J. G. A collaborative model for consultation and paraprofessional development. *Professional Psychology,* 1974, *5,* 191–197.

Thorndike, E. L. *Animal intelligence.* New York: Macmillan, 1911.

Thorndike, E. L. *Educational psychology: The psychology of learning* (Vol. 2). New York: Teachers College, 1913.

Thorndike, E. L. *The psychology of arithmetic.* New York: Macmillan, 1922.

Thorndike, E. L. *Human learning.* New York: Century, 1931.

Thorndike, E. L. *The fundamentals of learning.* New York: Teachers College, 1932.

Tidwell, R. Informal assessment to modify the role and image of the school psychologist. *Psychology in the Schools,* 1980, *17,* 210–215.

Ullmann, L. P., & Krasner, L. *A psychological approach to abnormal behavior.* Englewood Cliffs, N.J.: Prentice-Hall, 1969.

Walker, H. M., & Hops, H. The CLASS program for acting out children: R & D procedures, program outcomes and implementation issues. *School Psychology Digest,* 1979, *8,* 370–381.

Walker, V. S. Efficacy of the resource room for educating retarded children. *Exceptional Children,* 1974, *40,* 288–289.

Waters, L. G. School psychologists as perceived by school personnel: Support for a consultant model. *Journal of School Psychology,* 1973, *11,* 40–46.

Wenger, R. D. Teacher response to collaborative consultation. *Psychology in the Schools,* 1979, *16,* 127–131.

Williams, D. L. Consultation: A broad, flexible role for school psychologists. *Psychology in the Schools,* 1972, *9,* 16–24.

Yoshida, R. K., Fenton, K. S., Maxwell, J. P., & Kaufman, M. J. Group decision making in the planning team process: Myth or reality? *Journal of School Psychology,* 1978, *16,* 237–244.

Ysseldyke, J. E. Who's calling the plays in school psychology? *Psychology in the Schools,* 1978, *15,* 373–378.

Ysseldyke, J. E. Issues in Psychoeducational assessment. In G. D. Phye & D. J. Reschley (Eds.), *School psychology: Perspectives and issues.* New York: Academic, 1979.

Ysseldyke, J. E., & Salvia, J. Diagnostic-prescriptive teaching: Two models. *Exceptional Children,* 1974, *41,* 181–185.

Zubin, J. Classification of behavior disorders. *Annual Review of Psychology,* 1967, *18,* 373–406.

CHAPTER 8

Exceptional Individuals and the Family: Interactional Processes

BARCLAY MARTIN

Helen: He's (retarded sibling) the only person who gets attention around our house. Mother has to work with him day and night. After he goes to bed is about the only time I get to talk to her. I never ask her anything unless it's an emergency until _____'s in bed. Last year before school started I saw the first movie I had seen in three years! . . . Two of my best girl friends have large families, but still their mothers have more time for them than mine does for me.
Teresa: (asked to describe what makes her unhappy or mad) When I have to leave her (retarded sibling) and she's crying. I start out the door to play and I have to shut the door in her face and she's crying. It makes me feel awful but I always go on out to play. . . . And sometimes I start to leave the yard and she follows me and I have to go back and put her in the house. It makes me feel mad and guilty.
(L. S. TAYLOR, 1980)

Helen and Teresa both have retarded siblings and their comments give us a small glimpse of the impact that a retarded child can have on a family. This chapter focuses on family systems which include a handicapped child.

It is commonplace now to view families as systems in which each member is affecting the others' behavior as well as being affected by it (e.g., Watzlawick & Weakland, 1977). The impact of this conceptualization on research, however, remains somewhat limited. Perhaps the greatest body of research reflecting this orientation is that studying the effects of children's or infants' characteristics on parents or caretakers. Researchers have indeed been busy on that topic, and we will take a look at some of those findings shortly. But showing that parents, usually the mother, react differently to different infants (or children) by no means exhausts the heuristic implications of a systems view. Two additional areas of study are implied. First, the systems perspective suggests that the *whole* family is an interacting system and, for example, that when the infant affects the mother's behavior this in turn may affect the mother's relationship with the father and the rest of her children. Research on the larger family system that goes beyond the parent–child dyad is meager.

Second, the systems view is dynamic. An infant or young child at risk for developing a disability, for example, may produce certain changes in parental behavior. These changes in parental behavior in turn affect the child, and these new changes in the child may again affect the parent. After these kinds of interactive exchanges have gone on for a while it becomes difficult to determine what in the parent's current behavior reflects a response to the early precursors of the child's disability and what is a response to the child's response to the parent.

Sameroff and Chandler (1975) and Sameroff (1975) stress the importance of studying these kinds of transactions between child and caretaker in order to understand how childhood disorders develop. They propose that not only must one obtain information about the child's constitutional makeup and the caretaking environment but, just as important, one must study the continuing transactions between child and caretakers as they mutually influence each other. These authors use the somewhat awkward term *continuum of reproductive casualty* to refer to a dimension of infant constitutional characteristics or complications associated with pregnancy or birth that might contribute to later difficulties in development. At one end of this continuum, for example, would be relatively mild traits of troublesome temperament; at the other end are more severe conditions such as mental retardation, cerebral palsy, or other forms of brain damage. Similarly, the term *continuum of caretaking casualty* refers to the dimension characterized by positive environmental influences at one end and negative environmental influences at the other end. Examples of extreme negative conditions would be severe parental abuse or neglect.

It is not surprising that research on the dynamic development of the current interactive patterns is quite limited. The valid measurement of the appropriate interactive sequences over a period of time is a challenge few researchers can meet. In the following discussion of the exceptional individual in the family empirical research is emphasized when available, but an effort is made not to forget the other implications of a family systems view even when there is little systematic research to go on.

PARENTAL RESPONSES TO EARLY DIFFERENCES

That parents respond differently to infants with different behavioral characteristics has been well documented. Thomas, Chess, and Birch (1968) assessed individual differences in infant temperament and found that a higher percentage of those infants labeled "difficult" later developed behavior disorders than did nondifficult infants. Temperamental characteristics of infants labeled difficult included biological irregularity, especially with respect to sleep, feeding, and elimination cycles; withdrawal and distress to new stimuli such as the first bath or new foods; slow adaptability to change; generally negative mood state involving a readiness to fuss and cry with high intensity (see Chapter 6 for more detail on this research). The authors trace the way in which the development of several children's disturbances reflected the interaction between child temperament and parent reaction. In one example they describe two children who as infants had similar difficult temperaments but only one subsequently developed a behavior problem. Differences in parental response to the same traits were thought to account for the difference in development. For the child who developed a behavioral disorder, the father had disciplined her in a punitive way, spent little or no recreational time with her, and reacted angrily to her difficulties in adjusting to nursery school. There was, in Sameroff and Chandler's (1975) words, a difference in the continuum of caretaking casualty.

There is a growing body of literature based on direct observation of infants very early in life that further identifies individual differences in temperament; for example, frequency and duration of crying (Beckwith, 1978; Thoman, Becker, & Freese, 1978), ease of soothing when crying (Birns, Blank, & Bridger, 1966; Korner, 1971), state of alertness or wakefulness (Korner & Grobstein, 1967; Osofsky, 1976; Thoman, Becker, & Freese, 1978), responsiveness to stimulation (Birns, 1965; Osofsky & Danzger, 1974; Osofsky, 1976) and cuddliness (Schaffer & Emerson, 1964). However, when longer time periods are considered, the consistency of traits of temperament found in the first month or so of life decreased or in some cases disappeared altogether (Thomas, et al., 1968; Bell & Ainsworth, 1972).

Osofsky (1976) found that neonates who showed greater responsivity on the Brazelton assessment procedure (measures various functions in the newborn such as orienting to animate and inanimate visual and auditory stimuli, consolability, and cuddliness) also showed greater responsivity when interacting with their mothers, and their mothers were more attentive and responsive to them than were mothers of less responsive infants. Cause and effect between infant and maternal variables cannot be determined in this study, but the strong consistency on measures of infant responsivity obtained in the first two to four days of life suggests that the infants' responsiveness did not develop entirely as a result of interacting with responsive mothers.

Parents do, of course, have variations in personality present before the birth of a child that will affect their subsequent interactions with the child. Moss and his colleagues have shown that several measures obtained from mothers *before* the birth of their infant predicted maternal behavior with the infant. Moss (1967) found an interview measure of "acceptance of nurturant role" predicted directly observed maternal responsiveness when the infant was 3 weeks old; Robson, Pedersen, and Moss (1969) found "interest in affectionate contact" correlated with frequency of mother-infant mutual gazing at 1 month; and Moss, Robson, and Pedersen (1969) reported that ratings of animation in a mother's voice correlated with the amount of stimulation she provided the infant at 1 and 3 months of age.

There is, then, evidence which suggests that mothers and infants have characteristics from the outset that will have some continuing effect on their relationship. These initial characteristics may or may not be influenced much by subsequent interaction. Thus a mother's strong initial feeling of dislike for an infant or an infant's extreme fussiness may or may not be reduced by subsequent interactions. Both of these traits might, in fact, become even more extreme. If, for example, the mother's dislike results in the infant becoming more irritable, then she may find even more grounds for dislike. Or if fussiness in the infant results in increased unresponsiveness or annoyance in the mother, this could produce even greater fussiness in the infant. With less extreme initial traits both mother and infant may be able to influence each other in a direction toward moderation of their responses.

THE AT-RISK INFANT

Thus far we have seen how variations in child temperaments and maternal attitudes might lead via interactive exchanges to different kinds of mother–child relationships. We now focus more specifically on those infants who are considered to be at risk for the later development of a disability. For present purposes the term at-risk refers to infants whose mothers experienced prenatal (before birth) or perinatal (at or shortly after birth) complications and/or to infants born with deviant physical or behavioral characteristics. I am not referring to major or gross disorders such as clear-cut brain damage, blindness, or physical deformities, and it is well to keep in mind that although these at-risk infants are somewhat more likely to have later difficulties, most of these infants develop normally.

Infants that would seem to carry some increased risk for interactional difficulties are the prematurely born. One characteristic that may contribute to a difference in the mother–infant relationship is the premature infant's cry, which tends to be of shorter duration and higher pitch than the nonpremature infant's cry (Zeskind & Lester, 1978). These distinctive cries are also found in infants with more clearly identifiable illness or brain damage (Lester, 1976; Wolff, 1969), and would seem to have functional significance in arousing concern and attention from caregivers. Several studies have shown that adults respond differently to the cries of premature infants (Frodi, Lamb, Leavitt, Donovan, Neff, & Sherry, 1978; Zeskind, 1980; Zeskind & Lester, 1978). For example, Frodi et al. had half of a sample of 32 married couples look at videotapes of normal, full-term newborns and the other half look at videotapes of prematurely born infants. Sound tracks were dubbed so that half of the normal and half of the premature infants "emitted" the cry of a normal infant, while the other half emitted the cry of a premature infant. The cry of the premature infant produced greater autonomic nervous system arousal and was reported to be more annoying and disturbing than was the cry of the normal infant. This effect was even more pronounced when the premature cry was paired with the face of a premature infant, suggesting that the physical appearance of the premature baby was distinctive in a way that produced less accepting reactions.

In the early weeks of interaction premature infants are less responsive, less vocal, and more fretful than nonpremature infants and mothers show less face-to-face and physical contact and less smiling to their premature babies (DiVitto & Goldberg, 1979; Klaus & Kennell, 1970; Leifer, Leiderman, Barnett, & Williams, 1972. Mothers of prematures around 4 to 6 months of age, are more vocal and attentive than mothers of nonprematures, apparently in an attempt to get their infants to respond. The premature infants, however, remain relatively less responsive and more fretful (Crawford, 1982; Field, 1977). When the babies are 12 to 14 months, however, mother–child interaction for prematures is no longer different from that for nonprematures on most measures (Crawford, 1982; Goldberg, Brachfeld, & DiVitto, 1980). Bakeman and Brown (1980) found that prematures showed a cognitive deficit (Stanford Binet IQ) at 3 years but no deficit in social interaction.

It is not clear how much the forced separation of mother and infant which usually accompanies prematurity contributes to later disturbances in mother–infant interaction as opposed to infant characteristics such as the nature of the cry and physical appearance. In a widely cited study Kennell, Jerauld, Wolfe, Chesler, Kreger, McAlpine, Steffa, and Klaus (1974) randomly assigned mothers of normal infants to an extended contact group (an additional 16 hours of contact) and a control group that received the routine amount of contact during the first few days after birth. They reported results indicating greater attachment of the extended contact mothers when the infants were 1 month and 1 year of age. Subsequent research, however, with both normal term and premature infants has not consistently supported this finding (deChateau & Widberg, 1977; Field, 1977; Grossman, Thane, & Grossman, 1981; Schaller, Carlsson, & Larsson, 1979; Svejda, Campos, & Emde, 1980). Nor does time spent in an intensive care unit necessarily affect later attachment. Rode, Chang, Fisch, and Sroufe (1981) found that infants who had spent an average of 27 days in the intensive care unit showed no difference in attachment at 12 to 19 months from a normal comparison group. In general, the research indicates that the amount of contact between mother and infant routinely provided in hospitals or the amount of deprivation of contact ordinarily associated with prematurity or other perinatal complications does not have longlasting effects. Given a reasonably adequate experience of parenting, most early effects of contact deprivation will have disappeared by the end of the first year. This, of course, is not to say that more prolonged separations of mothers from infants, without adequate substitutes, may not have more lasting effects.

A longitudinal study conducted by Werner and Smith (1977, 1982) is a good example of research that attempts to identify both infant and parental characteristics associated with the future development of psychopathology. These authors followed from birth to age 18 all of the 698 youth on the island of

Kauai, Hawaii, born in 1955. At age 10 there were 25 children who were considered in need of long-term mental health services. A large majority of these children were showing acting-out problems—fighting, destructiveness, truancy, stealing, and so on. A smaller number had chronic nervous habits or anxiety-withdrawal symptoms. As a group these children tended to come from families rated low or very low in socioeconomic status (SES)—88% compared to 56% for the total population. SES was found to have strong associations with psychological disorders throughout this study and accordingly a control group matched with the deviant group on SES, sex of child, and ethnicity was selected. Compared to the control group a higher proportion of children in the deviant group had been low-birthweight babies, had suffered from moderate to severe perinatal complications, had been rated by their mothers at age 1 as "not cuddly, not affectionate," and had mothers rated by interviewers when the child was age 1 as less relaxed, affectionate, energetic, happy, and intelligent. At age 2 a higher proportion of future deviant children came from homes rated low in stability, as indicated by such characteristics as illegitimacy of child, absence of father, marital discord, alcoholism, emotional disturbance of parents, and long-term separation of child from the mother without an adequate substitute caretaker. These findings suggest that a higher proportion of the deviant 10-year-olds were born with constitutional tendencies to be "difficult" infants. The results also strongly suggest that the mothers, and probably also the fathers, brought characteristics to the relationship with the child that were not entirely reactive to having a "difficult" child. Even with SES controlled, stressful life circumstances were more often present that would be likely to make adequate parenting difficult.

Not all infants who experienced risk factors of the above types before age 2 developed later mental health problems. The authors identified a group of *resilient* children, as they were called, who also lived in chronic poverty and had experienced at least four risk factors before age 2 but had not developed subsequent adjustment problems by either age 10 or age 18. Roughly similar percentages of these resilient children had experienced perinatal stresses, had low birth weights, and had conditions requiring further hospital care after the mother was discharged. Compared to the children who had developed serious mental health problems at age 18 the resilient children were more often first-born, especially the males, had fewer congenital defects, were more often perceived by their caretakers as active and socially responsive infants, elicited and received more attention during the first year of life, and less often experienced prolonged separations from their mothers during the infancy period. This matching does not allow us to separate all constitutional characteristics from factors in the social environment. However, the results do suggest that perinatal complications and low birth weight occurring in a context of chronic poverty do not inevitably lead to later mental health problems. The factors that remain after this matching continue to suggest the importance of infant temperament (and in a small number of cases, congenital defects) and an attentive, available caretaker during the first two years of life. In addition, resilient children continued to be rated as experiencing more emotionally supportive family relationships between ages 2 and 10. The authors speculate that the positive effect of being first-born for males may be due to the greater amount of individual attention these infants could be given in these poor and usually large families. Although the authors comment anecdotally on the interactional results of infant and parent characteristics—a mother becoming increasingly erratic, careless, ambivalent, or overprotective in response to an infant's difficult temperament—no systematic data are provided on this important aspect of development.

In conclusion, both infants and parents bring dispositions to the relationship that can effect the subsequent interactional history for better or worse. Infants who experienced prenatal or perinatal difficulties, such as prematurity, have a somewhat higher risk for disturbed early parent–child interaction, but research suggests that for most mother–infant pairs these difficulties have largely disappeared by 12–14 months of age. For some children, however, these difficulties do not go away and instead escalate to more troublesome behavior problems at a later age (Thomas et al, 1968; Werner & Smith, 1977) and it is in these children and their families that we have a special interest.

THE ABUSED CHILD

Many factors can contribute to the final outcome of child abuse and they are by no means the same in each case. Broad sociological variables such as community acceptance of severe physical punishment, individual personality characteristics of the parents, attributes of the child, and the dynamic interaction of these factors in the family setting can all play a role. Perhaps most relevant for our concern with the exceptional child are the characteristics of the child that increase the risk for abuse. These characteristics turn out largely to be many of those factors we have just been discussing: prematurity, low birth weight, congenital birth defects or brain damage, illness during infancy (Friedrich & Boriskin, 1976), and delays in cognitive and motor development (Applebaum, 1980). These are the conditions that are likely to make a child more difficult to live with, and, as Parke and Collmer (1975) suggest, the child may be so different from what parents had expected that the parents' frustration eventually results in physical abuse. It is essential to take an interactive view though. Only a very small percentage of these at-risk children are, in fact, abused. Their "difficultness" provokes eventual abuse only in those parents who have a readiness for such a reaction.

Some parents no doubt have generally low thresholds for aggressive responses (not just toward their children), and some communities have relatively accepting attitudes about hitting children. Under these conditions a difficult infant or child might be all that is necessary to provoke an abusive response. For example, an infant may be more than usually difficult to soothe when crying. The parent tries various techniques to stop the infant's crying but nothing works. In time the parent's frustration and anger mount and he or she resorts to a physical attack.

The parent's own predisposition to violence can have many roots. It has been found repeatedly that abusing parents were themselves more often abused as children than were nonabusing parents (Spinetta & Rigler, 1972), a learning experience that would seem to increase the likelihood that they will respond to their own children in the same manner. Rejecting attitudes toward the child and lack of emotional bonding with the child early in life can increase the probability of later abuse. For example, Fanaroff, Kennell, and Klaus (1972) counted the frequency of hospital visits of 146 mothers of low-birth-weight infants. Thirty-eight of these mothers visited their babies less than three times in a two-week period. Subsequently 11 of the infants from the total sample were abused or "failed to thrive." The mothers of 9 of these babies were in the infrequent visiting group. If low frequency of visiting reflects negative attitudes on the part of the mothers, then these results illustrate how a child characteristic, low birth weight, and a maternal attitude can interact to produce the outcome of abuse—an excellent example of the contributions from the continuum of both reproductive and caretaking casualty.

In a similar study, Hunter, Kilstrom, Kraybill, and Loda (1978) prospectively studied 255 infants who were either premature or ill at birth. Ten were subsequently reported as victims of child abuse during the first year of life. Characteristics that separated the families of these 10 infants from the remainder of the sample were social isolation, serious marital problems, inadequate child care arrangements, apathetic and dependent personality styles of parents, and less adequate spacing between children. Evidently these parents brought different dispositions to the relationship than most of the other parents.

That interaction styles are different in abusive and nonabusive families has been documented by several studies using direct observation techniques. Burgess and Conger (1978), for example, found higher levels of negative interchanges and lower levels of positive interchanges between parents and children in abusive than in nonabusive families. Exchange of negative behavior, both verbal and physical, was twice as high in single-parent abusing families than in two-parent abusing families (Kimball, Stewart, Conger, & Burgess, 1980). Dietrich, Starr, and Kaplan (1980) found abusing mothers to provide less tactile and auditory stimulation to their infants. The control mothers more actively touched, rubbed, kissed, nuzzled, and engaged in baby talk with their infants.

Abused children are more often found to be developmentally retarded than nonabused children (Gill, 1970; Sandgrund, Gaines, & Green, 1974). Most of these children probably had their developmental disability before they were abused, but some small proportion of abused children may have become intellectually impaired as a result of head injuries suffered during abuse (Elmer & Gregg, 1967).

THE MENTALLY RETARDED CHILD

In this section we focus on intellectual deficits that result from some definite organic impairment (such as Down's syndrome) and not on the so-called cultural–familial retardation in which factors such as psychosocial deprivation may play an important role. Family dynamics may well contribute in a primary way to the intellectual deficit in the latter but probably do not in the former. Family-interaction correlates of cultural–familial retardation are discussed in some detail in Chapters 10 and 12.

It is self-evident that the presence of a retarded child represents a major stress for a family. More specific dimensions of this stress have been documented by several researchers. Holt (1958) interviewed 201 families of the severely retarded in England and found many of them adversely affected by such factors as limitations on family activities, the need for constant supervision, extra expenses, and exhaustion of the mother resulting in neglect of the father and normal siblings. Farber (1968) has emphasized two aspects of the stress of having a mentally retarded child: (1) the frustration and disappointment associated with the violation of parental expectancies for future accomplishments and (2) the everyday problems in caring for a retarded person over a period of time. Roles within the family may undergo changes in the course of adjusting to the presence of a retarded child; for example, the retarded child may be treated as the youngest regardless of actual age or some normal siblings may be asked to assume certain parental roles with respect to the retarded sibling.

Before considering the long-term effects on the entire family let us restrict our view to the early mother–infant relationship and see what effects there may be when retardation is apparent soon after birth as is the case, for example, with Down's syndrome. There is evidence that these infants show certain behavioral deficits that may affect parent–child interaction. They smile less or begin smiling at a later date than do normal infants (Buckhalt, Rutherford, & Goldberg, 1978; Schmitt & Erickson, 1973; Stone & Chesney, 1978). They may also vocalize less (Buckhalt et al., 1978) and be more limp when picked up (Stone & Chesney, 1978). The smiling response is a powerful reinforcer of parental interaction, and these results suggest that parents of Down's syndrome infants may experience fewer rewards for interacting with their infants. There is, however, no evidence that these parents as a group actually show less responsiveness, especially in the first year of life. In their laboratory-based assessment procedure, Buckhalt et al. (1978), for example, did not find their mothers of Down's syndrome infants to be less active. In fact, on a direct teaching task they seemed to be trying harder to encourage their infants to perform better.

Further evidence for a communication deficit in slightly older Down's syndrome children (aged 8 to 24 months) comes from a study by Jones (1980). Directly observing mother–child interaction for six Down's syndrome children matched with six normal children, he found the former to show less "referential" eye contact, meaning eye contact that is used as a communication signal. For example, a child bangs a drum and looks up to mother as if to communicate, "Did you hear that?" or "That was a loud noise, wasn't it?" and mother may respond verbally by saying, "Yes, you banged it, didn't you?" Jones also found that the Down's syndrome infants did not use their vocalizations for communicative purposes to the same degree as normal infants. Their vocalizations were more repetitive and closer together so that it was difficult for mothers to respond contingently to them. He suggests that part of the cognitive deficit in Down's syndrome infants is an impairment in the ability to learn that their responses can serve as signals to the mother. The mothers in this study seemed to experience difficulty interacting with their Down's syndrome babies, which the author speculated might result in their feeling ignored or rebuffed by their child. On the other hand, the mothers of the Down's syndrome infants spent a greater proportion of time guiding and teaching than did mothers of normal infants. The kind of guiding done, however, was not of an interactive sort in which the infants could learn to affect the mother's behavior actively by their own signals.

It would seem, then, that from very early in their children's lives parents are likely to experience frustration in interacting with severely retarded children and they may, perhaps unwittingly, contribute further to a kind of passive orientation to the world of learning by being unusually directive in their teaching efforts. Jones suggests that parents of retarded infants might be urged to provide lots of opportunities for contingent, informative feedback. For example, whenever the infant initiates eye contact the parent might respond in some exaggerated, exciting way.

That these early difficulties may have cumulatively negative effects on parent–child relations is suggested by the findings of studies of somewhat older retarded children. Kogan, Wimberger, and Bobbitt (1969) directly observed 3- to 7-year-old retarded children interacting with their mothers. Compared to mother–normal child dyads, the mothers of retarded children were more controlling and the retarded children more submissive. When retarded children did attempt to assert control, their mothers were more likely to respond in either a hostile or neutral manner. Mothers of retarded children more often asked questions to which they themselves then gave answers or gave orders. Mothers of normal children more frequently stated their own thoughts and feelings and acknowledged the child's activity. O'Conner and Stachowiak (1971) also found both fathers and mothers of retarded children to be more controlling (use more overt and covert power) than parents of either normal or psychologically maladjusted children. In this study the authors had selected two-child families in which the oldest sibling was either well adjusted, poorly adjusted, or retarded. Age-related roles were different in families with a retarded child, namely that the parents made a higher frequency of emotional expressions to the retarded sibling even though he was chronologically older, whereas in the other families the youngest sibling received the greater frequency of emotional messages.

In directly observed interaction, Kogan (1980) found that 3- to 5-year-old developmentally delayed or mildly retarded children (IQs not lower than 60) and their mothers showed less positive affect and more negative affect than did normal children and their mothers. She also attempted an intervention procedure involving weekly guided practice sessions and at a one-year follow-up found that the mothers in the treatment groups showed more positive affect, less negative affect, less control, and greater acceptance; the delayed children became less submissive. Specifically, the mothers watched more, engaged in separate activity less, took the lead less, gave fewer orders, and followed more. Although there was relatively little effect on the child's basic developmental delays, these results suggest that the difficult and negative features of the parent–child relationship that sometimes emerge can be reversed with appropriate interventions.

Although the presence of a retarded child puts a strain on almost all families, there is considerable variation in the extent to which family functioning is adversely affected. Fotheringham, Skelton, and Hoddinott (1972) compared families who institutionalized their retarded child (average age about 8.7 years) with families who kept their retarded child at home. During the following one-year period the general adjustment of those families which had institutionalized their children remained the same on the average, whereas functioning in families who kept their retarded child showed some deterioration. For example, in the latter families the physical and mental health of parents and siblings decreased and the relationships between the siblings and the retarded child became more troubled. Of course general trends of this kind obscure variations in family adaptation. The authors do not use those results as a basis for advocating the wholesale institutionalization of retarded children. We do suggest that alternatives to large impersonal institutions may provide opportunities for part-time or temporary separation of a retarded child from the family when family relationships become unusually stressed.

Is there good evidence that the siblings of mentally retarded children are more maladjusted than other children? In one of the few studies using a control group, Gath (1973) found that 20% of the siblings of retarded children were rated as showing psychological problems by either parents or teachers compared to 10% in a control group. For those siblings rated as showing psychological problems the most common symptom was unpopularity with peers, followed by restlessness, disobedience, misery, and temper tantrums. Only one parent attributed the sibling's disturbance to having a retarded sibling; the rest tended to stress the bonds of affection existing between the retarded child and other family members—highly suggestive that, in some parents at least, a good deal of denial was going on. We should, however, not lose sight of the fact that in 80% of the families neither parents nor teachers reported psychological problems in the siblings. Gath's findings must also be tempered by the fact that in an earlier study (Gath, 1972) she had found no significant differences in adjustment between siblings of retarded children and siblings of normals.

A number of uncontrolled studies, however, strongly suggest that probably a small minority of children are adversely affected by the presence of a retarded sibling. Holt (1958) concluded that 15% of the 430 siblings included in his study were affected negatively in various ways: afraid of physical attack, resented the attention given to the handicapped child, felt they had to help too much in the care of the retarded child or felt ashamed, and were teased by their peers. A finding especially relevant to a family systems view is that of Graliker, Fishler, and Koch (1962), who found that when both mother and father had the same attitude toward the retarded child, the siblings showed no disturbance at home or at school. When there was conflict between the parents on issues involving the retarded child, the siblings were more likely to show some psychological distress.

Grossman (1972) did use a matched control group and found no significant differences in the academic and social functioning of her college-age subjects. She also assessed the extent to which these college-age siblings had been effective in coping with the presence of a retarded sibling in the family and concluded that 45% of the siblings had *benefited* from the experience of having a retarded sibling, 45% were harmed, and 10% were neither harmed or benefited. Some of the benefits Grossman noted were a greater understanding of people, more tolerance of people in general and of handicapped people in particular, more compassion, more sensitivity to prejudice and its consequences, more appreciation of their own good health and intelligence, and a sense that the experience had drawn the family closer. McHale (1983) and Turnbull, Brotherson, and Summers (1983) have also reported positive effects. McHale, for example, found that mothers rated siblings of mentally retarded and autistic children as more supporting and less hostile than siblings of nonhandicapped children.

To return to Grossman's (1972) study, some of the harmful effects were: "shame about the handicapped child . . . ; a sense of being somehow tainted or defective; a sense of guilt for being in good health and, more often, for harboring negative feelings about the retarded child; a feeling of having been neglected by their parents, who were preoccupied with the handicapped child" (p. 96).

Disturbance in normal siblings may be affected by the extent to which parents fail to communicate factual information about the nature of the retarded child's disorder and by a lack of openness to talk about the emotional impact of the retarded child upon the family.

Grossman (1972) had judges rate openness of communication between normal siblings and their parents from interviews with the normal siblings. Normal siblings who described their parents as permitting and encouraging open discussion about the retarded sibling and who reported themselves to have been curious about the nature of the retardation were rated to be coping more effectively with the presence of a retarded sibling. Also, the normal siblings who described open communication reported less embarrassment at being seen with the retarded siblings, more frequent talks with friends about the retarded sibling, and higher scores on a test of information about retardation and brain damage. Difficulties in communication in families with retarded children have also been reported by Kramm (1963) and by Turnbull, Brotherson, and Summers (1983). Kramm, for example, interviewed 50 families of Down's syndrome children and found that 34% of the parents had never used the term Down's syndrome (or mongoloid) and had not provided basic information about the syndrome to the normal siblings. In 16% of the families the parents said they still felt too emotional to talk even with each other about the retarded child.

L. S. Taylor (1974) further confirmed the importance of clear communication between mothers and normal siblings of retarded children and also provided some initial evidence on the effectiveness of a brief intervention designed to enhance communication. She developed a questionnaire to measure siblings' questions, problems, and concerns centering around their retarded sibling. Items were grouped into subscales such as concern about favoritism, burden of care, parental rejection, concerns for the future, genetic fears, unacceptable feelings toward the retarded sibling, sensitivity to others' reactions, and so on. The normal siblings filled out the questionnaire and the mothers filled out the questionnaire as they thought the normal sibling would. Thus the discrepancy between the normal siblings' responses and the mothers' responses reflected the extent to which the mothers understood their children's concerns, resentments, and fears. Taylor found that the more positive were the mothers' interaction behaviors with their normal child in a standardized assessment situation the more accurate were their perceptions of the normal siblings' concerns. In addition, there was some evidence that the more open exchange of information was related to better sibling adjustment. Taylor also found that improvement in open communication could be accomplished in some of the mother–child dyads in a brief two-session intervention emphasizing practice in expressing and listening to others. For mothers, however, whose defensiveness was more deeply rooted it was apparent that a longer intervention would be required.

The marital relationship may also be affected by the presence of a retarded child. Love (1973) reported divorce and suicide rates higher than the national average among parents of retarded children. Farber (1959), comparing families with retarded children of different ages, found higher levels of marital tension in families of older children. This finding suggests that either older retarded children put more strain on family functioning or that there is a cumulative negative effect over time, or both. Holt (1958) and Lonsdale (1978) also reported adverse effects on the marital relationship, but Kramm (1963) did not find a negative impact.

All in all the research would suggest the not too startling conclusion that families will respond differently to the presence of a retarded child. Although mean trends may suggest a slight adverse effect overall on sibling mental health and marital functioning, these means hide the many variations in response and coping styles used by families.

AUTISM AND CHILDHOOD PSYCHOSIS

Autism

The consensus of contemporary opinion is that early childhood autism, narrowly defined by current diagnostic criteria, is the result of some organic defect and not the result of aberrant parent–child relationships (e.g., Cantwell, Baker, & Rutter, 1978; Folstein & Rutter, 1977). Mothers report retrospectively that their infants who were later to be diagnosed autistic were nonresponsive, did not cuddle in a normal way, and smiled unfrequently if at all (Clancy & McBride, 1969; Rendle-Short, 1969). These retrospective reports rely on memory and are anecdotal in nature. Kubicek (1980), however, was able to obtain films of a mother interacting with a 16-week-old male infant who was diagnosed autistic two years after the film was made. The mother was also filmed interacting with the same-aged fraternal twin, who developed normally. These films had been obtained as part of a larger study of genetic influences (Freedman, 1965) and for the episode used in this study the mother had been given the standard instruction to "elicit a smile from her infant." The author summarizes the differences between the two twins as follows:

> The normal twin was attentive to his mother and his surroundings. His posture was normal, and he generally held his extended or slightly flexed arms comfortably at his sides. The mother picked him up at the beginning of their interaction and held him in that same way for its entirety. She and the twin spend much of their time mutually attending and in social play.

> The autistic twin, on the other hand, did not establish eye contact with his mother during their interaction. His face was without expression. His head was either turned away from her or held back, his gaze directed upwards at the ceiling. For most of their interaction, his back was arched, his arms were rigidly flexed or extended and held up and away from his body, and his hands were fisted . . . The mother continually changed how she was holding him and moved herself and/or the infant, always attempting to position herself within his line of vision. (pp. 102–103)

The mother of the autistic infant seemed to be trying, more or less appropriately, to make visual and affective contact but without success.

Coping with an autistic child becomes progressively more difficult following infancy. The extreme nonresponsiveness, lack of communicative speech, and sometimes bizarre or self-injurious behavior pose management problems of the first magnitude. Holroyd and McArthur (1976) compared the difficulties involved in raising autistic, Down's syndrome, and psychiatric outpatient children. Although mothers of both autistic and Down's syndrome children reported more problems and concerns associated with general intellectual impairment than did mothers of outpatient children, there were a number of areas in which mothers of autistic children reported greater difficulty than did mothers of Down's syndrome children. For example, mothers of autistic children said they were more upset and disappointed about the child, more concerned about the effect of the child on the rest of the family, and more bothered by personality problems of the child. These results confirm the general notion that Down's syndrome children are frequently sociable and affectionate and thus more readily integrated into the family system than an autistic child.

Bristol (1979) used the same questionnaire employed by Holroyd and McArthur and found that mothers reported greater stress associated with older than younger autistic children (ages ranged from approximately 5 to 19 years), and more stress with boys than with girls. Specific child characteristics that were most predictive of the degree of stress reported by the mothers were difficult personality characteristics, degree of child's dependency on others for everyday functions, and degree of child's physical incapacitation. Bristol also found that mothers who received more social support (from spouses, relatives, neighbors, and so on) reported less difficulty in coping with the problems associated with an autistic child.

Schopler and Reichler (1971) developed a program to help parents interact more effectively with an autistic child and to maximize the child's potential for cognitive-perceptual-motor development. Parents, for example, are taught to communicate with the child at a level that is meaningful to the child and the use of reinforcement and mild punishments such as time-out. Short (1980) found that after only two to three months of this program there were significant improvements in parent–child relationships. Home observations, for example, showed that the percentage of times in which the child engaged in appropriate play or work following attention or guidance from the parent nearly doubled, going from 23% to 43%, the percentage of times the child responded with meaningful communication following parental attention or guidance rose from 12 to 24%, and the percentage of times the child remained unresponsive following parental attention or guidance dropped from 20 to 8%. These results provide encouragement for parents who must face the demanding task of coping with an autistic child.

Childhood Psychosis

There are other severe psychological disorders of childhood, sometimes called childhood psychoses, in which the interplay of organic and psychosocial causative factors is more complex than in autism. In some of these disorders disturbances in parent–infant and parent–child interaction may contribute in a primary way. Massie (1978, 1980), like Kubicek, was able to obtain films of early parent–infant interaction for babies who were later diagnosed as psychotic, schizophrenic, or autistic. In this case, however, the films were home movies and lacked the standardized situation introduced by Kubicek. The films are nonetheless of considerable interest. In some instances the infants would seem to be the primary cause of the disturbed interaction; in other cases, it would seem to be the mother.

Edward and his mother are an example of the latter. The family dynamics involved a father who was gentle and responsive and a mother who was brusque and demanding. The mother was insensitive to the tempo of her son's attention to people or objects and would push or pull him away from one activity, prematurely terminating it, and push him toward something else. One interaction at age 21 months involved the father. Edward was sitting on the edge of a swimming pool and the mother "brusquely pulled the boy off the edge of the pool and toward her chest; however, he twisted his face away. After a moment the father approached and reached his hands out to his son seated on the side of the pool. After 3–4 seconds, while the father had waited patiently, Edward extended his arms toward his father, leaned off the edge of the pool and into his father's waiting arms with a smile on his face. After another 3 seconds, the mother interrupted and pulled Edward away from his father and into her arms. The boy's face showed a grimace, and his body twisted away from his mother toward his father" (p. 88).

At age 4 Edward was diagnosed as having a symbiotic psychosis when he was unable to separate from his mother to enter preschool. The author suggests that the mother's insensitive controlling and intrusive behaviors inhibited the development of his own individuation and autonomy. Other kinds of deviant maternal styles described by Massie included emotional unresponsiveness, avoidance of eye contact, and avoidance of close physical contact. Spitz and Cobliner (1965), on the basis of clinical observations, had previously emphasized the pathological consequences to the infant of mothers who are unusually unresponsive, tense, and insensitive with their infants. More recently Tronick, Als, Adamson, Wise, and Brazelton (1978) have experimentally demonstrated with normal infants the distressing effect that maternal nonresponsiveness can have. In this study each mother was asked to briefly avoid smiling back at her infant when the baby smiled or brightened at the mother's face. In a matter of seconds the infant became restless, irritable, confused, and dejected. If such a brief interlude of maternal nonresponsiveness can have such a strong effect, one can imagine the more serious effects of chronic nonresponsiveness that continues for months or years.

It is extremely difficult to untangle genetic, organic, and psychosocial determinants in these cases. For example, unusual parenting behavior may reflect a genetically influenced trait in the parent that is passed along through the genes as well as through parent–child interactions. And in families in which the psychotic behavior has already developed one cannot be sure how much the parental behaviors are in response to the child's disturbed behavior as opposed to causing the child's disturbed behavior.

HYPERACTIVITY

In considering family interaction associated with hyperactivity (or hyperkinesis) we must, of course, be reasonably clear about what this term refers to.

See Chapter 13 for a discussion of definitions of this syndrome. In DSM-III (the third edition of the *Diagnostic and Statistical Manual of the American Psychiatric Association)* the term has been replaced with *attention deficit disorder with hyperactivity,* giving more prominence to the feature of distractability than to motor activity per se.

There have been several studies in which experimenters have directly observed hyperactive children and various comparison children with their mothers. Campbell (1973, 1975) and Campbell, Schleifer, Weiss, and Perlman (1977) found that mothers of hyperactive children in a structured problem-solving situation provided more physical help, verbal encouragement, and suggestions regarding impulse control than did mothers of normal or learning disabled children. The hyperactive children also more frequently asked for feedback from their mothers. Cunningham and Barkley (1979) observed hyperactive and normal children interacting with their mothers in both a structured and a free play situation. Hyperactive boys were more active, less compliant, and less likely to remain on task than were the nonhyperactive boys—confirming the hyperactive diagnosis. Of more interest, the authors coded the interactive sequences in a way that permitted them to see how mothers of one group might have responded differently to the same child behavior and found that mothers of hyperactive boys were less likely to respond positively to the child's social interactions, solitary play activities, or compliant on-task behavior. They were, in other words, providing less reinforcement for nonhyperactive behavior than were the mothers of nonhyperactive boys. The mothers of hyperactive boys also were more controlling of their children's play and task activities, as had been found by Campbell (1973, 1975). The mothers' controlling attempts were frequently in response to the child's failure to comply with instructions or to stay on task. At times, however, these mothers interrupted appropriate play sequences or made controlling comments when the child was engaging in on-task behavior.

We have the usual problem of not knowing how these patterns of interaction between hyperactive children and their mothers developed. Did the restless, inattentive behavior of the child come first and the mother's intrusive, controlling behavior develop secondarily as a response? Or did the mother's controlling comments, in response to inattentive child behavior and her lack of positive response to on-task or appropriate play behavior reinforce the development of the hyperactive behavior? The answer may well turn out to be both. The infant or young child may temperamentally or because of some mild organic dysfunction be more restless and inattentive, eliciting the more controlling reactions from parents. Parents may in time develop a generally negative expectation about these children and respond indiscriminately with controlling behavior and ignore the child's appropriate behaviors—further contributing to the behaviors in the child labeled hyperactive.

These interaction patterns can apparently be modified by using stimulant drugs to reduce the child's hyperactive behavior or by modifying the interaction directly. Using the former approach, Barkley and Cunningham (1979) found that stimulant drugs, in addition to reducing the usual characteristics of hyperactivity in the child, resulted in a decrease in the mother's negative or controlling comments, an increase in her facilitation of the child's play, and an increase in her positive response to the child's compliance to her requests. They conclude that many of these mothers are not rigid in their directive, intrusive reactions to their son's excessive, noncompliant behaviors. Many seem able to shift to a less coercive and more positive style of management when the children's hyperactivity and attentional deficits are reduced by the stimulant drugs.

Psychological interventions can also be effective with hyperactive children, although most research on these interventions has taken place in the classroom. O'Leary, Pelham, Rosenbaum, and Price (1976), for example, successfully reduced hyperactive behavior in the classroom by incorporating parents in a contingency program for nonhyperactive behavior. No data, however, were provided on the effect of the program on the parent-child interaction.

PSYCHOPHYSIOLOGICAL DISORDERS

Psychophysiological disorders, often referred to as psychosomatic disorders, involve physical symptoms in which emotional and psychological factors have contributed in an important way. Symptoms such as peptic ulcer, high blood pressure, headaches, diarrhea, and asthma *can* be significantly affected by psychological determinants but not necessarily in all cases. Studies of family interaction correlates of these disorders in children are limited in number, and we will consider primarily asthma because the research on this disorder is more extensive.

First, however, let us briefly consider two studies that look at family variables associated with a variety of psychophysiological disorders. Garner and Wenar (1959) directly observed mother–child interaction for a group of 21 children suffering from bronchial asthma, rheumatoid arthritis, ulcerative colitis (persistent diarrhea frequently accompanied by bleeding), or atopic eczema. They also obtained the same measures on a group of children with chronic illnesses such as polio, congenital cardiac disease, and nephrosis to control for the possibility that the mothers' reactions in the psychophysiological group were just secondary responses to a chronically incapacitated child. Mothers of children with psychophysiological disorders were rated as more irritable, angry, competitive, and domineering with the child. The child likewise responded to the mother in a more negative fashion. The authors characterized the mother–child interaction as one of mutual entanglement. "The mother cannot relinquish the techniques of competition and domination which keep her continually reacting to the child, nor can the child find relief in independent or encapsulated task-oriented activity" (p. 72). This study suggests that a continuing series of upsetting emotional interactions, probably in conjunction with particular biological susceptibilities, might contribute to the development of psychophysiological disorders in children.

Minuchin, Rosman, and Baker (1978) clinically studied three groups of psychosomatic families: 11 with children suffering from anorexia nervosa, 9 with psychosomatic diabetic children (control of the diabetis was greatly affected by the child's emotional state), and 10 asthmatic children. Anorexia nervosa is a disorder most commonly affecting teenage females in which they diet to an extreme degree, in some cases refusing to eat almost entirely, and lose weight to an extent that can be life threatening. In addition there were two control groups: seven families with normal or nonpsychosomatic diabetic children and eight families with diabetics whose illness was under good medical control but who had been referred for behavioral problems. On the basis of standardized assessment procedures and family therapy sessions they concluded that families with psychosomatic children were distinguished by four characteristics: enmeshment, overprotectiveness, rigidity, and avoidance of conflict resolution. Enmeshment refers to an extreme degree of togetherness and emotional overinvolvement. There tends to be a lack of privacy and family members intrude on each others' thoughts and feelings. The overprotective feature would seem to be an aspect of enmeshment involving an excessive degree of concern for each others' welfare. Family members are hypersensitive to signs of distress and act immediately to reduce it. For the sick child, the experience of being able to protect the family by using the symptoms may be a major reinforcement for the illness according to the authors. Rigidity in the psychosomatic families is shown in their great resistance to change. For example, issues surrounding an adolescent's bid for greater autonomy might not be allowed to surface enough to be explored. This feature is related to the last characteristic, avoidance of conflict resolution. Usually a strong religious or ethical code is used as a reason for not confronting disagreement.

The enmeshment of the psychosomatic families was demonstrated by data obtained in a three stage sequence of interactions. First the parents alone discussed a family problem, second an interviewer purposefully exacerbated a conflict between the parents, and third the child was brought into the room. In the third phase parents of the normal and behavior-problem diabetic children continued to interact with each other as well as with the child during this period. In the psychosomatic groups the parents turned their attention almost entirely to the child. In the anorectic group, 9 of the 11 parent pairs spoke to each other less than 10 minutes during this half hour. There would seem to be some parallel between the enmeshment described by Minuchin et al. and the mutual entanglement emphasized by Garner and Wenar. Minuchin et al., however, take a larger family systems view and introduce the concept of the child using the symptom to protect the family, thereby obtaining some family reinforcement for the symptom.

Asthma

The disorder of asthma is characterized by a narrowing of the air passages in the lungs, which especially impairs the expiration of air, leading to audible wheezing. The immediate trigger for the attack varies widely among different individuals but frequently is an external allergen, such as pollen, or a state of emotional arousal. Evidence suggests that three classes of causes may contribute to the development of asthma (Rees, 1964): (1) allergens such as pollen or dust, (2) infections of the respiratory tract, and (3) psychological variables. The weighting of these three causes apparently varies widely from case to case, and the research to be reviewed below suggests that it is only one subgroup of asthmatics in in which psychological factors play a significant and primary role.

The identification of a subgroup of asthmatic children whose symptoms seem primarily associated with family interaction variables has resulted largely from the work of Purcell and his colleagues at the Children's Asthma Hospital and Research Institute in Denver. Purcell, Bernstein, and Bukantz (1961) found that asthmatic children could be divided into two broad groups: (1) a rapidly remitting type (RR), who become free of all attacks within three months of hospitalization without steroid drug therapy, and (2) a steroid-dependent type, who continued to require steroid drugs in order to prevent attacks. Further research showed the rapidly remitting children more often than the steroid-dependent children reported that emotions such as anger, anxiety, or excitement triggered asthma attacks at home and that both mothers and fathers of the rapid remitters obtained higher scores on child-rearing questionnaire measures of authoritarian and punitive attitudes (Purcell & Metz, 1962). These results suggest that asthmatic attacks in the rapidly remitting children are often linked to emotionally upsetting interactions in the family, which would explain why hospitalization involving removal from the family context is associated with an almost immediate decrease in asthmatic attacks. The attacks of the steroid-dependent children, on the other hand, may be more determined by allergic dispositions and respiratory infections. Purcell and his colleagues point out that the distinction between these two groups is a relative one and that both factors may be present to varying degrees in a given child.

Block, Harvey, Jennings, and Simpson (1964) also identified two subgroups of asthmatic children using a somewhat different procedure. They assessed degree of allergic potential on the basis of such factors as family history of allergy, skin test reactivity, and relation to specific allergens. When children were divided into those with high and those with low allergic potential, they found greater emotional disturbance in the children with low allergic potential, more psychopathology and marital conflict in their parents, and more conflicted parent–child relationships. These results also suggest that family relationships may be more important in the development of some cases of asthma and allergic dispositions may be more important in other cases.

It turns out that Purcell's rapid remitting and steroid-dependent groupings are not exactly the same as Block et al.'s low and high allergic potential groupings. For example, a child whose susceptibility to asthma resulted largely from respiratory infections might score low on allergic potential and the attacks might not necessarily show any relationship to family interaction. Purcell, Muser, Miklich, and Dietiker (1969) combined both of these measures in one study.

When rapid remitters were further subdivided into children with high and low allergic potential it was found that the rapid remitters with low allergic potential showed even more indicators of family pathology than did the rapid remitters with high allergic potentials. Thus the low allergic potential, rapid remitters were found to be significantly more timid, anxious, and depressed and their mothers were more authoritarian and intrusive. It should be noted that Gauthier, Fortin, Drapeau, Breton, Gosselin, Quintal, Weisnagel, Tetreault, and Pinard (1977) studied very young asthmatic children (14–30 months of age) and did not find the inverse relationship between allergic potential and disturbed mother–child interaction. Whether this discrepancy in findings results from the major difference in age levels or something else is not clear.

Purcell, Brady, Chai, Muser, Molk, Gordon, and Means (1969) dramatically demonstrated the relevance of family interaction to the frequency of asthmatic attacks in a subgroup of children whose attacks had been reported by their parents to be largely precipitated by emotional reactions. These children stayed in their homes so that there was no change in the presence of any allergic materials, and their families temporarily moved to a motel while a substitute mother moved in. For this group of children the daily frequency of asthmatic attacks dropped sharply while the family was away and began to increase again as soon as the family returned. For another group of children whose attacks were not reported to be associated with emotional reactions, the removal of the family had no effect on the frequency of attacks.

Purcell (1975) concludes from these and other research findings that there is no one type of child personality or style of parent–child interaction that is associated with asthma in those children for whom family variables are important. He suggests that the common denominator in these cases is an emotional reaction (the kind can vary widely) that has come to trigger the attacks. Any number of family interactional styles can be associated with these emotional reactions. One example is given by a mother:

> You know how Mike used to get asthma at almost every meal when I tried to get him to eat. I'd scold him and he would get angry and choke up and then start to cough and then, bingo, he would have asthma. Well, I decided if Mike didn't finish his food we would just leave him at the table to clean up the dishes and not say anything. Since we started that he hasn't coughed once at mealtime—and no asthma at those times. (p. 117)

PHYSICAL DISABILITIES

A child with a severe and chronic disability such as cerebral palsy, spina bifida, hemophilia, blindness, or deafness certainly represents a stressful circumstance that a family must cope with, but there is no reason to believe that family interaction plays any kind of causative role in the basic disorder. However, as with organically based mental retardation such as Down's syndrome, family interaction may have a lot to do with the personality and social development of these children.

Drotar, Baskiewicz, Irvin, Kennell, and Klaus (1975) studied the reactions of parents to the birth of a child with a congenital malformation, and suggested that parental reactions tended to progress throught successive stages: (1) shock, accompanied by irrational behavior, crying, and feelings of helplessness, (2) denial in which the parents refuse to believe the information about the malformation or minimize its significance, (3) sadness, anger, and anxiety in which parents grieve over the loss of a normal baby, are angry at themselves, the baby, or the hospital staff, or are fearful for the baby's life, and (4) adaptation and reorganization, in which there is a gradual reduction of intense emotional reactions and an increase in the parents' comfort with their situation and confidence in their ability to care for their babies. They begin to develop a more rewarding level of interaction with the infant.

A concern voiced by many writers is the possibility that parents may be too protective and thus hinder these children from reaching their potential for independence and self-confidence. There is some evidence that this may be true. Boles (1959), for example, found in a questionnaire study that mothers of cerebral palsied children scored significantly higher on a scale of overprotection than did a control group of mothers. Mothers of cerebral palsied children did not, however, score higher on scales of anxiety, guilt, or rejection. Cook (1963), using the same questionnaire, also found that mothers of blind, Down's syndrome, and cerebral palsied children scored high on scales related to control.

Schaffer (1964) describes a subgroup of families with a cerebral palsied child who were excessively cohesive. These families (13 out of a total of 30) spent almost all of their time together, except when at work or school, and much of their life centered around an intense concern for the handicapped child. The mothers, especially, were extremely overprotective of the child. For example, if the cerebral palsied child in one family was outside playing in the garden, the mother would stand at the window watching him, unable to get on with her housework. These parents were unwilling to leave the child with babysitters and in many cases the child slept in the parental bed.

This kind of extreme "togetherness" is strikingly similar to the concept of the "enmeshed" family system described by Minuchin et al. (1978) as being characteristic of psychosomatic families. There is no way of knowing to what extent these families' overcohesiveness would have been present without the handicapped child and perhaps have spawned a psychological disturbance in another child, or the extent to which the handicapped child precipitated the reaction in a family that would not otherwise have become so overly enmeshed. Is this excessive involvement with the handicapped child serving some psychological purpose in these families? Schaffer suggests that the great fear that harm will befall the child may reflect underlying feelings of anger and rejection that are unacceptable and guilt-producing. The parents defend against these hostile impulses by becoming compulsively concerned about the child's welfare. Or taking a systems point of view one might ask if the family enmeshment is serving as an acceptable way of avoiding other issues such as marital dissatisfactions. An anecdote from one family suggests that possibility. When the cerebral palsied child went for a few weeks to a convalescent home, the parents went on their first holiday in five years. After two days they came back. "My husband and I were like strangers together, we did not know what to do with ourselves or what to say to each other."

The handicapped child pays a price for this excessive togetherness. The children in the overly cohesive families were more socially immature, helpless, emotionally dependent, reluctant to make contacts outside of the family, and played less well with peers than did the cerebral palsied children in the other families. Whether or not this high degree of enmeshment will be found with the same frequency in other samples of families with a cerebral palsied child, this style of family coping with a handicapped child is an important one for professionals to be aware of.

We turn now to a study by Kogan, Tyler, and Turner (1974), who directly observed mothers interacting with their young cerebral palsied children at three times during a two-year period of comprehensive training for the children. They found that when the mothers were performing physical therapy with their children, both mothers and children showed more negative behavior than when they were playing and that mothers became excessively controlling during the therapy. Perhaps the most important finding was that the mothers showed a progressive decrease in friendly, warm behaviors during both play times and physical therapy sessions over the two-year period. The children showed no change in their positive or negative expressions, which makes it unlikely that the mothers' changes reflected an interactive response to the child being less positive. Physical therapists working with these children showed a similar decrease in warmth over the two-year period. The magnitude of the child's gross motor handicap significantly predicted the degree of decrease in positive affect in the mothers. These data suggest that the more severe the gross motor handicap and the less improvement in this area that occurs, the less positive the mothers (and therapists) become. On a more cheerful note, Kogan (1980) reports that in eight sessions of behavioral interventions focusing directly on mother–child interaction, she was successfully able to reduce negative interaction between cerebral palsied children (aged 21–61 months) and their mothers. At a one-year follow-up the reduction in negative interactions was maintained and measures of positive interaction had not changed (but they had not decreased as in the previous study). In general, the mothers made more changes than did the children.

Dorner (1975) interviewed the mothers of 63 adolescents who had spina bifida (a disorder in which the spinal nerves are partially exposed at birth, resulting in various long-term physical disabilities). More than half (57.5%) of the mothers reported they were able to lead an unrestricted social life of their own, but 20% found it difficult or impossible to accomplish this. Thirty-two percent of the mothers were judged to have experienced marked feelings of depression compared with 15% in a roughly comparable group without physically handicapped children assessed in Rutter's Isle of Wight study (Rutter, Cox, Tupling, Berger, & Yule, 1975). These mothers, however, rarely attributed their depression to the handicapped child, ususally giving other reasons such as bereavement, serious illness in the family, or marital problems. Perhaps, as Dorner suggests, these mothers may be more vulnerable to depression when a traumatic life circumstance occurs because they live for years with the chronic stress of having a severely handicapped child. Such an interpretation is consistent with the findings of Brown, Bhrolchain, and Harris (1974) that the onset of depression often occurs after the accumulation of stressful events rather than after just one traumatic episode.

According to the mothers, about 66% of the adolescents were considered to have experienced "definite and recurring feelings of misery" in the preceding year. This compares with a rate of 44% for a roughly comparable group of adolescents on the Isle of Wight (Rutter et al., 1975). Lack of mobility and loneliness were the most common reasons given by mothers to account for their child's misery or depression. Dorner also reports anecdotally that some mothers seemed to deny the existence of depressed feelings in their child even when they were present, and some adolescents made it clear that they withheld expression of such feelings, knowing that their mothers did not want to hear about their distress. One boy who was interviewed jointly with his mother made blatant attempts to tell her he did often feel miserable, despite her insistence that he was a "happy boy." A mother's defensive avoidance of her child's unhappiness is understandable. It does raise the question of whether families should be encouraged, with professional help, to face more realistically the child's emotional distress or whether some degree of denial is a desirable thing. Recall that L. S. Taylor (1974) had some success in improving communication between mothers and the siblings of retarded children, especially when the mothers' defensiveness was not extreme.

As was the case for mental retardation there is evidence for both positive and negative impacts on siblings of chronically ill children (S.C. Taylor, 1980). Younger siblings, especially males, seem most vulnerable to adverse effects (Breslau, Weitzman, & Messenger, 1981; Lavigne & Ryan, 1979) and also closeness of age to the chronically ill sibling seems to be related to greater maladjustment in the well sibling (S.C. Taylor, 1980). What effect does a physically handicapped child have on the marriage relationship? The evidence is a bit inconsistent on this point. Boles (1959) in his study of cerebral palsied children found that their mothers reported more marital conflict than did the comparison group of mothers of nonhandicapped children. This was a relative difference, however, and most mothers of these handicapped children did not report unusual degrees of marital conflict. Dorner (1975) concluded that marital disharmony was not greater in families with a spina bifida child than in the general population. Two other studies that did not have a control group suggest that the marital relationship is adversely affected, at least in some families with a spina bifida child (Richards & McIntosh, 1973; Walker,

Thomas, & Russell, 1971). Walker et al., for example, reported that 26% of 106 mothers reported that the marriage relationship had deteriorated as a result of the birth of the handicapped child. Seventeen percent of the fathers felt this was the case. One father said, "We get on each other's nerves now. She pays too much attention to the baby." The mother said, "I am too tired after working with the baby all day. We quarrel. Marriage relations are not what they used to be." Ten percent of the mothers and 14% of the fathers felt that the handicapped child had improved the marital relationship, that it brought the family closer together. Recall, however, that in the case of Schaffer's (1964) overly cohesive families being brought "closer together" could mean in some cases a masking of underlying marital dissatisfaction. The data in these various studies would seem to point out again the commonsense conclusion that different families will respond differently to the stress of a severely handicapped child.

SOME SUBJECTIVE VIEWS OF THE EXCEPTIONAL CHILD'S EMOTIONAL IMPACT ON THE FAMILY

The quantitative studies emphasized thus far hardly capture the varied dimensions of psychological impact that a handicapped child can have on a family—and vice versa. Featherstone (1980) richly describes, with many direct quotations from parents and siblings, some of the emotional consequences of having such a child. She considers several common emotional reactions that are experienced by both parents and siblings: fear, anger, loneliness, guilt, and self-doubt. I would add only grief and sadness to this list. Most parents feel an acute sense of loss for the normal child they expected. And although in time the intensity of the grief subsides, it is not quite the same as with the death of a child, since the handicapped child continues to be a living reminder of the loss.

With respect to fear, parents commonly have apprehensions about the child's future. A mother of a severely handicapped 3-year-old says,

> Sometimes I think I will die from hurting to think of his future without us. For now he has love, good health, happy times and lots of work (therapy) to do. What does he have to look forward to if he cannot improve, but a bed with bad smells and only a dimness of life around him? (Golden, 1974).

Or parents may fear their own old age in which with diminished capacities they will still have responsibility for their handicapped child. Siblings may have various irrational and unspoken fears: Will they "catch" the handicap as one might catch an infectious disease? When they become parents, will they have a defective child?

Parents experience anger—anger at the fates for inflicting this burden upon them, anger at other people for having normal children or for not appreciating what it means to have a defective child, or anger at professionals because they either overplayed or underplayed the severity of the disorder, or, provoked by a hundred frustrations, anger at the child.

Siblings, like those quoted at the beginning of this chapter, can become angry because parents give a disproportionate share of attention to the disabled child or because they are made to take on certain "babysitting" responsibilities for their sibling that interfere with their own activities.

The time and energy necessary to cope with a severely handicapped child can isolate parents and siblings from outside contacts and create loneliness. Loneliness can also result from being cut off psychologically, if not physically, from other people who unintentionally say things that are experienced as hurtful. A sibling describes some of the events that contributed to her loneliness:

> Mindy's "differentness" rubbed off on me in the eyes of my playmates. I was the sister of "that deaf kid." Mindy was a "drag" for me and my playmates. She was difficult to communicate with, wild and stubborn. I was often excluded from neighborhood games because of my sidekick. And then there was the unwritten family rule that I was to leave with Mindy whenever my playmates made fun of her. They often did mock her, of course, and we would leave—except for one time which to this day gives my conscience no rest, when I joined in. I lost many playmates by having to side with Mindy. I felt neglected by my family and shunned by my peers. I was a very lonely little girl. (Hayden, 1974)

Guilt, no matter how irrational, is a common accompaniment to having a handicapped child. No doubt some parents are more vulnerable to feelings of guilt as a function of their own psychological dynamics but most probably experience some self-recrimination as does this mother of a child with cerebral palsy remembering the night following the diagnosis:

> What had I done wrong? How had I hurt my baby? During the fourth month of pregnancy I started staining slightly. Under doctor's orders I stayed in bed for two months. Should I have stayed in bed? Maybe Nature knows best, and I was wrong to challenge her decision. No, no, then I wouldn't have Debby, and a hurt Debby is better than no Debby. Perhaps I could have postponed the birth for just a couple of weeks, and then Debby would have had enough strength to withstand the trauma of labor. . . . Why did I give in to pain and agree to medication? (Segal, 1966, pp. 18–19)

To varying degrees most parents in time come to some sort of terms with this difficult circumstance. Not that the pain and distress ever goes away completely, but the handicapped child becomes woven into the pattern of their life and they come to appreciate the positive qualities and limited successes of the child. Featherstone, for example, describes her own increased appreciation for the "miracle of development":

Some mothers and fathers also find themselves re-examining feelings about handicap and difference. For me this happened slowly. I did not realize I had changed until I started looking at schools for Jody.

On the way to the first preschool I got lost and nearly ran out of gas. I was nervous. I knew the children would be handicapped and I wondered how they would look to me. I was afraid I would want to turn away in embarrassment.

When I entered the classroom I was astonished. It was not the children's disabilities that struck me. It was their vitality and beauty. I marveled at the miracle of mobility and the achievement of human communication. A little girl hitched herself across the floor to offer me a toy and a smile. I was touched. Driving home I thought, "This was a gift from Jody. If I had visited this school three years ago, I would have recoiled from the kids. Now they look beautiful to me." (Featherstone, 1980, p. 227)

AN OVERALL PERSPECTIVE

Each family is unique and how a particular family system responds to or helps produce a given disability is a function of a number of factors:

1.   *The degree and nature of the disability.* Clearly the relatively slight at-risk status of a premature infant will have far less impact on a family than an autistic child. And, although an autistic child and a Down's syndrome child are both severely impaired, the nature of the autistic child's disability, the extreme nonresponsiveness and occasional bizarre behavior, will cause more family disruption.

2.   *Personality dynamics of individual family members.* The meaning and impact of an exceptional child will be partially determined by the psychological makeup of the individual family member. For some parents, for example, the disabled child will "hook" into neurotic patterns and the parent may feel irrationally guilty or respond with a rigidly held denial of the disability or other distorted beliefs about the handicapped child. Extremes of rejecting or overly intrusive tendencies probably reflect individual dispositions that were present before the birth of the child.

3.   *Family interaction.* As Sameroff (1975) indicated, it is necessary to study the ongoing transactions between constitutional characteristics in the child and environmental circumstances, primarily in the family, if we are to understand and predict later developmental outcomes. The focus here can range from the parent–child, two-person system, to the entire family. Much of the research has been limited to two-person systems; for example, studies on attachment and synchrony in at-risk infants, or the development of overcontrolling tendencies in mothers of mentally retarded or physically disabled children. These dyadic relationships develop in a larger family (and cultural) context that is usually ignored. That fact does not negate the findings; it only means that the findings may be incomplete in many cases. Child abuse, for example, may be

partially determined by the vicissitudes of the interaction between a mother and an at-risk infant but the larger family context and surrounding culture may be at least as important in affecting the final outcome.

There is some research in which the larger family perspective is taken but it is meager and frequently not as tightly controlled as the parent–infant dyadic research. Clinical studies suggest that the way the family copes with a handicapped child will be influenced by family "rules" (e.g., Satir, 1964) or expectations about how the family should function. Some examples of family rules that would effect the adaptation to an exceptional child might be: don't talk about emotionally distressing things; don't express anger openly; we should keep this within the family. Another aspect of the family system that could be involved in a family's response to a disabled child would be the degree of enmeshment. This factor was dramatically demonstrated in Schaffer's (1964) study of the excessively cohesive families with a cerebral palsied child and also in Minuchin et al.'s (1978) study of psychosomatic families. Yet another factor could be the separateness of the parenting and child roles, and the clarity of the intergenerational boundaries (Minuchin, 1974). If one or both parents become relatively inadequate in coping with the disabled child, a sibling might take on parental responsibilities at some emotional cost to himself or herself. The marriage relationship probably has implications for all of these family systems effects. A psychologically healthy marriage is likely to be correlated with openness of communication throughout the family, optimal degrees of cohesiveness, and appropriate intergenerational boundaries, all of which should be advantageous in coping with a handicapped child.

4. *Exacerbating or moderating effects of external circumstances.* Financial and occupational stresses and nonaccepting attitudes from friends, neighbors, and relatives can all add to the difficulty of coping with a disabled child. Unfortunately there have also been occasions when reactions from professionals have had negative impacts on families; for example, parents being made to feel psychologically responsible for their autistic child. On the other hand, some environmental circumstances can be constructive. There is a growing body of literature which suggests that social support can have beneficial effects on both physical and psychological health (Cobb, 1976). Families that have positive emotional ties to relatives and friends are likely to cope more effectively with the stress of having an exceptional child (Bristol, 1979). There is a cause and effect problem here. It is likely that families with basically healthy modes of interaction will be more motivated and find it easier to develop friendships and a social support network. It may, in other words, be the basically healthy modes of interaction that produce both the better coping and the extensive social support network. Nevertheless it seems likely that the presence of a good social support network does serve as a buffer against the effects of stress whatever the degree of general family adequacy.

Can families be helped in efforts to cope and come to terms with having an exceptional child? The answer would seem to be a qualified yes. For younger handicapped children behaviorally oriented interventions focused on parent–child interaction and parent management would seem to have considerable promise (Kogan, 1980 and Tavormina, 1975 with mentally retarded children; Schopler & Reichler, 1971 and Short, 1980 with autistic children; and Kogan, 1980 with cerebral palsied children). Interventions that emphasize structured communications training may be especially useful in helping husband and wife and older siblings cope with this stress. There are a few research studies in this area but L. S. Taylor's (1974) findings showed considerable promise with respect to improving communication between mothers and the siblings of retarded children. The use of family therapy approaches such as those of Satir (1964) and Minuchin (1974) has not been systematically researched for families with handicapped children, although Minuchin et al. (1978) reported considerable effectiveness in treating families with an anorectic child. These family therapy approaches might be especially useful in helping families that are overly enmeshed and that have poorly drawn intergenerational boundaries.

Both our understanding of and our efforts to improve quality of functioning in families with a handicapped child should benefit from continuing research on those transactions between child and family which influence the developmental process.

REFERENCES

Applebaum, A. S. Developmental retardation in infants as a concomitant of physical child abuse. In G. J. Williams & J. Money (Eds.), *Traumatic abuse and neglect of children at home.* Baltimore: Johns Hopkins University Press, 1980.

Bakeman, R., & Brown, J. V. Early interaction: Consequences for social and mental development at three years. *Child Development*, 1980, *51*, 437–447.

Barkley, R. A. , & Cunningham, C. E. The effects of methylphenidate on the mother-child interactions of hyperactive children. *Archives of General Psychiatry*, 1979, *36*, 201–208.

Beckwith, L. Caregiver-infants interaction and the development of the high risk infant. In G. P. Sackett (Ed.), *Observing behavior: Theory and application in mental retardation.* (Vol. 1). Baltimore: University Park Press, 1978.

Bell, S. M., & Ainsworth, M. D. S. Infant crying and maternal responsiveness. *Child Development*, 1972, *43*, 1171–1190.

Birns, B. Individual differences in human neonates' responses to stimulation. *Child Development*, 1965, *36*, 249–256.

Birns, B. Blank, M., & Bridger, W. H. The effectiveness of various soothing techniques on human neonates. *Psychosomatic Medicine*, 1966, *28*, 316–322.

Block, J., Harvey, E., Jennings, P., & Simpson, E. Interaction between allergic potential and psychopathology in childhood. *Psychosomatic Medicine*, 1964, *26*, 307–320.

Boles, G. Personality factors in mothers of cerebral palsied children. *Genetic Psychology Monographs*, 1959, *59*, 159–218.

Breslau, N., Weitzman, M., & Messenger, K. Psychologic functioning of siblings of disabled children. *Pediatrics,* 1981, *67,* 344–353.

Bristol, M. H. Maternal coping with autistic children: Adequacy of inter-personal support and effects of child's characteristics. Unpublished doctoral dissertation, University of North Carolina at Chapel Hill, 1979.

Brown, G. W., Bhrolchain, M., & Harris, T. Social class and psychiatric disturbance in young women in urban population. *Sociology,* 1974, *9,* 225–233.

Buckhalt, J. A., Rutherford, R. D., & Goldberg, K. E. *American Journal of Mental Deficiency,* 1978, *82,* 337–343.

Burgess, R. L., & Conger, R. D. Family interaction in abusive, neglectful and normal families. *Child Development,* 1978, *49,* 1163–1173.

Campbell, S. Mother-child interaction in reflective, impulsive, and hyperactive children. *Developmental Psychology,* 1973, *8,* 341–347.

Campbell, S. Mother-child interaction: A comparison of hyperactive, learning disabled, and normal boys. *American Journal of Orthopsychiatry,* 1975, *45,* 51–57.

Campbell, S. B., Schleifer, M., Weiss, G., & Perlman, T. A two-year follow-up of hyperactive preschoolers. *American Journal of Orthopsychiatry,* 1977, *47,* 149–162.

Cantwell, D. P., Baker, L., & Ruter, M. Family factors. In M. Rutter & E. Schopler (Eds.), *Autism: A reappraisal of concepts and treatment.* New York: Plenum, 1978.

Clancy, H., & McBride, G. The autistic process and its treatment. *Journal of Child Psychology and Psychiatry,* 1969, *10,* 233–244.

Cobb, S. Social support as a moderator of life stress. *Psychosomatic Medicine,* 1976, *38,* 300–314.

Cook, J. J. Dimensional analysis of child-rearing attitudes of parents of handicapped children. *American Journal of Mental Deficiency,* 1963, *68,* 354–361.

Crawford, J. W. Mother-infant interaction in premature and full-term infants. *Child Development,* 1982, *53,* 957–962.

Cunningham, E.E., & Barkley, R. A. The interactions of normal and hyperactive children with their mothers in free play and structural tasks. *Child Development,* 1979, *50,* 217–224.

deChateau, P., & Widberg, B. Long-term effect on mother-infant behavior of extra contact during the first hour post partum. 2. A follow-up at three months. *Acta Paediatricia Scandinavia,* 1977, *66,* 145–151.

Dietrich, K. N., Starr, R. H., & Kaplan, M. G. Maternal stimulation and care of abused infants. In T. M. Field, S. Goldberg, D. Stern, & A. M. Sostek (Eds.), *High-risk infants and children.* New York: Academic, 1980.

DiVitto, B., & Goldberg, S. The development of early parent-infant interaction as a function of newborn medical status. In T. Field, A. Sostek, S. Goldberg, & H. H. Shuman (Eds.), *Infants born at risk.* Holliswood, N.Y.: Spectrum, 1979.

Dorner, S. The relationship of physical handicap to stress in families with an adolescent with spina bifida. *Developmental Medicine and Child Neurology,* 1975, *17,* 765–776.

Drotar, D., Baskiewicz, A., Irvin, N., Kennell, J., & Klaus, M. *Pediatrics,* 1975, *56,* 710–717.

Elmer, E., & Gregg, G. Developmental characteristics of abused children. *Pediatrics,* 1967, *40,* 596–602.

Fanaroff, A. A., Kennell, J. H., & Klaus, M. H. Follow-up of low birth-weight infants—the predictive value of maternal visiting patterns. *Pediatrics,* 1972, *49,* 288–290.

Farber, B. Effects of a severely mentally retarded child on family integration. *Monographs of the Society for Research in Child Development,* 1959, *24,* (2, Serial No. 71).

Farber, B. *Mental Retardation: Its social context and social consequences.* Boston: Houghton Mifflin, 1968.

Featherstone, H. *A difference in the family.* New York: Basic Books, 1980.

Field, T. Effects of early separation, interactive deficits, and experimental manipulations on Mother-Infant interaction. *Child Development,* 1977, *48,* 763–771.

Folstein, S., & Rutter, M. Infantile autism: A genetic study of 21 twin pairs. *Journal of Child Psychology and Psychiatry,* 1977, *18,* 297–321.

Fotheringham, J. B., Skelton, M., & Hoddinott, B.A. The effects on the family of the presence of a mentally retarded child. *Canadian Psychiatric Association Journal,* 1972, *17,* 283–289.

Freedman, D. G. An ethological approach to the genetic study of human behavior. In S. G. Vanderberg (Ed.), *Methods and goals in human behavior genetics.* New York: Academic, 1965.

Friedrich, W. N., & Boriskin, J. A. The role of the child in abuse: A review of the literature. *American Journal of Orthopsychiatry,* 1976, *46,* 580–590.

Frodi, A. M., Lamb, M. E., Leavitt, L. A., Donovan, W. L., Neff, C., & Sherry, D. Fathers' and mothers' responses to the faces and cries of normal and premature infants. *Developmental Psychology,* 1978, *14,* 490–498.

Garner, A. M., & Wenar, C. *The mother-child interaction in psychosomatic disorders.* Urbana: University of Illinois Press, 1959.

Gath, A. The mental health of siblings of congenitally abnormal children. *Journal of Child Psychology and Psychiatry,* 1972, *13,* 211–218.

Gath, A. The school-age siblings of Mongol children. *British Journal of Psychiatry,* 1973, *123,* 161–167.

Gauthier, Y., Fortin, C., Drapeau, P., Breton, J. J., Gosselin, J., Quintal, L., Weisnagel, J., Tetreault, L., & Pinard, G. The mother-child relationship and the development of autonomy and self-assertion in young (14–30 months) asthmatic children. *Journal of the American Academy of Child Psychiatry,* 1977, *16,* 109–131.

Gill, D. G. *Violence against children: Physical child abuse in the United States.* Cambridge, Mass.: Harvard University Press, 1970.

Goldberg, S., Brachfeld, S., & DiVitto, B. Feeding, fussing, and play: Parent-infant interaction in the first year as a function of prematurity and perinatal medical problems. In T. M. Field, S. Goldberg, D. Stern, & A. M. Sostek (Eds.), *High-risk infants and children.* New York: Academic, 1980.

Golden, S. Letter. *Exceptional Parent,* July/August 1974, *4,* 18.

Gralicker, B., Fishler, K., and Koch, R. Teenage reactions to a mentally retarded sibling. *American Journal of Mental Deficiency,* 1962, *66,* 838–843.

Grossman, F. K. *Brothers and sisters of retarded children.* Syracuse, N.Y.: Syracuse University Press, 1972.

Grossman, K., Thane, K., & Grossman, K. E. Maternal tactual contact of the newborn after various postpartum conditions of mother-infant contact. *Developmental Psychology,* 1981, *17,* 158–169.

Hayden, V. The other children. *Exceptional Parent,* July/August 1974, *4,* 26–29.

Holroyd, J., & McArthur, D. Mental retardation and stress on the parents: A contrast between Down's syndrome and childhood auitism. *American Journal of Mental Deficiency,* 1976, *80,* 431–436.

Holt, K. S. The influence of a retarded child on family limitation. *Journal of Mental Deficiency,* 1958, *2,* 28–36.

Hunter, R. S., Kilstrom, N., Kraybill, E. N., & Loda, F. Antecedents of child abuse and neglect in premature infants: A prospective study of newborn intensive care unit. *Pediatrics,* 1978, *61,* 629–635.

Jones, O. H. M. Prelinguistic communication skills in Down's syndrome. In T. M. Field, S. Goldberg, D. Stern, & A. M. Miller (Eds.), *High-risk infants and children.* New York: Academic, 1980.

Kennell, J. H., Jerauld, R., Wolfe, H., Chesler, D. Kreger, N. C., McAlpine, W., Steffa, M., & Klaus, M. H. Maternal behavior one year after early and extended post-partum contact. *Developmental Medicine and Child Neurology,* 1974, *16,* 172–179.

Kimball, W. H., Stewart, R. B., Conger, R. D. & Burgess, R. L. A comparison of family interaction in single- versus two-parent abusive, neglectful, and control families. In T.M. Field, S. Goldberg, D. Stern, & A. M. Sostek (Eds.), *High-risk infants and children.* New York: Academic, 1980.

Klaus, M. H., & Kennell, J. H. Mothers separated from their newborn infants. *Pediatric Clinics of North America,* 1970, *17,* 1015–1037.

Kogan, K. L. Interaction systems between preschool and handicapped or developmentally delayed children and their parents. In T. M. Field, S. Goldberg, D. Stern, & A. M. Sostek (Eds.), *High-risk infants and children.* New York: Academic, 1980.

Kogan, K. L., Tyler, N. & Turner, P. The process of interpersonal adaptation between mothers and their cerebral palsied children. *Developmental Medicine and Child Neurology,* 1974, *16,* 518–527.

Kogan, K. L., Wimberger, H. C. , & Bobbitt, R. A. Analysis of mother-child interaction in young mental retardates. *Child Development,* 1969, *40,* 799–812.

Korner, A. F. Individual differences at birth: Implications for early experience and later development. *American Journal of Orthopsychiatry,* 1971, *41,* 608–619.

Korner, A., & Grobstein, R. Individual differences at birth: Implications for mother-infant relationship and later development. *Journal of American Academy of Child Psychiatry,* 1967, *6,* 676–690.

Kramm, E. R. *Families of mongoloid children.* Washington, D.C.: U.S. Government Printing Office, 1963.

Kubicek, L. G. Organization in two mother-infant interactions involving a normal infant and his fraternal twin brother who was later diagnosed autistic. In T. M. Field, S. Goldberg, D. Stern, & A. M. Sostek (Eds.), *High-risk infants and children.* New York: Academic, 1980.

Lavigne, J. V., & Ryan, M. Psychologic adjustment of siblings of children with chronic illness. *Pediatric,* 1979, *63,* 616–622.

Leifer, A. D., Leiderman, P. H., Barnett, C. R., & Williams, J.A. Effects of mother-infant separation on maternal attachment behavior. *Child Development,* 1972, *43,* 1203–1218.

Lester, B. M. Spectrum analysis of the cry sounds of well-nourished and malnourished infants. *Child Development,* 1976, *47,* 237–241.

Lonsdale, G. Family life with a handicapped child: The parents speak. *Child: Care, Health and Development,* 1978, *4,* 99–120.

Love, H. *The mentally retarded child and his family.* Springfield, Ill.: Charles C. Thomas, 1973.

Massie, H. Blind ratings of mother-infant interaction in home movies of prepsychotic and normal infants. *American Journal of Psychiatry,* 1978, *135,* 1371–1374.

Massie, H. N. Pathological interactions in infancy. In T. M. Field, S. Goldberg, D. Stern, & A. M. Sostek (Eds.), *High-risk infants and children.* New York: Academic, 1980.

McHale, S. M. Children with handicapped brothers and sisters. In E. Schopler & G. Mesibov (Eds.), *Issues in autism. 2. The effects of autism on the family.* New York: Plenum, 1983.

Minuchin, S. *Families and family therapy.* Cambridge, Mass.: Harvard University Press, 1974.

Minuchin, S., Rosman, B. L. & Baker, L. *Psychosomatic families: Anorexia nervosa in context.* Cambridge, Mass.: Harvard University Press, 1978.

Moss, H. A. Sex, age, and state as determinants of mother-infant interaction. *Merrill-Palmer Quarterly,* 1967, *13,* 19–36.

Moss, H. A., Robson, K. S., & Petersen, F. Determinants of maternal stimulation of infants and consequences of treatment for later reactions of strangers. *Developmental Psychology,* 1969, *1,* 239–246.

O'Conner, D., & Stachowiak, J. Patterns of interaction in families with low adjusted, high adjusted, and mentally retarded family members. *Family Process,* 1971, *10,* 229–241.

O'Leary, K. D., Pelham, W. E., Rosenbaum, A., & Price, G. H. Behavioral treatment of hyperkinetic children. *Clinical Pediatrics,* 1976, *15,* 510–515.

Osofsky, J. D. Neonatal characteristics and mother-infant interaction in two observational situations. *Child Development,* 1976, *47,* 1138–1147.

Osofsky, J. D., & Danzger, B. Relationships between neonatal characteristics and mother-infant interaction. *Developmental Psychology,* 1974, *10,* 124–130.

Parke, R. D., & Collmer, C. Child abuse: An interdisciplinary review. In E. M. Hetheringon (Ed.), *Review of child development research* (Vol. 5) Chicago: University of Chicago Press, 1975.

Purcell, K. Childhood asthma, the role of family relationships, personality, and emotions. In A. Davids (Ed.), *Child personality and psychopathology: Current topics* (Vol. 2). New York: Wiley, 1975.

Purcell, K., Bernstein, L., & Bukantz, S. A preliminary comparison of rapidly remitting and persistently "steroid dependent" asthmatic children. *Psychosomatic Medicine,* 1961, *23,* 305–310.

Purcell, K., Brady, K., Chai, H., Muser, J., Molk, L., Gordon, N., & Means, J. The effect on asthma in children of experimental separation from the family. *Psychosomatic Medicine,* 1969, *31,* 144–164.

Purcell, K., & Metz, J. Distinctions between subgroups of asthmatic children: Some parent attitude variables related to age of onset of asthma. *Journal of Psychosomatic Research,* 1962, *6,* 251–258.

Purcell, K., Muser, J., Miklich, D., and Dietiker, K. A comparison of psychologic findings in variously defined asthmatic subgroups. *Journal of Psychosomatic Research,* 1969, *13,* 67–75.

Rees, L. The importance of psychological, allergic, and infective factors in childhood asthma. *Journal of Psychosomatic Research,* 1964, *7,* 253–262.

Rendle-Short, J. Infantile autism in Australia. *Medical Journal of Australia,* 1969, *2,* 245–249.

Richards, I. D. G., & McIntosh, H. T. Spina bifida survivors and their parents: A study of problems and services. *Developmental Medicine and Child Neurology,* 1973, *15,* 293–302.

Robson, K. S., Pedersen, F. A., & Moss, H. A. Developmental observations of diadic gazing in relation to the fear of strangers and social approach behavior. *Child Development,* 1969, *40,* 619–627.

Rode, S. S., Chang, P. N., Fisch, R. O., & Sroufe, L. A. Attachment patterns of infants separated at birth. *Developmental Psychology,* 1981, *17,* 188–191.

Rutter, M., Cox, A., Tupling, C., Berger, M., & Yule, W. Attachment and adjustment in two geographical areas. *British Journal of Psychiatry,* 1975, *126,* 493–509.

Sameroff, A. J. Early influences on development: Fact or fancy? *Merrill-Palmer Quarterly,* 1975, *21,* 267–294.

Sameroff, A. J., & Chandler, M. J. Reproductive risk and the continuum of caretaking casualty. In F. D. Horowitz (Ed.), *Review of child development research* (Vol. 4). Chicago: University of Chicago Press, 1975.

Sandgrund, A., Gaines, R. W., & Green, A. H. Child abuse and mental retardation: A problem of cause and effect. *American Journal of Mental Deficiency,* 1974, *79,* 327–330.

Satir, V. *Conjoint family therapy.* Palo Alto, Calif: Science and Behavior Books, 1964.

Schaffer, H. R. The too cohesive family: A form of group pathology. *International Journal of Social Psychiatry,* 1964, *10,* 266–275.

Schaffer, H. R., & Emerson, P. E. Patterns of response to physical contact in early human development. *Journal of Child Psychology and Psychiatry,* 1964, *5,* 1–13.

Schaller, J., Carlsson, S. G., & Larsson, K. Effects of extended post-partum mother-child contact on the mother's behavior during nursing. *Infant Behavior and Development* 1979, *2,* 319–324.

Schmitt, R., & Erickson, M. T. Early predictors of mental retardation. *Mental Retardation,* 1973, *11,* 27–29.

Schopler, E., & Reichler, R. J. Developmental therapy by parents with their own autistic child. In M. Rutter (Ed.), *Infantile autism: Concepts characteristics and treatment.* London: Churchill-Livingstone, 1971.

Segal, M. *Run away, little girl.* New York: Random House, 1966.

Short, A. Evaluation of short term treatment outcome using parents as co-therapists for their own psychotic children. Unpublished doctoral dissertation, University of North Carolina, 1980.

Spinetta, J. J., & Rigler, D. The child-abusing parent: A psychological review. *Psychological Bulletin,* 1972, *77,* 296–304.

Spitz, R., & Cobliner, W. G. *The first year of life.* New York: International University Press, 1965.

Stone, N. W., & Chesney, B. H. Attachment behaviors in handicapped infants. *Mental Retardation,* 1978, *16,* 8–12.

Svejda, M. J., Campos, J. J., & Emde, R. N. Mother-infant "bonding": Failure to generalize. *Child Development,* 1980, *51,* 775–779.

Tavormina, J. B. Relative effectiveness of behavioral and reflective group counseling with parents of mentally retarded children. *Journal of Consulting and Clinical Psychology,* 1975, *43,* 22–31.

Taylor, L. S. Communications between mothers and normal siblings of retarded children: Nature and modification. Unpublished doctoral dissertation, University of North Carolina at Chapel Hill, 1974.

Taylor, L. S. Personal communication, 1980.

Taylor, S. C. The effect of chronic childhood illnesses upon well siblings. *Maternal-Child Nursing Journal,* 1980, *9,* 109–116.

Thoman, E. B., Becker, P. T., & Freese, M. P. Individual patterns of mother-infant interaction. In G. P. Sackett (Ed.), *Observing behavior: Theory and application in mental retardation* (Vol. 1). Baltimore: University Park Press, 1978.

Thomas, A., Chess, S., & Birch, H. G. *Temperament and behavior disorders in children.* New York: New York University Press, 1968.

Tronick, E., Als, H., Adamson, L., Wise, S., & Brazelton, T. B. The infant's response to entrapment between contradictory messages in face-to-face interaction. *Journal of the American Academy of Child Psychiatry,* 1978, *17,* 1–13.

Turnbull, A. P.. Brotherson, J. J., & Summers, J. A. The impact of deinstitutionalization on families: A family systems approach. In R. H. Bruininks (Ed.), *Living and learning in the least restrictive environment.* Baltimore: Paul H. Brookes, 1983.

Walker, J. H., Thomas, M., & Russell, I. T. Spina bifida—and the parents. *Developmental Medicine and Child Neurology,* 1971, *13,* 462–475.

Watzlawick, P., & Weakland, J. H. *The interactional view: Studies of the Mental Research Institute, Palo Alto, 1965–1974.* New York: W. W. Norton, 1977.

Werner, E. E., & Smith, R. S. *Kauai's children come of age.* Honolulu: University Press of Hawaii, 1977.

Werner, E. E., & Smith, R. S. *Vulnerable but invincible.* New York: McGraw-Hill, 1982.

Wolff, P. The natural history of crying and other vocalizations in infancy. In B. M. Foss (Ed.), *Determinants of infant behavior* (Vol. 4). London: Methuen, 1969.

Zeskind, P. S. Adult responses to cries of low and high risk infants. *Infant Behavior and Development,* 1980, *3,* 167–177.

Zeskind, P. S., & Lester, B. M. Acoustic features and auditory perceptions of the cries of newborns with prenatal and perinatal complications. *Child Development,* 1978, *49,* 580–589.

PART THREE

Perspectives on Specific Areas of Exceptionality: Characteristics, Etiologies, and Treatments

CHAPTER 9

Positive Exceptionality: The Academically Gifted and the Creative

GEORGE S. WELSH

Anyone departing markedly from what is usual or expected attracts our attention. Children who begin to read when they are 2 years old or those who have not learned to read when they are 12 are equally remarkable and may be referred to as "exceptional." Yet until recently the term exceptional more often was applied to positively evaluated characteristics rather than negative ones even though from an etymological point of view both directions of departure are equally justified. An illustrative quotation dated 1868 from the *Oxford English Dictionary* clearly shows the direction originally implied: "The founders of the thirteen colleges . . . were almost all of them exceptional men." The same directional intent is shown also in the definition given by the *New International Dictionary,* 2nd ed., 1934: "Forming an exception: not ordinary; uncommon; rare; hence, better [*sic*] than the average; superior; as exceptional talents or opportunities."

It may be noted, however, that the bidirectionality of the word had been recognized in an older book on the psychology of children. In a chapter entitled "exceptional children" the authors differentiated between the ordinary child and the exceptional child making it clear that the latter fell at either end of various continua that they discussed. But as the authors stress, "It is noteworthy that as so many more causes are likely to bring people down in the scale than to send them up, so our attention has been centered more on those who deviate in a minus direction from what we regard as the norm, and even our nomenclature is fuller here than in the upper end of the range" (Norsworthy & Whitley, 1923, p. 311).

The fact that the title for this chapter selected by the editors of this book includes the modifier positive before the term exceptionality is not only an indication of current convention in word usage but also a reflection of a more open attitude. A. A. Roback, in *A History of American Psychology,* reveals his own negative views about one end of the continuum of exceptionality. In discussing the early work of Lewis M. Terman and Frederick Kuhlman, who translated and adapted the Binet-Simon scales of intelligence, he comments:

> Yet, while Kuhlman was taking the low road exploring feeblemindedness, Terman, through most of his life, was travelling the high road, spotting, through tests, the upper limits of human mentality . . . . Dullness could conceivably be the basis of an interesting study, but compared with talent and genius it can hardly make a popular appeal. The drab life in government institutions for the half-witted would be reflected in the mandatory reports and monographs dealing with the subject. (Roback, 1964, p. 457)

HISTORICAL BACKGROUND

Although many persons have been concerned with giftedness in one way or another, there are three names preeminently associated with the area: Sir Frances Galton in England, Alfred Binet in France, and Lewis M. Terman in the United States. A good summary of the work of these three men is given by Goodenough (1949, Part 1) and interesting material related to the contribution of other less well-known individuals to what is generally called "mental testing" is also included. The work of contemporary contributors as well as that of the pioneeers is reported in detail by Edwards (1971, 1972, 1975), by Butcher (1968), and more briefly by DuBois (1970). Detailed historical accounts of the gifted child movement itself may be found in Hildreth (1966, Chapter 3) and in Gowan (1977).

Galton is termed the "father of mental testing" by Goodenough (1949, p. 40), and although he did not study gifted children in their own right, many of his observations have influenced our own views of giftedness. He was interested in the heredity and environment problem and introduced in 1874 the phrase that we still use, "nature and nurture." His belief in the importance of "nature" in this controversy is strongly asserted in the 1892 edition of one of his most influential works, *Hereditary Genius,* first published in 1869:

> "I propose to show . . . that a man's natural abilities are derived by inheritance . . . [and that] it would be practicable to produce a highly-gifted race of men by judicious marriages during several consecutive generations. I shall show that social agencies of an ordinary character, whose influences are little suspected, are at this moment working toward the degradation of human nature, and that others are working toward its improvement. (Galton, 1892/1962, p. 45)

His influence is seen also in quantitative methods of investigation, and he devised many ingenious methods of measuring human behavior accurately. While it is true that profoundly retarded individuals show diminished sensory discrimination, Galton was wrong in his belief that this faculty "would on the whole be highest among the intellectually ablest" (Galton, 1883, p. 27). Thus easily and accurately measured sensory experiences do not differentiate the gifted from the average.

We still tend to think of attributes in terms of frequency as he did. That is, he defined an "eminent man" as one achieving a position attained by only one in 4000 and one who is "illustrious" appears as one in a million. No matter how we may define giftedness, a child we believe to be gifted will be one out of many.

Further, he stressed differences along a continuum of ability that parallels our own observations today. "Eminently gifted men are raised above mediocrity as idiots are depressed below it; a fact that is calculated to considerably enlarge our ideas of the enormous differences of intellectual gifts between man and man" (Galton, 1892/1962, p. 76).

It is to the French psychologist Alfred Binet that we are indebted for the first practical method of assessing intelligence in an individual child. He saw clearly the need to measure a complex characteristic like intelligence by a complex kind of task (rather than simple sensory measurement) and to show that such "tests" as he termed them, were in fact related to performance in school and in dealing with the affairs of everyday life. It was not that he was uninterested in theory or in experimental measurement, but rather that he was eminently empirical; this was a consequence of practical research at home with his two daughters as well as his work in the public schools. Of the pure theoreticians he comments:

> Theirs is an amusing occupation, comparable to a person's making a colonizing expedition into Algeria, advancing only upon the map, without taking off his dressing gown. We place but slight confidence in the tests invented by these authors and we have borrowed nothing from them. All the tests which we propose have been repeatedly tried, and have been retained from among many, which after trial have been discarded. We can certify that those which are here presented have proved themselves valuable. (Binet & Simon, 1905, p. 193)

He arranged the tests of mental ability in order of difficulty as determined by the percentage of children at successive ages who could satisfactorily complete the task. In 1908 he introduced the concept of "mental level" although we now use the more familiar term "mental age," to refer to the number of items passed in terms of age standards. This was later modified by a comparison with the actual age of a child and popularized by Terman in the 1916 "Stanford Revision," although this metric had been suggested earlier by a German, William Stern, and by Frederick Kuhlman in the United States.

The quantitative form of this comparative ratio, the intelligence quotient or IQ, and its convenience in referring to a child's performance led to an unfortunate departure from Binet's insight that the metric must be a psychological one and not an objective physical measurement. That is, the IQ has been reified as some kind of direct measure of intelligence, indeed it has become for psychologists as well as for laypersons a vague synonym for intelligence itself. Thus we are told that a student failed because "he didn't use his IQ," or are informed that control and experimental groups were "matched in IQ."

It is important to restate the original meaning and implication of this metric. First, it must be kept in mind that an IQ is basically a score on some test; that is, a number given to a subject on the basis of how many items are answered correctly. The number of correct items—mental age (merely a score) — can be divided by the number of items a child of the same age *ought* to answer correctly—chronological age (again, merely a score). In this context ought means merely a statistical average. These two numbers, actually based on the number of items arbitrarily included in the test but conveniently converted to units based in terms of time (months and years), are divided and the quotient then multiplied by 100 to get rid of the decimal point. The formula shows this clearly:

$$\frac{\text{obtained score (MA)}}{\text{expected score (CA)}} \times 100 = \text{IQ score}$$

If the ratio is 1, it becomes an IQ of 100. If it is .75, it is an IQ of 75 and indicates that the subject did not get as many items right as the average child at the same age. To say that a child with an IQ of 75 is below average in intelligence and that one with an IQ of 125 is above average is an inference, justified perhaps by experience with the test and by acknowledging the psychometric assumptions, but an inference nonetheless, that is a long way from observations of the child's actual behavior when taking the test. An even more distant inference is that the test behavior as reflected in the IQ score will be related to some nontest behavior such as progress in school or the ability to prosper in the world of everyday experience.

It must be pointed out that the use of the term IQ is not even accurate psychometrically at the present time because most standard intelligence tests have abandoned the use of ratio scores (which had serious drawbacks, both numerical and conceptual, from the beginning). They now use standard scores derived by completely different statistical procedures even though these scores are usually expressed in the same kind of numerical values (see Anastasi, 1982, pp. 59-60, 81-83).

The systematic study of gifted children really began with the longitudinal study of high IQ children by Terman and his associates, reported in *Genetic Studies of Genius* (Terman, 1925; Cox, 1926; Burks, Jensen, & Terman, 1930; Terman & Oden, 1947 and 1959) and by Oden (1968).

It is of interest that Terman first studied both kinds of exceptionality, and his doctoral dissertation at Clark University (Terman, 1906) was an experimental study of 14 boys, "seven of them picked as the brightest and seven as the dullest in a large city school" (Terman, 1954, p. 222).

At Stanford University he pursued this interest in intellectual behavior and, after several tentative translations and adaptations of Binet and Simon's tests, in 1916 he published the famous Stanford Revision of their work, which became "the standard for all testing in the United States" (Goodenough, 1949, p. 62). Reliance on Stanford-Binet scores as a universal metric is still a common practice.

In the standardization, Terman noted at each age level the contrast in behavior between the highest and the lowest scoring children. These observations reinforced and intensified the interest that had been aroused by a college report he gave on genius and mental deficiency and by his dissertation. He resolved to study the gifted end of the intellectual continuum and in 1921 he received a grant from the Commonwealth Fund of New York for research on subjects of superior intelligence. By means of individual and group intelligence tests given in school classes from kindergarten level to the eighth grade, more than 1500 subjects were identified in California schools who averaged about 150 in IQ score. His aims in this research were typically straightforward: "First of all to find what traits characterize children of high IQ, and secondly, to follow them for as many years as possible to see what kind of adults they might become" (Terman, 1954, p. 222).

The high IQ children turned out to be high IQ adults. They seem to be successful academically, occupationally, socially, and personally. Yet in a review of these studies on the gifted and talented, it is pointed out that "most strikingly, the group [Terman's subjects] did not produce any great creative artists" (Fliegler & Bish, 1959, p. 410). A high degree of intellectual ability as was demonstrated by Galton can lead to success in life but, if that ability is manifest only in a high IQ score, then not much may be shown in the way of imagination, originality, or creativity.

It must be indicated, however, that Terman himself recognized the importance of factors other than intellectual ones related to high IQ scores. In a study of "success in life" as defined by "the extent to which a subject had made use of his superior intellectual ability" (Terman, 1954, p. 229) two groups were defined: 150 "A's," who were rated highest, and 150 "C's," rated lowest. Although they were similar in elementary school performance the A's began to do better in high school and performed at a much higher level in college. Ratings by teachers and parents showed the two groups similar in general health but they differed in most other ways. The A's were superior in "four volitional traits: prudence, self-confidence, perseverance, and the desire to excel," as well as "leadership, popularity, and sensitivity to approval or disapproval" (p. 229). Thus when subjects are already selected by high IQ scores, differential performance seems to be more a function of personality traits than cognitive ones.

CONCEPTION AND DEFINITION

The term "gifted" certainly connotes positive exceptionality and is no doubt understood in this sense by most persons working in this area. Yet one must agree that "a review of the literature on children with superior cognitive abilities, the academically talented, the superior, the able and ambitious, the talented, the gifted, the creative, etc., reveals confusion, to say the least" (Payne, 1974, p. 191). Rather than singling out some particular definition or trying to force some consensus, it may be more useful to put giftedness into a general framework of intelligence as a mental function.

A general model of intelligence in terms of "intelligent behavior" suggested by Webb, Oliveri, & Harnick (1977) and adapted by Hogan (1980) distinguishes three aspects of the mind that they term "power," "structure," and "style." These three aspects have been modified and elaborated by the present writer to serve as organizing principles for a general model of giftedness and as an heuristic paradigm for the study of persons displaying positive exceptionality. This model is set forth in Table 9.1.

Table 9.1. A General Model of Intelligent Behavior

Conceptual term	Definition	Theoretical Basis

Intelligence
  General mental ability
    Spearman's g
	Level of intellectuality	General neurological efficiency (largely heritable)

Talent Specific mental capacities and special aptitudes	Structure of intellectual functions	Innate cognitive organization (probably genetically controlled)
Style Manner in which ability and capabilities are expressed	Form of intellectual performance	Basic temperamental dispositions (may be learned, possible genetic component)

General Characteristics	Psychometric Index	Behavioral Manifestation
Speed of acquiring knowledge of one's culture	Stanford-Binet or similar IQ test; for example, Otis, Henmon-Nelson, WISC-R	General brightness, quickness in learning academic course content, likelihood of early scholastic success
High level of skill in particular area; for example, language, music, mathematics, spatial relations, memory	Specific test: PSAT V & Q, Seashore Music or Art, Minnesota Formboard, and so on (dimensions often identified through factor analysis)	Outstanding achievement in actual performance: painting, playing musical instruments, writing poetry, winning science awards, and so on
General approach to experience, preferred method of problem solving, way of interacting with other people	Personality assessment tests such as ACL, CPI, MMPI, WFPT; teacher nomination; peer sociometrics	Recognition in terms of creativity, originality, intellectuality, practicality, artistry, leadership, risk-taking, and so on

The first aspect of mind is here referred to as "intelligence" rather than as power and the second as "talent" rather than structure. Both ideas are relatively well understood and comprehended by the terms employed in the present context and probably make more sense on a pragmatic level since most lay-persons as well as professionals are familiar with the terminology used here. Indeed Sternberg and his associates have shown that the conceptions of intelligence held both by experts and by the public are remarkably similar (Sternberg, Conway, Ketron, & Bernstein, 1980).

The present model proposes a definition for each conceptual term and suggests a theoretical basis for the general characteristics of the three aspects of mental functioning. It also indicates a method of identifying gifted children by means of psychometric procedures or in terms of overt accomplishments.

Intelligence is seen here as general mental ability in the sense of Spearman's *g* (Spearman, 1904) and is defined in terms of level of intellectuality. That is, intelligence is ordinarily thought of as falling along a continuum from low to high. Children at the high end will be expected to prosper in school since they learn rapidly and should be better able to respond appropriately to demands of living in their own society. An IQ score from the Stanford-Binet (S-B) or any of the myriad of general intelligence tests developed in the S-B image can serve as an index of intellectual level.

The gifted child can be identified in terms of a high score on such a test; thus the number of gifted will depend on the elevation of the score used and the number of cases above the cutting score in the sample being studied. That is, in a given sample of children there will be fewer gifted if an IQ score of 135 rather than 125 is used as a cutoff score. The exact number of cases falling above a given score level cannot be stated precisely in an abstract statistical sense because norms are based on different subjects for different tests and, more important, the numerical value adopted for the standard deviation varies from test to test. For the S-B it is 16, for the Wechsler scales it is 15, while for the Otis group test it is only 12. This means that children with S-B IQ scores of 116, Wechsler IQ scores of 115, and Otis IQ scores of 112 would all lie equally distant above the mean of their norm groups and would be superior to approximately 84% of the subjects in those groups.

Further, the actual distribution of scores varies from one subject pool to another. There will be proportionately more scores above any particular level in a sample of students from a school in an affluent, middle-class suburb than from one located in an inner-city ghetto.

In the model, for the sake of completeness, a theoretical basis is ascribed to each of the three conceptual components which follows the initial proposal of Webb and Hogan. For intelligence this is given as general neurological efficiency and it is suggested that this is largely heritable. Earlier in the chapter reference was made to the nature/nurture controversy in which Galton argued for the importance of nature. This controversy is exceedingly complex and the reader is referred to Vernon's (1979) *Intelligence: Heredity and Environment* for a thorough analysis of the problem. In a summary of 30 main points of evidence he concludes that "although the total number of items favoring genetic influences . . . is roughly balanced by the number of environmental points . . . , more of the highly convincing items are G [genetic] than E [environmental]" (p. 319).

It is well to keep in mind that the human mind as well as the human body is a resultant of many components complexly interacting. Even though an obvious and easily measured characteristic like height can be shown to vary according to genetic differences, it is also modifiable by environmental factors such as nutrition or disease. To say that intelligence is largely hereditable does not mean that it cannot be changed—up or down—by training and experience.

The second component in the model, talent, is seen here in terms of two delimited aspects of mental functioning: first, as specific factors such as memory or perceptual speed, and second, as manifest in some particular area such as art, music, or language. The method of factor analysis is often used to elucidate the structure of intellectual functions as shown, for example, in the "Primary Mental Abilities" (PMA) identified by Thurstone and Thurstone (1941). But it may be noted that a PMA factor like memory does not operate abstractly in the human mind; rather it is made manifest in some content area. That is, one has a good (or poor) memory for words, numbers, faces, and so on. Musical talent, for example, may be vocal or instrumental, the latter may be displayed on wind or on stringed instruments.

Although gifted have been often identified on this basis, there is evidence that PMA factor test scores on V (verbal meaning) and R (inductive reasoning) are useful in predicting academic success. In selecting gifted artists and musicians, on the other hand, tests of these abilities are not usually employed and identification is made by means of demonstrated excellence in actual performance.

It must be noted that it is possible for a child to be gifted in terms of talent and yet not be gifted in the sense of having a high IQ score. Indeed a child may be exceptional positively on one dimension and negatively on the other. It has been pointed out above that Terman's gifted subjects were not particularly talented.

The opposite pattern of low IQ score with outstanding talent may be seen in cases of the so-called idiot savant, mentally retarded individuals with exceptional ability of a specific nature. Some can tell immediately on what day of the week any given date in the past or future falls. Others have perfect musical pitch and can reproduce exactly any musical phrase or melody after hearing it once (Scheerer, Rothman, & Goldstein, 1945). Although less common, a severely retarded and autistic child has shown remarkable drawing ability (Selfe, 1977). Cases have been reported of retarded children who could read fluently not only in their native tongue but in many foreign languages as well, yet without any comprehension of the words at all. Many mathematical prodigies can almost instantly give the cubes of 12 digit numbers or can add at a glance an entire page of numbers; in general intelligence they are average at best and most of them actually retarded (Bryan, 1970).

It is apparent that the two components are relatively independent and that one can be intelligent but untalented or talented but unintelligent; the chances of finding someone who is both very intelligent and very talented is relatively low. This may account for the reported lack of creative artists in Terman's high IQ subjects referred to above. If the selection procedures were changed so that only children with outstanding artistic skills were identified, how many would have IQs above 150?

The third component of the model, style, is seen here as the manner in which ability and capabilities are expressed, that is, the form of the intelligent behavior in dealing with life's experiences. Just as we can listen to two persons play the same tune on a piano and recognize differences in their style of playing the instrument, so we can identify differences in the way individuals behave toward all of the problems that confront them.

The importance of this aspect of behavior is stressed by Getzels and Jackson in their landmark study of creativity and intelligence where they state that "the concept of style of cognitive functioning is much more central to the objectives of this study than any linear notion of 'more or less' intellective ability or even the concept of 'level' of cognitive functioning" (Getzels & Jackson, 1962, p. 21).

A concrete example given by Gough makes the point very clearly. The problem of whether or not the number 1,000,008 is divisible by 9 can be solved in three different ways, all three being accurate and equally fast. The first and most obvious method is to employ conventional division and divide the first number by the second; the result—111,112—shows that the correct answer is, in fact, "yes." A less obvious method is to observe that the digits in the given number sum to 9 and that the original number must therefore be divisible by 9. Gough goes on,

> The third way is the most elegant or aesthetic way, and begins with an analysis which says something like this: "that number is wrong somehow, or it obscures something about the problem; if I express it as 999,999 + 9 then the question 'can it be divided by 9?' has a special relevance and meaning." . . . The answer to the question is not just "yes" but something like "yes, of course," or "to be sure." There is an elegance and an appropriateness to the third solution which transcends anything found in the first two. Creative thinking seems always to be characterized by a movement toward solutions of this third type, and by a preference for them. (Gough, 1964)

It may be possible, then, to identify a gifted child in terms of stylistic preferences for problems and for approaches to problems that go beyond the conventional right-or-wrong solutions ordinarily possible in standard intelligence tests. In fact the child who does give original, unusual, or clever responses may be penalized rather than rewarded. No credit on one widely used intelligence test is given for responding that wood and alcohol are alike because "both can knock you out" or that a fly and a tree are alike because "they both have limbs."

If—as asserted above for the second component of the model, talent—the same independence of intelligence and style is found, further implications for selection of gifted persons is apparent. This bears directly on the problem of the relationship of creativity and intelligence. It must be pointed out that most of the work done in this area has taken an approach which sees creativity as a cognitive function akin to intelligence and to intellectual aspects of talent. Identification of creative persons has been made by means of so-called creative thinking tests. An approach to creativity in terms of personality which is related to style will be discussed below.

CREATIVITY AND INTELLIGENCE

Probably the landmark study of the relationship between creativity and intelligence is that of Getzels and Jackson (1962). Their basic position was set forth directly: "Giftedness in children has most frequently been defined as a score on an intelligence test, and typically the study of the so-called gifted child has been equated with the study of the single [sic] IQ variable" (p. 6). They studied, in addition, subjects high on what are often called "creative thinking" tests.

Intelligence scores were "either a Binet or a Henmon-Nelson IQ . . . although perhaps a dozen were WISC. All scores were converted by regression equation to comparable Binet IQs" (p. 16). Thus the Stanford-Binet as the prototypical test of intelligence and its method of expressing IQ scores as a standard metric was followed.

Creativity scores were determined by a battery of tests related to, but also differing in some ways from, classic IQ measures. "In this study, the term 'creativity' refers to a fairly specific type of cognitive ability reflected in performance on a series of paper-and-pencil tests" (p. 16). The five tests in the battery were:

1. *Word association.* Give as many definitions as possible to stimulus words such as "bolt" or "bark." It may be pointed out that this differs from the assessment of vocabulary as typically employed in standard intelligence tests by virtue, first, of using relatively common and easily defined words as items and, second, by awarding points for the total number of different definitions supplied by the subject rather than for one "correct" answer.

2. *Uses for things.* This requires the subject to give as many different uses as can be thought of for some common object such as "brick." This test, derived from the work of J. P. Guilford, has frequently been used as a creativity measure in the sense of "divergent production" and it is sometimes called "Unusual Uses" or "Alternate Uses." (see Guilford, 1959).

3. *Hidden shapes.* This is basically a perceptual test in which the subject has to locate a simple geometric figure that is "hidden" in one of the four

complex figures which follow each stimulus item. The test is derived from the work of R. B. Cattell.

4. *Fables.* The subject has to make up different endings for the omitted last line of four different fables.

5. *Make-up problems.* This is a mathematical task which requires the subject to derive as many different kinds of problems as he can from a paragraph containing a series of numerical statements.

Scores on the five tests were summed to give a single creativity score since all of the tests were positively correlated with each other. The values ranged from .16 to .53. It must be noted that these scores were also correlated almost to the same degree with intelligence scores. In other words, creativity scores were not independent of intelligence scores.

Subjects were selected from about 500 students in the sixth to the twelfth grades in a private school. A "high intelligence" group of 17 boys and 11 girls scored in the upper 20% on IQ scores but not on creativity scores. A "high creativity" group of 15 boys and 11 girls was in the top 20% on creativity scores but not in IQ scores. It may be noted that the IQ mean for the entire school was 132 (SD 15), for the high intelligence group it was 150 (SD 6.6), while the high creativity group had 127 (SD 10.6). The latter was certainly highly intelligent by ordinary psychometric standards.

Both groups showed scholastic achievement superior to the rest of the students although they did not differ on need for achievement. Even so there was a slight preference by the teachers for the high intelligence group. The most marked differences were reported to be in the area of personality and stylistic features.

> The high I.Q.'s tend to converge upon stereotyped meanings, to perceive personal success by conventional standards, to move toward the model provided by teachers, to seek out careers that conform to what is expected of them. The high creatives tend to diverge from stereotyped meanings, to produce original fantasies, to perceive personal success by unconventional standards, to seek out careers that do not conform to what is expected of them. (Getzels & Jackson, 1963, p. 172)

Many of these stylistic preferences can be assessed by personality tests or by observations of behavior shown to be related to the preferences; specific methods will be outlined below.

Another pair of workers, Wallach and Kogan (1965), studied all four possible groups of subjects rather than just two; that is, they added subjects high on both kinds of test scores and those low on both since the incomplete type of research design employed by Getzels and Jackson had been strongly criticized in this regard. Although they offered a somewhat different theoretical rationale from that of Getzels and Jackson, their orientation was essentially cognitive. The creative thinking battery consisted of five tests each comprising from 4 to 10 items:

1. *Instances.* Name all the (round) things you can think of.
2. *Alternative uses.* Tell all the different ways you could use a (newspaper).
3. *Similarities.* Give the ways in which a (potato and a carrot) are alike.
4. *Pattern meanings.* Tell the different things the drawings (see Wallach & Kogan, 1965, Figure 2) could be.
5. *Line meanings.* Tell the different things the line (Wallach & Kogan, 1965, Figure 3) makes you think of.

These tasks were presented to their subjects, a group of 151 fifth grade pupils, more in the nature of games to be enjoyed rather than tests to be endured. They felt that "an attitude of playfulness rather than evaluation" would be more likely to maximize the "generation of associate material" (Wallach & Kogan, 1965, p. 19). This was necessary since they subscribed to the associative concept of creativity set forth by Mednick, which is discussed below. It has been found, however, that the gamelike approach is not required in creativity studies and that conventional test conditions seem optimal (Hattie, 1980).

Intelligence was measured by three subtests of the Wechsler Intelligence Scale for Children (WISC), Vocabulary, Picture Arrangement, and Block Design; two scores, Verbal and Quantitative, from the School and College Ability Tests (SCAT); and five tests from the Sequential Tests of Educational Progress (STEP) -- Mathematics, Science, Social Studies, Reading, and Writing.

The entire fifth grade of a middle-class school was studied; there were 70 boys and 81 girls who were divided on the basis of their scores on the tests enumerated above into four groups of from 36 to 39 subjects each. Although there were some sex differences, a summary of clinical information and experimental findings supports the conclusion of four basic types of cognitive functioning:

High creativity-high intelligence: These children can exercise within themselves both control and freedom, both adultlike and childlike kinds of behavior.

High creativity-low intelligence: These children are in angry conflict with themselves and with their school environment and are beset by feelings of unworthiness and inadequacy. In a stress-free context, however, they can blossom forth cognitively.

Low creativity-high intelligence: These children can be described as "addicted" to school achievement. Academic failure would be perceived by them as catastrophic, so they must continually strive for academic excellence in order to avoid the possibility of pain.

Low creativity-low intelligence: Basically bewildered, these children engage in various defensive maneuvers ranging from useful adaptations such as intensive social activity to regressions such as passivity or psychosomatic symptoms. (Wallach & Kogan, 1965, p. 303)

MEDNICK'S REMOTE ASSOCIATES TEST

As indicated previously Wallach and Kogan utilized a different theoretical framework from the general cognitive one employed by Getzels and Jackson. They followed Mednick, who had defined "the creative thinking process as the forming of associative elements into new combinations which either meet specified requirements or are in some ways useful. The more mutually remote the elements of the new combination, the more creative the process of solution" (Mednick, 1962, p. 221).

Scoring of the tests to assess creativity was based on this conceptual framework but they did not use Mednick's specific test. The Remote Associates Test (RAT) comprises 30 items that "are intended to require the testee to perform creatively. That is, he is asked to form associative elements into new combinations by providing connective links. Since the test situation is contrived, the combination must meet specified criteria that are experimenter imposed" (Mednick, 1962, p. 228). Each item contains three words such as rat, blue, and cottage; the subject has to supply a fourth word "which could serve as a specific kind of associative connective link between these disparate words" (p. 229). The required answer is cheese. The RAT is thus quite similar to conventional measures of intelligence in the sense of convergent thinking since it requires the subject to give a response which has been determined in advance by the tester and can be achieved by cognitive functions on the basis of information supplied.

In practice the RAT has indeed proved to be highly correlated with conventional tests of intelligence for many different kinds of subjects. There is little evidence to show that subjects nominated on the basis of demonstrated creativity differ from noncreative control subjects; even the conceptual basis of Mednick's work has been challenged (Jacobson, Elenewski, Lordahl, & Liroff, 1968).

A PERSONALITY APPROACH

A different kind of typology related to creativity and intelligence was developed by the present writer in a study of gifted adolescents attending a special summer program, the Governor's School of North Carolina. Rather than using the cognitive kinds of tasks employed by Getzels and Jackson and by Wallach and Kogan described previously the Revised Art Scale (RA) of the Welsh Figure Preference Test (WFPT) was employed as an index of creative potential (Welsh, 1980). The WFPT is a nonlanguage test and it is suitable for children as well as adults in different cultures. Figure 9.1 gives examples of items from the WFPT; the subject's task is a simple one—to decide for each item either "like" or "don't like." Of crucial importance is the fact that there is a good deal of empirical evidence that the Art Scale does relate to actual creative

Figure 9.1. Items from the Welsh Figure Preference Test (WFPT). Subjects are asked to indicate whether they "like" or "don't like" each item by marking L or DL on the answer sheet.

performance not merely psychometric test scores (Welsh, 1975, Appendix A). This is in contrast to the many studies showing that the so-called creative thinking tests which employ cognitive tasks really do not identify persons who have truly manifested creativity in terms of some overt accomplishment in science or in art (Hudson, 1966; MacKinnon, 1965; Nicholls, 1972).

As an index of intellectual ability a very difficult intelligence test, the Concept Mastery Test (CMT), developed by Terman (1954, 1956) in the course of his well-known study of gifted children was used. For students at the Governor's School the CMT and RA proved to be uncorrelated (Welsh, 1966), and subsequent studies have shown other intelligence tests to be uncorrelated with RA as well (Welsh, 1975).

Thus it was possible to use a fourfold design as Wallach and Kogan had, but rather than selecting subjects with a median split on each dimension, the method of extreme groups was possible since a total of 1163 students had been tested. Groups of 60 (30 of each sex) falling high or low on RA and high or low on the CMT (see Welsh, 1975, for cutting scores employed and for norms on these tests with other subjects) were studied in terms of personality characteristics. The test battery included the Adjective Check List (ACL) (Gough, 1960), the Minnesota Multiphasic Personality Inventory (MMPI) (Dahlstrom & Welsh, 1960), and the Strong Vocational Interest Blank (SVIB) (Strong, 1959).

There were, then, four different groups selected on the basis of scores on two independent tests, RA as a measure of creativity and the CMT as a measure of intelligence:

1. High RA, low CMT
2. High on both
3. Low on both
4. Low RA, high CMT

The pool of items in each of the three personality tests was analyzed to locate subsets of items that each group had answered differently from the other three groups looked at conjointly. Next, features common to each group across the different tests were used for a psychological interpretation of the basic typology. A summary of these personality characteristics is given in Table 9.2. Finally, two hypothetical personality dimensions were proposed to account for the fourfold typology generated from the item analysis (see Welsh, 1975, pp. 78–80).

These dimensions are construed as independent in the conceptual model just as the uncorrelated original test scores could be arrayed on orthogonal axes for the psychometric analysis. The vertical dimension, initially measured by RA, is called "origence" because of the relation of that scale to originality in studies of creative persons. A counterpart term, "intellectence" was coined for the horizontal dimension to indicate its inception in CMT score differences.

Intellectence is related to personality characteristics, temperamental dispositions, and interests associated with a dimension conceptualized as extending from the concrete to the abstract. That is, at the low (left) end of intellectence emphasis is placed on literal and specific events which may be expressed in concrete terms and may have practical or pragmatic applications for the usual experiences of life.

At the high (right) end of intellectence, on the other hand, an abstract attitude is evident, leading to concern for figurative or symbolic expression and generalized principles of comprehension. This attitude is also manifested in

Table 9.2.   Summary of Characteristics for Origence/Intellectence Typology

```
                              ┌──────────────┐
                              │ Unstructured │
                              │  Irregular   │
  1. High Origence-           │  Implicit    │        2. High Origence-
     Low Intellectence        └──────────────┘           High Intellectence

     "Imaginative type"                                   "Intuitive type"

       Non-conforming                                       Unconventional
       Dissenter                                            Risktaker
       Fantasy                                              Insight
       Extroversive                                         Introvert
       Interactive                                          Autonomous
       Outgoing               ORIGENCE                      Isolative
       Self-seeking                                         Self-centered
       Sales and business                                  Arts and humanities


┌──────────┐                                                        ┌──────────┐
│Practical │                                                        │Structured│
│Concrete  │────────── INTELLECTENCE ──────────                     │Regular   │
│Literal   │                                                        │Explicit  │
└──────────┘                                                        └──────────┘

  3. Low Origence-                                        4. Low Origence-
     Low Intellectence                                       High Intellectence

     "Industrious type"                                   "Intellective type"

       Conforming                                           Conventional
       Acquiescer                                           Rule follower
       Persistence                                          Logic
       Extrovert                                            Introversive
       Dependent                                            Independent
       Friendly                                             Guarded sociality
       Self-effacing                                        Self-confident
       Commercial and service                              Sciences and professions

                              ┌──────────────┐
                              │ Theoretical  │
                              │  Abstract    │
                              │  Symbolic    │
                              └──────────────┘
```

differences between the ends of the dimension in regard to social behavior. The high end seems more impersonal and unsocial while the low end is much more directly personal in outlook and more socially participative.

It must be emphasized that this personality dimension has to be kept separate from the concept of general intelligence. Persons at the low end of intellectence may be just as intelligent as those at the high end and may be just as successful in dealing with ordinary problems of life. It is likely, however, that there is a positive relationship between scores on conventional intelligence tests and the dimension of intellectence because such tests are loaded with the kind of content requiring abstractions for correct response. These tests are biased against the person who expresses his intelligence and ability in practical ways. Furthermore, these tests have been developed for the most part to predict academic achievement rather than success in the pragmatic world of every-day affairs.

Origence, by contrast, is not so directly related to intellectual performance either in terms of conventional intelligence tests or academic performance per se. The dimension seems to distinguish those at the low end who prefer and are more at home in an explicit and well-defined world which can be grasped by the application of objective rules. This is quite different from those at the high end who find congenial an implicit and open universe which they can structure and order in their own subjective way. The high origent person resists conventional approaches that have been predetermined by others and would rather do things his own way, even if it is unpopular or seems rebellious or nonconforming. This person is often interested in artistic, literary, and aesthetic matters that do not have a "correct" answer agreed upon by consensus, because these matters allow him or her more individualized interpretation and expression.

At the low end of origence are those who are more at ease in an orderly, structured, and regular environment where problems can be solved by conventional methods and by conforming to the status quo. In academic settings that stress rote memory and course content oriented to facts and figures these individuals may seem to achieve more than those at the upper end of this dimension. Some success in grade-getting may also accrue to them because of stylistic features related to persistence and planfulness as well as personal characteristics of deference to authority and self-effacement. This seeming advantage is probably countered in courses requiring initiative and imagination, where the high origent person would be rewarded for atypical or unusual performance and for independent study. Although uncorrelated with scores on conventional intelligence tests, origence is positively related to measure of fantasy, divergent thinking, and originality.

Since these dimensions are orthogonal they generate four basic personality types as summarized in Table 9.2. They have been identified alliteratively for convenience as:

1. Imaginative
2. Intuitive
3. Industrious
4. Intellective

These terms are descriptive labels and are not intended to define all of the implications of the fourfold origence/intellectence (O/I) typology, although they do epitomize some basic tendencies. For example, in a problem-solving situation the type 1 person will rush ahead with unusual ideas and may influence others by enthusiam and cleverness; but if there is only one correct answer this type may lose out because of careless errors. The type 2 individual is likely to prefer working along and will risk novel solutions that may seem illogical to others; verbal tasks are particularly favored. The type 3 person enjoys working with others and responds favorably to leadership asserting that hard work and application of known principles is the best way to get things done. Leadership is often shown by type 4 individuals particularly in areas where logic and rationality can lead to solutions; they are consistent and careful workers and make the fewest errors of all the types.

A detailed account of the O/I typology is given in Welsh (1975) with suggestions for research in different kinds of settings. An analysis of teachers' ratings of gifted adolescents in terms of origence and intellectence may be found in Welsh (1977). These ratings are consistent with findings from other reports and studies of adults that persons high on both dimensions are more likely to manifest behavior that will be seen as creative than the other three types. However, this is not a matter of absolute score level; comparison must be made within a peer group. That is, the persons in any group who score relatively higher than those of similar status will be seen as more original and creative.

The items on the personality tests answered differentially by the four selected groups can be employed as measurement scales. They have been studied at length psychometrically and have been cross-validated on other groups of children and adults (Welsh, 1975, 1981). In subsequent work, counterpart scales have been developed for the California Psychological Inventory (CPI) and for the WFPT (Welsh 1980). The latter test has the advantage that it does not require literacy or reading ability and has been used successfully with mentally retarded subjects (Krop, 1970; Mitchell, 1971a, 1971b; Watson, 1964).

It was pointed out above that cognitive tests, whatever their value in assessing cognitive functions, have not satisfactorily identified truly creative persons. In addition to shortcomings in application and to implications for research (Nicholls, 1972), there is an obvious problem for the subject. On any test that requires specific kinds of knowledge—word meaning or items of information, for example—a person who lacks that background is at a disadvantage. The subject may not be able to answer these items and will get a lower score on such a cognitively based measure whether it is called a test of creativity, divergent thinking, or even general intelligence. Thus a subject may be classified as "uncreative" or "unintelligent" merely because of a lack of some specific bit of knowledge required by such a test.

On personality scales, however, like those discussed above, the subject is not disadvantaged because of a requirement to give responses to cognitive items that must be answered in a certain way to be scored as "correct." Rather the individual describes his or her own attitudes and personality characteristics. It is entirely possible for the subject to be recognized as having traits associated with intelligent behavior or creativity as manifested outside of a test situation. That is, the subject will not be handicapped per se because background or education has deprived him or her of specific content required by conventional tests.

RELATION OF INTELLIGENCE, TALENT, AND STYLE

To understand the implications of the threefold model of intelligent behavior proposed above, it may be helpful to exemplify each of the three pairs of elements with some empirical data drawn from the present writer's experience. There are three different combinations of these elements: intelligence and talent, intelligence and style, and talent and style.

Intelligence and Talent

Reference has been made above to the Governor's School of North Carolina. Students are selected for this program who are highly gifted and talented in one of five academic areas: English, French, Mathematics, Natural Science, and Social Science; or in one of the five arts areas: Painting, Drama, Dance, Vocal Music, and Instrumental Music (see Welsh, 1969, 1971, 1975). To what extent will intelligence be related to the specific kind of talent required for 1 of the 10 special areas? Comparison can be made by means of the scores on Terman's Concept Mastery Test (CMT). Suppose that the CMT by itself had been used instead of the demonstrated talent, academic or artistic, required for selection to the school. How successful would identification have been? If we take one of the academic areas, Social Science, and one of the Arts areas, Painting, markedly different results are apparent. A count of the number of students scoring above the mean for the entire school (raw score 57) shows that 98 of 148 students, 66.2%, in Social Science do so while only 13 of 51, 25.5%, of those in Painting score at that level. In other words, if the CMT had been the selection criterion and the only index of giftedness used, two-thirds of those in Social Science would have been found but three-fourths of those in Painting would have been missed.

Intelligence and Style

An example of the relationship of these two elements of the model may be seen in data from a group of ninth and tenth graders in an ordinary high school tested with the Otis Test of Mental Ability and the Welsh Figure Preference Test (WFPT). We can use IQ scores from the Otis for intelligence and determine style from scores on the WFPT for origence (WOR) and for intellectence (WIN). Although, as noted above, the origence/intellectence model postulates that "basic intelligence" (were it possible to measure it directly) is theoretically independent of the two dimensions, it is predicted that scores on the usual IQ test will be related to the model. Achievement of high scores on tests such as the Otis requires the subject to respond in a prescribed and delimited manner avoiding clever or unusual responses and to answer accurately without making careless answers. Thus high origent subjects will be at a disadvantage because of imagination and impulsivity while high intellectent subjects will have an advantage because of conventional ideation and response. Otis IQs were available for 389 subjects who were divided into nine groups or "novants" on the basis of their scores on WOR and WIN into high, medium, and low thirds on each dimension conjointly. Table 9.3 shows that there is a significant relationship to both of the dimensions, and the marginal totals indicate the postulated decrease in scores along origence and an increase along intellectence. Thus subjects of type 1, high origence/low intellectence, have the lowest IQ, 98; whereas type 4, low origence/high intellectence achieved the highest IQ, 103. It may be noted that the overall mean and standard deviation are almost identical to the general norms for this test.

It is of interest that a test which does not require any special knowledge like vocabulary and information or cognitive skills like memory and reasoning shows a systematic relationship to a test that does.

Table 9.3. Mean IQ and Analysis of Variance Summary for Origence/Intellectence Novant Grouping of High School Students

	Low Intellectence WIN 22–	Medium Intellectence WIN 23–27	High Intellectence WIN 28+	
	(1)	(1–2)	(2)	
High origence WOR 40+	$N = 52$ 97.87	$N = 40$ 99.63	$N = 39$ 98.21	$N = 131$ 98.50
	(1–3)	(0)	(2–4)	
Medium origence WOR 20–39	$N = 51$ 99.67	$N = 38$ 98.34	$N = 40$ 100.70	$N = 129$ 99.60
	(3)	(3–4)	(4)	
Low origence WOR 19–	$N = 30$ 101.60	$N = 42$ 100.86	$N = 57$ 103.25	$N = 129$ 102.09
	$N = 133$ 99.40	$N = 120$ 99.65	$N = 136$ 101.05	$N = 389$ 100.05 SD = 12.60

Analysis of Variance Summary

Source	df	MS	F	p
Origence	2	1437.01	9.84	.0001
Intellectence	2	1106.23	7.58	.0005
Interaction	4	801.23	5.49	.0005
Error	380			

Talent and Style

This combination of model elements can be illustrated by returning to the Governor's School and arraying data in the novant system used above. The novant location was based on composite scores from the three personality tests referred to above—ACL, MMPI, and SVIB. A count was made of the numbers of students from each area of study falling into each of the origence/intellectence novants; these are summarized in Table 9.4 for two representative areas, one academic, Mathematics, and one arts, Dance. If we take the three novants in the upper left of the table, high origence/low intellectence, high origence/medium intellectence, and medium origence/low intellectence, it can be seen that for Mathematics only 8 of 111 students, 7.2%, fall here. By contrast, 58.9% of the Dance students, 43 out of 73, lie in this corner. In three novants for medium origence/high intellectence, low origence/medium intellectence, and low origence/high intellectence the values are reversed; there are 65, or 58.6%, from Mathematics and 5, 6.8%, from Dance. For the diagonal novants extending from that low on both through medium on both to high on both, the two areas have an identical proportion, 34.2%.

These examples suggest that it would be helpful in any program for the gifted to investigate the relationships among the three elements of the model to make sure that appropriate selection procedures are being employed.

NURTURING THE GIFTED

Once the academically gifted and creative have been identified by any of the means suggested above, a basic and crucial question remains—What should be done with such children?

At one extreme, a do-nothing attitude is expressed, the argument being that youngsters of high ability can fend for themselves and are better left to their own devices. Sometimes a more sophisticated form of this position is made by citing inconclusive or inconsistent research reports about giftedness and arguing that since we are not completely certain, it is better not to interfere with their own "natural" progress.

A sophistical position is sometimes adduced that it is unfair to offer special

Table 9.4. **Numbers of Students in Mathematics and Dance Falling into Origence/Intellectence Novants**

	Mathematics Intellectence				Dance Intellectence			
Origence	Low	Medium	High		Origence	Low	Medium	High	
High	2	4	6	12	High	19	11	5	35
Medium	2	15	16	33	Medium	13	10	0	23
Low	17	26	23	66	Low	10	5	0	15
	21	45	45	111		42	31	5	73

experience to the gifted and that it is a form of snobbishness and elitism to single them out.

> Curiously the critics never seem to object to partial segregation or special instruction for outstanding members of athletic teams. . . . Provisions for students talented in music or drama are also not regarded as undemocratic. Nor are objections raised to the almost universal practice of grouping children within the class for the early stages of teaching reading, or to special classes for backward pupils. . . . It is only grouping on the basis of high intelligence which is attacked, presumably because it is so value laden. (Vernon, Adamson, & Vernon, 1977, p. 168)

A corollary of the points made by Vernon et al. is that for the three kinds of intellectual functioning described in Table 9.1—general intelligence, talent, and style—it would probably be easier in most circumstances to utilize the concept of talent to select children for special programs. It is the present writer's experience that it is even more difficult than in the case of intelligence to argue for selection in terms of style despite evidence (Domino, 1968; Roid, 1967) of the effectiveness of this approach.

Another point of view commonly expressed is the citation of specific cases of intellectual precocity gone awry; the prime exemplar of this "case history" approach is William James Sidis (Montour, 1977). Sidis read before he was 3 and at the age of 11 attracted national attention in 1910 when he gave, as a special student at Harvard, a lecture on higher mathematics. He died at 46 after working most of his adult life in obscure clerical jobs.

These few tragic cases are used to argue generally against early recognition or encouragement of intellectual giftedness on the assumption that the prodigal child is better off without special attention. Yet most studies have shown that

> with the exception of Sidis and Colburn [Zerah Colburn, a mathematically precocious individual] whose childhoods were exploited ruthlessly by their parents, the early and rapid educational development by these prodigies demonstrated no consistent relationship to social maladjustment or emotional problems . . . [in fact] for those whose lives were problematic, possessing extraordinary intellectual abilities served to help them survive. (Cohn, 1979, p. 8)

In sum, arguments against doing anything for the gifted are made in terms of "benign" neglect, active discouragement, uncertainty about results, and "democratic" leveling of experience for all children.

The other end of the spectrum takes the position that indeed something should be done; the question now becomes, what specifically? The answers range from private personalized experience for an individual child all the way to vast reforms in the entire educational system. In general, however, two primary methods have been advocated, enrichment and acceleration, both having many variations in their form and application. *Enrichment* provides a quantitative or qualitative different kind of experience for gifted children while maintaining age-grade status. *Acceleration* is "progress through an educational program at rates faster or ages younger than conventional" (Pressey, 1949, p. 2).

"Lateral" or "horizontal" enrichment is seen in the common practice of assigning more of the same kind of work in a given class to the highly able. Many consider this mere busywork (Stanley, 1976) and stultifying to gifted students. It may also take the form of additional classes in other fields although at the ordinary level; that is, a mathematically precocious child might take an extra course in social studies or typewriting (Sidis was able to type before the age of four). Stanley refers to this practice as *irrelevant* academic enrichment. He considers *cultural* enrichment more appropriate even though not specifically tailored to the individual abilities of the gifted. In cultural enrichment the child is offered experience in art, drama, music, creative writing, or dance, for example, that is intended to broaden or extend the academic curriculum beyond the ordinary school subjects.

"Vertical" enrichment refers to higher level or more complex experience afforded on an in-grade basis to students with special aptitudes. A mathematically precocious youngster, for example, might be given advanced topics in this subject while maintaining his or her peer status in other subjects in the school system. For Stanley this constitutes *relevant* academic enrichment.

Acceleration takes two major forms: (1) starting in a school system at an earlier age than usual, or (2) skipping grades in the system. It is in a sense vertical but differs from the in-grade emphasis found in academic enrichment because ability rather than age determines the child's placement. Both aspects of acceleration may overlap since a child who starts school early may also move through the system faster by skipping one or more grades. Often enrichment by any of the methods listed here may be conjoined with acceleration.

A comparative evaluation of the merits of enrichment and acceleration was undertaken in the Ninth Annual Hyman Blumberg Symposium on Research in Early Childhood Education. Revised and expanded proceedings of this symposium were edited by George, Cohn, and Stanley (1979). In their preface to the edited volume they point out that

> early entrance and "double promotions" seemed more natural in the context of the one-room schoolhouse than they do today. The issue [of acceleration versus enrichment] has led to a great deal of argument, most of it unsupported by firm empirical evidence. Seldom is it even recognized explicitly that there are about as many different ways to speed up the educational progress of an intellectually talented youth as there are ways to "enrich" his or her educational experiences. (p. 13)

Of particular value in the volume is a review of the literature by Daurio. He concludes that

> according to the findings of most of the studies reported here [221 references are given], acceleration appears to be the more feasible method for meeting the needs

of gifted students. We would expect to find diminishing adherence to the age-grade lock step as more educators, administrators, and parents become aware of the facts as opposed to the myths. (Daurio, 1977, p. 53)

Acceleration has the advantage that no special provisions are necessary; the gifted individual is moved ahead into a class or a grade appropriate for his or her level of ability. All that is required is an accurate identification and assessment of the intellectual gift, willingness on the child's part, support from the parents, and concurrence of the school administration. Enrichment in the form of special classes or special programs necessarily does entail some changes or modification of the ordinary procedures in a school system which may bring added costs for instruction, materials, and administration.

One major roadblock to the use of acceleration is the firmly entrenched practice of age-grade grouping in American school systems. Kett (1974) has outlined the evolution of this administrative procedure which came about in the late nineteenth century, although it did not become solidly established until the 1930s. Thus insisting on chronological homogeneity in school grades is relatively recent and seems to rest more on a modern "tradition" than on the social, economic, and political needs that originally brought it about.

Some of the reasons for resistance to special treatment for the gifted have been outlined above but it may be that insistence on what has been called the age-grade lockstep is the most difficult to deal with. In discussing the refusal of a school to accelerate a 7-year-old girl, Montour comments: "These same educators would agree that to keep a retardate in his chronologically 'right' grade would be cruel and harmful to him, but they are unwilling to reverse this line of reasoning and apply it to the fortunate deviates who can be equally harmed—namely the gifted" (Montour, 1977, p. 266). Apparently these refractory attitudes are widespread (see Fox, 1976, pp. 202–204; Haier & Solano, 1976, pp. 215–222; Pyrt, 1976).

Another problem facing those who would help the gifted is a practical one; the lack of money either for the development of special programs or for research into the nature of giftedness. In the Blumberg Symposium this problem was frequently brought up for discussion. An indication of the depth of this difficulty is seen "in the traditional pattern of expenditure for the handicapped and the gifted in state legislatures, about $20 for the handicapped to $1 for the gifted. At the federal level it has run a little more sharply against the gifted, about $100 for the handicapped for every dollar earmarked for the gifted. . . . This expenditure pattern [reflects] a very deep value implanted in our society that we help the underdog but remain pretty wary of someone who has the initial advantage of intellectual talent" (George, Cohn, & Stanley, 1979, p. 212).

The obverse of the gifted/handicapped coin is pointed out by the remarks of Anastasi:

The social value of any effort to identify and cultivate outstanding talent should need no justification. Yet in the present humanitarian surge of interest in the mentally retarded, the brain-damaged, and the physically disabled, we may lose sight of society's continuing need for the talented. Remember that it is discoveries by the talented researchers in biochemistry, neurology, psychology, and other sciences that underlie current improvements in the condition and functioning level of the handicapped. Good intentions without the requisite knowledge base are not enough. Society needs the maximum cultivation and utilization of human talent—wherever found and in all fields of human endeavor—in order to improve the quality of life for all of us. (Anastasi, 1974, p. 87)

It must be emphasized at the same time that despite all of the problems and difficulties enumerated above, there have been notable attempts to make appropriate education available to the gifted. Indeed there have been special classes in American school systems since at least 1914 (Hildreth, 1966, p. 301) mostly in urban areas. A summary of these various efforts made on behalf of the gifted is given by Hildreth with some evaluation of the effectiveness of different kinds of approaches.

A more recent discussion of programs in California, Florida, New Jersey, North Carolina, and Wisconsin may be found in *Educational Programs and Intellectual Prodigies* (Stanley, George, & Solano, 1978), which was a supplement to *The Gifted and the Creative: A Fifty-Year Perspective* (Stanley, George, & Solano, 1977). Mention might be made of the Governor's School of North Carolina, a special summer program for high school students gifted and talented in academic arts areas (Welsh, 1969; 1975). Also in the same state are two special schools, North Carolina School of the Arts (Getlein, 1981), and North Carolina School of Science and Mathematics (Office of the Governor, 1978).

Notable in terms of conception and conduct is the Study of Mathematically Precocious Youth (SMPY) directed by Julian C. Stanley at the Johns Hopkins University. Although the focus is on identifying, encouraging, and educating one specific talent—mathematics—the program might well serve as a model for other kinds of talents as well. A series of publications report in detail many of the different aspects of their program which seem to the present writer to be applicable *mutatis mutandi* to other programs for the gifted and talented. Especially recommended for this purpose are Stanley, Keating, and Fox (1974); Keating (1976); Stanley (1977); Fox, Brody, and Tobin (1980); and Benbow and Stanley (1983).

The work of SMPY as reported in their first book-length publication, *Mathematical Talent: Discovery, Description, and Development* (Stanley et al., 1974), is abbreviated by the group in the form of a pseudo-mathematical reference, $MT:D^3$. "Discovery is the identification phase during which the talent is found. Description is the study phase during which the most talented students are tested further and otherwise studied a great deal" (Stanley, 1977, p. 89). It might be stressed that standard tests are much better at discovering outstanding mathematical talent than teachers are. In fact one study showed that tests given two or three years earlier were more effective than nominations by current math teachers (Stanley, 1976).

Emphasis is placed on the third D, development. "During it the youths who were found and studied are continually helped, facilitated and encouraged. Each is offered a smorgasbord of educational possibilities from which to choose whatever combination, *including nothing*, that best suits the individual" (Stanley, 1977, p. 89, emphasis added)

One last point seems particularly important to the present writer and should be pondered by all who make provisions for the gifted. SMPY has always dealt directly with the talented youths directly rather than through parents or teachers; test results, percentile ranks, and other material go to the individuals themselves. The group believes that contacts "should be mainly through the youth, even though he or she may be only nine or ten years old. After all, a child that age whose Stanford-Binet IQ is 170 or more . . . has a mental age [sic] of at least fifteen years. . . . We want the youths to take charge of their own academic planning early and to use their parents and us as a means for implementing their own decisions" (Stanley, 1977, p. 95). This would imply a fourth D (really a double-D) in the program, *decision* and *determination* for development on the part of the gifted individuals themselves.

PERSONAL PERSPECTIVE

The term academically gifted seems clear enough in the sense that it refers to those students doing outstandingly well in school work. But generally it has the implication of "academic" subjects only, that is, science and math, for example, rather than art and music or athletics. The term gifted by itself ought to refer to all kinds of different abilities and skills but generally it has been used in a more restricted sense. As the work of Getzels and Jackson discussed previously stressed, the term gifted has most often been used to indicate a student with high IQ scores. But, as I have illustrated with data from the Governor's School, if giftedness is defined solely in terms of IQ scores, many students with special competence or abilities will be excluded. These talented students may not be identified.

One obvious solution is a two-step selection procedure in programs for the gifted: first, some general IQ-like measure could be administered to assess the general level of intelligence; second, special tests related to the area of talents could be given. The contrast between the first and the second relates to the orientation of the school system.

> The problem becomes whether something like Spearman's g should be the central consideration, or whether something like Thurstone's primary mental abilities should play the central role in determining educational policy. In principal, pure g seems to argue for acceleration of the whole child. Purely separate traits seems to argue for enrichment to deal with the special talent. (George, Cohn, & Stanley, 1979, p. 209)

I would suggest using a general test of intelligence and setting the cutting score at a level to ensure that students of at least average to high average ability would be identified. Then a battery of special tests either for content areas like math and science or performance areas like music and art to identify those who are highly talented. These special tests and the appropriate cutting scores would have to be determined by experience and be related to the goals of the program.

Finally, I would include some kind of personality assessment since, in my judgment, creativity (in contrast to straightforward intellectual ability) is more likely to be manifested in this way than by cognitive tests.

Elsewhere I outlined three basic features of creativity: competence, diligence, and intelligence (Welsh, 1975, pp. 14–16).

Competence

This refers to what I call *talent* in the present chapter, some special kind of ability displayed in a particular modality. This would include, among others, kinesthetic skills of athletes, gustatory skills of chefs, social skills of leaders, as well as conventional academic skills needed in ordinary school systems. Creativity cannot be manifested abstractly, it must be displayed in some modality. Most children seem to possess enough academic talent to progress satisfactorily through the typical school system since such little demand is made of them. Special talent may be overlooked or not recognized if there is no opportunity for its expression. It is tragic that in many school systems such courses as music and art are seen as ''frills'' that can be sacrificed when budgets are tight. An aesthetic attitude might be engendered by participation in these areas or in drama and personal poetry writing, for example. I believe that these special talents should be encouraged by school classes not only for the abilities themselves, but also to stimulate aesthetic approaches to problems. The example given by Harrison Gough speaks to this latter point.

Diligence

This refers to motivational characteristics of perseverance and what I have called the ''capacity for sustained endeavor'' (Welsh, 1977, p. 213). No person who has attained more than superficial success has done so without a lot of hard work. This is true for creative accomplishment as well as for intellectual achievement and has long been recognized by psychologists. Terman's coworker Catherine Cox wrote that ''high but not the highest intelligence, combined with the greatest degree of persistence will achieve greater eminence than the highest degree of intelligence with somewhat less persistence'' (Cox, 1926, p. 187). Some students are self-motivated and move ahead on their own, but too many seem unwilling or unable to exert themselves. The problem of how to motivate the slothful and indolent is very difficult. One proposal often heard is to increase both the amount and the level of difficulty of school work required. It is my opinion that if students had to work harder on assigned tasks—tasks that were appropriately challenging, not mere busywork—it might lead to diligence in other matters as well.

Intelligence

This includes not only the kinds of abilities tapped by IQ tests but also to its organizational and directional attributes. Just being bright is not enough, as we read in the sad case of William James Sidis. But what might have happened if he had access to a good school counselor to help him "get his head on straight?" I believe that many students would behave more intelligently and more creatively if they had this kind of help.

Personality

To these three features I have added two personality dimensions and have continued the suffix"–ence" nomenclature by calling them *origence* and *intellectence*. They are easily assessed by the tests discussed above. Their importance in positive exceptionality has been summarized by one writer: "The intellectence-origence distinction and the typologies derived from it is the end point and high water mark of the intelligence-creativity debate that lasted through the 1960s. His data strongly suggest that he has identified two important and fundamental dimensions of intellectual style that have important consequences for understanding the performance of gifted adolescents" (Hogan, 1980, p. 553).

Finally, I would like to comment on the concept of "minimal competency" and its relation to positive exceptionality. Many states have instituted minimal competency testing with some score level required as a condition for receiving a high school diploma. If the score level is set high enough so that it truly reflects enough ability to prosper in the everyday world, then such testing serves a useful function. But if it is set too low and is not in fact related to the abilities needed outside school, then it is a psychometric sham. The ordinary student as well as the gifted will see such testing as a waste of time and a joke. It can only inquinate meaningful and legitimate testing.

I have tried to summarize in Table 9.5 some of the relationships between instruction and the student as well as score level on tests and performance levels. The continuum of exceptionality will have the positive end at the top and the gifted and highly talented should be able to achieve excellence. At the bottom will fall the negatively exceptional and some will be incompetent to deal with the world alone; some will require custodial care and direct personal supervision. But many, with proper training, will be able to achieve minimal competence of a meaningful kind.

A good testing program should be able to identify correctly a student's level of ability so that instruction appropriate to that level can be given. A student of high ability should obtain high scores on tests related to that ability, should

Table 9.5. Summary of Relationship among Student, Instruction, Test Scores, and Accomplishment

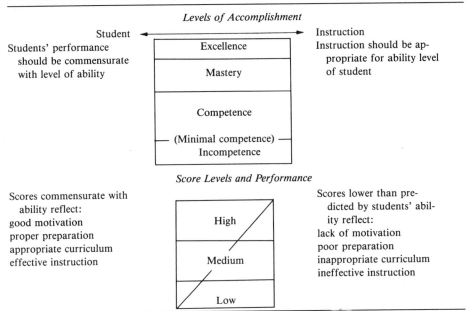

Levels of Accomplishment

Student ⟷ Instruction

Students' performance should be commensurate with level of ability

Instruction should be appropriate for ability level of student

| Excellence |
| Mastery |
| Competence |
| ⎯ (Minimal competence) ⎯ Incompetence |

Score Levels and Performance

Scores commensurate with ability reflect:
good motivation
proper preparation
appropriate curriculum
effective instruction

Scores lower than predicted by students' ability reflect:
lack of motivation
poor preparation
inappropriate curriculum
ineffective instruction

| High |
| Medium |
| Low |

be given challenging classes in the area, and should perform at a level of excellence. Scores and performance related to medium and lower levels should be considered similarly. The goal of any school system should be to enable the students to achieve the highest level that they are capable of — not merely to manifest minimal competency.

REFERENCES

Anastasi, A. *Psychological testing* (5th ed.). New York: Macmillan, 1982.

Anastasi, A. Commentary on the precocity project. In J. C. Stanley, D. P. Keating, & L. H. Fox (Eds.), *Mathematical talent: Discovery, description, and development* (pp. 87–100). Baltimore: Johns Hopkins University Press, 1974.

Benbow, C. S., & Stanley, J. C. (Eds.). *Academic precocity: Aspects of its development*. Baltimore: Johns Hopkins University Press, 1983.

Binet, A., & Simon, T. New methods for the diagnosis of the intellectual level of subnormals. *L'Annee Psychologique,* 1905, *11,* 191–244.

Bryan, J. Who needs computers with mathematical prodigies like these? *Horizon,* 1970, *12,* 46–47.

Burks, B. S., Jensen, D. W., & Terman, L. M. *Genetic studies of genius. 3. The promise of youth.* Stanford, Calif. Standford University Press, 1930.

Butcher, H. J. *Human intelligence: Its nature and assessment.* London: Methuen, 1968.

Cohn, S. J. Acceleration and enrichment: Drawing the base line for further study. In W. C. George, S. J. Cohn, & J. C. Stanley (Eds.), *Educating the gifted: Acceleration and enrichment* (pp. 3–12). Baltimore: Johns Hopkins University Press, 1979.

Cox, C. M. *Genetic study of genius. 3. The early mental traits of three hundred geniuses.* Stanford, Calif. Stanford University Press, 1926.

Dahlstrom, W. G., & Welsh, G. S. *An MMPI handbook: A guide to its use in clinical practice and research.* Minneapolis: University of Minnesota Press, 1960.

Daurio, S. P. Educational enrichment versus acceleration: A review of the literature. In W. C. George, S. J. Cohn, & J. C. Stanley (Eds.), *Educating the gifted: Acceleration and enrichment* (pp. 13–63). Baltimore: Johns Hopkins University Press, 1977.

Domino, G. Differential prediction of academic achievement in conforming and independent settings. *Journal of Educational Psychology,* 1968, *59,* 256–260.

DuBois, P. H. *A history of psychological testing.* Boston: Allyn & Bacon, 1970.

Edwards, A. J. *Individual mental testing. 1. History and theories.* Scranton, Pa.: International Textbook, 1971.

Edwards, A. J. *Individual mental testing. 2. Measurement.* Scranton, Pa.: International Textbook, 1972.

Edwards, A. J. *Individual mental testing. 3. Research and interpretation.* New York: Intext International Publishers, 1975.

Fliegler, L. A., & Bish, C. E. The gifted and talented. *Review of Educational Research,* 1959, *29,* 408–450.

Fox, L. H. Sex differences in mathematical precocity: Bridging the gap. In D. P. Keating (Ed.), *Intellectual talent: Research and development* (pp. 183–214). Baltimore: Johns Hopkins University Press, 1976.

Fox, L. H., Brody, L., & Tobin, D. (Eds.). *Women and the mathematical mystique.* Baltimore: Johns Hopkins University Press, 1980.

Galton, G. *Inquiries into human faculty and its development.* New York: Macmillan, 1883.

Galton, F. *Hereditary genius: An inquiry into its laws and consequences* (2nd ed.). (originally published 1892) New York: Meridian Books, 1962.

George, W. C., Cohn, S. J., & Stanley, J. C. (Eds.). *Educating the gifted: Acceleration and enrichment.* Baltimore: Johns Hopkins University Press, 1979.

Getlein, F. Where homework might be dance or music or theater. *Smithsonian,* 1981, *11,* (12), 54–65.

Getzels, J. W., & Jackson, P. W. *Creativity and intelligence.* New York: Wiley, 1962.

Getzels, J. W., & Jackson, P. W. The highly intelligent and the highly creative adolescent: A summary of research findings. In C. W. Taylor & F. Barron (Eds.), *Scientific creativity: Its recognition and development* (pp. 161–172). New York: Wiley, 1963.

Goodenough, F. L. *Mental testing: Its history, principles, and applications.* New York: Rinehart, 1949.

Gough, H. G. The Adjective Check List as a personality assessment research technique. *Psychological Reports,* 1960, *6,* 107–122.

Gough, H. G. Identifying the creative man. *Journal of Value Engineering,* 1964, *2,* 5–12.

Gowan, J. C. Background and history of the gifted child movement. In J. C. Stanley, W. C. George, & C. H. Solano (Eds.), *The gifted and the creative: A fifty-year perspective* (pp. 5–27). Baltimore: Johns Hopkins University Press, 1977.

Guilford, J. P. *Personality.* New York: McGraw-Hill, 1959.

Haier, R. J., & Solano, C. H. (1976). Educators' stereotypes of mathematically gifted boys. In D. P. Keating (Ed.), *Intellectual talent: Research and development* (pp. 215–222). Baltimore: Johns Hopkins University Press, 1976.

Hattie, J. Should creativity tests be administered under test-like conditions? An empirical study of three alternative conditions. *Journal of Educational Psychology,* 1980, *72,* 87–98.

Hildreth, G. H. *Introduction to the gifted.* New York: McGraw-Hill, 1966.

Hogan, R. The gifted adolescent. In J. Adelson (Ed.), *Handbook of adolescent psychology* (pp. 536–559). New York: Wiley, 1980.

Hudson, L. *Contrary imaginations: A psychological study of the young student.* New York: Schocken, 1966.

Jacobson, L. L., Elenewski, J. J., Lordahl, D. S., & Liroff, J. H. Role of creativity and intelligence in conceptualization. *Journal of Personality and Social Psychology,* 1968, *10,* 431–436.

Keating, D. P. (Ed.). *Intellectual talent: Research and development.* Baltimore: Johns Hopkins University Press, 1976.

Kett, J. History of age grouping in America. In J. S. Coleman et al. (Eds.), *Youth: Transition to adulthood,* (report to the panel of youth—President's Science Advisory Committee): Chicago: University of Chicago Press, 1974.

Krop, H. Perceptual preference of the mentally retarded. *Training School Bulletin* (American Institute for Mental Studies), 1970, *66,* 188–190.

MacKinnon, D. W. Personality and the realization of creative potential. *American Psychologist,* 1965, *20,* 273–281.

Mednick, S. A. The associative basis of the creative process. *Psychological Review,* 1962, *69,* 220–232.

Mitchell, M. M. Analysis of Welsh Figure Preference Test scores of educable mentally handicapped children. *Training School Bulletin* (American Institute for Mental Studies), 1971, *67,* 214–219.(a)

Mitchell, M. M. Personality assessment of retarded children. *Training School Bulletin* (American Institute for Mental Studies), 1971, *68,* 186–191. (b)

Montour, K. M. William James Sidis, the broken twig. *American Psychologist,* 1977, *32,* 265–279.

Nicholls, J. G. Creativity in the person who will never produce anything original and useful: The concept of creativity as a normally distributed trait. *American Psychologist,* 1972, *27,* 717–727.

Norsworthy, N., & Whitley, M. T. *The psychology of childhood.* New York: Macmillan, 1923.

Oden, M. H. The fulfillment of promise: 40-year follow-up of the Terman gifted group. *Gifted Psychology Monographs,* 1968, *77,* 3–93.

Office of the Governor. *The North Carolina School of Science and Mathematics.* Raleigh, N.C.: Office of the Governor, July 14, 1978.

Payne, J. The gifted. In N. G. Haring (Ed.), *Behavior of exceptional children: An introduction to special education* (pp. 189–214). Columbus, Ohio: Merrill, 1974.

Pressey, S. L. *Educational acceleration: Appraisal and basic problems* (Bureau of Educational Research Monographs, No. 31). Columbus: Ohio State University Press, 1949.

Pyrt, M. Attitudes toward teaching the gifted child. *Intellectually Talented Youth Bulletin,* 1976, *2*, (6), 1–2.

Roback, A. A. *A history of American psychology* (2nd ed.). New York: Collier, 1964.

Roid, G. H. *Welsh Figure Preference Test scores and student reactions to various college teaching methods.* Unpublished master's thesis, University of Oregon, 1967.

Scheerer, M., Rothman, E., & Goldstein, K. A case of "idiot savant": An experimental study of personality organization. *Psychological Monographs,* 1945, (4, Whole No. 269).

Selfe, L. *Nadia: A case of extraordinary drawing ability in an autistic child.* London: Academic, 1977.

Spearman, C. E. "General Intelligence" objectively defined and measured. *American Journal of Psychology,* 1904, *15*, 72–101.

Stanley, J. C. Test better finder of great math talent than teachers are. *American Psychologist,* 1976, *31*, 313–314.

Stanley, J. C. Rationale of the study of mathematically precocious youth (SMPY) during its first five yars of promoting educational acceleration. In J. C. Stanley, W. C. George, & C. H. Solano (Eds.), *The gifted and the creative: A fifty-year perspective* (pp. 75–112). Baltimore: Johns Hopkins University Press, 1977.

Stanley, J. C., George, W. C., & Solano, C.H. (Eds.). *The gifted and the creative: A fifty-year perspective.* Baltimore: Johns Hopkins University Press, 1977.

Stanley, J. C., George, W. C., & Solano, C. H. (Eds.). *Educational programs and intellectual prodigies.* Baltimore: Johns Hopkins University Press, 1978.

Stanley, J. C., Keating, D. P., & Fox, L. H. (Eds.). *Mathematical talent: Discovery, description, and development.* Baltimore: Johns Hopkins University Press, 1974.

Sternberg, R. J., Conway, B. E., Ketron, J. L., & Bernstein, M. *People's conceptions of intelligence* (Tech. Rep. No. 28). Washington, D.C.: Office of Naval Research, 1980.

Strong, E. K., Jr. *Manual for the Strong Vocational Interest Blanks for men and women, revised blanks (Forms M and W).* Palo Alto, Calif.: Consulting Psychologists Press, 1959.

Terman, L. M. Genius and stupidity: a study of some of the intellectual processes of seven "brighter" and seven "stupid" boys. *Pedagogical Seminars,* 1906, *13*, 307–373.

Terman, L. M. *Genetic studies of genius. 1. Mental and physical traits of a thousand gifted children.* Stanford, Calif.: Stanford University Press, 1925.

Terman, L. M. The discovery and encouragement of exceptional talent. *American Psychologist,* 1954, *9*, 221–230.

Terman, L. M. *Manual, the Concept Mastery Test*. New York: Psychological Corporation, 1956.

Terman, L. M., & Oden, M. H. *Genetic studies of genius. 4. The gifted child grows up*. Stanford, Calif.: Stanford University Press, 1947.

Terman, L. M., & Oden, M. H. *Genetic studies of genius. 5. The gifted group at midlife*. Stanford, Calif.: Stanford University Press, 1959.

Thurstone, L. L., & Thurstone, T. G. Factorial studies of intelligence. *Psychometric Monographs*, 1941, (2).

Vernon, P. E. *Intelligence: Heredity and environment*. San Francisco: Freeman, 1979.

Vernon, P. E., Adamson, G., & Vernon, D. G. *The psychology and education of gifted children*. London: Methuen, 1977.

Wallach, M. A., & Kogan, N. *Modes of thinking in young children*. New York: Holt, Rinehart & Winston, 1965.

Watson, W. G. *An analysis of responses to the Welsh Figure Preference Test to evaluate its effectiveness as a measure of mental ability*. Unpublished doctoral dissertation, University of North Carolina at Chapel Hill, 1964.

Webb, R. A., Oliveri, M. E., & Harnick, F. S. The socialization of intelligence: Implications for educational intervention. In R. A. Webb (Ed.), *Social development in childhood: Day-care programs and research* (pp. 111–140). Baltimore: Johns Hopkins University Press, 1977.

Welsh, G. S. Comparison of D-48, Terman CMT, and Art Scale scores of gifted adolescents. *Journal of Consulting Psychology,* 1966, *30,* 88.

Welsh, G. S. *Gifted adolescents: A handbook of test results*. Greensboro, N.C.: Prediction Press, 1969 (Distributed by Consulting Psychologists Press).

Welsh, G. S. Vocational interests and intelligence in gifted adolescents. *Educational and Psychological Measurement,* 1971, *31,* 155–164.

Welsh, G. S. *Creativity and intelligence: A personality approach*. Chapel Hill, N.C.: Institute for Research in Social Science, 1975.

Welsh, G. S. Personality correlates of intelligence and creativity in gifted adolescents. In J. C. Stanley, W. C. George, & C. H. Solano (Eds.), *The gifted and the creative: A fifty-year perspective* (pp. 197–221). Baltimore: Johns Hopkins University Press, 1977.

Welsh, G. S. *Manual for the Welsh Figure Preference Test* (rev. ed.). Palo Alto, Calif.: Consulting Psychologists Press, 1980.

Welsh, G. S. Personality assessment with Origence/Intellectence scales. *Academic Psychology Bulletin,* 1981, *3,* 299–306.

CHAPTER 10

General Cognitive Deficits: Mental Retardation

BAHR WEISS AND JOHN R. WEISZ

Mental retardation has almost certainly been recognized for as long as human society has existed; but popular notions of what retardation is and societal treatment of retarded people have varied widely over the course of history. Roman parents reportedly threw their retarded children into the Tiber River to avoid the burden of caring for them (Maloney & Ward, 1979), and the Spartans are known for having killed or abandoned anyone who was "defective" (Scheerenberger, 1983). Retarded people who survived these early hurdles frequently served as fools or jesters for the rich.

In the Middle Ages, with the rise of Christianity and its doctrine of love and kindness for the unfortunate, there was an increase in the compassion shown to some retarded persons. One such example is Gheel, a religious shrine in Belgium, which became established as an asylum for the mentally disabled. Here retarded persons worked with the other inhabitants and lived in private homes. This practice continues today in Gheel. The majority of retarded persons during this period were less fortunate, however. More often they were superstitiously regarded as "infants of the good God" or as divine prophets and left to fend for themselves in the streets of Europe (Kanner, 1964).

Retarded persons received perhaps their most inhumane treatment in the 1600s, during what is known (rather ironically for the retarded) as the period of "enlightenment." With the prevailing belief in demonism, retarded persons came to be seen as "infants of the Devil" and were physically tortured or murdered, often in the course of "exorcism." Martin Luther believed that retarded people lacked souls and were possessed by Satan; he recommended that they be drowned (Kanner, 1964).

It was not until the nineteenth century that truly scientific efforts to study and care for retarded people emerged. In 1801 Jean-Marc Itard, a student of Philippe Pinel, attempted to train and civilize a "wild boy" who had been found in the forests of Aveyron. Victor, as Itard named the boy, was incapable of speech and appeared to be more animal than human. Pinel believed Victor

344

to be an "incurable idiot," but Itard believed that Victor's deficiencies were the result of a severe lack of social contact and educational neglect. Against Pinel's advice, Itard devoted himself to teaching Victor speech and the customs of human society. At first Victor made rapid progress in his education. After five years, though, he was still unable to speak, and Itard gave up in disappointment. Although Itard felt that he had failed with Victor, the French Academy of Science commended him for his efforts. They praised the relative success he had achieved with Victor and the systematic teaching methods that he had developed in the process.

Despite this early failure the period of Itard and the other early pioneers was generally one of great optimism, founded on the belief that mental retardation could be "cured." Much energy was expended in the pursuit of this goal. The French physician Edouard Séguin further developed and systematized the techniques and procedures of Itard, who was his teacher. At the time of Itard's death in 1838, he and Séguin were collaborating on the instruction of a retarded child. Then, distrusting the new government that followed the 1848 revolution in France, Séguin emigrated to the United States and helped to found the mental retardation movement in this country. In 1876, four years before he died, Séguin was elected president of The Association of Medical Officers of American Institutions for Idiotic and Feebleminded Persons. This organization was the forerunner of the American Association on Mental Deficiency (AAMD), currently the foremost professional organization concerned with mental retardation.

The surge of public optimism about retardation had begun to fade by the time of Séguin's death. Repeated efforts to cure retardation had failed, a sense of disillusionment spread, and society's attitudes toward retarded people underwent a radical change. Mental retardation came to be seen as "incurable" and therefore best dealt with by institutionalization. Because retarded persons evidently could not be "cured" by educational means, belief in an environmental etiology began to shift to belief in the importance of hereditary factors. Reports began to appear purporting to show that retardation "ran in families" (e.g., *The Kallikak Family: A Study in the Heredity of Feeblemindedness*, Goddard, 1912). Other reports linked retardation to immorality and criminal behavior (e.g., *The Jukes, A Study in Crime, Pauperism, Disease and Heredity,* Dugdale, 1877). Among the scientific shortcomings of these and similar studies was a failure to recognize that family members generally share similar environments as well as heredity.

In the United States belief in the hereditary transmission of mental retardation and a concomitant fear of the intellectual and moral deterioration of the species gave rise to the eugenics movement. Many influential politicians and scientists came to view retarded people as degenerate and undesirable people who should be prevented from breeding either by sterilization or social isolation (Kamin, 1974; Sarason & Doris, 1969). By 1926, 23 states had passed laws allowing involuntary sterilization of retarded persons. Not all of these

laws were upheld in the state courts; however, "properly drawn" sterilization laws were found constitutional by the U.S. Supreme Court (Kanner, 1964).
A similar though less extreme movement developed in Europe.

Prior to the advent of intelligence testing there was little awareness of the
milder and less obvious forms of mental retardation. This state of affairs began to change in 1904, when test developers Alfred Binet and Theophile Simon
received an important assignment from the French Minister of Public Education. They were commissioned to develop a means of identifying children
likely to fail in school. With this objective in mind, Binet and Simon developed
the first successful intelligence test. This test, in turn, led to the "discovery"
of the mildly mentally retarded, which greatly increased the number of known
retarded persons. Given the volatility of the times, this "discovery" further
fueled the eugenics fire by giving evidence of the magnitude of the supposed
decline in the species.

It was not until the 1930s that a relatively humane and rational attitude
toward retarded people reemerged. New and better designed research failed
to substantiate the previous claims that retardation caused diverse social ills.
The simplistic view that retardation was purely hereditary began to be questioned. In the United States attention turned to the more pressing problems
of the Great Depression and then to World War II, and interest in retarded
people waned.

After the end of World War II there was a resurgence of interest in retarded
persons in the United States. The federal government began to fund research
and direct service programs for this part of the population. During the depression millions of people had been jobless; regardless of their efforts to remain
self-sufficient many had required governmental assistance to survive. This experience helped many to see that one might need assistance without necessarily
being shiftless or immoral; popular support for a laissez-faire policy by the
government toward its needy citizens diminished accordingly. This newfound
attitude influenced the public's orientation toward retarded persons, and by
the late 1950s the shifting orientation began to show up in legislation. A public
policy of "normalization" developed, whereby retarded persons were accorded the right to live in the least restrictive environment possible and to have
as "normal" a life as they were capable of leading. Normalization has meant
a number of changes, including a shift from institutionalization to community
placement and training.

Despite shifts in legal policy, discrimination and prejudice remain; one can
still see reflections of past stereotypes in current attitudes toward retarded
persons. Reviewing the research literature related to the attitudes of children
toward their retarded peers, Corman and Gottlieb (1977) found that in most
cases, retarded children were less well liked or accepted than nonretarded children.

As adults, retarded persons are confronted with both nonaccepting attitudes and outright discrimination. In a study by Trippi, Michael, Colao, and
Alvarez (1978), for example, only 1 landlord out of 100 expressed a willingness

to even consider renting a room to a retarded person. More than half the landlords falsely stated that the apartment advertised was no longer available. The remainder voiced serious concerns; for example, that the retarded person "would play with matches," might be vicious and bad tempered, might steal and damage property, or would be incapable of independent living. While these fears may not have been totally unfounded in all cases, few of the landlords sought any confirming or disconfirming information; only 2 of the 100 requested any information about the applicant's severity of retardation, or the training that the retarded individual had received.

Comparable though less pronounced attitudes have been found toward group homes. Thirty-five percent of group homes surveyed by Baker, Seltzer, and Seltzer (1977) initially faced community opposition. Furthermore, this figure is an underrepresentation of the true level of opposition, since group homes which never opened or were closed because of community resistance were not included in the study.

People do tend, however, to show more acceptance of retarded persons when the issues are stated in broad, hypothetical terms rather than in specific, personal, and real terms. In a Gallup survey in 1974, 85% of those questioned stated that they would not object to a group home for retarded individuals on their block. This high level of acceptance in the abstract, compared to actual levels of resistance in concrete situations, suggests a certain discrepancy; many people seem to feel that retarded persons should be accepted and treated fairly, but many also seem opposed to taking what they see as a personal risk.

Findings like those cited above suggest that more humane treatment of retarded individuals may be fostered by a better understanding of what retardation is and is not. In this chapter we review a number of efforts to improve understanding of retardation. We focus on several broad issues that have surged and resurged in the public forum and among professionals in the area. The issues include definition and assessment, etiology, personality and behavioral correlates, and approaches to prevention and intervention. We now turn to the first of these issues, focusing on a key question: What is mental retardation?

DEFINITION AND ASSESSMENT OF MENTAL RETARDATION

> Mental Retardation refers to significantly subaverage general intellectual functioning existing concurrently with deficits in adaptive behavior, and manifested during the developmental period. (Grossman, 1973, p. 11)

This definition by the American Association on Mental Deficiency is generally recognized as the most widely accepted definition of mental retardation. The American Psychiatric Association (APA) in its *Diagnostic and Statistical Manual* (3rd ed., APA, 1980) has defined mental retardation in accordance with the AAMD definition:

> The essential features [of mental retardation] are: (1) significantly subaverage general intellectual functioning, (2) resulting in, or associated with, deficits or impairments in adaptive behavior, (3) with onset before the age of 18. (APA, 1980, p. 36)

These two definitions suggest that the two major professional organizations involved with retarded people agree as to how mental retardation should be conceptualized. However, current consensus is by no means unanimous. In fact, for as long as mental retardation has been studied scientifically professionals have debated how it should be defined and assessed. Various alternative models have been proposed, some apparently evolving from the AAMD definition (e.g., Zigler & Balla, Note 1), and some radically departing from it (e.g., Mercer, 1973).

The system that Zigler and Balla proposed is based on the supposition that a valid and useful classification system must have two features. The first is reliability. For a system to be reliable, the system must afford consistent categorization of individuals, regardless of who is using the system. Zigler and Balla suggested that intelligence tests are the most practical and reliable psychological measures relevant to mental retardation and therefore chose IQ score as their first classificatory axis.

The second feature identified as essential by Zigler and Balla is the usefulness of the system. A classification system that is reliable but of little practical use is pointless. The utility of a system, according to these authors, depends on the amount of information its categories yield about the individuals being classified. Such information is largely a function of the number of meaningful correlates of class membership.

A retarded individual's IQ score gives important information about the likely cognitive functioning of the individual. However, according to the Zigler and Balla position, more precise information can be obtained if retarded people are differentiated on the basis of etiology as well as IQ. Zigler and Balla cite evidence indicating that retarded persons with similar IQ scores but different etiologies perform differently under certain conditions. For this reason the second axis of their proposed system is etiology: retarded persons are classified as being of organic, familial (nonorganic), or undifferentiated (indeterminable) etiology.

This system has been proposed on a heuristic basis and exact behavioral and cognitive correlates of the categories have not been specified. Zigler and Balla have argued that adoption of their two axis system would enhance the professionals' efforts to assist mentally retarded people by increasing the precision with which retarded people could be categorized. At present, however, a single axis typology favored by the AAMD and APA is most often used when a need is felt to subclassify retarded individuals.[1]

The intellectual and adaptive abilities of retarded people vary over a wide range. In an effort to take this into account, both the AAMD and the APA classify mental retardation into four subcategories on the basis of degree of intellectual impairment.

Mild Mental Retardation (IQ 55-69)

Approximately 80% of retarded persons are in this category (APA, 1980). Retarded children at this level usually look and act normal; ordinarily, it is only when they face school and its intellectual demands that their mental deficiency becomes apparent. As children they are able to interact cooperatively and develop social and communication skills. As adults they are capable of acquiring academic skills up to about the sixth grade level. Most retarded persons in this category can become self-supporting, albeit at jobs that most people consider mundane.

Moderate Mental Retardation (IQ 40-54)

Approximately 12% of individuals classified as mentally retarded fall into this category (APA, 1980). Moderately retarded children frequently appear clumsy and may show observable physical abnormalities. As preschool children they are able to talk or communicate but show limited awareness of social conventions. While many moderately retarded adults are able to work at unskilled or semiskilled jobs in sheltered settings, few are able to be entirely self-supporting and live independently.

Severe Mental Retardation (IQ 25-39)

This group constitutes approximately 7% of the population of retarded persons (APA, 1980). As children, these people usually show signs of pronounced speech and motor deficits. It is not until they are school age that they may begin to talk and learn elementary personal hygiene. The focus of training is on self-help skills, rather than academic or vocational training. Many severely retarded adults are able to perform simple occupational tasks under close supervision.

Profound Mental Retardation (IQ < 25)

Less than 1% of mentally retarded persons are in this category. Profoundly mentally retarded children are frequently nonambulatory and unable to speak more than a few words. They often show multiple physical handicaps and suffer from neurological abnormalities. Constant supervision is required but through the use of behavior modification techniques rudimentary self-care skills may be learned. Profoundly mentally retarded persons usually remain in custodial care their entire lives.

Knowing that a person fulfills the criteria for inclusion in a certain group may be helpful in initially developing an idea of what can be expected of this person. There is a danger, however, that once the person has been labeled, he or she will be perceived and treated as a member of this category rather than as a unique individual. The characteristics that he or she has in common with the group may be focused on to the exclusion of the individual's unique qualities that are not characteristic of the group in general. This process, which can have significant consequences for retarded persons, will be discussed more fully in our later section on "labeling."

The danger of overgeneralization exists with any classification system. The four-level system described above also has specific problems of its own. As Maloney and Ward (1979) point out, our current classification system for the retarded is expected to fulfill a number of different scientific, clinical, legal, social-administrative, educational, and political functions. Yet a system that would be appropriate for use in a social-administrative context (i.e., where subgroups must be identified) may yield adverse results when applied to an individual in a clinical setting (i.e., where individual case planning is required).

Despite these problems, diagnosis and classification remain essential. If one is to study the causes of retardation and investigate methods of education and prevention, one's population must be clearly defined. Diagnosis and classification are also necessary in order to determine the extent of the population and the types of services needed so that society may most efficently distribute its resources to aid this population.

Theoretical Models of Mental Retardation

Most definitions and categorization systems for mental retardation have been based on either a medical or statistical model of deviation (Mercer, 1973). The medical model, or pathological model as it is sometimes known, views mental retardation as analogous to physical disorders. Such conditions may exist and affect the individual whether or not anyone is aware of them. From the medical model perspective, "mental retardation" is conceptualized as an underlying disorder that results in symptoms such as academic failure; "normality" is viewed as an absence of pathological symptoms.

The statistical model, on the other hand, conceptualizes mental retardation as below average intelligence. A person receives the label "mentally retarded" if his or her score on an IQ test is a certain distance below the mean. Under the statistical model, "normality" means being of average intelligence (i.e., scoring within a certain range of the mean on an IQ test). One can see that the AAMD definition (Grossman, 1973) of mental retardation is primarily a statistical model, while the Zigler and Balla (Note 1) definition contains elements of both the medical and the statistical model.

Mercer (1973) proposed an alternative model for conceptualizing mental retardation, which is based on neither the medical nor statistical model. She refers to her model as a "social system" perspective. She believes that a person is labeled "mentally retarded" as punishment for inadequate social role performance and views mental retardation as an acquired social role, rather than as an attribute of the individual. She feels "a mental retardate is one who occupies the status of mental retardate and plays the role of the mental retardate in one or more of the social systems in which he participates" (p. 27). According to this view, one is "mentally retarded" if and only if one has been labeled as such by the social system that one lives in. As an illustration of this perspective we mention the case of Daniel Hoffman, who was incorrectly labeled as mentally retarded by a school board psychologist (Payne & Patton, 1981). It was ultimately discovered that he was of above average intelligence but incapacitated by a serious speech defect. So well did Hoffman accept the role of a mentally retarded person that for 12 years he himself believed that he was retarded.

Within this framework the role or label of "mentally retarded person" is construed as social system-specific. Other societies have defined different roles, such as the prophet or buffoon, for persons who would be labeled as "mentally retarded" in Western culture. In agrarian societies, where formal intellectual skills are of little value, persons labeled as mildly mentally retarded by industrialized society would not necessarily be seen as performing their social roles inadequately and hence might not be labeled as deviant (Maloney & Ward, 1979). Thus "mental retardation" involves relationships of individuals to their society. From this perspective it is important to study not only the characteristics of people labeled "mentally retarded" but also the society doing the labeling and society's basis for the labeling.

Despite continuing discussion of these and other definitional issues, the AAMD definition remains by far the most widely used. It is, in fact, the legal definition of mental retardation in the Education for All Handicapped Children Act (PL 94–142). Under the AAMD definition a person must satisfy two criteria to justify the diagnosis of mental retardation. The first of these is significantly subaverage intellectual functioning. In practice this means receiving a low score on an individually administered intelligence test; an IQ score more than two standard deviations below the mean[2] has frequently been used as the cutoff point (Robinson & Robinson, 1976). When the AAMD originally defined mental retardation (Heber, 1959, 1961), an IQ score of 85 (one standard deviation below the mean) was specified as the cutoff point. Because IQ scores show an approximately normal distribution, almost one-sixth of the population of the United States would have been below this cutoff point. Dissatisfaction with the inclusiveness of this level led to the lowering of the cutoff point back to the traditional level of 70 when the AAMD definition was revised (Grossman, 1973). With this change the number of people who could be labeled as mentally retarded on the basis of their IQ score dropped drastically from about 17 to 3% of the population.

Criticisms of Intelligence Tests

The arbitrariness of the cutoff point is just one of many criticisms that have been directed toward the use of intelligence tests in diagnosis of mental retardation. Ultimately, however, most people agree that any system of diagnosis must have some type of cutoff point, be it quantitative or qualitative, and that any such point must be somewhat arbitrary. There is much less agreement, though, on the fairness of intelligence tests used in conjunction with a cutoff point to diagnose retardation.

Over the past several decades an acrimonious debate has developed over an issue of major importance in U.S. society: whether standardized intelligence tests discriminate against nonwhite and non–middle-class individuals. It has repeatedly been found that IQ correlates significantly with both socioeconomic status and race, and that blacks on the average score about 15 points lower on intelligence tests.[3] Critics of intelligence tests feel this is indicative of the white, middle-class biases inherent in the tests and the testing situation. It is no wonder that white middle-class children do better on the tests, the critics say, since theirs is precisely the group for whom the tests were designed; moreover, the designers themselves were white and middle-class. Yet the tests are used to make decisions about children who are not white and middle-class, and critics charge that this is unfair.

A number of specific points have been raised in relation to the alleged unfairness of intelligence tests. First, IQ tests have frequently been criticized for the unrepresentativeness of their standardization samples; the normative group for the 1937 Stanford-Binet was all white, as was the norm group for the Wechsler Intelligence Scale for Children. It did seem unfair to compare individuals to a group that they are not part of; partly for this reason, recent restandardizations of both of these tests have used in their norm groups roughly the same proportion of blacks as found in the general population. However, as Vernon (1979) points out, this does not make a difference in the relative standings of different racial groups. Though the IQ scores reflect somewhat different raw scores than before, the relative score and percentile rank for each individual remains the same, as do the relationships between various racial and ethnic groups. The restandardizations did have one significant effect: they effectively lowered the cutoff point and decreased the number of children of all racial groups who would attain "mentally retarded" status on the basis of their score.

Probably the most hotly debated question is whether or not the item content of intelligence tests is culturally biased. There are several issues involved here. One is whether the same answer can always be considered "correct" for children from different backgrounds. As Williams (1970) points out, the "correct" answer for a white middle-class child to the Stanford-Binet question "What's the thing to do if another boy hits you without meaning to do it?" may be "walk away." However, for a child in a black ghetto this response could be interpreted as a sign of weakness and lead to future physical aggression. The most adaptive response for such a child might actually be "hit him back," a response that would be scored incorrect on the test. Similar examples can be found for the Wechsler Intelligence Scale for Children–Revised.

A second issue concerns the exposure of children to test-relevant materials and learning opportunities. The concept of standardized intelligence tests assumes that all children are about equally familiar with the test materials and have had roughly similar opportunities to develop the skills related to the test. Under this assumption differences in children's performances can be attributed to their abilities and not their backgrounds (MacMillan, 1977). Verbal ability and abstract reasoning are a large part of most intelligence tests. Although these qualities may be highly valued by the dominant culture, this may not be the case with certain subcultures; a child who has grown up in a subculture that places less emphasis on abstract, verbal abilities may not have highly developed skills in this area, and his or her test score may reflect this fact. In such cases the test is measuring not just ability but also experience and background.

There has been much research attempting to ascertain whether intelligence tests are in fact biased. Sandoval and Miille (1980), for example, had minority persons judge which items on the WISC-R they thought were biased. Interrater reliability was quite low. This indicates that it is not clear even to members of minority groups which items, if any, are biased. Further, removing items that appear on their face to be biased ("facial bias") has had little effect on any group's test scores (Cole, 1981). Reschly (1981) reviewed studies assessing item bias using objective techniques such as similarity of factor structure between various groups, internal psychometric properties, and relative item difficulties for different groups. Reschly concluded that "conventional tests are nearly always found to be largely unbiased on the basis of the technical criteria" (p. 1098). If we accept this conclusion, then the question of bias becomes a matter of defining the purpose of the tests, specifying what they are used for, and determining whether they are being misused.

As we noted earlier, the first intelligence test was developed by Binet and Simon to predict academic performance. Such prediction is still crucial. The ultimate test of whether current measures are biased in diagnosing mental retardation is this: Do the measures have equal predictive validity for both black and white children? If the tests consistently predicted less accurately (and in the negative direction) for minority groups, then the tests would indeed be biased. However, Cleary, Humpherys, Kendrick, and Wesman (1975) weighed the evidence available in the research literature and concluded that differential predictive validity for minority groups has yet to be established. In fact Cole (1981) notes that when the same tests and standards are used to predict achievement in black and white students, the tests tend to overestimate the performance of the black students. (See Reynolds, Chapter 4 of this volume, for an extended discussion of this issue.)

There is finally the issue of the misuse of intelligence tests. The case of Daniel Hoffman, mentioned earlier, is merely one of the more extreme examples of misuse that many believe is quite widespread. Use becomes misuse when intelligence tests are administered improperly, when they are assumed to be infallible, when they are presumed to measure a person's total and enduring intellect, when they are used to make decisions that should be based on something other than academic potential, and when they are seen as somehow measuring a person's worth. However, these misuses do not reside in the tests themselves, and the tests have in many respects enhanced the fairness with which children are treated. As Robinson and Robinson (1976) point out,

> There can be no doubt that many individuals have been incorrectly labeled and have been adversely affected by decisions based on the faulty assessment of mental level. It is perhaps unnecessary to point out that such errors are almost always the result of misuse of the tests rather than of the tests themselves. There is little doubt that a much higher percentage of individuals were inappropriately labeled as mentally retarded, or, conversely, not retarded, when such labels depended completely on the subjective appraisal of teachers and physicians. (p. 23)

There would perhaps be less misuse of intelligence tests and fewer problems associated with their use if their name more accurately reflected what they measure. Though they are among the best predictors of academic potential, the heavy importance placed on scholastic ability in the definition and diagnosing of mental retardation can itself be seen as a form of bias. Not all segments of our society have such an emphasis, and it may be unfair to judge nonmembers of the majority culture on this basis. For this reason there has been an increasing interest in the second widely recognized criterion for mental retardation, failure of adaptive behavior, to which we now turn.

Assessment of Adaptive Behavior

Despite, or perhaps because of, the various controversies surrounding intelligence tests, there has been an enormous amount of research on the tests during the past 80 years. This is not the case with the assessment of adaptive behavior. Only since 1959 has failure in adaptive behavior been a criterion for mental deficiency; the conceptualization of what constitutes adaptive behavior and the development of tests for its assessment have lagged far behind that of intelligence and intelligence testing (Maloney and Ward, 1979). Clausen (1972) has gone so far as to suggest that adaptive behavior be removed from the definition of mental retardation until such time as there are reliable and valid means for assessing it. He believes that its inclusion in the definition leads to subjectivity in diagnosis; this in turn, he argues, interferes with the scientific study of mental retardation and may also be unfair or detrimental to retarded persons in clinical settings.

The first instrument designed to measure adaptive behavior is still among the most popular. It is the Vineland Social Maturity Scale (VSMS; Doll, 1936), which has undergone several revisions since first being published (e.g., Doll, 1964). The VSMS was developed to aid in the diagnosis of mental retardation, and Doll was among the first to argue that low social competency should be included in the definition and diagnosis of mental deficiency.

The Vineland differs from intelligence tests in that it does not measure an individual's response to standardized stimuli. It is rather a checklist of 117 behaviors or skills that a child normally would be expected to have developed by a certain age; the behaviors range from asking to go to the toilet to involvement in community activities. The majority of the items deal with self-help and independence or with social responsiblity. The examiner interviews a person who is intimately familiar with the individual being assessed and then decides which behaviors the individual being assessed performs or is capable of in his or her daily life. The interview yields a "social age" (SA); this is then divided by the individual's chronological age (CA) and multiplied by 100 (SA/CA × 100) to yield a "social quotient" (SQ). The Social Quotient is akin to the Intelligence Quotient in that it is designed so that the average child should receive a score of 100, and similar scores at different ages are supposed to have comparable meaning.

Unfortunately this is not the case. The mean score and standard deviation are not the same for different age groups; therefore, scores are not directly comparable across age groups. Silverstein (1971) has developed a table to convert the Social Quotient to Deviation Social Quotient which compensates for this limitation. Another shortcoming of the VSMS is that the standardization sample was relatively small and not representative of the general population. A total of 620 individuals were used, all of whom were white and living in New Jersey. Further, the VSMS was standardized in the 1930s, and child-rearing conventions have surely changed since then. In effect, children rated on the VSMS in 1985 are being compared to white New Jersey children from almost half a century ago; such comparisons are of questionable validity.

Finally, there is also a potential problem in that the Vineland does not rely on direct observation of behavior but rather on the opinion of someone other than the examiner. Since the person whom the examiner obtains the information from must be intimately familiar and hence involved with the individual being assessed, the potential for bias exists. The validity of the assessment, then, is largely dependent on the reliability of the informant. The AAMD Adaptive Behavior Scale (Nihira, Foster, Shellhaas, & Leland, 1974) circumvents this problem to some extent. Unlike the VSMS, the Adaptive Behavior Scale (ABS) may be administered by direct observation or by formal or informal interview. This allows the examiner the freedom to utilize the technique that appears best suited to the specific situation. However, although direct observation in some instances may be a more accurate method of assessment, it is also very time consuming; moreover, the validity of observations can be undermined by the effects of the observer on the child being assessed, by the choice of unrepresentative observation times, or by observer bias. Interpretation of results must take into account the manner in which the information was obtained, as different assessment approaches may not yield comparable results (Millham, Chilcutt, & Atkinson, 1978).

The ABS is divided into two parts. Part I was designed to assess an individual's capacity for functioning independently. Included in the 10 areas are physical development, economic activity, language development, and domestic activity. Part II assesses maladaptive behavior patterns related to personality and behavioral disorders. Included in the 14 areas are violent and destructive behaviors, stereotyped behavior and odd mannerisms, self-abusive behavior, and sexually aberrant behavior.

Although the size of the standardization sample for the ABS was respectable (approximately 4000 people), its breadth was limited. Only retarded, institutionalized persons were used in the normative group. To overcome the limitaton that this poses for the test's valid use, a modified version of the ABS, the public school version (PSV-ABS), was developed (Lambert, Windmiller, Cole, & Figueroa, 1975). Probably the most significant modification was the standardization of the new form; the normative group for the PSV-ABS was a large group of retarded and nonretarded public school children. With the exception of areas that would not be applicable to the school setting, the public school version of the ABS assesses most of the same behavioral domains as the original version.

The authors of the ABS wisely warn against using the ABS alone to determine an individual's level of adaptive functioning. They suggest that the measure be accompanied by other assessment devices. Further, the authors have arranged for the ABS to yield a score on 24 different scales, rather than a global rating. This makes the ABS especially useful for evaluation and planning, though it may complicate its use in screening. However, this latter point may be moot; the measurement of adaptive behavior in the diagnosis of retardation may be the exception rather than the rule. At this early stage in the development of adaptive behavior scales, there is no clear consensus on how they should be used, or which measures to use (some institutions, in fact, use nonstandardized scales of their own devising), or even whether they should be used at all. The idea that a deficit in adaptive behavior should be one criterion for mental retardation has much to recommend, but much remains to be done before this idea fulfills its promise.

PREVALENCE OF MENTAL RETARDATION IN THE UNITED STATES

Estimates of the prevalence of mental retardation in the United States (the number of people who currently meet the criteria for mental retardation and would be so diagnosed if tested) vary from 3% (Farber, 1968; Goodman, Gruenberg, Downing, & Rogot, 1956) to 1% (APA, 1980; Birch, Richardson, Baird, Horobin, & Illsley, 1970). Given the size of the present population, this means that there may be anywhere from 2.3 to 6.9 million retarded persons in the United States. There are several reasons for the disparity of these estimates; we will consider some of the most significant.

While the full definition of mental retardation requires that a person score two standard deviations below the mean on an intelligence test *and* show a deficit in adaptive functioning, most diagnoses are, as we noted above, still made solely on the basis of the individual's IQ score. However, not everyone who scores significantly below average on an intelligence test also scores significantly below average on a measure of adaptive behavior. In fact, Mastenbrook (1978, cited in Sattler, 1982) found that of the 300 children in his study who scored between 50 and 70 on the WISC-R, less than 35% also scored lower than two standard deviations below the mean on a test of adaptive behavior. Thus different prevalence estimates may be arrived at depending on whether one utilizes both tests in making the diagnosis of mental retardation.

Many estimates of prevalence have been based on studies of circumscribed geographical regions. It is known, however, that academic and intellectual attainments differ somewhat according to region (Roberts, 1972). Prevalence estimates may therefore vary as a result of the geographical area studied. This is also true in regard to the type of community (urban or rural) upon which the prevalence estimate is based. Further, since IQ is correlated with socio-economic status (SES) and race, the SES or ethnic mixture of a sample may influence the estimation of the prevalence rate.

One purpose of studying the demographics of mental retardation is to aid in the identification of etiological factors. This knowledge should ultimately enhance our ability to prevent some forms of mental retardation. We will now look at what is currently known about some of the causes of mental retardation.

ORGANIC SYNDROMES

At present there are several hundred known causes of mental retardation; many professionals, however, believe this to be only a fraction of the total number of actual causes. Though the causative agents are numerous and diverse, it is possible to separate them into two broad categories. In some cases mental deficiency is a result of known organic abnormalities and/or damage or malformation in the nervous system. The various causes that fall within this category are frequently referred to as "organic" syndromes. On the other hand in some cases there is no evidence of organic impairment or damage; these causes are often called "nonorganic." We will now look at some of the known organic sources of retardation.

Mental Retardation Caused by Chromosomal Aberrations

Down's Syndrome

This syndrome was first described by the British physician Langdon Down in 1866 and was originally labeled "mongolism" because the facial features of some of the afflicted persons led Down to believe that the syndrome was an evolutionary throwback to the Mongoloid race. However, because of the racist connotations of the term and because the syndrome is not related to the Mongoloid peoples, the term "mongolism" has been replaced by the term "Down's syndrome."

Down's syndrome occurs when a child is born with three #21 chromosomes instead of the normal two; this defect is also known as Trisomy 21. At present there are three known causes for Trisomy 21. The most frequent cause, nondisjunction, accounts for about 90% of the diagnosed cases. In nondisjunction the child receives an extra chromosome 21 from one parent, usually the mother (Uchida, 1973; see Brown, Chapter 6 of this volume, for details.)

Although the exact reason is not clear, there is a strong relationship between maternal age and the probability of having a nondisjunction Down's syndrome child. The chances of having a Down's syndrome child are only about 1 in 2500 for a woman who is 19 years old, while the chances rise to 1 in 45 if the woman is 45 or older (Gibson, 1978); there is a sharp increase in the probability after a woman reaches 35. Overall about 1 in 600 children is born with Down's syndrome. However, in recent years there has been a decrease in the incidence due both to abortion law reform (Hansen, 1978) and to a decrease in the number of women over 35 having children (Penrose, 1967).

Two forms of Down's syndrome each account for about 5% of the cases. Mosaicism occurs when the #21 chromosome pair fails to divide properly after the first cell division subsequent to fertilization. In contrast to nondisjunction, only a portion of the child's cell will have three #21 chromosomes; this usually results in less severe mental retardation and less pronounced physical stigmata (Rynders, Spiker, & Horrobin, 1978).

Only the third form of Down's syndrome, translocation, has the potential for genetic transmission to future generations. Translocation occurs when all or part of two different chromosomes is accidentally joined together during cell division. If this occurs with the #14 and #21 chromosomes during the formation of the parent's gamete or during the first cell division of the fertilized egg, the child may have three #21 chromosomes (but only a total of 46 chromosomes) and manifest Down's syndrome. It is also possible for people to be carriers of the 14-21 translocation without having Down's syndrome themselves. There is about a 10% chance that the child of such a person will have Down's syndrome. A person with translocation Down's syndrome will show a degree of intellectual impairment intermediate between that of nondisjunction Down and mosaic Down.

Stereotypically, Down's syndrome children have been pictured as more affable, affectionate, and docile than other mentally retarded children. Empirically, however, it has been found that there is much variation in personality types between Down's syndrome children and that no one description or stereotype can accurately describe the majority of cases (Gibson, 1978). Similarly, the stereotype that all Down's syndrome children show moderate to severe intellectual impairment has not been substantiated. Rynders, Spiker, and Horrobin (1978) report that in their sample of Down's syndrome children, IQ scores ranged from 14 to 100 and that, in general, mild mental retardation was much more frequent in Down's syndrome children than was commonly believed.

Certain physical features are often associated with Down's syndrome. The hands of persons with Down's syndrome are usually small and the fingers short. The neck, skull, mouth, and nose are also frequently small; the latter lends the face a flat appearance. Often the most noticeable facial feature is upward slanting eyes. There is, however, a wide range of variation among individuals for the presence and severity of these stigmata and any particular person afflicted with Down's syndrome may or may not show any of these features (see Figure 10.1).

Other Chromosomal Aberrations

Occasionally a trisomy of the #13 or #18 chromosome may occur. About 90% of persons born with Trisomy 18 and 80% of those born with Trisomy 13 die before they are 1 year old. Those that survive are severely retarded. Partial deletion of the #5 chromosome may result in the *cri du chat* (cat's cry) syndrome. Because of abnormal development of the larynx, children afflicted with this disorder emit a high-pitched, catlike cry. Individuals suffering from this disorder are usually severely retarded.

Mental Retardation Caused by Single Genes

Recessive genes are responsible for the large majority of single gene conditions causing mental retardation. When a defective (or any other) gene is dominant and follows Mendelian laws of heredity, it is not possible for an individual to

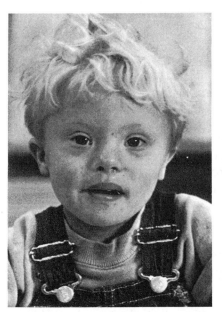

Figure 10.1. Not all children with Down's syndrome are this appealing but many are. (Reprinted with permission from Smith & Wilson, 1973.)

be a carrier of the gene without manifesting the disorder. If the gene controls a trait or condition that is maladaptive, people with this gene will be less likely to successfully adapt, develop, reproduce and pass on the gene. Thus dominant defective genes tend to die out. If, on the other hand, a defective gene is recessive, a person may carry the gene without manifesting the condition. A person will manifest the maladaptive trait only if he or she has received the gene from both parents. If the individual receives the recessive defective gene from only one parent, he or she will be a carrier of the gene but will not manifest the trait and will likely survive to pass on the gene.

There are exceptions to this pattern. Not all genetic traits follow simple Mendelian laws of inheritance. Certain dominant genes show weak penetrance; that is, only a small percentage of persons who possess the dominant gene manifest the trait. This is believed to be due to the effect of other genes on the expression of the dominant gene. In other cases the onset of the symptoms of a defective dominant gene does not occur until after an individual has had children; in such cases the defective gene may be passed on. This is usually not applicable to mental retardation, however, since the full definition of mental retardation requires that the mental deficiency be manifested during the individual's developmental period (APA, 1980; Grossman, 1973).

Phenylketonuria

Phenylketonuria (PKU) is a rare disorder (approximately 1 in 15,000 babies born have PKU) that is the result of a single recessive gene. Infants born with this disorder lack the proper enzymes to metabolize phenylalanine, an amino acid found in many foods, which normally is converted into tyrosine, another amino acid. Excess phenylalanine is converted into phenylpyruvic acid, which causes extensive damage to the nervous system. Individuals who have suffered PKU damage have been described as hyperirritable, psychoticlike and fearful, and usually are severely retarded (Pitt, 1971; Wright and Tarjan, 1957).

Fortunately it is relatively easy to screen newborn infants for PKU through blood or urine tests. Newborn infants who show excessive phenylalanine in their blood or phenylpyruvic acid in their urine can be placed on restricted diets to prevent damage to their nervous system. If the diet is started before the child is 3 months old, retardation can be avoided; if the diet is begun after 3 months, retardation probably will occur (Berry, 1969). However, normal development requires a certain amount of phenylalanine which varies from individual to individual and proper control of the diet is a tricky matter, especially when one is dealing with children who may not fully understand the necessity of the dietary restrictions. Even once dietary decisions have been successfully implemented, the difficulties are not necessarily ended; phenylalanine is found in many foods, and the rigid control which must be exercised over many aspects of the child's food intake may result in personality and behavioral problems.

A further difficulty is that some infants who initially show elevated blood levels of phenylalanine do not have PKU; a number of factors other than PKU may be responsible for this. Care must be exercised so that youngsters are not misdiagnosed and unnecessarily subjected to the dangers of phenylalanine deprivation and the secondary problems that may result from strict dietary control.

Tay-Sachs Disease

This disorder results from a recessive gene that is unusually frequent among Jewish people, particularly those of Ashkenazic (East European) origin. It consists of an inability to properly metabolize lipids (fats), and it results in profound mental retardation and ultimately death, usually occurring by age 3. There is no known cure.

Hypothyroidism

This syndrome in the past has been known as "cretinism," a term that seems likely to follow mongolism into obscurity. Insufficient levels of thyroxin (thyroid hormone) result in underdevelopment of the nervous system, moderate to severe mental retardation, and physical stigmata characteristic of the eighteenth-century stereotype of the "cretin" (i.e., small stature, a relatively large head with coarse, heavy features, and dry, scaly, ashen skin). Besides genetically determined thyroid deficiency, there are numerous other causes of hypothyroidism. Physical damage to the thyroid gland occurring during the birth trauma or resulting from infectious diseases such as diphtheria and insufficient dietary intake of iodine all may cause hypothyroidism.

Hypothyroidism does not always result in mental deficiency, however; only at certain developmental levels will hypothyroidism result in mental retardation. If hypothyroidism occurs after the brain has developed, retardation seldom occurs. If, however, the condition develops in utero or in infancy and is untreated, mental retardation will result. Certain other potential causes of mental retardation (e.g., maternal illnesses) may similarly exert their damaging effect only when they occur at certain developmental levels. In general, one must take into consideration the developmental level of the individual when predicting the consequences of some trauma or abnormal environmental condition.

In the case of hypothyroidism, treatment with thyroid extract can prevent mental retardation if initiated before damage occurs, and severe cases are becoming rare. However, early detection is essential; permanent damage begins to occur by the end of the first year of life (Coleman, Butcher, & Carson, 1980).

Nongenetic Organic Causes of Mental Retardation

A developing fetus is vulnerable to a wide variety of aversive conditions. Rubella (German measles) during the first three months of pregnancy, syphilis, radiation from X-rays, and various drugs including alcohol (Chernoff, 1980) have all been shown to cause mental retardation. Blood type incompatibility, anoxia (oxygen shortage) due to prolonged labor or a tangled umbilical cord, and bodily injury sustained during the birth process also may result in neurological damage and intellectual deficit.

Postnatal factors account for a relatively small percentage (6%) of organic mental retardation (Yannet, 1950). Exposure to heavy metals (i.e., lead and mercury) or pesticides, infections such as meningitis or rabies, and physical injury to the head may also cause retardation. Sadly, the two main sources of head injuries to children are unnecessary byproducts of modern society: child abuse and automobile accidents.

Malnutrition, both prenatal and postnatal, has frequently been studied as a possible cause of mental deficiency and retardation. Studies utilizing infrahuman species have shown that undernourishment and unbalanced diets can result in improper brain development and deficits in learning ability (e.g., Goldberger, Ausman, & Boelkins, 1980; Joffe, 1969). Similar effects may result from the severe malnutrition that sometimes occurs in underdeveloped nations (Ricciuti, 1977; Vernon, 1969). The effects of the mild and moderate forms of improper nourishment that exist in Western countries are more difficult to ascertain, however. It is hard to separate the effects of malnutrition from the general effects of poverty, with which malnutrition is highly correlated. Further, collecting accurate information on people's food consumption is very difficult.

Despite these methodological complexities, most experts believe that the malnutrition found in the United States is generally not severe enough to cause permanent neurological deficiencies (Ingalls, 1978). However, the possibility exists that undernourishment may indirectly cause mental deficiency and retardation. Children who are preoccupied with obtaining food or apathetic because they are hungry may not be motivated to pay attention to academic activities or develop their mental abilities.

PSYCHOSOCIAL CONDITIONS RELATED TO MENTAL RETARDATION

Severe Sensory and Social Deprivation

Extreme impoverishment of social and sensory stimulation is known to result in mental retardation. Itard's "Wild Boy of Aveyron" is a classic example (assuming that Itard and not Pinel was correct as to the cause of Victor's condition). A number of cases have been reported more recently in which children placed under extreme environmental restrictions by their guardians showed moderate to severe mental retardation (eg., Koluchova, 1972; Patton & Gardner, 1963). Curtiss (1977) relates the poignant case of a young girl named Genie whose father was unable to tolerate noise and forced her to remain isolated in a small bedroom in the back of their house for 11 years. When she was finally discovered and released at age 13, she was functioning at the level of a 1-year-old child. Two years after being released her intellectual ability had increased to the level of about a 7-year-old. Though she has made impressive gains in overcoming her early history and at present lives in a board and care facility, most consider it unlikely that Genie will ever be able to fully compensate for her early experiences or be able to live independently.

Deprivation experiences less extreme than those of "attic" children like Genie may also inhibit mental development. In the past, children raised in institutions where they received minimal physical and social stimulation have been found to show intellectual deficits when compared to children raised at home (Dennis & Narjarian, 1957; Spitz, 1945). It has been found, however, that the quality and amount of stimulation that the child receives within the institution makes a critical difference. Skeels and Dye (1939) studied 24 children originally diagnosed as mentally retarded while living in an orphanage where they interacted minimally with adults or other children. Thirteen of these children were transferred to another institution where they became the focus of attention for a group of mentally retarded young women. Subsequently it was found that the mean IQ score of the 11 children who had remained in the institution decreased by approximately 26 points, while the mean score of the 13 children who had been transferred and received the extra attention increased by about 27 points. In a 30 year follow-up, Skeels (1966) found that all 13 of the children who had been transferred were either holding skilled jobs or were married women and were leading "normal" lives, while the 11 who had remained in the orphanage were either holding menial labor jobs or still institutionalized.

There were several methodological shortcomings in this study, however. Subjects were not randomly assigned to conditions; in fact, the control group was created post hoc, after the data for the experimental group had been collected and analyzed. Further, the average IQ score for the mothers of the experimental group children (for those mothers for whom it was possible to obtain scores) was 8 points higher than that of the control group mothers. However, the average initial IQ for the control children was 22 points higher than that of the experimental group; it would probably be unreasonable to conclude that the difference in outcomes for the two groups was caused primarily by the methodological shortcomings.

Mental Retardation Accompanying Psychiatric Disorder

Included in the AAMD etiological classification system is a category for mental retardation following a psychiatric disorder when there is no evidence of neuropathology (Grossman, 1973). This is based on the supposition that emotional problems can sufficiently interfere with cognitive functioning to cause significant impairment in intellectual functioning and adaptive behavior (i.e., mental retardation). Methodological complexities have made this a difficult issue to study. Psychiatric disturbances often make it a demanding or impossible task to assess an individual's intelligence accurately. The fact that these disturbances may disrupt the assessment of intelligence does not, however, necessarily mean that intellectual functioning itself has been disrupted. Maloney and Steger (1972), in fact, found no relationship between severity of mental illness and general intelligence.

The subjects of this study were not children, however. It is possible that the effects of psychiatric disturbances on intelligence may be dependent on the developmental level of the afflicted individual, much as the effects of hypothyroidism are. Maloney does state elsewhere (Maloney & Ward, 1979) that low intelligence may result from psychiatric disturbances such as autism or childhood schizophrenia. But as Achenbach (1982) points out, "while emotional problems no doubt can interfere with cognitive functioning, we do not know whether they actually do reduce functioning to the retarded range in many cases" (p. 229).

SOCIOCULTURAL OR CULTURAL-FAMILIAL RETARDATION

The causes of mental retardation that we have discussed thus far have all been pathological in nature. That is, they represent some environmental or biological element that is dysfunctionally aberrant. In these cases the resulting degree of intellectual impairment is usually moderate, severe, or profound; mental retardation resulting from these sources occurs with about the same frequency in all social classes. However, the majority (approximately 75%) of mental deficiency is not associated with any specific, identifiable pathology (Table 10.1). The level of severity in these cases is usually mild and is generally associated with subaverage intellectual functioning in some immediate family members and a substandard environment. This type of mental retardation has been known as "cultural-familial retardation" or, more recently, as "retardation associated with psychosocial disadvantage" (Grossman, 1973). Unlike pathologically based retardation, cultural-familial retardation is most prevalent in lower SES groups. The question of why this relationship occurs has not been satisfactorily resolved, and disagreement over this question has continued to fan the flames of the nature/nurture controversy.

When Heber (1959, 1961) first described cultural-familial retardation in the AAMD manual, he noted that at that time it was not known whether this form of mental deficiency resulted from environmental or genetic factors or a combination of the two. Despite the fact that there is now no more of a consensus among professionals than there was then as to relationship between genetics and mild mental retardation (Payne & Patton, 1981), the more recent AAMD manuals (Grossman 1973, 1977) appear to assume an exclusively environmental etiology.[4] Many professionals in the field believe this assumption to be premature. We now will review evidence relevant to this issue.

It should be kept in mind while studying this issue that it would be conceptually incorrect to state that either heredity or the environment is responsible for "intelligence." It is only possible to say that in a specifically defined

Table 10.1.   Estimated Prevalence of Mental Retardation According to Etiology

Etiology	Number	Percentage
Phenylketonuria (PKU)	17,900	0.27
Hypothyroidism	10,200	0.15
Other disorders of metabolism	63,900	0.95
Fiberous growths	33,200	0.49
Down's syndrome	199,400	2.95
Cranial anomalies	63,900	0.95
Undetermined congenital cerebral defect	214,800	3.18
Maternal infections and intoxications	117,700	1.74
Physical prenatal injury	35,800	0.53
Other prenatal causes	210,000	3.11
Prematurity	135,000	2.00
Mechanical injury at birth	53,700	0.80
Anoxia at birth	135,500	2.01
Postnatal physical injury	63,900	0.95
Other postnatal causes	102,300	1.52
Unknown structural reactions	258,300	3.83
Cultural-familial or psychosocial disadvantage	5,062,500	75.00

Source: Adapted from Ingalls (1978). Assumes a U.S. population of 225 million, a prevalence rate of 3% for mental retardation, and that 25% of retardation is organically based. This table is not presented as a definitive statement on exact prevalence rates; its purpose is rather to give the reader a general idea of the number of retarded persons of each etiology.

population within a particular environment a certain proportion of the variability in intelligence test scores between groups or individuals is attributable to variability in one factor or the other. The proportion of variance in intelligence (or any other trait) attributable to variance in genetic factors is known as the "heritability" of the trait, and will vary across different racial groups and different environments. If the individuals and groups being studied were to live in an environment that was completely homogeneous (clearly impossible), any variability in intelligence would have to be attributable to genetic factors. This decreased environmental effect is analogous to the attenuation of a correlation coefficient by restriction of range. With increases in the heterogeneity of the environment, the variability of intelligence would also increase as the environment began to have an impact; the proportion of variability attributable to environmental factors would thus increase accordingly. The same is true in regard to heredity. The more genetically similar individuals or groups are, the less the differences in heredity could contribute to variability in intelligence and the smaller the proportion of variability in the trait that could be attributed to genetics. Thus the heritability of a trait is not merely an attribute of the trait but is also a function of the population and the environment that this population lives in.

Most of the evidence for the existence of genetic effects on intelligence comes from research with pairs of individuals who have different degrees of genetic and environmental similarity. Some of the strongest evidence comes from twin studies, which utilize the fact that monozygotic twins share identical genetic backgrounds. Intelligence test score correlations for monozygotic twins who were raised together in the same household (MZT) will reflect the fact that they share similar environments and identical heredities. A correlation between monozygotic twins who were raised apart (MZA; i.e., one or both adopted out) should be a result of only their shared genes, since they have not shared environmental effects. One can compare the correlation between dizygotic twins who were raised together (DZT) and the correlation between unrelated siblings (i.e., one or both are adopted) raised together (URT). The former share on the average 50% of their genes while the latter would share environments but no genes.

Vernon (1979) reports the average intelligence test score correlation coefficient as .87 for MZT twins, .74 for MZA twins, .56 for same-sex DZT twins, and .24 for URT children. There are several important comparisons here.

1. MZA share identical heredities but not environments, whereas URT share environments but no genes. Thus the correlation for the former should be a reflection of genetic factors, while the correlation for the latter should be a function of environmental factors. The MZA correlation (.74) is more than three times that of the URT correlation (.24).

2. MZT and DZT twins and URT children all share similar environments (within pairs) but varying degrees of heredity. Thus if environmental factors were the only ones affecting intelligence, the three types of pairs should show similar correlation. However, as one increases the amount of shared heredity from .00 (URT) to .50 (DZT) to 1.00 (MZT) there is a concomitant increase in the correlation (.24–.56–.87).

3. A third important comparison is between the MZT and MZA twins. The correlational value for the MZA (.74) twins, contrasted to that of the MZT (.87) twins, shows that the effect of increasing similarity of environments is apparently less than that of increasing heredity.

These comparisons appear to indicate a substantial genetic component for intelligence, apparently larger than the environmental component. There are several difficulties in interpreting these figures, however. First, it is possible that since MZT twins are more similar to each other than DZT twins, they may be treated more similarly by their guardians. Thus the larger MZT correlation could occur because they have more similar environments than the DZT pairs. Second, twins who are adopted out may not be randomly placed in their new environments (i.e., their adoptive homes). Adoption agencies tend to place children in environments that are similar to that of their biological families. The correlation for MZA twins' intelligence may therefore also be a function of environmental as well as genetic similarities. Finally, two children raised in the same family may experience somewhat different environments, particularly when one is adopted, so the URT correlation may underestimate the true effect of the environment. One must remember that while it is possible for certain children to share identical genetic backgrounds (i.e., monozygotic twins), it is impossible for any two children to share completely identical environmental backgrounds; nor is it possible to accurately quantify the similarity between two environments. Thus the similarity of genetic backgrounds can range from .00 (URT) to 1.00 (MZA and MZT), whereas the range for the similarity of environmental backgrounds must be shorter. This restriction of range will artificially decrease the size of environmental correlations.

A second strategy for assessing genetic effects on intelligence is to ascertain whether adopted children's IQ correlate more highly with that of their adopted or biological parents. (In practice it is usually not feasible to obtain the biological father's score and only the mother's is used.) All children receive and share 50% of their genes with each of their biological parents; adopted children share similar environments but no genes with their adoptive parents. Thus a correlation between an adopted child and his biological parents would reflect the role of genetic factors, while a correlation between the child and his or her adopted parents would reflect the role of environmental factors.

Once again one must take into account the possibility of selective adoption placement. However, in this case the effect would be to artificially raise the environmental correlation (i.e., the correlation between the children and their adopted parents). Despite potential biasing in the direction of environmental factors, it has been found rather consistently that children's IQ scores are more highly correlated with those of their biological parents than those of their adoptive parents (Achenbach, 1982).

Taken together, the evidence from twin and adoption studies indicates that any claim that IQ scores reflect "environment only" would be premature. While the exact proportions that environmental and genetic factors each contribute to the development of intelligence in the populations studied are far from being specified, it does seem clear that it is unjustified to claim that genetic factors are not involved. Based on the current state of knowledge, the most valid model would include both environmental and genetic factors affecting the development of intelligence, with the latter apparently contributing somewhat more than the former, at least in most populations and environments studied thus far.

These findings have important implications for the study and prevention of mental retardation, since subaverage intellectual functioning is a major part of the definition of mental retardation. On the other hand, the definition also requires a deficit in adaptive functioning and little is known thus far about the environmental and genetic effects on adaptive behavior. It would not be surprising, however, if environmental effects played a somewhat larger role in determining adaptive behavior than IQ scores.

Thus far we have discussed two general types of mental retardation: retardation resulting from various pathological influences and cultural-familial (nonpathological) retardation. The latter has sometimes been viewed as essentially the low end of the normal distribution of intelligence, a completely integral part of that distribution (e.g., Zigler, 1967). From this viewpoint, cultural-familial retarded persons are seen, in terms of intelligence, as quantitatively different from nonretarded persons, not qualitatively different.

A normal distribution is the result of a myriad of factors influencing the variable in question (Hays, 1981). In the case of intelligence, a vast constellation of nonpathological environmental and genetic factors are believed by many to interact with each other to shape a person's intellectual abilities (Robinson & Robinson, 1976). (The random sources of error associated with the assessment of IQ also contribute to the formation of a normal distribution.) However, sometimes something radically out of the ordinary (e.g., Down's syndrome or brain damage) occurs in an individual's genetic or environmental background and exerts a disruptive influence on the intellectual potential that this individual has received from the constellation of nonpathological environmental and genetic factors. If this pathological abnormality is sufficiently intense, mental retardation will result.

Overall, the distribution of IQ scores is in fact fairly normal (Vernon, 1979). However, at the low end of the IQ distribution (below 55) there is an abnormally high proportion of the population (see Table 10.2). It is evidently the inclusion of these retarded persons with neuropathological etiologies (e.g., brain damaged persons, persons with chromosomal abnormalities, etc.) that results in this bulge or excess beyond the expectation based on the normal curve. The distribution of IQ scores would be about normal if the curve included only those people without signs of organic abnormality (i.e., nonretarded persons and cultural-familial retarded persons). Zigler (1967) has suggested that the curve for the actual distribution of IQ scores is in fact a combination of two separate curves, one representing persons with organic abnormalities, the other representing persons without organic abnormalities. If the curve representing the organic group had a mean IQ of about 35 and the curve representing the nonorganic group a mean IQ of about 100 and both were distributed normally with the same standard deviation, combining the two curves would result in a curve closely paralleling the actual IQ distribution (see Figure 10.2).[5] Thus there may be two different basic etiological types of mental retardation and two different populations of retarded persons each,

Table 10.2.   Theoretical and Estimated Prevalence of Mental Retardation in the United States

IQ	Expectations Based on Normal Curve	Estimated Prevalence	Excess Number	Excess Percentage
0–20	64	112,500	112,440	175,688
20–50	199,996	450,000	250,020	125
50–70	6,716,900	6,784,400	67,500	1
Total	6,916,960	7,346,900	429,960	6

Source: Adapted from Dingman and Tarjan (1960), assuming a U.S. population of 225 million. Excess percentage refers to the excess over the normal expectations divided by the normal expectation, multiplied by 100.

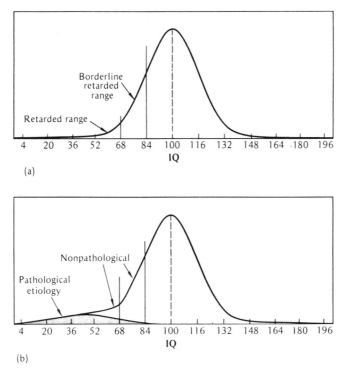

Figure 10.2. Comparison of the theoretical distribution of Stanford-Binet IQs with the approximate form of the distribution actually found.(Reprinted by permission from Achenbach, 1982.) (*a*) Distribution of Stanford-Binet IQs expected from the normal curve. (*b*) Approximate distribution of IQs actually found, with individuals having signs of pathological etiology separated from those not having signs of pathological etiology.

perhaps, with different potentials and needs. This, at least, is Zigler's suggestion, and it is one part of the rationale offered by Zigler and Balla (Note 1) for their proposed biaxial classification system.

PERSONALITY, BEHAVIORAL, AND COGNITIVE DEVELOPMENTAL CORRELATES OF MENTAL RETARDATION

The primary attribute common to these diverse forms of retardation is an intellectual deficit. This is true by definition. However, certain behavioral and personality characteristics also tend to occur more frequently in retarded than in nonretarded persons. Some of these appear to be secondary consequences of mental deficiency and some may result, in part, from being labeled "mentally retarded."

This is not to ignore what we have previously warned about overgeneralizing. There is much heterogeneity and variability among retarded people and the dangers of stereotyping are real. However, there do appear to be certain behavior and personality patterns that arise more frequently in retarded groups. The important point to remember is that we are talking here about groups of retarded persons and what is said may or may not apply to any specific individual.

For many retarded children one result of mental deficiency may be frequent failure; such experiences may be prolonged until the youngsters are identified as mentally retarded and accorded special treatment. Before a retarded child is identified as such the expectations of teachers and other adults may be unrealistic in relation to the child's actual abilities; as a consequence, the child may be given tasks that are essentially out of reach intellectually. Once a child has been identified as mentally retarded, expectations can be adjusted to accord with the child's ability. (There is then a danger that adult expectations may become excessively pessimistic. This issue will be addressed shortly).

One consequence of early exposure to failure is that retarded children often lack confidence in their ability to succeed, even at tasks they could master (Zigler & Balla, 1982). It is possibly a result of this pattern that retarded children sometimes settle for partial success rather than attempting to find complete solutions (Balla & Zigler, 1979). Retarded children can become so concerned with avoiding failure that they do not persist in efforts to succeed (Weisz, 1982). This lack of self-confidence and the concomitant self-defeating and "helpless" behavior can apparently be affected by current success and failure experiences. Further failure may exacerbate these problems (Weisz, 1981a), while success experiences may mitigate them (Ollendick, Balla, & Zigler, 1971). Thus one important reason for identifying and understanding retarded children is to help ensure that realistic expectations may be set for them and that the potentially debilitating effects of repeated failure may be avoided.

Labeling

One hypothesized effect of labeling has been its effect on peer acceptance. As we noted earlier, Corman and Gottlieb (1977) found that in most cases retarded children were less accepted than their nonretarded peers. It was unclear, however, whether these peer attitudes were the result of the "mentally retarded" label or something about the appearance or behavior of the retarded youngsters. Some evidence suggests that the label alone may have significant effects.

Dent (1967) found that college students were less interested in interacting with a hypothetically described person when this person was labeled "mentally retarded" than when the hypothetically described person was unlabeled. However, some researchers (e.g., Gottlieb, 1974) have found that the "mentally retarded" label does not seem to have a significant effect on attitudes toward retarded children, while other researchers (e.g., Foley, 1979) have found that the "mentally retarded" label results in an increase in positive responses from other children. Thus it appears that the effects of the label vary according to the specific circumstances in which it is used (i.e., in this case the different research methodologies).

Gottlieb (1975) attempted to delineate this effect more precisely. He had young children rate a child they observed on a film. Half saw a film of a passive boy and the other half a film of an aggressive boy. Within each of these conditions, half the subjects were told the boy was mentally retarded and half just that he was a fifth grader. The label had no effect on how the children rated the passive boy. However, the "mentally retarded" aggressive boy was more negatively rated than the unlabeled aggressive boy. Budoff and Siperstein (1978) found that nonretarded children react less negatively to the incompetent behavior of a labeled child than they do that of an unlabeled child. Thus it appears the effect of the label depends in part on the behavior of the person labeled.

It may, however, be an oversimplification to interpret the results of the above studies as strictly effects of the label. The expectations people have about someone labeled "mentally retarded" may in part be based on prior contact with retarded persons. Thus the reaction people have to the label may be more than just a response to a stereotype; their response may be also based on prior experience with the actual behavior of retarded individuals.

There is evidence that labeling may have significant effects on the manner in which adults think about and respond to retarded children. Bromfield (Note 2) showed young adults a film in which a child attempted but was unable to solve a puzzle; his subjects were more likely to ascribe the child's failure to low ability and to predict future failure when the child was labeled "mentally retarded" than when the child was unlabeled. This occurred despite the fact that written descriptions portrayed the "retarded" and unlabeled child as identical in mental age, general achievement, and ability on the specific task shown on the film. And, of course, the same film was shown to both groups. Other evidence suggests that the "mentally retarded" label can decrease the amount an adult feels a child should be encouraged to persist at a difficult task (Weisz, 1981b; Yeates & Weisz, in press). A disinclination to encourage a retarded child to persist could have an impact on the child that goes beyond the original task. It could adversely influence the child's self-concept, undermine motivation to persevere when the going gets tough, and encourage the development of what has been called "learned helplessness" (Abramson, Seligman, & Teasdale, 1978).

It appears, however, that these labeling effects are not equally strong for all groups of people. Yeates and Weisz (in press) found that unlike college undergraduates and regular classroom teachers, special education teachers and graduate students in special education were not strongly influenced by the "mentally retarded" label. In contrast to the responses of the first two groups, the special education teachers and graduate students rated themselves equally likely to urge a child to persist in the face of failure regardless of whether the child was labeled "mentally retarded." The authors concluded that experience with retarded children apparently moderates labeling effects.

Developmental Delay Versus Difference Controversy

An important assumption of the Bromfield (Note 2), Weisz (1981a, 1981b), and Yeates and Weisz (in press) studies is that a retarded and a nonretarded child matched on mental age (MA) will have similar cognitive abilities. This assumption is one part of what has been called the "developmental" position on mental retardation (Zigler, 1969). This position includes the view that the cognitive and intellectual development of retarded and nonretarded individuals follows the same sequence of steps or stages (similar sequence hypothesis), but that retarded individuals develop at a slower rate and that their cognitive development ceases at a lower ceiling than nonretarded individuals. Further, it is hypothesized that at each different stage or level of development there is a similar structure or pattern of cognitive abilities for both groups (similar structure hypothesis). Thus when retarded and nonretarded children have been equated for developmental level (by matching them on MA), their cognitive abilities should be similar, except for the effect of differential life experiences.

The "difference" hypothesis, on the other hand, postulates that even when retarded and nonretarded persons have been equated for developmental level, the retarded individuals are deficient in certain cognitive areas, and that the formal reasoning processes of retarded and nonretarded individuals are not the same (see, e.g., Milgram, 1973). Some who hold this view also argue that the cognitive development of retarded persons is not merely slower and subject to a lower ceiling but is innately different from that of nonretarded persons. According to this hypothesis, the sequence of development and the structure of cognitive abilities within a given stage or level of development are different for retarded and nonretarded persons.

Weisz and Yeates (1981) and Weisz and Zigler (1979) reviewed studies in which MA-matched retarded and nonretarded children were compared for performance on Piagetian-type tasks. They found that the preponderance of evidence appeared to support the developmental position for both the similar structure and the similar sequence hypotheses. However, when studies which failed to exclude organically impaired persons from the subject pool were included, the evidence was inconsistent, particularly with regard to the similar structure hypothesis. It appears that the developmental position holds reasonably well for retarded individuals who are not organically impaired, at least in relation to Piagetian measures of cognitive development.

If this finding is in fact valid, an important implication is that nonorganically impaired retarded persons should not be regarded as "abnormal" but instead as manifesting a developmental delay. In other words, intellectually nonorganically retarded individuals are quantitatively different from nonretarded individuals, not qualitatively different.

INSTITUTIONAL AND COMMUNITY ADJUSTMENT

Effects of Institutionalization on Mentally Retarded Children[6]

The effects of institutionalization appear in part to be a function of the characteristics of the particular institution involved. Zigler and Williams (1963), for example, studied retarded people three years after admission to an institution described as "depriving"; these individuals showed a decrease in IQ together with an increased desire for and responsiveness to social reinforcement (i.e., increased dependency). However, at another institution described as one of the finest in the country, retarded residents showed an increase in IQ and a decrease in dependency after three years (Zigler, Balla, & Butterfield, 1968). One factor apparently affecting how dependent residents become on adult attention is the size of the institution (Zigler & Balla, 1977); the larger the institution, the more dependent the residents became. The authors hypothesized that this occurs because large institutions are less personal and residents are more deprived of adult attention and support. Surprisingly, the amount of money spent per day on each resident evidently was not a significant factor affecting the dependency of residents.

Other characteristics of institutions also appear to have an impact on the behavior of retarded residents. From the same study, Zigler and Balla report that the higher the employee turnover rate, the higher the ratio of aides to residents, and the larger the number of individuals in a living unit, the more wary of adults retarded residents were. Wariness was gauged by observing how close retarded individuals sat to a stationary adult and how this distance changed over time. Contrary to what we might expect, lower levels of wariness were found in institutions with institution-oriented care practices (e.g., where there were rigidly structured routines to make the functioning of the institution easier for the institution) than in resident-oriented settings (e.g., where there was flexibility in the routine that took account of individual circumstances). Zigler and Balla hypothesized that this may have occurred because the structure of the institution-oriented care practices may have made the residents' lives more predictable, increasing their sense of security. However, the institution-oriented practices were also associated with what the authors believe to be an excessive degree of conformity.

Critical in the current climate of normalization is the extent to which institutions foster or hinder self-sufficiency and independent functioning. Institutions apparently vary widely in regard to this variable. Klaber (1969) found that across institutions the average score on the Hartford Self-Sufficiency Scale for subjects matched on intellectual ability varied by almost 50%. The institutions that showed the lowest levels of resident self-sufficiency also showed the lowest levels of resident adjustment or happiness.

Klaber also found that in "effective" institutions (i.e., where the residents were happier and more self-sufficient) the attendants devoted more time to actual care and direct contact with the retarded youngsters than the attendants in "ineffective" institutions. However, the self-reported attitudes of attendants at the two types of institutions toward the residents and the institution did not vary significantly; nor did the "effective" institutions differ from the "ineffective" institutions in regard to employee-patient ratio, institutional size, or salary of the attendants. Finally, there was no relationship between frequency or even existence of in-service training and the "effectiveness" of an institution.

These findings, in conjunction with those of Zigler and Balla, indicate that the effects of institutionalization are complex. Increasing the amount of money spent or the number of personnel evidently does not guarantee improvements in the quality of institutions. More research is needed to discover means for truly improving institutional care for retarded children.

Personal Factors Affecting Success in Community Placements

A number of different characteristics are apparently related to how successful or unsuccessful a retarded person is in living in the community and/or remaining employed. Vocational failure is apparently more often a result of improper work attitudes than lack of work skills (McCarver & Craig, 1974). IQ (within the mildly retarded range, at least) does not appear to be related to vocational success (Schalock & Harper, 1978). The mental health of the retarded individual does seem to make a difference, though. Fulton (1975) compared demographic characteristics (e.g., gender, IQ, presence of previous work history) of vocationally successful and unsuccessful retarded persons. The only factor he found significantly related to job success was the absence of secondary emotional or psychiatric disturbance. There was, however, a nonsignificant tendency for vocationally successful individuals to reside with their families. Finally, Brolin (1982) recommends that for vocational success retarded individuals must be eager to work, have proper work attitudes, dress appropriately, and act responsibly. In sum, it appears that for mildly retarded persons the key to keeping a job lies not in IQ points but rather in a capacity to act in a responsible and socially appropriate manner.

Successful community living does, however, appear to be related to intellectual level. Schalock and Harper (1978) found that retarded individuals who were successful in independent community living averaged almost 12 points higher in IQ than those who were not successful. They also found that successful individuals were younger (average age of 31 versus 40) and during training had acquired higher levels of independent living skills (clothing care, personal maintenance, etc.) than the unsuccessful individuals. Length of training was related to success in both independent living and employment. It appears then that general intelligence and specific independent living skills are important determinants of a retarded person's adjustment in the community.

However, even those retarded individuals most successful in adjusting to life in the community may not really be that successful compared to nonretarded individuals. In the classic study *The Cloak of Competence*, Edgerton (1967) examined in detail the lives of 48 retarded individuals released from an institution with a good prognosis for independent community living. He found them to be successful in that they had managed to survive in the community; but by most other standards the quality of their lives was poor. Most of these individuals had little job security or stability and few had achieved what could be considered adequate social functioning; few had much of a sense of personal security in their lives. In general, he found that what success a retarded individual was able to achieve in the community was largely dependent on how well he or she was able to enlist the aid of a "benefactor" (a nonretarded spouse, landlady, etc.). Thus even the more "successful" of this group did not appear to be truly living independently.

A major finding of this study was that many of these ex-patients expended a great deal of energy attempting to appear "normal" (i.e., nonretarded and competent). They went to great lengths to deny to their neighbors and themselves that the "mentally retarded" label was in any way appropriate for them. Many blamed their inadequacies on their institutionalization or hid the fact that they had ever been institutionalized and labeled. One individual unable to tell time wore a "broken" watch in order to have an excuse for asking the time. Another excused her inability to read labels in a grocery store by claiming to be too intoxicated to focus her eyes properly. In general, their self-esteem was dependent on how well they could convince themselves and others that they were "normal."

Twelve years later Edgerton and Bercovici (1976) located and revisited 30 members of the original sample. The life circumstances (economic security, social competence, etc.) of almost a third of the group (8) had improved; for a full third of the group (10), though, conditions had deteriorated. The authors did note, however, that many of the group appeared and claimed to being enjoying life more.

Passing for "normal" was much less of a concern than before for many of these individuals; for most of the group this appeared to be an issue of the past. They seemed to be more concerned with enjoying their leisure time and friends. And the group as a whole appeared to be less dependent on the assistance of benefactors. Over half of the group was rated more independent, while none was rated more dependent; and for the large majority of those rated more independent, the decreased reliance on others appeared to be the result of decreased need, rather than a decreased availability of assistance.

The authors concluded that the passage of time may not be sufficient in and of itself to increase the quality of life for retarded individuals in the community. They also, however, raised an important question: whose assessment of success is more valid, the professional's or the retarded individual's?

PREVENTION, EDUCATION, AND CARE ALTERNATIVES FOR MENTALLY RETARDED CHILDREN

As noted earlier, one ultimate goal of much of the etiological research in mental retardation is prevention. Several basic strategies may be employed in pursuing this goal. Current knowledge of the causes of organic mental retardation may be implemented and public awareness of this knowledge increased. For example, through the use of genetic counseling and procedures such as amniocentesis and chorionic villi sampling,[7] persons planning to have children may evaluate the chances of having certain types of retarded children. Their decision whether or not to have the child can thus be made in the context of maximum information. To maximize the utility of our knowledge in this area, it will be necessary to increase public awareness of the availability of genetic counseling and when it is advisable. Similarly, if we can assure that all segments of our society are aware of the pre- and postnatal dangers discussed above and that mothers routinely receive adequate perinatal services, we may be able to decrease the number of children born mentally retarded. Finally, important contributions may be made by efforts to control such potential sources of mental retardation as pesticides and heavy metals in the environment; the success of such efforts, though, may depend more on shifts in the structure and priorities of our society than on individual awareness.

Such pathologically based forms of mental retardation are easier to cope with than the problem of cultural-familial retardation. This should not be surprising, since the nature and cause of cultural-familial retardation are less clearly established. One strategy used thus far to combat cultural-familial retardation has been to target the environment—that is, to increase the quality of the social and physical environment of children considered at risk for retardation. Of all these efforts the most massive has been Head Start.

The Head Start program was initiated during the mid-1960s and was designed to compensate for the environmental deprivation that lower-class children were thought to suffer. Descriptive accounts of the positive effects of Head Start rapidly appeared and optimism was at first high. Substantial gains in IQ were found for participating children. However, it soon began to be reported that these gains were "washed out" once the children were no longer enrolled in Head Start (Cicirelli, 1969; Jensen, 1972). "The Westinghouse Report," as Cicirelli's 1969 report became known, found few significant differences in language development or on achievement tests between children who had been in Head Start one to three years previously and those who had never attended. It was concluded that if Head Start programs were to be successful, they would have to increase the stress on language development, begin with younger children, and lengthen the programs. It was noted, however, that the study did not take account of the variability among programs in terms of design and effectiveness and that the design of the study was entirely post hoc (i.e., all testing was done after the fact, and there was no random assignment of subjects to conditions).

Many proponents of compensatory early education agreed that one reason for the less than hoped for success of Head Start may have been that it was too little, too late; they maintained that interventions lasting a few hours a day for a year or so could not compensate for years of life in a less-than-optimal environment. Following this reasoning, a number of investigations have tried to determine if early and intensive compensatory education can make a difference. Perhaps the best-known study of this type was the Milwaukee Project.

The Milwaukee Project (Strickland, 1971; Garber & Heber, 1977) involved an intervention with children believed to be at high risk for mental retardation. Forty families in Milwaukee, each with a high-risk infant, were divided into control and experimental families. The educational program for experimental children focused on cognitive and language skills. It began soon after the child reached the age of 3 months and was designed to last until the child reached school age. Initially the child was visited daily in his or her home by a teacher; later small groups met at a neighborhood center. Experimental group mothers were trained in child-rearing and domestic skills and also received vocational rehabilitation. Control children were tested at the same regular intervals as the experimental children but received no intervention.

At first there were no measured differences between the experimental and control groups. By age 18 months, however, the mean IQ scores for the groups reportedly began to diverge; by age 9 the experimental group's IQ stabilized a few points above 100, while the control group's mean IQ score was slightly less than 80.

Initially this study was hailed in both professional journals and the popular press. It was viewed as a landmark, showing that intensive efforts could compensate for an impoverished environment. However, a serious question has been subsequently raised as to the validity of the study. Page (1972) notes that the skills the experimental group children were trained in were similar to those specifically measured by the IQ tests used to assess the program's effects. Thus the superiority of the experimental group's IQ scores may have been a reflection of their skill at taking IQ tests rather than of greater intelligence.

More carefully designed and executed studies have found significant positive effects for early compensatory education; however, the effects have not been as dramatic as those reported for the Milwaukee Project (see, e.g., Robinson & Robinson, 1971; Sprigle, 1972). While large, lasting effects on IQ may not be common, it does appear that early compensatory education can decrease the likelihood that a child will be placed in a special class or retained in grade and may also increase pride in academic achievement (Lazar & Darlington, 1982). There are also indications that these programs may increase achievement test scores, though the evidence is somewhat contradictory.

Spicker (1971) attempted to determine what elements were critical to the success of early intervention programs. Reviewing outcome reports for a number of early compensatory projects, he concluded the following:

1.   In general, the programs which produced the largest gains in intellectual development were well supervised and structured and stressed cognitive and academic skills. It also appears important that programs have well defined short- and long-term goals.

2.   One difficulty with many preschool programs has been that they are not geared to the realities of the public school curriculum that the child will eventually face. For example, children may need to be taught the techniques necessary for rote memory tasks, since such tasks are common in most elementary schools. It also may be more valuable for disadvantaged children to improve their general langauge skills than to learn abstract reasoning or critical thinking.

3.   Home intervention contributes little to intellectual development if the child is part of an extended, full-time curriculum. If, however, he or she is part of a more limited program, home intervention can be valuable. It is also possible that home intervention may indirectly have positive effects on siblings who are not part of the program.

4.   Though it has been generally assumed that the earlier intervention starts the more effective it will be, it is not clear that this is actually the case. What evidence there is in support of this position needs to be carefully qualified; it indicates, for example, that for earlier intervention to be more successful, it may be important to take into account the Piagetian stage of the children when planning the curriculum.

5.   If the duration of intervention is to magnify the positive outcome, the program must provide for more advanced skills to be learned in sequence. "More of the same" is probably not sufficient to cause further meaningful increases in development.

6.   Low child/teacher ratios appear to be essential; individualized attention is critically important for disadvantaged children. Teacher aides should as much as possible be used for academic instruction, rather than nonacademic chores (i.e., cleaning up messes, supervising free playtime).

Education of Retarded Children

Realistically it is unlikely that we will ever be able to prevent all or even the majority of cases of mental retardation. There will probably always be individuals needing assistance in compensating for their mental deficiency. While the specific objectives and purposes of education and training for retarded persons will vary according to each individual's circumstances, the overall objective should always be to aid the retarded person in leading as "normal" a life as possible, and to make certain that he or she lives with as few restrictions as possible.

The focus of a retarded child's education and training will depend in part on how severely retarded he or she is. Children who are "educable mentally retarded" (EMR; IQ from about 50 to 70) generally are able to learn basic academic skills such as reading and writing. Their education is usually more pragmatically oriented than that of nonretarded children, however, and an emphasis is commonly placed on developing skills designed to help them live independently (e.g., vocational training or how to use the bus). Children who are "trainably mentally retarded" (TMR; IQ from about 30 to 50), on the other hand, are believed to be generally unable to benefit from an academic education. These children instead are taught self-help skills, simple vocational skills that may be utilized in a sheltered setting and guided toward increased social adjustment. The education of the "profoundly mentally retarded" (PMR; IQ less than 30)[8] generally consists of training in basic self-care skills such as use of the toilet and feeding oneself. Efforts are usually made to develop communication skills. In some cases, however, the individual may be unable to accomplish these goals.

The training and education that a retarded youngster receives may be in part a function of society's willingness to expend the necessary resources. For example, as a result of shifting priorities and efforts to reduce federal spending, the amount of money available for human services such as vocational training of retarded persons has been decreased. As a consequence, many retarded individuals who could benefit from vocational training are not receiving such training.

Beyond the human cost, this policy may actually be fiscally shortsighted and uneconomical. Conley (1973) estimated that the vocational rehabilitation of mildly retarded male adolescents yields an increased lifetime productivity of $14 for every dollar spent (using $2468, in 1970 dollars, as the average cost of vocational rehabilitation for individuals in this group). This ratio is smaller for moderately retarded individuals and for females and obviously decreases as the age of the rehabilitant increases. However, the ratio always was greater than one for the populations Conley studied (which included mildly and moderately retarded men and women) and was usually much greater than one. Thus in the long run it might well be less expensive for society to expend the financial resources necessary to help retarded citizens become productive citizens than it would be to refrain from spending the money.

Regular versus Special Classes

With the push toward "normalization" during the 1970s, there has been a concomitant shift toward placing EMR children who are in public schools in regular classes rather than in separate special education classes. Because random assignment of subjects to treatments is difficult in educational settings, however, the value of "mainstreaming" versus placement in special classes has been difficult to determine. The move toward educating retarded children in regular classes may have been based more on ideological principles than on the empirical evidence available at the time.

Research attempting to delineate the comparative effects of mainstreaming versus special classes has focused on two broad areas: effects on academic achievement and effects on social adjustment (self-concept, peer acceptance, etc.). In regard to the former it appears that the relative effects of regular and special classes depend in part on the ability level of the child (e.g., Budoff & Gottlieb, 1976; Goldstein, Moss, & Jordan, 1965). Children who are more severely impaired intellectually tend to do better academically in special education classes, whereas those who are less impaired and closer to the "average" child in intellectual ability tend to do better in regular classrooms.

This same relationship has been found for retarded children's self-concept. In Budoff and Gottlieb's (1976) study, "low-able" children had more favorable attitudes toward themselves when they were in special classes, whereas "high-able" children had better attitudes when they were in regular classes. The acceptance of retarded children in regular and special classes by their nonretarded peers appears to be partly a function of the labeling effects we discussed earlier and partly a function of sheer contact. Evidence indicates that at least in some cases peer acceptance decreases as the degree of contact between retarded and nonretarded children increases (Goodman, Gottlieb, & Harrison, 1972; Gottlieb & Budoff, 1973). In general, retarded children in special classes appear to be more accepted than those in regular classes.

At least two independent factors may be affecting the social integration of retarded children. Gottlieb, Semmel, and Veldman (1978) found that peer acceptance was related to peer perceptions of academic competence, while peer rejection was related to inappropriate behavior; these two dimensions appeared to be independent. The increased contact between retarded and nonretarded children that results from regular class placement probably also results in an increased awareness by the nonretarded children of any academic deficiencies or misbehavior on the part of the retarded children. This may be partly responsible for the low level of social integration of the retarded children into regular classes.

There are alternatives for retarded children, intermediate between "mainstreaming" and self-contained special classes. Children may remain a part of their regular class while sometimes visiting a "resource room" where they receive extra instruction. The amount of time spent in the resource room may vary from an hour or so a day to the entire day excluding nonacademic periods (lunch, recess, physical education, etc.). The child can thus maintain contact with his or her age peers yet still receive needed attention. Although the use of resource rooms is a fairly new innovation, there is evidence for their value. Walker (1974) compared the effect of the resource room to that of special classes on the academic and social progress of matched groups of retarded children in Philadelphia public schools. After two years she found that the resource room children surpassed the special class children in reading, vocabulary, and social behavior; the groups did not differ in self-concept, arithmetic, or social adjustment. She concluded that the resource room was at least as effective a method as special classes for helping educate retarded children, and that it reduces both the stigma and expense involved in special class placement.

In schools where the number of children needing special services is not sufficient to justify a resource room or special classes, services may be provided by an "itinerant teacher." This teacher may visit the school periodically and work with children individually or in small groups. A school may also utilize the services of a consultant who has minimal direct contact with pupils but instead assists regular class teachers in planning instruction for retarded children.

In addition to the educational methods traditionally used in classrooms, recently developed techniques such as behavior modification may be used in the education and training of retarded persons (Thompson & Grabowski, 1972). Operant conditioning principles such as response shaping and extinction may effectively and efficiently help retarded children learn desired new behaviors and reduce unwanted maladaptive behaviors. The broad variety of behaviors that may be affected by these techniques includes academic and language proficiencies, self-care, vocational skills, and social behaviors. For example, O'Brien and Azrin (1972) used behavioral techniques to teach institutionalized retarded individuals to feed themselves in a socially acceptable manner. The individuals received one daily training meal in a private room with a trainer. During this meal, shaping and imitation, time-outs and extinction, and verbal reinforcement were used to establish and then maintain proper eating habits. At the end of training the "eating errors" had decreased significantly from the baseline rate and were well below the rate of a control group who had received no training. Moreover, the rate of "eating errors" did not significantly differ from an important external criterion—the behavior of nonretarded diners in a public restaurant.

As a final test the training group was evaluated under more normal, group eating conditions, where they in fact maintained their improved behavior. Such responses generalization does not always occur, however. A major difficulty with many operant programs is that responses learned under one set of conditions may not be maintained when conditions or settings change. There is also a danger with operantly conditioned responses: unless external reinforcement of the response is carefully shifted to internal self-reinforcement, the individual may stop responding when the specific, external reward contingencies are dropped. It is possible, though, to teach behavioral techniques to parents so that a child's behavioral changes may be sustained, even if the child is not capable of self-reinforcement.

Another recently developed technique gaining in popularity is the "therapeutic pyramid" (Whalen & Henker, 1971). Professional therapists train and then supervise retarded adolescents and young adults, who in turn teach more severely retarded children new adaptive behaviors. This strategy can economically increase the effectiveness of professionals and help severely retarded youngsters as well. In addition, significant gains have been found in the behavior and self-concept of the "assistants" (Coleman et al., 1980).

Care Alternatives Outside the Home

Sometimes, however, despite the efforts expended and the techniques used, it may not be possible for a child to be successfully educated in public schools or to remain with his or her family in the community; in these cases a decision to institutionalize the child may be made. This decision is sometimes the result of an inability (or occasionally an unwillingness) on the part of the family to properly care for the child. The severity of retardation is one factor that may determine whether a family institutionalizes a particular retarded child (MacMillan, 1977). As the degree of mental deficiency increases, the amount of time and money that the family must expend caring for a child also increases. The family's resources may be taxed beyond their limits, and the decision to institutionalize the child may become almost unavoidable. In other cases, the decison to institutionalize may be made because the retarded child has serious behavioral or emotional problems; these may make it difficult or impossible for the parents to manage the child at home. Sometimes the decision is made because the parents fear that a retarded child living at home may have a negative effect on nonretarded siblings.

Today there are alternatives to the traditional high-density state institution. One of these, the regional center, is now being widely utilized. Such centers usually house a smaller number of individuals (approximately 50–500 residents) and serve a more restricted geographic area than state institutions. This allows children to reside closer to their parents and preserves the possibility of continuing contact with the family neighborhood. Even smaller than regional centers are community or group homes; these sometimes admit school-age children, who may continue to attend public school. These facilities tend to be less structured and to allow more freedom than either the state institutions or the regional centers. Group homes are usually more similar to private residences than institutions (e.g., more comfortable furnishings, inside locks on bathroom doors); but certain quasi-institutional practices frequently remain (e.g., residents typically share bedrooms and have curfews; Baker et al., 1977).

Further, it is possible that some of the benefits believed to be associated with these smaller residential options may not actually materialize. Balla (1976), in a review of some of the relevant literature, concluded that the distance parents and friends resided from the institution was a relatively minor factor in determining the frequency of visits. He did note, though, that retarded individuals in group homes were more likely to visit their families than those living in institutions.

Finally, we should note that some retarded children are placed in foster homes. The state reimburses the foster parents (usually at a rather modest rate) for caring for the retarded child and supplying needed guidance. However, as Robinson and Robinson (1976) pointed out, the level of support and advisory assistance provided to the foster parents is almost always inadequate. To rear a retarded child properly foster parents may need more than a couple of hundred dollars a month and a warm heart. They will probably also need continuing advice and guidance regarding the care of their young charge; they may also need the support of other adults to carry them through the trials and tribulations of raising a child who, after all, has proven too difficult to remain at home.

Concluding Comments

Although much remains to be done, it does seem that we have progressed quite a distance from the days when treatment for retarded infants consisted of being thrown into a river. We have made progress in understanding what retardation is and is not and some of the conditions that cause it. Further extension and implementation of our knowledge about the prevention of retardation is necessary, particularly in the area of cultural-familial retardation. Perhaps most important, it appears that in some cases society is beginning to give retarded persons the human respect and assistance they deserve, so that someday retarded individuals should be able to live as full, productive, and happy lives as their potential allows them, without receiving the further burdens of society's neglect or abuse.

NOTES

1. Even though the current AAMD and APA definitions of retardation suggest a two axis typology (i.e., IQ and level of adaptive behavior), the categorization systems for both groups are based solely on IQ. It appears that this is in part due to the lack of a generally accepted method for assessing adaptive behavior. This issue will be discussed in more detail in our section on the measurement of adaptive behavior.

2. Throughout the rest of this chapter all references to IQ scores assume a standard deviation of 15, the standard deviation of the most widely used tests, the Wechsler intelligence tests.

3. A recent study (Burton & Jones, 1982) indicates that the gap between black and white youths may be narrowing, at least in achievement test scores. The difference between 13 year-old black and white youths' percent correct scores has diminished from about 18% in 1970 to about 13% in 1980. This held true for writing, science, social studies, and reading achievement. The gap for mathematics, the most difficult subject for 13-year-old blacks, decreased from about 25% to 21% in a similar time period.

4. In this edition of the manual, cultural-familial (retardation) is declared an "obsolete term" (p. 130). The category replacing cultural-familial is "psycho-social disadvantage," which has been placed under the general heading of "Environ-

mental Influences.'' These categories specify that only environmental influences have been involved in the etiology.

5. There are two other deviations between the actual distribution of IQ scores and the theoretical distribution derived from the normal curve (Jensen, 1969). There is an excess of IQ scores in the 70–90 range and an excess at the very top of the distribution. At present the reason for these deviations is not known.

6. The large majority of retarded children live in the community and attend public schools rather than residing in institutions. Because the effects of institutionalization traditionally have been discussed under the heading of personality development, they are reviewed here. Other settings and their effects (e.g., public schools) will be discussed in the subsequent section on the care and education of retarded children.

7. Chorionic villi sampling (CVS) is a recently developed technique similar in purpose to amniocentesis. However, instead of inserting a needle into the abdomen of a pregnant woman to obtain amniotic fluid, a tube is inserted through the woman's vagina into her uterus. A few chorionic villi, which are small, fingerlike projections that aid the transportation of food and oxygen from the mother to the fetus, are removed. This tissue is part of the preplacenta, and genetically identical to that of the fetus. Once the tissue has been removed, chromosomal analyses similar to those performed on the fluid withdrawn through amniocentesis may be performed. The advantages of this procedure are that it can be performed earlier than amniocentesis (approximately 5 instead of 16 weeks after conception) and that there is less delay in receiving the results (overnight versus 4 weeks).

8. This system of classification (EMR, TMR, PMR) overlaps with the AAMD and APA classification system (mild, moderate, severe, profound retardation). EMR corresponds roughly to mild retardation while TMR corresponds roughly to moderate retardation; the two systems are somewhat redundant. The former system however, was developed and is used primarily by educators and is based on the type of education program in which the child is placed rather than on IQ. Though there is a relationship between IQ and the type of program in which a child is placed, the latter should not be based strictly on the former.

REFERENCE NOTES

1. Zigler, E., & Balla, D. *On the definition and classification of mental retardation.* Book in preparation, Yale University, 1983.
2. Bromfield, R. N. *Effects of the "mentally retarded" label on perceptions of a child's failure.* Unpublished Master's Thesis, University of North Carolina at Chapel Hill, 1983.

REFERENCES

Abramson, L.Y., Seligman, M. E. P., & Teasdale, J. D. Learned helplessness in humans: Critique and reformulation. *Journal of Abnormal Psychology,* 1978, *87,* 49–74.

Achenbach, T. M. *Developmental psychopathology* (2nd ed.). New York: Wiley, 1982.

American Psychiatric Association. *Diagnostic and statistical manual of mental disorders* (3rd ed.). Washington, D.C.: APA, 1980.

Baker, B. L., Seltzer, G. B., & Seltzer, M. M. *As close as possible: Community residences for retarded adults.* Boston: Little, Brown, 1977.

Balla, D. A. Relationship of institution size to quality of care: A review of the literature. *American Journal of Mental Deficiency,* 1976, *81,* 117–124.

Balla, D., & Zigler, E. Personality development in retarded persons. In N. R. Ellis (Ed.), *Handbook of mental deficiency, psychological theory and research* (2nd ed.). Hillsdale, N.J.: Erlbaum, 1979.

Berry, H. K. Phenylketonuria: Diagnosis, treatment and long-term management. In G. Farrell (Ed.), *Congenital mental retardation.* Austin: University of Texas Press, 1969.

Birch, H. G., Richardson, S. A., Baird, D., Horobin, G., & Illsley, R. *Mental subnormality in the community: A clinical and epidemiological study.* Baltimore: Williams & Wilkins, 1970.

Brolin, D. E. *Vocational preparation of persons with handicaps.* Columbus, Ohio: Charles E. Merrill, 1982.

Budoff, M., & Gottlieb, J. Special-class EMR children mainstreamed: A study of an aptitude (learning potential) × treatment interaction. *American Journal of Mental Deficiency,* 1976, *81,* 1–11.

Budoff, M., & Siperstein, G.N. Low income children's attitudes toward mentally retarded children: Effects of labeling and academic behavior. *American Journal of Mental Deficiency,* 1978, *82,* 474–479.

Burton, N. W., & Jones, L. V. Recent trends in achievement levels of black and white youths. *Educational Researcher,* 1982, *11,* 10–17.

Chernoff, G. The fetal alcohol syndrome: Clinical studies and strategies for prevention. In M. K. McCormack (Ed.), *Prevention of mental retardation and other developmental disabilities.* New York: Marcel Dekker, 1980.

Cicirelli, V. *The impact of Head Start: An evaluation of the effects of Head Start on children's cognitive and affective development.* Springfield, Va.: U.S. Dept of Commerce Clearinghouse, 1969.

Clausen, J. Quo Vadis, AAMD? *Journal of Special Education,* 1972, *6,* 51–60.

Cleary, T. A., Humpherys, L. G., Kendrick, S. A., & Wesman, A. Educational uses of tests with disadvantaged students. *American Psychologist,* 1975, *30,* 15–41.

Cole, N. S. Bias in testing. *American Psychologist,* 1981, *36,* 1067–1077.

Coleman, J. C., Butcher, J. N., & Carson, R. C. *Abnormal psychology and modern life.* Glenview, Ill.: Scott, Foresman, 1980.

Conley, R. W. *The economics of mental retardation.* Baltimore: John Hopkins University Press, 1973.

Corman, L., & Gottlieb, J. Mainstreaming mentally retarded children: A review of research. In N. R. Ellis, *International review of research in mental retardation.* (Vol. 9). New York: Academic, 1977.

Curtiss, S. R. *Genie: A linguistic study of a modern-day "Wild Child."* Ann Arbor, Mich.: University Microfilms International, 1977.

Dennis, W., & Narjarian, P. Infant development under environmental handicap. *Psychological Monographs,* 1957, *71,* (436).

Dent, H. E. An investigation of the influence of mental retardation on college students' judgements of social distance. *Dissertation Abstracts,* 1967, *28,* 1899–1900.

Dingman, H. F., & Tarjan, G. T. Mental retardation and the normal distribution curve. *American Journal of Mental Deficiency,* 1960, *64,* 991–994.

Doll, E. A. *The Vineland Social Maturity Scale: Revised condensed manual of directions.* Vineland, N. J.: Vineland Training School, 1936.

Doll, E. A. *Vineland Scale of Social Maturity.* Minneapolis: American Guidance Service, 1964.

Dugdale, R. *The Jukes: A study of crime, pauperism, disease, and heredity.* New York: Putnam, 1877.

Edgerton, R. B. *The cloak of competence.* Berkeley: University of California Press, 1967.

Edgerton, R. B., & Bercovici, S. M. The cloak of competence: Years later. *American Journal of Mental Deficiency,* 1976, *80,* 485–497.

Farber, B. *Mental retardation: Its social context and social consequences.* Boston: Houghton Mifflin, 1968.

Foley, J. M. Effect of labeling and teacher behavior on children's attitudes. *American Journal of Mental Deficiency,* 1979, *83,* 380–384.

Fulton, R. W. Job retention of the mentally retarded. *Mental Retardation,* 1975, *13*(2), 26.

Gallup Organization report for the President's Committee on Mental Retardation. *Public attitudes regarding mental retardation.* In R. Nathon (Ed.), *Mental retardation: Century of decision* (No. 040-000-00343-6). Washington, D.C.: U.S. Government Printing Office, 1976.

Garber, H. & Heber, F.R. The Milwaukee Project: Indications of the effectiveness of early intervention in preventing mental retardation. In P. Mittler (Ed.), *Research to practice in mental retardation.* Baltimore: University Park Press, 1977.

Gibson, D. *Down's syndrome: The psychology of mongolism.* Cambridge, Mass.: Cambridge University Press, 1978.

Goddard, H. H. *The Kallikak family: A study in the heredity of feeblemindedness.* New York: Macmillan, 1912.

Goldberger, L. I., Ausman, L. M., & Boelkins, R. C. Incidental learning, attention, and curiosity in squirrel monkeys calorie deprived as infants. *Learning & Motivation,* 1980, *11,* 185–207.

Goldstein, H., Moss, J., & Jordan, L. *The efficacy of special class training on the development of mentally retarded children.* Urbana: University of Illinois Press, 1965.

Goodman, M. B., Gruenberg, E. M., Downing, J. J., & Rogot, E. A prevalence study of Mental Retardation in a metropolitan area. *American Journal of Public Health,* 1956, 46, 702–707.

Goodman, H., Gottlieb, J., & Harrison, R.H. Social acceptance of EMRs integrated into a nongraded elementary school. *American Journal of Mental Deficiency,* 1972, 76, 412–417.

Gottlieb, J. Attitudes toward retarded children: Effects of labeling and academic performance. *American Journal of Mental Deficiency,* 1974, *79,* 268–273.

Gottlieb, J. Attitudes toward retarded children: Effects of labeling and behavioral aggressiveness. *Journal of Educational Psychology,* 1975, *67,* 581–585.

Gottlieb, J., & Budoff, M. Social acceptability of retarded children in nongraded schools differing in architecture. *American Journal of Mental Deficiency,* 1973, *78,* 15–19.

Gottlieb, J., Semmel, M. I., & Veldman, D. J. Correlates of social status among mainstreamed mentally retarded children. *Journal of Educational Psychology,* 1978, *70,* 396–405.

Grossman, H. J. *Manual on terminology and classification in mental retardation* (rev. ed.). Washington, D.C.: American Association on Mental Deficiency, 1973.

Grossman, H. J. *Manual on terminology and classification in mental retardation* (rev. ed.). Washington, D.C.: American Association on Mental Deficiency, 1977.

Hansen, H. Decline of Down's syndrome after abortion reform in New York State. *American Journal of Mental Deficiency,* 1978, *83,* 185–188.

Hays, W. L. *Statistics* (3rd ed.). New York:Holt, Rinehart & Winston, 1981.

Heber, R. F. *A manual on terminology and classification in mental retardation.* Washington, D.C.: American Association on Mental Deficiency, 1959.

Heber, R. F. A manual on terminology and classification in mental retardation (rev. ed.). *American Journal of Mental Deficiency Monograph,* 1961.

Ingalls, R. P. *Mental retardation: The changing outlook.* New York: Wiley, 1978.

Jensen, A. R. How much can we boost IQ and scholastic achievement? *Harvard Educational Review,* 1969, *39,* 1–123.

Jensen, A.R. *Genetics and education.* New York: Harper & Row, 1972.

Joffe, J. M. *Prenatal determinants of behavior.* New York: Pergamon, 1969.

Kamin, L. J. *The science and politics of IQ.* Potomac, Md.: Erlbaum, 1974.

Kanner, L. *A history of the care and study of the mentally retarded.* Springfield, Ill.: Charles C. Thomas, 1964.

Klaber, M. M. The retarded and institutions for the retarded—A preliminary research report. In S. B. Sarason & J. Doris, *Psychological problems in mental deficiency* (4th ed.). New York: Harper & Row, 1969.

Koluchova, J. Severe deprivation in twins: A case study. *Journal of Child Psychology and Psychiatry,* 1972, *13,* 107–114.

Lambert, N. M., Windmiller, M., Cole, L., & Figueroa, R. A. Standardization of a public school version of the AAMD Adaptive Behavior Scale. *Mental Retardation,* 1975, *13*(2), 3–7.

Lazar, I., & Darlington, R. Lasting effects of early education: A report from the consortium for longitudinal studies. *Monographs of the Society for Research in Child Development,* 1982, *47*(2–3, Serial No. 195).

MacMillan, D. L. *Mental retardation in school and society.* Boston: Little, Brown, 1977.

Maloney, M. P., & Steger, H. G. Intellectual characteristics of patients in an urban community mental health facility. *Journal of Consulting and Clinical Psychology,* 1972, *38,* 299.

Maloney, M. P., & Ward, M. P. *Mental retardation and modern society.* New York: Oxford University Press, 1979.

Mastenbrook, J. Future directions in adaptive behavior assessment: Environmental adaptation measure. In A. T. Fisher (Chair), *Impact of adaptive behavior: ABIC and the environmental adaptation measure.* Symposium presented at the meeting of the American Psychological Association, Toronto, Canada, 1978.

McCarver, R. B., & Craig, E. M. Placement of the retarded in the community: Prognosis and outcome. In N. R. Ellis, *International review of research in mental retardation* (vol. 7). New York: Academic, 1974.

Mercer, J. R. *Labeling the mentally retarded.* Berkeley: University of California Press, 1973.

Milgram, N. A. The rationale and irrational in Zigler's motivational approach to mental retardation. *American Journal of Mental Deficiency,* 1969, *73,* 527-532.

Milgram, N. A. Cognition and language in mental retardation: Distinctions and implications. In D. K. Routh (Ed.), *The experimental psychology of mental retardation.* Chicago: Aldine, 1973.

Millham, J., Chilcutt, J., & Atkinson, B. L. Comparability of naturalistic and controlled observation assessment of adaptive behavior. *American Journal of Mental Deficiency,* 1978, *83,* 52-59.

Nihira, K., Foster, R., Shellhaas, M., & Leland, H. *AAMD Adaptive Behavior Scale* (rev. ed.). Washington, D.C.: American Association on Mental Deficiency, 1974.

O'Brien, F., & Azrin, N. H. Developing proper mealtime behaviors of the institutionalized retarded. *Journal of Applied Behavior Analysis,* 1972, *5,* 389-399.

Ollendick, T., Balla, D., & Zigler, E. Expectancy of success and the probability learning of retarded children. *Journal of Abnormal Psychology,* 1971, *77,* 275-281.

Page, E. B. Miracle in Milwaukee: Raising the IQ. *Educational Researcher.* 1972, *1,* 8-16.

Patton, R. G., & Gardner, L. I. *Growth failure in maternal deprivation.* Springfield, Ill.: Charles C. Thomas, 1963.

Payne, J. S., & Patton, J. R. *Mental retardation.* Columbus, Ohio: Charles E. Merrill, 1981.

Penrose, L. S. The effects of change in maternal age distribution upon the incidence of mongolism. *Journal of Mental Deficiency Research,* 1967, *11,* 54-57.

Pitt, D. B. The natural history of untreated phenylketonuria. *Medical Journal of Australia,* 1971, *1,* 378-383.

Reschly, D. J. Psychological testing in educational classification and placement. *American Psychologist,* 1981, *36,* 1094-1102.

Ricciuti, H. Adverse social and biological influences on early development. In H. McGurk (Ed.), *Ecological factors in human development.* Amsterdam: North-Holland, 1977.

Roberts, J. Intellectual development of children by demographic and socioeconomic factors. *Vital and Health Statistics, Series II.* Washington, D.C.: U.S. Government Printing Office, 1972.

Robinson, H. B., & Robinson, N. M. Longitudinal development of very young children in a comprehensive day care program: The first two years. *Child Development,* 1971, *42,* 1673-1683.

Robinson, N. M., & Robinson, H. B. *The mentally retarded child* (2nd ed.). New York: McGraw-Hill, 1976.

Rynders, J. E., Spiker, D., & Horrobin, J. M. Underestimating the educability of Down's syndrome children: Examination of methodological problems in recent literature. *American Journal of Mental Deficiency,* 1978, *82,* 440–448.

Sandoval, J., & Miille, M. P. W. Accuracy of judgments of WISC-R item difficulty for minority groups. *Journal of Consulting and Clinical Psychology,* 1980, *48,* 249–253.

Sarason, S. B., & Doris, J. *Psychological problems in mental deficiency.* New York: Harper & Row, 1969.

Sattler, J. M. *Assessment of children's intelligence and special abilities* (2nd ed.). Boston: Allyn & Bacon, 1982.

Schalock, R. L., & Harper, R. S. Placement from community-based mental retardation programs: How well do clients do? *American Journal of Mental Deficiency,* 1978, *83,* 240–247.

Scheerenberger, R. C. *A history of mental retardation.* Baltimore: Paul Brooks, 1983.

Silverstein, A. B. Deviation social quotients for the Vineland Social Maturity Scale. *American Journal of Mental Deficiency,* 1971, *76,* 348–351.

Skeels, H. M. Adult status of children with contrasting early life experiences. *Monographs of the Society for Research in Child Development,* 1966, *31,* (105).

Skeels, H. M., & Dye, H. B. A study of the effects of differential stimulation on mentally retarded children. *Proceedings of the American Association on Mental Retardation,* 1939, *44,* 114–136.

Smith, D. W., & Wilson, A. A. *The child with Downe's syndrome (mongolism). Causes characteristics and exceptance.* Philadelphia: Saunders, 1973.

Spicker, H. H. Intellectual development through early childhood education. *Exceptional Children,* 1971, *37,* 629–640.

Spitz, R. A. Hospitalism: An inquiry into the genesis of psychiatric conditions in early childhood. *Psychoanalytic Study of the Child,* 1945, *1,* 53–74.

Sprigle, H. A. The learning to learn program. In S. Ryan (Ed.), *A report of longitudinal evaluations of preschool programs.* Washington, D.C.: Office of Child Development, 1972.

Strickland, S. P. Can slum children learn? *American Education,* 1971, *7,* 3–7.

Thompson, T., & Grabowski, J. *Behavior modification of the mentally retarded.* New York: Oxford University Press, 1972.

Trippi, J., Michael, R., Colao, A., & Alvarez, A. Housing discrimination toward mentally retarded persons. *Exceptional Children,* 1978, *44,* 430–433.

Uchida, I. A. Paternal origin of the extra chromosome in Down's syndrome. *Lancet,* 1973, *2,* 1258.

Vernon, P. E. *Intelligence and cultural environment.* London: Methuen, 1969.

Vernon, P. E. *Intelligence, heredity and environment.* San Francisco: Reeman, 1979.

Walker, V. S. The efficacy of the resource room for educating retarded children. *Exceptional Children,* 1974, *40,* 288–289.

Weisz, J. R. Learned helplessness in black and white children identified by their schools as retarded and nonretarded: Performance deterioration in response to failure. *Developmental Psychology,* 1981, *17,* 499–508.(a)

Weisz, J. R. Effects of the "mentally retarded" label on adult judgments about child failure. *Journal of Abnormal Psychology,* 1981, *90,* 371–374.(b)

Weisz, J. R. Learned helplessness and the retarded child. In E. Zigler, & D. Balla (Eds.), *Mental retardation: The developmental-difference controversy.* Hillsdale, N.J.: Erlbaum, 1982.

Weisz, J. R., & Yeates, K. O. Cognitive development in retarded and nonretarded persons: Piagetian tests of the similar structure hypothesis. *Psychological Bulletin,* 1981, *90,* 153–178.

Weisz, J. R., & Zigler, E. Cognitive development in retarded and nonretarded persons: Piagetian tests of the similar sequence hypothesis. *Psychological Bulletin,* 1979, *86,* 831–851.

Whalen, C. K., & Henker, B. A. Pyramid therapy in a hospital for the retarded. *American Journal of Mental Deficiency,* 1971, *75,* 414–434.

Williams, R. L. Black pride, academic relevance, and individual achievement. *Counseling Psychologist,* 1970, *2,* 18–22.

Wright, S. W., & Tarjan, G. Phenylketonuria. *American Journal of Diseases of Children,* 1957, *93,* 405–419.

Yannet, H. Mental deficiency due to prenatally determined factors. *Pediatrics,* 1950, *5,* 328–336.

Yeates, K. O., & Weisz, J. R. On being called mentally retarded: Developmental and professional perspectives limit labeling effects? *American Journal of Mental Deficiency,* in press.

Zigler, E. Familial mental retardation: A continuing dilemma. *Science,* 1967, *155,* 292–298.

Zigler, E. Developmental versus difference theories of mental retardation and the problem of motivation. *American Journal of Mental Deficiency,* 1969, *73,* 536–556.

Zigler, E., & Balla, D. A. Impact of institutional experience on the behavior and development of retarded persons. *American Journal of Mental Deficiency,* 1977, *82,* 1–11.

Zigler, E., & Balla, D. Introduction: The developmental approach to mental retardation. In E. Zigler & D. Balla (Eds.), *Mental retardation: The developmental-difference controversy.* Hillsdale, N.J.: Erlbaum, 1982.

Zigler, E., Balla, D., & Butterfield, E. C. A longitudinal investigation of the relationship between preinstitutional social deprivation and social motivation in institutionalized retardates. *Journal of Personality and Social Psychology,* 1968, *10,* 437–445.

Zigler, E., & Williams, J. Institutionalization and the effectiveness of social reinforcement: A three-year follow-up study. *Journal of Abnormal and Social Psychology,* 1963, *66,* 197–205.

CHAPTER 11

Specific Learning Deficits: The Learning Disabled

JAMES E. YSSELDYKE AND LINDA J. STEVENS

This chapter presents a historical perspective on learning disabilities, an account of various efforts to define learning disabilities, a discussion of defining characteristics identified in the literature and problems in differentiating the learning disabled (LD) from other low-achieving students or other mildly handicapped students, and prevalence and related demographic information. Also discussed are current approaches to assessment of learning disabilities, problems in identifying the etiology of learning disabilities, and current promising efforts to identify major syndromes associated with the condition. Information is presented on manifestations of learning disabilities, including reading problems, locus of control, the relationship between learning disabilities and juvenile delinquency, and communicative competence and social interactions of LD individuals. A discussion of theoretical formulations concerning underlying processes is also provided, along with information on trends in interventions with learning disabled children and adolescents. Finally, the authors' personal perspective on the issues of definition, assessment, and intervention is presented.

HISTORICAL PERSPECTIVE

Although the term learning disability is a relatively recent one, professionals have been concerned with individuals who exhibit learning problems despite sensory intactness and normal intelligence since at least the early 1800s. In a detailed review of the history of efforts to educate the learning disabled, Wiederholt (1974) described three developmental phases: a foundation phase, a transition phase, and an integration phase.

The *foundation phase* (approximately 1800–1930) involved the formulation of theoretical perspectives based on information collected from clinical accounts of the behavior of adults who exhibited focal brain damage (acquired from gunshot wounds or strokes), on attempts to describe the sensory, perceptual-motor, and language characteristics of these patients, and on efforts to relate the characteristics to specific lesions in the brain. Gall, Broca, and Wernicke studied disorders of spoken language; Hinshelwood and Orton studied written language disorders; and Goldstein, Werner, and Strauss focused on brain injury in children and disorders of perceptual-motor processes. Werner and Strauss postulated specific disabilities in attention, behavior, body awareness, perception, and reasoning; their work later significantly affected the direction of the field of learning disabilities.

The *transition phase* (approximately 1930–1960) was characterized by attempts by educators and psychologists to translate early laboratory-based findings into remedial education programs. Concerns shifted from etiology to intervention as major contributors concentrated on specific types of disabilities—spoken language, written language, and perceptual and motor processes—to a greater extent than did their predecessors in the foundations phase. A test-based approach was used in which efforts were made to develop instruments to measure the traits, characteristics, or behaviors identified as associated with brain injury by early researchers and to develop interventions for elementary age children who evidenced either suspected brain damage or "minimal cerebral dysfunction." Wepman, Samuel and Winifred Kirk, Johnson and Myklebust, and Eisenson focused on spoken language disorders; Fernald, Samuel and Winifred Kirk, Gillingham, and Stillman focused on written language disorders; and Lehtinen, Cruickshank, Kephart, Barsch, and Frostig focused on the development of programs and materials to assess and remediate perceptual-motor disorders.

What Wiederholt (1974) termed the *integration phase,* from about 1960 to the present, is characterized by eclecticism and the use of developmental and remedial programs borrowed from psychology, general education, and other areas of special education. During this 25-year period there has been a dramatic increase in the number of public school programs for learning disabled students.

The first use of the term "learning disabilities" is generally attributed to Samuel Kirk, who used the term in April 1963 at a conference sponsored by the Fund for Perceptually Handicapped Children, Inc. Yet Lambert (1981) noted that the term appeared in the legal literature in late 1960 in a summary of research that she and Bower prepared in support of legislative proposals for intervention programs for handicapped students in California. Whatever its origin, within a few years a series of three task force reports concerned with terminology and identification of learning disabled students was issued (Chalfant & Scheffelin, 1969; Clements, 1966; Haring & Miller, 1969).

In 1971 the first major federal effort to provide services for learning disabled students was instituted by the Bureau of Education for the Handicapped (BEH). Authorized under PL 91–230, Title 6, Part G, eight grants totaling 1 million dollars were awarded to state departments to develop Child Service Demonstration Projects (CSDPs). Additional states received grants or contracts for CSDPs (later called Child Service Demonstration Centers or CSDCs) over the next six years until by 1977 every state had received at least one such award. At peak level of funding in 1977, 53 CSDCs were operating.

With passage of PL 94-142, the Education for All Handicapped Children Act, learning disabilities became a recognized handicapping condition and separate legislative authority for demonstration projects in learning disabilities was ended.

In addition to an infusion of federal dollars and tremendous increases in the number of public school programs, the integration phase has been described as characterized by both divisiveness among learning disabilities professionals and critical evaluation of unidimensional conceptualizations of learning disabilities. The field has consisted of two basic approaches: the neuropsychological orientation, focusing on neuropsychological dysfunctions thought to underlie learning disabilities, and the educational orientation, less concerned with etiology and focusing instead on provision of educational services.

Learning disabilities is still a young and developing field. Wiederholt (1974) observed,

Although the field has a considerable history of development, it is still in its infant stages. It was only christened and incorporated into the larger educational community during the last decade. But, in that short period of time it has become one of the most rapidly expanding and controversial fields in education. (p. 148)

Formal Definition

Educators consistently have been frustrated by an inability to reach consensus on a formal definition of "learning disability." The subject has been the focus of multiple task forces, Congressional testimony and intervention, and spirited professional debate. In response to confusion about prevalence rates in learning disabilities Congress established specific requirements for the definition of learning disabilities as part of PL 94-142. Until final regulations were established which included criteria for determining the existence of learning disabilities, appropriate diagnostic procedures, and compliance monitoring procedures, state and local education agencies were prohibited from identifying for purposes of reimbursement more than 2% of their school-aged population as learning disabled.

In response to that mandate the U.S. Office of Education proposed guidelines stating that in order to be classified as having specific learning disabilities a child must demonstrate a severe discrepancy between achievement and intellectual ability. Severe discrepancy was defined as performance at or below 50% of the expected achievement level when intellectual ability, age, and previous educational experiences were considered. In addition, the following formula for determining the severe discrepancy was proposed:

$$CA \left(\frac{IQ}{300} + 0.17 \right) - 2.5 = \text{severe discrepancy level}$$

A severe discrepancy could exist in one or more of several areas: oral expression, written expression, listening comprehension or reading comprehension, basic reading skills, mathematics calculation, mathematics reasoning, or spelling. In addition, the "definition by exclusion" notion which had characterized earlier attempts to define learning disabilities was retained: a child could not be identified as LD if the learning problem was "primarily the result of visual, hearing, or motor handicaps, mental retardation, emotional disturbance, or environmental, cultural, or economic disadvantage" (USOE, 1976, p. 52405).

Overwhelming opposition to the use of a formula became apparent during a 120-day review period and led to the elimination of both the formula and the requirement of a severe discrepancy level of 50%. Field testing during that review period indicated some specific technical problems with the formula; for example, children under 8 years old were more likely to be identified as learning disabled, and children with lower IQs were more likely to be identified than children with higher IQs (Danielson & Bauer, 1978). Algozzine, Forgnone, Mercer, and Trifiletti (1979) applied the proposed BEH formula to a sample of hypothetical cases and found that the severe discrepancy level was differentially influenced by IQ (with discrepancy levels in excess of 50% found more frequently when IQs were lower than 100 and less often when IQs were higher than 100). However, no such differential effects were found with variations in age, and the differential effects of IQ were not supported when the formula was applied to a sample of 125 Florida children identified as LD. Algozzine and his colleagues concluded that if the severe discrepancy level was used as the sole criterion for identification as learning disabled, 30% of the low IQ children and 54% of the high IQ children would be misidentified.

The final version of the regulation omitted the formula and requirement for a 50% severe discrepancy level but retained seven of the original eight areas in which that discrepancy could be demonstrated (spelling was considered to be subsumed under the other seven areas of function). The exclusionary provisions remained and responsibility for identifying a child as learning disabled was placed with a multidisciplinary team. The final definition closely parallels the guidelines established in 1968 by the National Advisory Committee on Handicapped Children (NACHC), and is as follows:

> Specific learning disability means a disorder in one or more of the basic psychological processes involved in understanding or in using language, spoken or written, which may manifest itself in an imperfect ability to listen, think, speak, read, write, spell, or do mathematical calculations. The term includes such conditions as perceptual handicaps, brain injury, minimal brain dysfunction, dyslexia, and developmental aphasia. The term does not include children who have learning problems which are primarily the result of visual, hearing, or motor handicaps, of mental retardation, of emotional disturbance, or of environmental, cultural, or economic disadvantage. (USOE, 1977, p. 65083)

The final regulations omit any attempt at operationally defining "process variables"; the omission suggests that learning disability is primarily (or only) an achievement discrepancy (Algozzine et al., 1979).

In January 1981, in an effort to address some of the problems associated with the NACHC definition, the National Joint Committee on Learning Disabilities drafted a position paper on issues of definition of learning disabilities. The Joint Committee is made up of representatives of the governing boards of six professional organizations concerned with learning disabilities. There were concerns that the NACHC definition led many to view learning disabilities as a homogeneous disorder, that the use of "children" was too restrictive, that etiology was only implied, and that the exclusion clause implied that LD individuals could not be multihandicapped or be from different cultural or linguistic backgrounds. All the member associations of the Joint Committee except the Association for Children and Adults with Learning Disabilities approved the position paper and the following definition:

> Learning disabilities is a generic term that refers to a heterogeneous group of disorders manifested by significant difficulties in the acquisition and use of listening, speaking, reading, writing, reasoning or mathematical abilities. These disorders are intrinsic to the individual and presumed to be due to central nervous system dysfunction. Even though a learning disability may occur concomitantly with other handicapping conditions (e.g., sensory impairment, mental retardation, social and emotional disturbance) or environmental influences (e.g., cultural differences, insufficient/inappropriate instruction, psychogenic factors), it is not the direct result of those conditions or influences. (Leigh, 1983, pp. 43–44)

Defining Characteristics

Keogh and her colleagues (Keogh, Major, Omori, Gandará, & Reid, 1980) noted the wide range of symptoms associated with learning disabilities in the 408 research studies they reviewed. They observed that included were

> emotional, attentional, perceptual-motor, neurological, learning, linguistic, and activity-related symptoms. LD subjects in the sample articles were frequently described as evidencing symptoms of frustration, aggression, inappropriate affect, poor social and/or school adjustment, and behavior disorders. They were also described as immature and irritable, and as having sleep disorders and emotional problems. Symptoms related to learning problems included specific achievement deficits, general low achievement, and school failure. (p. 24)

Despite the expansion of interest in the phenomenon called learning disabilities, relatively few large-scale studies to date have investigated characteristics of children labeled LD. One of the most frequently cited studies is that by Kirk and Elkins (1975), who surveyed 24 federally funded Child Service Demonstration Centers (CSDCs) in 21 states in an attempt to describe the more than 3000 children labeled and served as learning disabled. Information was collected on the ages of children served, intellectual level, sex distribution, percentage of local school population served, major emphasis in remediation, degree of disability (as rated by the teacher), degree of discrepancy between expectancy for age and academic achievement, setting, and methods used for delivery of services. Kirk and Elkins found that the majority of children served came from kindergarten and the lower elementary grades and that the sex ratio was three boys to one girl. Reading problems were rated as the primary remedial focus for approximately two-thirds of the children, followed by arithmetic, spelling, and language. The most commonly used method for delivery of special services was the resource room, followed by the itinerant teacher and the self-contained classroom. The median educational retardation (when compared to chronological age expectancy) was a 1.7 grade discrepancy for reading, a 1.3 grade discrepancy for arithmetic, and a 1.8 grade discrepancy for spelling. Kirk and Elkins indicated that approximately 35% of the children served by the projects had IQs below 90 (compared to an average population where 25% are below 90); the median IQ across all projects was 93.

In a later similar study, Norman and Zigmond (1980) collected and analyzed intake placement data from the files of 1966 children labeled and served as LD by a different set of CSDCs located in 22 states. Information collected included age, IQ and achievement data, grade, sex, and ethnic origin. Again there were between three and four times as many boys as girls labeled LD. The mean age was 11.83 years, indicating a larger proportion of CSDCs serving students at the secondary level than at the time of the Kirk and Elkins study. The mean IQ (92.5) and median IQ (91.3) for the total sample were similar to the median of 93 found by Kirk and Elkins. Norman and Zigmond found a wide range of IQs (58–141) with 54% of the CSDCs classifying students with IQs of 69 or lower as learning disabled. Younger students (ages 6–8) had significantly higher IQs than older students (ages 15–17); older students demonstrated greater underachievement relative to age than younger students. Reading and math levels of younger students were almost at grade level, whereas mean grade scores for 17-year-olds were 5.7 in reading and 6.8 in math. Considerable variability in IQ range and degree of academic retardation was found across CSDCs, leading Norman and Zigmond to conclude that a "heterogeneous and ill-defined population of students is being labeled as learning disabled" (p. 542).

Although the majority of research to date has addressed learning disabilities at the elementary level, there has been increasing interest since the mid-1970s in the characteristics and needs of the learning disabled adolescent. Researchers at the University of Kansas Institute for Research in Learning Disabilities (IRLD) established an epidemiological data base on learning disabled adolescents, comparing more than 300 LD adolescents of varying socioeconomic status with similar numbers of low achieving students and normally achieving students (Schumaker, Deshler, Alley, & Warner, 1983; Warner, Schumaker, Alley, & Deshler, 1980). Data were collected on academic, social, medical, and environmental variables from parents, teachers, and administrators, as well as the adolescents themselves, through the use of formal tests, laboratory tasks, interviews, and surveys. Considerable overlap was apparent in the distributions of ability and achievement scores for low achieving and LD students. Although behavioral, attitudinal, and test characteristics of low achieving and learning disabled students appeared to be more similar than dissimilar, LD adolescents were found to be the lowest of the low achievers, demonstrating poor performance in all academic areas and typically scoring below the tenth percentile on standardized tests of reading, written language, and mathematics. In addition, a substantial proportion of students labeled LD were characterized as substantially below the normative mean of 100 for estimated ability.

Learning disabled adolescents typically reached a plateau of basic skill levels during the secondary grades; their average achievement in reading and written language was at the high third-grade level in seventh grade and at the fifth-grade level in senior high, while mathematics achievement was at about the fifth-grade level in the seventh grade and reached a plateau at the sixth-grade level in senior high school. Learning disabled adolescents demonstrated deficiencies in study skills and strategies (e.g., note taking, test taking, scanning, monitoring writing errors, and listening comprehension), executive functioning (e.g., creating and applying a strategy to a new problem), and social skills (e.g., accepting negative feedback, conversing, giving negative and positive feedback, negotiating, social problem solving, and resisting peer pressure). Their skill deficits appeared exacerbated by the demands of the secondary school setting; teachers were found to rely predominantly on the lecture method and use few advance organizers or checks of student understanding, and the largest proportion of student time in junior high classes was spent in independent work requiring reading and writing skills (Schumaker et al., 1983).

One notable problem in defining characteristics of the learning disabled has been the inability of many researchers to differentiate LD students from emotionally disturbed (ED) or educable mentally handicapped (EMH) students. Hallahan and Kauffman (1976) observed that for the majority of children identified as LD, ED, or EMH, there is no known cause of the condition, although different theorists hold particular viewpoints concerning the contribution of heredity, environment, or the combination of the two. In addition, there is considerable overlap in the teaching methods used with these three populations; successful teaching strategies are more dependent on the specific behaviors exhibited by the child than the diagnostic category in which he or she has been placed. Hallahan and Kauffman suggested that with the exception of the fact that EMH students have lower IQs, no behaviors are specific to any of the three conditions.

Webster and Schenck (1978) found little diagnostic utility of norm-referenced objective test data and personal information in differentiating LD from ED, EMH, or multihandicapped students; between 69% and 86% of the children from the other three groups were predicted to be LD on the basis of the most commonly used standardized intelligence and achievement test data (the WISC-R and WRAT). In an effort to determine the relevance of characteristics in distinguishing among LD, ED, and EMH children, Gajar (1980) found some measures to be useful in classifying exceptional children but raised the question of their instructional relevance, noting that they yield little useful information for the design of interventions.

Recent research at the University of Minnesota Institute for Research on

Learning Disabilities (IRLD) has further documented problems in differentiating learning disabled from other low-achieving students. Ysseldyke, Algozzine, Shinn, and McGue (1982) compared the performance of 49 learning disabled and 50 low achieving students on 49 separate cognitive, achievement, personality, perceptual motor, and behavior rating measures. They were unable to discriminate between the two groups, finding an average 96% overlap in the performance of the two groups on the psychometric measures.

Similarly, when Ysseldyke, Algozzine, and Epps (1983) applied 17 frequently used definitions of learning disabilities to test data from 350 normal, low-achieving, or LD students, from 1 to 84% of normal students at a particular grade level (third, fifth, or twelfth grade) met criteria for classification as LD. These data are shown in Table 11.1. An average of 21% of the normal students were identified as LD. From 0 to 71% of the low achieving students could be classified as LD using any of the definitions, and from 1 to 78% of the students actually classified by their school systems as LD could be classified as LD using any one definition. As many as 4% of students identified by their schools as LD were not identified as such by any of the 17 operational definitions.

In a related study (Epps, Ysseldyke, & Algozzine, 1983), when 14 operational definitions were applied to approximately 150 school-identified LD and

Table 11.1.   Percentages of Regular Classroom, Low-Achieving, and School-Identified LD Students Classified as LD by 17 Operational Definitions

Definition	Regular Classroom Sample ($n = 248$)	Low-Achieving Sample ($n = 49$)	LD Sample ($n = 50$)
1	10	2	9
2	65	71	78
3	25	40	45
4	4	3	5
5	7	1	3
6	45	25	44
7	6	5	7
8	25	21	37
9	7	3	13
10	4	0	2
11	20	20	33
12	48	48	62
13	37	13	16
14	22	6	16
15	12	14	7
16	17	8	12
17	2	2	1

Note: Percentages are adjusted for cases missing information.
Source: Adapted from Ysseldyke et al., 1983, pp. 164–165.

non-LD children at the elementary level, different definitions identified significantly different numbers of students as LD. One definition classified only 7.3% of the school-identified LD group as LD, whereas another definition correctly classified 80.6% of the LD students. Similarly, 3.3% of the non-LD children were classified as LD using one definition, while another identified 64.6% of the non-LD subjects as learning disabled. The addition of even a single subtest to an operational definition changed the number of students identified as LD. As Epps et al. noted, "a student may or may not be classified depending on which definition is selected, how it is operationalized, the idiosyncratic approach to assessment by the diagnostician, the degree of curriculum bias, and the extent to which information on exclusionary criteria are used" (p. 350).

A recent survey of 150 professionals identified by their peers as on the "cutting edge" of research and programming in learning disabilities (Tucker, Stevens, & Ysseldyke, 1983) found considerable agreement concerning the viability of learning disabilities as a classification for handicapped children (82.6%) and the belief that learning disabilities be differentiated clinically from other problems associated with learning (88%). However, there was less agreement on the prevalence of learning disabilities among school-aged children or the age at which identification was possible. Prevalence estimates ranged from 0 to 70%; nearly 60% of the sample indicated prevalence figures of less than 3% of the school-aged population. Approximately half of those surveyed indicated that learning disabilities could not be clearly identified until a child was at least 6 years old, while half believed learning disabilities could be diagnosed before the typical age of entrance to school. Estimates of age at diagnosis ranged from infancy to 9 years.

Prevalence and Related Demographic Figures

Recent prevalence figures transmitted to Congress by the U.S. Department of Education, Office of Special Education (USDE, 1984) indicated that LD children ages 3–21 represent the largest category of handicapping condition served in the 1982–1983 school year, followed by speech impaired and mentally retarded children. Learning disabled children constituted approximately 4.4% of school enrollment in 1982–1983, an increase from 3% in 1979–1980; they represented about 42.5% of all handicapped children, an increase from about 22% in 1976–1977, and the largest increase of any handicapping condition in that time period. As shown in Table 11.2, there was an average increase of 119% in the number of LD children ages 3–21 in the states and territories in those six years, compared with an average decrease of 19.5% in the number of mentally retarded children served in the same time period. Mississippi had the greatest increase in LD children—more than 500%. In 24 states and/or territories the number of LD children doubled during that time. Only the District of Columbia and American Samoa experienced declines in the number of children identified and served as LD during those six years.

Table 11.2. Number and Change in Number of Children Ages 3–21 Years Served Under PL 89–313 and PL 94–142

| | Learning Disabled | | | | |
| | Number | | Changes in Number Served | Percent Change in Number Served | |
State	1976–1977	1982–1983	1982–1983— 1976–1977	1982–1983— 1976–1977	1982–1983— 1981–1982
Alabama	5,436	20,899	15,463	284.5	5.2
Alaska	3,927	6,826	2,900	73.8	11.3
Arizona	17,214	25,710	8,496	49.4	1.3
Arkansas	5,072	19,436	14,365	283.2	4.8
California	74,404	198,696	124,293	167.1	4.2
Colorado	16,661	19,654	2,994	18.0	−6.1
Connecticut	19,201	29,352	10,152	52.9	−0.5
Delaware	4,392	6,670	2,279	51.9	2.3
District of Columbia	1,661	1,629	−32	−1.9	−15.0
Florida	31,850	58,105	26,256	82.4	4.2
Georgia	15,744	35,722	19,979	126.9	1.3
Hawaii	4,880	8,189	3,309	67.8	3.7
Idaho	5,604	8,233	2,630	46.9	0.1
Illinois	53,328	96,805	43,478	81.5	10.4
Indiana	5,422	27,434	22,012	406.0	9.2
Iowa	17,553	21,340	3,788	21.6	−4.5
Kansas	8,425	16,190	7,765	92.2	2.4
Kentucky	7,423	20,064	12,641	170.3	10.7
Louisiana	10,823	39,707	28,884	266.9	15.6
Maine	7,261	8,974	1,714	23.6	7.5
Maryland	29,093	48,366	19,274	66.2	−1.6
Massachusetts	18,542	48,884	30,343	163.6	−1.0
Michigan	28,143	55,467	27,325	97.1	6.0
Minnesota	21,456	34,748	13,292	62.0	−1.4
Mississippi	2,748	16,788	14,040	510.9	16.3
Missouri	22,862	36,224	13,362	58.4	0.2
Montana	2,883	7,208	4,326	150.1	10.9
Nebraska	5,433	12,227	6,794	125.1	−1.6
Nevada	4,782	7,041	2,260	47.3	5.5
New Hampshire	3,091	8,220	5,129	165.9	2.7
New Jersey	33,188	62,736	29,549	89.0	5.9
New Mexico	6,175	12,237	6,063	98.2	−0.7
New York	34,514	116,753	82,239	238.3	68.0
North Carolina	17,697	49,019	31,323	177.0	7.9
North Dakota	2,439	4,340	1,901	77.9	4.9
Ohio	32,399	72,031	39,632	122.3	0.5
Oklahoma	15,015	28,625	13,610	90.6	1.1
Oregon	11,146	23,459	12,313	110.5	5.5
Pennsylvania	19,772	63,413	43,641	220.7	9.8
Puerto Rico	1,012	1,852	841	83.1	5.2
Rhode Island	4,620	11,729	7,109	153.9	4.6
South Carolina	10,821	20,930	10,110	93.4	11.0
South Dakota	1,196	3,563	2,368	198.0	16.9
Tennessee	35,243	42,804	7,562	21.5	8.6

Table 11.2. (*continued*)

State	Number 1976-1977	Number 1982-1983	Changes in Number Served 1982-1983— 1976-1977	Percent Change in Number Served 1982-1983— 1976-1977	Percent Change in Number Served 1982-1983— 1981-1982
Texas	50,890	150,768	99,878	196.3	6.2
Utah	13,584	13,611	27	0.2	2.8
Vermont	2,026	2,973	947	46.7	−32.2
Virginia	16,211	38,614	22,403	138.2	6.8
Washington	10,129	31,286	21,157	208.9	3.8
West Virginia	5,743	14,719	8,976	156.3	14.5
Wisconsin	14,378	27,224	12,846	89.3	1.4
Wyoming	3,084	5,095	2,012	65.2	2.3
American Samoa	37	1	−36	−97.3	−99.1
Guam	148	530	382	258.1	19.1
Northern Marianas	—	—	—	—	—
Trust Territories	269	—	—	—	—
Virgin Islands	176	220	44	25.0	511.1
Bureau of Indian Affairs	—	2,531	—	—	1.2
United States and Territories	797,213	1,745,871	948,659	119.0	7.3

Source: Adapted from the U.S. Department of Education, 1984, p. 137.

While there has been relatively little research to date on racial and ethnic composition of the population labeled LD, a study by Tucker (1980) indicated that the increased proportion of blacks in LD classes in recent years (since the recent emphasis on protection in evaluation) was so pronounced that, despite a decreasing proportion of blacks in classes for the mentally retarded, the number of blacks in special education classes as a whole increased to a disproportionate number. Learning disabilities, then, may no longer be the white, middle-class suburban phenomenon that its critics have accused it of being but may be becoming the dumping ground for underachieving students or minority students who might more accurately (but with greater stigma) be placed in classes for the mentally retarded.

ASSESSMENT

Sarason and Doris (1979) eloquently described current practices in assessing students:

> The diagnostic process is always a consequence of somebody saying that someone has something wrong with him. We put it this way because frequently it is not the individual who decides to initiate the process. This is the case with children, but

there are also times when adults are forced by pressure from others or by legal action to participate in the process. In all of those instances people individually or society in general communicates four ideas: something may be wrong with someone; our lives are being affected; we should find out the source of the trouble; and we should come up with solutions to alter the individual's status and allow us to experience our lives in the way we wish. (p. 16)

Although two fundamentally different approaches characterize assessment of LD students, the dominant approach is based on assumptions that academic and social difficulties are caused by within-student deficits, dysfunctions, or disabilities, and that the purpose of assessment is to identify those within-student disorders. Assessment usually occurs outside the instructional context and focuses on the learner (Englemann, Granzin, & Severson, 1979). Sarason and Doris (1979) noted that such assessment is

a pathology oriented process activated by someone who thinks something is wrong with somebody else. It is a process in which objectivity and precision are sought, but it is permeated with personal values and judgments. (p. 39)

A second approach to assessment in the field of learning disabilities, one which Englemann et al. (1979) label "diagnosis of instruction" occurs considerably more infrequently. Such assessment is characterized by efforts to identify "(*a*) the extent to which a learner's failure is caused by poor instruction and (*b*) precisely what teachers could do to remedy an observed problem" (Englemann et al., 1979, p. 356).

Many norm-referenced tests are administered in the process of making decisions about LD students (Mardell-Czudnowski, 1980; Thurlow & Ysseldyke, 1979, 1982; Ysseldyke, Regan, Thurlow, & Schwartz, 1981). In an analysis of 579 questionnaires completed by assessment personnel in Illinois, Mardell-Czudnowski (1980) reported that LD children were the most frequently tested group of children, primarily for the purpose of classification for funding and/or placement. The children were assessed most often using norm-referenced tests, although there was a slight trend toward the use of criterion-referenced tests by professionals responsible for establishing curricular needs and classroom intervention strategies. Those tests used most often were inadequately constructed and standardized, and there was little evidence for their reliability and validity.

Research at the University of Minnesota IRLD has confirmed the existence of significant problems in current practice in assessing LD students. In a survey of 42 Child Service Demonstration Centers, Thurlow and Ysseldyke (1979) found that personnel in school districts associated with CSDCs used the same tests to make screening, identification, placement, intervention planning, and evaluation decisions, a practice for which there is no empirical support (Salvia & Ysseldyke, 1981; Ysseldyke & Algozzine, 1979, 1982). Thurlow and Ysseldyke also reported that the majority of tests used lacked the necessary reliability and validity to be used in decision making. In a later study, Thurlow and Ysseldyke (1982) investigated the congruence between assessment data collected by school psychologists for the purpose of instructional planning and data considered useful by teachers for instructional planning. Both groups assigned top priority to the Wechsler Intelligence Scale for Children–Revised, a device repeatedly shown to have limited utility for purposes of instructional planning (Ysseldyke, 1979; Ysseldyke & Algozzine, 1979).

In a study using computer-simulation methodology to examine the psychoeducational assessment and decision-making process, Ysseldyke, Algozzine, Regan, and Potter (1980) presented 159 educators and psychologists with assessment data indicative of normal performance by a fifth-grade student. Fifty-one percent of the decision makers declared the normal student eligible for special education services. Similarly, when three groups—school psychologists, special education teachers, and "naive" judges (university students enrolled in programs unrelated to psychology or education)—were asked to differentiate learning disabled students from low achievers by examining patterns of scores, all three groups were in agreement with school classification only about half the time (Epps, Ysseldyke, & McGue, 1984).

Ysseldyke, Algozzine, Richey, and Graden (1982) used a naturalistic observation methodology in which they videotaped placement team meetings and examined the relationship between placement decisions made by teams and the extent to which the data presented at team meetings supported the decisions made. These data are shown in Table 11.3. After using the data that teams presented and classifying students using three definitions of learning disabilities, Ysseldyke et al. (1982) found a negligible relationship between outcome decisions and the data to support the decisions.

In a review of validation studies on 10 most frequently recommended procedures used for diagnosing learning disabilities, Coles (1978) found serious methodological deficiencies, in particular inadequate demonstration of construct validity for these tests. Coles concluded that the tests fail to demonstrate that children categorized as LD are neurologically impaired and criticized the prevailing emphasis on biological explanations for performance deficits, to the neglect of concern for the academic and social demands of the settings in which LD children operate. He suggested that "the entire field of learning disabilities

Table 11.3.   Relationship between Number of Learning Disability Definitions Supported by Data and Placement Team Decisions

	Number of Definitions			
Decision made	0	1	2	3
Learning disabled	4	1	6	3
Non-learning disabled	1	3	2	0

Source: Adapted from Ysseldyke, Algozzine, Richey, & Graden, 1982, p. 42.

has an empirical foundation too frail for the ponderous structure that has been erected upon it" (p. 330), noted that professionals have acted "as if they had in their hands diagnostic instruments that could lay bare the cognitive processes of a child's mind" (p. 331), and called attention to the lack of scientific foundation for the learning disabilities battery.

Clearly there are major problems in current assessment practices with handicapped and potentially handicapped students. Nowhere are these problems more evident than in efforts to assess LD students.

ETIOLOGY AND DEVELOPMENT

The extremely heterogeneous group of students currently labeled "learning disabled" in public school settings have few characteristics in common. Yet professionals have spent an inordinate amount of time trying to identify *the* cause of learning disabilities. Learning disabilities have been said to result directly from a variety of medical problems, specifically by those who believe that neurological impairment is the fundamental cause of the academic and social difficulties evidenced by students. It has been argued that learning disabilities are caused by nutritional deprivation, environmental noise, anoxia, toxemia, rubella, premature birth, physical trauma, Rh factor, congenital malformations, unfavorable uterine environments, and heredity (Myers & Hammill, 1976).

Many of the early pioneers in this field (Getman, Cruickshank, Frostig, Kephart) attributed learning disabilities to perceptual-motor problems, although in most instances they too held that neurological disorders were the fundamental cause of the condition. Other pioneers (Kirk, McCarthy) argued that learning disabilities were caused by psycholinguistic disorders. Quay (1973) grouped these views together, stating that they are all characterized by the belief that learning disabilities are caused by within-child *process dysfunctions*.

Some professionals believe that learning disabilities are caused by *experience defects* (Quay, 1973). They believe that individuals demonstrate academic and social difficulties because of defective or harmful early experience.

A third group of professionals believe that learning disabilities are caused by what Quay labeled *experiential deficits*. Problems are seen as the direct result of inadequate opportunities to acquire the prerequisities for performing the tasks students are assigned in school. The emphasis here is not on harmful experience, as with experience defects, but on lack of appropriate experiences. A subgroup of those who ascribe to this view believes that learning disabilities result from inadequate teaching (Baer & Bushell, 1981).

A fourth view on the causes of learning disabilities is one that Quay (1973) labeled an *interactive view,* the belief that learning disabilities arise from an interaction between process dysfunctions, experience defects, and experience deficits.

To date, explanations for the specific causes of learning disabilities are based on correlational findings. Professionals find a variety of conditions *related* to learning disabilities. In far too many instances they have concluded that correlation is evidence for causation. For example, because many students labeled LD demonstrate perceptual-motor problems, many professionals have concluded that perceptual-motor problems *cause* learning problems and learning disabilities. Such a conclusion is, of course, unwarranted.

MAJOR TYPES OF SYNDROMES

The history of the field of learning disabilities is characterized by repeated efforts to identify major syndromes associated with the condition. This section focuses on some recent promising efforts to identify syndromes.

The concept of the LD student as an *inactive learner* (Torgesen, 1977) has received increasing attention in recent years. Originally derived from research on memory processes in LD children, Torgesen's work suggests that LD children have deficits in the spontaneous application of appropriate cognitive strategies to tasks but that they can be trained to use such strategies successfully. Torgesen argued that deficits in ability must be distinguished from deficits in performance and suggested that many of the performance deficits of LD children may result from general factors (rather than specific process disabilities) that affect performance in various task settings. One explanation proposed by Torgesen for the IQ-achievement discrepancy typically observed for LD children is that intelligence tests and school tasks place different demands on the learner. Intelligence tests sample primarily incidental learning and acculturation, whereas achievement tests sample specific factual material encoded during formal academic exposure. Torgesen suggested that LD students fail to adapt to new learning challenges (as represented in achievement tests) because of their inability to make efficient use of cognitive strategies (e.g., memorization, use of mnemonic devices, verbal rehearsal). The LD child as "inactive learner" is thought to be less aware of his or her cognitive processes or strategies (e.g., noting that he or she needs to write down a telephone number in order to remember it) and to show less goal-directedness and less intentional use of organization skills—in short, to respond to task demands differently from normal children.

Torgesen (1980) reviewed evidence supporting the notion that LD students fail to use appropriate task strategies spontaneously in a variety of situations. He noted that LD students, across different ages and different samples, have been shown to "demonstrate deficiencies in the use of verbal labeling and rehearsal strategies, the use of organizational structure to aid recall, and the active construction of implied parts of sentences" (p. 368). Hallahan and Reeve (1980) proposed that

the most parsimonious explanation for the learning disabled child's tendency to have problems in attending to relevant cues and ignoring irrelevant cues . . . is his inability to bring to the task a specific learning strategy. . . . Apparently, then it is not so much the learning disabled child's inability to attend selectively that is his/her basic problem so much as it is his inability to analyze the task in terms of the best strategies needed for performing it. (p. 156)

As demonstrated by investigations at the University of Virginia Learning Disabilities Research Institute, although LD students are slow to develop efficient encoding strategies such as labeling and verbal rehearsal, they can be trained successfully in the use of specific task strategies (Hallahan & Reeve, 1980). The primary problems to date with efforts to train LD students in the use of efficient learning strategies have been assuring adequate maintenance of those strategies and the appropriate generalization of strategies to new applications. The learning strategies notion recently has been applied as a programming approach (Schumaker et al., 1983) and preliminary results have been promising.

Another interesting approach has been proposed by Vellutino in his formulation of the verbal deficit hypothesis (Vellutino, 1977). He suggested that poor readers lack information about, and therefore fail to use, linguistic cues for labeling. He cited evidence on phonological, syntactical, and semantic components of language as possible areas of difficulty and suggested that LD individuals' encoding of stimuli is inefficient, affecting subsequent synthesis and retrieval of stimuli. As the poor reader labors over word decoding, his or her capacity to remember information from previous material is reduced and comprehension is adversely affected. The instructional implications of Vellutino's hypothesis are clear; he emphasizes direct instruction, calls for diagnostic and treatment procedures that focus on performance and task variables in units that closely correspond to the skill to be learned, and suggests avoidance of assumptions about the learner's ability or inability to acquire a skill which are based on etiological theories or which precede attempts to teach skills (Vellutino, Steger, Moyer, Harding, & Niles, 1977).

MANIFESTATIONS AND IMPACT

As Torgesen (1980) noted, "One of the few things that all learning disabled children have in common with one another is failure in school" (p. 369). Kirk and Elkins (1975) reported that LD students evidence significant reading problems, and a considerable body of research has focused on the reading difficulties of LD students. Research on the oral reading skills of LD students has demonstrated that they use context cues less often than do normal students, and that they rely more heavily on phonics cues (Bryan, 1980). Cawley and his colleagues (Cawley, Fitzmaurice, Shaw, Kahn, & Bates, 1979) have focused on the math difficulties experienced by LD students and have emphasized the implications of deficits in math for daily living and vocational skills.

Research by Bryan and her colleagues (Bryan, Pearl, Donahue, Bryan, &

Pflaum, 1983) indicated that learning disabled children were more likely than their nondisabled peers to believe that success at a task was the result of external factors such as luck, other people, or task characteristics. They were also less likely to adopt an internal locus of control—to attribute success to their own efforts and abilities. Thus LD children may not necessarily interpret successes as reflecting something positive about themselves, nor may they view failures as something that they can overcome with effort.

Research on locus of control among LD adolescents, however, has indicated no significant differences from non-LD adolescents in responses to general self-esteem and attribution questionnaires (Tollefson, Tracy, Johnson, Borgers, Buenning, Farmer, & Barke, 1980). Learning disabled adolescents did report that effort was a factor that explained success or failure in academic tasks but explained their personal success or failure on a specific spelling task by factors other than effort.

The belief that there is a link between learning disabilities and juvenile delinquency has received increasing attention recently. Prevalence estimates of learning disabilities among juvenile delinquents have ranged from 26 to 73% (Zimmerman, Rich, Keilitz, & Broder, 1980), substantially above estimates for prevalence of learning disabilities in the normal population. One of the few rigorous empirical studies in this area was recently completed by the Association for Children with Learning Disabilities and the National Center for State Courts (Broder, Dunivant, Smith, & Sutton, 1981; Keilitz & Miller, 1980; Keilitz, Zaremba, & Broder, 1979; Lane, 1980; Zimmerman et al., 1980). The study was designed to determine the prevalence of learning disabilities in groups of adjudicated delinquent and nondelinquent 12- to 15-year-old males. Preliminary findings of the study, which involved records review and extensive testing of more than a thousand public school students and adjudicated youths in the metropolitan areas of Baltimore, Phoenix, and Indianapolis, revealed that of the public school (nonadjudicated) youth, 18.9% were identified as LD; approximately double that prevalence rate, or 36.5% of the adjudicated youth, were determined to have learning disabilities (Broder et al., 1981).

It is also interesting to note the relative proportion of LD youths who are adjudicated delinquent. Of the youths classified as LD by the investigators, 55.6% were adjudicated; 33.7% of the non-LD youths were in the delinquent group. When prevalence figures were weighted, based on the assumption that adjudicated boys represent approximately 4% of the 12- to 15-year-old male population, the rate of adjudication among LD youths (7.4%) was more than twice that among non-LD youths (3.2%). These figures support the existence of a significant relationship between learning disabilities and adjudication. It should be noted, however, that there appeared to be no relationship between learning disabilities and incarceration; of the adjudicated youth, LD and non-LD subjects demonstrated equal rates of incarceration. Subjects also completed a 28-item self-report questionnaire assessing frequency of delinquent activities. When the effects of potentially confounding background variables were controlled, LD youths reported less delinquent behavior than non-LD youths. Learning disabled public school youth reported being picked up by the police at about the same rate as non-LD youth, and charges for conviction for LD and non-LD youth followed the same patterns.

Numerous theories have been proposed to account for the fact that although LD youth do not evidence more delinquent behavior than non-LD youth, they are more likely to be found delinquent by the courts. Broder et al. (1981) suggested that LD adolescents' expressive deficits, poor social skills, and poor abstract thinking skills may negatively affect their treatment in the judicial system. Zimmerman et al. (1980) proposed the *different treatment* model as an explanation for this phenomenon, in contrast to the *school failure* rationale and the *susceptibility* rationale. The different treatment model proposes that LD and non-LD youth engage in the same type and amount of delinquent behaviors but that one or more elements of the juvenile justice system treat LD and non-LD youth differently. The school failure rationale suggests that learning disabilities result in school failure leading to a negative self-image and association with a delinquency-prone peer group. The susceptibility rationale suggests that learning disabilities are accompanied by such behavioral characteristics as impulsivity, emotional lability, inability to conceptualize social relationships, and poor social perception, which increase the likelihood of delinquent behavior (Lane, 1980). It should be noted that the Zimmerman et al. study is not a direct test of the different treatment hypothesis but simply a set of correlational findings that suggest avenues for future research.

Difficulties in social interaction are also said to be related to learning disabilities. The most systematic research on the social problems of LD students has been conducted by the Bryans and their colleagues at the Chicago Institute for Learning Disabilities. Across time and using different samples, personality and social interaction studies have demonstrated personality and behavioral differences between LD and normally achieving youngsters. Learning disabled students, particularly girls, were found to be unpopular and to have difficulty developing friendships (Donahue, 1983). As Bryan and Sherman (1980) noted,

> However heterogeneous LD children may be in their performance on academic or cognitive tasks . . . they apparently share one commonality (i.e., their proclivity to alienate others, be they strangers or acquaintances, children or adults). Whether their academic deficiencies lead to the rejection, or their rejection leads to the deficiencies, or whether both are affected in yet unknown ways by other variables, remains to be seen. Clearly, however, they do share a common source of variance: social offensiveness. (p. 26)

The Bryans and their colleagues have investigated the communicative competence and social interactions of LD children. Although LD children were found to talk as much as nondisabled children, their exchanges differed on a number of dimensions. Learning disabled children functioned less well as listeners, and they made and received more negative statements than their normal achieving peers (Bryan & Bryan, 1978); they also appeared much less adaptive in their verbal interactions with younger children, neglecting to give instructional pointers to children to whom they were teaching a game (Bryan & Pflaum, 1978). Similarly, LD children were less tactful and less persuasive than nondisabled peers (Donahue, 1983).

Learning disabled children's conversational skills appeared to vary with the degree of contextual support provided in the conversation (Bryan et al., 1983). Although LD children performed as well as their nondisabled classmates when another speaker assumed responsibility for guiding the conversation or when there were clear cues about what responses were appropriate, LD students were significantly less able to initiate or be responsible for maintaining a conversation.

Learning disabled children also were significantly less accurate than normal children in understanding nonverbal communication (Bryan, 1977), a deficit that may affect others' attitudes toward them. They also have been found to demonstrate poorer role-taking skills than normal achieving children (Wong & Wong, 1980), a deficit which may be a possible source of their unpopularity. A diminished ability to put themselves in another's place may lead to a failure to understand and accommodate others' viewpoints, reducing the probability of successful social interaction between LD children and their normal peers.

Such social interaction problems also have been documented in adolescence and adulthood. In their review of social skills assessment and training for the learning disabled, Schumaker and Hazel (1984) noted that LD individuals

> tend to choose less socially acceptable behaviors for use in specifically named situations; they are less able to predict consequences for behaviors; they misinterpret social cues; they are less likely to adapt their behavior to the characteristics of their listener; they perform certain appropriate verbal and nonverbal skills at significantly lower levels than their peers; and they perform certain inappropriate skills at significantly higher levels than their peers. (p. 426)

Learning disabled adolescents were found to exhibit poorer social skills than non-LD students on seven of eight skills judged important for successful adjustment (accepting negative feedback, conversing, giving positive and negative feedback, negotiating, social problem solving, and resisting peer pressure) (Schumaker et al., 1983).

Observational studies indicated that LD junior high students were not social isolates in the classroom (Deshler, Schumaker, Lenz, & Ellis, 1984). But although LD adolescents interacted as frequently as normal students with peers and teachers, they more frequently violated classroom rules by being off-task, failing to comply with directions, or talking out. Learning disabled young adults also reported less satisfaction with their social lives than their non-handicapped peers and reported having significantly fewer close friends with whom they shared activities. They also were significantly less involved in recreational activities or social organizations than their non-LD peers (Deshler, Schumaker, Alley, Warner, & Clark, 1981).

However, Schumaker and Hazel (1984) noted that not all LD individuals exhibit such social skill deficits, and relatively few studies have related the apparent deficits and excesses noted above to peer popularity and social success. Similarly, it is unclear whether such deficits are skill or performance deficits: skill deficits are defined as problems resulting when needed skills are not in an individual's cognitive or behavioral repertoire, whereas performance deficits result when the skills are present in an individual's repertoire but are not performed when appropriate.

UNDERLYING PROCESSES

Although the notion of underlying process deficits in many respects has been the core of the notion of learning disabilities from its inception, and although the current federal definition of learning disabilities still includes an assumption of process deficits, this issue has been one of heated debate. It has been argued that processes do not exist, and that what does not exist cannot be trained (Mann, 1970, 1971a, 1971b; Mann & Phillips, 1967; Ysseldyke, 1978). Arter and Jenkins (1979) reviewed research on differential diagnosis and prescriptive teaching, efforts to assess and train processes, and concluded that there was no empirical support for the practice.

Largely in response to some of the criticisms of the process approach, behavioral theorists have addressed instructional variables in learning disabilities, concentrating on task analysis and concept analysis. These approaches are based on the premise that information on etiology, even if known, would not provide the teacher with direction on how to teach a specific skill, and that what is needed is an analysis of the prerequisite skills involved in a given task. The task analysis approach focuses on direct manipulation of the learning situation and emphasizes use of information that is directly relevant to instruction in academic skills. Such approaches have been effective in the instruction of discrete skills and tasks but generalization of skills has proven a problem.

The behaviorally oriented task-analytic approach has also come under its share of criticism in recent years, in part because the philosophy underlying such an approach appears too deterministic for some. As Mann (1980) noted,

We have been too long preoccupied with behavioral principles in special education. They have introduced a note of Prussian precision in our midst not entirely compatible with American principles. ("You vill complete three out of five four-number single-column addition problems.") (p. 416)

Or as Hammill (1980) commented in an address to members of the Division of Children with Learning Disabilities,

> Early in the 1970's the pendulum swung to something called criterion-referenced testing or what I call measurement of the tacky. I have a feeling that anything that can be reduced to 64 sequenced, behavioral objectives of skills is bound to have no relevance at all. (p. 5)

According to Torgesen (1979), the antiprocess revolution of behavioral objectives, contingency management, applied behavioral analysis, and criterion-referenced measurement neglects a conceptualization of individual differences in cognitive functioning that can affect both what particular skills and in what manner a child learns. This shortcoming has served as an impetus to a new approach to conceptualizing learning disabilities, one which bears striking resemblance to some features of the old process training notions.

This new "task-centered" approach (Torgesen, 1979) draws heavily on research in developmental psychology and information processing. Like behaviorally oriented task-analytic approaches, it incorporates a detailed breakdown of the child's competencies with regard to the skills required for successful completion of an academic task. But the task-centered approach goes beyond the pure behavioral approach in that research based on this model attempts to determine not only those kinds of processing deficiencies that can be addressed by direct instruction but also those that might require restructuring of academic activities (because of deficits resulting from structural impairment).

This rediscovery of cognitive principles, or recommitment to processes, is as yet largely untested in terms of implications for intervention, although it has indicated some interesting directions for research (Torgesen, 1980). Researchers from a variety of fields have embraced it as holding promise for solving the ills of learning disabilities.

> Special education's recommitment to processes, in any case, can justify itself (at least to me) simply on the basis that it washes the dusty-dry grit of instructional objectives out of our cerebral cortices and resists the legalistic-behavioristic graying of our field. (Mann, 1979, p. 417)

But as Hallahan (1980) noted in his introduction to a special issue on cognitive training, "good common sense combined with a penchant for scientific rigor" should encourage an "appropriate degree of caution," placing "cognitive training in the realm of ideas to be tested experimentally, not cast . . . as another in the long line of touted cure-alls for special education" (pp. xiv–xv).

Despite periodic swings of the pendulum, then, processes still appear to be the lifeblood of learning disability theory (Mann, 1980). And since educational practice typically follows new theoretical formulations, even as notions of process deficits fall in disfavor in the universities, they are incorporated into diagnosis and programming in the schools. Present alternatives to the notion of processes (e.g., use of discrepancy formulas) fail to distinguish learning disabilities from school failure, underachievement, or other handicapping conditions. It appears that process will continue to be with us:

> Process training has always made the phoenix look like a bedraggled sparrow. You cannot kill it. It simply bides its time in exile after being dislodged by one of history's periodic attacks upon it and then returns, wearing disguises or carrying new noms de plume, as it were, but consisting of the same old ideas, doing business much in the same old way. (Mann, 1979, p. 539)

TREATMENT AND INTERVENTION

Like all of special education, the field of learning disabilities has been characterized by diverse efforts to intervene in students' educational programs in an effort to ameliorate or alleviate academic or social problems. Treatment efforts in the field of learning disabilities have been implemented both rapidly and broadly before there is demonstrated research support for the efficacy of the interventions (Ysseldyke & Algozzine, 1982). The basis for adoption of specific interventions has been described by Ysseldyke and Algozzine, who noted five sources of decisions to intervene in students' programs:

1. *Bandwagon.* The tendency to adopt interventions because of their popularity in other settings, characterized by faddism.
2. *Tradition and history.* The adoption of treatments simply because "they have always worked" or because "they worked before."
3. *Cash validity.* The adoption of treatments because they sell well, or the creation of interventions for the purpose of financial gain.
4. *Testimonial evidence.* The selection of treatments or interventions on the basis of colleagues' testimony or because people were taught in university courses that the programs worked.
5. *"Doctor-tested."* The adoption of interventions because the interventions have been tested "and found effective in many cases."

Ysseldyke and Algozzine (1982) also described the kinds of interventions employed with LD students at the elementary school level. Most of those interventions, until very recently, were based on the belief that LD students' problems were evidenced because they had basic underlying within-student deficiencies. Intervention efforts have consisted of optometric training, visual-perceptual training, auditory-perceptual training, neurological organization training, perceptual-motor training, and psycholinguistic training. To date, however, there has been little empirical support for such efforts.

Within the past 15-20 years a promising trend has emerged in intervention efforts at the elementary level. Approaches derived largely from functional analyses of behavior have focused on instructional ecology. Emphasis was placed first on identifying those aspects of instruction that are under teacher control and can be modified to alleviate academic and social problems. The approach operates under assumptions that there is no way, *a priori,* to match instruction to assessment results, that any intervention decision is a hypothesis, and that data must be collected throughout the teaching process to verify the appropriateness of the intervention (Deno & Mirkin, 1977). The approach is promising because it is data-based, individualized, and cuts through the mystique associated with the notion that test results tell us how to teach students.

Programs for LD students at the secondary level have been relatively slow to develop and initially consisted primarily of upward extensions of elementary level remedial models. Increased attention to the particular needs of the LD adolescent in recent years, resulting in part from increased recognition of the new demands placed on a student moving to the junior high level and lack of evidence supporting the efficacy of the remedial model, has led to the development of a number of functional or coping skills curricula (Meyen & Lehr, 1980).

Deshler and his colleagues at the University of Kansas IRLD (Deshler et al., 1984; Lowrey, Deshler, & Alley, 1979) have identified a number of options in current programming for LD adolescents: the basic skill remediation approach, the tutorial approach, the learning strategies approach, the functional curriculum approach, and the work-study approach. The *basic skill remediation approach* is basically an upward extension of the predominant approach at the elementary level and was the most widely used service delivery model at the secondary level (about 51%) according to Lowrey et al.'s survey of 98 secondary LD teachers in 48 states. This approach is based on the assumptions underlying the diagnostic-prescriptive model; its implementation at the secondary level assumes that remediation of basic skills is prerequisite to content acquisition and that such instruction will be effective despite a history of failure at the elementary level.

The second most popular approach at the secondary level, the *tutorial approach,* emphasizes providing instruction in the regular academic curriculum. Short-term academic needs (e.g., passing a test) are addressed by the learning disabilities teacher to the possible neglect of generalization of skills to other materials and settings.

The *compensatory approach* uses nontraditional means of presenting content to help LD adolescents master secondary level subject matter. A variety of audio and visual formats (e.g., taping lectures, use of films to present content information, oral presentation of tests) are used to help the adolescent acquire information while circumventing skill deficits.

The *functional curriculum approach* is intended to help equip students to function effectively in society. This approach requires the development of a new curriculum, one which emphasizes consumer information and survival skills. It assumes that survival skills are identifiable and stable over time and that the LD student's chances of succeeding in a more traditional program are minimal.

The *work-study approach* is not as widely represented in learning disabilities programs as in programs for the educable mentally handicapped, in part because of the emphasis to date on normal intelligence of the LD student and subsequent development of postsecondary academic programs. This approach typically combines half-day instruction in job-related skills with half-day on-the-job experiences.

The *learning strategies approach* emphasizes teaching students *how* to learn rather than teaching them specific content. Students are taught to use existing academic skills in a strategic fashion to help them acquire, manipulate, store, retrieve, and express content information. This relatively recent approach, although used by only 4% of the teachers surveyed by Lowrey et al. (1979), has been increasing in popularity. The learning strategies approach has been employed for several years with promising results by researchers at the University of Kansas IRLD, who have validated an eight-step instructional methodology with more than 90 LD adolescents in both individual and group training situations (Deshler, Schumaker, & Lenz, 1984).

It is important to note that a single program rarely exemplifies any of the above approaches in the purest sense; rather, school systems generally include components from a number of approaches. Each of the above approaches is based on a different set of assumptions concerning the essential skills for LD adolescents to acquire. Appropriate program selection also requires consideration of age-related demands that are imposed by school and society.

Evidence supports some essential features of effective intervention programs, however, whether at the elementary or secondary level. Samuels (1981) described characteristics of exemplary reading programs which profitably could be applied to intervention programs in learning disabilities:

1. Strong administrative support, including encouragement, creation of a supportive organizational climate, provision of time for planning and implementing decisions, financial support, and liaison with the school and community.
2. High expectations for success and the belief that the school is largely responsible for the success and failure of its students.
3. Use of teacher aides in direct instruction and use of specialists in supportive roles (as consultants, trainers, resource people, etc.).
4. Teacher commitment to project goals.
5. Teacher training experiences that are concrete, teacher-specific, focused on practical problems, and that involve teachers in structured, skills-centered decision making.

6. A curriculum with clear and specific objectives and relevant materials.
7. Combination of a high task orientation with a positive classroom climate.
8. Efficient use of time.
9. High intensity of treatment.
10. Frequent evaluation of student progress.

Developers of intervention programs for LD children would do well to incorporate Samuels' list of features of effective programs into their planning activities.

PERSONAL PERSPECTIVES

Definition

The field of learning disabilities is characterized by considerable lack of agreement about *who* should be considered learning disabled and *how* they should be educated. The confusion exists because educators who identify interventions that work with a particular group of students labeled LD for the most part have been unable to replicate their interventions in new settings. Students labeled LD in one setting differ from those labeled LD in another setting and appear to have only one characteristic in common: they perform poorly in school.

The label LD is elusive and probably defies definition. Indeed Lovitt (1978) argued that it is as if someone perpetrated a great hoax by using the term and then challenging others to define it. Scores of professionals and task forces, he says, have taken the bait. The term defies definition for two reasons. First, an extremely heterogeneous group of students is now labeled LD. The academic and social problems experienced by those students are multidimensional, and the causes of the problems are multidimensional. Yet efforts to define "learning disabilities" have, for the most part, been unidimensional. We will never, in spite of all our efforts, define learning disabilities within an unidimensional model. Reger (1979) noted that "even a casual historical perspective suggests that the unidimensional single-factor trait discrepancy model of learning disability never will result in a satisfactory definition" (p. 530).

Second, at the present time the learning disability category is being used as a sociopolitical solution to an educational problem. Since the passing of compulsory education laws in the seventeenth century, educators have had difficulty figuring out what to do with students who failed to profit from the programs the schools (and society through its schools) designed for them. Early in American educational history students who failed to profit were simply excluded from school. The courts, in the late 1960s and early 1970s, ruled such "solutions" unconstitutional and forbade schools from excluding many different kinds of students, including the handicapped. Public Law 94–142 is a new kind of compulsory education law that mandates that schools provide an *appropriate* education for all handicapped students.

Significant numbers of students currently are failing in school. Educators, for the most part, believe that students fail either because of home and family problems or because of fundamental within-student disorders, deficits, or disabilities. Few—approximately 5%—attribute academic failure to the failure of schools and teachers to provide appropriate instruction. Although we believe that a proportion of students currently labeled LD do indeed have "learning disabilities," the majority are "teaching disabled," individuals for whom we simply have not identified appropriate interventions.

Senf (1977) talked about the sociopolitical nature of current efforts to serve LD students as follows:

> Learning disabilities were not empirically discovered in the early 1960's; rather, an economically relevant and politically viable coalition was formed which proved capable of instituting the term learning disabilities in law. While it is true that legislators had to be convinced of the reality of learning disabilities, it was the convincing, not the reality, that made LD law. In the extreme, one can even put forth the position that the convincing is the reality for all economic purposes for without the present law, who would quibble over whether a child did or did not have a learning disability? (p. 600)

Although this may be overly simplistic, we believe the only way currently to address the definitional dilemma is statistically. Until some better methodology is derived for doing so, we believe schools must decide what proportion of their population they have the necessary resources to serve and must then serve those who are worse off. Efforts to identify *a* unitary or unidimensional "condition" we believe will be unsuccessful.

Assessment

The state of the art in assessing LD students is incredibly problematic. It currently costs school systems between $500 and $700 simply to declare a student eligible for learning disabilities services. Assessment is completed using for the most part technically inadequate norm-referenced tests and decisions are probably wrong as often as they are right.

Currently assessment efforts exist as a kind of smokescreen to give alleged objectivity to a subjective process of declaring students eligible for learning disability services (Ysseldyke, Algozzine, Richey, & Graden, 1982). The state of the art is such that, by selecting from among several definitions of learning disabilities, using enough instruments, and selecting from a number of proposed cutoff scores, an assessor can label any student LD (Algozzine & Ysseldyke, 1981).

It is time to move more closely to the instructional scene, to discontinue efforts to assess students independently of the instructional ecology in which they learn, and to use data on intervention effectiveness for the purpose of making eligibility, classification, placement, and intervention decisions (Ysseldyke & Regan, 1980).

Intervention

Intervention efforts for LD students must, we believe, be based on data demonstrating their effectiveness. This belief has two immediate implications. Either we must, *a priori,* have data that indicate that a particular intervention is effective, or we must regularly gather data during intervention to provide evidence for the effectiveness of the intervention we use. Since the former is seldom the way things are, we strongly advocate a practice of formative evaluation of intervention effectiveness. We believe that if such practices were observed, we could end the ceaseless argumentation about interventions that were effective for LD students. Effective interventions would be defined as those for which the school has data on their effectiveness with individual students.

REFERENCES

Algozzine, B., Forgnone, C., Mercer, C., & Trifiletti, J. Toward defining discrepancies for specific learning disabilities: An analysis and alternatives. *Learning Disability Quarterly,* 1979, *2*(4), 25–31.

Algozzine, B., & Ysseldyke, J. E. Special education services for normal children: Better safe than sorry. *Exceptional Children,* 1981, *48,* 238–243.

Arter, J. A., & Jenkins, J. R. Differential diagnosis–prescriptive teaching: A critical appraisal. *Review of Educational Research,* 1979, *49,* 517–556.

Baer, D., & Bushell, D. The future of behavior analysis in the school? Consider its recent past, and then ask a different question. In J. Ysseldyke & R. Weinberg (Eds.), *The future of psychology in the schools: Proceedings of the Spring Hill Symposium* (Special issue). *School Psychology Review,* 1981, *10*(2).

Broder, P. K., Dunivant, W., Smith, E. C., & Sutton, L. P. Further observations on the link between learning disabilities and juvenile delinquency. *Journal of Educational Psychology,* 1981, *73*(6), 838–850.

Bryan, J., & Sherman, A. Immediate impressions of nonverbal ingratiation attempts by LD boys. *Learning Disability Quarterly,* 1980, *3,* 19–28.

Bryan, T. H. Learning disabled children's comprehension of nonverbal communication. *Journal of Learning Disabilities,* 1977, *10*(3), 501–506.

Bryan, T. H. The Chicago Institute for Learning Disabilities. *The Forum,* 1980, *6*(4), 4–5.

Bryan, T. H., & Bryan, J. H. Social interactions of learning disabled children. *Learning Disability Quarterly,* 1978, *1*(1), 33–38.

Bryan, T., Pearl, R., Donahue, M., Bryan, J., & Pflaum, S. The Chicago Institute for Learning Disabilities. *Exceptional Education Quarterly,* 1983, *444*(1), 1–22.

Bryan, T., & Pflaum, S. Social interactions of learning disabled children: A linguistic, social, and cognitive analysis. *Learning Disability Quarterly,* 1978, *1*(3), 70–79.

Cawley, J. F., Fitzmaurice, A. M., Shaw, R., Kahn, H., & Bates, H. LD youth and mathematics: A review of characteristics. *Learning Disability Quarterly,* 1979, *2*(1), 29–44.

Chalfant, J. C., & Scheffelin, M. A. *Central processing dysfunction in children: A review of research, phase three of a three phase project* (NINDS Monograph 9). Bethesda, Md.: U.S. Department of Health, Education and Welfare, 1969.

Clements, S. D. *Minimal brain dysfunction in children: Terminology and identification, phase one of a three-phase project* (NINDS Monograph 3, Public Health Service Bulletin No. 1415). Washington, D.C.: U.S. Department of Health, Education and Welfare, 1966.

Coles, G. S. The learning-disabilities test battery: Empirical and social issues. *Harvard Educational Review,* 1978, *48,* 313–340.

Danielson, L. C., & Bauer, J. N. A formula-based classification of learning disabled children: An examination of the issues. *Journal of Learning Disabilities,* 1978, *11*(3), 163–176.

Deno, S., & Mirkin, P. *Data-based program modification: A manual.* Reston, Va.: Council for Exceptional Children, 1977.

Deshler, D. D., Schumaker, J. B., Alley, G. R., Warner, M. W., & Clark, F. L. Social interaction deficits in learning disabled adolescents—Another myth? In W. M. Cruickshank & A. A. Silver (Eds.), *Bridges to tomorrow, Vol. 2, The best of ACLD.* Syracuse, NY: Syracuse University Press, 1981.

Deshler, D. D., Schumaker, J. B., & Lenz, B. K. Academic and cognitive interventions for LD adolescents (Part 1). *Journal of Learning Disabilities,* 1984, *17*(2), 108–117.

Deshler, D. D., Schumaker, J. B., Lenz, B. K., & Ellis, E. Academic and cognitive interventions for LD adolescents (Part 2). *Journal of Learning Disabilities,* 1984, *17*(3), 170–179.

Donahue, M. Learning-disabled children as conversational partners. *Topics in Language Disorders,* 1983, *4*(1), 16–27.

Englemann, S., Granzin, A., & Severson, H. Diagnosing instruction. *Journal of Special Education,* 1979, *13,* 355–365.

Epps, S., Ysseldyke, J. E., & Algozzine, B. Impact of different definitions of learning disabilities on the number of students identified. *Journal of Psychoeducational Assessment,* 1983, *1,* 341–352.

Epps, S., Ysseldyke, J. E., & McGue, M. "I know one when I see one"—Differentiating LD and non-LD students. *Learning Disability Quarterly,* 1984, *7,* 89–101.

Gajar, A. H. Characteristics across exceptional categories: EMR, LD, and ED. *Journal of Special Education,* 1980, *14,* 165–173.

Hallahan, D. P. Foreword. Teaching exceptional children to use cognitive strategies. *Exceptional Education Quarterly,* 1980, *1*(1), xiv–xv.

Hallahan, D. P., & Kauffman, J. M. *Introduction to learning disabilities: A psychobehavioral approach.* Englewood Cliffs, N.J.: Prentice-Hall, 1976.

Hallahan, D. P., & Reeve, R. E. Selective attention and distractibility. In B. K. Keogh (Ed.), *Advances in special education* (Vol. 1) (pp. 141–181). Greenwich, Conn.: JAI Press, 1980.

Hammill, D. D. The field of learning disabilities: A futuristic perspective. *Learning Disability Quarterly*, 1980, *3*(2), 2–9.

Haring, N. G., & Miller, C. A. (Eds.) *Minimal brain dysfunction in children: Educational, medical, and health related services, phase two of a three phase project* (NINDS Monograph, Public Health Publication No. 2015). Washington, D.C.: U.S. Department of Health, Education, and Welfare, 1969.

Keilitz, I., & Miller, S. L. Handicapped adolescents and young adults in the justice system. *Exceptional Education Quarterly*, 1980, *1*(2), 117–126.

Keilitz, I., Zaremba, B. A., & Broder, P. K. The link between learning disabilities and juvenile delinquency: Some issues and answers. *Learning Disability Quarterly*, 1979, *2*(2), 2–11.

Keogh, B. K., Major, S. M., Omori, H., Gandará, P., & Reid, H. P. Proposed markers in learning disabilities research. *Journal of Abnormal Child Psychiatry*, 1980, *8* (1), 21–31.

Kirk, S. A., & Elkins, J. Characteristics of children enrolled in the Child Service Demonstration Centers. *Journal of Learning Disabilities*, 1975, *8*(10), 630–637.

Lambert, N. School psychology training for the decades ahead. In J. Ysseldyke & R. Weinberg (Ed.), *The future of psychology in the schools: Proceedings of the Spring Hill Symposium* (special issue). *School Psychology Review*, 1981, *10*(2).

Lane, B. A. The relationship of learning disabilities to juvenile delinquency: Current status. *Journal of Learning Disabilities*, 1980, *13*(8), 425–434.

Leigh, J. The NJCLD position papers. *Learning Disability Quarterly*, 1983, *6*(1), 40–54.

Lovitt, T. *Reactions to planned research*. Paper presented at the Roundtable Conference on Learning Disabilities, Minneapolis, Minn., 1978.

Lowrey, N., Deshler, D., & Alley, G. Programming alternatives for learning disabled adolescents: A nationwide survey. *Academic Therapy*, 1979, *14*, 389–397.

Mann, L. Are we fractionating too much? *Academic Therapy*, 1970, *5*, 85–91.

Mann, L. Perceptual training revisited: The training of nothing at all. *Rehabilitation Literature*, 1971, *32*, 322–335.(a)

Mann, L. Psychometric phrenology and the new faculty psychology: The case against ability assessment and training. *Journal of Special Education*, 1971, *5*, 3–14.(b)

Mann, L. *On the trail of process*. New York: Grune & Stratton, 1979.

Mann, L. Divagations. *Journal of Special Education*, 1980, *14*, 415–417.

Mann, L. M., & Phillips, W. A. Fractional practices in special education: A critique. *Exceptional Children*, 1967, *33*, 311–317.

Mardell-Czudnowski, C. The four Ws of current testing practices: Who; what; why; and to whom—An exploratory survey. *Learning Disability Quarterly*, 1980, *3*(1), 73–83.

Meyen, E., & Lehr, D. H. Evolving practices in assessment and intervention for mildly handicapped adolescents: The case for intensive instruction. *Exceptional Education Quarterly*, 1980, *1*(2), 19–26.

Myers, P. I., & Hammill, D. D. *Methods for learning disorders* (2nd ed.). New York: Wiley, 1976.

Norman, C. A., & Zigmond, N. Characteristics of children labeled and served as learning disabled in school systems affiliated with Child Service Demonstration Centers. *Journal of Learning Disabilities,* 1980, *13*(10), 542–547.

Quay, H. C. Special education: Assumptions, techniques, and evaluative criteria. *Exceptional Children,* 1973, *40,* 165–170.

Reger, R. Learning disabilities: Futile attempts at a simplistic definition. *Journal of Learning Disabilities,* 1979, *12*(8), 529–532.

Salvia, J., & Ysseldyke, J. E. *Assessment in speical and remedial education* (2nd ed.). Boston: Houghton Mifflin, 1981.

Samuels, S. J. Characteristics of exemplary reading programs. In J. T. Guthrie (Ed.), *Comprehension and teaching: Research reviews* (pp. 255–273). Newark, Del.: International Reading Association, 1981.

Sarason, S. B., & Doris, J. *Educational handicap, public policy, and social history.* New York: Free Press, 1979.

Schumaker, J. B., Deshler, D. D., Alley, G. R., & Warner, M. M. Toward the development of an intervention model for learning disabled adolescents: The University of Kansas Institute. *Exceptional Education Quarterly,* 1983, *4*(1), 45–74.

Schumaker, J. B., & Hazel, J. S. Social skills assessment and training for the learning disabled: Who's on first and what's on second? (Part 1). *Journal of Learning Disabilities,* 1984, *17*(7), 422–431.

Senf, G. M. Are our differences truly questions of fact? *Journal of Learning Disabilities,* 1977, *10*(10), 599–600.

Thurlow, M. L., & Ysseldyke, J. E. Current assessment and decision-making practices in model LD programs. *Learning Disability Quarterly,* 1979, *2*(4), 15–24.

Thurlow, M. L., & Ysseldyke, J. E. Instructional planning: Information collected by school psychologists *v* information considered useful by teachers. *Journal of School Psychology,* 1982, *20,* 3–10.

Tollefson, N., Tracy, D., Johnson, E., Borgers, M. S., Buenning, M., Farmer, A., & Barke, C. *An application of attribution theory to developing self-esteem in learning disabled adolescents* (Research Report No. 23). Lawrence: University of Kansas, Institute for Research on Learning Disabilities, 1980.

Torgesen, J. K. The role of nonspecific factors in the task performance of learning disabled children: A theoretical assessment. *Journal of Learning Disabilities,* 1977, *10*(1), 27–34.

Torgesen, J. K. What shall we do with psychological processes? *Journal of Learning Disabilities,* 1979, *12*(8), 514–521.

Torgesen, J. K. Conceptual and educational implications of the use of efficient task strategies by learning disabled children. *Journal of Learning Disabilities,* 1980, *13*(7), 364–371.

Tucker, J. A. Ethnic proportions in classes for the learning disabled: Issues in non-biased assessment. *Journal of Special Education,* 1980, *14,* 93–105.

Tucker, J. A., Stevens, L. J., & Ysseldyke, J. E. Learning disabilities: The experts speak out. *Journal of Learning Disabilities,* 1983, *16*(1), 6–14.

U.S. Department of Education. *"To assure the free appropriate public education of all handicapped children." Sixth annual report to Congress on the implementa-*

tion of Public Law 94-142: The Education for All Handicapped Children Act. Washington, D.C.: U.S. Department of Education, Office of Special Education and Rehabilitative Services.

U.S. Office of Education. Education of handicapped children: Assistance to states: Proposed rulemaking. *Federal Register,* 1976, *41,* 52404-52407.

U.S. Office of Education. Assistance to states for education of handicapped children: Procedures for evaluating specific learning disabilities. *Federal Register,* 1977, *42,* 65082-65085.

Vellutino, F. R. Alternative conceptualizations of dyslexia: Evidence in support of a verbal-deficit hypothesis. *Harvard Educational Review,* 1977, *47,* 334-354.

Vellutino, F. R., Steger, B. M., Moyer, S. C., Harding, C. J., & Niles, J. A. Has the perceptual deficit hypothesis led us astray? *Journal of Learning Disabilities,* 1977, *10*(6), 375-385.

Warner, M. M., Schumaker, J. B., Alley, G. R., & Deshler, D. D. Learning disabled adolescents in the public schools: Are they different from other low achievers? *Exceptional Education Quarterly,* 1980, *1*(2), 27-36.

Webster, R. E., & Schenck, S. J. Diagnostic test pattern differences among LD, ED, EMH, and multi-handicapped students. *Journal of Educational Research,* 1978, *72*(2), 75-80.

Wiederholt, J. L. Historical perspectives on the education of the learning disabled. In L. Mann & D. A. Sabatino (Eds.), *The second review of special education.* Philadelphia: JSE Press, 1974.

Wong, B. Y. L., & Wong, R. Role-taking skills in normal achieving and learning disabled children. *Learning Disability Quarterly,* 1980, *3*(2), 11-18.

Ysseldyke, J. E. Remediation of ability deficits in adolescents: Some major questions. In L. Mann, L. Goodman, & J. L. Wiederholt (Eds.), *The learning disabled adolescent.* Boston: Houghton Mifflin, 1978.

Ysseldyke, J. E. Issues in psychoeducational assessment. In D. Reschly & G. Phye (Eds.), *School psychology: Methods and roles.* New York: Academic, 1979.

Ysseldyke, J. E., & Algozzine, B. Perspectives on assessment of learning disabled students. *Learning Disability Quarterly,* 1979, *2*(4), 3-13.

Ysseldyke, J. E., & Algozzine, B. *Critical issues in special and remedial education.* Boston: Houghton Mifflin, 1982.

Ysseldyke, J. E., Algozzine, B., & Epps, S. A logical and empirical analysis of current practice in classifying students as handicapped. *Exceptional Children,* 1983, *50*(2), 160-166.

Ysseldyke, J. E., Algozzine, B., Regan, R. R., & Potter, M. Technical adequacy of tests used by professionals in simulated decision making. *Psychology in the Schools,* 1980, *17,* 202-209.

Ysseldyke, J. E., Algozzine, B., Richey, L., & Graden, J. Declaring students eligible for learning disability services: Why bother with the data? *Learning Disability Quarterly,* 1982, *5,* 37-44.

Ysseldyke, J. E., Algozzine, B., Shinn, M., & McGue, M. Similarities and differences between underachievers and students labeled learning disabled. *Journal of Special Education,* 1982, *16,* 73-85.

Ysseldyke, J. E., & Regan, R. Nondiscriminatory assessment: A formative model. *Exceptional Children,* 1980, *46,* 465–466.

Ysseldyke, J. E., Regan, R., Thurlow, M., & Schwartz, S. Current assessment practices: The "cattle dip approach." *Diagnostique,* 1981, *6*(2), 16–27.

Zimmerman, J., Rich, W. D., Keilitz, I., & Broder, P. K. *Some observations on the link between learning disabilities and juvenile delinquency.* Williamsburg, Va.: National Center for State Courts, 1980.

CHAPTER 12

Economic and
Cultural Factors
in Childhood Exceptionality

DANIEL J. RESCHLY

The relationship between complex economic and cultural factors and childhood exceptionality has been the subject of considerable debate since the 1960s.
The central fact is that various types of exceptional classifications occur more
frequently with economically disadvantaged persons. The major controversy
has revolved around the classification of mild or educable mental retardation,
which, according to several studies, is several times more common among the
socially disadvantage.

The debate over the overrepresentation of minorities in programs for the
mildly retarded is often confused through failure to separate the effects of
poverty and culture. A further complication is the frequent assumption that
all poor persons are minorities or that all minority persons are poor. Throughout this chapter it is important for the reader to keep in mind that although
poverty and minority status overlap considerably in the present U.S. population, they are far from being perfectly correlated. Many minority persons
are not poor; in fact, the majority are not poor according to official standards.
Moreover, many white persons are poor; in fact, the majority of the poor in
the United States is white. Separation of the concepts of poverty and culture
is important in avoiding unnecessary stereotypes concerning the complex relationship between economic and cultural factors in childhood exceptionality.

CHARACTERISTICS OF THE ECONOMICALLY DISADVANTAGED

Perhaps the *only* characteristic that we can attribute with complete confidence
to the economically disadvantaged is that they are poor. This truism is important to understanding that group trends among the poor do not necessarily
apply to individuals. Official definitions of poverty released by government
agencies are based on somewhat arbitrary definitions of the economic re-

sources required in order to maintain a certain standard of living. Fairly small changes in these economic guidelines can lead to rather large variations in the percentages of people who may be defined as living in poverty circumstances. The guidelines used by the U.S. government since the mid-sixties suggest that from 10 to 15% of the U.S. population is characterized by poverty circumstances (Chan & Rueda, 1979). A variety of sociological, psychological, biomedical, and educational characteristics are associated with poverty circumstances, but, again, these charateristics should not be seen as synonymous with poverty.

Sociological Characteristics

During the 1960s discussions in the literature on the effects of poverty frequently used terms such as culturally deprived, culturally disadvantaged, culturally different. Although these terms may seem synonymous, the underlying assumptions behind the terms often were quite different. A typical discussion was provided by Havighurst (1964) concerning the characteristics of the socially disadvantaged. Havighurst suggested that the socially disadvantaged were most generally defined as persons who were disadvantaged in terms of coping effectively with the complex demands of a modern technological society. The general sociological characteristics of the disadvantaged, according to Havighurst, were that (1) they were at the bottom of American society in terms of income; (2) they often had a rural background; (3) many suffered from economic discrimination; and (4) although they were widely distributed in the U.S. population, many were concentrated either in large cities or in the rural South.

Although poverty is found in all sections and among all groups in the United States, the distribution is uneven. Specific groups are significantly overrepresented in povery circumstances (Chan & Rueda, 1979). Groups overrepresented include black Americans, found principally in large cities throughout the United States or the rural areas of the south; Hispanic Americans, who are concentrated in large cities throughout the United States and in both rural and urban areas of the southwest; Native Americans, located on reservations and occasionally in urban areas; and white Americans concentrated in the Appalachian Mountain regions of several states. Lest anyone think that poverty is concentrated only among minority groups, the reminder that significant numbers of Appalachian whites who, by and large, are Anglo-Saxon and Protestant, should dispel any such myth. Chan and Rueda (1979) cite data suggesting that approximately 35% of all black Americans, 24% of all Hispanic Americans, and nearly 40% of Native Americans are living in poverty circumstances. This rather large overrepresentation of specific minority groups in poverty circumstances is the source of unfortunate stereotypes that all minority persons are poor and that all poor persons have minority status.

Much of the literature concerning disadvantaged children has confused or failed to separate the effects of poverty and the effects of cultural group. Many of the characteristics discussed later in this section may be general effects of poverty, effects of cultural difference, or the interaction of both. In most of the research appearing on economically disadvantaged children the effects of poverty are hopelessly confounded with the possible effects of cultural differences. Moreover, nearly all of this literature involves results that are typical of groups of persons, often who are both poor and potentially culturally different. Results from groups do not necessarily hold true for individuals. Henderson (1980, 1981) pointed to the frequent use of stereotypes based on published literature concerning the characteristics of various minority persons. Some of these characteristics, such as the matriarchal family structure in black families, the male dominance supposedly characteristic of Hispanic families, and the fatalism allegedly found more often among Mexican Americans, are not typical of all, or perhaps even a majority of blacks or Mexican Americans. In reviewing this information it is important for us to recognize that variations *within* groups in the United States are usually greater than variations *between* different groups. For example, the matriarchal family structure supposedly typical of black families is not found among a majority of black families, nor is it unknown in white families. Perhaps it is best to conceptualize all of these characteristics as involving *overlapping* distributions among various economic and cultural groups.

Biomedical Effects of Poverty

One of the direct effects of poverty, regardless of cultural group, is unequal access to medical care, greater exposure to illness, injury, and environmental risks, and increased likelihood of poor nutrition. The effects of poverty on biomedical and health circumstances have been well documented in a large number of studies since the 1960s (see Brown, Chapter 6, this volume). Reports by Birch and Gussow (1970), Lilienfeld and Pasamanick (1956), and Pasamanick and Knobloch (1961), among others, have provided convincing documentation of the negative effects of poverty upon health status. Lilienfeld and Pasamanick suggested the concept of *continuum of reproductive casualty* to describe a variety of factors in the pre- and perinatal environment of poor women, which may be related to the ultimate health status of infants born in poverty circumstances. Throughout the prenatal period poor mothers have poorer health care, poorer nutrition, and less access to appropriate medical services. During the perinatal period poor mothers are more likely to experience difficulties with labor and delivery and are less likely to have access to medical care which mitigates various problems. In addition, poor women are likely to have pregnancies at either too young an age or too old an age than is optimum and to have pregnancies too frequently. Finally, the risk of prematurity is considerably greater among poor women than among women who have access to better medical care, better nutrition, and so on. All of these effects subsumed under Lilienfeld and Pasamanick's concept of reproductive casualty increase the risk that the child may suffer central nervous system insult and are associated with later educational and psychological problems. It is important to note, however, that not all poor children are at risk or suffer the consequences of the reproductive casualty factors. Further, many children who do suffer these risks do not display educational or psychological problems during childhood. The factors associated with reproductive casualty, like so many other variables that are associated with poverty and cultural differences involve increasing risk rather than any direct causal relationship.

The effects of poverty on biomedical status continue through infancy and early childhood. Throughout infancy and early childhood poor children, regardless of cultural group, are less likely to be provided with appropriate health care—regular physical examinations, routine vaccinations, and the like. Poor children suffer greater exposure to various accidents, injuries, and illnesses which have the effects of slightly increasing the risk of possible neurological dysfunction and have the indirect effects of reducing the child's energy level and opportunity to profit from other socialization experiences. Robinson and Robinson (1976) and Edgerton (1979) discuss a variety of environmental hazards, such as exposure to excessive amounts of lead, which are suffered by the poor. Nutritional status also varies by income level. It is rare in the United States for children to suffer from severe malnutrition, but many children apparently suffer from chronic subnutrition. North (1967) reported that a large proportion, perhaps half or more, of all children in Head Start programs suffer from anemia caused by poor diet. Although the nutritional status of these children was not poor to the extent of causing life-threatening circumstances, the subnutrition responsible for the anemia could very well translate into lower energy level, increased susceptibility to illness, and lowered participation in other socialization experiences.

The relationship of the subtle biomedical factors discussed in this section to school achievement is far from clear. In large scale investigations the biomedical factors account for a small but significant proportion of the variance in intelligence and achievement (Broman, Nichols, & Kennedy, 1975; Rutter, Tizard, & Whitemore, 1970). Other nonhealth variables such as socioeconomic status and maternal education are considerably stronger predictors of achievement. Biomedical factors alone are *not* sufficient to explain the overrepresentation of socially disadvantaged students in exceptional classifications such as mild mental retardation or the lower average performance of the socially disadvantaged on cognitive measures. However, it is important to note that the biomedical risks experienced by socially disadvantaged persons do not occur alone. They are associated with a wide variety of other circumstances and undoubtedly interact in complex ways with these other circumstances.

Psychological

The biomedical effects of poverty discussed in the previous section create serious factors of risk for poor children. Perhaps even more serious are the psychological effects of poverty. The practical difficulties of coping with the effects of poverty are described well in Robinson and Robinson (1976). Much of the literature since the 1960s on the psychological effects of poverty has emphasized cognitive development. The early literature, for example, Hunt (1961), suggested that extremely poor children were exposed to stimulus deprivation which, in turn, accounted for slower cognitive development. During much of the early 1960s, there was concern that extreme stimulus deprivation might be irreversible. Although some poverty situations may involve extreme sensory deprivation (see Gazaway, 1969), the typical environment associated with poverty does not involve anything akin to stimulus deprivation. In fact quite the opposite would appear to be the case. Rather than stimulus deprivation, the problem would appear to be insufficient opportunity for exposure to structured learning situations which would prepare the child for later school achievement. The possible effects of poverty on cognitive development have been discussed thoroughly in recent years. Generally the kinds of variables emphasized are the amount and quality of interaction between parent and child, the exposure to the kinds of skills that prepare for the development of literacy, and exposure to models for success and for language development. Poverty also has consequences for mental health and for the development of attitudes and values which are necessary for school performance. Nevertheless, the majority of attention concerning psychological effects of poverty has been devoted to concerns with the intellectual development and the acquisition of language competencies.

Intelligence

That intelligence is associated with socioeconomic status is one of the oldest and most controversial observations in Western psychology. In fact, this relationship was suggested even before the development of intelligence tests. Persons from low socioeconomic status backgrounds as a group obtain scores on conventional intelligence tests that are significantly below the population average regardless of cultural group. The typical relationship between social status and intelligence is far from perfect, usually a correlation of .3–.4. Again we see the phenomenon of considerable overlap of distributions and greater variability *within* social status groups than *between* social status groups.

The size of the differences between groups of poor children and the population averages varies somewhat by group and apparently by age level. Generally these differences, on the average, are in the range of 10–15 points on IQ scales where the mean is 100 and the standard deviation is 15 or 16. The source of these differences has not been entirely clear since many studies have confounded the effects of poverty and cultural group. Other studies have attempted to control for these separate variables through statistical manipulations, but it is doubtful that statistical controls are adequate. In one exception, Lesser, Fifer, and Clark (1965) separated the effects of poverty and cultural group through careful selection of samples. Lesser et al. suggested that social status influenced the level of intelligence, but cultural group influenced the pattern of intelligence, a finding at least partially replicated by Reynolds and Jensen (1980). These results suggest that it is highly likely that both social status and cultural group are important, and that they may interact to produce effects for individuals.

Considerable discussion has been devoted to various explanations for the lower performance of poor children on conventional measures of intelligence. The classic explanations of cultural disadvantage, cultural differences, and genetic inferiority have provoked a considerable amount of controversy. The presently available data do not lead to firm conclusions concerning any of these explanations (see Loehlin, Lindzey, & Spuhler, 1975). It should be noted that each of the explanations has implications for conceptions of exceptionality and for the kinds of services that might be provided to exceptional children. The implication of the genetic inferiority hypothesis would appear to be that many poor children are largely incapable of handling the current educational curriculum and should, therefore, be exposed to a markedly different curriculum with reduced cognitive demands which attempts to maximize their limited potential. The cultural disadvantage explanation suggests that early interventions and compensatory education programs are needed to overcome the deficiencies displayed by these children which are caused by inadequate environment. From this perspective nearly all socially disadvantaged children would be classified as exceptional and greater percentages would be expected to be handicapped. The purpose of educational interventions would be to compensate for these deficiencies to the greatest extent possible and, where necessary, to provide an alternative special education curriculum to enhance as much as possible their competencies for coping with modern, complex society. The third explanation, cultural differences, appears to be the one favored by many minority critics of current classification practices. This explanation would suggest that there is nothing wrong with the minority child, but rather current educational curricula and current assessment practices are largely irrelevant to the strengths and cognitive styles of these children. This explanation suggests radical revisions in current curriculum, in current assessment practices, and in current classification schemes for exceptional children.

Language

Language is often cited as a fundamental and unique characteristic of human beings. Language competence is viewed as a unique human facility and, in that context, all languages are regarded as equally good. However, competence with a specific language is learned. Intense controversy since the mid-1960s has been devoted to the subject of the language competencies of socially disadvantaged persons. The major questions in these debates have been whether the socially disadvantaged merely speak a different language or a different dialect of a language, which may not be understood by professional educators and psychologists, or whether the socially disadvantaged display various language deficits. Language development has enormous implications for and importance in overall cognitive development and educational achievement. Variations in language competence, whether they be differences or deficits, provide much of the basis for the differences in intellectual and academic performance among socially disadvantaged persons.

The language deficit point of view is based on studies of the language competencies of socially disadvantaged persons, observations typically made by professional educators and psychologists from the perspective of standard English. Perhaps the most important studies were conducted by Bernstein (1960, 1970), who suggested striking differences in language competence from comparisons of lower social status and middle-class children and parents in Britain. Bernstein described a typical language pattern of low social status British subjects as reflecting a *restricted code*. The critical features of the restricted code were (1) short and grammatically simple sentences which often were unfinished or reflected poor syntax; (2) restricted vocabulary and limited use of adjectives and adverbs; (3) repetitive use of conjunctions such as so, then, or because; (4) use of idiomatic phrases or sequences; and (5) imprecise meaning in the sentence organization or the message communicated. In contrast, the language typical of middle-class environments, called the *elaborated* code, had the characteristics of (1) accurate grammar and syntax; (2) use of adjectives and adverbs to modify the meaning of what was said; (3) frequent use of prepositions to indicate logical relationships as well as use of prepositions to indicate temporal and spatial relationships; and (4) communication of precise meaning. The concept of restricted versus elaborated code was applied by a number of scholars to studies of socially disadvantaged and minority children in the United States (Bereiter & Englemann, 1966; Hess, Shipman, & Jackson, 1965). The evidence gathered suggested an overall language deficit much like that described by Bernstein. This notion was an important influence on the development of compensatory education programs throughout the 1960s. Many of these programs, especially that of Bereiter and Englemann (1966), placed a considerable amount of emphasis on the development of language competencies.

Criticism of the language deficit view, particularly as it was applied to different cultural groups, has been prominent in the literature since 1970 (Bryen, 1974; Gonzalez, 1974; Hilliard, 1980). Studies establishing apparent language deficits among economically disadvantaged children, often children who had minority status as well, were criticized by Price-Williams (1975) as requiring minority students to perform unfamiliar tasks in an unfamiliar context using unfamiliar materials. Price-Williams, as well as others, contended that the language of economically disadvantaged minority children was just as elaborate, just as precise, and just as rich as the elaborated code of the middle-class child. The differences that were observed were largely a matter of the discrepancy between the language competencies of middle-class professionals, such as educators and psychologists, and lower-class children. For example, Labov (1970) studied the language competencies of urban black children under two conditions. First, conventional materials requiring standard English were used. Then different materials in a different context that was more consistent with the background and environment of urban black children were used. According to Labov the language displayed by these children was considerably different depending upon the task context and materials factors. The restricted code was apparently found only when standard English was required and elaborated code language was displayed when the situation and materials were familiar to the children. Labov suggested that the language deficit point of view needed to be reexamined, and that the alleged language deficiencies among economically disadvantaged black children were more a matter of the inability of white middle-class professionals to understand the language competencies that they possessed.

Bryen (1974) argued for the point of view that black English is a dialect of standard English which shares both similarities and differences with standard English. Bryen, as well as others, has argued strongly that black English is a unique language and that it is just as good a language as standard English. Moreover, Bryen (1974), Hilliard (1980), and Gonzalez (1974) have all argued that the major difficulty is not the language deficit on the part of disadvantaged minority children but rather differences in language that are *not* sufficiently appreciated in the context of formal education settings or in the services provided by psychologists and educators to minority children.

Social Skills and Affective Characteristics

Throughout the literature concerning the educational and psychological characteristics of economically disadvantaged students there is the suggestion that significant discrepancies in values, attitudes, and social behaviors create difficulties in the school environment which is assumed to be middle class. Most of the studies that have attempted to identify differences on these variables have confounded possible effects of social status and cultural group. An unfortunate misconception that has developed from this literature is the notion that economically disadvantaged and minority parents are less supportive and perhaps less interested in the educational achievement of their children. Although differences on social and affective variables probably do exist among low social status and/or minority children in comparison to middle-class children and families, these differences do not translate into lower expectations or less concern for educational achievement. The data from compensatory educational programs funded over the last 15 years or so suggest that low social status parents, whether they be minority or nonminority, are strongly supportive of the educational process and have high aspirations for the educational achievement of their children (Zigler, 1978). The differences in social skills and affective variables, therefore, are a matter of the kind of preparation provided in non–middle-class homes in comparison to the demands placed on children in the public school environment which, of course, is largely middle class.

The discontinuity in social skills and affective variables may affect the lower-class child's approach to learning tasks and the interaction between the lower-class child and the typical middle-class teacher. Pepper (1976) described a variety of value differences that may exist between traditional native American cultures and the typical middle-class school situation. Similar descriptions of these value differences have been provided for other groups and for low SES generally (McCandless, 1967). The kind of discontinuity in social skills and values that may well affect the educational process was described by Henderson (1980). Henderson described data from a wide variety of studies which led to speculation that socially disadvantaged students may develop a learned helplessness reaction in formal school settings. These differences in social skills and affective variables may constitute one of the most important discontinuities between the expectations in public education and the characteristics of disadvantaged children. Again, it is important to note, however, that most of the literature in this area has not separated the effects of social status and cultural group and that considerable variation exists within cultural groups and within social status.

Educational

The lower performance of socially disadvantaged students in educational settings became an intense national concern in the 1960s and continues to be the subject of considerable discussion today. Coleman, Campbell, Hobson, McPartland, Mood, Weinfeld, and York (1966) provided an extensive report documenting the lower educational performance of socially disadvantaged students, many of whom also had minority status. The actual size of the difference between the educational performance of socially disadvantaged students and population averages has not received as much attention as the size of the differences on conventional measures of intelligence. However, these differences apparently are in about the same range or about two-thirds to one standard deviation below population averages. Discussions of the educational performance of socially disadvantaged students have more often focused on differences in terms of grade equivalent scores. These differences generally range from about one-half to one grade below average in the early elementary years to as much as three to four grades below average in the high school years. The apparent increase in size of the difference between the performance of socially disadvantaged students as they went through the school years led Deutsch (1967) to suggest the notion of *cumulative deficit*. The apparent progressive decline of relative performance was noted earlier by Sherman and Key (1932) with respect to intelligence test scores of white children in the Appalachian Mountains of Tennessee. The notion of progressive decline in relative status has been criticized by Jensen (1974) as due to sampling and measurement artifacts. The metric often used, the grade equivalent score, does not have equal units throughout all grade levels. The units are large in the early grades and smaller in later grade levels. Thus a child who is one grade below in second grade is typically farther behind his or her age mates than a student who is three grades below in the eleventh grade.

Despite these problems the notion of cumulative deficit became part of the basis for the development of early intervention and compensatory education programs (Hunt, 1961; Mackie, 1968). The basic notion was that the educational disadvantage could be overcome more easily through early interventions when development was believed to be more malleable and when the deficit was relatively smaller. The effects of these programs have been debated rather intensely in recent years (see later discussion).

Perhaps the most widely accepted explanation for the lower educational performance of socially disadvantaged students was the notion of the *mismatch* between the preschool environment of socially disadvantaged students and the requirements of the traditional public school setting (Hunt, 1961; McCandless, 1967). The so-called hidden curriculum of the middle-class home was described by Chan and Rueda (1979) as providing four kinds of special preparation for school performance. These included rudimentary cognitive skills involving emphases on abstract cognitive processes and activities that were simulations of the kinds of tasks required in school. Second, motivation was seen as an important part of the hidden curriculum whereby children were strongly encouraged to engage in schoollike activities and reinforced for doing so by significant adults. Third, language development was seen as an important part of the hidden curriculum. The language development aspect involved emphasis on standard English, precise and complex verbal expression, and verbal abstraction. Finally, the hidden curriculum of the middle-class home was seen as providing social skills and affective characteristics which predisposed the child to doing well in the school environment. Sharp contrasts have been drawn between characteristics of the preschool environment in the middle-class home and the environment of socially disadvantaged children in terms of the amount and kind of preparation provided to children for school performance. Deutsch (1967) suggested that the low social status environment typically involved insufficient amounts and kinds of directed and sustained verbal interaction, insufficient emphasis on the use of language as a means of expressing and satisfying one's needs, and less emphasis by adults in those environments on verbal and abstract cognitive skills.

A sharply different perspective has been provided by a number of minority educators and psychologists over the past 10 years. Chinn (1979) suggested that many economically disadvantaged minority students suffered a double whammy in educational settings in that they were different because of minority status and many of them had to carry the additional stigma of being defined as handicapped as well (see later discussion). Jones and Wilderson (1976) suggested that the educational deficiencies of minority students were really artifacts of biases in the traditional educational system. These biases involved an irrelevant curriculum; that is, a curriculum that does not relate to the culture and values of minority students, and a curriculum that places undue stress on middle-class values and the use of standard English. Others (such as Castaneda, 1976; Dent, 1976; Hilliard, 1980; and Johnson, 1976) have suggested that the lower performance of socially disadvantaged minority students was due in a large degree to the failure of teachers to understand cultural differences and the failure of educators and psychologists generally to be sensitive to the unique characteristics of culturally different children. Symptoms of this lack of sensitivity included such things as biased teachers and administrators, inappropriate evaluation devices used to assess minority children, and the overrepresentation of minority students in lower ability tracks and special education programs. It is interesting to note that a fairly high degree of consistency exists across these critics concerning solutions to the problem. The typical recommendations involve increased sensitivity of teachers to cultural differences, revisions in the present curriculum so that the curriculum will be more consistent with the cultural background and values of minority students, emphasis on building self-concept, fostering motivation, and so on. It is unfortunate, however, that these general recommendations are rarely translated into suggestions for specific curricular objectives and materials. Finally, there is serious question as to whether changes toward a more culturally specific curriculum would, in fact, better serve the needs of minority students.

MODELS OF EXCEPTIONALITY

The current classification system for exceptional children involves a mixture of underlying constructs (Hobbs, 1975). In this section the underlying constructs of social system model and medical model are described as a means of clarifying the nature of the overrepresentation of the socially disadvantaged in exceptional classifications. As will be noted in this and later sections, the overrepresentation of socially disadvantaged persons occurs largely in the mildly handicapping classifications. These mildly handicapping classifications are probably best understood from the perspective of a social system model rather than the medical model. The failure to recognize the different underlying constructs associated with various exceptional classifications has caused a great deal of confusion and misunderstanding in the discussions of the overrepresentation of socially disadvantaged children. Moreover, some of the exceptional classifications, for example, mental retardation, reflect a mixture of the two models.

Medical Model

The term medical model is perhaps unfortunate in that it suggests that the assumptions and approaches to problems described as medical model are typical of how professionals in medicine solve problems. Kauffman and Hallahan (1974) pointed out large differences in the concept of medical model as used in psychology and education and the approach to solving problems actually used in medicine. Therefore, the term medical model should be seen as a heuristic device and not taken literally as indicative of practices in medicine.

The characteristics of "medical model" as an approach to the development of assessment devices and as an approach to conceptualizing child deviance were discussed by Mercer and Ysseldyke (1977) and Mercer (1979b). The most important characteristics of the medical model for our purposes are that abnormal patterns of behavior or development are attributed to underlying biological pathology. The etiology or the cause, direct or indirect, of deviant behavior is seen as stemming from biological anomalies. Other important characteristics of the medical model are that it is cross-cultural; that is, the same underlying biological abnormalities cause approximately the same deficits in behavior regardless of the social status or cultural group that might be involved. Further, the medical model is seen as a deficit model and the underlying biological anomaly is seen as an inherent part of the individual.

The medical model is probably useful in the description and classification of the low-incidence exceptional conditions. The low-incidence exceptional conditions involve classifications such as blind and visual impairments, deaf and hard of hearing, neuromotor disabilities, and the moderate, severe, and profound levels of mental retardation. In all of these classifications there is an underlying biological anomaly which is associated with and frequently the direct cause of observed deficits in behavior. Moreover, these underlying deficits cause approximately the same kinds of anomalies in patterns of development or behavior regardless of cultural context or social status. For example, Down's syndrome has the same underlying chromosomal aberration and causes approximately the same limitations in development regardless of social status and cultural group.

The emphasis on early diagnosis and intervention is universally agreed upon for medical model types of exceptionalities. There is no dispute concerning whether or not these children should be classified and no dispute on the importance of early diagnosis and intervention. Moreover, incidence data suggest that these medical model kinds of handicaps occur with approximately equal frequency regardless of social status or cultural group. In other words socially disadvantaged children are not overrepresented, at least to any significant degree, in any of the medical model handicaps.

Social System Model

In contrast to the medical model, the social system model uses a strongly ecological perspective (Mercer, 1979b). Deviant behavior or abnormal patterns of development are not seen as inherent characteristics of the organism but rather as reflecting a discrepancy between what the individual has learned in a cultural context and the expectations for normal behavior in a specific social role and social setting. Judgments about behavior or classification of certain patterns of behavior as being exceptional involve application of social norms within a particular social setting to observed patterns of behavior. The norms or expectations for behavior are determined by the larger society. Judgments of deviance are based on an interaction between the learned patterns of behavior on the part of the individual, the social setting in which a specific behavior is judged, the social role that the individual is engaged in, and the expectations for that behavior. The social system model suggests that social and cultural factors are extremely important in the determination of what the individual learns to be appropriate behavior and in the determination of expectations for behavior in a specific role or setting.

The vast majority of the so-called high-incidence handicaps, learning disabilities, emotional disabilities, and mild mental retardation, are best understood within the social system model. These three classifications account for 70% or more of all the children diagnosed officially as handicapped. To illustrate this distinction it might be useful for the reader to consider this question: Would we have a classification of learning disability or mild mental retardation if we did not have compulsory school attendance laws and nearly universal public education for children between the ages of approximately 5 and 17? In all likelihood, the kinds of deficits in behavior that are observed among learning disabled and mildly retarded children are a function of the sorts of demands and expectations that are placed on them in our culture, that is, demands and expectations for the development of abstract thinking and literacy skills. In another kind of culture, for example, a culture that did not place emphasis on literacy skills, it is highly unlikely that the children who now are regarded as deviant because of learning disabilities or mild mental retardation would be regarded as being unusual or exceptional. A similar kind of analysis would apply for the vast majority of children who are diagnosed as emotionally disturbed. It is important to note that some children, undoubtedly a small percentage, in the classifications of learning disability, emotional disturbance, and mild mental retardation, do in fact have underlying biological anomalies. However, for the vast majority there is no underlying biological anomaly that presently, at least, can be identified. It is therefore more accurate to regard these children as exhibiting a discrepancy between what is expected of them and the patterns of behavior that they exhibit.

The underlying values described by Mercer (1979b) for the social system model suggest that it is better to avoid early diagnosis and to be extremely cautious in classifying children as deviant so as to avoid establishing a "disabling trajectory." The debate over whether to classify children who exhibit these kinds of discrepancies involves an implicit, usually unrecognized, assumption about the effects of classification. Mercer and many other minority critics suggest that early diagnosis and intervention are damaging to the individual because the diagnosis is stigmatizing and humiliating and the interventions are largely ineffective. These criticisms have been made most often with regard to the classification of mild mental retardation. On the other hand, diagnosis might be regarded positively if the interventions are effective in improving educational competencies and expanding opportunities for individuals. Related to this controversy is the degree of stigma associated with the different mildly handicapping classifications. It appears that the greatest degree of stigma is associated with the classification of educable or mild mental retardation and considerably less stigma is associated with the classification of learning disability. These implicit assumptions concerning effects of classification and effectiveness of special education interventions have been important in concerns about overrepresentation of minorities.

The social system nature of the mildly handicapping classifications is illustrated well by the varying prevalence figures for different states. The official child count data obtained from states by the federal government indicates wide variations among states in prevalence of mental retardation, learning disabilities, and emotional disturbance (Patrick & Reschly, 1982). State department of education criteria may be inclusive or restrictive (MacMillan & Borthwick, 1980). Other system factors include variations in referral practices, in placement decisions, and in the regular student population (MacMillan, Meyers, & Morrison, 1980). The likelihood of exceptional classification for a specific child depends on an interaction between the characteristics of the child *and* a host of system factors. These system factors are much less likely to influence classification with the more severely handicapped or the medical model types of exceptionality.

THE ECONOMICALLY DISADVANTAGED AND CLASSIFICATION AS MILDLY EXCEPTIONAL

Many similarities exist in the characteristics attributed to the socially disadvantaged and to children who are classified as having mild handicaps such as learning disability, emotional disability, and mild mental retardation. In view of the similarities and apparent overlap in the characteristics of these groups of persons, it is therefore not surprising that overrepresentation of socially disadvantaged students in these classifications is found in most localities in the United States. However, it should be emphasized that the degree and pattern of overrepresentation often is misunderstood and exaggerated. The degree of overlap between socially disadvantaged as well as among the three most common categories of exceptional children has led to suggestions for reform in the classification system.

Overlap and Differences among Groups

Consider the following symptoms: a high rate of hyperactivity; low stimulus inhibition; perceptual deficits; deficits in perceptual motor processes; and low achievement. What group of children would these symptoms be typical of? In fact, this list of symptoms has been attributed to both socially disadvantaged and learning disabled children (Kavale, 1980). The overlap just illustrated is typical of the commonality and characteristics shared by many socially disadvantaged and mildly handicapped children. The criteria for classifying children as mildly handicapped typically involve the requirement that the child be achieving at a level that is significantly below the grade or age level expectancies (learning disability and mild mental retardation); that the child be significantly below average in measured intelligence (mild mental retardation) and/or that the child exhibit patterns of behavior that constitute significant interference with efficient learning or with the education of others in the environment (emotional disturbance). Economically disadvantaged children as a group typically are found to have higher rates of the kinds of behaviors that lead to classification as exceptional.

Overrepresentation of economically disadvantaged students is not evenly distributed across the mild exceptionality classifications. Economically disadvantaged and/or minority children tend to be overrepresented in the classification of mild mental retardation and, according to some data, overrepresented in the classification of emotional disturbance as well (Manni, Winikur, & Keller, 1980). Economically disadvantaged and/or minority children typically are underrepresented in programs for the learning disabled and for the gifted (Baca, 1980; Frasier, 1979; Jones & Wilderson, 1976).

The uneven distribution of minority students over the different exceptionality classifications has been part of the basis for suggestions that the classification system be reformed. Other have contended that the educational characteristics of the mildly handicapped are much more alike than different Hallahan & Kauffman, 1977; Neisworth & Greer, 1975). These concerns have led to suggestions that the classification system be reformed so that the types of services or the extent of services needed would form the basis for the classification rather than sorting children into categories according to presumably unique characteristics (Gutkin & Tieger, 1979; Hobbs, 1975).

Kavale (1980), in an extensive review of the literature on the socially disadvantaged and the learning disabled, reached the conclusion that there are many more similarities than differences across these groups. Kavale criticized the current trend of legislating away the relationship between learning disabled and the socially disadvantaged through what he regarded as improper use of exclusionary clauses. Gajar (1979) studied the characteristics of children classified as learning disabled, emotionally disturbed, and mildly retarded. A number of similarities were reported in the study including the fact that all three groups scored lower than average on measures of intelligence, although the mildly retarded were significantly lower than the other two groups. Moreover, all groups were significantly below grade level in achievement and all three groups were predominantly male and from lower socioeconomic status backgrounds.

The trend toward regarding the three major classifications of the mildly handicapped as being functionally similar was criticized by Becker (1978), who studied the intellectual and educational characteristics of educationally handicapped and mildly retarded children. The category of educationally handicapped in Becker's study included children who would typically be regarded as learning disabled or emotionally disturbed. Becker pointed to rather large differences in measured intelligence between the educationally handicapped and the mildly retarded. Perhaps more important, he suggested that significant differences existed in learning style and conceptual level. Contrary to the suggestion of combining the mildly handicapped classifications, Becker advocated continuation of the current distinctions because the children so classified have dissimilar needs, the educational programs to meet those needs should be different, and the same kind of training for teachers would not be appropriate across the three groups. In summarizing the information available on overlap across the groups discussed thus far, it is again important to note the social system nature of classification of mildly handicapped students. Depending on a variety of social system factors, children regarded as economically disadvantaged, learning disabled, mildly retarded, or emotionally disturbed, may have considerable commonality or may be quite different. Mild handicapped classification is not consistent, nor are universal criteria used across settings.

Disproportionate Classification Data

There is no question that economically disadvantaged children are overrepresented in the classification of mild mental retardation. From the perspective of the conventional literature on mild mental retardation, this is not at all surprising. For example, Robinson and Robinson (1976) suggested that the most common etiology of mild mental retardation is psychosocial disadvantage. Overrepresentation of poor children almost inevitably involves overrepresentation of minority children, at least in the present society. This overrepresentation of economically disadvantaged and minority children was severely criticized by Dunn (1968), who estimated that from 60 to 80% of all children placed in self-contained special classes for the mildly retarded were economically disadvantaged students. Samuda (1976) cited Dunn's estimates and speculated, probably erroneously, that over half of the students classified nationwide as mildly retarded were minority children.

Studies of the demographic characteristics of students placed in programs for the mildly retarded have indeed established that economically disadvantaged students are overrepresented in such programs regardless of cultural group (Franks, 1971; Neer, Foster, Jones, & Reynolds, 1973; Rubin, Krus, & Balow, 1973). A number of other studies and litigation in the 1970s have indicated that minority students are overrepresented in programs for the mildly retarded (Burke, 1975; *Diana v. State Board of Education*, 1970; *Larry P. v. Riles*, 1979; *Marshall v. Georgia*, 1984; *Mattie, T. v. Charles E. Holladay*, 1979: Mercer, 1973; *PASE, v. Joseph P. Hannon*, 1980). The studies on overrepresentation have typically involved relatively small samples or surveys across districts. Rarely has there been a careful analysis of all of the factors that might be related to or that might account for the overrepresentation. Of particular concern is the fact that few of the studies on overrepresentation have made an effort to clearly separate the effects of social status and cultural group. For example, Franks (1971) reported that socially disadvantaged children were overrepresented in the classification of educable mental retardation and underrepresented in the classification of learning disability. Prillaman (1975) reported the results of a survey of educable mental retardation special classes in Virginia. Prillaman reported a high degree of overrepresentation among socially disadvantaged students, black students, and males. Mercer (1973) reported overrepresentation of black and Hispanic students in self-contained EMR programs for the mildly retarded. Mercer reported that socioeconomic status accounted for a large part but not all of the overrepresentation of minority students. However, the actual data were not provided.

The litigation and a handful of studies on overrepresentation confirm that socially disadvantaged students, who often have minority status, are overrepresented in programs for the mildly retarded. The reasons for this overrepresentation, that is, whether it reflects the cultural differences or the effects of social status, have not been addressed sufficiently to date. Moreover, patterns of classification are highly variable across states, and low socioeconomic status and/or minority children are not always overrepresented in the classification of mild mental retardation. Tucker (1980) reported that minority children were overrepresented in programs for the learning disabled in the state of Texas, which may have been the result of emphasis on nonbiased assessment and Office for Civil Rights pressure on districts to reduce disproportionate classification of minority students in mild mental retardation.

It is important that the percentage data discussed in the litigation and in the literature be understood properly. The typical discussion of overrepresentation involves presenting the percentage of minority students in the total population and then comparing that with the percentage of minority students in educable mental retardation special classes. Numerous examples of these sorts of data could be provided. For example, in the *Larry P.* case, black students constituted approximately 10% of the total population in California and approximately 25% of students placed in educable mental retardation special classes. The totally incorrect assumption that apparently is made by some is that perhaps as many as 25% of all black students are placed in special class programs for the mildly retarded.

Data are presented in Table 12.1 from three studies on overrepresentation involving the Riverside, California Public Schools (Mercer, 1973), black students in the state of California (Reschly, 1980a, Yoshida, MacMillan, & Meyers, 1976), and minority students in special education programs in New Jersey (Manni, Winikur, & Keller, 1980). In all three cases, an entirely erroneous impression of the degree of overrepresentation might be developed from merely looking at the simple percentages of minorities in the total population and the percentage of minority students in the educable mental retardation special class population. In all instances simple comparison of these percentages suggests a high degree of overrepresentation with the implication that perhaps a large percentage of minority students are placed in self-contained special classes for the mildly retarded. However, in all instances the actual percentage of minority students classified and placed in these programs is a relatively low proportion of the total population of minority students.

Table 12.1.   Analysis of Overrepresentation Data

Riverside, California Public Schools[a]-1960s

Group	Percent of Total Population	Percent of EMR Enrollment	Number in Total Population	Number in EMR Classes	Percent of Each Group in EMR classes
White	82 %	53%	20,500	133	0.6%
Hispanic	9.5%	32%	2,375	80	3.4%
Black	7 %	12%	1,750	30	1.7%

State of California, 1968–1969 and 1976–1977[b]

Group	Percent of Total Population	Percent of EMR Enrollment		Percent of Each Group in EMR classes	
		1968–1969	1976–1977	1968–1969	1976–1977
White	72%	43 %	—	0.8%	0.4%
Black	10%	25.5%	25.4%	3.2%	1.1%
Hispanic	15%	29 %	—	2.6%	1.3%

State of New Jersey, 1979–1980[c]

	White	Black	Hispanic
Percent of total enrollment	73 %	18 %	7 %
Percent of total EMR enrollment	43 %	43 %	13 %
Percent of total handicapped enrollment	71 %	21 %	7 %
VS			
Percent of group in EMR	0.5%	1.9%	1.4%
Percent of group in TMR	0.2%	0.4%	0.3%
Percent of group in ED	0.8%	2.3%	0.7%
Percent of group in learning disabled	2.8%	2.3%	1.4%
Percent of group in handicapped	10.4%	12.5%	10.1%

[a]Based on data reported by Mercer (1973) and personal communication from Mercer (1979a) indicating that the total enrollment in the Riverside Public Schools in the mid-1960s was about 25,000 students, of which about 1% were in special classes for the mildly retarded.
[b]Based upon estimates derived from data reported in *Larry P. v. Riles* (1979), Yoshida et al. (1976), and personal communication with the California State Department of Education (1979).
[c]Data from Table 1, p. 10 of Manni et al., (1980).

Minority Criticism of Overrepresentation

Minority educators and psychologists have been increasingly harsh in their assessment of the overrepresentation issue. Jones and Wilderson (1976) suggested the overrepresentation reflects poor assessment practices, biased tests, and insensitive teacher attitudes and expectations that exist as a part of an overall pattern of institutional racism. Jones and Wilderson express concern about the impact of special education labels upon minority children as well as the apparent ineffectiveness of special education programs for minority students. A number of other minority commentators have been quite specific and equally severe in their criticism of overrepresentation. Here are some representative quotations from minority critics of special education practices:

> At any point where a certain cultural group is overrepresented in a particular category of special education, the special educator should spare no effort to review the system of assessment for cultural bias. The burden of proof in establishing the validity of any assessment process which yields a gross disproportion in the distribution of groups to categories must rest with the educator. It is a shame and a disgrace that the courts and the legislature are left to overrule the bad practices which are so widespread among us. (Hilliard, 1980, p. 587)

Hilliard also suggested that special education programs, to be successful, must develop culturally sensitive diagnostic procedures, a valid link between the assessment-diagnostic process and teaching strategies, and programs which are effective.

Johnson (1969) contended that overrepresentation was reflective of the failure of the educational system to meet its responsibilities to black Americans. With regard to special education Johnson commented:

> Its black clientele has been labeled delinquent and retarded, thus helping the general educational enterprise to avoid some of the responsibility for its failure to adapt to individual and collective needs. Basically, this labeling process imputes a lack of ability or lack of values in behavior which are acceptable to the schools. . . . The latest attempt at system maintenance is the generation of data to show blacks may actually be genetically less intelligent, and, therefore, less able to learn. Special education is implicated for it has cheerfully accepted the charge with little or no scrutiny of either the faulty conception upon which the IQ is grounded or the sociocultural environment of its clientele. (Johnson, 1969, p. 244)

Moreno advocated,

> that school districts place Mexican Americans in special classes (for both the gifted and the retarded) at the same proportion (or percent) that the school districts are placing majority children in special classes. School districts will claim that it is possible that some very needy children will be excluded from special education. We must remember that we are willing to take the chance that some children may be excluded from the program, but that the risk of a few children is far superior than living with a system that is misplacing thousands of our children every year. (Moreno, 1970)

Much of the criticism of overrepresentation identifies assessment practices as the major culprit leading to placement of more minority students in special education programs. For example, Williams (1970) asserted, "Ability testing is being utilized to dehumanize, damage, and destroy black children and youth through improperly labeling and classifying them" (p. 5). Samuda (1976) commented, "The implications and consequences of testing for minority group individuals are real, drastic, and pervasive in their effects at all stages in the lives of minority individuals" (p. 69).

The severe criticisms by minority representatives concerning classification practices were expressed in the placement litigation of the 1970s. This litigation has been discussed extensively by a number of authors (Bersoff, 1979, 1981, 1982; Reschly, 1979, 1980a). In most instances Federal District Courts have agreed with minority contentions that overrepresentation reflected a denial of equal educational opportunity and that the placement procedures were the major cause of the overrepresentation. The allegations of minority plaintiffs that intelligence tests were the principal basis for classification and that these tests are biased against minorities were generally accepted by the courts. Although extensive research and discussion of the problem of bias have appeared in the literature (see Jensen, 1980, and Reynolds, 1981, for reviews), the court cases have generally reflected rather simplistic notions of bias and, in some instances, have not been consistent with the results of empirical studies of bias (see Reynolds, Chapter 4, this volume). Perhaps more important than the issue of test bias and the concern about overrepresentation are various implicit assumptions made about the entire classification/placement process in special education.

Implicit Issues

Although the literature and litigation concerning overrepresentation of minorities in special class programs for the mildly retarded focused on alleged bias in intelligence tests, a number of implicit assumptions were made by the plaintiffs and accepted by the courts. These assumptions represent unresolved issues in the professional literature and are more important to the provision of fair and effective services to children than the narrow (and perhaps unresolvable) issue of bias in intelligence tests. Examination of these assumptions provides a better perspective on recent legislation as well as suggestions for different approaches to the problems of both bias in assessment and appropriate classification/placement decisions with minority students (Reschly, 1982, 1984).

Nature-Nurture

The debate over the relative effects of heredity and environment in determining intelligence predates the development of measures of intelligence. This very old debate has not been resolved and is not likely to be resolved in the foreseeable future. The controversy was increased dramatically in the 1970s with the extension of the hereditarian view to explain differences between racial groups (Jensen, 1969).

Since the debate over the source or cause of observed group differences in measured intelligence cannot be resolved with presently available data (Loehlin et al., 1975), minority critics have attempted to force a kind of resolution through the courts. Indirectly the real defendants in the court cases were the advocates of hereditarian explanations of race differences in measured intelligence, for example, Arthur Jensen and William Shockley. Their views were a major component in the motivation of plaintiffs to press these cases. However, most psychologists and educators are either neutral or strong advocates of the nurture (environmental) view in this debate. A comprehensive ban on IQ tests would accomplish little in resolving the debate and would not address the educational problems exhibited by minority students currently classified as handicapped (Heller, Holtzman, & Messick, 1982). Finally, an IQ test ban, if not accompanied by rigid quotas, would likely result in increasing rather than decreasing overrepresentation!

Meaning of IQ Test Results

A number of myths regarding the meaning of intelligence test results have been around for several decades. Of particular concern are the beliefs that IQ test results are predetermined by genetic factors, that intelligence is unitary and is measured directly by IQ tests, and that IQ test results are fixed. The available evidence clearly refutes these myths (Hunt, 1961; Reschly, 1982), and the vast majority of professional psychologists do not harbor such misconceptions. Kaufman (1979) provided an excellent discussion of the assumptions underlying and the meaning of intellectual assessment. His views are probably typical of most professional psychologists. However, many consumers of IQ test results such as teachers, parents, and the lay public generally hold these misconceptions. Recent suggestions to change the term IQ to School Functioning Level (Mercer, 1979b) or Academic Aptitude (Reschly, 1979) are designed to reduce these misconceptions.

A significant portion of the literature and litigation has been devoted to disproving these myths. The discussion has a "straw man" quality. The fact that these myths were an implicit isssue in the litigation provides further evidence for the need to clarify the meaning of IQ test results and, perhaps for renaming the construct. Reynolds (Chapter 4, this volume) provides a further discussion of these issues.

Labeling Effects

Implicit in all of the discussions was the assumption that classification as educable mentally retarded was stigmatizing and humiliating with probable permanent effects. The controversy over labeling is far from resolved. The available empirical evidence does not support the self-fulfilling prophecy notion, and direct effects of labels on the behavior of children or adults have been difficult to document (MacMillan, Jones, & Aloia, 1974; Reynolds, 1979). The dilemmas associated with classification have been prominent in the exceptional child literature for the past decade, but much of the discussion has not been guided by empirical data. The dilemma was described well by Gallagher (1972), who acknowledged the inevitability of classification but suggested that the crucial factor was whether the benefits of services provided as a result of the label were sufficient to justify the possible risks of the label. This risks/benefits criterion should guide efforts in the future to deal with this issue.

Meaning of Mild Mental Retardation

The reasoning of the *Larry P.* decision was that the plaintiffs were not "truly retarded" despite low IQs, low academic achievement, and teacher referral. The effort to identify "true" mental retardation appears to be related to confusion of mild with the more severe levels of mental retardation. The criteria for "true" mental retardation are apparently believed to require comprehensive incompetence, permanence, and evidence of biological anomaly (Mercer, 1973, 1979b). In contrast, the American Association on Mental Deficiency (AAMD) classification system does not specify etiology or prognosis. In addition, different domains of adaptive behavior are emphasized depending on the age of the individual. There was little doubt that the plaintiffs in the placement litigation had serious academic problems. The question was whether they were "truly" retarded, or whether they merely performed within the retarded range due to biases in the IQ tests. Confusion over the meaning of mild mental retardation and questions concerning the criteria for adaptive behavior were key issues in the cases.

Efficacy of Special Classes

The efficacy of special classes for the mildly retarded was challenged forcefully in the 1960s (e.g., Dunn, 1968; Johnson, 1962). The lack of clear evidence to support the effectiveness of special classes along with the allegations concerning the negative effects of labels created a difficult situation for the defendants (school districts and state departments of education) in the placement litigation. Further, the overrepresentation of minorities in segregated special classes raised questions about segregation of student groups by race. It should be noted that if the special class educational programs were as poor as alleged, then *no child regardless of race or social class should be placed in such programs.* The crucial issue, yet only implicit in the litigation, was effectiveness of special class programs. Unfortunately the plaintiffs and courts seemed to focus on the criteria for placement of students rather than the effectivenss of the programs as such. Additional research on the effectiveness of special education programs using longitudinal designs is clearly needed.

Meaning of Bias

Many definitions of bias in tests have been proposed in the psychological and educational measurement literature (see Reynolds, 1982; Chapter 4, this volume). Rather narrow and simplistic criteria have been used by critics. In all of the placement litigation the plaintiffs presented evidence on overrepresentation of minorities in special education programs. As noted earlier, the percentages concerning placement often are misinterpreted and exaggerated. The other definition of bias used by the courts is the rather simplistic notion of mean differences. On the basis of these criteria, all current measures of achievement and ability would be regarded as biased. However, other criteria for bias such as item content, predictive validity, and construct validity have been studied with minority samples using conventional tests. Current tests typically are not biased according to these criteria (see Reynolds, Chapter 4, this volume).

Special education placement litigation has been a significant influence in recent years. Unfortunately the courts, by their nature, are not a desirable mechanism for resolving disputes in the behavioral sciences. In contrast to the behavioral sciences and professions, the fundamental purposes and methods of resolving issues are quite different in the courts. The legal system in the placement litigation is concerned with abstract principles of justice, particularly as they apply to groups of persons. The sciences are devoted to "truth," which is recognized as being tentative and approximate. The perspectives of professional personnel such as special educators and school psychologists are typically focused on the individual student who is having significant learning or behavioral problems in the classroom. The explicit and implicit issues in the litigation are at best ambiguous. None of the issues can be resolved unequivocally through the scientific method of theory, research, and analysis of data. The available evidence is at the level of probability statements which would justify decisions using language such as "might" or "should." The professionals involved appear to operate in a manner consistent with this evidence. For example, not all children who meet eligibility criteria are placed in special programs and a few who perform above the criteria are placed. These decisions are based on a comprehensive view of the *individual* and the best estimates of what is best for that individual. The overrepresentation that has resulted has been the culmination of decisions about *individuals*, not decisions about groups. However, the status of *groups* of persons has been the focus of judicial inquiry. The courts by their nature reach decisions which pertain to groups and are stated in decisive, unequivocal language such as "shall" or "must." The court remedies are therefore rarely consistent with the scientific evidence or the approach of professionals and may be inconsistent with the best interests of individual students.

THE ASSESSMENT/PLACEMENT PROCESS

The process whereby students are classified as mildly handicapped is highly complex. It is rare, indeed, for students classified as mildly handicapped to be identified prior to school entrance. Mildly handicapped students typically are classified as such during the early elementary school years, most remain in that classification throughout their school careers, and most are not regarded officially as handicapped during their adult years. However, most probably continue to have problems as adults related to the original handicap (Edgerton, 1984). The vast majority of the mildly handicapped, typically in-

volving the classifications of educable mental retardation, emotional disturbance, and learning disability, have deficits that appear primarily in the school
setting. Earlier in this chapter there was a discussion of the complex system
factors which influence classification of children. Contrary to much of the
literature and litigation, intellectual assessment is not the most important factor in determining whether a child is classified as mildly handicapped or specifically as educable mentally retarded. For example, some children studied as
part of randomly selected samples are found to meet the eligibility requirements for special education classification (Mercer, 1971). However, if these
children are not referred, they are never classified and placed in special education programs. Studies of the assessment/placement process indicate that
some children who fail in the regular classroom are not eligible for special
education services, and some children who would be eligible for special education services are not referred by their teachers (Meyen & Moran, 1979). The
most important factor in determining whether or not a child is considered for
classification is educational failure in the regular classroom which, if coupled
with behavior problems as well, makes it highly likely that the child will be
referred.

Analysis of Referral Data

Despite the potential significance of careful analyses of referral characteristics
to the problem of overrepresentation, there have been surprisingly few studies
analyzing the entire process (Bickel, 1982). The studies that do exist suggest
rather clearly that males are overrepresented in the referral population (Cegalka, 1976; Nicholson, 1967; Mumpower, 1970). Other studies suggest that
in addition to males, socially disadvantaged and minority children also are
referred at considerably greater rates (Ashurst & Meyers, 1973; Richmond &
Waits, 1978; Tomlinson, Acker, Canter, & Lindborg, 1977). Unfortunately
most of these studies provided general percentages of minority students referred without a careful analysis of the reasons for referral, the school grades
in which these referrals occurred, as well as other factors. Tomlinson et al.
reported data suggesting that although approximately one-third of their sample was minority, about one-half of all of the referrals for classroom problems
during the elementary grades involved minority students. However, there were
no differences in the type of referral, that is, academic versus behavior problem, among minority and majority students.

The only exception in the literature concerning the trend toward considerably higher referral rates for socially disadvantaged students was Mercer's
(1973) analysis of referrals in the Riverside Public Schools. Mercer reported
equal referral rates among Anglo, black, and Hispanic students. The equal
referral rates, along with the overrepresentation of black and Hispanic students in special class programs for the mildly retarded, was interpreted by
Mercer as indicating that what happened *between* referral and placement, that

is, psychological and educational assessment, was responsible for the over-representation of minority students. Close examination of Mercer's data reveals that all referrals, including those for intellectual giftedness, were combined and then analyzed by group. Gordon (1980) severely criticized Mercer's findings, suggesting that if the referrals were properly analyzed by group and type of problem, the typical results of more minority students referred for academic problems would have been found. If this is the case, Mercer's attribution of psychological and educational assessment causing overrepresentation would have to be questioned seriously.

The referral process has not been examined sufficiently. It appears that several types of overrepresentation occur involving the factors of gender, socioeconomic status, and cultural group. Overrepresentation on these factors does not prove bias since these groups are known to exhibit more problems in the classroom. However, standards for best practices require careful examination of the reasons for referral *and* confirmation of the referral problem through classroom observation, examination of samples of daily work, review of previous records, and so on.

Psychoeducational Assessment

The typical purposes underlying psychoeducational assessment activities with referred children are to make decisions about classification/placement and program planning/intervention. The classification/placement purpose typically involves decisions about current level of performance, degree of discrepancy from grade or age expectancies, degree and type of need, and eligibility for classification as exceptional. The questions typically are addressed from the perspective of a comparison of the individual student's performance in relation to some group, usually a representative sample of other students. In recent years these comparisons have been called norm-referenced.

Assessment instruments and other data collection procedures for classification/placement decisions should meet certain requirements. The items should be *representative* of some relevant domain of behavior. A sample of items (or observations) should be sufficient to infer the individual's level of competence in the area. The inferences about the degree of discrepancy from expectations should be based on comparisons to the performance of a representative sample, that is, good norms. The scores used in these comparisons should have relatively equal units throughout the scale, and so on (e.g., Reynolds, 1981). The scores should be highly reliable when decisions are made about individuals. If the scores for a particular instrument are not highly reliable (e.g., $r = .9$ or above), then multiple sources of information using different instruments or data collection procedures should be developed and considered in making decisions. Finally, if inferences are made about underlying traits such as intelligence and psychological processes, the instrument must have good predictive validity relative to appropriate criterion behaviors in educational settings.

Program planning/intervention decisions require somewhat different types of assessment information and different types of instruments. Rather than general degree of need or overall strengths and weaknesses, information is needed on very specific skills or competencies. Data collection from this perspective, often called criterion referenced, is designed to pinpoint precisely what the child can and cannot do in some important domain of behavior. The items on such instruments should provide *thorough* coverage of the important skills or competencies anchored to very specific behavioral objectives rather than representative sampling. The items or observations should be related to important objectives and, ideally, to clearly specified interventions.

Most current instruments or observation procedures do not meet the necessary criteria for both purposes. In nearly all cases a particular instrument or observation procedure has desirable characteristics for norm-referenced classification/placement decisions, or criterion-referenced program planning/intervention purposes. Of course many instruments do not meet the criteria for either purpose.

Traditional psychoeducational practices used as part of the special education/placement process have been severely criticized in recent years (Shepard, 1983). One problem has to do with the limited scope of dimensions of behavior that are assessed during the preplacement evaluation. In all too many instances documentation indicated that about the only things assessed during the preplacement evaluation were the areas of intelligence, visual motor skills, and achievement. In addition, there are the criticisms directed at the quality of the instruments used, particularly in the area of visual motor skills assessment and assessment of achievement (Salvia & Ysseldyke, 1981). In many instances the preplacement evaluation has been restricted to instruments such as the Bender Motor Gestalt Test and the Wide Range Achievement Test, both of which may be seriously questioned with regard to their psychometric properties.

Critics of psychoeducational assessment who are part of minority groups have suggested that too much emphasis is placed on norm-referenced assessment for the purpose of classification/placement decisions. Minority critics see assessment for this purpose as resulting in stigmatizing labels, overrepresentation of minority students, and placement in ineffective programs. A number of critics have suggested that more emphasis be placed on edumetric, that is, criterion-referenced, kinds of tests and assessment. The typical norm-referenced instruments are often regarded as being biased. However, the allegation of bias appears to be largely unfounded with respect to most criteria for determining bias (see Reynolds, 1982; Chapter 4, this volume). In fact, the same kinds of skills are reflected on both norm-referenced and criterion-referenced achievement tests if these tests have a reasonable degree of content validity. Clearly there is much that needs to be done to improve psychoeducational assessment for all children, including socially disadvantaged children.

However, revisions of present instruments and greater use of criterion-referenced measurement are a small part of the overall problem.

Bias in Decision Making

In addition to alleged biases in tests, concern has been expressed in recent years about possible biases in classification/placement decisions that are made from assessment data and referral information. Ysseldyke (1978) contended, "I believe that if educators suddenly had *the* fair test, there would still be considerable bias in decision making. Recent research has demonstrated the extent to which naturally occurring characteristics act to bias the kinds of decisions made about pupils" (p. 156). Ysseldyke and Algozzine (1980) reviewed the literature concerning the possible biasing influences of various naturally occurring pupil characteristics on decisions. Some of these characteristics are physical attractiveness, gender, race or ethnicity, and socioeconomic status. It should be noted that nearly all of the studies cited as suggesting bias on the basis of naturally occurring characteristics were simulation or laboratory kinds of studies. These studies involved presenting individuals, teachers, or related service personnel with the same information concerning referral and results of psychoeducational assessment. The only difference was the information presented concerning some naturally occurring pupil characteristics. In these kinds of simulation studies it does appear that naturally occurring pupil characteristics may influence the kinds of decisions that are made. The question, however, is whether the same sorts of biases operate in actual situations. The data on this question are far from clear.

Classification

The studies cited by Ysseldyke and Algozzine suggest that naturally occurring pupil characteristics may influence classification decisions. One such study is typical of the kind of research done in this area. Neer, Foster, Jones, and Reynolds (1973) presented the same information to a group of psychologists concerning a pupil for whom they then were to make a classification decision. In all instances the child was described as having a low IQ, but in one condition the socioeconomic status (SES) was described as middle or upper class and in the other SES was described as lower class. Psychologists presented only with this information on IQ and SES were more likely to diagnose the low IQ–low SES child as being mentally retarded and less likely to diagnose the low IQ-middle or higher SES child as being retarded. Other studies conducted on children already placed in programs for the mildly retarded suggest that naturally occurring pupil characteristics were not a significant biasing factor. Meyers, MacMillan, and Yoshida (1978) studied a large sample of students who were "declassifed," that is, changed from special education classes to regular classes, as a result of the *Diana* court decision (*Diana* v. *State Board of Education*, 1970). Meyers et al. suggested that these students were properly classified according to the criteria in existence at the time that the placement decisions were made. They did not find any evidence that SES or race/ethnicity biased the original decisions.

The critical issue would seem to be whether the same decision is made about a pupil regardless of characteristics such as socioeconomic status, race, ethnicity, gender, and so on. Laboratory studies suggest that bias may exist depending on these characteristics. Studies of actual classification and placement decisions, although rare, do not support the existence of this sort of bias. Clearly additional research in this area is needed.

Placement

Bias might also enter into the kinds of decisions that are made after classification has been determined. For example, more restrictive or less restrictive educational programs may be selected on the basis of naturally occurring pupil characteristics. This sort of bias clearly would be inappropriate in terms of the principle of least restrictive environment. Recent federal rules and regulations require that decisions about classification and selection of program option should be made separately and related to the child's educational needs rather than special education classification. The full range of options, from full-time regular classroom placement with supportive services such as counseling to full-time placement in a self-contained special class, should be available to all mildly handicapped students regardless of their classification. Bias might enter in this process if minority students were more likely to be placed in more restricted, segregated programs such as special classes rather than part-time special education services, for example, resource programs.

Again the evidence in this area is far from clear. Rubin, Krus, and Balow (1973) reported that, although IQ per se was not the deciding factor in special class placement, SES was related to likelihood of special class placement. Low IQ, coupled with low SES, was more likely to result in a recommendation that the child be placed in a special class, whereas low IQ coupled with middle SES was less likely to result in special class placement. In contrast, Tomlinson et al. (1977) found that recommendations for special education services varied according to SES and minority status for the student, but the direction of the results was different. Tomlinson et al. reported that minority students who were determined to be eligible for special education services were more likely to be recommended for resource or part-time special education placement, whereas majority students also found to be eligible for special education services were more likely to be recommended for full-time special class placement.

Regardless of the position taken on the issue of bias in tests, I think that everyone would agree that if biases enter into the interpretation of information from tests or if naturally occurring pupil characteristics influence the kinds of classification or placement decisions that are made, such influences could constitute a very serious form of discrimination. Considerable research needs to be devoted to this topic and all individuals involved with classification/placement decisions need to be aware of the possibility of these sort of biases and need to guard against the influence of background information on the sorts of decisions that are made.

The Pluralistic Alternative

The publication of the System of Multicultural Pluralistic Assessment (SOMPA) by Mercer (1979b) represents one approach to removing possible biases in assessment procedures and classification/placement decisions. SOMPA represents several major innovations with respect to classification/placement procedures. Mercer describes three models of assessment, medical, social system, and pluralistic, along with the underlying values, appropriate measures, and so on, associated with each model. Second, several new instruments were provided as part of SOMPA, including the Physical Dexterity Battery, the Sociocultural Scales, the Adaptive Behavior Inventory for Children (ABIC), and the Estimated Learning Potential measure (ELP). The third major innovation is the use of pluralistic norms for intellectual assessment of children. Pluralistic norms were assumed by Mercer to remove the alleged socioeconomic and cultural biases in intelligence tests. Finally, SOMPA suggests the development of a more refined classification system. It is important to note that the information provided through use of SOMPA is of a classification, not educational programming, nature. This information ultimately will be useful to the degree to which the more refined classification decisions are related to specific educational interventions.

The background related to the development of SOMPA is important to understand. The epidemiology studies in Riverside, California (Mercer, 1973) formed the basis for the development of SOMPA. The Riverside epidemiology studies established that mild mental retardation was largely a school phenomenon and that most of the children classified as mildly retarded in the public schools were "six-hour retarded" children. The children classified as mildly retarded typically were regarded by their parents as functioning within normal limits outside of the school environment. The three major recommendations from the Riverside studies were to: (1) lower the IQ cutoff to the traditional criterion of two standard deviations below the mean, or an IQ of about 69 or 70; (2) to assess adaptive behavior outside of the school environment; and (3) to correct the alleged biases in conventional IQ tests. The most important measures in SOMPA with respect to these objectives are the ABIC and ELP.

The Adaptive Behavior Inventory for Children (ABIC) is seen by Mercer as a measure of the child's social role performance in a variety of social settings and social roles. The ABIC is part of the Social System model of assessment. The ABIC is a fairly extensive, structured interview in which questions are asked to the child's primary caretaker concerning the kinds of activities in which the child engages and the kinds of social roles performed by the child. The items on the ABIC have face validity. Major questions which still exist concerning the use of the ABIC include: (1) the generalizability of the ABIC norms to populations of children outside of California; (2) the narrow conception of adaptive behavior for school-age children that is used; and (3) the relatively low relationship of the ABIC to other measures of social role performance and to traditional measures of ability and achievement (Reschly, 1982). Meyers, Nihira, and Zetlin (1979) noted that the ABIC, in contrast to other measures of adaptive behavior, was not related to any substantial degree to other measures of competence. Although the ABIC items do have face validity, questions remain concerning construct, predictive, and concurrent validity.

The Estimated Learning Potential (ELP) measure that is used in SOMPA is perhaps the most controversial aspect of this entire approach. The ELP score is based on the child's sociocultural background, essentially a sophisticated measure of SES, which is used to adjust the child's conventional WISC-R score. The adjusted or ELP score is always equal to or higher than the conventional score. The difference between the conventional WISC-R score and the ELP score can be as high as 12–15 points on the average for specific groups of children and may range from 0–30 or more points for individuals. The questions concerning the use of the ELP are: (1) the generalizability of California norms to other locations, that is, generalizability of regression equations, and (2) the validity of the ELP measure. Sharp disagreement has appeared in the literature concerning whether the ELP score should be used in classification/placement decisions (see "SOMPA," 1979).

The debate concerning SOMPA has sometimes been acrimonious. The advertised purpose of SOMPA—that is, to separate ignorance from stupidity, or to identify the child's "true" learning potential—has contributed to the negative reactions of many professionals to this system. "True" learning potential in the sense of innate ability is impossible to assess. In some of the discussion, the lines seem to have been drawn sharply around the issue of whether or not SOMPA is a nondiscriminatory assessment procedure and whether those persons who are critical of SOMPA are at the same time advocating discriminatory assessment practices. This sort of polarization concerning the use of a specific assessment system, and the very important issue of bias or discrimination in assessment, is most unfortunate (Oakland, 1979).

One possible effect of using SOMPA measures is massive declassification of students currently placed in special education programs (Fisher, 1978; Reschly, 1981; Talley, 1979). The declassification effect occurs primarily through use of the ABIC rather than ELP and influences decisions about minority *and* majority students. Declassification is not a solution per se since the students affected have serious educational problems (Scott, 1979). Use of SOMPA leads to the conclusion that most of those currently placed in EMR programs are not "truly" retarded but provides no educational solution to their problems (Polloway & Smith, 1983). A more appropriate use of SOMPA measures may be in the selection of less restrictive programs (resource as opposed to special class) but the dilemma of classification still remains (Reschly, 1982).

Caution in use of SOMPA measures is needed. Direct application of these measures, or any other measures for that matter, in classification/placement decisions is unwise. Although trite, the needs of students must be the basis for classification/placement decisions rather than *a priori* percentages by student group. The efforts to ensure effective special education programming and prevention of the behavioral deficits that lead to classification are the most crucial issues.

PREVENTION OF EXCEPTIONAL CLASSIFICATION

Although not all socially disadvantaged or culturally different children need compensatory and remedial services, it is clear that greater percentages of these children do perform significantly below average on conventional measures of ability and achievement. Compensatory and remedial educational programs for these children are needed in order to maximize their educational opportunities. That socially disadvantaged and culturally different children need additional educational services is widely agreed upon by critics as well as advocates of current educational practices. The issues that remain, and perhaps cannot be resolved, have to do with the degree to which the conventional school curriculum is appropriate for socially disadvantaged and culturally different children. Opinions on this issue differ sharply. However, on the basis of data from studies of parents whose children were involved in compensatory programs such as Head Start and Follow Through, it appears that parents of the socially disadvantaged and culturally different children have about the same educational expectations and aspirations for their children (Zigler, 1978). These parents were strongly supportive of the traditional educational curriculum in terms of the emphasis on literacy skills and the emphasis on learning the requisite cognitive competencies required for social mobility within the present social and economic order.

A debate over the effects of compensatory education has been raging since the late 1960s. Jensen (1969) suggested that compensatory education had been tried and had failed largely because the cognitive abilities which formed the major objectives of compensatory education were determined more by hereditary than by environment. In recent years there has been a reexamination of Jensen's conclusion that Head Start and other compensatory education programs had failed (Zigler, 1978; Zigler & Trickett, 1978). First, Zigler pointed out that the vast majority, from 90 to 95%, of Head Start parents see the program as valuable and successful. Second, they addressed Jensen's criticism that the cognitive gains associated with Head Start were relatively small and tended to fade out after two or three years by pointing out (1) that achievement levels of children who have been through Head Start are slightly higher than similar children in control groups; and (2) that if these achievement gains fade out, it is an indictment of the schools rather than a failure of Head Start. Other educational gains associated with Head Start, according to Zigler, are that fewer children repeat grades or fail grades and fewer Head Start children end up in special education programs. However, the most important point made by Zigler is that cognitive gains, although important, are not the only basis on which Head Start should be evaluated. More emphasis should be placed on emotional and motivational development, particularly self-concept and self-image. Other variables that should be considered are dropout rate, rates of juvenile delinquency, and so on.

Although gains can be cited with respect to Head Start and other compensatory programs, overrepresentation of minority students continues in various special education programs. Prevention of this sort of overrepresentation may be possible based on the results of a study in Milwaukee (Garber, 1975; Garber & Heber, 1981; Heber, Garber, Harrington, Hoffman, & Falender, 1972). The Milwaukee project involved providing early and intensive cognitive stimulation for a sample of urban black children who were known to be at very high risk for the development of mild mental retardation. The intensive stimulation occurred from infancy throughout the preschool years. Initial results from the Milwaukee project indicated that the early intensive experiences were successful in preventing mild mental retardation. The long-term effects of this program as children go through the school years are not yet known. Unfortunately, the Milwaukee project results may not be credible (Sommer & Sommer, 1983). The preliminary results from another intensive, early cognitive stimulation project, also attempting to prevent mild mental retardation, are quite positive (Ramey & Campbell, 1984). The results of prevention studies have vast implications for research, theory, and practice in psychology and education.

TRENDS IN CLASSIFICATION AND SERVICES: PERSONAL PERSPECTIVE

Bias in assessment, particularly with respect to specific tests, has been a central issue in discussions of the overlap among the socially disadvantaged and exceptional classifications of persons. The issue of bias in assessment, especially as it pertains to the use of specific tests, probably cannot be resolved. Current tests appear to be largely free from many of the biases that are suggested in the professional literature. Moreover, as Ysseldyke and others have pointed out, even if the tests were completely free of bias, there still might be significant sources of discrimination in the decisions that are made before and after individual assessment data are collected. The implicit issues discussed earlier are more important to providing fair classification and effective services to the socially disadvantaged. Recognition of these implicit issues provides the basis for developing reforms in the present classification system. One final trend worthy of further emphasis has to do with the effort to prevent the development of exceptional conditions among socially disadvantaged students. The Milwaukee project, as well as compensatory education programs such as Head Start and Follow Through, hold promise for improving the educational services for all socially disadvantaged children and, in all likelihood, reducing the overrepresentation of socially disadvantaged children in various exceptional classifications.

Perspective on Bias

There have been numerous discussions of the question of bias in assessment in recent professional literature. The general trends in this literature have involved emphases on a number of reforms in traditional assessment practices. There is very little in these reforms which is new. Rather they involve better implementation of professional standards for assessment that have existed for many years.

One strong trend is an emphasis on collecting a broad variety of information prior to making classification decisions (Tucker, 1977). The discussion of a broad variety of information usually includes suggestions that the child's language competence be assessed very carefully, and that assessment devices that might be used as part of classification decisions be administered in the child's preferred language (Oakland, 1977). Much of the discussion about collecting a broader variety of information, as well as careful consideration of language competence, represents what might be regarded simply as common sense. It is difficult to believe that anyone would justify classification decisions made on limited and narrow information, or that the child's native language competencies would be ignored.

Further trends in this literature have to do with an emphasis on collection of adaptive behavior and social skills data, especially when classification decisions might involve the area of mental retardation (Bailey & Harbin, 1980; Coulter & Morrow, 1978; Gresham, 1985; Reschly, 1982). The emphasis on collection of adaptive behavior information usually implies more emphasis on out of school adjustment and may, unfortunately, imply a relatively narrow conception of adaptive behavior (Reschly, 1985). Another trend in this literature is the emphasis on the use of tests which are technically adequate in terms of norms, reliability, and validity (Duffey, Salvia, Tucker, & Ysseldyke, 1981). Finally, much of this literature has placed an emphasis on fairness in the entire decision making process (Bailey & Harbin, 1980; Duffey et al., 1981).

The importance of these trends and the reforms that they may represent should not be underestimated. I think everyone would agree that bias exists if a different decision is made, depending upon naturally occurring pupil characteristics, such as social status or race/ethnicity. However, the data now available on classification and placement decisions do not clearly indicate that this kind of bias or discrimination exists. These kinds of biases are poor professional practices and must be removed with respect to all children especially with respect to socially disadvantaged children. They might best be regarded as prerequisites to fairness in classification and effectiveness in educational services.

The very legitimate concerns raised by minority critics of the current classification/placement system regarding the diagnostic validity and effectiveness of services must be addressed in a comprehensive view of reforms that need to be made. Even if we could achieve universal implementation of the reforms suggested in the recent literature on bias in assessment, there would still be questions about whether the classification of socially disadvantaged children as exceptional was in the best interest of the child. These concerns led to the development of a definition of bias in assessment which emphasizes the fairness of classification decisions and the usefulness of the interventions that result.

> Assessment which does not result in effective interventions should be regarded as useless, and biased or unfair as well, if ethnic or racial minorities are differentially exposed to ineffective programs as a result of assessment activities. (Reschly, 1980b, p. 842)

The two essential components of this definition of bias are usefulness and fairness. Usefulness in the sense of assessment resulting in effective interventions that improve skills and competencies, and thereby enhancing opportunities, must be the paramount goal of classification services. Further, in this conception of bias the concern for fairness is closely related to the notion of usefulness. Assessment and accompanying classification decisions are seen as biased or unfair *if* they result in overrepresentation of minorities in programs that are ineffective or in no planned interventions at all. Assessment which leads to accurate descriptions of current behaviors, classifications which are essentially summary statements of these behaviors, and effective interventions should be regarded as fair or unbiased regardless of the ethnic or racial composition of student groups. Over- or underrepresentation of socially disadvantaged students in various exceptional classifications or programs is therefore not sufficient to establish bias from this conception.

The persepective on bias provided here is contradictory to some of the recent trends in the literature (Mercer, 1979b) and some of the views expressed in court decisions (*Larry P.* v. *Riles*, 1979). The definition of bias used by Mercer, by the *Larry P.* court, as well as in a number of other instances, is a highly simplistic notion requiring only that equal percentages of various groups be represented in exceptional classifications and special education programs. This simplistic notion of equal percentages appears to be a denial of the reality of the educational characteristics of socially disadvantaged students and a failure to recognize the legitimate educational needs represented by these students. Equal representation of all cultural groups and of socially disadvantaged students can be achieved through application of instruments published as part of SOMPA. Simple declassification will not lead to more effective educational services. However, the implicit assumption made by Mercer, the *Larry P.* court, and others is that classification into one of the mildly handicapping categories and placement in special education programs is not beneficial to students and, in fact, is damaging the students due to the stigma associated with classification. Again the implicit issues in this discussion should be regarded as the most important concerns in developing reforms in the current classification/placement system.

Prerequisites to Fairness

A number of prerequisites to achieving fairness and usefulness in the present classification process have been discussed previously (Reschly, 1979, 1982). These prerequisites emphasize appropriate assessment and effective educational programs. Some of the prerequisites include (1) good fundamentals in assessment and ethical practices; (2) clarification of the purposes of assessment and selection of assessment devices that are consistent with the purpose; (3) assessment which leads to interventions and evaluation of those interventions; (4) more emphasis on situational or behavioral assessment and use of that information in the development of educational and psychological interventions; and (5) the development of a broad variety of placement options and use of the least restrictive environment principle.

The concern for placement options is particularly important with respect to placement decisions with socially disadvantaged students. Previous data suggest that these students were overrepresented most often in self-contained, largely segregated special class programs for the mildly retarded. This degree of separation from the educational mainstream has been criticized as reflecting segregation practices and even viewed by the *Larry P.* court as stemming from an intent to segregate. At least some of the concern about overrepresentation of minorities and socially disadvantaged students would be reduced if these students were more often placed in less restrictive programs involving part-time special education services. The use of resource room options involving relatively short but intensive remediation may provide a much more acceptable and more effective way to deliver special education services to the socially disadvantaged.

Reforms in Classification

The validity and reliability of the present classification system used with exceptional children have been challenged forcefully in recent years. The area most in need of reform is the mental retardation classification system. The present system suggests that all levels of mental retardation exist on the same continuum, and the differences among levels of mental retardation are communicated through the adjectives mild, moderate, severe, and profound. Unfortunately, the adjectives attached to the classification of mental retardation have not been successful in communicating the very real differences that *do* exist between the mildly retarded and the more severe levels of mental retardation. Most persons interpret the classification of mental retardation, regardless of level, as implying comprehensive incompetence that is permanent and due to biological anomaly. These implications of permanence, comprehensiveness, and biological etiology, are largely accurate for the more severe levels of mental retardation, but they are quite inaccurate for most mildly retarded persons who constitute the vast majority of those classified as mentally retarded. The mildly retarded differ from the more severely retarded on a number of very important characteristics. The etiology of mild mental retardation typically is attributed to psychosocial disadvantage rather than some sort of biological anomaly. The age at which mild mental retardation is diagnosed typically involves the school-age years, most often between about 7 and 14. In contrast, the more severe levels of mental retardation usually are diagnosed during the preschool years, often before age 2. The mildly retarded typically are viewed as being incompetent only within the public school context. They typically are regarded as competent outside of school in various social roles in the home, neighborhood, and community. Again, in contrast, the more severely retarded usually are regarded as being incompetent in all social settings and in all important social roles. Socioeconomic status is strongly related to the classification of mild mental retardation regardless of cultural group (Robinson & Robinson, 1976). The more severe levels of mental retardation occur with about equal frequency regardless of social class membership or cultural group. Finally, the majority of the mildly retarded, as adults, function within normal limits, that is, they function independently in the community and are self-supporting. On the other hand, virtually all of the more severely retarded are unable to function independently or be entirely self-supporting at any time in the lifespan.

The recent concern represented in SOMPA with separating "true" from quasi or pseudo mental retardation reflects the confusion inherent in the current mental retardation classification system. A change in this system which would clearly separate the mildly retarded from the more severely retarded would go far in reducing the misconceptions about mild mental retardation and in resolving the dispute over whether socially disadvantaged students who obtain low IQs and perform significantly below average in educational settings are "truly" retarded or whether they are only quasi retarded (Polloway & Smith, 1983; Reschly, 1984). This kind of change in the classification system would not resolve all of the issues concerning overrepresentation of minorities in exceptional classifications. It would, however, address the most intense concern expressed in recent years.

SUMMARY

In summarizing this chapter it is again important to emphasize the avoidance of stereotypes. Not all socially disadvantaged children are minority; in fact, most are white. Moreover, not all minority students are socially disadvantaged; in fact, many are middle class and above in terms of social status. Much of the information that was reviewed in this chapter on the socially disadvantaged involves confounding of social status and cultural group effects. Very few studies have made any effort to separate the effects of social status and cultural group. It is therefore important that we avoid stereotypes about groups of persons as well as exercise caution in making generalizations either about social status effects or the effects of cultural group.

Much of what has been discussed in this chapter can best be understood from the perspective of the purposes of classification of persons as exceptional. Although classification, sometimes criticized as labeling, has been discussed extensively over the past 10 years, most would now agree that some sort of classification is not only inevitable but also desirable. However, realization of the purposes of classification is the most fundamental commitment that those of us who work with exceptional children need to make. The purposes of classification are to communicate, guide research, provide effective services, and prevent the development of maladaptive patterns of behavior that lead to classification. In the future we need to use the information that we have now to enhance the latter purposes of classification; that is, to develop effective services and to prevent the development of exceptional maladaptive behaviors on the part of socially disadvantaged students. Much remains to be learned about the socially disadvantaged, but much information is presently available which could be used in the social and political arena to enhance the educational and psychological development of socially disadvantaged children.

REFERENCES

Ashurst, D., & Meyers, E. Social system and clinical model in school identification of the educable retarded. In R. Eyman, C. E. Meyers, & G. Tarjan (Eds.), *Sociobehavioral studies in mental retardation.* Washington, D.C.: American Association on Mental Deficiency, 1973.

Baca, L. Issues in the education of culturally diverse exceptional children. *Exceptional Children,* 1980, *46,* 583.

Bailey, D., & Harbin, G. Nondiscriminatory evaluation. *Exceptional Children,* 1980, *46,* 590-595.

Becker, L. Learning characteristics of educationally handicapped and retarded children. *Exceptional Children,* 1978, *44,* 502-511.

Bereiter, C., & Engleman, S. *Teaching disadvantaged children in the preschool.* New York: Prentice-Hall, 1966.

Bernstein, B. Language and social class. *British Journal of Sociology,* 1960, *11,* 271-276.

Bernstein, B. A socio-linguistic approach to socialization: With some references to educability. In F. Williams (Ed.), *Language and poverty.* Chicago: Markham, 1970.

Bersoff, D. Regarding psychologists testily: Legal regulation of psychological assessment in the public schools. *Maryland Law Review,* 1979, *39,* 27-120.

Bersoff, D. The legal regulation of school psychology. In C. Reynolds & T. Gutkin (Eds.), *The handbook of school psychology.* New York: Wiley, 1981.

Bersoff, D. *Larry P.* and *PASE:* Judicial report cards on the validity of individual intelligence tests. In T. Kratochwill (Ed.), *Advances in school psychology* (Vol. 2). Hillsdale, N.J.: Earlbaum, 1982.

Bickel, W. E. Classifying mentally retarded students: A review of placement practices in special education. In K. A. Heller, W. A. Holtzman, & S. Messick (Eds.), *Placing children in special education: A strategy for equity.* Washington, D.C.: National Academy Press, 1982.

Birch, H., & Gussow, J. *Disadvantaged children: Health, nutrition, and school failure.* New York: Harcourt, Brace, & World, 1970.

Broman, S., Nichols, P., & Kennedy, W. *Preschool IQ: Prenatal and early developmental correlates.* Hillsdale, N.J.: Earlbaum, 1975.

Bryen, D. Special education and the linguistically different child. *Exceptional Children,* 1974, *40,* 589–599.

Burke, A. Placement of black and white children in educable mentally handicapped and learning disability classes. *Exceptional Children,* 1975, *41,* 438–439.

California State Department of Education. Personal communication, Sept. 17, 1979.

Castaneda, A. Cultural democracy and the educational needs of Mexican-American children. In R. Jones (Ed.), *Mainstreaming and the minority child.* Reston, Va.: Council for Exceptional Children, 1976.

Cegalka, P. Sex role stereotyping in special education: A look at secondary work study programs. *Exceptional Children,* 1976, *42,* 323–328.

Chan, K., & Rueda, R. Poverty and culture in education: Separate but equal. *Exceptional Children,* 1979, *45,* 422–428.

Chinn, P. The exceptional minority child: Issues and some answers. *Exceptional Children,* 1979, *45,* 532–536.

Coleman, J., Campbell, E., Hobson, C., McPartland, J., Mood, A., Weinfeld, F., & York, R. *Equality of educational opportunity.* Washington, D.C: Office of Education, U.S. Government Printing Office, 1966.

Coulter, A., & Morrow, H. *The concept and measurement of adaptive behavior.* New York: Grune & Stratton, 1978.

Dent, H. Assessing black children for mainstreaming placement. In R. Jones & F. Wilderson (Eds.), *Mainstreaming and the minority child.* Reston, Va., Council for Exceptional Children, 1976.

Deutsch, M. Learning in the disadvantaged. In M. Deutsch (Ed.), *The disadvantaged child.* New York: Basic Books, 1967.

Diana v. State Board of Education (No. C 70 37 RFP). United States District Court for Northern California, February 1970.

Duffey, J., Salvia, J., Tucker, J., & Ysseldyke, J. Nonbiased assessment: A need for operationalism. *Exceptional Children,* 1981, *47,* 427–434.

Dunn, L. Special education for the mildly retarded: Is much of it justifiable? *Exceptional Children,* 1968, *35,* 5–22.

Edgerton, R. *Mental retardation.* Cambridge, Mass.: Harvard University Press, 1979.

Edgerton, R. B. *Lives in process: Mentally retarded adults in a large city.* Washington, D.C.: American Association on Mental Deficiency, 1984.

Fisher, A. *Four approaches to classification of mental retardation.* Paper presented at the annual meeting of the American Psychological Association, Toronto, August 1978.

Franks, D. Ethnic and social characteristics of children in EMR and LD classes. *Exceptional Children,* 1971, *37,* 537–538.

Frasier, M. Rethinking the issues regarding culturally disadvantaged gifted. *Exceptional Children,* 1979, *45,* 538–542.

Gajar, A. Educable mentally retarded, learning disabled, and emotionally disturbed: Similarities and differences. *Exceptional Children,* 1979, *45,* 470–472.

Gallagher, J. The special education contract for mildly handicapped children. *Exceptional Children,* 1972, *38,* 527–535.

Garber, H. Intervention in infancy: A developmental approach. In M. Begab & S. Richardson (Eds.), *The mentally retarded and society: A social science perspective.* Baltimore: University Park Press, 1975.

Garber, H., & Heber, R. The efficacy of early intervention with family rehabilitation. In M. J. Begab, H. C. Haywood, & H. L. Garber, (Eds.), *Psychosocial influences in retarded performance. (Vol. 2). Strategies for improving competence.* Baltimore: University Park Press, 1981.

Gazaway, R. *The longest mile.* Garden City, N.Y.: Doubleday, 1969.

Gonzalez, G. Language, culture, and exceptional children. *Exceptional Children,* 1974, *40,* 565–570.

Gordon, R. Postscript, labelling theory, mental retardation, and public policy: *Larry P.* and other developments since 1974. In W. Gove (Ed.), *The labelling of deviance.* Beverly Hills, Calif.: Sage, 1980.

Gresham, F. Conceptual issues in the assessment of social competence in children. In P. Strain, M. Guralnick, & H. Salker (Eds.), *Children's social behavior.* New York: Academic, 1985.

Gutkin, T., & Tieger, J. Funding patterns for exceptional children: Current approaches and suggested alternatives. *Professional Psychology,* 1979, *10,* 670–680.

Hallahan, D., & Kauffman, J. Labels, categories, behaviors: ED, LD, and EMR reconsidered. *Journal of Special Education,* 1977, *11,* 139–149.

Havighurst, R. Who are the socially disadvantaged? *Journal of Negro Education,* 1964, *33,* 210–217.

Heber, R., Garber, H., Harrington, S., Hoffman, C., & Falender, C. *Rehabilitation of families at risk for mental retardation.* Madison: Rehabilitation Research and Training Center in Mental Retardation, University of Wisconsin, 1972.

Heller, K. A., Holtzman, W. H., & Messick, S. (Eds.). *Placing children in special education: A strategy for equity.* Washington, D.C.: National Academy Press, 1982.

Henderson, R. W. Social and emotional needs of culturally diverse children. *Exceptional Children,* 1980, *46,* 598–605.

Henderson, R. W. Nonbiased assessment: Sociocultural considerations. In T. O. Oakland, (Ed.), *Nonbiased assessment.* Minneapolis: University of Minnesota, National School Psychology Inservice Training Network, 1981.

Hess, R., Shipman, V., & Jackson, D. Early experience and the socialization of cognitive modes in children. *Child Development,* 1965, *36,* 869–886.

Hilliard, A. Cultural diversity and special education. *Exceptional Children,* 1980, *46,* 584–588.

Hobbs, N. *The futures of children.* San Francisco: Jossey-Bass, 1975.

Hunt, J. *Intelligence and experience.* New York: Ronald, 1961.

Jensen, A. How much can we boost IQ and scholastic achievement? *Harvard Education Review,* 1969, *39,* 1–123.

Jensen, A. Cumulative deficit: A testable hypothesis? *Developmental Psychology,* 1974, *10,* 996–1019.

Jensen, A. *Bias in mental testing.* New York: Free Press, 1980.

Johnson, G. The mentally handicapped: A paradox. *Exceptional Children,* 1962, *29,* 62–69.

Johnson, J. Special education and the inner city: A challenge for the future of another means of cooling the mark out? *Journal of Special Education,* 1969, *3,* 241–251.

Johnson, J. Mainstreaming black children. In R. Jones (Ed.), *Mainstreaming and the minority child.* Reston, Va: Council for Exceptional Children, 1976.

Jones, R., & Wilderson, F. Mainstreaming and the minority child: An overview of issues and a perspective. In R. Jones (Ed.), *Mainstreaming and the minority child.* Reston, Va.: Council for Exceptional Children, 1976.

Kaufman, A. *Intelligent testing with the WISC-R.* New York: Wiley-Interscience, 1979.

Kauffman, J., & Hallahan, D. The medical model and the science of special education. *Exceptional Children,* 1974, *41,* 97–102.

Kavale, K. Learning disability and cultural-economic disadvantage: The case for a relationship. *Learning Disability Quarterly,* 1980, *3,* 97–112.

Labov, W. The logic of non-standard English. In F. Williams (Ed.), *Language and poverty: Perspectives on a theme.* Chicago, Markham, 1970.

Larry P. v. Riles (No. C 71 2270 RFP). United States District Court for the Northern District of California, San Francisco, October 1979 (slip opinion).

Lesser, G., Fifer, G., & Clark, D. Mental abilities of children from different social-class and cultural group. *Monographs of the Society for Research in Child Development,* 1965, *30*(4), 1–115.

Lilienfeld, A., & Pasamanick, B. The association of maternal and fetal factors with development of mental deficiency. Relationship of maternal age, birth order, previous reproductive loss, and degree of mental deficiency. *American Journal of Mental Deficiency,* 1956, *60,* 557–569.

Loehlin, J., Lindzey, G., & Spuhler, J. *Race differences in intelligence.* San Francisco: Freeman, 1975.

Mackie, R. The handicapped benefit under compensatory education programs. *Exceptional Child,* 1968, *34,* 603–606.

MacMillan, D., & Borthwick, S. The new educable mentally retarded population: Can they be mainstreamed? *Mental Retardation,* 1980, *18,* 155–158.

MacMillan, D., Jones, R., & Aloia, G. The mentally retarded label: A theoretical analysis and review of research. *American Journal of Mental Deficiency,* 1974, *79,* 241–261.

MacMillan, D., Meyers, C. E., & Morrison, G. System identification of mildly mentally retarded children: Implications for interpreting and conducting research. *American Journal of Mental Deficiency,* 1980, *85,* 108–115.

Manni, J., Winikur, D., & Keller, M. *A report of minority group representation in special education programs in the state of New Jersey.* Trenton, N.J.: State Department of Education, 1980.

Marshall v. Georgia (CA 482-233), United States District Court for the Southern District of Georgia, June 28, 1984.

Mattie, T. v. Charles E. Holladay (C.A. No. DC-75-31-S). United States District Court for the Northern District of Mississippi, 1979.

McCandless, B. *Children: Behavior and development* (2nd ed.). New York: Holt, 1967.

Mercer, J. The meaning of mental retardation. In R. Koch & J. Dobson (Eds.), *The mentally retarded child and his family: A multidisciplinary handbook.* New York: Brunner/Mazel, 1971.

Mercer, J. *Labeling the mentally retarded.* Berkeley: University of California Press, 1973.

Mercer, J. Personal communication, July 29, 1979. (a)

Mercer, J. *SOMPA Technical Manual.* New York: Psychological Corporation, 1979. (b)

Mercer, J., & Ysseldyke, J. Designing diagnostic–intervention programs. In T. Oakland (Ed.), *Psychological and educational assessment of minority children.* New York: Brunner/Mazel, 1977.

Meyen, E., & Moran, M. A perspective on the unserved mildly handicapped. *Exceptional Children,* 1979, *45,* 526–530.

Meyers, C., MacMillan, D., & Yoshida, R. Validity of psychologists' identification of EMR students in the perspective of the California decertification experience. *Journal of School Psychology,* 1978, *16,* 3–15.

Meyers, C.E., Nihira, K., & Zetlin, A. The measurement of adaptive behavior. In N. Ellis (Ed.), *Handbook of mental deficiency: Psychological theory and research* (2nd ed.). Hillsdale, N.J.: Erlbaum, 1979.

Moreno, E. Special education and the Mexican-American. Unpublished paper, 1970. Quoted in R. Jones (Ed.), *Mainstreaming and the minority child.* Reston, Va.: Council for Exceptional Children, 1976.

Mumpower, D. Sex ratios found in various types of referred exceptional children. *Exceptional Children,* 1970, *36,* 621.

Neer, W., Foster, D., Jones, J., & Reynolds, D. Socioeconomic bias in the diagnosis of mental retardation. *Exceptional Children,* 1973, *40,* 38–39.

Neisworth, J., & Greer, J. Functional similarities of learning disability and mild retardation. *Exceptional Children,* 1975, *42* 17–21.

Nicholson, C. A survey of referral problems in 59 Ohio school districts. *Journal of School Psychology,* 1967, *5,* 270–279.

North, A. Project Head Start and the pediatrician. *Clinical Pediatrics,* 1967, *69,* 191–194.

Oakland, T. *Psychological and educational assessment of minority children.* New York: Brunner/Mazel, 1977.

Oakland, T. Research on the Adaptive Behavior Inventory for Children and the Estimated Learning Potential and Research on the ABIC and ELP: A revisit to an old topic. *School Psychology Digest,* 1979, *8,* 63–70, 209–213.

Pasamanick, B., & Knobloch, H. Epidemiologic studies on the complications of pregnancy and the birth process. In G. Caplan (Ed.), *Prevention of mental disorders in children*. New York: Basic Books, 1961.

(*PASE*) *Parents in Action on Special Education* v. *Joseph P. Hannon* (No. 74 3586). United States District Court for the Northern District of Illinois, Eastern Division, July 1980.

Patrick, J., & Reschly, D. Relationship of state education criteria and demographic variables to prevalence of mental retardation. *American Journal of Mental Deficiency*, 1982, *86*, 351–360.

Pepper, F. Teaching the American Indian child in mainstream settings. In R. Jones (Ed.), *Mainstreaming and the minority child*. Reston, Va.: Council for Exceptional Children, 1976.

Polloway, E. A., & Smith, J. D. Changes in mild mental retardation: Population, program, and perspectives. *Exceptional Children*, 1983, *50*, 149–159.

Price-Williams, D. *Explorations in cross-cultural psychology*. San Francisco: Chandler & Sharp, 1975.

Prillaman, D. An analysis of placement factors in classes for the educable mentally retarded. *Exceptional Children*, 1975, *42*, 107–108.

Ramey, C. T., & Campbell, F. A. Preventive education for high risk children: Cognitive consequences for the Carolina Abecedarian Project. *American Journal of Mental Deficiency*, 1984, *88*, 515–523.

Reschly, D. Nonbiased assessment. In G. Phye & D. Reschly (Eds.), *School psychology: Perspectives and issues*. New York: Academic, 1979.

Reschly, D. Psychological evidence in the Larry P. opinion: A case right problem—wrong solution? *School Psychology Review*, 1980, *9*, 136–148. (a)

Reschly, D. School psychologists and assessment in the future. *Professional Psychology*, 1980, *11*, 841–848. (b)

Reschly, D. Evaluation of the effects of SOMPA measures on classification of students as mildly retarded. *American Journal of Mental Deficiency*, 1981, *86*, 16–20.

Reschly, D. Sociocultural background, adaptive behavior, and concepts of bias in assessment. In C. Reynolds & T. Gutkin (Eds.), *The handbook of school psychology*. New York: Wiley, 1982.

Reschly, D. Beyond IQ test bias: The national academy panel's analysis of minority EMR overrepresentation. *Educational Researcher*, 1984, *13*(3), 15–19.

Reschly, D. Adaptive behavior. In J. Grimes & A. Thomas (Eds.), *Best practices in school psychology*. Washington, D.C.: National Association of School Psychologists, 1985.

Reynolds, C. Should we screen preschoolers? *Contemporary Educational Psychology*, 1979, *4*, 175–181.

Reynolds, C., & Jensen, A. *Patterns of intellectual abilities between blacks and whites matched on "g."* Paper presented to the annual meeting of the American Psychological Association, Montreal, September 1980.

Reynolds, C. The fallacy of two years below grade level for age as a diagnostic criterion for reading disorders. *Journal of School Psychology*, 1981, *19*, 250–258.

Reynolds, C. The problem of bias in psychological assessment. In C. Reynolds & T. Gutkin (Eds.), *The handbook of school psychology*. New York: Wiley, 1982.

Richmond, B., & Waits, C. Special education—Who needs it? *Exceptional Children,* 1978, *44,* 279–280.

Robinson, N., & Robinson, H. *The mentally retarded child* (2nd ed.). New York: McGraw-Hill, 1976.

Rubin, R., Krus, P., & Balow, B. Factors in special class placement. *Exceptional Children,* 1973, *39,* 525–532.

Rutter, M., Tizard, J., & Whitemore, K. *Education, health and behavior.* London: Longmans, 1970.

Salvia, J., & Ysseldyke, J. *Assessment in special and remedial education* (2nd ed.). Boston: Houghton Mifflin, 1981.

Samuda, R. Problems and issues in assessment of minority group children. In R. Jones (Ed.), *Mainstreaming and the minority child.* Reston, Va. Council for Exceptional Children, 1976.

Scott, L. *Identification of declassified students: Characteristics and needs of the population.* Paper presented at the annual meeting of the American Psychological Association, New York, August 1979.

Shepard, L. The role of measurement in educational policy: Lessons from the identification of learning disabilities. *Educational Measurement: Issues and Practice,* 1983, *2,* 4–8.

Sherman, M., & Key, C. The intelligence of isolated mountain children. *Journal of Consulting Psychology,* 1932, *3,* 279–290.

Sommer, R. & Sommer, B. A. Mystery in Milwaukee: Early intervention, IQ, and psychology textbooks. *American Psychologist,* 1983, *38,* 982–985.

SOMPA: A Symposium. *School Psychology Digest,* 1979, *8* (1 & 2).

Talley, R. *Evaluating the effects of implementing SOMPA.* Bloomington: University of Indiana, School of Education, Center for Innovation in Teaching the Handicapped. Unpublished manuscript, 1979.

Tomlinson, J., Acker, N., Canter, A., & Lindborg, S. Minority status, sex, and school psychological services. *Psychology in the Schools,* 1977, *14,* 456–460.

Tucker, J. Operationalizing the diagnostic–intervention process. In T. Oakland (Ed.), *Psychological and Educational Assessment of Minority Children.* New York: Brunner/Mazel, 1977.

Tucker, J. Ethnic proportions in classes for the learning disabled: Issues in nonbiased assessment. *Journal of Special Education,* 1980, *14,* 93–105.

Yoshida, R., MacMillan, D., & Meyers, C. The decertification of minority group EMR students in California: Student achievement and adjustment. In R. Jones (Ed.), *Mainstreaming and the minority child.* Reston, Va.: Council for Exceptional Children, 1976.

Ysseldyke, J. Implementing the "Protection in Evaluation Procedures" provisions of Public Law 94–142. In L. Morra (Ed.), *Developing criteria for the evaluation of protection in evaluation procedures provisions.* Washington, D.C.: Office of Education, Bureau of Education for the Handicapped, 1978.

Ysseldyke, J., & Algozzine, B. *Diagnostic classification decisions as a function of referral information* (Res. Rep. No. 19). Minneapolis: Institute for Research on Learning Disabilities, University of Minnesota, 1980.

Williams, R. Danger: Testing and dehumanizing black children. *Clinical Child Psychology Newsletter,* 1970, *9,* 5–6.

Zigler, E. The effectiveness of Head Start: Another look. *Educational Psychologist,* 1978, *13,* 71–77.

Zigler, E., & Trickett, P. IQ, social competence, and evaluation of early childhood intervention programs. *American Psychologist,* 1978, *33,* 789–798.

CHAPTER 13

Attention Deficit Disorder

DONALD K. ROUTH

Attention deficit disorder (ADD) is the new terminology used by the American Psychiatric Association's DSM-III, *Diagnostic and Statistical Manual of Mental Disorders* (APA, 1980), for the problem previously known as hyperkinetic reaction or, more simply, hyperactivity. It is very difficult to keep up to date on the current thinking on this disorder because of the high rate at which new published research, chapters, and books appear. When I previously attempted a comprehensive review of the topic of hyperactivity (Routh, 1978), I found myself working with a stack of reprints and photocopies over a foot high. In writing this chapter the emphasis was given to materials which have appeared since about 1977: even so, there turned out to be a stack of materials even higher than for the previous review.

This chapter begins by sketching the historical background of our present concept of attention deficit disorder, including its often hypothesized relationship to "brain damage" in children and the discovery and rediscovery of stimulant drug effects on children's attention and related behaviors. Next, issues concerning the conceptual and operational definition of attention deficit disorder are dealt with, followed by the prevalence of the condition as now defined. Then the procedures most commonly used in assessing attention deficit disorder are described, including the Conners Teacher Rating Scale (Conners, 1969), the Werry-Weiss-Peters Parent Rating Scale (Routh, Schroeder, & O'Tuama, 1974), and direct observational measures.

Attention deficit disorder and its core problem, attention, do not exist in isolation in children, and therefore the discussion turns next to the "four A's" (Loney, 1980)—activity, attention, aggression, and achievement—and how they are interrelated.

Next the etiology and development of attention deficit disorder are discussed, including the question of genetic factors, normal variations of temperament, the relationship of attention deficit disorder to "brain damage," and the evidence for the importance of certain physical and chemical envi-

The author would like to thank Margaret Cavanaugh for her help in obtaining library materials for the literature review involved in writing this chapter.

ronmental factors. Follow-up studies are reviewed in order to examine the implications of childhood attention deficit disorder for adolescent and adult functioning.

The phenomena associated with attention deficit disorder have long been of interest to research psychologists as well as clinicians. The underlying psychological and physiological deficits involved have been the subject of a great deal of laboratory research. Therefore, the most recent findings concerning attention deficit disorder on the part of experimental psychologists are described in the next section of the chapter.

It is now clear also that attention deficit disorder involves not only difficulty staying "on task" in academic situations but also the child's social interactions with parents, siblings, peers, and teachers, and thus the following section of the chapter deals with the social aspects of attention deficit disorder.

The most common treatment chosen for attention deficit disorder is pharmacological. The recent stimulant drug research that is reviewed here involves children with attention deficits and includes comparative drug studies of normal children and adults. Behavioral approaches have also proven effective in dealing with attentional and behavioral problems in children; one focus of research at this time is on the comparison of drug and behavioral treatments.

The chapter ends with a statement of the author's personal views on attention deficit disorder, which are the product of many years' involvement in research on this and related topics (Routh, 1980a) and a continuing attempt to stay abreast of the relevant literature (Routh, 1978; Routh & Mesibov, 1980).

HISTORICAL BACKGROUND

Still (1902), in his lectures to the Royal College of Physicians, described certain "defects in moral control," which very much resemble the modern concept of attention deficit disorder. He found that these problems were more common in boys than in girls, that they tended to run in families, and that they were sometimes associated with certain congenital anomalies. He tried to document their association with mental retardation, seizure disorders, and with progressive and static neurological disease, or, in other words, with many conditions we would call developmental disabilities today. He also noted that these behavior disorders could occur in the absence of any evident neurological condition. His writings set the stage for the recurrent hypothesis that these behavioral problems were essentially a manifestation of abnormality of the central nervous system.

At the time of World War I there was a world-wide epidemic of encephalitis which left in its wake a variety of postencephalitic behavior disorders in children, some of which had a remarkable resemblance to what is now called attention deficit disorder.

During and after World War II a group of neurologists, psychologists, and educators working at the Wayne County Training School in Northville, Michigan popularized the idea of "brain injury" as the explanation for certain disorders of behavior and perceptual functioning in children. The most influential of their writings was Strauss and Lehtinen's (1947) *Psychopathology and Education of the Brain-Injured Child.* In retrospect, it was evident that this group of investigators had made a serious error of circularity in their research. They defined groups of children as "brain injured" or not by using behavioral criteria and then tried to validate tests of brain injury by using them to contrast the two behaviorally defined groups.

Subsequent to Strauss and Lehtinen's work there was a great proliferation of new technology and assessment procedures which eventually were brought together under the heading of minimal brain dysfunction (MBD). A U.S. government task force headed by Clements (1966) tried to bring some order to this chaos by attempting a formal definition of MBD and reviewing the burgeoning literature related to this concept. In the Clements monograph, 99 separate "symptoms" of MBD were listed, with the most frequently cited one being that of hyperactivity. Empirical studies attempting to confirm the existence of an MBD syndrome (e.g., Langhorne, Loney, Paternite, & Bechtoldt, 1976; Routh & Roberts, 1972; Werry, 1968) were, however, unsuccessful. The editors (and most of the authors) of a recent authoritative handbook on MBD (Rie & Rie, 1980) concluded that there was, in fact, no such syndrome and that this terminology should be abandoned. The main problems for the MBD concept were seen as twofold: (1) the lack of evidence for any clustering of the behaviors subsumed by the concept, and (2) the lack of evidence that "brain dysfunction" necessarily was an underlying etiological factor in the behavior disorders.

The official committees of the American Psychiatric Association responsible for its diagnostic terminology have resisted jumping on the bandwagon of such global concepts as MBD or its less organic sounding counterpart, learning disabilities (LD). The DSM-II manual (APA, 1968) stuck to a more narrowly defined behavioral concept of hyperkinetic reaction of childhood (or adolescence) characterized by overactivity, restlessness, distractibility, and short attention span. As will be discussed in the following section of this chapter, the more recent DSM-III manual (APA, 1980) has moved with the prevailing consensus in the field that attentional problems are a more constant feature of this disorder than hyperactivity; thus the new terminology, attention deficit disorder.

Any historical account of attention deficit disorder would be incomplete without mention of related developments in child psychopharmacology. Bradley (1937) was the first to report clinical findings of favorable effects of a stimulant drug (the drug he used was Benzedrine) on the behavior of children. This was a serendipitous discovery in that Bradley used the drug with delinquent boys in residential treatment in an attempt to forestall headaches when doing pneuomoencephalographic studies. The children, however, were soon referring to the Benzedrine tablets as "smart pills" and viewed them as helping them to concentrate on academic tasks. This led Bradley to attempt the more systematic clinical study of these behavioral effects, which he then reported.

Bradley's initial clinical reports and those of some others were not followed up by any systematic or controlled research at the time. Rather, the systematic research had to await the more recent era of psychopharmacology beginning in the 1950s. In fact, the researchers who did the earliest controlled studies on stimulant drugs in children—Eisenberg and Conners—first set out to study the effects of phenothiazines on children; they got into the stimulant drug research as a side issue. As with Bradley's work, what started as a sort of sideshow turned out to be the main event. Eventually stimulant drug effects with hyperactive and attention-deficit children turned out to be among the best documented of clinical treatments for behaviorally disturbed children (e.g., Barkley, 1977a).

The increasing use of stimulant drugs with children in the United States occurred in the context of the common view that hyperactivity (as it was then called) was an aspect of MBD; thus drug treatment was viewed as a medical treatment of what was basically an organic disorder. Despite this view, the use of drugs with behaviorally disordered children elicited considerable public controversy. An article in the *Washington Post* on June 30, 1970 alleged that 10% of the school children in Omaha, Nebraska were receiving amphetamines (a very exaggerated report, as it turned out). This triggered a congressional hearing. There has also been a continuous stream of popular articles and books expressing concern about the misuse of psychotropic drugs for the control of the behavior of school children. The general lack of consensus on the definition of the behavioral problems for which the prescription of stimulant drugs may be considered appropriate has made the discussions on public policy all the more difficult.

Most of the important historic issues concerning attention deficit disorder (and its various outmoded synonyms) are still being debated. Their current status is what the remainder of this chapter is about.

Definition and Prevalence

DSM-III, the *Diagnostic and Statistical Manual of Mental Disorders* (APA, 1980), provides the following diagnostic criteria for "Attention Deficit Disorder with Hyperactivity."

> The child displays, for his or her mental and chronological age, signs of developmentally inappropriate inattention, impulsivity, and hyperactivity. The signs must be reported by adults in the child's environment, such as parents and teachers. Because the symptoms are typically variable, they may not be observed directly by the clinician. When the reports of teachers and parents conflict, primary consideration should be given to the teacher reports because of greater familiarity with age-appropriate norms. Symptoms typically worsen in situations that require self-appli-

cation, as in the classroom. Signs of the disorder may be absent when the child is in a new or a one-to-one situation.

The number of symptoms specified is for children between the ages of eight and ten, the peak age range for referral. In younger children, more severe forms of the symptoms and a greater number of symptoms are usually present. The opposite is true for older children.

A. Inattention. At least three of the following:
    (1) often fails to finish things he or she starts
    (2) often doesn't seem to listen
    (3) easily distracted
    (4) has difficulty concentrating on schoolwork or other tasks requiring sustained attention
    (5) has difficulty sticking to a play activity

B. Impulsivity. At least three of the following:
    (1) often acts before thinking
    (2) shifts excessively from one activity to another
    (3) has difficulty organizing work (this not being due to cognitive impairment)
    (4) needs a lot of supervision
    (5) frequently calls out in class
    (6) has difficulty awaiting turn in games and group situations

C. Hyperactivity. At least two of the following:
    (1) runs about or climbs on things excessively
    (2) has difficulty sitting still or fidgets excessively
    (3) has difficulty staying seated
    (4) moves about excessively during sleep
    (5) is always "on the go" or acts as if "driven by a motor"

D. Onset before the age of seven

E. Duration of at least six months

F. Not due to schizophrenia, affective disorder, or severe or profound mental retardation. (APA, 1980, pp. 43–44)

The DSM-III also lists criteria for two other related conditions: attention deficit disorder without hyperactivity, and attentional deficit disorder, residual type, but these will not be discussed to any great extent in this chapter since there is much less evidence as to the validity of these categories (Rutter & Shaffer, 1980). The only empirical study on attention deficit disorder without hyperactivity known to the author, that by Maurer and Stewart (1980), suggests that this may not be an independent syndrome.

The DSM-III definition of attention deficit disorder with hyperactivity is still too new to have been the subject of much research on its reliability, the clustering of its subcategories into syndrome(s), or its validity.

A recent review by Barkley (1982) examined 210 scientific papers on hyperactivity published over the last 20 years in order to discover the actual subject selection criteria they used. The vast majority, over 64%, used nothing more than the opinion of the investigators without specifying any particular criteria. Clearly the explicit use of the DSM-III criteria would be superior to this practice. However, 70% of the studies did at least specify the age range of their subjects, with the modal range being from 6 to 12 years, and 43% of them required that their subjects' IQs be greater than 70. Also, 29% of the studies required the absence of neurological disorders or of psychosis, which would be in line with Part F of the DSM-III definition. Although standardized parent and teacher scales have for some time been available to assist in diagnosis, only 10% of the studies reviewed by Barkley used standardized parent questionnaires, and only 13% used standardized teacher questionnaires. Whatever the faults of the DSM-III diagnostic criteria may prove to be, they are at least more explicit than any previous consensual criteria have been, and they encourage the use of teacher opinions and ratings, which may be the most valid single source of information concerning attention deficit disorder (e.g., Rapoport & Benoit, 1975).

How prevalent is attention deficit disorder? Bosco and Robin (1980) carried out a teacher and parent survey in the Grand Rapids, Michigan school system. According to the parent data, 3.16% of these elementary and junior high school students had ever been diagnosed as hyperkinetic, and it was verified by phone calls to the parents that 2.92% had been so diagnosed by a physician. The teacher data (collected separately) indicated that 3.38% of these students had ever been diagnosed as hyperkinetic. The percentage of children currently being treated with stimulant drugs was 0.72 according to the parents and 0.81 according to the teachers, with the most frequently prescribed drug being methylphenidate (Ritalin). Almost 75% of the physician-diagnosed hyperkinetic children had been treated with Ritalin at some time; about 32% of these children received counseling and about 10% behavior modification treatment.

Another community prevalence survey was carried out by Lambert, Sandoval, and Sassone (1978, 1979). In a large, representative sample of children in kindergarten through the fifth grade in California public and private schools, they attempted to estimate the numbers considered hyperactive by parents, by physicians, and by schools, or by any combination of these three "definers." A total of 4.92% were considered hyperactive by one or more definers (with 3.30% considered so by the school only). Only 1.19% were considered hyperactive by all three definers. Boys were identified as hyperactive from six to eight times as frequently as girls. Of the children identified as hyperactive by home, school, and physician, it was estimated that 86% will be given medication at some time, usually Ritalin.

Is attention deficit disorder more prevalent in the United States or in North America than in other countries? There certainly have been some gross discrepancies in the frequency with which it is diagnosed here as compared, for example, to Britain. Rutter, Tizard, and Whitmore (1970) found only 1 in 1000 children to be hyperkinetic in a general population survey on the Isle of Wight. It is interesting that despite the supposed small number of such children in Britain, a Hyperactive Children's Support Group with over 70 branches exists there (Colquhoun & Bunday, 1981). British norms on the Conners Teacher

Rating Scale have been collected, and they are at least roughly comparable to American figures (Sandberg, Rutter, & Taylor, 1978). As Glow (1980) showed by applying both U.S. and British diagnostic criteria to the same population of Australian children, the explanation for the discrepancies in prevalence figures seems to lie in different philosophies of diagnosis, that is, the much narrower British concept of hyperkinesis (and correspondingly broader concept of conduct disorder).

Minde and Cohen (1978) also present some preliminary information suggesting that a hyperactive syndrome exists in Uganda similar to the one with which they are familiar in Canada.

ASSESSMENT

The Conners Teacher Rating Scale (Conners, 1969) in its various versions is by far the most frequently used diagnostic instrument. Norms for this scale have been collected in the United States, Canada, New Zealand, Germany, and Britain. In fact, a fair degree of consensus is emerging that a mean item score exceeding 1.5 on the Conners Abbreviated Teacher Rating Scale (where 0 stands for "not at all," 1 for "just a little," 2 for "pretty much," and 3 for "very much") is a meaningful criterion for the selection of research subjects with attention deficit disorder. This score approximates two standard deviations above the mean for most normative samples. However, a problem with the use of the Conners and other such teacher rating scales is that the sample of children selected will generally include those who have aggressive conduct disorders in addition to those who are more purely representative of attention deficit disorder in the absence of aggressive behavior. Loney and Milich (1982) recently developed a modified teacher rating scale called IOWA Conners (Inattention-Overactivity With Aggression) with separate, relatively independent subscales for inattentive and active versus aggressive behavior. The importance of the distinction is discussed under the heading of Major Syndromes.

Parent rating scales are also quite frequently used in the assessment of attention deficit disorder, for example, the Werry-Weiss-Peters Activity Scale (Routh et al., 1974) and the Conners Parent Rating Scale (Conners, 1970). There is good reason to believe that as informants fathers do not generally provide as much useful information about their children as do mothers. Earls (1980), for example, found that with fathers as informants the prevalence of behavior disorders among 3-year-olds would be estimated as only one-third as high as that based on information from mothers (8 versus 24%); this is probably understandable simply on the basis that fathers ordinarily spend considerably less time with their children than mothers. Even mothers seem to be less able than teachers or clinicians to provide useful diagnostic information in the form of rating scales; Rapoport and Benoit (1975) found that there was good agreement among teachers and clinicians' ratings concerning hyperactive boys with home observations and even with mothers' daily diaries but not with maternal ratings. Apparently the mothers lacked the kind of normative framework provided by teachers' and clinicians' observations of many children of the particular age. Also, parents' ratings have generally proven to be less sensitive indices of stimulant drug effects than those of teachers (Barkley, 1977a). Nevertheless, parents' opinions and feelings are clinically important in themselves and should surely continue to be attended to, even if for that reason alone.

Ratings by peers and self-ratings by children with attention deficit disorder have so far been little used sources of information. It is possible that we have been overlooking a good bet. Glow and Glow (1980) found good convergent and discriminant validity in their study of ratings of hyperkinetic impulse disorder in regular classrooms by self and peers. In fact, in this study there was good convergence among self, peer, and teacher ratings of hyperkinetic behavior. Only the parents' ratings were divergent from those of other sources. This study was, however, carried out with a nonclinical sample and it would be interesting to replicate it with attention deficit disorder children.

Although direct observations of the behavior of children with attention deficit disorder may be too cumbersome and expensive for everyday clinical purposes, there is simply no other way to obtain information about what the children actually do. Studies using only ratings will never provide this. Previous research using direct observation had most often taken place in somewhat artificial laboratory or clinic playroom situations (e.g., Routh & Schroeder, 1976). Brief observation periods in such a situation may suffice where some developmental change or experimental effect is being studied (e.g., Routh et al., 1974; Routh, Walton, & Padan-Belkin, 1978); such studies, in effect, solve the problem of instability in the behavior of individuals by aggregating across many subjects. However, Plomin and Foch (1981) found rather disappointing test–retest reliabilities of measures of hyperactive children's locomotion and toy-touching behaviors based on playroom observations two months apart (correlations of .23 and .19, respectively). They used only a 10 minute observation time on each occasion; perhaps we have all been naive in expecting such brief samples of behavior to show high temporal stability or correlation with external criteria. Epstein (1980) argues cogently that in order to get stable estimates of important individual difference variables, it is important to aggregate our observations either over occasions, or over situations, or both. Thus to get at stable individual differences and their correlates, we should apply to our behavioral observation techniques the well known psychometric principle that the reliability of a test can be increased by "adding more items," that is, lengthening the period of observation. Aggregating two-hour actometer-based activity scores across three occasions about a week apart, Buss, Block, and Block (1980) found both substantial correlations between actometer-based and teacher-based activity scores and considerable consistency of activity measures even across a four-year time span. With a clinical population, Stevens, Kupst, Suran, and Schulman (1978) used actometers to collect 40 one-hour samples of activity for children in the class-room and in other settings. They found appreciable correlations between ratings of clinic staff and objectively measured classroom activity. Mothers' ratings were more highly correlated with the children's activities outside the classroom, for example, in the gymnasium or woodshop.

Another general principle from the field of personality research which might have applicability in the study of attention deficit disorder is Bem and Allen's (1974) scheme for "predicting some of the people some of the time". Briefly, Bem and Allen suggest that for a given "trait," some people may be quite consistent and others not. If we can find out about an individual (by asking the individuals, asking others about them, or studying the variability of their behavior over time), we can then predict the behavior of such individuals with greater accuracy (say, with correlations nearer to .6 than to the usual .3 obtained in such research). The research of Kenrick and Stringfield (1980) suggests the possibility that all people may be consistent only for different "traits." The implication is simply that if we can identify those children whose attentional characteristics are consistent across time and across situations, we will be much more successful than at present in predicting their long-term prognosis.

Another important development in the assessment of attention deficit disorder is the validation of direct behavioral observational codes for the classroom. Abikoff, Gittelman-Klein, and Klein (1977) validated such a 14-category observation code for hyperactive and normal children, finding that children referred for hyperactivity had significantly higher scores on 12 of the categories than control subjects. In confirmation of playroom observational research (Routh et al., 1974, 1978), Abikoff et al. found that motor activity for both groups was inversely related to age. In a more recent study, Abikoff, Gittelman, and Klein (1980) cross-validated these findings. In both of the Abikoff studies, the behaviors of interference (calling out, interruption of others during work periods, and clowning) and off-task behavior were the most discriminating ones.

MAJOR RELATED SYNDROMES

As Loney (1980) states, there are several terms that deserve careful consideration by clinicians—the "four A's" of activity, attention, aggression, and achievement. The best current evidence suggests that there may be at least three overlapping but separable syndromes here: attention deficit disorder with hyperactivity, aggressive conduct disorder, and learning disabilities, with somewhat different antecedents, correlates, treatment response, and prognosis.

Although the DSM-III attempts to distinguish between attention deficit disorders with and without hyperactivity, the available evidence suggests to this author that only the former category may have validity. Although attention deficit disorder children do seem to be more active in certain situations (Routh & Schroeder, 1976; Ullman, Barkley, & Brown, 1978), attentional problems are a much more discriminating feature of their behavior in the classroom (Abikoff et al., 1977, 1980) and elsewhere. Also, attentional measures have proven to be much more sensitive to stimulant drug effects than activity measures are. For the time being, it seems most useful to lump activity and attention together into the hypothesized syndrome of attention deficit disorder with hyperactivity.

On the other hand, there are abundant reasons to maintain the distinction between attention deficit disorder and aggressive behavior. Loney, Langhorne, and Paternite (1978) developed an empirical basis for subgrouping child psychiatry patients along the separate dimensions of hyperactivity and aggression, using chart review criteria. The hyperactivity dimension subsumed hyperactive and inattentive behaviors, while the aggression dimension included control deficits, negative affect, and aggressive interpersonal behavior. The correlates of these two dimensions were quite different. For example, only the hyperactivity factor was related to errors on the Bender Gestalt test and to the child's response to medication. Only the aggression dimension was related to low family socioeconomic status and high hostility and low control ratings for both parents on the Schaefer (1971) scale. Paternite (1980) found, in addition, that the child's aggression was related to parental disturbance and to urban residence. In a longitudinal study, Loney, Kramer, and Milich (1979) found that the predictive values of hyperactivity and aggression were quite different. Childhood hyperactivity and aggression were quite different. Childhood hyperactivity was a significant predictor only of adolescent academic achievement. Aggression predicted adolescent hyperactive symptoms (better than did childhood hyperactivity), adolescent aggressive symptoms, and delinquent behavior.

Assessing children separately on attention deficit disorder and aggression permits one to separate a clinical population into four groups: those who have attention deficit only, those who are aggressive only, those with both attention deficit and aggression, and those with neither disorder. Following this general strategy, Stewart, Cummings, Singer, and DuBlois (1981) found that two-thirds of the hyperactive children in a child psychiatric sample were also characterized as unsocialized aggressive; conversely, three-fourths of the unsocialized aggressive children were also hyperactive. A previous study by Stewart, DeBlois, and Cummings (1980) had found that it was a child's conduct disorder rather than hyperactivity which was related to psychiatric disorder in the parents.

One of the most interesting studies contrasting the dimensions of attention deficit disorder and aggression is that of Roberts (1979). Roberts observed children of the four different groups (hyperactive only, aggressive only, hyperactive and aggressive, and controls) in a "restricted" academic situation in a clinic playroom in which the child was left alone in the room to complete worksheets similar to the WISC-R coding task. As expected, children in the hyperactive group were off-task significantly more than Control subjects. The purely aggressive children, however, were indistinguishable from controls in their on-task behavior. The hyperactive and aggressive group, however, was on task even less than the purely hyperactive group.

Also, Milich (1980), using a four-group design, found that it was hyperactivity rather than aggression which was correlated with children's problems in sociability as rated by their teachers.

The last of the four A's, achievement (learning disabilities), also should be regarded as a set of factors which are separable from, but overlapping with, attention deficit disorder. Although most children with attention deficits have learning difficulties, not all do. Delamater, Lahey, and Drake (1981) reviewed literature which suggested that perhaps 80% of hyperactive children have learning disabilities, whereas about 50% of learning disabled children are hyperactive. In their own sample of 36 learning disabled children, 21 were found to be hyperactive and 15 not. Somewhat in contrast, Lambert and Sandoval (1980) found that only about half of their sample of hyperactive children had learning disabilities. In a teacher rating scale study, Lahey, Stempniak, Robinson, and Tyroler (1978) found evidence for independent dimensions of hyperactivity and learning disabilities.

Attention deficit disorder and learning disabilities may have somewhat separate correlates. In a study of children with language and academic problems, for example, Idol-Maestas (1981) found that the subgroup diagnosed hyperactive was significantly more likely to have relatives with alcoholism and behavior disorders, whereas the nonhyperactive subgroup was significantly more likely to have relatives with learning problems. Similarly, Singer, Stewart and Pulaski (1981) compared hyperactive and specific reading disabled children and found that the hyperactive children had more relatives with psychopathology and criminal behavior, while reading disabled children had more relatives with histories of reading disability. Also, not only did the children have different cognitive profiles, but so did their relatives. Another reason to distinguish between attention deficit disorder and learning disabilities is that stimulant drugs have clear-cut effects on attentional problems but no documented influence on a child's long-term academic achievement (Aman, 1980; Rie, Rie, Stewart, & Ambuel, 1976a, 1976b).

The existence of separate syndromes of attention deficit disorder, aggressive conduct disorder, and learning disabilities with different antecedents, correlates, response to treatment, and typical outcomes has very important implications for future research in this field. We need much more careful delineation of these different pure and mixed subgroups in order to know *which* of the syndromes is related to the particular variables examined in a given investigation. Research in the past has dealt with samples of differing and often unknown mixtures of attentional deficits, aggression, and learning difficulties.

ETIOLOGY AND PROGNOSIS

In most cases of attention deficit disorder we have few clues as to the actual etiological factors. Perhaps with improvements in selection criteria, some reliable information will emerge in this area.

Genetic Factors

Past research (reviewed by Routh, 1978) indicated considerable support for the idea that the so-called St. Louis triad of alcoholism, sociopathy, and hysteria as well as child hyperactivity and conduct disorder were more common among the biological relatives of hyperactive children than the relatives of control subjects. More evidence of this kind has continued to accumulate. However, many of the family studies previously done (e.g., Cantwell, 1972; Morrison & Stewart, 1971, 1973) did not distinguish clearly between the overlapping childhood disorders here labeled as attention deficit disorder and aggressive conduct disorder. When this important distinction is made, it may turn out to be the relatives of children with conduct disorder, *not* those with attention deficit disorder only, who manifest these types of psychopathology. Thus in their study of 126 boys attending a psychiatric clinic, Stewart et al. (1980) found that antisocial personality and alcoholism were significantly more common in the natural fathers of aggressive antisocial boys than in the remainder of the sample. There was no association, however, between these parental disorders and childhood hyperactivity.

Nevertheless, there still may be reason to continue the search for specific familial correlates of activity and attention deficits, independent of aggressive conduct disorder. For example, a recent infant study by Torgersen and Kringlen (1978) found significantly greater similarity in monozygotic than in dizygotic twins on the temperamental attributes of activity level of distractibility measured according to the methods of Thomas and Chess (1977). Cunningham, Cadoret, Loftus, and Edwards (1975) found that the adopted children of psychiatrically disturbed biological parents were more likely to have problems themselves, particularly hyperactivity, than adoptees whose biological parents were normal.

Noxious Physical and Chemical Influences

As already noted, there is a long history of a hypothesized relationship between brain damage or brain dysfunction and hyperactivity and attention deficits. Current evidence suggests, however, that although frank brain damage in children is associated with manifold increase in risk for all kinds of behavioral disturbance (Rutter, Graham, & Yule, 1970), the relationship of brain damage and these behavior disorders is rather nonspecific. That is, there is no reason to expect a brain damaged child to show attention deficit disorder more frequently than some other kind of disburbed behavior.

Other studies reviewed by Routh (1978) suggested the possibility that some cases of hyperactivity and attentional deficit might be the result of lead poisoning, symptomatic or asymptomatic. Indeed there is now further confirmation that overt lead encephalopathy is associated with increased activity level in affected children. Rummo, Routh, Rummo, and Brown (1979) found that children with a history of lead encephalopathy were rated as significantly more active by their parents on the Werry-Weiss-Peters Activity Scale than comparison subjects with either no lead exposure or exposure of a subclinical degree.

The debate over whether subclinical lead exposure is a significant contributor to developmental deficits or psychopathology in children still continues unabated. Needleman (1982), citing his own recent study in which child estimates of children's bodily lead burden were obtained from analysis of their deciduous teeth, argues for significant effects. Others point to various sources of confounding in the available data. For example, Milar, Schroeder, Mushak, Dolcourt, and Grant (1980) found that deficits in maternal IQ and in the quality of the caregiving environment were significant correlates of children's lead burden. Ernhart, Landa, and Schell (1981) similarly argued that the small effects of subclinical lead levels which they found were hopelessly confounded with group differences in parental IQ level, providing a plausible alternative interpretation of their findings.

On the topic of diet and attention deficit disorder, there are some important new findings. Feingold's (1975) popular book had suggested (on the basis of uncontrolled case history information) that many children's hyperactive behaviors were due to allergic reactions to foods, particularly artificial colors and flavors. However, the initial attempts of researchers to confirm the efficacy of the Feingold diet (which excluded the presumably offending substances) were either negative or contradictory in their findings.

Swanson and Kinsbourne (1980) decided that the difficulty might lie in relatively low dosage levels of food dyes used as challenge substances in the previous research on diet and hyperactivity. In their study, they used larger doses of these dyes, 100 or 150 mg, estimated by the Food and Drug Administration to be at the 90th percentile for daily consumption by children from 5 to 12 years of age. They also selected subjects who were not only hyperactive but who had shown a favorable response to stimulant medication in terms of their performance on a paired associate learning test. These children were placed on the Feingold diet for three days; then on days 4 and 5 they received capsules containing either the blend of food dyes or placebo, in a double blind crossover design. These children's performance was significantly impaired by the food dyes relative to their performance on placebo. Their reactions to the food dyes became evident within a half hour and appeared to be at maximum by one and a half hours, suggesting to the investigators that the effect was a pharmacologic or toxic one rather than an immunological one as Feingold had hypothesized. However, another study by Tryphonas and Trites (1979) found evidence of a significant association between food allergies and teacher ratings of hyperactivity and inattention, especially among children with learning disabilities and subtle neuropsychological impairments.

Some individual children appear to respond adversely to food dyes at a dosage level nearer to the average child's daily intake of these substances. Using rigorous single-subject designs with 22 separate children, Weiss, Williams, Margen, Abrams, Caan, Citron, Cox, McKibben, Ogar, and Schultz (1980) documented significant adverse effects of a 35 mg dose of a blend of food dyes as compared to placebo. For one subject, a 3-year-old boy, the behavioral effects of the dyes were very specific: biting, kicking, hitting, and throwing things inappropriately. A second subject, a $2\frac{1}{2}$-year-old girl, responded dramatically; she was significantly worse on five of seven selected aversive behaviors and on all global measures including the Conners Parent Questionnaire after ingesting the food dyes as compared to placebo.

It is clear that we will be hearing much more in the future about attention deficit disorder and children's diet. Crook (1980) interviewed a sample of parents of children with behavior problems and found that 70% of them were convinced that diet had some role in their child's problem. A recent study on this general topic by Prinz, Roberts, and Hantman (1980) emerged with intriguing findings which call for follow-up studies. These investigators obtained seven-day dietary records for 28 hyperactive children. They found that the amount of sugar products consumed (desserts, candy, snacks containing sugar, beverages containing sugar, etc.) was significantly correlated with the amount of destructive-aggressive and restless behavior observed during free play. The data are insufficient at this point for us to be sure whether it was the sugar that was somehow causing the misbehavior, whether aggressive, restless children just happen to eat a different diet than others, or whether some third variable was influencing both behavior and diet.

There is still another type of chemical influence that has been mentioned in the past as a cause of hyperactivity and other behavior disorders; phenobarbital, most commonly administered as an anticonvulsant medication. These possible effects of phenobarbital were recently documented in a well-done clinical study by Wolf and Forsythe (1978). Of 109 children treated with daily phenobarbital following a first febrile convulsion, 42% developed a behavior disorder, usually hyperactivity, as compared to only 18% of a similar group which did not receive phenobarbital, a significant difference. These behavioral problems were sufficiently disruptive that the parents were in many cases willing to accept the risk of further seizures rather than the child's continued hyperactivity. The behavior problems improved immediately when phenobarbital was discontinued.

Follow-up Studies

It was once thought that hyperactivity and attention deficit were outgrown by the age of 12. However, actual longitudinal studies, when they began to appear, proved otherwise (for a review of the older follow-up studies, see Routh, 1978). These children are at risk for continued poor academic achievement; Helper (1980) stated that the most common educational "intervention," applied to at least half of hyperactive or learning disabled children, was requiring them to repeat a grade in school. In Weiss, Hechtman, and Perlman's (1978) 10-year follow-up study, young adults who had been hyperactive children were rated as markedly inferior to normal controls by teachers. It is interesting, however, that their employers did not rate them as inferior. The former hyperactive subjects also appeared to have low self-esteem. In a separate report on these follow-up data, Weiss, Hechtman, Perlman, Hopkins, and Wenar (1979) indicated that as young adults, their hyperactive subjects had less education than controls and a history of more car accidents and more geographical moves. In terms of actual psychopathology, one of the possible risks for the formerly hyperactive adult may be that of alcoholism. Tarter, McBride, Buonopane, and Schneider (1977) found that severe problem drinkers retrospectively reported more symptoms of childhood "minimal brain dysfunction" than did less severe problem drinkers, other psychiatric patients, or nonpatient controls. In a prospective study, Blouin, Bornstein, and Trites (1978) reported that adolescents who had been hyperactive children were found to drink alcohol more frequently than control subjects. A 25-year follow-up study of children retrospectively diagnosed as hyperactive from child guidance clinic records (Borland & Heckman, 1976) used the subjects' brothers as controls. More than half the clinical group continued to have symptoms of hyperactivity and attentional problems in adulthood. For example, many had a hard time sitting through a television show. Their achieved socioeconomic status was less than that of their brothers or fathers.

Of course, research on long-term outcomes is always limited by the validity of the criteria originally used to select the subjects. As has already been made clear, the selection criteria used in the past were in general neither explicit nor very specific (Barkley, 1982). What we now need to find out is what are the differential outcomes of the various subgroups, such as children with attention deficit disorder only, those with mixed attention deficit and aggressive conduct problems, those with learning disabilities unaccompanied by attention deficit disorder, and so on. Research already reviewed under the heading of Major Related Syndromes suggests that the different facets of a child's problems may enable much more specific predictions to be made for different outcome criteria. If the best prediction of the future is the past, we might expect childhood aggression to predict adult antisocial behavior (Robins, 1966), childhood attention deficit to predict adult attentional problems, childhood learning disabilities to predict low adult academic attainments, and so on. However, when the necessary research is actually carried out there may be some more surprises in store for us, like Loney et al.'s (1979) finding that childhood aggression predicts adolescent hyperactivity better than childhood hyperactivity does.

RESEARCH ON BASIC PROCESSES

Much of the research related to attention deficit disorder attempts to get at basic psychological processes involved rather than addressing clinical issues directly.

Obviously the different kinds of attention and factors which affect these constitute one important issue. Rosenthal and Allen (1978) point out that there is considerable conceptual confusion here. Experimental psychology recognizes many kinds of attentional processes, for example, selective attention, span, vigilance, and so on. It is hardly clear yet which of these processes are awry in attention deficit disorder and which are not.

Consider, for example, the notion of distractibility. In agreement with clinical tradition, the DSM-III diagnostic criteria for attention deficit disorder include the statement "easily distracted." However, the evidence for this usually consists only of the observation that the child is "off-task" a lot, rather than any rigorous demonstration of a greater than average decrement in performance as a result of extraneous stimulation. In fact some have started to doubt that the attention deficit disorder child is excessively distractible (e.g., Douglas, 1980).

We do not really know a lot about distraction even among normal children. For example, one might think that having a child engage in two complex activities simultaneously would impair the optimum performance on each; yet when Lorch, Anderson, and Levin (1979) had young children watch Sesame Street on television with or without toys to play with, they found intriguing results. As expected, children in the no-toys group showed nearly twice as much visual attention to television as those in the toys group, yet there turned out to be no difference in the two groups' measured comprehension of the television program. Patton, Routh, and Offenbach (1981) demonstrated that the presence of videotaped classroom sights and sounds impaired the performance of normal and reading disabled children equally on academic tasks. The only difference was that when given the opportunity to avoid this distraction, the reading disabled children were significantly more likely not to do so or to make the distraction even worse by turning up the sound!

The laboratory research on distractibility in children with attention deficit is getting more sophisticated, however, and is beginning to overcome some of our doubts about the distractibility hypothesis. Denton and McIntyre (1978), for example, presented a span of apprehension task to normal and hyperactive boys and found that in the absence of visual "noise," the span of both groups was the same. In the presence of increasing "noise" in the form of irrelevant letters in the display, the hyperactive children's performance was significantly more impaired compared to that of the normal subjects. Similarly, Rosenthal and Allen (1980) demonstrated that hyperkinetic children were significantly more distractible than normal children on a speeded classification task when high salience distractors (irrelevant stimulus dimensions) were presented within the task context.

Another active area of research has concerned children's "impulsivity," usually assessed by Kagan's Matching Familiar Figures task (MFFT). This task has undergone significant criticism in the last few years (Block, Block, & Harrington, 1974) and partly in response to this some new developments have occurred. For one thing, a longer and therefore more reliable version of the MFFT has emerged (Cairns & Cammock, 1978), with reported test–retest correlations over a five week period of .85 and .77 for latency and errors, respectively. Also, Salkind and Wright (1977) suggested a new method using continuous numerical variables of efficiency and impulsivity on the MFFT, derived from error and latency scores, rather than the traditional double median split that resulted in discarding so many subjects from research studies. Further developmental study of the MFFT has been carried out (e.g., the study of Salkind & Nelson, 1980) confirming the expectation that children get more reflective as they get older.

Although it did not directly concern children with attention deficit disorder, some of the recent MFFT research has uncovered some interesting new correlates of "conceptual tempo." Brodzinsky, Tew, and Palkovitz (1979), for example, found that children with high MFFT error rates had less control of their affective responses than others: their humor responses to jokes were significantly more strongly facilitated by audience laughter added to a television presentation. Messer and Brodzinsky (1979) found that impulsive children, especially boys, exercised less control over their aggressive thoughts on a TAT-like task than did other subjects.

Research in the area of psychophysiology continues with attention deficit disorder children. In reviewing this area Hastings and Barkley (1978) concluded that neither the underarousal nor the overarousal hypothesis concerning hyperactive children had been confirmed in terms of the children's resting levels of autonomic functions. There is some evidence that these children are underreactive autonomically to environmental stimulation and that stimulant drugs not only increase resting arousal levels but also enhance the impact of external stimulation on the nervous system.

SOCIAL IMPACT OF ATTENTION DEFICIT DISORDER

The studies of Abikoff and his colleagues, reviewed under the heading of Assessment, indicated that it was not only off-task behavior which was characteristic of these children but also a number of behaviors that are bound to have greater impact on people in the surrounding environment—calling out, interruption of others' work, clowning, and so on. Whalen, Henker, Collins, Finck, and Dotemoto (1979) also identified some low-frequency but highly socially salient behaviors characteristic of hyperactive children, such as pulling down an easel or making unusual, high-pitched warbling sounds. One of the most interesting aspects of recent research with attention deficit disorder is its careful documentation of the strong negative impact such behavior has on other people, including parents, siblings, teachers, and peers.

Cunningham and Barkley (1979) studied the interactions of normal and hyperactive children and their mothers in a playroom situation using both free play and structured tasks. They found that the mothers were less likely to respond positively to hyperactive children's social interactions, solitary play activities, and even to their on-task behavior. These mothers imposed more structure and attempts to control their child's play, social interactions, and task-oriented activities than did the mothers of normal boys. The authors interpreted the mothers' behaviors as consistent with Bell and Harper's (1977) concept of upper-limit controls, that is, as a response to the child's behavioral style rather than as the cause of the child's deviance. This interpretation is supported by other research to be discussed later suggesting that medicating the child tended to normalize the *mother's* behavior.

Mash and Johnston (1980) carried out a behavioral assessment of the sibling interactions of hyperactive and normal children. The children's mothers were also present during the laboratory playroom observations. The interactions of hyperactive children and their siblings were characterized by high social conflict in comparison to those of control subjects and their siblings. The mothers of the hyperactive children were less responsive and more negative with *both* the hyperactive children and their siblings than were mothers of control subjects. Thus the study suggested that not only is hyperactive children's own behavior deviant; they also function in behaviorally disturbed family systems. Presumably much of the family disturbance is a result of the attention deficit disorder child's behavior rather than being its cause.

As one would expect, the behavior of these children in the classroom also elicits certain kinds of responses from their teachers. Whalen, Henker, and Dotemoto (1981) found that teacher behavior was more intense and controlling toward hyperactive boys on placebo than toward either those on medication or normal control subjects. Campbell, Endman, and Bernfeld (1977) found that the presence of a hyperactive child even increased the amount of negative feedback teachers gave to *normal* children in the same classroom.

Recent studies using sociometric ratings, for example, Klein and Young (1979) and Mainville and Friedman (1976), have uniformly found hyperactive children to receive greater peer rejection than other children. This confirms the results of other research which had used parent and teacher reports to make judgments about the poor quality of these children's peer relationships (Campbell & Paulauskas, 1979; Riddle & Rapoport, 1976). These findings of difficulties in peer relationships are of special concern in view of the fact that peer problems are one of the best known predictors of adult psychopathology (e.g., Cowen, Pederson, Babigian, Izzo, & Trost, 1973). Future work in this area will no doubt be expanded to include direct behavioral observation of the peer interaction of children with attention deficit disorder. This kind of study is needed in order for us to understand precisely what transactions occur between these children and their peers which earns them the kind of rejection they so often receive.

TREATMENT

Pharmacological Approaches

If it is true, as the data of Lambert, et al. (1979) suggest, that 86% of children consensually identified as hyperactive by parents, teachers, and physicians will at some time be given medication, then it is hardly surprising that most treatment research in this area has to do with stimulant drugs. At this point the short-term effectiveness of stimulant drugs, particularly on attentional processes, is well established (Barkley, 1977a), and it is no doubt difficult for alternative approaches to compete with the relatively low cost of medications, which Whalen and Henker (1980) estimate at 20 cents per day.

Nevertheless, controversy continues over the appropriateness of and guidelines for the use of stimulant drugs for the treatment of attention deficit disorder and related conditions. Even if Ritalin is not being used in wholesale quantities to tranquilize children or suppress legitimate dissent (Conrad, 1975; Whalen & Henker, 1977), there are many complexities involved in its proper use. In the next several pages there will be an attempt to deal with the following topics: the effects of such drugs on the attention deficit disorder child, the social impact of drug use, effects on learning, side effects, prediction of drug effects, the effects of stimulant drugs on normal children and adults, and the long-term effects of these drugs.

Drug Effects on the Attention Deficit Disorder Child

Although research continues with a number of alternative prescription and nonprescription drugs, for example, imipramine (Werry, Aman, & Diamond, 1980) and caffeine (Harvey & Marsh, 1978), the mainstays in both treatment and research remain methylphenidate (Ritalin) and to a lesser extent dextroamphetamine (Dexedrine). Research on stimulant drugs with children continues to increase in sophistication. One recent example is Henker, Whalen, and Collins' (1979) triple blind study of methylphenidate, in which not only were the child and the investigators blind as to drug and placebo conditions, but the teachers providing some of the ratings were even unaware that a medication study was underway at all.

One area in which research findings in the past have been somewhat equivocal concerns the effects of stimulant drugs on hyperactive children's motor activity. Barkley (1977b) was thus somewhat surprised to find in his dissertation research that methylphenidate significantly decreased hyperkinetic children's wrist, ankle, locomotor, and seat movement activity regardless of the type of setting in which measures were taken. Rapoport, Tepsic, Grice, Johnson, and Langer (1980) even found that dextroamphetamine decreased hyperactive children's motor activity during an active program in a gymnasium. Because of the sensitive measuring device used in this study and the large number of test periods (eight one-hour sessions), these results have to be taken as serious evidence for the possibility of a direct effect of amphetamine on the motor system (as opposed to an indirect one mediated by improved attentional processes). Among the motor effects of stimulant drugs is one decreasing "high-energy" behaviors in which the child's behavior is intense, vehement, rapid, or loud (Collins, Whalen, & Henker, 1982).

Another way in which stimulant drug research with hyperactive children has gotten more sophisticated is in the determination of the dosages used. Rather than titrating dosages according to intuitive clinical impressions of their effects on the child or using fixed amounts, as in the past, contemporary studies have at last begun to administer medication in graded amounts according to the child's body weight (in milligrams per kilogram). Using this approach Sprague and Sleator (1977) demonstrated that for the learning task they used, the optimal dosage of methylphenidate approximated 0.3 mg/kg and higher dosages such as 1.0 mg/kg, which had greater effects on teacher ratings, were less optimal for learning. (However, a recent study by Weber, 1980, indicated that for certain other learning tasks, i.e., operant schedules, improvements in efficiency were directly dose-related, with 1.0 mg/kg being more optimal than 0.3 mg/kg.) An important new development is that it is now possible to measure serum concentrations of such drugs as dextroamphetamine and pemoline (Brown, Ebert, Mikkelson, & Hunt, 1980; Tomkins, Soldin, MacLeod, Rochefort, & Swanson, 1980). By using these measures it should be possible to specify the therapeutic range of the drugs with considerably greater precision.

The most typical laboratory task used in studying stimulant drug effects is one involving vigilance, in which the subject must monitor and attempt to detect certain infrequent events over a sustained time interval. Sostek, Buchsbaum, and Rapoport (1980) used this kind of task with older and younger normal and hyperactive boys in which the child had to observe digits displayed and to signal whenever a 6 appeared followed by a 4. The investigators applied signal detection analysis to the results and were able to show effects of age, diagnosis, and drug on d', a measure of sensitive detection of these infrequent digit sequences. The drug increased such sensitivity. It also increased children's conservative response bias (beta), making them less ready to report that they had detected the specified digit sequences.

Stimulant drugs do not necessarily facilitate performance on tasks in the psychological laboratory. In fact they can make performance worse under specifiable conditions. For example, Hiscock, Kinsbourne, Caplan, and Swanson

(1979) gave hyperactive children a dichotic listening task. If the children reported all the digits heard in one ear, then all those heard in the other ear, methylphenidate helped them keep their attention on input to a particular ear and thus facilitated performance under those circumstances. On the other hand, when the child tried to switch frequently from one ear to the other and back again, the drug actually seemed to make this more difficult.

Stimulant drug research using psychophysiological response measures also continues apace. For example, Porges and Smith (1980) found that an 0.5 mg/kg dosage of methylphenidate seems to be more optimal than a 1.0 mg/kg dose in facilitating the hyperactive child's control of heart rate via the parasympathetic nervous system.

Social Impact of Stimulant Drugs

The fact that ratings by other people are among the most sensitive measures of drug effects must mean that the drugs have an impact on the child's social behavior. The interesting additional discovery of recent research is that medicating the child also affects the behavior of other people in the social environment. Studying hyperactive twins, Cunningham and Barkley (1978) found that methylphenidate increased the children's amount of solitary play and decreased the number of social interactions initiated. However, the mother was more responsive to the interactions that the children did initiate, suggesting that these were more socially appropriate. Barkley has come to emphasize the importance of noncompliant behaviors in attention deficit disorder and, in reporting on two larger scale studies, Barkley and Cunningham (1980) stated that not only did methylphenidate increase the child's rate of compliance, it also decreased the frequency of maternal commands and led to more positive interactions of the mother with the child.

Other research by Whalen et al. (1980, 1981) already mentioned has documented the effects of medicating the child on the behavior of a teacher— that is, decreasing the number of intense behaviors—leading to less calling of the child's name to get his attention and generally to fewer control behaviors (guidance, commands, admonitions).

As Riddle and Rapoport (1976) suggest, a very important area for future drug research is on the child's peer interactions and ratings by peers.

Effects on Learning

Stimulant drugs usually are given to children in an attempt to affect their classroom performance. A major disappointment in this research has thus been the lack of any evidence for lasting effects on children's academic achievement. Gittelman (1980) studied a group of children with a specific reading disability but no behavior problems and found no significant effects of 12 weeks of methylphenidate on their academic achievement. Rie and Rie (1977) found that though one might find temporary effects of a sitmulant drug on a child's academic performance, the effect was not maintained over the long run. Lerer, Lerer, and Artner (1977), in a double blind study of the effects of methylphenidate of 50 children with handwriting deficits, found that the handwriting of 26 of them was better with methylphenidate versus only 1 who was better on placebo. However, the children's handwriting deteriorated immediately when the drug was discontinued.

A second source of embarrassment has been the poor quality of the liaison between physician and teacher in the prescription and monitoring of drugs. A survey by Okolo, Bartlett, and Shaw (1978) suggests that the most likely person to be able to break through this communication barrier might be the school nurse, who (unlike the physician) is on the school scene and (unlike the teacher) is likely to be informed about the child's medication status.

Other drug research related to learning falls within the category of basic science rather than aiming at immediate clinical or educational utility. An example is the search for the somewhat elusive phenomenon of state dependent learning. This refers to the situation in which something learned while on drug is retained better when on drug, and something learned while off drug is retained better when off drug. A number of earlier attempts to demonstrate state dependent learning were unsuccessful. Swanson and Kinsbourne (1976) did demonstrate state dependent learning with a stimulant drug (methylphenidate) in hyperactive children, using a very sensitive, within-subjects design in which each child learned some paired associate items on drug and other items on placebo on one day and then on the next day was tested on both sets of items on drug and on placebo. State dependent learning was shown, but only children whose initial learning was facilitated by the drug showed the effect. These findings were replicated in a doctoral dissertation by Shea (1977) using a somewhat different paired associate task. In Shea's study it was also true that the only children who showed state dependent learning were those whose learning was facilitated by the drug in the first place.

Another important theoretical issue in the field of stimulant drugs and learning involves rate dependency, the idea that the effect of a drug on behavior depends on the baseline frequency of the behavior, that is, that a given dosage might increase the frequency of low-rate behaviors and decrease the frequency of high-rate behaviors. Among individuals who are knowledgeable in the animal psychopharmacology literature, this has seemed to be an appealing explanation for the apparently "paradoxical" calming effects of stimulants on hyperactive children's behavior. The rate dependency hypothesis was tested in a recent doctoral dissertation by Weber (1980), who administered placebo and 0.3 mg/kg and 1.0 mg/kg of methylphenidate to hyperactive children who were performing a button pressing task on a high-rate (FR) schedule and a low-rate (DRL) schedule of reinforcement (the reinforcers were nickels). Counter to some of the rate dependency predictions, there was a dose-related increase in the high-rate behavior on drug, as well as a dose-related improvement in the child's discrimination between the two schedules and in the precision of timing of responses (but not an overall increase in rate) of the DRL responding. A certain more specific and quantitative version of the rate dependency hypothesis involving the correlation of drug and control rates under different drug dosages did, however, receive strong support from Weber's (1980) data. The "drug" and control rates were positively correlated under placebo, slightly negatively correlated under the lower dosage, and highly negatively correlated under the higher dosage.

Side Effects

In his review of the effects of stimulant drugs with children, Barkley lists the following as the most common side effects mentioned: insomnia, decreased appetite, weight loss, irritability, abdominal pain, headaches, drowsiness, sadness, and proneness to crying. Other side effects were mentioned by less than 10% of the studies reviewed. Of course it is more difficult to assess all of the subjective side effects of a drug when it is administered to children, for they are not as articulate as adults in their complaints. Rapoport and others (Whalen & Henker, 1980) in fact found a correlation of .33 between the number of side effects reported and the child's verbal IQ.

Probably the single most worrisome side effects of stimulant drugs have been those involving decreased appetite, weight loss, and abdominal pain, for they suggest the possibility that long-term stimulant prescription might permanently retard a child's growth. Recent research, though not ideal in experimental design, has provided reassurance that at dosages commonly used, stimulant medications produce only temporary effects on children's growth (i.e., only during the first year of treatment; Satterfield, Cantwell, Schell, & Blaschke, 1979) and not long-term ones. An FDA subcommittee which reviewed the question agreed with this conclusion (Roche, Lipman, Overall, & Hung, 1979). The subcommittee's conclusion is also in line with the generalization that stimulant drugs are not useful as diet pills for reducing obesity because their effects are only temporary.

One possible mechanism underlying the growth inhibiting effects of stimulant drugs was studied by Puig-Antich, Greenhill, Sassin, and Sachar (1978). They found that chronic dextroamphetamine maintenance significantly suppressed children's sleep-related secretion of prolactin, and there was a .88 correlation between inhibition of this prolactin secretion and growth inhibition (height) at one year after drug treatment was initiated.

Another side effect of stimulant drugs is a cardiovascular one, that is, increased pulse rate and blood pressure. However, this seems to be strictly a temporary phenomenon related to drug ingestion and no long-term cardiovascular sequelae have been found (Cannon & Compton, 1980).

In some individual children, of course, side effects of a more serious kind may be observed which require immediate termination of stimulant drug use. For example, Golden (1974) reported the occurrence of Gilles de la Tourette's syndrome following methylphenidate administration to a 9-year-old hyperactive boy. When medication was begun the child's behavior improved immediately, but about eight weeks later he suddenly began to produce loud explosive noises and to make multiple tic movements involving the face, arms, and body.

Prediction of Drug Response

Since only about 75% of children respond favorably to stimulant drugs, it would be of considerable practical as well as theoretical interest to know how to predict drug response. Barkley (1977), in his review of research on this issue, concluded that the presence of attentional deficits was the most promising predictor but not many new findings in this area have been reported in the years since that review. One study by Loney, Prinz, Mishalow, and Joad (1978) found that older children tended to respond more favorably than younger ones ($r = .36$), and children with more perinatal complications responded better than those with fewer of them ($r = .25$).

Stimulant Drug Effects in Normal Children

In the past, the effects of the stimulant drugs on hyperactive children had often been regarded as paradoxical ones, and some clinicians have even viewed favorable drug response itself as confirmation of abnormality. Thus it was quite important to have evidence that normal, healthy boys with no behavioral problems show the same kinds of responses to stimulant drugs as do hyperactive children, that is, a decrease in motor activity and reaction time and improved performance on cognitive tasks (Rapoport, Buchshaum, Zahn, Weingartner, Ludlow, & Mikkelsen, 1978). Normal and hyperactive children also show similar physiological response to stimulant drugs for example, greater heartrate slowing during the foreperiod of a reaction time task.

A question which was raised even before the Rapoport et al. (1978) findings with normal boys was why stimulant drug use is restricted (by consensus rather than empirical demonstration) to those with hyperactivity or "minimal brain dysfunction" (Werry, Aman, & Lampen, 1975). If drug response does not depend on pathophysiological abnormality in the child, there seems to be every reason to regard stimulant drugs as more general purpose psychopharmacological agents. Perhaps their use among children with aggressive conduct problems in the absence of attention deficit disorder should be further explored.

Differential Drug Effects in Adults and Children

Drugs such as dextroamphetamine have been studied with normal adult subjects for some time, and it is well known that many of their effects are similar in adults and children, for example, facilitation of performance on attentional and cognitive tasks. What is new is research comparing drug response in normal men and boys (Rapoport, Buchsbaum, Weingartner, Zahn, Ludlow, & Mikkelsen, 1980). The most important differential effects of dextroamphetamine seemed to be that the men reported significant euphoria with drugs as compared to placebo, while boys only reported that the drug made them feel "tired" or "different,"

In fact, a major reason for stopping the prescription of stimulant drugs for adolescents may be the increasing probability that this adult type of euphoric reaction will develop, increasing the danger of abuse. Recently a case of a 13-

year-old boy was reported who met research criteria for hyperkinesis, did demonstrate a therapeutic effect of methylphenidate, but after two years of treatment began to abuse his prescribed medication (Goyer, Davis, & Rapoport, 1979). Although this case is very interesting on theoretical grounds, it should not be taken to imply that children treated with stimulant drugs are at any higher risk than others for adult substance abuse, for this does not seem to be the case according to Kramer and Loney's (1982) review.

Long-Term Effects of Stimulant Drugs

In this chapter it has been possible to put to rest a number of fears regarding possible long-term ill effects of stimulant drug treatment of children, for example, on the child's growth or the likelihood of substance abuse. On the other hand, it still must be said that there is no evidence that these medications have favorable long-term effects either. The conclusions of the Montreal studies of children who did or did not receive such drugs still stand (e.g., Weiss, Minde, Douglas, Werry, & Sykes, 1971).

Behavioral Approaches

Among the psychological approaches to treating children with attention deficit disorder, or indeed all kinds of other problems, the behavior therapies are certainly the best represented and most often cited in the research literature (Routh, 1980b). However, many behavioral researchers object to any "medical model" and do not design their studies to be relevant to groups with narrowly delimited psychiatric diagnoses. Thus in order to appreciate the variety and quality of the behavioral therapeutic approaches available, a wider net needs to be cast. A review of some of this broader but highly relevant material is provided by Routh and Mesibov (1980).

A great deal of child behavior therapy research is school-based. As an example of one kind of issues it addresses, consider the following: behavioral research, unlike drug research, targets particular responses, and therefore involves important decisions as to what behavior is to be changed. As Routh and Mesibov's (1980) review concluded, it is easy enough to induce children to sit in their seats and keep their eyes on their schoolwork, if that is the behavioral goal. However, as a number of studies have demonstrated, reinforcing a child for "paying attention" does not guarantee that any more academic work will thereby be accomplished (Ferritor, Buckholdt, Hamblin, & Smith, 1972). A generally more successful approach is to apply contingency management to the child's academic performance, which can decrease disruptive behavior as a side effect (Ayllon & Roberts, 1974).

The pattern in which stimulant drugs are used as part of the attention deficit disorder child's treatment usually involves a morning and perhaps a noon dose, each with effects on behavior lasting about four hours. This leaves the child's behavior at home in the late afternoon and evening relatively unaffected, in order to avoid the problem of insomnia (the most frequent side effect of stimulant drugs). The child's behaviors at home thus provide rather clear and exclusive territory for behavior-oriented treatment. Dubey and Kaufman carried out a controlled experimental study of a 10-week workshop program training parents in behavior modification and child management skills. The behavior of hyperactive children whose parents attended such a workshop improved significantly at home by several measures, compared to the behaviors of children in a control group. Another purpose of this kind of home-based behavioral treatment program can be to use home reinforcements to modify the child's classroom behavior. A number of programs of this kind have been carried out with positive results, but as Atkeson and Forehand (1979) point out, there needs to be better monitoring of the actual behavioral events at home and longer term follow-up data. The same criticisms could be made of available home-based behavioral treatment programs for children with attention deficit disorder. Although there are no strikingly new developments to report here, cognitive behavioral research with attention deficit disorder has been an active area for the last several years. Much of this research unfortunately involves analogue or laboratory tasks rather than more clinically relevant measures, whether at home or at school. A review of such research may be found in Routh (1978).

The current behavioral literature is filled with new ideas for treating children's problems which simply are in need of further research and development to establish how feasible they might be. For example, there is a case study of a 4-year-old "hyperactive" boy who was given medication (actually, haloperidol rather than a stimulant drug) to enable him to enact certain role behaviors which were videotaped. Video editing was then used to produce a modeling tape in which the child appeared to perform at a level of which he was actually incapable. Watching this tape evidently had a favorable therapeutic effect on the child (Dowrick & Raeburn, 1977). A single study by Redfering and Bowman (1981) described how Benson's meditative-relaxation technique was taught to a group of behaviorally disturbed children. Compared to a randomly assigned group merely instructed to rest, the meditative treatment group improved significantly in their observed off-task behaviors in the classroom. Another new type of behavioral treatment which needs to be given thorough trials with attention deficit disorder children, in view of their serious peer problems, is social skills training.

In concluding this brief section on behavioral treatment approaches to attention deficit disorder, the author would like to make a plea for long-term follow-up studies. As O'Leary (1980) noted, behavior therapy has been shown to effect positive behavioral changes in children's academic and social behavior but only in studies of one to four months' duration.

Educational Approaches

Eisenberg (1978), one of the most experienced clinicians and researchers in this field, provides a balanced view of the usefulness and limitations of drugs for hyperkinetic children. He espouses the view that behavior modification when properly applied can reduce disruptive symptoms both in the classroom and at home, but then concludes that "remedial education must be viewed as the central component in care" (p. 320). If this is true, why are we not investing considerably more of our scientific resources into this area?

One pioneering study of this kind, by Arnold, Barnebey, McManus, Smeltzer, Conrad, Winer, and Desgranges (1977), actually involved a preventive approach. Eighty-six first graders were screened from a larger group as being vulnerable to academic failure and behavioral difficulty using the SEARCH procedures of Silver and Hagin (1976). Then they were assigned to either an intervention group which received individually tailored educational tutoring from Silver and Hagin's (1976) TEACH program, a contact control group, or a no-contact control group. At the conclusion of treatment, and even to a larger extent at follow-up one year later, the intervention group surpassed the others on IQ measures, in reading performance, and had lower hyperactivity and conduct disorder scores on three teacher rating scales (the Conners, Davids, and Quay-Peterson measures).

More good educational research with attention deficit disorder children should be a high priority. If Eisenberg is correct, the scientific neglect of such remedial education must be considered a scandal.

Comparative Treatment Research

For the most part, the two treatments which have been compared are pharmacological and behavioral approaches. Wolraich, Drummond, Salomon, O'Brien, and Sivage (1978) simultaneously examined the effects of 0.3 mg/kg methylphenidate and two different behavioral approaches (group and individual) in the classroom with hyperactive children. There was no apparent interaction between drug and behavioral approaches, both of which had significant effects. Medication affected several behavioral measures, especially during individual work. Behavior modification was effective only during the group period, but it affected academic performance (which the drug did not change) as well as classroom behaviors. Another comparative study, by Gittelman, Klein, Abikoff, Katz, Pollack and Mattes (1980), did not include a control group with neither drug nor behavioral treatment, but it did find a significant drug effect on classroom behavior (the addition of behavioral treatment to drug did not make a significant difference). These investigators considered their findings to weigh largely on the side of the drug as the more effective treatment, but the Wolraich et al. study seems to provide a more definitive assessment of the merits and disadvantages of the two approaches (which are, after all, not at all incompatible with each other except perhaps for those who are philosophically averse to one or the other).

The most provocative discussion of comparative treatment effects in the current literature may be that accompanying the study of Bugental, Whalen, and Henker (1977), who compared a self-control treatment and a social reinforcement treatment of medicated versus unmedicated hyperactive children.

In this study children who attributed high personal causality to themselves and unmedicated children did better on the experimental task (Porteus mazes) under the self-control intervention. In contrast, children who attributed low causality to themselves and medicated children showed a trend toward more error reduction under the social reinforcement condition. It seems that the child's own attributional style may be an important moderator of which is the treatment of choice. Behavioral change may be optimized when the child's causal attributions match the implicit attributional emphasis of a given intervention. Perhaps there are ways of presenting even pharmacological or behavioral treatments to the high personal causality child in such a way that the child can see them as aides to get to his or her own goals, appropriately taking personal credit for at least some of the outcome.

A PERSONAL VIEW OF ATTENTION DEFICIT DISORDER

First of all, let me say that on the whole I applaud the new terminology. We should get used to speaking of attention deficits and begin to regard "hyperactivity" as an outmoded term. It is too bad, however, that DSM-III emerged with the heretofore unheard of distinction between attention deficit disorder with and without hyperactivity. As the reader will be well aware by now, I would much prefer that the committee distinguish between attention deficit disorder with and without aggression, or attention deficit disorder with and without learning disabilities, so to speak. As I have tried to show, these are the distinctions that really make a difference in terms of empirically documented antecedents, correlates, response to treatment, and prognosis.

Also, while the DSM-III definition is clearly an advance over previous official definitions in specifying the criteria to be met for a diagnosis of attention deficit disorder, it is not yet as operational as it might be. It would have been more in line with the best current research and clinical practice if it had specified that the child must have a teacher rated attentional problem two standard deviations above the mean for age. Of course even this operational definition, if based on commonly used teacher rating scales, is increasingly subject to criticism in that the scales do not adequately distinguish attention deficit disorder from aggressive conduct problems. The IOWA Conners Scale developed by Loney and Milich (1982) is an excellent step in the right direction, and I hope it will now be widely used.

In terms of basic psychological processes, what do these children's problems consist of? I would describe them in terms of different varieties of developmental immaturity. The normal child steadily improves in the ability and disposition to sustain attention in the multiple senses of increased span of apprehension, vigilance, and resistance to distraction, and in the tendency to be appropriately selective. The motor restlessness of normal children also tends to decline with age (Abikoff et al., 1977, 1980; Routh et al., 1974, 1978). The attention deficit disorder child lags in all these respects, generally to the detriment of both the child's academic performance and social relationships. Either stimulant drugs or appropriate behavioral contingency management can overcome these difficulties for at least short periods of time or in particular situations, but we have yet to come up with self-control or remedial strategies that are helpful over the long term.

The normal child steadily increases in the empathic appreciation of the effects of his or her behavior on other people's feelings. Thus tantrums, noncompliance, physical and verbal aggression, and frequent violations of social norms generally give way to greater sensitivity to other people and better socialized behavior. The child with conduct problems seemingly does not develop such empathic sensitivity, or at least impulsively disregards such considerations in his or her behavior. The child may also develop a bias to attribute hostile motives to others (e.g., Nasby, Hayden, & DePaulo, 1980) and to act on the basis of such attributions. Obviously if such a child has attentional problems as well, it can only lead to even more impulsive and uncontrolled conduct. Behavioral treatment approaches have generally focused directly on contingency management of the aggressive or delinquent youth's behavior (e.g., Patterson, 1974; Phillips, 1968) rather than the underlying affective and cognitive processes that I presume to be the more fundamental difficulty here. At any rate, the effectiveness of the available treatments has not yet been shown to alter the unfavorable long-term prognosis of children's conduct problems.

The developmental prerequisites for complex academic skills such as reading, spelling, and mathematics are legion. In fact, at different stages of skill development in reading (to take but one important academic area), there are shifts in which subskills are the most important. Thus among the earliest challenges may be the phonemic analysis and synthesis of spoken language (Fox & Routh, 1975, 1976, 1980) and letter–sound associations such as are involved in decoding written words to speech. Later the challenge may involve the high-speed visual processing so difficult for the child identified by Boder (1973) as "dyseidetic." Still later the challenge may involve reading as a language comprehension task. The ultimate limits on "reading skill," when the reader confronts high-level, difficult material, whether it be poetry or science, are probably general cognitive ones rather than being linguistic in any narrow sense. Thus there are many ways in which a child can have difficulty in the process of learning to read, and children with specific reading disabilities are therefore a psychologically heterogeneous group. Nevertheless, the combination of attention deficit disorder and any of these perceptual, linguistic, or cognitive difficulties can only make things more difficult for the child academically and socially. Stimulant drugs do not seem at all helpful in remediating learning disabilities, and behavioral approaches have so far been studied mostly in the short term. Special education for children with learning disabilities is still a chaotic field. Although it includes a number of vulnerable philosophies of remediation, such as Orton-Gillingham-Stillman (Gillingham, 1970), and Fernald (1943) approaches to reading problems, there is as yet little in the way of systematic, empirical research on their effectiveness.

Going beyond basic psychological processes, what can one say about the etiology of attention deficit disorder and related conditions? Here I think we must begin by recognizing that in the individual case, we usually do not have an answer.

The evidence that certain behavioral and learning disorders tend to run in families is actually quite strong. Although research has generally confounded the conditions of attention deficit disorder and aggressive conduct disorder in children, it is clear that one or the other of these (or both) is related to the frequency of such problems as antisocial personality, alcoholism, and hysteria in biological (but not adoptive) relatives. Similarly, the relatives of children with specific reading disorders are more likely to have had reading problems than persons in the general population. Also, twin studies have generally supported the hypothesis of significant genetic variance in such temperamental variables as activity level, however defined. What is so far completely lacking, however, is any knowledge of just what genes or enzymes might be involved in the hereditary transmission of factors relevant to attention deficit disorder, aggressive conduct disorder, or learning disabilities.

What about the role of "brain damage" or more generally of biological environmental factors in attention deficit disorder and related problems? There is little doubt that there is a role, but it seems to be a nonspecific one. An example is lead poisoning. Children with lead encephalopathy who survive its acute effects do not just have attentional problems; they may also suffer from seizures, cerebral palsy, mental retardation, poor academic achievement, decreased visual acuity, and so on. As Rutter has so effectively argued, any kind of overt neurological disorder increases the probability of all kinds of child behavioral problems, not just of those traditionally grouped under the umbrella of "minimal brain dysfunction." Although research in the area of food additives and attention deficit disorder is really just beginning, this may provide an exception to the above "nonspecificity" rule, that is, there could be a direct relationship (toxicological or immunological) between certain food dyes and attentional problems for the susceptible child. Much more research is needed to determine whether this is so.

The etiological role of experiential factors is probably clearest in the case of aggressive conduct disorders. One can cite a considerable number of rigorous laboratory and field studies on modeling effects on children's aggression and also naturalistic studies on how young children learn specific aggressive and antisocial behaviors from peers. To the extent that specific behavioral or remedial educational procedures are helpful for any of these behavioral or learning disorders, their presence or absence in the repertoires of parents and teachers may be regarded as an important set of environmental factors. Sameroff and Chandler's (1975) important review of the continuum of caretaking casualty and considerable subsequent research (e.g , the Kauai study by E. Werner and her associates) supports the idea of an interaction between biological risk factors and the supportiveness of the home environment in determining a whole variety of behavioral and educational outcomes. Similarly, the work of Chess, Thomas, and their colleagues at New York University highlights the importance of the match or mismatch between the child's emerging temperament and the child rearing styles of the parents.

In conclusion, I would like to stress the recency of important developments in this field. The quantity of research and writing on attention deficit disorder and related problems over the last several years has been so great that it is impossible to stay current. More important, it has included some new and valuable concepts and findings regarding stimulant drug effects, child behavior therapy, rating scales and behavioral observation codes, and the differential prognosis for certain subgroups. In the past, the area was too often characterized by diverse views not well grounded in empirical findings and a lack of effective communication. I hope that soon there will be the kind of moving consensus in this field that is characteristic of more mature scientific disciplines.

REFERENCES

Abikoff, H., Gittelman, R., & Klein, D. F. Classroom observation code for hyperactive children: A replication of validity. *Journal of Consulting and Clinical Psychology,* 1980, *48,* 555–565.

Abikoff, H., Gittelman-Klein, R., & Klein, D. F. Validation of a classroom observational code for hyperactive children. *Journal of Consulting and Clinical Psychology,* 1977, *45,* 772–783.

Aman, M. G. Psychotropic drugs and learning problems: A selective review. *Journal of Learning Disabilities,* 1980, *13,* 87–97.

American Psychiatric Association. *DSM-II. Diagnostic and statistical manual of mental disorders* (2nd ed.). Washington, D.C.: APA, 1968.

American Psychiatric Association. *DSM-III. Diagnostic and statistical manual of mental disorders* (3rd ed.). Washington, D.C.: APA, 1980.

Arnold, L. E., Barnebey, N., McManus, J., Smeltzer, D. J., Conrad, A., Winer, G., & Desgranges, L. Prevention of specific perceptual remediation for vulnerable first graders. *Archives of General Psychiatry,* 1977, *34,* 1279–1294.

Atkeson, B. M., & Forehand, R. Home-based reinforcement programs designed to modify classroom behavior. *Psychological Bulletin,* 1979, *86,* 1298–1308.

Ayllon, T., & Roberts, M. D. Eliminating discipline problems by strengthening academic performance. *Journal of Applied Behavior Analysis,* 1974, *7,* 71–76.

Barkley, R. A. A review of stimulant drug research with hyperactive children. *Journal of Child Psychology and Psychiatry,* 1977, *18,* 137–165. (a)

Barkley, R. A. The effects of methylphenidate on various types of activity level and attention in hyperkinetic children. *Journal of Abnormal Child Psychology,* 1977, *5,* 351–369. (b)

Barkley, R. A. Guidelines for defining hyperactivity in children (attention deficit disorder with hyperactivity). In B. Lahey & A. Kazdin (Eds.), *Advances in clinical child psychology. Vol. 5.* New York: Plenum, 1982.

Barkley, R. A. & Cunningham, C. E. The parent-child interactions of hyperactive children and their modification by stimulant drugs. In R. M. Knights & D. J. Bakker (Eds.), *Treatment of hyperactive and learning disordered children.* Baltimore: University Park Press, 1980.

Bell, R. Q., & Harper, L. V. *Child effects on adults.* Hillsdale, N.J.: Erlbaum, 1977.

Bem, D. J., & Allen, A. On predicting some of the people some of the time. *Psychological Review,* 1974, *81,* 506–520.

Block, J., Block, J. H., & Harrington, D. M. Some misgivings about the Matching Familiar Figures Test as a measure of reflection-impulsivity. *Developmental Psychology,* 1974, *10,* 611–632.

Blouin, A. G. A., Bornstein, R. A., & Trites, R. L. Teenage alcohol use among hyperactive children: A five year follow-up study. *Journal of Pediatric Psychology,* 1978, *3,* 188–194.

Boder, E. Developmental dyslexia: A diagnostic approach based on three atypical reading-spelling patterns. *Developmental Medicine and Child Neurology,* 1973, *15,* 663–687.

Borland, B. L., & Heckman, H. K. Hyperactive boys and their brothers. *Archives of General Psychiatry,* 1976, *33,* 669–675.

Bosco, J. J., & Robin, S.S. Hyperkinesis: Prevalence and treatment. In C. K. Whalen & B. Henker (Eds.), *Hyperactive children: The social ecology of identification and treatment.* New York: Academic, 1980.

Bradley, C. The behavior of children receiving benzedrine. *American Journal of Psychiatry,* 1937, *94,* 577–585.

Brodzinsky, D. M., Tew, J. D., & Palkovitz, R. Control of humorous affect in relation to children's conceptual tempo. *Developmental Psychology,* 1979, *15,* 275–279.

Brown, G. L., Ebert, M. H., Mikkelsen, E. J., & Hunt, R. D. Behavior and motor activity response in hyperactive children and plasma amphetamine levels following a sustained release preparation. *Journal of the American Academy of Child Psychiatry,* 1980, *19,* 225–239.

Bugental, D. B., Whalen, C. K., & Henker, B. Causal attributions of hyperactive children and motivational assumptions of two behavior-change approaches: Evidence for an interactionist position. *Child Development,* 1977, *48,* 874–884.

Buss, D. M., Block, J. H., & Block, J. Preschool activity level: Personality correlates and developmental implications. *Child Development,* 1980, *51,* 401–408.

Cairns, E. & Cammock, T. Development of a more reliable version of the Matching Familiar Figures Test. *Developmental Psychology,* 1978, *14,* 555–560.

Campbell, S. B., Endman, M. W., & Bernfeld, G. A three-year follow-up of hyperactive preschoolers into elementary school. *Journal of Child Psychology and Psychiatry,* 1977, *18,* 239–249.

Campbell, S. B., & Paulauskas, S. Peer relations in hyperactive children. *Journal of Child Psychology and Psychiatry,* 1979, *20,* 233–246.

Cannon, I. P. & Compton, C. L. School dysfunction in the adolescent. *Pediatric Clinics of North America,* 1980, *27* (1), 79–96.

Cantwell, D. P. Psychiatric illness in the families of hyperactive children. *Archives of General Psychiatry,* 1972, *27,* 414–417.

Clements, S. D. *Minimal brain dysfunction in children: Terminology and identification.* Washington, D.C.: U.S. Department of Health, Education and Welfare, 1966.

Collins, B. E., Whalen, C. K., & Henker, B. Ecological and pharmacological influences on behaviors in the classroom: The hyperkinetic behavioral syndrome. In J. Antrobus (Ed.), *The eco-system of the "sick kid."* 1982.

Colquhoun, I., & Bunday, S. A lack of essential acids as a possible cause of hyperactivity. *Medical Hypotheses,* 1981, *7,* 673–679.

Conners, C. K. A teacher rating scale for use in drug studies with children. *American Journal of Psychiatry,* 1969, *126,* 884–888.

Conners, C. K. Symptom patterns in hyperkinetic, neurotic, and normal children. *Child Development,* 1970, *41,* 667–682.

Conrad, P. The discovery of hyperkinesis: Notes on the medicalization of deviant behavior. *Social Problems,* 1975, *23,* 12–21.

Cowen, E., Pederson, A., Babigian, H., Izzo, L., & Trost, M. Long-term follow-up of early-detected vulnerable children. *Journal of Consulting and Clinical Psychology,* 1973, *41,* 438–446.

Crook, W. G. Can what a child eats make him dull, stupid, or hyperactive? *Journal of Learning Disabilities,* 1980, *13,* 281–286.

Cunningham, C. E., & Barkley, R. A. The effects of methylphenidate on the mother-child interactions of hyperactive identical twins. *Developmental Medicine and Child Neurology,* 1978, *20,* 634–642.

Cunningham, C. E., & Barkley, R. A. The interactions of normal and hyperactive children with their mothers in free play and structured tasks. *Child Development,* 1979, *50,* 217–224.

Cunningham, L., Cadoret, R. J., Loftus, R., & Edwards, J. E. Studies of adoptees from psychiatrically disturbed biological parents: Psychiatric conditions in childhood and adolescence. *British Journal of Psychiatry,* 1975, *126,* 534–549.

Delamater, A. M., Lahey, B. B., & Drake, L. Toward an empirical subclassification of "learning disabilities": A psychophysiological comparison of "hyperactive" and "nonhyperactive" subgroups. *Journal of Abnormal Child Psychology,* 1981, *9,* 65–77.

Denton, C. L., & McIntyre, C. W. Span of apprehension in hyperactive boys. *Journal of Abnormal Child Psychology,* 1978, *6,* 19–24.

Douglas, V. I. Treatment and training approaches to hyperactivity: Establishing internal or external control. In C. K. Whalen & B. Henker (Eds.), *Hyperactive children: The social ecology of identification and treatment.* New York: Academic, 1980.

Dowrick, P. W., & Raeburn, J. M. Video editing and medication to produce a therapeutic self model. *Journal of Consulting and Clinical Psychology,* 1977, *45,* 1156–1158.

Earls, F. The prevalence of behavior problems in 3-year-old children: Comparison of the reports of fathers and mothers. *Journal of the American Academy of Child Psychiatry,* 1980, *19,* 430–452.

Eisenberg, L. Hyperkinesis revisited. *Pediatrics,* 1978, *61,* 319–321.

Epstein, S. The stability of behavior. 2. Implications for psychological research. *American Psychologist,* 1980, *35,* 790–806.

Ernhart, C. B., Landa, B., & Schell, N. B. Subclinical levels of lead and developmental deficit: A multivariate follow-up reassessment. *Pediatrics,* 1981, *67,* 911–919.

Feingold, B. F. *Why your child is hyperactive.* New York: Random House, 1975.

Fernald, G. M. *Remedial techniques in basic school subjects.* New York: McGraw-Hill, 1943.

Ferritor, D. E., Buckholdt, D., Hamblin, R. L., & Smith, L. The noneffects of contingent reinforcement for attending behavior on work accomplished. *Journal of Applied Behavior Analysis,* 1972, *5,* 7–17.

Fox, B., & Routh, D. K. Analyzing spoken language into words, syllables, and phonemes: A developmental study. *Journal of Psycholinguistic Research,* 1975, *4,* 331–342.

Fox, B., & Routh, D. K. Phonemic analysis and synthesis as word-attack skills. *Journal of Educational Psychology,* 1976, *68,* 70–74.

Fox, B., & Routh, D. K. Phonemic analysis and severe reading disability in children. *Journal of Psycholinguistic Research,* 1980, *9,* 115–119.

Gillingham, A. *Remedial training for children with specific disability in reading, spelling and penmanship* (7th ed.). Cambridge, Mass.: Educators Publishing Service, 1970.

Gittelman, R. Indications for the use of stimulant treatment in learning disorders. *Journal of the American Academy of Child Psychiatry,* 1980, *19,* 623–636.

Gittelman, R., Klein, D. G., Abikoff, H., Katz, S., Pollack, E., & Mattes, J. A controlled trial of behavior modification and methylphenidate in hyperactive children. In C. K. Whalen & B. Henker (Eds.), *Hyperactive children: The social ecology of identification and treatment.* New York: Academic, 1980.

Glow, R. A. How common is hyperkinesis? *Lancet,* 1980, *1,* 89.

Glow, R. A., & Glow, P. H. Peer and self-rating: Children's perception of behavior relevant to hyperkinetic impulse disorder. *Journal of Abnormal Child Psychology,* 1980, *8,* 471–490.

Golden, G. S. Gilles de la Tourette's syndrome following methylphenidate administration. *Developmental Medicine and Child Neurology,* 1974, *16,* 76–79.

Goyer, P. F., Davis, G.C., & Rapoport, J. L. Abuse of prescribed stimulant medication by a 13-year-old hyperactive boy. *Journal of the American Academy of Child Psychiatry,* 1979, *18,* 170–175.

Harvey, D. H. P., & Marsh, R. W. The effects of de-caffeinated coffee versus whole coffee on hyperactive children. *Developmental Medicine and Child Neurology,* 1978, *20,* 81–86.

Hastings, J. E., & Barkley, R. A. A review of psychophysiological research with hyperkinetic children. *Journal of Abnormal Child Psychology,* 1978, *6,* 413–447.

Helper, M. M. Follow-up of children with minimal brain dysfunctions: Outcomes and predictors. In H. E. Rie & E. D. Rie (Eds.), *Handbook of minimal brain dysfunction.* New York: Wiley, 1980

Henker, B., Whalen, C. K., & Collins, B. E. Double-blind and triple-blind assessments of medication and placebo responses in hyperactive children. *Journal of Abnormal Child Psychology,* 1979, *7,* 1–13.

Hiscock, M., Kinsbourne, M., Caplan, B., & Swanson, J. M. Auditory attention in hyperactive children: Effects of stimulant medication on dichotic listening performance. *Journal of Abnormal Psychology,* 1979, *88,* 27–32.

Idol-Maestas, L. Behavior patterns in families of boys with learning and behavior problems. *Journal of Learning Disabilities,* 1981, *14,* 347–349.

Kenrick, D. T., & Stringfield, D. O. Personality traits and the eye of the beholder: Crossing some traditional philosophical boundaries in the search for consistency in all of the people. *Psychological Review,* 1980, *87,* 88–104.

Klein, A. R., & Young, R. D. Hyperactive boys in their classroom: Assessment of teacher and peer perceptions, interactions, and classroom behaviors. *Journal of Abnormal Child Psychology,* 1979, *7,* 425–442.

Kramer, J., & Loney, J. Childhood hyperactivity and substance abuse: A review of the literature. In K. Gadow & I. Bialer (Eds.), *Advances in learning and behavioral disabilities* (Vol. 1). Greenwich, Conn.: JAI Press, 1982.

Lahey, B. B., Stempniak, M., Robinson, E. J., & Tyroler, M. J. Hyperactivity and learning disabilities as independent dimensions of child behavior problems. *Journal of Abnormal Psychology,* 1978, *87,* 333–340.

Lambert, N. M., & Sandoval, J. The prevalence of learning disabilities in a sample of children considered hyperactive. *Journal of Abnormal Child Psychology,* 1980, *8,* 33–50.

Lambert, N. M., Sandoval, J., & Sassone, D. Prevalence of hyperactivity in elementary school children as a function of social system definers. *American Journal of Orthopsychiatry,* 1978, *48,* 446–463.

Lambert, N. M., Sandoval, J., & Sassone, D. Prevalence of treatment regimens for children considered to be hyperactive. *American Journal of Orthopsychiatry,* 1979, *49,* 482–490.

Langhorne, J. E., Loney, J., Paternite, C. E., & Bechtoldt, H. P. Childhood hyperkinesis: A return to the source. *Journal of Abnormal Psychology,* 1976, *85,* 201–209.

Lerer, R. J., Lerer, M. P., & Artner, J. The effects of methylphenidate on the handwriting of children with minimal brain dysfunction. *Journal of Pediatrics,* 1977, *91,* 127–132.

Loney, J. The Iowa theory of substance abuse among hyperactive adolescents. In D. J. Lettieri, M. Sayers, & H. W. Pearson (Eds.), *Theories on drug abuse* (NIDA Research Monograph, No. 30). Rockville, Md.: National Institute of Drug Abuse, 1980.

Loney, J. & Milich, R. The IOWA Conners Teacher Rating Scale. In M. Wolraich & D. K. Routh (Eds.), *Advances in behavioral pediatrics* (Vol. 3). Greenwich, Conn.: JAI Press, 1982.

Loney, J., Kramer, J., & Milich, R. *The hyperkinetic child grows up: Predictors of symptoms, delinquency, and achievement at follow-up.* Paper presented at the meeting of the American Association for the Advancement of Science, Houston, January 1979.

Loney, J., Langhorne, J. E., Jr., & Paternite, C. An empirical basis for subgrouping the hyperkinetic/minimal brain dysfunction syndrome. *Journal of Abnormal Psychology,* 1978, *87,* 431–441.

Loney, J., Prinz, R. J., Mishalow, J., & Joad, J. Hyperkinetic/aggressive boys in treatment: Predictors of clinical response to methylphenidate. *American Journal of Psychiatry,* 1978, *135,* 1487–1491.

Lorch, E. P., Anderson, D. R., & Levin, S. R. The relationship of visual attention to children's comprehension of television. *Child Development,* 1979, *50,* 722–727.

Mainville, F., & Friedman, R. J. Peer relations of hyperactive children. *Ontario Psychologist,* 1976, *8,* 17–20.

Mash, E. J., & Johnston, C. *A behavioral assessment of sibling interactions in hyperactive and normal children.* Paper presented at the meeting of the Association for the Advancement of Behavior Therapy, New York, November 1980.

Maurer, R. G., & Stewart, M. A. Attention deficit without hyperactivity in a child psychiatry clinic. *Journal of Clinical Psychiatry,* 1980, *41,* 232–233.

Messer, S. B. & Brodzinsky, D. M. The relation of conceptual tempo to aggression and its control. *Child Development,* 1979, *50,* 758–766.

Milar, C. R., Schroeder, S. R., Mushak, P., Dolcourt, J. L., & Grant, L. D. Contributions of the caregiving environment to increased lead burden of children. *American Journal of Mental Deficiency,* 1980, *84,* 339–344.

Milich, R. *Hyperactivity, aggression, and peer status.* Paper presented at the meeting of the American Psychological Association, Montreal, September 1980.

Minde, K. K., & Cohen, N. J. Hyperactive children in Canada and Uganda. *Journal of the American Academy of Child Psychiatry,* 1978, *17,* 476–487.

Morrison, J. R., & Stewart, M. A. A family study of the hyperactive child syndrome. *Biological Psychiatry,* 1971, *3,* 189–195.

Morrison, J. R., & Stewart, M. A. The psychiatric status of the legal families of adopted hyperactive children. *Archives of General Psychiatry,* 1973, *28,* 888–891.

Nasby, W., Hayden, B., & DePaulo, B. M. Attributional bias among aggressive boys to interpret unambiguous social stimuli as displays of hostility. *Journal of Abnormal Psychology,* 1980, *89,* 459–468.

Needleman, H. Effects of low level lead exposure on children. In M. Wolraich & D. K. Routh (Eds.), *Advances in behavioral pediatrics* (Vol. 3). Greenwich, Conn.: JAI Press, 1982.

Okolo, C., Bartlett, S. A., & Shaw, S. F. Communicative between professionals concerning medication for the hyperactive child. *Journal of Learning Disabilities,* 1978, *11,* 647–650.

O'Leary, K. D. Pills or skills for hyperactive children. *Journal of Applied Behavior Analysis,* 1980, *13,* 191–204.

Paternite, C. E. Childhood hyperkinesis: Relationships between symptomatology and home environment. In C. K. Whalen & B. Henker (Eds.), *Hyperactive children: The social ecology of identification and treatment.* New York: Academic, 1980.

Patterson, G. R. Interventions for boys with conduct problems: Multiple settings, treatments, and criteria. *Journal of Consulting and Clinical Psychology,* 1974, *42,* 471–481.

Patton, J. E., Routh, D. K., & Offenbach, S. I. Televised classroom events as distractors for reading disabled children. *Journal of Abnormal Child Psychology,* 1981, *9,* 355–370.

Phillips, E. L. Achievement Place: Token reinforcement procedures in a home-style rehabilitation setting for "pre-delinquent" boys. *Journal of Applied Behavior Analysis,* 1968, *1,* 213–223.

Plomin, R., & Foch, T. T. Hyperactivity and pediatrician diagnoses, parental ratings, specific cognitive abilities, and laboratory measures. *Journal of Abnormal Child Psychology,* 1981, *9,* 55–64.

Porges, S. W., & Smith, K. M. Defining hyperactivity: Psychophysiological and behavioral strategies. In C. K. Whalen & B. Henker (Eds.), *Hyperactive children: The social ecology of identification and treatment.* New York: Academic, 1980.

Prinz, R. J., Roberts, W. A., & Hantman, E. Dietary correlates of hyperactive behavior in children. *Journal of Consulting and Clinical Psychology,* 1980, *48,* 760–769.

Puig-Antich, J., Greenhill, L. L., Sassin, J., & Sachar, E. J. Growth hormone, prolactin and cortisol responses and growth patterns in hyperkinetic children treated with dextro-amphetamine. *Journal of the American Academy of Child Psychiatry,* 1978, *17,* 457–475.

Rapoport, J. L., Buchsbaum, M., Zahn, T. P., Weingartner, H., Ludlow, C., & Mikkelsen, E. J. Dextroamphetamine: Cognitive and behavioral effects in normal prepubertal boys. *Science,* 1978, *199,* 560–563.

Rapoport, J. L., & Benoit, M. The relation of direct home observations to the clinic evaluation of hyperactive school age boys. *Journal of Child Psychology and Psychiatry,* 1975, *16,* 141–147.

Rapoport, J. L., Buchsbaum, M. S., Weingartner, H., Zahn, T. P., Ludlow, C., & Mikkelsen, E. J. Dextroamphetamine: Its cognitive and behavioral effects in normal and hyperactive boys and normal men. *Archives of General Psychiatry,* 1980, *37,* 933–943.

Rapoport, J. L., Tepsic, P. N., Grice, N., Johnson, C., & Langer, D. Decreased motor activity of hyperactive children on dextroamphetamine during active gym program. *Psychiatry Research,* 1980, *2,* 225–229.

Redfering, D. L., & Bowman, M. J. Effects of a meditative-relaxation exercise on nonattending behaviors of behaviorally disturbed children. *Journal of Clinical Child Psychology,* 1981, *10,* 126–127.

Riddle, K. D., & Rapoport, J. L. A 2-year follow-up of 72 hyperactive boys. *Journal of Nervous and Mental Disease,* 1976, *162,* 126–134.

Rie, E. D., & Rie, H. E. Recall, retention, and Ritalin. *Journal of Consulting and Clinical Psychology,* 1977, *45,* 967–972.

Rie, H., & Rie, E. D. (Eds.). *Handbook of minimal brain dysfunctions: A critical view.* New York: Wiley, 1980.

Rie, H. E., Rie, E., Stewart, S., & Ambuel, J. P. Effects of methylphenidate on underachieving children. *Journal of Consulting and Clinical Psychology,* 1976, *44,* 250–260. (a)

Rie, H. E., Rie, E., Stewart, S., & Ambuel, J. P. Effects of Ritalin on underachieving children: A replication. *American Journal of Orthopsychiatry,* 1976, *46,* 313-322. (b)

Roberts, M. A. *A behavioral method for differentiating hyperactive, aggressive, and hyperactive plus aggressive children.* Unpublished doctoral dissertation, University of Wisconsin, Madison, 1979.

Robins, L. *Deviant children grown up.* Baltimore: Williams & Wilkins, 1966.

Roche, A. F., Lipman, R. S., Overall, J. E., & Hung, W. The effects of stimulant medication on the growth of hyperkinetic children. *Pediatrics,* 1979, *63,* 847-850.

Rosenthal, R. H., & Allen, T. W. An examination of attention, arousal, and learning dysfunctions of hyperkinetic children. *Psychological Bulletin,* 1978, *85,* 689-715.

Rosenthal, R. H., & Allen, T. W. Intratask distractibility in hyperkinetic and nonhyperkinetic children. *Journal of Abnormal Child Psychology,* 1980, *8,* 175-187.

Routh, D. K. Hyperactivity. In P. R. Magrab (Ed.), *Psychological management of pediatric problems. 2. Sensorineural conditions and social concerns.* Baltimore: University Park Press, 1978.

Routh, D. K. Developmental and social aspects of hyperactivity. In C. K. Whalen & B. Henker (Eds.), *Hyperactive children: The social ecology of identification and treatment.* New York: Academic, 1980. (a)

Routh, D. K. Child treatment citation classics. *Professional Psychology,* 1980, *9,* 901-906. (b)

Routh, D. K., & Mesibov, G. B. Psychological and environmental intervention: Toward social competence. In H. Rie & E. D. Rie (Eds.), *Handbook of minimal brain dysfunctions.* New York: Wiley, 1980.

Routh, D. K., & Roberts, R. D. Minimal brain dysfunction in children: Failure to find evidence for a behavioral syndrome. *Psychological Reports,* 1972, *31,* 307-314.

Routh, D. K., & Schroeder, C. S. Standardized playroom measures as indices of hyperactivity. *Journal of Abnormal Child Psychology,* 1976, *4,* 199-207.

Routh, D. K., Schroeder, C. S., & O'Tuama, L. A. Development of activity level in children. *Developmental Psychology,* 1974, *10,* 163-168.

Routh, D. K., Walton, M. D., & Padan-Belkin, E. Development of activity level in children revisited: Effects of mother presence. *Developmental Psychology,* 1978, *14,* 571-581.

Rummo, J. H., Routh, D. K., Rummo, N. J., & Brown, J. F. Behavioral and neurological effects of symptomatic and asymptomatic lead exposure in children. *Archives of Environmental Health,* 1979, *34,* 120-124.

Rutter, M., Graham, P. & Yule, W. *A neuropsychiatric study in childhood.* London: Spastics International Medical Publications/Heineman, 1970. (Clinics and Developmental Medicine #35 & 36.)

Rutter, M., & Shaffer, D. DSM-III: A step forward or back in terms of the classification of child psychiatric disorders. *Journal of the American Academy of Child Psychiatry,* 1980, *19,* 371-394.

Rutter, M., Tizard, J., & Whitmore, K. (Eds.), *Education, health, and behavior.* London: Longman, 1970.

Sameroff, A. J., & Chandler, M. J. Reproductive risk and the continuum of caretaking casualty. In F. D. Horowitz (Ed.), *Review of child development research.* Chicago: University of Chicago Press, 1975.

Salkind, N. J., & Nelson, C. F. A note on the development nature of reflection-impulsivity. *Developmental Psychology,* 1980, *16,* 237–238.

Salkind, N. J., & Wright, J. C. The development of reflection-impulsivity and cognitive efficiency. *Human Development,* 1977, *20,* 277–287.

Sandberg, S. T., Rutter, M., & Taylor, E. Hyperkinetic disorder in psychiatric clinic attenders. *Developmental Medicine and Child Neurology,* 1978, *20,* 279–299.

Satterfield, J. H., Cantwell, D. P., Schell, A., & Blaschke, T. Growth of hyperactive children treated with methylphenidate. *Archives of General Psychiatry,* 1979, *36,* 212–217.

Schaefer, E. Development of hierarchical configurational models for parent behavior and child behavior. In J. P. Hill (Ed.), *Minnesota symposium on child psychology.* Minneapolis: University of Minnesota Press, 1971.

Shea, V. T. *State dependent learning in children receiving methylphenidate.* Unpublished doctoral dissertation, University of North Carolina, 1977.

Silver, A. A., & Hagan, R. A. *SEARCH and TEACH.* New York: Walker, 1976

Singer, S. M., Stewart, M. A., & Pulaski, L. Minimal brain dysfunction: Differences in cognitive organization in two groups of index cases and their relatives. *Journal of Learning Disabilities,* 1981, *14,* 470–473.

Sostek, A. J., Buchsbaum, M. S., & Rapoport, J. L. Effects of amphetamine on vigilance performance in normal and hyperactive children. *Journal of Abnormal Child Psychology,* 1980, *8,* 491–500.

Sprague, R. L., & Sleator, E. K. Methylphenidate in hyperkinetic children: Differences in dose effects on learning and social behavior. *Science,* 1977, *198,* 1274–1276.

Stevens, T. M., Kupst, M. J., Suran, B. G., & Schulman, J. L. Activity level: A comparison between actometer scores and observer ratings. *Journal of Abnormal Child Psychology,* 1978, *6,* 163–173.

Stewart, M. A., Cummings, C., Singer, S., & DeBlois, C. S. The overlap between hyperactive and unsocialized aggressive children. *Journal of Child Psychology and Psychiatry,* 1981, *22,* 35–45.

Stewart, M. A., DeBlois, C. S., & Cummings, C. Psychiatric disorder in the parents of hyperactive boys and those with conduict disorders. *Journal of Child Psychology and Psychiatry,* 1980, *21,* 283–292.

Still, G. F. Some abnormal physical conditions in children. *Lancet,* 1902, *1,* 1008–1012, 1077–1082, 1163–1168.

Strauss, A. A., & Lehtinen, L. E. *Psychopathology and education of the brain-injured child.* New York: Grune & Stratton, 1947.

Swanson, J. M., & Kinsbourne, M. Stimulant-related state-dependent learning in hyperactive children. *Science,* 1976, *192,* 1354–1357.

Swanson, J. M., & Kinsbourne, M. Food dyes impair performance of hyperactive children on a laboratory learning test. *Science,* 1980, *207,* 1485–1487.

Tarter, R. E., McBride, H., Buonopane, N., & Schneider, D. U. Differentiation of alcoholics: Childhood history of minimal brain dysfunction, family history, and drinking pattern. *Archives of General Psychiatry,* 1977, *34,* 761–768.

Thomas, A., & Chess, S. *Temperament and development.* New York: Brunner/Mazel, 1977.

Tomkins, C. P., Soldin, S. J., MacLeod, S. M., Rochefort, J. G., & Swanson, J. M.

Analysis of pemoline in serum by high performance liquid chromatography: Clinical application to optimize treatment of hyperactive children. *Therapeutic Drug Monitoring,* 1980, *2,* 255–260.

Torgersen, A. M. & Kringlen, E. Genetic aspects of temperamental differences in infants: A study of same-sexed twins. *Journal of the American Academy of Child Psychiatry,* 1978, *17,* 433–44.

Tryphonas, H., & Trites, R. Food allergy in children with hyperactivity, learning disabilities, and/or minimal brain dysfunction. *Annals of Allergy,* 1979, *42,* 22–27.

Ullman, D. G., Barkley, R. A., & Brown, H. W. The behavioral symptoms of hyperkinetic children who successfully responded to stimulant drug treatment. *American Journal of Orthopsychiatry,* 1978, *48,* 425–437.

Weber, K. *Effects of methylphenidate on operant responding in hyperactive boys.* Unpublished doctoral dissertation, University of Iowa, 1980.

Weiss, G., Hechtman, L., & Perlman, T. Hyperactives as young adults: School, employer, and self-rating scales obtained during ten-year follow-up evaluation. *American Journal of Orthopsychiatry,* 1978, *48,* 438–445.

Weiss, G., Hechtman, L., Perlman, T., Hopkins, J., & Wenar, A. Hyperactives as young adults: A controlled prospective ten-year follow-up of 75 children. *Archives of General Psychiatry,* 1979, *36,* 675–681.

Weiss, G., Minde, K., Douglas, V., Werry, J., & Sykes, D. Comparison of the effects of chlorpromazine, dextroamphetamine, and methylphenidate on the behavior and intellectual functioning of hyperactive children. *Canadian Medical Association Journal,* 1971, *104,* 20–25.

Weiss, B., Williams, J. H., Margen, S., Abrams, B., Caan, B., Citron, L. J., Cox, C., McKibben, J., Ogar, D., & Schultz, S. Behavioral responses to artificial food colors. *Science,* 1980, *207,* 1487–1489.

Werry, J. S. Studies on the hyperactive child. 4. An empirical analysis of the minimal brain dysfunction syndrome. *Archives of General Psychiatry,* 1968, *19,* 9–16.

Werry, J. S., Aman, M. G., & Diamond, E. Imipramine and methylphenidate in hyperactive children. *Journal of Child Psychology and Psychiatry,* 1980, *21,* 27–35.

Werry, J. S., Aman, M. G., & Lampen, E. Haloperidol and methylphenidate in hyperactive children. *Acta Paedopsychiatrica,* 1975, *42,* 26–40.

Whalen, C. K., & Henker, B. The pitfalls of politicization: A response to Conrad's "The discovery of hyperkinesis: Notes of the medicalization of deviant behavior." *Social Problems,* 1977, *24,* 590–595.

Whalen, C. K., & Henker, B. The social ecology of psychostimulant treatment: A model for conceptual and empirical analysis. In C. K. Whalen & B. Henker (Eds.), *Hyperactive children: The social ecology of identification and treatment.* New York: Academic, 1980.

Whalen, C. K., Henker, B., Collins, B. E., Finck, D., & Dotemoto, S. A social ecology of hyperactive boys: Medication in structured classroom environments. *Journal of Applied Behavior Analysis,* 1979, *12,* 65–81.

Whalen, C. K., Henker, B., & Dotemoto, S. Methylphenidate and hyperactivity: Effects on teacher behaviors. *Science,* 1980, *208,* 1280–1282.

Whalen, C. K., Henker, B., & Dotemoto, S. Teacher response to methylphenidate (Ritalin) versus placebo status of hyperactive boys in the classroom. *Child Development,* 1981, *52,* 1005–1014.

Wolf, S. M. & Forsythe, A. Behavior disturbance, phenobarbital, and febrile seizures. *Pediatrics,* 1978, *61,* 728–731.

Wolraich, M., Drummond, T., Salomon, M. K., O'Brien, M. L., & Sivage, C. Effects of methylphenidate alone and in combination with behavior modification procedures on the behavior and academic performance of hyperactive children. *Journal of Abnormal Child Psychology,* 1978, *6,* 149–161.

CHAPTER 14

The Emotionally Exceptional

SUSAN M. JAY, DIANA BROWN WATERS, AND DIANE J. WILLIS

The purpose of this chapter is to provide a broad overview of emotional disturbance in children. The chapter is organized to give the reader at least a cursory understanding of the major issues, methods, and orientations in the field of child mental health. Such a broad perspective precludes detailed discussion of major issues, but we have attempted to highlight the most poignant, providing both theoretical concerns and relevant research data. The chapter is organized into eight major sections: historical perspective, conceptualization and definition of emotional disturbance, incidence, etiology, classification, syndromes, treatment, and a personal perspective concerning child psychopathology.

Throughout the chapter varying orientations are presented. For instance, neuroses are conceptualized in traditional psychodynamic terms, personality disorders in a social-environmental framework, psychoses are presented in a biological framework, and psychosomatic disorders are defined in empirical, behavioral terms. This eclecticism reflects the bias among the authors regarding etiological factors and treatment alternatives. Classification of emotional disorders developed out of a traditional psychodynamic approach in which parent–child relationships, early experiences, and instinctual drives were conceptualized as the primary influences in shaping personality. Such factors may be influential in shaping certain personality patterns, but no single orientation seems sufficient in explaining all types of emotional disorders. Furthermore, because of multiple and unknown etiological factors, no one treatment approach is effective for all disorders. The underlying assumption we present in this chapter is that emotional disturbance is a complex phenomenon, not fully understood, that is influenced by interactions among biological characteristics of a child, his or her environmental circumstances and demands, and the nature of the child's interpersonal transactions during development. Different syndromes of psychopathology may reflect varying contributions from these biological, environmental, and social factors. Our presentation of issues, methods, and research will reflect this underlying premise.

DEFINITION AND CONCEPTUALIZATION

Before pursuing the topic of emotional disturbance further, one must ask what we mean when we refer to an "emotionally disturbed" child. What criteria define emotional disturbance? Where do we draw the line between a normal child who is experiencing problems and a child labeled as emotionally disturbed? In answering these questions one must take into account several considerations: (1) the rubric "disturbed behavior" includes a seemingly infinite variety of excessive as well as deficient behaviors ranging from mild to profound; (2) many children who are considered "normal" exhibit disturbed behaviors (tantrums, phobias, hyperactivity, aggression) to some degree at some time during their development; (3) children's behavior problems often are transitory; and (4) disturbed behavior often occurs in conjunction with other handicapping conditions which makes differential diagnosis difficult (Kauffman, 1977). Such factors complicate the definition process considerably.

The definition of emotional disturbance depends on a definition of normality. Although there is no clear consensus as to what constitutes normality, Offer and Sabshin (1966) summarized alternative concepts of normality used in mental health. The first view defines normality as health or absence of pathology. Normality represents a wide range of functioning characterized by the absence of disturbing symptoms or behaviors which warrant professional attention. In this view health constitutes a "reasonable" state shared by most people rather than an "optimal" state (Korchin, 1976). The second concept defines normality in terms of an ideal, "utopian" state. Normality is an ideal state of functioning and variations from this ideal are considered disturbances. This view is held by those who emphasize self-actualization and optimal psychological health (Korchin, 1976). A third concept defines normality in statistical terms. Behaviors are viewed as falling along a normal, or bell-shaped, curve and normality encompasses behaviors that fall within the middle, or "average," range. Extreme or infrequent behaviors are viewed as disturbed or deviant. A fourth perspective views normality in the context of societal norms and standards. Behavior which conforms with societal expectations is considered normal, whereas behavior that does not meet with societal approval is considered disturbed.

All of these views are commonly used in conceptualizing emotional disturbance. Each concept has its limitations and none offers concise, mutually exclusive criteria for the definition of normality versus emotional disturbance. At this time in our field, it is impossible to define "normal" adjustment due to conflicting concepts of normality and insufficient study of normal development (Nagera & Benson, 1979). Therefore any attempts at defining emotional disturbance will be problematic and likely insufficient.

Hewett and Forness (1974) and Kauffman (1977) summarized a number of definitions of emotional disturbance that have arisen from various theoretical orientations. One of the most practical definitions of emotional disturbance was presented by Bower (1969). He discussed five characteristics, one or more of which emotionally disturbed children exhibit *to a marked extent* and *over a period of time:* (1) learning difficulties which cannot be explained by intellectual, sensory, or health factors; (2) difficulties in interpersonal relationships with peers and teachers; (3) inappropriate behavior; (4) a general mood of unhappiness; and (5) a tendency to develop somatic symptoms. Bower established a continuum of disturbance with one end of the continuum representing mild, transient disturbance and the other end representing severe, fixed pathology. Bower's definition is useful because it includes behavioral criteria and mild disturbances are distinguished from severe types of psychopathology. Through its usefulness for educators as well as psychologists, Bower's definition strongly influenced that adopted in PL 94-142.

INCIDENCE AND RELATED FACTORS

It is difficult to determine the prevalence of emotional disturbance in children because there is no consensus regarding definition of normality versus pathology. Depending on the definition and criteria used, estimates of emotional disturbance in children vary from 0.05 to 15% (Schultz, Salvia, & Feinn, 1974). The U.S. Office of Education (1975) estimated the percentage of emotionally disturbed children to be 2%. Bower (1969) estimated that 10% of school-aged children need special attention for some behavioral difficulty.

Boys tend to outnumber girls three to one in being labeled emotionally disturbed (Clarizio & McCoy, 1976). Boys exhibit more aggressive conduct disorder patterns than girls (Schultz et al., 1974). Although referral rates to psychiatric clinics are highest during preadolescent and adolescent years, evidence indicates that incidence of emotional disturbance is unrelated to age (Clarizio & McCoy, 1976). Emotional disturbance tends to be highly correlated with educational difficulty (Gilbert, 1957; Morse, Cutler, & Fink, 1964). The cause and effect relationship is not clear, although it is not difficult to see how disturbance in one area could adversely affect adjustment in the other. A higher number of behavior disorders are reported in nonwhite populations, which can possibly be linked to the influences of prejudice, discrimination, and limited opportunities for advancement (Clarizio & McCoy, 1976). A higher incidence of disturbed children has been reported among lower socioeconomic groups (Bower, 1961; Hollingshead & Redlich, 1958).

ETIOLOGY

Discussion of etiologic factors in the genesis of psychopathology is an extremely broad topic. A panoply of theories and conceptual schemes have been generated to explain how and why children and adults develop behavioral and emotional disturbances. The scope of this chapter allows only an outline of possible contributing factors. Discussion of etiologic factors are subsumed under the following categories: genetic, neurological, temperamental, and socioenvironmental.

Genetic Factors

There is little or no evidence that genetic factors are related to the development of mild or moderate emotional disturbance in children; however, genetic mechanisms have been postulated for severe forms of psychopathology, particularly psychosis (Kauffman, 1977). Studies have indicated that the closer the genetic relationship of a person to a schizophrenic, the higher the likelihood of that person becoming schizophrenic (Kallman, 1946). The risk of developing schizophrenia is 8–10 times higher in children who have a biological parent who is schizophrenic than in children of healthy parents (Chess & Hassibi, 1978). However, no genetic model has been developed to account for the exact mechanism of genetic transmission. As Rutter (1972) concluded, "The mode of inheritance and what is inherited remain unknown. Is it a predisposition in terms of personality traits which is inherited or is it a direct vulnerability to a disease which is handed on genetically? We do not know" (p. 322). Although genetic concordance rates are high enough to indicate genetic components, they do not account for the total variance, and it appears that nongenetic environmental variables (such as perinatal complications and stressful separation experiences) also play a part in the causation of schizophrenia (Mednick & Schulsinger, 1974).

Although theorists disagree as to whether autism is a separate entity from childhood schizophrenia, genetic factors reportedly do not operate to the same degree in autism as in schizophrenia. The incidence of psychosis in relatives of autistic children is lower than in the relatives of children diagnosed as schizophrenic (Rutter, 1972). Neurological deficits and dysfunction are considered by most theorists to be more important in the etiology of autism than genetic factors. However, a twin study conducted by Folstein and Rutter (1977) suggested a possible genetic linkage between autism and cognitive disorders involving speech and language. The results suggested that in some cases genetic factors alone may be sufficient to produce autism, in others brain injury alone may be causative, while in still other cases biological hazards and a genetic predisposition for a cognitive language disorder may combine to produce autism.

Neurological Dysfunction

Neurological dysfunction or brain damage has been posited as a possible etiological factor in many behavior disorders. Research conducted by Pasamanick and his co-workers (Pasamanick & Knobloch, 1960) suggests a causal relationship between complications in pregnancy, neurological damage, and behavioral disorders. A statistically significantly higher number of pre- and perinatal complications, notably prematurity and abnormality of pregnancy, were found in the medical histories of a large group of children referred for behavior disorders as compared to a control group. Hyperactivity was the most frequently associated syndrome. Further research led Pasamanick and Knobloch to develop a "continuum of reproductive casualty" in which the effect of brain damage on behavior depends on the extent of brain damage. Prematurity and other complications may result in death, massive brain damage, or minimal brain damage. Children who exhibit minimal central nervous system deficits, according to Pasamanick and Knobloch, may be predisposed to develop behavior disorders depending on socioenvironmental experiences.

Pasamanick's research has been widely cited as evidence of the etiological importance of brain injury in child psychopathology. However, the studies have been criticized on the grounds that socioeconomic factors were not controlled (Pond, 1961). Because of the high preponderance of lower SES and socially disorganized families in one of the subsamples, it is unclear whether the behavior disorders in children resulted from brain damage or from social pathology, which was also shown to be highly correlated with pre- and perinatal complications (Werry, 1979).

There are mounting indications, but as yet no conclusive evidence, of neurophysiologic disturbances which are etiologically related to autism (Piggott, 1979). Abnormalities have been reported in anatomical structures (Hauser, Delong, & Rosman, 1975; Steg & Rappaport, 1975), electrophysiological responses (LeLord, Laffont, Jusseanume & Stephant, 1973; Ornitz, Ritvo, Brown, LaFranchi, Parmelee, & Walker, 1969; Student & Sohmer, 1978; Tanguay, 1976; White, DeMyer, & DeMyer, 1964), autonomic monitoring system (Hutt, Forrest, & Richer, 1975), the vestibular system (Colbert, Koegler, & Markham, 1956; Ritvo, Ornitz, Eviator, Markham, Brown, & Mason, 1969), biochemical processes (Boullin, Coleman & O'Brien, 1970; Schain & Freedman, 1961), and the immunologic system (Fowle, 1968; Stubbs, 1976). No single etiology has been established and it seems likely that there are probably a number of subgroups that stem from different basic pathological processes but which collectively manifest a similar clinical presentation.

In addition to basic etiological research, numerous studies have addressed the nature of the primary and fundamental deficit in autistic symptomatology. Three major theories have been proposed. All assume an organic etiology, with one focusing on subcortical processes and two on cortical processes. These theories will be discussed in the section on autism.

Many authors have inferred organic etiology in child psychopathology on the basis of studies which document a higher proportion of neurological abnormalities, particularly EEG abnormalities, in behaviorally disturbed children than in normal children (Rutter, Graham, & Yule, 1970; Wikler, Dixon,

& Parker, 1970). Studies have indicated a higher frequency of EEG abnormalities in children with psychoses, organic brain syndrome, and conduct disorders than in normal children or children diagnosed as neurotic (Werry, 1979). There is no clear relationship between EEG patterns and CNS functioning (Freeman, 1967); the evidence is circumstantial and inconclusive. Werry stated, "Although suggestive of organic etiology, these findings do not preclude adverse social experience, psychophysiological effects, or normal variation as etiological factors, alone or in concert with physical factors" (p. 110).

Temperament

Thomas, Chess, and Birch (1968) reported evidence that children are born with unique temperaments, that is, an innate tendency to behave in certain ways. They identified nine categories of temperamental characteristics which may differ among children: activity level, rhythmicity, approach-withdrawal, adaptability, threshold, intensity, mood, distractibility, and attention span and persistence. These characteristics were grouped under three major constellations of temperament: the difficult child, the easy child, and the slow-to-warm-up child. The difficult child is characterized by biological irregularity, negative mood, high intensity of expressiveness, withdrawing reactions to new stimuli, and slow adaptability. Thomas and Chess (1977) found that the temperamental characteristics of the difficult child create a higher risk for stressful environmental interactions and for the development of behavior disorders. They emphasized, however, that a child with any temperamental pattern may, under certain environmental conditions, prove vulnerable to the development of behavior disorders. A child's adjustment is dependent on "goodness of fit" or the match between the child's temperamental characteristics and the properties, expectations, and demands of the environment. Their results indicate that children with intellectual or physical defects plus mild manifestations of the difficult child constellation were especially vulnerable to the development of behavior disorders. A study conducted by Graham, Rutter, and George (1973) supported the findings of Thomas, Chess, and Birch; results indicated that temperamental characteristics were predictive of later development of psychiatric disorders.

Socioenvironmental Factors

The nature and quality of a child's family life and experiences are important in determining his or her adjustment, since early primary relationships provide the foundation for social, emotional, and intellectual development. Conceptual models including psychoanalytic, behavioral, and transactional models have been generated to explain the relationships between family factors and child psychopathology. Unfortunately there is a lack of sound research evidence relating specific familial interactions and origins of emotional disorders in children (Kauffman, 1977). However, research and descriptive studies have identified particular familial factors that appear to be correlated with the development of certain emotional disorders.

One of the most consistent findings in the literature concerns the relationship between maternal deprivation and psychopathology. Long-term institutionalization has been associated with intellectual and language retardation, personality disturbances, and impaired capacity for interpersonal relationships in children (Goldfarb, 1955). Separation from the mother or primary caretaker can result in progressive deterioration in physical, social, and intellectual development if the relationship with the caretaker is not restored (Spitz & Wolf, 1946). Spitz called this syndrome "anaclitic depression" and it is often referred to in pediatric settings as the "failure to thrive" syndrome. Bowlby (1944) related maternal deprivation in infancy or early childhood to antisocial behavior and delinquency in later years. His conclusions were based on clinical findings that 12 out of 14 "affectionless characters" in his sample had suffered early separation or deprivation experiences. These early classic studies have documented the disastrous effects of extreme deprivation on child development. There is more recent evidence that less extreme forms of deprivation may cause problems in social development. A large body of research on attachment behavior in infants and young children indicates the importance of a positive consistent relationship with a maternal figure for normal behavioral development (Ainsworth, 1973; Bowlby, 1969). Disruptions in this primary relationship can result in social and behavioral disturbances. Bowlby (1969), in his two-volume work *Attachment and Loss,* documents children's reactions to separations from maternal figures. Bowlby vividly describes the stages of protest, despair, and detachment that children exhibit behaviorally when separated from their primary caretaker even for a short period of time. The intensity of these reactions and the long-term effects of separation depend on a number of factors including the age of the child, the length of separation, the quality of the parent–child relationship, the quality of substitute parental figures, and the constitutional capacities of the child (Yarrow, 1961).

Distortions in parent–child relationships can hinder normal development. Parental psychopathology may be manifested in hostile rejection of the child, overprotection and emotional "smothering," or ambivalent swings between affection and rejection. Such extreme behaviors may result in delayed or distorted personality development in the child. The battered child syndrome is an extreme example of a distorted parent–child relationship. The effects of chronic physical abuse on emotional development are pervasive; psychological studies document depression and severe deficits in impulse control, cognitive functioning, reality testing, interpersonal relationships, and body image in children who have been abused (Green, 1978).

Relationships between parents may be deviant and/or disharmonious causing conflicts of allegiance and guilt for the child. Incest is an example of a grossly deviant family coalition. Children of incest may develop very distorted views of their sexual identity and role assignment. Deviant parental coalitions may result in divorce that, if turbulent and exploitative, can contribute to child maladjustment (Chess & Hassibi, 1978). Broken homes have been found more often in the background of psychopaths and schizophrenics than in other groups (Lidz, Fleck, & Cornelison, 1966). Studies have shown a higher rate of juvenile delinquency in broken, disorganized families in which parents are neglectful, hostile, and cruel in punishing their children (Cavan & Ferdinand, 1975; Robins, West, & Herjaniz, 1975).

A vast literature exists on the consequences of different parental discipline and childrearing techniques. The findings from these studies have been somewhat contradictory (Becker, 1964). There has been some agreement, however, that inconsistent parental discipline may be related to delinquency (Becker, 1964; Beiser, 1972). Research conducted by Minuchin, Montalvo, Guerney, Rosman, and Schumer (1967) on disorganized lower-class urban families indicated that parental inconsistency and lack of stable identification models may result in personality disturbances in children manifested through antisocial and aggressive behavior.

Enculturation or learning of communication patterns may be faulty within a family. Children learn maladaptive as well as adaptive behavior and interactional styles. Minuchin et al. (1967) found in their studies of interactions within disturbed lower-class families that children learned negative and coercive communication styles, poor conflict resolution, and reactive rather than contemplative responses to situations. "Double-bind" communication has been indicated as a factor in the genesis of schizophrenia (Weakland, 1960). According to double-bind theory, the child receives conflicting communications which he or she is unable to resolve; any action or response would be wrong or ineffective. Following repeated exposure to such conflicting messages, the child loses or fails to grasp the distinction between what is real and rational and what is not, resulting in distorted views of reality. Families of children with psychosomatic disorders have been characterized as being overly enmeshed, overly protective, overly rigid, with inadequate methods of conflict resolution (Minuchin, Rosman, & Baker, 1978). The interaction between the physiological vulnerability of the child and these familial characteristics may make children high-risk for psychosomatic disorders.

Most studies relating family factors to child disorders are correlational in nature and do not indicate a unilinear cause-and-effect relationship. Recent literature on parent–child interactions has emphasized the reciprocal nature of the relationship between parent and child (Bell, 1968; Clarke-Stewart, 1973). Behavioral, temperamental, and social characteristics of a child influence the responsiveness of parental figures toward the child. As the work of Thomas, Chess, and Birch (1968) indicates, the children who are at "high risk" for later difficulties are those children who have "difficult" temperaments and who elicit negative rather than positive responses from their environment. Children with physical defects, chronic illness, or terminal illness may precipitate family crises which are not resolved adequately, resulting in rejection, scapegoating, or overprotection of the child. Kauffman (1977) suggested that undesirable family interactions or parental behaviors may be as much a reaction of family members to a deviant child as they are a cause of the child's disturbed behavior.

Although no direct correlation between socioeconomic status (SES) and psychopathology has been demonstrated, it has been speculated that adverse sociological conditions and extreme poverty may have pervasive effects on children's personality development. A higher incidence of behavior disorders, particularly delinquency, has been documented in lower SES families (Hollingshead & Redlich, 1958; McDermott, Harrison, Schrager, & Wilson, 1965). Authors have pointed to the higher incidence of broken homes in delinquents' histories as etiologic factors (Short, 1966; Waldrup, 1967). Jauch (1977) suggested, however, that the stress of poverty in lower SES families may be a stronger causal factor in the higher incidence of child abuse, child neglect, and delinquency than the fact that the home is broken. Malone (1966) indicated that slum children develop a "danger orientation" through constant exposure to real threats of physical harm that results in distrustfulness, hyperalertness, and constant need for self-protection. The fact that sociocultural deprivation and lack of stimulation results in cognitive delays has been well documented in the literature (Deutsch, 1967). Disadvantaged children may consequently experience failure early in their school careers which may lead to lowered self-esteem and to what has been termed the "disparagement syndrome" by Cleveland and Longaker (1957).

Beiser (1972) presents a very thorough and enlightening review of sociocultural etiologic factors in child psychopathology. Beiser makes the point that the focus on etiologic studies in the literature has been one-sided; developmental forces, internal personality factors, and early life experiences have been emphasized to the exclusion of *current* environmental stresses which may precipitate psychopathological responses. Beiser notes that the literature on events or situations which may precipitate psychological disorders is very scant. Studies do indicate that a child's response to stress is mediated by familial factors; children who remain with their parents in an intact, supportive family unit are much less likely to respond to external stresses with disordered behavior (Bloch, Silber, & Perry, 1956; Freud & Burlingham, 1944). Divorce, death of a loved one, birth of a sibling, and serious physical illness are all stressful situational events which may cause adjustment problems in children, ranging from mild to severe.

Beiser (1972) discusses the implications of negative and stressful school experiences for child mental health. Lower-class children, in particular, are susceptible to failure because of lack of readiness and middle-class teacher biases (Deutsch, 1967). Burt and Howard (1952) demonstrated a relationship between school conditions and adjustment, particularly an uncongenial teacher and assignment to a class in which work is too difficult. These findings suggest that failure experiences may lead to disordered behavior and psychopathology. High self-esteem and self-confidence may provide an important buffer for a child as he or she grows older and confronts various life difficulties.

When one considers the evidence concerning the etiology of emotional disorders in childhood, it becomes evident that there are no clear-cut causal relationships between particular etiological factors and development of emotional disturbance. Although certain familial and biological factors appear to be highly correlated with certain forms of disturbance, the actual causal mechanisms and the direction of causation are unclear. It is safe to assume that no set of factors (genetic, neurological, temperamental, or socioenvironmental) operates in isolation, with each factor independent of each other. As Kauffman (1977) stated, "The most tenable view at this time is that biological and environmental factors interact with one another in the causation of behavior disorders and that either biological or environmental variables may be manipulated in order to exacerbate or attenuate many behavioral difficulties" (p. 113).

CLASSIFICATION

Classification of emotional disorders involves the categorization of emotional-behavioral phenomena according to certain established criteria for the purpose of providing a conceptual framework by which professionals can communicate ideas and concepts. Traditional classification systems are based on the concept of diagnosis. In medicine, conditions are diagnosed and distinguished from one another according to certain criteria: (1) a common set of observable signs and symptoms, (2) a common specific etiology, (3) a known course, and (4) a known outcome that can be altered through specific interventions (Clarizio & McCoy, 1976). The application of this "medical model" approach to emotional disturbance has created controversy and confusion in the field of mental health because such criteria have not been met by proposed emotional-behavioral classification systems. These criteria have been questioned as to their validity and applicability in relation to mental health problems.

Reliability, or agreement between clinicians as to the diagnosis of a given patient, has not been established for most classification schemes (Clarizio & McCoy, 1976). Ideally a diagnostic category should describe a set of symptoms in such a way that a consensus between clinicians can be obtained as to classification. Traditional classification schemes have been criticized because of poorly defined and inconsistent criteria of various categories.

Specification of etiological factors is often very difficult in the diagnostic process because most psychological problems do not arise from specific etiological agents. Emotional problems may result from complex, bidirectional interactions between genetic, constitutional, psychological, and social-environmental factors rather than from simple, unilinear causal relationships. Futhermore, identical symptoms may have different etiologies.

Ideally, diagnosis should lend information concerning prognosis and future outcome. However, in a review of studies regarding the prediction of adult mental health from childhood behavior, Kohlberg, LaCrosse, and Ricks (1972) indicated there is no research evidence that diagnoses predict future course or outcome of early psychological disorders. MacFarlane (1963) indicated that 50% of the children in the Berkeley Guidance Study had much more favorable outcomes as adults than predicted by psychologists; 20% failed to do as well as predicted; and only about 30% turned out as predicted. Such results suggest that, in addition to being unduly pessimistic, psychologists do not have sufficiently valid criteria to predict how well a given child will do in the future (Clarizio & McCoy, 1976).

Mental health diagnoses do not imply a specific treatment of choice. No logical or defined relationship exists between diagnostic categories and treatment modalities. In practice the type of therapy depends more on the theoretical orientation of the clinician and/or clinic policies than on the diagnoses of clinicians (Bahn, Chandler, & Eisenberg, 1962; Patterson, 1959). Certain types of therapy have been shown to be more effective for certain disorders (i.e., behavior therapy for encopresis) but currently we do not have clear-cut matches between therapies and most disorders.

Because of the lack of relevance of the aforementioned criteria to mental health classification schemes, the practice of classification has been seriously questioned on ethical grounds. One of the major criticisms has been that diagnosis or "labeling" stigmatizes a child and serves no beneficial function for the child. Others argue that labeling has made legislation and government programs possible that provide services for children with specialized problems and needs. Diagnoses must be made with much caution, with knowledge of a child's cultural background, and with an awareness of the implications for a given child (May, 1979).

Despite the limitations in current classification systems, some form of taxonomy is necessary. Classification systems provide a common frame of reference as well as a common language with which to communicate. Diagnostic classifications are essential for studying the epidemiology of emotional disorders, for developing research priorities, and for evaluating treatment programs (Fish, 1971). Although much improvement is needed in our current classification systems, their practical utility generally outweighs the shortcomings. However, one must be extremely careful in using labels on children. Further discussion of classification can be found in chapters by Edelbrock and by McDermott in this text.

In the following sections specific diagnostic syndromes will be discussed including neuroses, behavior disorders, psychoses, psychosomatic disorders, and other problem behaviors. Syndromes will be defined and specific subtypes delineated. Behavioral characteristics associated with each syndrome will be discussed and etiological considerations taken into account for specific syndromes. Treatment alternatives will be discussed in a separate section following the discussion of syndromes.

NEUROSES

Neuroses are probably the most frequent disorders observed in children (Shaw & Lucas, 1970). Although the term is used frequently, definitions are vague and discrepant and differential diagnosis is often difficult due to the vague distinctions along the continuum of normal–neurotic–behavior disorder. Definitions differ depending on theoretical orientations. Learning theorists view neurosis as a learned adjustment reaction to a conflictual situation. Psychoanalytically oriented theorists view neuroses as disorders based on conflicts over unconscious sexual and aggressive impulses. The conflicts produce anxiety, which in turn precipitates defensive maneuvers by the ego resulting in symptom formation (Group for the Advancement of Psychiatry, 1966). Thus symptoms are conceptualized as being a partial although unhealthy solution of the underlying conflict. Diagnoses of neuroses usually are not made prior to school age due to the fact that the child's development is not sufficiently stable to warrant a clear diagnostic picture of neurosis as opposed to reactive or adjustment disorders.

Neuroses may develop from normal developmental conflicts which are external, that is, the young child's needs may conflict with external environmental demands (Anthony, 1971). If the external demands do not change, the conflict may gradually become internalized and partially resolved through symptom formation as the child grows older and his personality and character structure become more crystallized. In certain instances neuroses may be precipitated by an overwhelmingly stressful or traumatic event in a child's life.

The major symptom common to all neurotic disorders is the presence of *anxiety.* The formulation of symptoms (compulsions, phobias, aggression) may serve to alleviate anxiety to some extent but anxiety remains prominent. Children with neurotic disorders generally display unhappiness and dissatisfaction. Kessler (1972) points out that neurotic children tend to suffer internally whereas children with more severe behavior disorders create suffering for others through acting-out behaviors. Academic failure is a secondary symptom of neurosis (Shaw & Lucas, 1970). Reasons for academic failure are numerous and vary according to the child; overwhelming anxiety, preoccupation, acting-out behavior, inhibitions, isolation, low self-esteem, and retribution to parents are a few possible contributing factors.

Children with neurotic disorders may display a number of varying symptoms as well as behavioral difficulties. Neurotic disorders are often classified according to the most prominent symptoms and behaviors. Different types of neuroses can be distinguished by the way anxiety is handled by the child, that is, whether it is free-floating, displaced onto external objects, converted into somatic dysfunctions, or discharged through compulsive rituals or dissociative reactions (reactions that involve temporary personality disorganization). The Group for the Advancement of Psychiatry (1966) classified neuroses into six categories: (1) anxiety type, (2) phobic type, (3) conversion type, (4) dissociative type, (5) obsessive-compulsive type, and (6) depressive type.

Anxiety Type

These children exhibit intense, diffuse, and free-floating anxiety which is not tied to a specific situation or object. Defenses and symptom formation are not present or are inadequate in binding the anxiety. Children suffering from anxiety neurosis may exhibit the following: fear of impending doom, feelings of inadequacy, indecisiveness, insomnia, irritability, restlessness, and school problems (Adams, 1979). Physiological symptoms may include diarrhea, heart palpitations, sweating, trembling, nausea, dizziness, and dilation of pupils (Adams, 1979).

Phobic Type

Phobias are characterized by irrational and severe anxiety aroused in specific situations or by specific objects (Kessler, 1972). Phobias should be distinguished from the typical fears observed in young children at particular stages of development (examples: fear of separation in the 2- to 3-year-old, fear of the dark in preschool children, fear of large animals in children 3 to 8 years old). In phobias the reaction is more severe and is characterized by overwhelming panic. Phobias often have an obsessional quality, so that the child is constantly worrying about the feared object or situation (Kessler, 1972). Phobias, psychodynamically interpreted, represent a defensive reaction against unacceptable impulses or conflicts. The phobic child tries to detach himself or herself from the anxiety aroused by a forbidden or conflicting wish by displacing the anxiety onto a situation, person, idea, or thing that holds symbolic significance (Adams, 1979). For instance, a child who has strong destructive urges may develop a phobia of lions and tigers to the point where he or she cannot sleep for fear of being attacked. The symbolic significance of lions and tigers is that they represent wild, ferocious feelings which can get out of control resulting in physical injury (Kessler, 1972). Thus the child displaces his or her own fear of getting out of control onto external animals.

The conditioning model of phobia acquisition holds that phobias are learned responses, acquired through classical conditioning in which a noxious stimulus is paired with an originally benign object. If these two stimuli are continually associated with each other, the benign object becomes fear-inducing. Once there becomes sufficient fear to avoid the now phobic object, the phobia is maintained by the anxiety reduction which occurs as a result of the avoidance of the feared object. Other theorists contend that phobias can result from the occurrence of specific events which are highly traumatic in nature. Bandura (1969) suggests that phobias may be acquired as a result of modeling or vicarious learning. In other words, a child may become fearful of thunderstorms because he or she observes a parent exhibiting highly fearful behavior in such circumstances.

School phobia is one of the more common phobias observed in school-aged children. School-phobic children typically exhibit severe anxiety about going to school and may exhibit somatic complaints such as abdominal pain, headaches, or nausea before going to school in the morning (Kauffman, 1977). Specific aspects of the school (teacher, janitor, bus, schoolmates, cafeteria, classroom) may elicit severe panic attacks in the child. School phobia should be distinguished from truancy and school refusal by the neurotic, conflictual nature of the reaction. The onset of a school-phobic reaction may be precipitated by specific negative events at school or at home and may be maintained by parents who wish to protect their child from the manifest anxiety (Clarizio & McCoy, 1976).

Many writers view school phobia as a specific form of separation anxiety shared by mother and child (Eisenberg, 1958; Johnson, 1957). Studies of school phobia have identified a mutually dependent relationship between mother and child (Leton, 1962; Levinson, 1962). In such cases the mother reinforces the child's dependence and separation anxiety out of her own need to be nurtured by allowing the child to stay home from school (Kelly, 1973).

Fears of abandonment and death are often the underlying conflict in school phobia. Such children fear the death of or harm of the parent while they are at school. Not all school phobias represent mutual neurosis by parent and child related to separation. One may observe children who displace fears of aggression or sexual impulses onto some aspect of the school situation and thus attempt to avoid the conflict through such symptom formation. School phobias can also result from anxiety related to various aspects of the school situation, including fear of failure, fear of teachers, fear of classmates, and evaluation anxiety (Kessler, 1972).

Kennedy (1965) classified school phobias into two major types which have different etiologies and require different intervention strategies. Type I school phobia is characterized as a "true phobic reaction" that has an acute onset in younger children from families in which communication is good. Type II school phobia is characterized by Kennedy as a "way of life phobia" with a very complex pattern of fearful reactions to almost any situation. The school phobia is only one aspect of this complex of phobias. Type II phobias are generally found in upper grades, and they come from families which have poor communication.

Treatment for Type I school phobias involves establishing close liaisons among school, medical, and mental health professionals, along with parental consultation. The child is forced in a matter-of-fact manner to attend school, and somatic complaints are minimized. Treatment for Type II phobias is more complex and generally involves more intensive, multimodal intervention.

Conversion Type

In conversion disorders children express unconscious conflict through somatic dysfunction, involving organs operated by the voluntary portion of the central nervous system. These bodily disturbances may include motor dysfunction (tics, paralysis), hysterical blindness or deafness, anorexia, vomiting, and various other somatic disturbances. The symptom may symbolically express the conflict as in the example of a child who developed conversion blindness after witnessing a traumatic incident. Secondary gain from attention, dependence, and so on, may reinforce symptoms and make treatment much more difficult.

Dissociative Type

This disorder is similar to the conversion disorder. Neurotic anxiety leads to temporary disorganization of the personality resulting in amnesia, narcolepsy, stuporous states, and somnambulism.

Obsessive-Compulsive Type

In these disorders the child attempts to counteract the anxiety aroused by unconscious conflict by repetitive thoughts (obsessions) and acts (compulsions) or both. The child seems compelled to repeat rituals such as counting, cleaning, or handwashing. The external behavior may represent the opposite of the unconscious wish as in the child who controls his impulse to soil and mess by excessive cleaning and washing rituals. Another example is that of the child with a learning disability who carefully and slowly prints or draws, frequently erasing, and never being completely satisfied with his or her production. Many children exhibit obsessive ideation and compulsive behavior at certain stages of development; it is only when such behaviors interfere seriously with the child's ability to function that obsessive-compulsive neurosis would be considered as a diagnosis.

Depressive Type

Depression in children is exhibited differently from depression manifested in adults and is not well understood as a diagnostic entity in children. Symptoms may include crying spells, flat affect, somatic complaints, loss of appetite, hyper- or hypoactivity, accident proneness, acting-out, and suicidal threats. Self-deprecation is often evident.

BEHAVIOR DISORDERS

The term "behavior disorder" has been used in the literature to describe a very broad range of problem behaviors and maladaptive behavioral syndromes. Some theorists conceptualize behavior disorders as personality disorders that are on a continuum ranging from relatively normal to severe pathology (Group for the Advancement of Psychiatry, 1966). Others use the term to describe only severe, antisocial, norm-violating behavior, implying serious deficiencies in moral judgment. The authors of this chapter conceptualize behavior disorders as disorders which include aggressive, acting-out, norm-violating behavior. Behavior disorders are divided into two major categories, the primary distinction between the two being the absence or presence of moral-conscience development (guilt, remorse, etc.).

Antisocial Behavior Disorder

This category includes disorders referred to by other authors as unsocialized psychopathic (Schwartz & Johnson, 1981), sociopathic (Rosen & Gregory, 1965), unsocialized aggressive (Hewitt & Jenkins, 1946), psychopathic delinquency (Peterson, Quay, & Cameron, 1959), and tension-discharge personality disorder (Group for the Advancement of Psychiatry, 1966). Behavioral and personality characteristics of children falling in this category include poor impulse control resulting in uninhibited discharge of aggressive or sexual impulses towards peers, parents, teachers, and social institutions; lack of anxiety or guilt concerning such behavior; poor frustration tolerance; failure to learn from consequences of behavior; inability to form meaningful interpersonal relationships; poor self-esteem; and manipulative, deceitful behavior (Rosen & Gregory, 1965; Schwartz & Johnson, 1981; Shaw & Lucas, 1970).

Specific behaviors may include vandalism, arson, stealing, fighting, truancy, sexual acting-out, assaultive-aggressive, and other delinquent acts that often result in conflict with the law. Shaw and Lucas (1970) aptly described the child with an antisocial behavior disorder: "There is something about his whole demeanor: an air of emptiness, of hopelessness, of defeat; a total disinterest and absence of motivation towards anything" (p. 233).

The most important etiological factor in the development of antisocial behavior disorders is the absence of mature and consistent parental love and nurturance (Shaw & Lucas, 1970). These children usually have experienced severe early parental rejection and fail to become socialized as a consequence. Moral-conscience development is severely delayed in these children resulting in an inadequate understanding of "right" versus "wrong." Inconsistencies and unpredictability in parental behaviors, uncontrolled and punitive aggression, pathologic sexual experiences, and broken homes are often found in the histories of children with antisocial behavior disorders (Shaw & Lucas, 1970). These children often grow up to be criminals if not treated effectively. Attitudes toward effective treatment of such children have historically been rather pessimistic. However, treatment successes have been reported in the literature (Cohen, Filipczak, Slavin, & Boren, 1971; Fixsen, Phillips, Phillips, & Wolf, 1972; Jesness, DeRisi, McCormick, & Wedge, 1972). Meeks (1979) contends that such professional pessimism has resulted from ignorance, insufficient study, and punitive attitudes due to the discomfort aroused by the behaviors of children diagnosed with antisocial behavior disorders.

Aggressive Behavior Disorders

Aggressive behavior disorders are disorders characterized by behaviors that may result in personal injury (physical or psychological) or destruction of property (Bandura, 1973). Specific behaviors may include hitting, fighting, biting, throwing, disruption, destroying, verbal abuse, and opposition (Patterson, Cobb, & Ray, 1972). The behaviors of the child diagnosed with an aggressive behavior disorder may superficially resemble the behaviors of the child with an antisocial behavior disorder. However, differential diagnosis can be made on the basis of several criteria: (1) presence of anxiety or guilt; (2) etiology, and (3) responsiveness to treatment. Children with aggressive behavior disorders may exhibit anxiety, conflict, guilt, and remorse concerning their aggressive behavior. Aggressive behavior may arise from intense internal conflicts or frustration (Group for the Advancement of Psychiatry, 1966) rather than from unbridled, impulsive aggression as in the antisocial behavior disorder.

Aggressive behavior may be motivated by unconscious desires to punish others, particularly parents, by a need to gain attention, by a need to be punished, or by a need to act out parental antisocial attitudes (Clarizio & McCoy, 1976). Children who exhibit aggressive behavior because of such motivating factors have been called "neurotic delinquents" (Schwartz & Johnson, 1981) and are reportedly more responsive to treatment than children with antisocial behavior disorders (Quay, Peterson, & Consalvi, 1960).

Some children exhibiting aggressive, antisocial behavior are merely conforming to the norms established in their cultural subgroup, neighborhood, or family. Such children may learn to fight, lie, and steal to survive within their social subculture. These children may exhibit healthy psychological development despite behaviors that deviate from the larger society (Clarizio & McCoy, 1976; Group for the Advancement of Psychiatry, 1966). This category of aggressive behavior has been referred to as sociosyntonic personality disorder (Group for the Advancement of Psychiatry, 1966) or the subcultural delinquent (Clarizio & McCoy, 1976; Schwartz & Johnson, 1981). Unlike the antisocial behavior disorder, these children may experience guilt and anxiety if they violate the norms of their subgroup and they are able to form close, meaningful attachments with others (Clarizio & McCoy, 1976).

Aggressive acting-out behavior can take many forms and may result from numerous environmental as well as internal personality factors. A child's display of aggression may be mild and sporadic or persistent, eventually resulting in apprehension by law-enforcement officials. Juvenile delinquency is not discussed as a separate entity in this chapter because the authors view juvenile delinquency as a legal rather than a psychological category. Although juvenile delinquents may exhibit behaviors that have aggression as the common denominator, the personality makeup of such individuals is quite diverse, ranging from mild neuroticism to severe psychopathy, and the etiological factors motivating juveniles toward delinquent vary considerably.

PSYCHOSES

Psychotic disorders appearing in childhood are characterized by severe distortion in the development of basic psychological functions involving perception, reality testing, cognition, language, and affect. Until around 1970, the various diagnostic labels of autism, atypical development, symbiotic psychosis, and childhood schizophrenia were used interchangeably and synonymously under the general heading of childhood psychosis. In recent years, however, significant progress has been made in delineating and refining diagnostic criteria for various separate syndromes. Of particular importance in this refinement has been the separation of infantile autism from childhood schizophrenia and its establishment as a separate category. Although some controversy still exists concerning the continuity or discontinuity of autism and childhood schizophrenia, currently available evidence points to childhood schizophrenia as an early onset variant of adult schizophrenia and autism as a distinct diagnostic entity. Particularly strong evidence for the discontinuity position was obtained in a systematic comparative study by Kolvin and his colleagues in Britain (Kolvin, Ounstead, Humphrey, & McNay, 1971) in which differences were established between the two groups in regard to symptomatology, parental socioeconomic and intellectual characteristics, family history and genetic background, and pattern of seizure disorders. In addition, frequency distributions of childhood psychoses by age of onset show graphic illustration of discontinuity. Generally such distributions show one peak of onset before age 2 followed by a scarcity of onsets from ages 3–6, rising from 7 years on to another peak in late childhood and early adolescence (Kolvin et al., 1971; Markita, 1966). Figure 14.1, as depicted in Rutter (1974), illustrates this distribution. Those psychoses with onset between 3 and 6 years usually have been found to be associated with clear-cut organic processes (Rutter, 1968, 1972; Kolvin et al., 1971).

The following discussion of types of childhood psychoses will focus on the two major categories of childhood schizophrenia and infantile autism. Because of the comparatively greater amount of recent research in autism, more attention will be devoted to autistic symptomatology and possible underlying deficits.

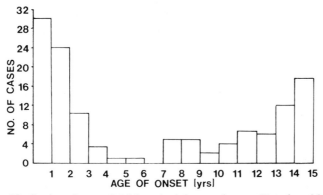

Figure 14.1. Distribution of cases of child psychosis by age of onset. (Data from Markita, 1966, and Kolvin et al., 1971.)

Childhood Schizophrenia

The diagnosis of schizophrenia occurring in childhood is now reserved for those children showing the classic schizophrenic signs seen in adult schizophrenia (American Psychiatric Association, 1980). Onset of a fully developed schizophrenic syndrome in children occurs most commonly after the age of 11 with a decreased incidence of onset between 7 and 11 and extremely rare onset prior to 7. The symptomatology is basically similar to that seen in adult schizophrenia and is characterized by severely impaired reality testing, disorders of thought association, thought blocking, delusions, and hallucinations, particularly of an auditory nature (Ekstein, 1975; Kolvin et al., 1971). Intellectual functioning is generally within the low average to average range although substantial inter- and intrasubtest scatter is often present on formal intellectual tests (Kolvin et al., 1971).

Although presentation of the full complement of classic schizophrenic symptoms is rarely seen in early childhood, there is a group of children who fall in the age range of 3½ to 12 years who show evidence of disturbance in the areas of body boundaries, self-identity, sensory reactions, and symbol formation. These disturbances are manifested behaviorally by sudden excessive anxiety, impaired social relatedness, and inappropriate affect. In the past the diagnosis of childhood schizophrenia was also applied to this group of children even though frankly psychotic behavior (e.g., delusions, hallucinations, thought disorder) was not always present at the time of diagnosis or in the child's later development into adolescence and adulthood. Currently these children are classified in the diagnostic category of childhood onset pervasive developmental disorder. Although it is presumed that many of the children diagnosed in this category will later develop schizophrenia, the actual percentage of cases in which this occurs is unknown.

Retrospective reports of development in infancy often reveal abnormalities of personality or behavior from an early age. The reliability of such reports depends on the accuracy of parents' memories and thus may be biased in some respects. However, the consistency of parents' retrospective accounts of their autistic children's infancy as well as the difficulty in obtaining prospective data lend importance to the information. In infancy the child often has difficulty in establishing a regular rhythm for bodily functions of sleeping, eating, and elimination and may be either extremely passive or irritable. Uneven developmental patterns are often seen with advanced development in some areas and delayed functioning in others. Unusual sensitivities to sensory stimuli are frequently noted with frightened, paniclike behavior in response to sounds or sights that realistically pose no harm. Although these abnormalities are noted retrospectively, the child does not appear grossly impaired in cognitive or affective development as does the autistic infant. Onset of frankly deviant behavior is not seen prior to 30 months of age.

As the children enter the toddler and preschool ages, basic difficulties of self-identity, body image, and boundaries of self often become evident with intense anxiety as a predominant response. The persistent anxiety about body and self boundaries may be manifest in multiple phobias, psychosomatic complaints, obsessive-compulsive symptoms, and persistent questioning about identity and orientation. As a result of the anxiety and lack of consolidation of identity, these children may cling excessively to parents and others with whom they are familiar as though to reestablish a self–other fusion. In some cases they may quickly establish inappropriately intense attachments to relative strangers, again as if to establish a fusion state that will stabilize the precarious nature of their own self-identity. They are often especially vulnerable and sensitive to separation experiences, moving, and even mild rejection. In many cases they react to these common experiences as if they were catastrophic events that signify a complete loss of love and security.

Emotions in general are experienced intensely and may be overwhelming for children with resultant severe temper tantrums and panic reactions. Rapid shifts in ego functioning may occur, often in response to real or feared loss of relationships without which they feel unable to continue in a frightening world. Relatively mild stress often leads to rapid regression and disorganization of behavior with frantic activity and complete withdrawal. Anger, in particular, is a difficult emotion and children may envision their own anger as an omnipotent, destructive force or become terrified by their own feelings of hostility and strike out blindly at a world believed to be dangerous and destructive.

As children enter school age and communication skills improve, disorders of thinking and idiosyncratic usage of language often become apparent. Especially under stress, children's speech and language often will be fragmented and incoherent with tangential associations and missing logical links in the sequence of thoughts. Frequently children have difficulty separating reality, fantasy, and dreams with intense affect and illogical associations between objects and thoughts. Symbol formation may be distorted so that words and objects take on idiosyncratic meanings. Bender (1947) provides an example of the language and thought processes of an early school-aged child:

> I say, hello, doctor, have you any new toys? Let me open your radiator with this screw driver. I say let me open it. I say, so what! Can I copy your animals? I am in a doctor's office. You and I are twins, aren't we? I am coloring this camel brown. I said I am coloring it brown. I said I am coloring this camel brown. Have you a little scissors? Have you a big scissors? I say, have you a big scissors? Well here's what I will use, what do you think? It is called a knife. How does my voice sound? What? What? Judy what? Is that your name? I'm cutting out this camel. Is it pretty enough to hang on the wall? Can you cut as pretty as this? My sister says, camel talk. Isn't that funny? Camel talk. My voice sounds like up in the library. Doesn't it? In the hospital my voice sounds like up in the library. Can you say li-bra-ri-an? The library is where you get books.

The thought disorder, rapid regression under stress, and pervasive anxiety characterize the school-aged child. In the prepubertal period and continuing through adolescence, delusions and hallucinations may begin to occur and the clinical picture becomes increasingly similar to that seen in adults diagnosed with schizophrenia.

Major differential diagnostic criteria for childhood onset pervasive developmental disorder and infantile autism include age of onset, degree and type of disturbance in speech, language and symbolic functioning, and profile of intellectual abilities (American Psychiatric Association, 1980). Onset of infantile autism is seen prior to 30 months of age while onset of childhood onset pervasive developmental disorder is after 30 months. Speech and language development are much more severely impaired in autistic children. Similarly, while children with childhood onset pervasive developmental disorder tend to show *distorted,* idiosyncratic symbolic functioning, autistic children are more likely to show a severe *deficit* in the capacity for symbolic thought. Finally, autistic children have a characteristic profile of intellectual abilities with high scores on visuospatial and motor tasks and low scores on verbal, symbolic, or sequencing tasks. Children with childhood onset pervasive developmental disorder do not tend to show this profile of abilities and may, in fact, show the reverse with deficits in visual motor tasks. In addition, while two-thirds of autistic children fall in the retarded range of intelligence, children with childhood onset pervasive developmental disorder are more likely to fall in the average to low average range.

Infantile Autism

In his original description of the syndrome of infantile autism, Kanner (1943) viewed the essential features as a combination of extreme aloneness from the beginning of life, delay in speech acquisition and noncommunicative use of speech after it develops, repetitive behavior with acute distress at changes in the environment, good rote memory, and generally normal appearance. In addition to the originally described symptoms, peculiarities in autistic children's responses to sensory stimuli and in their motor movements have been noted as common symptoms (Ornitz & Ritvo, 1968). However, these disturbances of perception and motility have been established as universally present in all autistic children (Rutter, 1966). Each of the major symptom areas is discussed here, followed by consideration of the major theories regarding the underlying deficits.

Disturbances in Social Relationships

Autistic children's failure to develop appropriate social relationships has received a great deal of attention. Several distinctive features have been noted, particularly the lack of attachment behavior and relative failure of bonding, deviant use of eye-to-eye gaze, and lack of anticipatory posture and body molding when being picked up as an infant or young child. Wing (1972) aptly described the behavioral features that characterize the social withdrawal and aloofness of autistic children.

Most (though not all) young autistic children behave as though other people did not exist. It is possible to list the points in the behavior of an autistic child which make him seem so aloof and distant—such a "changeling child." He does not come when he is called, he does not listen if you speak to him, his face may be empty of expression, he rarely looks straight at your face, he may pull away if you touch him, he does not put his arms around you if you pick him up, and he may walk past you (or over you, if you are sitting on the floor) without pausing in his stride. If he wants something he cannot reach for himself he grabs you by the back of your hand or wrist (not sliding his hand inside yours like a normal child) and pulls you along to do the work for him. Once he has the object you are ignored again. He shows no interest or sympathy if you are in pain or distress. He seems cut off, in a world of his own, completely absorbed in his own aimless activities. (p. 24)

As autistic children grow older, they tend to become more affectionate, but serious social difficulties continue with particular difficulties in cooperative group play, making personal friendships and understanding others' feelings and responses (Rutter, 1978). Their naivete and lack of empathy frequently lead to socially embarrassing behavior as the children talk in public about topics that are usually either ignored or discussed in private.

Disturbances of Speech and Language

A variety of abnormalities in speech and language development have been reported (Bartak, Rutter, & Cox, 1975; Fay & Schuler, 1980; Ricks & Wing, 1975; Rutter, 1965, 1966). Autistic children usually show marked delays in the acquisition of speech as well as deviant patterns of prelinguistic and language skills. In normal development, social imitation, meaningful use of objects, and the capacity for imaginative play are thought to be important determinants of appropriate development of the symbolic function, which is, in turn, crucial for language development (e.g., Piaget, 1946/1962). Each of these functions is seriously impaired in autistic children.

Comprehension of the language spoken to them is almost always seriously impaired. Many autistic children seem unaware that spoken words have meaning, although they may attend to a few simple words which are linked to pleasant experiences (e.g., dinner, Coke). At a later age they may acquire limited comprehension of simple and short commands or phrases (e.g., put your coat on).

Slightly less than half of all autistic children never acquire useful language. Those who do learn to speak at all usually begin much later than normal and, for a long while after speech develops, their speech consists primarily of repeating words spoken by others (echolalia). Echolalia may be immediate or delayed repetition of phrases heard in the past and is often accompanied by I–You pronominal reversal. In most cases the repeated words seem to have little meaning to the child, although they often give a misleading impression of the child's level of expressive language.

Generation of spontaneous language is a difficult and confusing process for autistic children. Even for those who begin to generate appropriate language, retrieval of words usually continues to be difficult and understanding the concept of multiple meanings for a single word is often an impossible task.

Resistance to Change and Repetitive Behavior

Many autistic children insist on rigid adherence to established routines. For example, a child may insist on taking exactly the same route each time he or she goes with mother to the grocery store, or he or she may insist that each member of the family sit in the same chair in the living room or at mealtimes. Similarly rigid play patterns with limited variety or ritualistic compulsive behaviors are often established. For example, an autistic child may ritualistically line up his or her toys in a certain pattern or collect string or stones that are repetitively arranged in the same pattern. The rituals also may be verbal as when the child has to ask a certain sequence of questions and insists on specific answers. If these routines and rituals are disturbed, tantrumous or panicked behavior usually results.

Disturbance of Perceptual Integration

Parents of autistic children often suspect at some point that their child is deaf because of the lack of response to some sounds. They may report that their child does not even blink when heavy books are dropped on the floor behind him or her. Usually, however, this same child shows a heightened sensitivity to other sounds. For example, he or she may detect the crinkling of a candy wrapper, or he or she may show distress and cover his or her ears at the roar of an airplane or the barking of a dog. This alternation between hypo- and hyperresponsive states is apparent in all sensory modalities (hearing, vision, touch, taste, and smell).

Ornitz and Ritvo (1968) proposed a theory of perceptual inconstancy which they feel accounts for the symptoms seen in autistic children. These authors postulate a deficit in the homeostatic regulation of sensory input and motor output. Thus the level of sensory input is at times too high and, at other times, too low. Because of this breakdown in regulation of the level of sensory input, it is hypothesized that the autistic child is unable to construct a stable, internal representation of his environment and thus is unable to learn to interact normally or to use communicative speech. Support for the theory comes from several electrophysiological studies which have focused on the oculomotor response to vestibular stimulation. On the basis of the experimental model, Ornitz and Ritvo proposed a dysfunction of the central vestibular system.

A second major theory of an underlying defect in cross-modal associations has been proposed by several authors. In normal development, children are adept at receiving information in one modality, such as the auditory, visual, or tactile, and responding in another. In addition, normal children are typically able to integrate information from different sensory input modalities. Autistic children have severe difficulties with both of these processes (e.g., Bryson, 1970; LeLord et al., 1973; Lovaas, Schreibman, Koegel, & Rehm, 1971).

A deficit in cross-modal associations would have profound effects on all areas of the child's development beginning very early in life. For example, successful bonding between mother and infant requires that the child be able to process information from the diverse modalities of taste, touch, smell, audition, and vision. Eventually these various sensory inputs must be integrated into a schema of "mother." The autistic child's concept of "mother," however, is likely to be a fragmented collection of body parts, different tones of voice, and other dissociated traces of taste, touch, and smell.

The third major theory of underlying deficit is that of Rutter and his colleagues (Rutter, 1968), who hypothesized that autistic children suffer from a central cognitive defect which prevents them from comprehending symbolic or sequenced information, and that this central cognitive defect is closely similar to other developmental disorders of language. To focus on the role of language impairment in autism, Rutter, Bartak, and Newman (1971) compared autistic children with children showing a developmental receptive language disorder. Results showed many similarities between the groups, but the cognitive impairment in the autistic children was "deeper and wider" than in the language-disordered children. Specifically, impairment of comprehension in general was more severe in the autistic group, and autistic children's comprehension of gesture was impaired whereas understanding and use of gesture was intact in the language-disordered group. The findings of a possible genetic linkage between autism and language disorder (Folstein & Rutter, 1977) further emphasize the importance of a central cognitive defect.

PSYCHOSOMATIC DISORDERS

Traditionally, psychosomatic disorders have been defined as those disorders involving physical dysfunction resulting from the interaction between chronic emotional stress and biological predisposition or vulnerability. This traditional view of psychosomatic disorders is considered by many theorists to be outdated and reductionistic due to research advances which indicate that all illness is caused by an interaction among social, psychological, and biological factors (Selby & Calhoun, 1978). Some theorists argue that because of the multidetermined nature of all illness the delineation of psychosomatic disorders as a separate entity creates a false and useless dichotomy of disease (Lipowski, 1968). Wright (1977) suggested that to do justice to the interface between physical and psychological factors, the term psychosomatic should refer to all behavioral concomitants of illness and all physical concomitants of psychological disturbance. Wright (1977) and Jay and Wright (1981) delineated categories of psychosomatic disorders based on this broadened definition of psychosomatic disorders. Following is a discussion of these types of psychosomatic disorders.

Physical disorders caused by difficulties in learning and development constitute one category of psychosomatic disorders. Tracheotomy addiction in children is an example. Tracheotomy addiction is most likely to occur in children less than 1 year of age who have breathed through tracheotomies for more than 100 days (Jackson, 1963). Such children *learn* to breath through a tracheotomy, and this response is strengthened neurologically through habit and practice while the normal breathing response is extinguished through disuse. The result is a physical problem created by difficulty in learning and development. Encopresis is another example of a physical problem which may be caused by problems of learning and development. Children who withhold their feces over a prolonged period of time develop a permanently distended colon (megacolon). Normal amounts of fecal material can no longer stimulate the colon to trigger neurologically a defecation reflex. The child remains impacted, the colon remains distended, the anus becomes dilated, and gradually seepage or staining occurs (Wright, 1977). The habit of defecating normally and regularly is extinguished because of the development of a megacolon.

A second category of psychosomatic disorders involves physical problems created by deviations in personality or character development. Examples include self-mutilation, including scratching, biting, cutting, and puncturing one's flesh, as well as trichotillomania (excoriation of hair). Self-mutilating behavior may be the result of a masochistic personality which has developed through reinforcement. However, the genetic disorder Lesch-Nyhan syndrome must be ruled out as a causative agent before this disorder can be considered in this category of psychosomatic disorders. Deviations in the development of autonomy in young children may cause physical problems. In pediatric settings, young children may refuse oral medications and may regurgitate medicine administered through a nasogastric tube (Wright, 1977). Such pathological expressions of autonomy can create potentially lethal medical problems.

A third category of psychosomatic disorders includes the traditionally defined psychophysiological disorders mentioned previously. Psychophysiological disorders are those disorders created by an interaction between biological predisposition and psychological factors such as chronic emotional stress (Group for the Advancement of Psychiatry, 1966). These disorders usually involve organ systems innervated by the autonomic nervous system and, in severe disorders, structural changes may occur to a point that is irreversible and life-threatening. Psychophysiological disorders include disorders such as asthma, ulcerative colitis, peptic ulcers, and eczema.

A fourth category of psychosomatic disorders refers to physical symptoms and reactions created primarily by psychological factors. Such symptoms often occur in young children and are usually physiological responses to stressful stimuli, life changes, or interpersonal conflicts. These disorders are usually transient situational and may disappear without treatment. Examples of such disorders include eating disturbances, regressive behavior (thumbsucking), tics, panic states, diurnal enuresis, and nonretentive encopresis (Prugh, 1963). Symptoms in this category of psychosomatic disorders are distinguished from neurotic disorders in that they tend to be transient-adjustment reactions and do not represent internal conflict or pathology.

The aforementioned categories refer to disorders in which psychological factors (stress, learning, personality development) precipitate or perpetuate physical disorders. The complement of these disorders involves a set of psychological problems caused by physical illness. Lachman (1972) referred to these disorders as "somatopsychic," although Wright (1977) and Jay and Wright (1981) included them all as falling under the rubric of psychosomatic disorders.

Psychological problems may result indirectly from physical illness. Concomitants of chronic illness including hospitalization, traumatic medical procedures, physical disfigurement, and loss of independence may result in acute emotional crises or long-term psychological problems. Hematologists have observed reckless and dangerous behavioral tendencies in hemophiliacs. Such self-destructive behaviors may be counterphobic reactions to the fear of being injured and bleeding to death, or they may be expressions of hostility and anger at having such a disease (Wright, 1977). Another example of psychological problems resulting indirectly from illness can be found in cases of congenital heart defects. Medical literature suggests that children with congenital heart defects exhibit more delays in intellectual and emotional growth, although there is no medical reason for such delays. The mechanism involved may be parental tendencies to infantize and shelter such children, thus preventing optimal growth and stimulation (Wright, 1977).

A final category of psychosomatic disorders includes psychological problems caused directly by physical illness. Meningitis may cause deficits in perceptual motor functioning and abstract thinking abilities (Wright & Jimmerson, 1971). Patients who had Rocky Mountain spotted fever have exhibited depression, deficits in full scale IQ, perceptual-motor functioning, and abstract-thinking abilities (Wright & Jimmerson, 1971). Other organic diseases may result in mental retardation.

TREATMENT

Although diagnosis and classification do not imply a specific type of treatment, decisions as to therapy for a child should be made on the basis of diagnostic procedures which reveal relevant information concerning the exact nature of a child's problem, strengths and deficits, and the likelihood of therapeutic compliance. A number of factors must be assessed including the following: Is the etiology primarily organic or psychosocial in nature? Can the symptoms be easily unlearned or reconditioned, or do they seem to be manifestations of unconscious internal conflicts? What family factors are operating in perpetuating the symptoms? How resistant is the family and the child to treatment? What resources do the child and family possess—intellectually, economically, and emotionally? What are the available treatment resources? (Jay & Wright, 1981).

In considering these questions, one crosses the theoretical boundaries among several schools of psychotherapy. Unfortunately, strong theoretical biases operate among mental health professionals in choosing therapeutic interventions. Behavior therapists and psychodynamically oriented therapists often view each other as polar opposites and are blinded to mutual and complementary aspects of their work with children. Similarly, individually oriented therapists often exclude relevant family factors which may need addressing before the child improves. A more global open-minded eclectic approach would seem to be most appropriate in deciding what type of treatment a child should receive. Schaefer and Milman (1977) used the term "prescriptive eclecticism" to describe an individualized, nonbiased approach to treatment planning. In a prescriptive approach to therapy, the practitioner tries to determine what intervention approach will be most feasible and most effective for a specific disorder in a given child. The assumption underlying the eclectic approach is that no one therapeutic approach is superior across all disorders.

Treatment approaches commonly used with children having emotional-behavioral difficulties are discussed next.

Psychodynamic Psychotherapy

The traditional therapeutic approach for psychological disorders is the psychodynamic approach generated by Freud and other psychoanalytic theorists. In psychodynamic therapy, underlying psychological causes rather than overt symptoms are treated. The major assumption of psychodynamic theory is that an individual's symptoms are a result of internal personality conflicts which have been ineffectively resolved at an unconscious level through defense mechanisms such as repression, denial, and somatization. Fears, anxieties, and impulses may be denied and repressed by the individual resulting in symptom formation. The aim of psychodynamic therapy is to explore feelings, attitudes, and fears and to gradually bring the unconscious and warded-off feelings into conscious awareness. The rationale is that once an individual becomes able to recognize and cope with internal tensions and conflicts in a more conscious constructive manner, the symptoms which precipitated the referral for therapy will gradually diminish (Carek, 1979).

The main therapeutic ingredients in psychodynamic therapy with children include a trusting child–therapist relationship, parent consultation, expression of feelings and fantasies through spontaneous play, and interpretation by the therapist (Schaefer & Milman, 1977). Through a warm, empathic relationship with the therapist, the child is encouraged to openly express feelings, fantasies, and fears. Play is usually the medium for the child's communication since the child spontaneously conveys messages, feelings, and preoccupations through his or her play activities. The therapist may enter the child's play as an active participant and/or make dynamic interpretations concerning the child's communication. The aim of interpretation is to make the child more aware of unconscious thoughts and feelings which are influencing his or her behavior. Interpretations may be made on a subconscious level through nondirective techniques such as Gardner's mutual storytelling technique (Gardner, 1971), Lynn's structured doll play (Lynn, 1959), Ekstein's metaphorical techniques (Ekstein, 1966), or Bettelheim's use of fairy tales (Bettelheim, 1976).

The therapist may attempt to intervene on a more conscious level by confronting the child as to consequences of certain behaviors and by educating the child to use more adaptive ego functions such as impulse control and critical thinking. Catharsis, interpretation confrontation, and education are all psychodynamic techniques aimed at increasing the child's awareness of emotions so that they can be expressed in a conflict-free, nondestructive manner (Carek, 1979). Parent consultation is an important adjunct to individual psychodynamic psychotherapy (Lesser, 1972). Parents can obtain insights concerning their children's behavior as well as their own behavior, and they can be taught more effective parenting skills.

Individual psychodynamic psychotherapy is probably most appropriate for disorders in which internal (rather than external-environmental) conflicts are precipitating and maintaining maladaptive behavior. Children with serious deficiencies in intellectual functioning, reality testing, impulse control, and object relationships may not benefit from psychodynamic therapy since the capacity for meaningful relationships, self-reflection, and frustration tolerance are requisite for success (Carek, 1979).

Behavior Therapy

Behavior therapy is a therapeutic modality based on principles derived from learning theory. The behavioral model holds that *all* behavior is learned and the principles are the same for maladaptive as well as adaptive behavior. Children with behavior disorders may have learned maladaptive responses to environmental situations or may have failed to learn appropriate behaviors and social skills. Behavior therapists treat psychological disorders by (1) identifying target behaviors to be increased or decreased, (2) determining the functional relationships between target behaviors and environmental events, and (3) manipulating these relationships so as to encourage certain behaviors (Werry & Wollersheim, 1973).

The term behavior therapy refers to a wide array of methods rather than a specific therapeutic technique. Werry and Wollersheim (1973) categorized behavioral methods into one of four groups depending upon the focus of attention: (1) stimulus manipulation (systematic desensitization, modeling, aversion therapy); (2) response manipulation (reciprocal inhibition, shaping); (3) reinforcement manipulation (withholding reward, punishment); or (4) manipulation of intraorganismic drive states (pharmacotherapy, hypnosis, muscle relaxation). These techniques are diverse in nature, the common characteristics being an emphasis on *behavior* change and the application of principles derived from learning theory.

Behavior therapy differs from psychodynamic therapy in practice as well as conceptualization. Behavior therapists focus on modification of symptoms rather than underlying causes. The emphasis is on the *present* environmental contingencies rather than contributing historical factors. Behavior therapy is a directive form of therapy by which the therapist actively attempts to manipulate, rather than analyze, behavior. Relationship factors (rapport, nurturance, acceptance) although important, are not regarded as essential prerequisites for successful behavior change (Franks, 1965). Behaviorists are concerned with *outcome* rather than process and employ objective evaluative criteria more often than psychodynamic psychotherapists (Clarizio & McCoy, 1976).

Specific considerations should be taken into account when deciding whether or not to choose behavior therapy as the form of treatment for a given disorder. Werry and Wollersheim (1973) suggested behavior therapy as a treatment of choice with disorders in which discrete symptoms are present and/or with patients who lack verbal insight skills or who are symptom- rather than insight-oriented. An advantage of behavior therapy is that years of training are not necessarily required, making it possible for paraprofessionals, teachers, and parents to employ behavior techniques.

Cognitive behavior therapy has developed from recent trends in behavioral psychology. Some behaviorists include cognitive and motivational factors as intervening variables between environmental stimuli and consequent behavior. Cognitive behaviorists emphasize the importance of an individual's internal cognitions and perceptions in determining his or her behavior. If these cognitions are faulty, illogical, or irrational, disorders or maladaptive behavior may occur. In cognitive behavior therapy, a patient's cognitions are examined and corrected if faulty. Correction of faulty cognitions then should lead to clinical improvement. Meichenbaum (1977) has been the leading cognitive behaviorist in the treatment of behavior disorders in children.

Group Psychotherapy

Group therapy is a psychotherapeutic method which involves group meetings of two or more children with one or more therapists. The nature and goals of therapy groups differ according to the orientation of the leader; groups may be behavioral, psychodynamic, transactional, or supportive in nature. The primary difference between individual and group therapy is that the child in a therapy group learns in an interpersonal context and receives multiple inputs from therapist and peers. Therapeutic components of group therapy for children include interpersonal and social-skills experience, the opportunity for modeling of adaptive behavior, catharsis and expression of feelings, and attainment of information and feedback concerning one's behavior in a social setting (Kraft, 1979). The goal of most therapy groups, regardless of orientation, involves increased awareness and control of emotions (Rosenbaum & Kraft, 1972).

Group therapy occurs in a variety of settings including outpatient clinics, residential treatment centers, hospitals, and schools. Groups are composed of children spanning almost every diagnostic category. They are usually divided according to age groups, with those for preschool-aged children usually involving structured play activity while those for older children may be activity-oriented, activity- and discussion-oriented, or solely discussion-oriented.

Advantages of group therapy include its economy and the opportunity to work in an interpersonal context. Children who need to develop social skills are particularly suitable referrals for group therapy.

Family Therapy

In family therapy the identified patient is treated within the context of his or her family. Although one family member, often the child, manifests the symptoms, the therapist perceives the entire family as the patient and intervenes at a family-systems level rather than at an individual level. The family is seen as a biosocial system with deeply entrenched transactional patterns which function to preserve equilibrium (Brown, 1972). However, the transactional patterns may be maladaptive and family equilibrium may be achieved at the expense of a family member, usually the identified patient. The underlying assumption of the family-therapy approach is that the development of symptoms in any member of the family is a manifestation of transactional problems within the family (Whiteside, 1979). These symptoms may mask the actual difficulties and may serve to maintain equilibrium within the family system. For example, a child's symptoms may be related to covert marital problems between the parents but the symptoms may serve to protect the parents from their own conflict by maintaining a focus on the child. As long as the child remains the "patient," the family equilibrium is maintained.

Family therapy involves a process of identifying and modifying maladaptive familial patterns that perpetuate emotional problems in the child. Through various techniques, the therapist attempts to make gradual shifts in the family equilibrium and encourages healthier interactional modes of communication between family members. The goal of family therapy is to help families adopt stable, healthy transactional patterns by which conflicts are resolved in ways that do not involve symptom formation in the child.

Biofeedback

Biofeedback training is a therapeutic technique by which the patient learns to exercise control over physiological responses which are not ordinarily under voluntary control by receiving information or feedback arising from those responses (Blanchard & Epstein, 1978).

In biofeedback training electrodes connected to a biofeedback machine are placed on a particular part of the patient's body. Detailed information concerning physiological responses such as heartbeat, blood pressure, muscle tension, and brain waves are mirrored back to the patient through an electronic monitoring system. The physiological feedback may be auditory (buzzer, clicks) or visual (meter readings or lights). The goal of biofeedback is to learn self-control over certain physiological states, particularly maladaptive ones (headaches, high blood pressure, etc.).

Although biofeedback has been used primarily with adults, it is rapidly gaining acceptance as a therapeutic alternative with children. Walker (1979) suggested biofeedback as a viable treatment method in children with tension-related disorders. Biofeedback is particularly appropriate for psychosomatic disorders in children (Jay & Wright, 1981). Biofeedback has been reported as a successful treatment of pediatric disorders including asthma (Feldman, 1976), seizures (Seifert & Lubar, 1975), speech disorders (Roll, 1973), and spastic movements (Sachs, Martin, & Fitch, 1972).

Relaxation Training

Relaxation training is considered by many to be a behavioral treatment method although it can be used in conjunction with other forms of psychotherapy. The rationale behind relaxation training is that stress and tension-related symptoms can be alleviated through the reduction of anxiety and tension. It is often used in conjunction with systematic desensitization, biofeedback, and/or hypnosis. Children can be taught relaxation procedures and should be encouraged to practice the exercises frequently at home and in other settings. Tape recorded relaxation series are available (Lupin, 1974) for use at home. Walker (1979) reviewed uses of relaxation training with children.

Hypnotherapy

Olness and Gardner (1978) in an article on uses of hypnotherapy in pediatrics defined hypnosis as "an altered state of consciousness, usually involving relaxation, in which a person develops heightened concentration on a particular idea or image for the purpose of maximizing potential in one or more areas" (p. 228). The literature indicates that children are generally more easily hypnotized than adults (Ambrose, 1968). Even very young preschool children have responded to hypnotherapy for a wide range of physical and psychological problems (Gardner, 1977). Such hypnotizability is likely due to the ease with which many children engage in fantasy and imagination. Because of this inclination, many children may be less resistant to hypnotherapy than other more traditional intervention techniques.

One of the primary values of hypnotherapy with children is the capacity to generate a new sense of mastery that can in turn facilitate rapid relief of disabling symptoms (Williams, 1979). Hypnotherapy has been used with chronically ill children for counteracting pain, anxiety, and nausea (Gardner, 1974a); for enuresis (Olness, 1975); encopresis (Olness, 1976); conduct disorders (Gardner, 1978); and psychogenic epilepsy (Gardner, 1973). Children can be taught to use hypnotic techniques themselves and parents can be used as allies in the treatment (Gardner, 1974b).

Like biofeedback and relaxation therapy, hypnotherapy is not a substitute for comprehensive therapy aimed at modifying environmental influences or resolving intense conflicts (Williams & Singh, 1976). Whether it is used as a conjunctive technique or as a treatment in itself depends on the nature of the problem and the treatment goals.

Parent Consultation

Parent consultation can be a most effective therapeutic intervention for pediatric problems. Advantages over other methods include economy of time and expense, practicality, and the ability to closely monitor a child's psychological condition (Wright, Schaefer, & Solomons, 1979). Parents are often less resistant to consultation than to individual therapy for their child. Parent consultation may take a variety of forms: general advice on childrearing practices, explanations of how and why children react to particular life events, explanations of how family factors affect children's adjustment, teaching of behavioral management techniques, and/or supportive reassurance and guidance. Parent consultation may be used as an indirect method of treatment for the child, or as an adjunct to individual child therapy. Parent consultation is often conducted in a time-limited series of group sessions for parents.

Reviews of parent consultation methods generally indicate that it is an effective intervention modality (Johnson & Katz, 1973; O'Dell, 1974). Barnard (1976) found that a training program in which parents were taught to implement a behavioral approach was more effective than conventional treatment strategies. Research also has demonstrated that parents of autistic children can effectively use operant techniques to remove maladaptive behavior and to improve communication in their own children (Lovaas, Schreibman, & Koegel, 1974; Schopler, 1971).

Special Education

Psychotic children often need a multifaceted treatment approach which includes special educational approaches as well as more traditional psychologically oriented intervention. Educational approaches with psychotic children are usually based on a highly structured program which uses behaviorally oriented methodology. Specific training is directed toward improving basic perceptual, cognitive, and language skills. Goals for training are selected after a thorough and systematic evaluation of developmental functioning in a variety of areas. Rutter (1970) suggested three aims of education for the autistic child: (1) preventing the development of secondary handicaps; (2) finding approaches to education that circumvent the primary handicaps; and (3) finding techniques to aid the development of functions involved in the primary handicaps.

For example, a child with good visual discrimination skills and no language might be taught language through visual stimuli. Such a procedure might entail teaching the child to match pictures with common objects and then gradually use the picture to request that the child go to get the objects. Later written words might be paired with the pictures and then used to communicate simple instructions.

Residential Treatment

For severely disturbed children, residential treatment may be the treatment of choice. It is indicated for children with antisocial disorders, severe impulse disorders, and psychotic disorders who cannot be managed on an outpatient basis (Stone, 1979) and is usually recommended after a number of outpatient interventions have been tried unsuccessfully.

Residential treatment centers provide a structured environment in which limits are placed on behavior and acting-out behavior is dealt with therapeutically as it occurs. The organization and clinical functions of many residential programs are based on principles of behavior modification and behavior therapy. Individual, group, and family therapy are often built into the program. Children in residential settings attend school and specialized instructions may be offered to those with learning problems. "Therapeutic tutoring," an approach which combines academic and emotional-therapeutic learning, is often a part of residential educational programs. The goal of residential treatment programs is to improve the child's emotional and social adjustment so that he or she can function adaptively at home and in the community. Follow-up and outpatient treatment after discharge can be critical in maintaining treatment gains.

PERSONAL PERSPECTIVE

At the beginning of this chapter, objections to current criteria for defining and diagnosing the emotionally exceptional child were considered. Controversy over diagnostic categories focuses on the general issue of diagnosis on the basis of overt behavior versus diagnosis on the basis of intrapsychic dynamics. Those advocating the use of overt behavior as the guideline for classification are frankly skeptical of the unmeasurable processes postulated by the psychodynamic group. The psychodynamic group, on the other hand, criticizes the superficiality of a classification system that fails to account for the fact that similar behavior may arise from different motives. Similar controversies are apparent in the differing opinions regarding treatment.

Underlying the controversy over diagnosis is the more crucial issue of defining the emotionally exceptional child. Central to the resolution of the issue is an understanding of normal development not only in terms of what behaviors or knowledge children display at certain ages but also how they understand that behavior and how they acquire their knowledge at differing stages. An abundance of empirical and theoretical information concerning the normal development of cognitive processes and concept formation has been accumulated by psychologists operating out of the cognitive developmental frameworks of Piaget (1936/1963, 1937/1971, 1946/1962) and Werner (1948). However, this abundance of information seems to have been disregarded for the most part by child clinicians, first because of the traditional insularity between child-clinical practice and academic-developmental research. Santostefano (1980), in a discussion of this problem, reviewed major handbooks on child psychopathology and noted the minor role assigned to the developmental view. Similarly, he found a scarcity of topics with direct clinical relevance in primary texts on child development research. A second factor which has hindered the integration of cognitive developmental views with clinical practice is the strong emphasis of Piagetian research on the child's understanding of the physical environment as opposed to interpersonal or intrapsychic processes.

Studies of psychotic children have been conducted using concepts derived from Piaget's original work on the child's developing understanding of the physical environment (Marks, 1972; Neal, 1966; Serafica, 1971). These studies have been used to present a Piagetian approach to understanding psychotic disorders and to suggest intervention techniques (Cowan, 1978). More recently, however, investigators have begun to use the cognitive-developmental methods and theoretical models to explore the child's developing understanding of social and psychological experiences (Damon, 1977; Flavell, Bottan, Fry, Wright, & Jarvis, 1968; Jurkovic & Selman, 1980; Shantz, 1975; Youniss, 1978). These investigations of the child's developing social cognition have included studies of peer relations, parent–child relations, methods of coping with aggressive feelings, ability to take the perspective of another person, and intrapsychic understanding. The knowledge of the individual's way of structuring interpersonal and intrapsychic processes has been used, in turn, to predict behavior (Gilligan & Belenky, 1980) or to specify treatment approaches (Jurkorvic & Selman, 1980; Santostefano, 1980).

While each of these areas has definite relevance for the study of psychopathology in children, two studies seem of particular interest for clinicians. In the first, Jurkovic and Selman (1980) described five stages of intrapsychic understanding derived from empirical analysis of semistructured interviews with children of varying age levels (preschool to late adolescence). In the earliest stages, the child does not appear to view inner or psychological experience as different from the nature of outer experience and exhibits little awareness that one may intentionally misrepresent inner thoughts or feelings or that one may actually manipulate inner experiences. Children at these lower levels are likely to attribute events or their own feelings to external events (e.g., "The chair was in my way"; "The other kids made me be bad"). Through a series of developmental steps, the child shifts to a view of the self as an active agent in the generation and control of thoughts and feelings but with limitations on self-control imposed by unconscious motives.

The distinctions between the lower and higher levels of intrapsychic understanding are strikingly similar to the differentiating factors between neuroses and personality disorders cited by psychodynamically oriented clinicians (Group for the Advancement of Psychiatry, 1966). Both systems stress the importance of determining the degree to which the child externalizes or internalizes the source of conflict. Unlike the theoretical psychodynamic formulation, however, the developmental stages offered by Jurkovic and Selman are open to empirical replication and offer more precise and consistent knowledge about the sequences and patterns of intrapsychic understanding.

Although many children may show age-appropriate levels of reasoning about interpersonal and intrapsychic processes in general, their reasoning about specific issues which are associated with stressful experiences may be at a lower developmental level. Because of the anxiety associated with the issue, they may then avoid reexamining their reasoning even though the reasoning itself is a continuing source of anxiety. For example, children whose parents divorce during the preschool years may maintain, at a later age, residuals of lower level preoperational thinking in regard to this specific issue, but show higher level reasoning in other areas. Two characteristics of preoperational thought which might be important in this regard are the tendency to attribute causal power over external events to one's own internal feeling states, and the difficulty in distinguishing one's own thoughts and feelings from those of others. The child's affective-cognitive organization of divorce, then, might include such thoughts as being mad at daddy, wishing for an exclusive relationship with mommy, and fearing daddy because he must be angry in return. While this would likely be a common hypothesis of the psychodynamically oriented therapist with such children, the cognitive developmental tradition provides a methodology of empirically verifiable investigation as well as a framework for interpretation of results.

A second study illustrates the potential for predicting clinical outcome by applying cognitive developmental theory to crisis situations. Gilligan and Belenky (1980) compared the psychodynamic view of crisis as a precipitant of regression with the cognitive developmental view of crisis as an impetus for further growth and development. They interviewed pregnant adolescent girls who were in the process of making decisions about abortion. Measures derived from cognitive developmental research on moral judgment were obtained for the girls' level of reasoning about hypothetical situations as well as the actual abortion decisions. Discrepancies between these two measures were calculated yielding three groups: transitional, stable, and at-risk. The transitional group consisted of women whose understanding of the actual decision they made showed more mature structures of thoughts (regardless of whether their decision was for or against an abortion) than were apparent on their responses to the hypothetical dilemmas presented. The stable group showed no structural differences in their thinking about real and hypothetical dilemmas. The women considered at-risk demonstrated thinking about the abortion decision at a less mature level than their thinking about hypothetical problems. In accordance with predictions, one-year follow-up data for the transitional group generally showed increased maturity in reasoning about hypothetical dilemmas *as well as improvement in life situations* (status of educational or occupational roles, interpersonal relationships and overall psychological state). The stable group showed little evidence of change on either dimension while the at-risk group evidenced decrements in reasoning about hypothetical dilemmas along with deterioration in life situation. Although this study is certainly important for its theoretical contribution to the understanding of individuals in crisis, it also suggests that similar techniques could be used to identify those persons in crisis who will require therapeutic intervention to prevent deterioration in functioning. Such an approach might prove helpful in many areas such as rape, divorce, or perhaps even effective contraceptive usage in adolescents.

In addition to predicting clinical outcome of crisis, understanding the patterns and sequences of children's thought should be helpful in planning intervention at an appropriate level. For example, interpretive or reflective statements about feelings or motives which may be associated with a child's actions in therapy may vary in their impact depending upon the child's capacity for social cognitive reasoning. A child functioning at the lower levels of intrapsychic understanding may not grasp even reflective comments about simple feeling states, let alone interpretive statements regarding internal motivation. Rather than labeling the child's lack of response as resistance, a careful analysis of the child's developmental level will enable the therapist to frame comments in a structure which is at or just above the child's level. Again, experienced child therapists may intuitively accomplish such a matching of intervention with developmental level, but a thorough knowledge of cognitive-developmental stages enables the therapist to make this match with more precision.

Finally, the established stages of social cognitive reasoning offer promise as outcome measures for psychotherapy with children. While the content of a child's disturbance may vary infinitely according to various environmental factors, the study of the underlying structure of the child's thought yields common characteristics for children at different levels. Most important, these levels rest on an empirical foundation, can be reliably demonstrated, and appear to be related to a wide range of positive developmental factors.

The current thinking among cognitively oriented clinicians (Arnold, 1970; Lazarus, 1968) is that cognition rather than emotion is basic to the regulation and maintenance of behavior. For these theorists, emotions are a function of cognitive appraisal or the individual's interpretation and evaluation of a situation. The understanding of psychological disorders must then be sought in cognition. Although the importance of cognitive appraisal has been recognized in work with children (e.g., cognitive behavior therapy; Meichenbaum, 1977), a developmental understanding of the changing structure of cognition at different ages has been notably lacking. It seems likely the inclusion and integration of a cognitive developmental framework can only serve to increase the reliability of classification as well as the specificity of treatment approaches. As a side benefit, it may also help to bridge the remaining gap between the cognitive behaviorists and the psychodynamicists.

SUMMARY

Emotional disturbance in children is a generic term encompassing a wide range of problem behaviors and symptom clusters. Disturbance may be manifested in mild, encapsulated forms or in grossly maladaptive patterns. A characteristic common to most forms of emotional disturbance is maladaptive behavior concomitant with internal distress for the child and/or external conflict with the environment (peers, parents, teachers). Classification in childhood psychopathology is controversial since most classification systems do not satisfy the criteria of adequate reliability and validity. Furthermore, the placing of diagnostic labels on children has become a major issue of controversy because of the potential abuses and negative implications reported in the literature. Numerous diagnostic syndromes (neuroses, psychoses, etc.) are described which differ according to behavioral characteristics, etiology, and treatment potential. A broad-based eclectic treatment approach is advocated since no one approach has been proven superior across disorders. Furthermore, family and clinical resources may dictate one treatment approach as opposed to another.

The literature is replete with descriptions and reports of various treatment approaches ranging from long-term intensive intervention to brief, narrowly defined treatment, many of which offer promise and optimism concerning effective remediation. Carefully controlled research is sorely needed to document the efficacy and cost/benefit ratios of various treatment approaches. Finally, understanding of psychopathology in children can be enhanced by more extensive integration of knowledge concerning normal developmental cognitive processes with traditional psychodynamic views. Furthermore, cognitive theories are more amenable to empirical verification and offer promise in designating treatment planning and treatment outcome measures.

REFERENCES

Adams, P. L. Psychoneuroses. In J. D. Noshpitz (Ed.), *Basic handbook of child psychiatry* (Vol. 2). New York: Basic Books, 1979.

Ainsworth, M. D. S. The development of infant-mother attachment. In B. M. Caldwell & H. N. Riccuitt (Eds.), *Review of child development research* (Vol. 3). Chicago: University of Chicago Press, 1973.

Ambrose, G. Hypnosis in the treatment of children. *American Journal of Clinical Hypnosis*, 1968, *11*(1), 1–5.

American Psychiatric Association DSM-III. *Diagnostic and statistical manual of mental disorders*. Washington, D.C.: APA, 1980.

Arnold, M. B. *Feelings and emotions*. New York: Academic, 1970.

Anthony, E. J. Neuroses of children. In A. M. Freedman & H. I. Kaplan (Eds.), *The child: His psychological and cultural development* (Vol. 2). New York: Atheneum, 1971.

Bahn, A., Chandler, C. A., & Eisenberg, L. Diagnostic characteristics related to services in psychiatric clinics for children. *Milbank Memorial Fund Quarterly*, 1962, *15*, 289–318.

Bandura, A. *Principles of behavior modification*. New York: Holt, Rinehart, & Winston, 1969.

Bandura, A. *Aggression: A social learning analysis*. Englewood Cliffs, N.J.: Prentice-Hall, 1973.

Barnard, J. D. *The family training program: Short and long-term evaluations*. Paper presented at the Annual Meeting of the American Psychological Association, Washington, D.C., September 1976.

Bartak, L., Rutter, M., & Cox, A. A comparative study of infantile autism and specific developmental receptive language disorder. 1. The children. *British Journal of Psychiatry*, 1975, *126*, 127–145.

Becker, W. C. Consequences of different kinds of parental discipline. In M. L. Hoffman & L. W. Hoffman (Eds.), *Review of child development research*. New York: Russell Sage, 1964.

Beiser, M. Etiology of mental disorders: Sociocultural aspects. In B. Wolman (Ed.), *Manual of child psychopathology*. New York: McGraw-Hill, 1972.

Bell, R. O. An interpretation of the direction of effects in studies of socialization. *Psychological Review*, 1968, *75*, 81–95.

Bender, L. Childhood schizophrenia: Clinical study of 100 schizophrenic children. *American Journal of Orthopsychiatry*, 1947, *17*, 40–56.

Bettelheim, B. *The uses of enchantment: The meaning and importance of fairy tales*. New York: Knopf, 1976.

Blanchard, E., & Epstein, L. Clinical applications of biofeedback. In M. Hersen, R. M. Eisler, & P. M. Miller (Eds.), *Progress in behavior modification* (Vol. 4). New York: Academic, 1978.

Bloch, D. A., Silber, E., & Perry, S. E. Some factors in the emotional reaction of children to disaster. *American Journal of Psychiatry*, 1956, *113*, 416–422.

Boullin, P., Coleman, M., & O'Brien, A. Abnormalities in platelet 5-hydroxytryptamine efflux in patients with infantile autism. *Nature*, 1970, *226*, 371–372.

Bower, E. *The education of emotionally handicapped children*. Sacramento: California State Department of Education, 1961.

Bower, E. M. *Early identification of emotionally handicapped children in school* (2nd ed.). Springfield, Ill.: Charles C. Thomas, 1969.

Bowlby, J. Forty-four juvenile thieves. *International Journal of Psychoanalysis*, 1944, *25*, 1–57.

Bowlby, J. *Attachment and loss*. New York: Basic Books, 1969.

Brown, S. L. Family group therapy. In B. Wolman (Ed.), *Manual of child psychopathology*. New York: McGraw-Hill, 1972.

Bryson, C. Q. Systematic identification of perceptual disabilities in autistic children. *Perceptual and Motor Skills*, 1970, *31*, 239–246.

Burt, C., & Howard, M. The nature and causes of maladjustment among children of school age. *British Journal of Psychology*, 1952, *5*, 39–59.

Carek, D. J. Individual psychodynamically oriented therapy. In J. D. Noshpitz (Ed.), *Basic handbook of child psychiatry* (Vol. 3). New York: Basic Books, 1979.

Cavan, R. S., & Ferdinand, T. N. *Juvenile delinquency* (3rd ed.). New York: Lippincott, 1975.

Chess, S., & Hassibi, M. *Principles of practice of child psychiatry*. New York: Plenum, 1978.

Clarizio, H. F., & McCoy, G. F. *Behavior disorders in childhood* (2nd ed.). New York: Thomas Crowell, 1976.

Clarke-Stewart, A. K. Interactions between mothers and their young children: Characteristics and consequences. *Monographs of the Society for Research in Child Development* (Serial No. 153), 1973, *38*, 6–7.

Cleveland, E. J., & Longaker, W. D. Neurotic patterns in the family. In A. H. Leighton, J. A. Clausen, & R. N. Wilson (Eds.), *Explorations in social psychiatry*. New York: Basic Books, 1957.

Cohen, A., Filipczak, J., Slavin, J., & Boren, J. *Programming interpersonal curricula for adolescents*. Silver Spring, Md.: Institute for Behavioral Research, 1971.

Colbert, E. G., Koegler, R. R., & Markham, C. H. Vestibular dysfunction in childhood schizophrenia. *Archives of General Psychiatry*, 1956, *1*, 600–617.

Cowan, P. *Piaget with feeling: Cognitive, social and emotional dimensions*. New York: Hold, Rinehart & Winston, 1978.

Damon, W. *The social world of the child*. San Francisco: Jossey-Bass, 1977.

Deutsch, M. P. (Ed.). *The disadvantaged child*. New York: Basic Books, 1967.

Eisenberg, L. School phobia: A study in the communication of anxieties. *American Journal of Psychiatry*, 1958, *114*, 712–718.

Ekstein, R. (Ed.). *Children of time and space, of action and impulse*. New York: Appleton-Century-Crofts, 1966.

Ekstein, R. Functional psychosis in children. In A. M. Freedman, H. Kaplan, & B. Sadock (Eds.), *Comprehensive textbook of psychiatry* (Vol. 2). Baltimore: Williams & Wilkins, 1975.

Fay, W. H., & Schuler, A. L. *Emerging language in autistic children*. Baltimore: University Park Press, 1980.

Feldman, G. M. The effect of biofeedback training on respiratory resistance of asthmatic children. *Psychosomatic Medicine*, 1976, *38*, 27–34.

Fish, B. Limitations of the new nomenclature for children's disorders. In A. M. Freedman & H. I. Kaplan (Eds.), *The child: His psychological and cultural development* (Vol. 2). New York: Atheneum, 1971.

Fixsen, D. L., Phillips, E. L., Phillips, E. A., & Wolf, M. M. *The teaching-family model of group home treatment.* Paper presented at the annual meeting of the American Psychological Association, Honolulu, Hawaii, September 1972.

Flavell, J. H., Bottan, P., Fry, C., Wright, J., & Jarvis, P. *The development of role-taking and communication skills in children.* New York: Wiley, 1968.

Folstein, S., & Rutter, M. Infantile autism: A genetic study of 21 twin pairs. *Journal of Child Psychology and Psychiatry,* 1977, *18,* 297–321.

Fowle, A. Atypical leukocyte patterns of schizophrenic children. *Archives of General Psychiatry,* 1968, *8,* 666–680.

Franks, C. Behavior therapy, psychology, and the psychiatrist: Contributions, evaluations, and overview. *American Journal of Orthopsychiatry,* 1965, *85,* 145–151.

Freeman, R. Special education and the EEG: Marriage of convenience. *Journal of Special Education,* 1967, *2,* 61–73.

Freud, A., & Burlingham, D. T. *Infants without families.* New York: International Universities Press, 1944.

Gardner, G. G. Use of hypnosis for psychogenic epilepsy in a child. *American Journal of Clinical Hypnosis,* 1973, *15*(3), 166–169.

Gardner, G. G. Hypnosis with children. *International Journal of Clinical and Experimental Hypnosis,* 1974, *22,* 20–38. (a)

Gardner, G. G. Parents: Obstacles or allies in child hypnotherapy. *American Journal of Clinical Hypnosis,* 1974, *17*(1), 44–49. (b).

Gardner, G. G. Hypnosis with infants and preschool children. *American Journal of Clinical Hypnosis,* 1977, *19*(3), 158–162.

Gardner, G. G. Hypnotherapy in the management of childhood habit disorders. *Journal of Pediatrics,* 1978, *92*(5), 838–840.

Gardner, R. A. Therapeutic communication with children: *The mutual story-telling technique.* New York: Science House, 1971.

Gilbert, G. M. A survey of "referral problems" in metropolitan child guidance centers. *Journal of Clinical Psychology,* 1957, *13,* 37–42.

Gilligan, C., & Belenky, M. F. A naturalistic study of abortion decisions. In R. L. Selman & R. Yando (Eds.), *New directions for child development: Clinical developmental psychology* (No. 7). San Francisco: Jossey-Bass, 1980.

Goldfarb, W. Emotional and intellectual consequences of psychologic deprivation in infancy: A reevaluation. In P. M. Hoch & J. Zubin (Eds.), *Psychopathology of childhood.* New York: Grune & Stratton, 1955.

Graham, P., Rutter, M., & George, S. Temperamental characteristics as predictors of behavior disorders in children. *American Journal of Orthopsychiatry,* 1973, *43*(3), 328–339.

Green, A. M. Psychopathology of abused children. *American Academy of Child Psychiatry,* 1978, *17*(1), 92–103.

Group for the Advancement of Psychiatry. *Psychopathological disorders in childhood: Theoretical considerations and a proposed classification* (Vol. 6, Report No. 62). New York: GAP, 1966.

Hauser, S., Delong, G., & Rosman, N. Pneumographic findings in the infantile autism syndrome: A correlation with temporal lobe disease. *Brain,* 1975, *98,* 667–688.

Hewett, F. M., & Forness, S. R. *Education of exceptional learners*. Boston: Allyn & Bacon, 1974.

Hewitt, L. E., & Jenkins, R. L. *Fundamental patterns of maladjustment: The dynamics of their origin*. Springfield: State of Illinois, 1946.

Hollingshead, A. B., & Redlich, F. C. *Social class and mental illness: A community study*. New York: Wiley, 1958.

Hutt, C., Forrest, S. J., & Richer, J. Cardiac arrhythmia and behavior in autistic children. *Acta Psychiatrica Scandinavica, 1975, 51,* 361–372.

Jackson, B. Management of the tracheostomy in cases of tetanus neonatorum treated with intermittent positive pressure respiration. *Journal of Laryngology,* 1963, *77,* 541–554.

Jauch, C. The one-part family. *Journal of Clinical Child Psychology,* 1977, *6,* 30–32.

Jay, S., & Wright, L. Psychosomatic disorders in children. In C. J. Golden, B. Graber, F. Strider, M. A. Strider, & S. Alcaparras (Eds.), *Applied techniques in behavioral medicine and psychology*. New York: Grune & Stratton, 1981.

Jesness, C. F., DeRisi, W. J., McCormick, P. M., & Wedge, R. F. *The youth center research project*. Sacramento, Calif.: American Justice Institute, 1972.

Johnson, A. M. School phobia workshop, discussion. *American Journal of Orthopsychiatry,* 1957, *27,* 307–309.

Johnson, C. A., & Katz, R. C. Using parents as change agents for their children: A review. *Journal of Child Psychology and Psychiatry,* 1973, *14,* 181–200.

Jurkovic, G. J., & Selman, R. J. A developmental analysis of intrapsychic understanding: Treating emotional disturbances in children. In R. L. Selman & R. Yando (Eds.), *New directions for child development: Clinical-developmental psychology* (No. 7). San Francisco: Jossey-Bass, 1980.

Kallman, J. F. The genetic theory of schizophrenia: An analysis of 691 schizophrenic twin index families. *American Journal of Psychiatry,* 1946, *103,* 209–322.

Kanner, L. Autistic disturbances of affective contact. *Nervous Child,* 1943, *2,* 217–250.

Kauffman, J. M. *Characteristics of children's behavior disorders*. Columbus, Ohio: Charles E. Merrill, 1977.

Kelly, E. W. School phobia: A review of theory and treatment. *Psychology in the Schools,* 1973, *10,* 33–41.

Kennedy, W. A. School phobia: Rapid treatment of fifty cases. *Journal of Abnormal Psychology,* 1965, *70,* 285–289.

Kessler, J. W. *Psychopathology of childhood*. Englewood Cliffs, N.J.: Prentice-Hall, 1966.

Kessler, J. W. Neurosis in childhood. In B. Wolman (Ed.), *Manual of child psychopathology*. New York: McGraw-Hill, 1972.

Kohlberg, L., LaCrosse, J., & Ricks, D. The predictability of adult mental health from childhood behavior. In B. Wolman (Ed.), *Manual of child psychopathology*. New York: McGraw-Hill, 1972.

Kolvin, I., Ounsted, C., Humphrey, M., & McNay, A. The phenomenology of childhood psychoses. *British Journal of Psychiatry,* 1971, *118,* 385–395.

Korchin, J. G. *Modern clinical psychology*. New York: Basic Books, 1976.

Kraft, I. A. Group therapy. In J. D. Noshpitz (Ed.), *Basic handbook of child psychiatry* (Vol. 3). New York: Basic Books, 1979.

Lachman, S. J. *Psychosomatic disorders: A behavioristic interpretation*. New York: Wiley, 1972.

Lazarus, R. S. Emotions and adaptation: Conceptual and empirical relations. In W. J. Arnold (Ed.), *Nebraska symposium on motivation*. Lincoln: University of Nebraska Press, 1968.

LeLord, G., Laffont, F., Jusseanume, P., & Stephant, J. L. Comparative study of conditioning of averaged evoked responses by coupling sound and light in normal and autistic children. *Psychophysiology,* 1973, *10,* 415–425.

Lesser, S. R. Psychoanalysis with children. In B. B. Wolman (Ed.), *Manual of child psychopathology*. New York: McGraw-Hill, 1972.

Leton, D. A. Assessment of school phobia. *Mental Hygiene,* 1962, *46,* 256–264.

Levinson, B. Understanding the child with school phobia. *Exceptional Children,* 1962, *28,* 393–398.

Lidz, T., Fleck, S., & Cornelison, A. *Schizophrenia and the family*. New York: International Universities Press, 1966.

Lipowski, Z. J. Review of consultation psychiatry and psychosomatic medicine. 3. Theoretical issues. *Psychosomatic Medicine,* 1968, *30*(4), 395–422.

Lovaas, O., Schreibman, L., Koegel, R., & Rehm, R. Selective responding by autistic children to multiple sensory input. *Journal of Abnormal Psychology,* 1971, *77,* 211–222.

Lovaas, I., Schreibman, L., & Koegel, R. A behavior modification approach to the treatment of autistic children. *Journal of Autism and Childhood Schizophrenia,* 1974, *4,* 111–129.

Lupin, M. *Peace, harmony, and awareness*. Houston: Self-Management Tapes, 1974.

Lynn, B. *Structured doll play test*. Denver: Test Developments, 1959.

MacFarlane, J. From infancy to adulthood. *Childhood Education,* 1963, *39,* 336–342.

Malone, C. A. Safety first: Comments on the influence of external danger in the lives of children of disorganized families. *American Journal of Orthopsychiatry,* 1966, *36,* 3–12.

Markita, K. The age of onset of childhood schizophrenia. *Folia Psychiatric et Neurologica Japonica,* 1966, *20,* 111–121.

Marks, E. Slow learning children. *Australian Journal on the Education of Backward Children,* 1972, *19,* 92–101.

May, J. G. Nosology and diagnosis. In J. D. Noshpitz (Ed.), *Basic handbook of child psychiatry*. New York: Basic Books, 1979.

McDermott, J., Harrison, S., Schrager, J., & Wilson, P. Social class and mental illness in children: Observation of blue-collar families. *American Journal of Orthopsychiatry,* 1965, *35,* 500–508.

Mednick, S. A., & Schulsinger, F. Studies of children at high risk for schizophrenia. In S. A. Mednick & F. Schulsinger (Eds.), *Genetics environment, and psychopathology*. New York: American Elsevier, 1974.

Meeks, J. E. Behavioral and antisocial disorders. In J. D. Noshpitz (Ed.), *Basic handbook of child psychiatry* (Vol. 2). New York: Basic Books, 1979.

Meichenbaum, D. *Cognitive behavior modification,* New York: Plenum, 1977.

Minuchin, S., Montalvo, B., Guerney, B. G., Rosman, B. L., & Schumer, F. *Families of the slums: An exploration of their structure and treatment.* New York: Basic Books, 1967.

Minuchin, S., Montalvo, B., Guerney, B. G., Rosman, B. L., & Schumer, F. *Families context.* Cambridge, Mass.: Harvard University Press, 1978.

Morse, W. C., Cutler, R. L., & Fink, A. M. *Public school classes for the emotionally handicapped: A research analysis.* Washington, D.C.: Council for Exceptional Children, 1964.

Nagera, H., & Benson, R. M. Normality as a syndrome. In J. D. Noshpitz (Ed.), *Basic handbook of child psychiatry* (Vol. 2). New York: Basic Books, 1979.

Neal, J. Egocentrism in institutionalized and noninstitutionalized children. *Child Development,* 1966, *37,* 97–101.

O'Dell, S. Training parents in behavior modification: A review. *Psychological Bulletin,* 1974, *81,* 418–433.

Offer, D., & Sabshin, M. *Normality: Theoretical and clinical aspects of mental health.* New York: Basic Books, 1966.

Olness, K. N. Treatment of enuresis with self-hypnosis: An evaluation of forty cases. *Clinical Pediatrics,* 1975, *14,* 273–279.

Olness, K. N. Autohypnosis in functional megacolon in children. *American Journal of Clinical Hypnosis,* 1976, *19,* 28–32.

Olness, K. N., & Gardner, G. G. Some guidelines for uses of hypnotherapy in pediatrics. *Pediatrics,* 1978, *62*(2), 228–233.

Ornitz, E. M., & Ritvo, E. R. Perceptual inconstancy in early infantile autism. *Archives of General Psychiatry,* 1968, *18,* 79–98.

Ornitz, E. M., Ritvo, E. R., Brown, M. D., LaFranchi, S., Parmelee, T., & Walker, R. D. The EEG and the rapid eye movments during REM sleep in normal and autistic children. *Electroencephalography and Clinical Neurophysiology,* 1969, *26,* 167–175.

Pasamanick, B., & Knobloch, H. Brain damage and reproductive causality. *American Journal of Orthopsychiatry,* 1960, *30,* 298–305.

Patterson, C. M. *Counseling and psychotherapy: Theory and practice.* New York: Harper, 1959.

Patterson, G. R., Cobb, J. A., & Ray, R. S. Direct intervention in the classroom: A set of procedures for the aggressive child. In F. W. Clark, D. R. Evans, & L. A. Hammerlynck (Eds.), *Implementing behavioral programs in schools and clinics.* Champaign, Ill.: Research Press, 1972.

Peterson, D. R., Quay, H. C., & Cameron, G. R. Personality and background factors in juvenile delinquency as inferred from questionnaire responses. *Journal of Consulting Psychology,* 1959, *23,* 392–399.

Piaget, J. *The origins of intelligence in the child.* New York: Norton, 1963 (originally published, 1936).

Piaget, J. *The construction of reality in the child.* New York: Ballantine, 1971 (originally published, 1937).

Piaget, J. *Play, dreams and imitation in childhood.* New York: Norton, 1962 (originally published, 1946).

Piggott, L. A. Overview of selected basic research in autism. *Journal of Autism and Developmental Disorders,* 1979, *9,* 199–218.

Pond, D. Psychiatric aspects of epileptic-brain damaged children. *British Medical Journal,* 1961, *2,* 1377–1382, 1454–1459.

Prugh, D. Toward an understanding of psychosomatic concepts in relation to illness in children. In A. J. Solnit & S. Provence (Eds.), *Modern perspectives in child development.* New York: International University Press, 1963.

Quay, H. C., Peterson, D. R., & Consalvi, C. The interpretation of three personality factors in juvenile delinquency. *Journal of Consulting Psychology,* 1960, *24,* 555.

Ricks, D. N., & Wing, L. Language communication and the use of symbols in normal and autistic children. *Journal of Autism and Childhood Schizophrenia,* 1975, *5,* 191–222.

Ritvo, G. R., Ornitz, E. M., Eviator, A., Markham, C. H., Brown, M. B., & Mason, A. Decreased postrotatory nystagmus in early infantile autism. *Neurology,* 1969, *19,* 653, 658.

Ritvo, E., Yuwiler, A., Geller, E., Ornitz, E., Saeger, K., & Plotkin, S. Increased blood serotonin and platelets in early infantile autism. *Archives of General Psychiatry,* 1970, *23,* 566–572.

Robins, L. N., West, P., & Herjaniz, B. Arrests and delinquency in two generations: A study of urban families and their children. *Journal of Child Psychology and Psychiatry,* 1975, *16,* 125–140.

Roll, D. L., Modification of nasal resonance in cleft palate children by informative feedback. *Journal of Applied Behavioral Analysis,* 1973, *6,* 397–403.

Rosen, E., & Gregory, I. *Abnormal psychology.* Philadelphia: Saunders, 1965.

Rosenbaum, M., & Kraft, I. A. Group psychotherapy for children. In B. Wolman (Ed.), *Manual of child psychopathology.* New York: McGraw-Hill, 1972.

Rutter, M. Speech disorders in a series of autistic children. In A. W. Franklin (Ed.), *Children with communication problems.* London: Pitman, 1965.

Rutter, M. Behavioral and cognitive characteristics of a series of psychotic children. In J. Wing (Ed.), *Early childhood autism.* London: Pergamon, 1966.

Rutter, M. Concepts of autism: A review of research. *Journal of Child Psychology and Psychiatry,* 1968, *9,* 1–25.

Rutter, M. Autism: Educational issue. *Special Education,* 1970, *59,* 6–10.

Rutter, M. Childhood schizophrenia reconsidered. *Journal of Autism and Childhood Schizophrenia,* 1972, *2,* 315–337.

Rutter, M. The development of infantile autism. *Psychological Medicine,* 1974, *4,* 147–163.

Rutter, M. Diagnosis and definition. In M. Rutter & E. Schopler (Eds.), *Autism: A reappraisal of concepts and treatment.* New York: Plenum, 1978.

Rutter, M., Bartak, L., & Newman, S. Autism: A central disorder of cognition and language? In M. Rutter (Ed.), *Infantile autism: Concepts, characteristics, and treatment.* Edinburgh: Churchill and Livingstone, 1971.

Rutter, M., Graham, P., & Yule, W. *A neuropsychiatric study in childhood.* Philadelphia: Lippincott, 1970.

Sachs, D. A., Martin, J. E., & Fitch, J. L. The effect of visual feedback on a digital exercise in a functionally deaf cerebral palsied child. *Journal of Behavior Therapy and Experimental Psychiatry,* 1972, *3,* 217–222.

Santostefano, S. Clinical child psychology: The need for developmental principles. In R. L. Selman & R. Yando (Eds.), *New directions for child development: Clinical-developmental psychology* (No. 7). San Francisco: Jossey-Bass, 1980.

Schaefer, C. E., & Milman, H. L. *Therapies for children.* San Francisco: Jossey-Bass, 1977.

Schain, R., & Freedman, D. Studies on 5-hydroxyindole metabolism in autistic and other mentally retarded children. *Journal of Pediatrics,* 1961, *58,* 315–320.

Schopler, E. Developmental therapy by parents with their own autistic child. In M. Rutter (Ed.), *Infantile autism: Concepts, characteristics and treatment.* London: Churchill, 1971.

Schultz, E. W., Salvia, J. A., & Feinn, J. Prevalence of behavioral symptoms in rural elementary school children. *Journal of Abnormal Child Psychology,* 1974, *2,* 17–24.

Schwartz, S., & Johnson, J. H. *Psychopathology of childhood.* New York: Pergamon, 1981.

Seifert, A. R., & Lubar, J. F. Prediction of epileptic seizures through EEG biofeedback training. *Biological Psychology,* 1975, *3,* 157–184.

Selby, J. W., & Calhoun, L. G. Psychosomatic phenomena: An extension of Wright. *American Psychologist,* 1978, *33*(4), 396–398.

Serafica, F. C. Object concept in deviant children. *American Journal of Orthopsychiatry,* 1971, *41,* 473–482.

Shantz, C. U. The development of social cognition. In E. M. Hetherington (Ed.), *Review of child development research* (Vol. 5). Chicago: University of Chicago Press, 1975.

Shaw, C. R., & Lucas, A. R. *The psychiatric disorders of childhood* (2nd ed.). New York: Appleton-Century-Crofts, 1970.

Short, J. K. Juvenile delinquency: The sociocultural context. In L. W. Hoffman & M. L. Hoffman (Eds.), *Review of child development research* (Vol. 2). New York: Russell Sage, 1966.

Spitz, R. A., & Wolf, K. Anaclitic depression. *Psychoanalytic Study of the Child,* 1946, *3,* 313–342.

Steg, J. P., & Rappaport, J. L. Minor physical anomalies in normal neurotic, learning disabled and severely disturbed children. *Journal of Autism and Childhood Schizophrenia,* 1975, *5,* 299–307.

Stone, L. A. Residential treatment. In S. I. Harrison (Ed.), *Basic handbook of child psychiatry* (Vol. 3). New York: Basic Books, 1979.

Stubbs, E. G. Autistic children exhibit undetectable hemagglutination-inhibition antibody titers despite previous rubella vaccination. *Journal of Autism and Childhood Schizophrenia,* 1976, *6,* 269–274.

Student, M., & Sohmer, H. Evidence from auditory nerve and brainstem evoked responses for an organic brain lesion in children with autistic traits. *Journal of Autism and Childhood Schizophrenia,* 1978, *8,* 13–20.

Tanguay, P. Clinical and electrophysiological research. In E. Ritvo, B. Freeman, E. Ornitz, & P. Tanguay (Eds.), *Autism: diagnosis, current research, and management.* New York: Spectrum, 1976.

Thomas, A., & Chess, S. *Temperament and development.* New York: Brunner/ Mazel, 1977.

Thomas, A., Chess, S., & Birch, H. G. *Temperament and behavior disorders in children.* New York: New York University Press, 1968.

U.S. Office of Education. *Estimated number of handicapped children in the United States, 1974–1975.* Washington, D.C.: U.S. Office of Education, 1975.

Waldrup, K. R. Delinquent teenage types. *British Journal of Criminology,* 1967, *714,* 371–380.

Walker, C. E. Behavioral intervention in a pediatric setting. In J. R. McNamara (Ed.), *Behavioral approaches to medicine.* New York: Plenum, 1979.

Weakland, J. The "double-bind" hypothesis of schizophrenia and three-party interaction. In D. D. Jackson (Ed.), *The etiology of schizophrenia.* New York: Basic Books, 1960.

Werner, H. *Comparative psychology of mental development.* New York: Follett, 1948.

Werry, J. S. Organic factors. In H. C. Quay & J. S. Werry (Eds.), *Psychopathological disorders of childhood* (2nd ed.). New York: Wiley, 1979.

Werry, J. S., & Wollersheim, J. P. Behavior therapy with children: A broad overview. In H. H. Barton & S. S. Barton (Eds.), *Children and their parents in brief therapy.* New York: Behavioral Publications, 1973.

White, P., DeMyer, W., & DeMyer, M. EEG abnormalities in early childhood schizophrenia: A double-blind study of psychiatrically disturbed and normal children during promazine sedation. *American Journal of Psychiatry,* 1964, *120,* 950–958.

Whiteside, M. F. Family therapy. In S. I. Harrison (Ed.), *Basic handbook of child psychiatry* (Vol. 3). New York: Basic Books, 1979.

Wikler, A., Dixon, J., & Parker, J. Brain function in problem children and controls: Psychometric, neurological, and electroencephalographic comparisons. *American Journal of Psychiatry,* 1970, *127,* 634–655.

Williams, D. T. Hypnosis as a psychotherapeutic adjunct. In S. I. Harrison (Eds.), *Basic handbook of child psychiatry* (Vol. 3). New York: Basic Books, 1979.

Williams, D. T., & Singh, M. Hypnosis as a facilitating therapeutic adjunct in child psychiatry. *Journal of American Academy of Child Psychiatry,* 1976, *15(2),* 326–342.

Wing, L. *Autistic children: A guide for parents and professionals.* New York: Brunner/Mazel, 1972.

Wright, L. Conceptualizing and defining psychosomatic disorders. *American Psychologist,* 1977, *32*(3), 625–628.

Wright, L., & Jimmerson, S. Intellectual sequelae of hemophilus influenzis meningitis. *Journal of Abnormal Psychology,* 1971, *77,* 181–183.

Wright, L., & Jimmerson, S. Intellectual sequelae of Rocky Mountain spotted fever. *Journal of Abnormal Psychology,* 1972, *80,* 315–316.

Wright, L., Schaefer, A. B., & Solomons, G. *Encyclopedia of pediatric psychology.* Baltimore: University Park Press, 1979.

Yarrow, L. J. Maternal deprivation: Toward an empirical and conceptual reevaluation, *Psychological Bulletin,* 1961, *38*(6), 459–490.

Youniss, J. Peer conceptions and peer relations. In W. Damon (Ed.), *New directions for child development research: Social cognition* (No. 1). San Francisco: Jossey-Bass, 1978.

CHAPTER 15

Children with Auditory and Visual Impairment

T. ERNEST NEWLAND

In this chapter we consider jointly psychological, social, and educational aspects of children who have auditory and/or visual impairments. Doing so has merit because many important similarities can be identified and certain significant differences can be more sharply delineated. We are concerned primarily with psychological perspectives and their implications rather than with specific educational procedures and general research summarization.

First, we identify the populations with whom we are concerned—their natures and incidences. Next we identify certain underlying psychological "givens" that must be kept in mind regarding these children. When we consider the crucial nature of their information processing in terms of similarities and differences, the paramount importance of these givens becomes apparent. Ensuing implications figure largely in our consideration of their social and emotional adjustments. We conclude with some beliefs regarding the impaired that we hold important and some comments on research.

OUR POPULATIONS

The age range of the children with whom we are concerned, which in terms of PL 94–142 is from the age of 3 to 21, suggests at once the complexity of what confronts us—a range both from essential dependence to at least the beginning of presumed independence and from the early stages of acquiring symbolic adequacy to that which is vital to effective social functioning. It would seem logical to explore equally fully the psychosocioeducational problems of these children at the pre- and primary-school range, at the later educational range up to high school, and at the high school, beginning-adulthood range. However, because of their importance, major attention will be given to the first two levels; carryover implications regarding the third level will receive some attention.

Reprinted by permission of Bo Brown.

The overall procedure used to identify children who are auditorially and visually impaired is fundamentally the same as that used with respect to all exceptional children: first, a gross screening, formal or otherwise, in order to identify candidates for the exceptionality of concern and, second, more refined individual ascertainment of the nature and extent of their acuity problems. Basically the approach involves ascertaining whether the subject responds to a stimulus (or stimuli) of known character(s) and magnitude(s). This commonality aside, it is necessary to consider separately our two kinds of populations. In doing so, we consider only rather grossly the examination procedures and problems. Doing so more fully has been the concern of books.

The Auditorially Impaired

Hearing is a phenomenon that too quickly tends to be regarded as a totality—we hear or we don't hear. For some, like the totally deaf, such a perception is reasonably valid. But hearing is actually a matter of degree. Auditory acuity is a continuum ranging from full and complete sensitivity to sound at one end to complete lack of that sensitivity at the other end. But it is more complicated that that. Spoken speech is composed of sounds which involve a mixture of frequencies. A high-pitched speaker may not be heard by one person even though that person hears sounds at lower frequencies; or the reverse may be true—a person may not hear all or most of the speech of a low-pitched talker even though he hears sounds at higher frequencies. A still further possible complication exists with respect to the time at which hearing loss occurs: children who have no hearing before they are conventionally exposed to speech communication (the prelingual deaf) have more serious problems than do those whose hearing loss occurs after that. Excluding times when they are fully asleep, children may not react or respond to conventional auditory stimuli because they are deeply involved in what they are doing. Conditions such as these must be kept in mind when judgments are made informally about children's hearing.

The existence of conditions such as these makes particularly important the formal determination of the nature of a child's hearing. With very young children, failure to respond, under suitable nondistracting conditions, to the speech of others or to bells, snappers, and the clashing of physical objects can be taken as suggestive of hearing loss, but the possibilities of false positives or false negatives must be recognized. Wax or objects in the ear canal and the presence of certain ear infections can yield false positives; and there was that mother of a seven-year-old who had to be placed behind a one-way screen before she would recognize that her child was a very clever speech reader who had a severe hearing loss. Provided the proper facilities are available, infants can be tested audiometrically either by conditioning them to respond to auditory stimuli or by observing their galvanometric responses to sounds. An audiometer is an instrument by means of which sounds of variable intensity can be applied at different frequencies to a subject, which are designated as hertz (Hz) units. In less formal audiometric screening practice, the subject is presented with sounds at four frequencies within the speech range and usually at an intensity of 30 decibels (dB). The more intensive individual examination can yield an audiogram for each ear which shows the amount of loudness needed at each frequency for the subject to hear each sound. Such audiograms can be obtained by both air and bone conduction. In otological clinics, the hearing of speech also is examined.

Limitation in auditory acuity can contribute to serious problems, particularly at the early age levels. Teacher and parental sensitivity to the possibility of a hearing impairment is a must in the case of any child who does not "pay attention." Probably more often than not, other distracting stimuli may be operating, but at times audition can be the factor. Errors in words involving certain letters can be significant cues—those involving high-frequency sounds such as in "e," "i," "a," as in "say," "t," and "d," or low-frequency ones of "m," "n," and "o." But as in other areas of exceptionality, it is indefensible essentially to wait until such children identify themselves. Systematic, formal screening is the better strategy.

In 1940 Pennsylvania had a legally mandated program to test each schoolchild's hearing every three years. (Massachusetts also was doing wide auditory testing of its school children but not under a mandated program.) The children's hearing was screened by means of a group audiometer, and those who appeared to have hearing losses of 30 dB or greater later were examined by means of an individual audiometer. From that time forward the practice of auditory screening has grown, albeit slowly and spottily. Often the screening is done by the speech correctionist. An increasing practice that merits recognition and extension is the involvement of parents who help audiometrists or speech correctionists in systematically locating children having suspected hearing loss. Whether the children thus identified receive the necessary individual examination in the schools or in local clinics depends on the nature of the local facilities available.

Such formal screening is least likely at the high school and adult level. Here more intensive individual audiometric examinations tend to result from individual referrals, which in turn result from the subject's having had particular difficulties in school learning or occupational placement. Diagnostic and placement services under the auspices of vocational rehabilitation become theoretically available; the availability and quality of such services vary considerably.

The extent to which any condition or phenomenon exists depends upon how it is measured and how it is defined. How severe a hearing loss should a child have in order to be regarded as hearing impaired? In only one or both ears? How will that loss be determined? By an audiometric sweep test? By a full audiometric evaluation? Quite generally a child would be regarded as a *candidate* for the impaired category if found, on formal audiometric screening, to have an apparent hearing loss of 30 dB or more in the better ear. Formal individual audiometric examination then determines whether the child still qualifies technically as impaired. It should be noted that a high percentage of children who "qualify" in terms of the 30 dB criterion in the screening examination are later found to have wax, chalk, peas, beans, marbles, or water in their ears, or to have temporary health conditions which reduce their acuity.

The Conference of Executives of American Schools for the Deaf agreed on the definition of a deaf person as one whose hearing is disabled to an extent (usually 70 dB or greater) that precludes the understanding of speech through the ear alone, with or without the use of a hearing aid, and of a hard-of-hearing person as one who is disabled to an extent (usually 35–69 dB) that makes difficult, but does not preclude, the understanding of speech through the ear alone, with or without a hearing aid. It identified the following categories of hearing loss for educational and research purposes: Level I, 35–54 dB—not needing special class or school placement but routinely needing special speech and hearing assistance; Level II, 55–69 dB—occasionally needing special class or school placement but routinely needing special speech, hearing, and language assistance; Level III, 70–89 dB, and Level IV, 90 dB and beyond—needing special placement and routinely requiring special speech, hearing, language, and educational assistance (Frisina, 1974).

The habilitative implications of any such characterization will vary in terms of whether the measurement has been made by means of air conduction or of bone conduction. But from a psychological standpoint the matter of working effectively with hearing impaired children is still more complex since the needs of those who are born with severe hearing impairment are very different from those who have later acquired hearing loss as a result of illness or accident. Although it is possible thus to think of the hearing impaired as a group in terms of such different paramenters, the child with a hearing impairment has to be thought of and worked with predominantly as an individual with a unique pattern of characteristics.

For practical purposes it seems justifiable to anticipate that, generally, some 3% of children of school age can be expected to have hearing loss sufficient to impair their educational performance and social adjustment. This suggests a possibility, overall, of one child in each class of some 30 pupils. Corrective and adjustive aspects are, of course, matters for the otologist and audiometrician. Tremendous advances have been made in the development of individually adapted hearing aids. Interesting and challenging findings have emerged in surveys by the U.S. Health Resources Administration: acuity generally is better in the right ear than in the left ear; acuity is slightly inversely related to annual family income and to family educational level (Roberts, 1975a); hearing trouble is at least twice as frequent in the South as in the Northeast (Roberts, 1975b).

The Visually Impaired

Visual impairment in children is an even more varied condition than is auditory impairment. The term includes: (1) limitation in visual acuity as such; (2) impairments in the field of vision, as when there is scotoma or a spot with no vision or seriously impaired visual reception, and when there is "tunnel vision" with impaired peripheral vision; and (3) impaired color vision, caused by a limitation in the end organs in the retina which are sensitive to different colors.

There are certain visual anomalies with which we are not particularly concerned. *Strabismus,* loosely referred to as "crosseyedness," although it includes internal and external divergence and other conditions, denotes that binocular focusing is abnormal due to faulty eye muscle functioning. Although not technically regarded as a visual impairment, it plays an important role in the young child's learning depth perception, often causing the child to be considered clumsy in running and/or in negotiating steps. Later, if uncorrected, it becomes a socially distracting characteristic of the individual.

In the carefully controlled National Health Administration study (Roberts, 1974) *color vision deficiencies* were found in some 7.5% of the boys and in 0.6% of the girls in the 12–17 age range. The screening was done by means of the Ishihara Test for Color-Blindness (Ishihara, 1960) and the more intensive diagnosis by means of the Hardy-Rand-Rittker Pseudoisochromatic Plates (Hardy, Rand, & Rittker, 1957). Red-green deficiencies were more prevalent than blue-yellow defects. Red-green deficiency was not related significantly to race, age, or income level.

Astigmatism, for which firm prevalence data are lacking, is an impairment of vision which is caused by irregular curvature of the refractive surfaces of the eye causing blurring. It is potentially correctable by glasses.

Nystagmus, perceived by the uninformed as "shiftyeyedness," involving involuntary movement of the eyeballs (horizontal, vertical, rotary, and mixed), accompanied by nearsightedness, and usually part of an albino syndrome, has been found in 0.51% of the 12–17 age population (Roberts, 1975c).

Fortunately the flurry of an alarmingly high incidence of blindness in prematurely born infants around 1963–1964 (and not attributable to heredity) is no longer with us. The condition causing the blindness was *retrolental fibroplasia* (RLF), which resulted from a faulty high-level supply of oxygen provided those infants. Sophisticated systems for monitoring blood-oxygen level have now virtually eliminated the condition. Also brought under at least potential control was rubella, which in 1968–1969 resulted in the birth of large numbers of multiply impaired infants, many of whom had serious visual impairments.

We are concerned primarily with the more prevalent condition of impaired visual acuity. Grossly perceived, there are two major categories of such children—those who are born blind or partially sighted and those who become blind or partially sighted after birth. Heredity has been regarded as responsible for approximately one-half of those who are born blind (Hatfield, 1975).

Visual acuity, like auditory acuity, can be thought of in terms of a continuum from complete absence (literal blindness) to normal vision. To delineate just where a child's visual acuity falls along this continuum involves problems that are more complex than in the case of auditory acuity. At first the approach seems simple: confront the child with stimuli of known magnitudes, under specified conditions, and characterize his acuity in terms of the smallest magnitude to which he responds correctly. The well-known Snellen chart, and its adaptations for small children, has a series of rows of letters which vary systematically in size. One line can be reacted to correctly at 20 feet by a child with "normal" visual acuity, leading to a designation of visual acuity by the Snellen fraction 20/20. Another child who performed satisfactorily only at the line intended for 70 feet would have performance denoted by 20/70. And still another may not perform accurately until reaching the letter normally read at 200 feet and would have acuity designated as 20/200. Since this testing is done with only one eye at a time, performance is recorded for each eye separately. The child who can read is then confronted with text which is to be read, binocularly, at a fixed distance, and this near-distance acuity is recorded in terms of the smallest print read on the card. Legally, performance at 20/200 or worse in the better eye, with maximal correction, is regarded as indicating blindness. Essentially performance in the 20/70 to 20/200 range, with correction, technically qualifies a child for characterization as "partially sighted," one clearly in need of large-type texts and other major visual aides.

Formal screening in this manner, usually done by school nurses and sometimes by parents who are supervised by them, is generally employed. In some instances such screening is accomplished by means of the Keystone Telebinocular, which involves binocular vision. The fact that such formal screenings occur fairly regularly in a moderate number of places should not cause the conscientious teacher or parent to overlook responsibility for noting child behavior that could suggest the possible presence of visual impairment. Children who have bumped into objects have been regarded by their teachers or parents as clumsy when in reality they had serious visual impairment. Compensatory squinting has been attributed to poor lighting when it really accompanied efforts at focusing. Failure to read printed material has been called "inattention" when the child just was not able to see properly what was to be read. On the other hand, the kindergarten or primary teacher must realize that it is not always poor vision that causes the beginning learner to write "with his nose."

Once any child has been identified, formally or otherwise, as seeming to have a visual impairment, it is necessary—as it is in the cases of all exceptional child candidates—to have a competent individual examination, preferably by an opthalmologist or oculist, or at least by an optometrist. Examination by a medically qualified eye specialist is particularly important because the eye is such a great diagnostic channel to the nervous system and because many visual problems have physiological bases.

The effectiveness of the vision of visually impaired children is considerably more complex than the results of formal screening procedures might suggest. While children meeting the Snellen 20/200 criterion may be regarded as technically blind, some of them can see well enough to read large print when it is held close to their eye(s). In fact, characterizations of visually impaired children range from this technical definition of blindness: "Central visual acuity of 20/200 or less in the better eye, with correcting glasses, or central visual acuity of more than 20/200 if there is a field defect in which the peripheral field has contracted to such an extent that the widest diameter of visual field subtends an angular distance of no greater than 20 degrees" (Hurlin, 1962) to this functional educational definition: "A visually handicapped child is one whose visual impairment interferes with his optimal learning and achievement, unless adaptations are made in the methods of presenting learning experiences, the nature of the materials used, and/or in the learning environment" (Barraga, 1964, p. 16). Functional visual acuity is such a complex condition, even when it is not deteriorating, that the parent and teacher must seek to work with the child in the terms of the most competent diagnosis possible. And it must be remembered that some quantified degree of visual acuity (especially in even the better eye) may not be truly synonymous with the extent of functional vision.

As in the case of the auditorially impaired, the determination of the incidence of visual impairment among children involves the population examined, the measures and procedures used, and the degrees which are specified. Probably the best data in the case of vision are those of the National Health Survey (Roberts, 1977). Based on a systematically collected sample of 9263 persons, aged 4–74, the data show monocular "corrected vision" (the subjects using whatever correction they had) as reflected by screening performances in the Snellen letter (94.8%), the illiterate E (3.9%), pictures (1.1%), and the Landolt rings (0.2%). In terms of Snellen ratios the overall findings were: 20/20 and better, 72.8%; 20/25, 12.7%; 20/30, 8.0%; 20/40, 3.2%; 20/50, 1.5%; 20/70, 2.0%, 20/100, .4%; and 20/200 and worse, 0.4% (Table 4). For children aged 6–11 the findings were: 20/20 or better, 72.5%; 20/25 and 20/30, 21.1%, 20/40, 2.9%, 20/50–20/70, 2.8%, 20/80–20/100, 0.5%; and 20/200 and worse, 0.2% (Table 13). There was a somewhat higher incidence among black people; higher education and income was found among the whites.

SOME IMPORTANT GIVENS

Since the primary intent of this chapter is to consider learning and adjustment aspects of auditorially and visually impaired children in terms of major psychological perspectives, we need to consider at the outset certain fundamental psychological "givens." These are basic and therefore apply potentially to all children, but our concern is factors or conditions that can facilitate or interfere with their effects. Our two groups of children are obviously differentially sensitive to environmental stimuli, and these givens have important implications for our later examination of their similarities and differences in actual and potential cognitive, social, and emotional adjustments. These givens are our perceptions of the principles underlying the adjustment—normal and abnormal—of the visually and aurally impaired children with whom we are concerned.

These givens are highly interrelated. At any moment any one of them can be observed in any child, depending on the frame of reference of the observer, just as a physical object can be observed to have weight, color, chemical constituency, and the like. In contrast to the physical characteristics of a relatively inert object, our first two premises have to do with constantly interrelated conditions within the organism (child), the third speaks to the social context within which the first two operate, and the last is a methodological admonition largely with respect to the observer but potentially affecting the one observed. Each is considered separately, but their coexistence and probable interaction must be recognized.

Activity

The child is active. At first this may seem to be just another way of saying that the child is alive. But this principle has important ramifications, some of which long have been recognized but some of which are receiving deserved attention only relatively recently.

Children react to stimuli, both external and internal, responding to pin pricks, hits, different temperatures, and conditions of internal malaise. But, by definition, our impaired children do not respond to or respond differently to certain external stimuli than do nonimpaired children—as in the case of the blind child's responding to "ruby" in terms of texture rather than in terms of color. Important as is this simple aspect of activity, other aspects are even more important.

Because the organism is active, even before birth, it tends to act after birth in ways that are variously characterized by observers of that behavior. Some see the organism as "outgoing": it presses into its environment, thus encountering objects, persons, and conditions. Some regard such behavior teleologically: it seeks stimulation. Whether regarded technically as "purposeful" or not, healthy children tend to push into their environment, "getting into" things in the home and even "running away." Later they physically explore their environment more widely, seeking both more raucous auditory and visual stimuli (that so many adults find intrusive) and problem-solving experiences as in puzzles, games, and mysteries. Such behaviors in children may be nurtured by tolerance or encouragement of them by significant others or adversely affected by physical conditions, such as sensory impairment, or by restrictive attitudes or actions by those significant others.

Certainly one of the major advances in psychology during the last generation has been the increasing recognition and study of the extent to which and the manner in which the organism reacts to stimuli. Understandable though it may be, it has been an embarrassingly long period between the concept of the seemingly passive "mind" as something on which experiences left impressions, and the current belief that the organism, when stimulated, actually did things to and with those stimuli. That a surprisingly complex response can occur to a simple stimulus supports the inference that the nervous system is put together to process stimuli actively.

When talking about organisms' behavior, we deal with two parts of the picture—what is observed and what is inferred. Stimuli and most responses are observable. What happens in between, especially cognitively, in the "black box" between stimulus and response, is inferred. This "central processing" is being intensively explored, albeit still basically inferentially, under the rubrics of cognition, metacognition, retrieval, and the like, even with ramifications regarding the possible differential rules of the cerebral hemispheres. (The research literature in this area is tremendously varied. See, for instance, Estes, 1975; Gagné, 1968; Jacobs & Vandeventer, 1971; Luria, 1973; and Sternberg, 1977.) The understanding of central processing is of major importance in understanding the learning of all children. But it is of particular importance for the sensorially impaired, especially those with pronounced hearing loss. Hence our rather extended consideration of it here.

Input Processing

The child "makes" his or her responses in the sense that how he or she responds depends not only upon his or her being stimulated but also upon what he or she does to those stimuli. The response of any individual is a function of three kinds of conditions:

1.   The nature of the stimulus (input)
   1.1   Its frequency
   1.2   Its strength (loudness, brightness, pressure)
   1.3   Its quality, which is a function of
      1.31   Its psychological import (percept, concept, "meaning") to him or her
      1.32   Its social import/value, which then activates
2.   The processing of that stimulus/information, which involves
   2.1   The processing capability of the individual, which determines
   2.2   The nature of the end result of that processing, which becomes
3.   The response (output) of the individual, which is affected by
   3.1   The capability of the individual to respond overtly
      3.11   Which can be motorically influenced
   3.2   The social milieu in which the response occurs

Assume that a child is asked "Do you like school?" Put most simply, one of three possible situations could arise.

1.   If he is asked this orally and he cannot hear it, he may process the fact of aural stimulation in terms of prior similar experiences and respond (assuming no motor involvement) by gesturing that he does not hear.

2.   If he is then asked this question in writing, three possibilities exist:

a. If he has not learned to read, he may respond in much the same manner as in number one.

b. If he can read, he will determine (process) whether "like" means to tolerate or to enjoy whatever "school" means to him, which may be either the particular school he attends or, in the sense in which the inquirer may have meant, that he liked or doesn't like learning itself. His response will be determined by his interpretations of the meanings of "like" and "school" and by his recalled related experiences.

c. If he is asked this question by an adult educationally significant to him and understands it, his response may be either acquiescent or negativistic, depending on what was involved in the processing; if he is asked it by some child outside of school, his response may be influenced by how he processes the inquiry in terms of his perception of what the social climate suggests is appropriate.

d. If he is asked this question and hears it, he responds to it in the same manner as the child who comprehendingly reads it.

This example is crucial to the full understanding of part of what is involved in learning—incidental and formal—by auditorially and visually impaired children. The greater the degree of impairment, the greater the reduction in input. Therefore, certain links in the stimulus–response chain become more crucial. Further, many fewer stimuli impinge on the severely auditorially impaired than on the functionally blind. Sound amplification can be an important factor in the case of the hearing impaired as can large print size and quality of lighting for the partially sighted. And the nature of stimulation by others may be either reduced because of lowered expectations or exaggerated because of compensatory efforts.

The inference that the organism, without formal training, processes information (stimuli) it receives can be drawn from observations of everyday behavior of young children as well as of their behavior under experimental conditions. Take, for instance, the case of the four-year-old who ran crying to his mother "He hitted me." He had certainly not been taught that the past tense of "hit" was "hitted." On the contrary, enough past tense of stimuli had impinged upon him in the course of everyday living that he "just knew" how to communicate his problem. Put another way, without verbalizing what had taken place when pastness was communicated to him usually with "ed" added to the present tense of a verb, he perceived a commonality that made possible a generalization with respect to the use of "ed." Extrapolating backward in age level, a similar type of event sequence "caused" the one-year-old to cry every time a white-coated person attempted to pick him up. In later years and in like manner the child manifests aversive behavior when confronted with certain academic demands, as in reading or arithmetic. These understandable responses then result from a processing of stimuli called "generalization." Children differ in their capability to generalize. In fact it could be maintained that the capacity to generalize is a major component in school learning aptitude.

It is important to understand the functioning of generalization in children's learning. There are differences in this learning between acoustically and visually impaired children and between them and nonimpaired children. We examine generalization analytically, since our approach has been more "lumpy" than many and possibly more relevant to early learning.

Put simply, the problem basically is this: How does a child on whom many stimuli impinge identify certain aspects of some of those stimuli and come to respond in a certain way to a still different stimulus situation which also has one of those aspects of earlier stimuli? In the case of our four-year-old, the present tense of a verb plus "ed" occurred frequently enough in the denotation of pastness that he used it in a new situation. He had "seen"/"perceived"/ "discovered" a relationship between "edness" and pastness and then had extrapolated that relationship to a new situation. Actually this illustrates Spearman's (1927) eduction of relationships and of correlates—processes which, while logically differentiable, are as inseparable as are the two sides of a coin.

We may identify the following subprocesses of the larger phenomenon of generalization:

1.   The perception of differences among stimuli—one stimulus is different from others which themselves may have something in common. (The doll is different from the toy house, the wagon, the ball, and the dress.)

2.   The perception of identities between or among stimuli. (One five-inch, blue rubber ball is the same as another similar ball but different from the baby doll, the toy dog, the rattle, and the flat shining disc in the stimulus field.)

3.   The perception of similarities among stimuli due to the fact that, whereas each is literally different, some have characteristics in common (The toy stuffed dog is relatable to the toy stuffed cat but not to the toy airplane, the doll house, or the five-inch ball.)

4.   On the basis of a perception of a progressive relationship among stimuli, the further perception that another stimulus extends or continues that progression. (The child is confronted with two pools of objects. One is a row of round objects arranged in order of increasing or decreasing size. The other pool contains miscellaneous objects, two of which are round but one of which is larger or smaller than the largest or smallest in the presented pool.)

5.   On the basis of a perception, either discovered by or provided for the child, of a relationship existing between two (or more) stimuli, identifying a fourth stimulus that has an identical (or similar) relationship to a third stimulus. (A boy doll is presented with a father-figure doll. A girl doll is then presented with a mother-figure doll which is part of a pool of objects, such as a toy dog, a ball, a wagon, etc.

6.   Discerning a stimulus that is missing from some identifiable pattern of stimuli. (Present three of the stimuli in a four-figure matrix, the fourth figure completing the matrix to be selected from the pool of possible response objects. Nine-figure matrices can be concocted, making certain that both the horizontal and vertical relationships are valid. Or a situational matrix can be conceived, as when the child is caused to complete a setting by adding an obviously missing table to a kitchen.)

Two things are apparent in this description of generalization. First, the subprocesses are in order of increasing difficulty. Each presumes the child's comprehension of the nature of the stimuli involved; analogs which may be developed for training in these processings must reflect this fact. Second, they are highly interrelated: 1, 2, and 3 are involved in the operation of 4, 5, and 6, and 5 clearly is involved in 6. It must be recognized then that failure with 4, 5, and 6 could be due to failure in 1, 2, and/or 3. Because they are more truly inferred, other kinds of processing such as information storage and retrieval in remembering, imaging, and the like, are intentionally omitted from consideration here.

Development

The child manifests an identifiable pattern of development or maturation. An identifiable sequence of behavior in the development or maturation of the organism was first seen in motor area (Coghill, 1929). The organism reacts as a totality to a stimulus—the mass response stage. Later responses of parts of the organism to stimulation appear—the differentiated response stage. Finally, the differentiated responses become patterned parts of the total organism's responding—the integrated stage. More important for our consideration, cognitive development shows an analogous progression. The organism initially perceives a stimulating phenomenon (the physical event itself, a gesture for it, or a word for it) as a totality. Immature children live in a world of just "somethings." They totally "accept" or "reject." As they mature, they react to aspects of these somethings. Their differentiated responses at this stage are limited to the stimuli involved, not having become parts of a larger conceptual structure—they have not become "abstracted." The response is essentially perceptual or of a very elementary conceptualization. In the integrative stage reactions to events or their equivalents are characterized by evidence of a conceptualization of the stimulus—a more integrated patterning of the response. Young children just accept or reject the pet; later they perceive it as something to be played with and patted during its interaction with them, or they perceive it as a biting or scratching stimulus; still later they understand it as a member of the canine or feline world that has both positive and negative possibilities. Children initially react to confrontations in reading or arithmetic as totally challenging or as totally threatening; later they see such confrontations as involving specific things that can or can't be done; still later, they regard them in terms of demands that can provide means to certain ends. In a test situation children at the mass stage respond to the request to define, say, a triangle by just shaking their heads or saying only "something." Later they report their perception of it as a "pointed figure"; and still later will define it in terms of its basic class characterization and also its logically differentiating characteristics. The individuated response that chair and table are alike because they both have legs is clearly cognitively different from the integrated response that they both are furniture.

This developmental/maturational sequence has been dealt with rather fully because its cognitive aspects are highly relevant to learnings by our impaired children. Our concern is with the extent to which they are able to progress from a perceptual (individuated) level to a conceptual (integrated) level.

Social Milieu

The child grows/matures/develops in a social milieu that may have neutral, negative, or facilitative effects. This seemingly trite statement will take on considerable significance with respect to auditorially and visually impaired children. Strictly speaking, it is unlikely that any social milieu can be regarded as having a literally neutral effect on the development of a child. Logically, though, the impacts of the social milieu on the development of the child can range from those having highly positive nurturant effects through a theoretically zero influence to those having grossly negative, limited, or harmful effects.

In an overall sense, the varied impacts of the child's social milieu have a beneficial, nurturant effect. Whether these stimulations are intentional on the parts of others or are only incidental to his social commingling and physical growth, they are multitudinous and, it may be argued, essential to his effective development. From the intentional physical and psychological stimulation in babyhood, through admonitions in early childhood, to formal schooling by parents and social agencies the child learns as his potential permits. All learning resulting from this array of stimulation is supplemented significantly by incidental learnings, as illustrated by our four-year-old. Not to be overlooked is the fact that all of these learnings are made possible by the child being able to hear and see. But to the degree that the child's hearing or vision is impaired, he is deprived of this important nurturance.

Both nonimpaired and impaired children can be deprived of potentially important nurturance by a passively neglectful social milieu. In the case of more seriously impaired children, many well-intentioned actions and practices by others actually can be detrimental to the nurturance which such children need. All too often, things done for impaired children to protect them or ease their way actually may deprive such children of valuable incidental learning. It is a fine line, and always an individual one, that separates an impaired child's nurturant social milieu from one that, albeit unwittingly, seriously reduces his opportunities to interact with important incidental stimuli in his environs. Such is the case with those children with high degrees of either auditory or visual impairment, and particularly so in the case of seriously hearing impaired children.

Although these considerations have been highly slanted with respect to the impact of the social milieu upon the child's cognitive development, emotional and social attitudinal aspects cannot be ignored. The deleterious effects of adults' overcompensatory behavior, adults misconstruing gushy sympathy for a calm understanding and acceptance of impairment, or their despairing reaction of surrender to perceived awfulness of such impairment can contribute most adversely to both the child's emotional adjustment and attitudes toward others.

Learning

The child learns. To state that teachers teach too often contributes to the impression that they implant knowledge in a (hopefully) receptive pupil. The impression thus is fostered that the child is a passive receiver of what the culture regards as appropriate. In fact the teacher's "teaching" consists of the manipulation of the stimulation of the child, recognizing (and, it is hoped, understanding at least in part) that the child then processes the information in that stimulation—perceiving, storing, organizing, and retrieving that information or something evolving from the processing of that information. The contention that the child (or anyone) learns to do by doing early pertained to overt (observed) behavior; now the statement has broader applicability in that it pertains also to covert (inferred) behavior—particularly to whatever central neural processing is involved in cognizing.

Teaching takes place largely with children who are nicely susceptible to such stimulation. But the limited sensitivity to conventional stimuli of our impaired children presents unique challenges, particularly in the cases of those with profound hearing loss. For these, especially if the hearing loss has occurred during the prelingual stage, there are special problems with respect to their processing of whatever information they are able to receive.

THE LEARNING SITUATION

The term learning is used here to denote the child's reacting to those experiences, intentional, structured, or otherwise, which he or she encounters in the process of growing up. Without denying the important role played by incidental experiencing, our primary concern is with that learning intentionally nurtured by parents and/or society's parent surrogates. Learnings in connection with emotional, social, and vocational adjustment are dealt with later. The primary focus of concern here is cognitive learning since it is fundamental to such other learnings, even in the learning by the blind to move about in their environs. It is recognized that the effectiveness of this cognitive learning can be influenced by children's emotional, social, and physical condition.

The basic learning process is neurologically the same for auditorially and visually impaired children. Since the early learnings of all children are so crucial, they are our major concern. Attention is given primarily to psychological aspects of learning rather than to educational methodologies per se. It is assumed that appropriate correction has been provided the visually impaired and that appropriate hearing amplification has been provided those needing it. The most frustrating—those who are both deaf and blind—are considered briefly.

The Auditorially Impaired

Rather than consider separately the learning situation for each of the gradations of hearing loss, we concern ourselves first with children with lesser degrees of hearing loss, and then turn to those with severe and extreme impairment. The nature of the learning problems of those having intermediate degrees of hearing loss can be conceptualized by interpolation.

Children in our first group are those whose hearing losses can range as high as 55 dB and for whom sound amplification can be relatively easily provided. (Unfortunately, a distractingly large percentage of these children so often are not identified and therefore have no such help.) Input and output aspects of their learning situations merit particular attention. When duly attended to by parents, teachers, and others, no particular problems should arise in central processing.

For both the preschool and the school child with even a slight hearing loss, the adult must consistently make certain that auditory stimuli "get through" to the child. The greater the child's hearing loss the more the adult must communicate in face-to-face situations. (Obviously the blind child can hear what is said to him or her even though facing away from the speaker.) If the child's hearing has been properly evaluated, the adult should know from the audiogram which high- and low-frequency sounds should be capitalized on or stressed. In the early stages of their relationship, the adult can have the child respond in ways that will indicate clearly whether the child is receiving what the adult is sending; later only occasional checks need be made. The adult will need to make sure why the child is not "attending": Is the child really not hearing? Has he or she already learned to "tune out" that adult, or all adults? Were there other distracting, concomitant auditory stimuli? Is the child playing with the adult? In the classroom, the child should be seated so that he can hear and see both the teacher and his/or her fellow pupils. (In one situation, a teacher appreciatively accepted the suggestion that her hearing-impaired pupil be seated in the front of the room instead of in the back, but most of the time the teacher was found to stand clear across the room from the child!)

It is assumed that such hearing-impaired children probably will do their school learning in a regular classroom—probably through unintentional "mainstreaming." If the school district they are in happens to have resource facilities relative to their impairment, they probably will spend intervals getting specialized help appropriate to their needs. The parents may need to enlist the aid of the children's teacher(s) in helping the children adjust to the use and maintenance of the hearing aid—the extent to which they can and should wear it during play, keeping it at proper amplification, and, indeed, that they actually wear it. Particularly important is the teacher's, as well as the parents', calmly helping the children to be perceived by classmates as just children with an understandable difference rather than as different. These factors are essentially basic maintenance ones, but they are important in assuring the adequacy and quality of input.

For the learning situation of children with severe hearing losses, who have markedly lower input, it is important to examine more closely the role played by their central processing of the stimuli/information which they do receive. Since these children are usually "normally" neurologically "wired," normal processing of input could be possible. But in sharp contrast to our four-year-old who socially and "intellectually" benefited from a plethora of incidental stimulation, this kind of child receives much less incidental information. By virtue of the fact that fewer stimuli effectively impinge on these children, the processing of which they initially are capable is not stimulated to the same extent as that of the fully hearing child. In the belief that normal stimulation is, in effect, nurturant to normal processing we presume that decreased effective stimulation contributes to decreased processing, and that this decrease contributes to a "withering on the vine" of that processing of which the child originally was capable. This would seem to be the case most clearly with those who were born with extreme hearing loss. In discussing the personality development of the deaf, Levine (1971) maintained that they suffer from "educational and psychological malnutrition otherwise known as cultural deprivation," pointing out that this is a result of the failure by teachers, parents, and peers to provide the information and experiences deaf children need for development. But it should be recognized that in addition to not receiving as much information as the hearing, they may not process effectively what they do receive.

Certain evidence supports this contention. In a nationwide study at Gallaudet—the college for the deaf—Stanford Achievement Test results on 16,908 hearing-impaired students at all levels from primary through advanced revealed that they did consistently less well on tests involving verbal relationships than on the more rote tests of spelling and arithmetic computation (Moores, 1978, adapted from Gentile, 1972). Oleron (1953) observed less conceptual and more perceptual functioning in deaf children's thinking. Suggestive support exists in the finding that understimulated young mice did not later process stimuli as effectively as the more "normally" stimulated ones did. Certain observers of deaf education long have noted what seemed to be a dominance of perceptual over conceptual outcomes. That such children might be capable of the higher-functioning level even though they do not manifest it is beside the point; their education has been such that they, as a group, just do not. Moores (1978) points out that the Gallaudet data indicate that the hearing impaired, over nine years of schooling, improved in arithmetic computation at an average rate of a half grade per year, whereas their scores in paragraph comprehension increased at only half that rate. Furth (1973) is highly critical of educational programs for the deaf from the standpoint of the limited improvement in language proficiency.

Making much of the inevitability of reduced input in the case of the more acutely hearing impaired is important for at least three reasons. First, most people just do not realize sufficiently that such children have this problem to a greater extent than do any other impaired children, except, of course, those who are both deaf and blind. Second, the fact that there is lowered input means that such children do less central processing of information, and this can result in less effective cognitive functioning because their intellectual diet has been restricted. Finally, if no preventive or corrective efforts are exerted by adults in the preschool experiences of these children, either the children will later function below their potential, resulting in cognitive stunting, or those who later properly educate these children must provide learning opportunities that will at least arrest that stunting or, preferably, provide stimulation and follow-through that will alleviate it.

Such nurturance of cognitive functioning—either the prevention of further deterioration or the restoration and maintenance of normal functioning—must be recognized as of prime importance in the education of deaf children. Actually this problem is by no means unique to the deaf. Children reared in environments of lower intellectual expectations are allowed (reinforced) to function at perceptual or lower conceptual levels than their basic capabilities indicate are possible. Clinical work with the parents and teachers of such psychoeducationally disadvantaged children has shown that the children respond quickly to such nurturant remediation. Providing this kind of educationally nurturant climate for children with severe or extreme hearing loss makes stringent demands on the adults in such children's environs. Not only are carefully planned programs of stimulation (input) needed, but special attention must be paid to the nature of the children's responses to make certain that the information that the children received was processed effectively. That some improvement of this sort is possible, at least for a short period of time, was shown by Rudio (1972), whose experimental treatment involved elementary processing of figural stimuli and outcome measurement of semantic material. The extent to which such restorative nurturance can be truly effective is not at all clear. Elliott and Ambruster (1967), having studied the effectiveness of delayed diagnosis and remediation, observed that "hearing-impaired children who are not identified at an early age and who are not provided with sound amplification or placed in an appropriate educational setting may experience a special type of sensory deprivation, the effects of which are only partly reversible" (p. 223). Any successful remedial or nurturant effort must involve a psychologically sound program and a consistent, conceptually insightful checking by all the child's significant adults on the nature of the children's responses. Whether and how the way the deaf communicate may affect this will be considered later.

The need for process training will differ depending on the age and degree of impairment of the child. Young children need a patterning of stimulation that will lead essentially to normal development. This involves stimuli which can be comprehended by and are appropriate to each child. The kind of processing to be involved should progress through the levels identified earlier. Older children probably will need remediation or resuscitation of processing, and the pattern of stimulation will have to start with that kind of processing of which the child is at first capable and then progress gradually into and through the more complex kinds.

The Visually Impaired

The learning situations of these children are considered in terms of three major groups—those who have moderate impairment which is essentially correctible, those who are regarded technically as partially sighted, and those who are blind. This last category actually includes four differentiable subgroups: those who are functionally blind—having sufficient vision to get around but needing to learn as though they actually are blind, and those who are totally blind, each of these groups having the condition from birth or having had it develop subsequent to birth. Since visually impaired children as a group have no typical central nervous system pathology, no problems in the processing of input are expected; when serious visual impairment is part of a larger syndrome, some attending pathology can impair cognitive functioning, as in the case of a validly established "brain-injured" blind child.

Assuming that proper correction has been provided for the children in our moderately impaired category, which unfortunately too often is not the case, the learning situation is not markedly different from that of other children. Younger children need help to get used to their glasses, to make proper use of them, and even to take care of them. Proper seating for maximum benefit from natural and artificial lighting plus freedom to change their seating in order to get closer to important visual material should be routine considerations. Lest thinking about such needs be too conveniently confined to the presumed existence of modern, up-to-date lighting facilities in classrooms, some actual potential detrimental conditions are worth identifying: smudged, dirty reading materials, dirty windows, especially in mining and factory areas, dirty and nonfunctional light fixtures, windows obstructed on the outside by bushes and/or on the inside by displays of pupil productions, and even dirty, ill-lighted Snellen charts. Light meter readings for pupils' reading surfaces should be at least 50 foot-candles. Actually, these concerns are as important for children with normal vision as for those with impaired vision. And it is to be remembered that the eyes are not harmed by extended normal reading.

For the partially sighted, those with Snellen ratios 20/70 to 20/200 in the better eye after correction, the major problem is the adequacy of visual stimuli. For these children large-type reading materials, including dictionaries, now are generally available. Also available are various kinds of magnifiers needed particularly for children looking at illustrative materials; such aids should be used only with the specific approval of each child's ophthalmologist or optician. From the standpoint of the verbal output of these children, no unique problem exists, obviously, in oral production. For written expression they need special materials, including large-type typewriters. In terms of input in communication the blind must depend on hearing voice inflections, whereas the deaf can benefit from seeing the gesturings and facial expressions of the communicator.

Functionally and totally blind children, of course, have the greatest difficulties, but not as great as do children with severe and extreme hearing loss. Two groups of these children—those who are born blind and those who become blind after birth—have quite different kinds of problems.

The learning problems of those who become blind after birth—the adventitiously blind—vary with the age and rate, sudden or gradual, at which sight is lost. The extent to which an infant or young child can have usable vision and benefit from it in his later learning is essentially a matter of conjecture. A child's perception of his world is a function of the nature of the stimuli which he or she receives from it plus what emerges when those stimuli are processed in terms of what is remembered. Contributive to the effectiveness of the child's processing of input, of course, are the extent to which his or her nervous system has matured and the "quality" of that nervous system—the number of nerve cells, nature of neuronal processes, and functioning synapses. The richer his or her prior stored information, the more fully he or she tends to respond to subsequent stimulation. Obviously then the earlier in life that vision is lost, or seriously impaired, the less full the responses to later stimuli tend to be.

Lowenfeld (1980) finds acceptable Toth's (1930) and others' observations that children who have lost their sight before about the age of five are unable to benefit from visual imagery. In light of this the born blind category of children is here regarded as including not only those who were born blind but also those who had lost their sight on or before reaching the age of five. Children who have lost their sight after that age will constitute the adventitiously blind. Although the learning problems of children in both groups have important commonalities, those of the adventitiously blind will be attenuated to the extent to which their loss of vision has been delayed. The later in life children lose vision, the more they can capitalize on prior visual input and the more relevantly they can process that information with, or in terms of, what they remember having seen—dimensional, configurational, and color perceptions. To the extent that this learning has been reinforced or supplemented by accompanying cutaneous, kinesthetic, olfactory, and even abstract verbal stimuli, the richer becomes the supply of information in terms of which, after losing sight, information can be processed. In spite of the value of preloss input to the adventitiously blind, their underlying learning problems and those of the born blind have much in common. In fact, in certain situations seeing and partially seeing children who have firm diagnoses of future blindness are forthwith placed in educational programs for the blind.

The importance of first considering input problems of blind children is apparent. A comparison of the input of blind and deaf children will help sharpen the picture. Both can respond to customary cutaneous, kinesthetic, and olfactory stimuli, as do other children. Whereas blind children are capable of responding to and benefiting from a vast array of auditory stimuli from a variety of sources, deaf children have to depend heavily on those stimuli they can see. Blind children can respond to sound stimuli whether their sources are in front of them, beside them, or behind them; deaf children must see the source of their crucial stimulation. Without in any way denying the important contributive value of stimulation through other possible sensory channels, certainly a major input channel of the blind is tactual. Except relatively recently developed and developing techniques for making printed material accessible to the blind (which tend to be limited in use because of their costs), the unit of input is the braille cell, which can represent a letter or symbol—a configuration of from one to six embossed dots in a space 10 centimeters high and 5 centimeters wide.

It will help in understanding how the blind accomplish their reading by the bits of information in braille units if we consider how sighted children learn to read by means of letters, words, phrases, and sentences. The sighted look at a line of printed characters and eyes fixate on a certain point in the line of letters. The total input at the moment may be just one letter, say the "o" in the word "boy." They gradually learn to acquire a fixation span such that the whole word "boy" is taken in at once. With improvement in their reading skill, the fixation span can come to widen such that "The boy has" is taken in as a unit. This is "stored" in the processing and the next fixation span can include "a dog." This is stored in the processing either to be recalled as a unit or to be processed in relation to prior and subsequent input that has been and will be received. In like general manner, but much more atomistically in nature, the bits of input for the blind are reacted to. Each braille cell or group of braille cells is reacted to, "received" or perceived, stored, and subsequently further processed in terms of others.

Whereas the efficient sighted reader develops relatively wide spans on which he fixates in rapid succession, perhaps having occasionally to go back and pick up some overlooked or uncomprehended element, the blind reader is limited, at least at first, to single-finger inputs which have to be taken in serially. Just as the picture image which a sighted person perceives is the resulting integration of many individually looked-at bits in the actual picture, so is the word or sentence perceived by the blind child by means of braille cells. (There are at least 180 braille contractions which have evolved in the shortening and condensing of the process.) Without including the higher cognitive operations that also are involved, the "mechanics" of braille assimilation are a complex part of the central processing by the blind.

Considering at such length the nature of brialle input for the blind must not in any way distract from the tremendous part played by their auditory input. Hearing not only enables them to learn much generally but also facilitates their acquisition of braille reading skill. Looking with their fingers and hands (and they *do* "look") supplements their examining and exploring fields of objects and areas, and in a gross sense they perceive movement. This situation is paralleled in their output. Although most of it is vocal, a part tends to be in braille writing. With special assists, some handwriting is taught and encouraged, largely for writing signatures. For quite some time the blind wrote by means of a hinged metal or plastic template, called a slate, which had braille-sized cells within which the writer, using a stylus, made embossing impressions in the paper underneath to represent letters or contractions. This meant that writing was from right to left in order that subsequent reading could be from left to right. To check what was written the paper had to be taken out of the slate, turned over, and read. The development of a braille writer improved this situation. This machine has six keys, each for a dot in the braille cell, one or more of which are depressed simultaneously creating the braille character on a tape or paper. Goldfish (1967) reported that, as of 1965, there were 28,000 Perkins Braillers in use. "A good braillist completes an average of five braille pages of straight prose per hour" (Goldfish, 1967, p. 5).

The cumbersome problem of input for the blind has been and is being tackled in a variety of ways. Whereas the braille writer was developed for children, the others were started with adults, with adaptations and benefits filtering down to children. The most widely known of these is the talking book program, started through the American Printing House for the Blind with federal funding and now being carried on also elsewhere. Paid and volunteer workers read book material which is recorded and then made available in record and tape form. Many schools utilize volunteer readers for their pupils.

Technologically and psychologically the most intriguing efforts involve the conversion of printed verbal material into a modality which the blind can respond to. One, the Optacon Print Reading System,[1] converts the image of a printed letter or symbol into an enlarged tactile form that can be felt with one finger. A different kind of approach involves an electronic element which is passed over printed material, producing sounds which vary in pitch and duration depending upon the height and width of the letter. Both of these require that the blind learn to use them. Technically much more complex but simpler for the blind to use is the Kurzweil Reading Machine for the Blind,[2] which converts printed text into full-sound synthetic speech. Some training in the use of this machine is required.

With the exception of unique problems of input and possibly a greater demand in processing, the fundamental learning procedures of blind children do not differ from those of nonimpaired children. Even skilled readers of braille read discernibly more slowly than do sighted readers. This is due to the nature of the input of the blind and the attending greater demand in processing—in integrating the units of input. The young blind child has a small finger area with which to look at the braille cell, sometimes having to explore even the single cell and to assimilate the resulting perception in order to perceive what the whole cell is; older children have larger finger areas and soon come to use more than one finger. The good sighted reader can perceive at least 10–15 letters in a single fixation. In light of the limitation in the reading material that is available in braille and the complications attending the reading of braille, it is quite understandable that great effort has been put forth to develop the technology by means of which printed text is converted to auditory form.

The Deaf Blind

It would be simple forthrightly to regard children as deaf-blind if they had literally no auditory and visual acuity. Such would be the stereotypic view. However, it would be in keeping with what has thus far been developed to regard any child as both deaf and blind if his or her autitory acuity in the better ear after correction was 70 dB or less and visual acuity in the better eye after correction was 20/200 or less, assuming that such degrees of impairment had existed from the prelingual age of 3 years for hearing and from the age of 5 for sight. Any such child would be regarded as "born deaf-blind"; any who became so impaired after those ages, in those modalities, would be regarded as adventitiously deaf-blind. The learning problems of the former group would, of course, be the more severe.

Firm knowledge of the incidence of these children is elusive for two reasons: (1) parents of such children tend to keep them out of circulation, and (2) once they are located, diagnosis of them often is ambiguous. The increasing social concern for "handicapped" children of the 1970s should help improve their discovery. In 1960 it was believed that there were only 372 such children, but the 1969 figure was stated as 2461 (U.S. Office of Education, 1970).

Obviously extremely difficult problems exist with respect to both input and output. Unless the limitations are part of some complex impairment syndrome it seems reasonable to assume that processing is not hampered by neuropathology. The primary channel for the stimulation of these children is tactual, a mixture of cutaneous and kinesthetic, with some possible olfactory and gustatory supplementation. The seeming inaccessibility of these children constitutes the initial problem. Actually, as in any learning but so much more obvious and crucial in the bases of these children, the evocation of that very first discriminative response to a stimulus serves as the cognitive beachhead. Through slow learning, the gross motor nature of the initial response becomes differentiated from gesturing and progresses slowly into signing and/or finger spelling. The tonal quality of any vocal response that later may be cultivated depends on the degree of residual hearing which the child has. The tremendous gap between the establishment of the initial learning and the adult performance of such as Helen Keller is very difficult for the ordinary hearing and seeing person to comprehend.

THE LEARNINGS

The Acoustically Impaired

In considering the unique problems of these children we shall bear in mind our premise that their learning is not hampered by neuropathology. The area of greatest psychological concern for the hearing impaired is communication. How communication should be accomplished has long been in contention. There are cognitive ramifications of their manner of communicating that are important. And these aspects of the communication problem have important bearing on the social behavior of the acoustically impaired, varying with the degree of impairment. They will be considered in terms of the deaf, recognizing that to the extent that hearing is present they can be attenuated. Whatever additional learning difficulties they might have which validly could be attributed to faulty brain structure and/or functioning would call for special attention to and compensatory efforts in enhancing both input and output.

But the basic psychoeducational assumptions and techniques employed with such children would be essentially the same as for otherwise nonimpaired children. Similarly, the basic principles and applications of educational psychology would operate in their being taught and in their learning—with, of course, special attention being given to input and output problems.

Just as so many problems seem to call for an either-or solution, thereby creating vigorous proponents and opponents, so has controversy arisen over the manner of communication by the deaf. In this case, however, three kinds of advocates have pressed their cases, each with plausible claims of social and psychological merit: those who have contended that finger spelling should be the means of communication, those who have maintained that signing is best, and those who have insisted that lip reading is the preferred mode. Each group has recognized that whatever oral speech could be cultivated would help. All have recognized the possible facilitation of facial and/or bodily gesturing. And for each group the literature of the field has reflected "research evidence" purportedly supporting the validity of its position. Each has its own validity as well as its unique limitations. As Birch (1964, p. 13) observed, "The literature, while voluminous, has almost invariably reflected strong bias, pro and con." Moores (1978, p. 175) concluded that "most of the available literature still consists primarily of position papers in favor of one or another of the various methodologies." As will be seen, the resolution of these contentions lies not just in this, that, or the other approach. A good source for the early history of communication by the deaf can be found in Wallin (1924). Furth (1973, pp. 34–42) provides an interesting discussion of the oral-manual problem. Moores (1978) gives a concise summary of deaf communication procedures (pp. 15–18) and of Gallaudet's recommended "combined" method as contrasted with Bell's preference for the oral method (pp. 57–64). We consider each of these means of communication by the deaf in the light of three factors: (1) its implications in terms of the age of the receiver (input) and the sender (output), (2) social implications of its use, and (3) implications regarding its "conceptual adequacy."

Finger Spelling

From a developmental standpoint it can be argued that the young deaf child at first perceives the total visual configuration of, say, the word "cat" and later comes to differentiate the letters as separates which make up that configuration. Such being the case, the child need not "know his alphabet" before learning to communicate by finger spelling. The child's "yield" in thus learning to communicate would seem to be greater at first in terms of input—his perceiving holistically the finger-spelled word. The child's output—his finger spelling of a word—would be determined by his later-developing finger motor skills and his comprehension of the letter configuration of words. Acquisition of motor competency in communicating by finger spelling is a straightforward motor developmental/learning matter. However, deaf persons so communicating must be in visual range; one cannot communicate with another behind him or in another room the way the blind can.

It is apparent that finger spelling admits the fullest possible communication between skilled deaf persons in visual contact. Any thing, action, or relationship for which there is a word can be so communicated if the words are known by the sender and receiver. Certain nuances or inflections can be communicated by facial expressions and gesturings that can and do accompany finger spelling. There can be limitations, however. One member of the communication link may not know how to send or receive in that manner. This has major social implications in that the deaf are thus disposed to communicate within their own clusterings, apart from the "mainstream." The conceptual adequacy of what is thus communicated is necessarily a function of not only the nature of the input received but also of the nature of the central processing that has been evoked, and the nature of the learning by the deaf has been much criticized as resulting excessively in perceptual or low conceptual output. Fullness of meaning and depth and scope of comprehension are communicated with words only so long as the words are known by the communicators. Since all words can be communicated by finger spelling, under appropriate conditions (adequate visibility and motor skills), finger spelling has maximal potential for conceptual adequacy in communication by and with the deaf. A major limitation in communicating by finger spelling is that, when it is used exclusively, it is too protracted; to spell out every word in every sentence would be extremely time-consuming. As in any communication, contractions occur, certain words are omitted, and condensations are made. One type of condensation is accomplished by signing.

Signing

Signing, the other kind of manual communication, is accomplished by gesturing with one or both hands, such gesturing being accompanied by facial expressions and bodily movements. Signing is the most primitive means of giving and receiving information—it is the least common denominator of communication. This is both its strength and its weakness.

Since signing is more molar than finger spelling, since a sign is a simpler stimulus (more "compact" than a spelled-out word), and since young children begin their perceiving at a mass level, signing would, from a psychological point of view, seem to be the preferred means of communication for *young* deaf children, particularly with respect to input. From the standpoint of output, signing would seem to have the edge in childhood since gross motor manual facility would be more suited to the larger movements involved in signing, as contrasted with finger movements called for in finger spelling.

As in the use of any language form, signing plays an important part in determining a relatively tight social structure among the deaf. Barring exceptional situational forays, the social clustering of those who thus communicate understandingly among themselves is inevitable.

When signing is considered in terms of its conceptual adequacy in communicating, its limitation becomes apparent. As the least common denominator of communication, it can convey clearly simple expressions but fall short when complex concepts have to be communicated. With young deaf children this causes no serious problems, but problems increase with age. The latter situation is nicely illustrated by what happens when a speaker who has hearing talks to a deaf audience: there usually is a "translator" who converts the oral speech into input appropriate to the deaf. Skilled translators generally use the following combination. The bulk of the speech is communicated by signing or by a mixture of signing and finger spelling. When words occur for which signs are not available/suitable, one of three things occurs: (a) they are finger spelled, (b) a synonym for the obstreperous word is substituted (which may not communicate precisely the thought the speaker wished to convey), or (c) the term actually is omitted in the translation. The extent to which signing is conceptually adequate depends, of course, on the extent to which the deaf have developed a higher level of conceptualization in terms of which they think/communicate. Conveying nuances by accompanying gestures and facial expressions has only limited possibilities so far as this is concerned. Synonyms and shadings of meaning can be elusive, as, for instance, in the use of the same sign for the words believe, think, opine, and ponder. And, as in finger spelling, visual contact is essential.

Lipreading

In place of this more generally used term those working with the deaf prefer the term "speech reading" because facial expressions are so much a part of this means of communicaton. Gesturing and posturing, of course, also can contribute.

Speech reading is ardently advocated by certain workers with the deaf because they believe its use can be conducive to a fuller social integration of the deaf with the hearing. The validity of this contention involves two important assumptions: (1) that the speech of others can be read effectively by the deaf (input) and (2) that the production of speech by the deaf can be read effectively by others (output). Underlying these is the presumption that effective, generalizable speech is reasonably producible. Individual differences in speech reading skills by the deaf and in speech production by both the deaf and the hearing can influence the effectiveness of speech reading. Also, the production of certain vowels, in particular, is visually elusive.

In the case of the very young deaf child, learning speech reading requires much finer discrimination of visual stimuli than does either finger spelling or signing. The more severe the hearing loss, the greater the difficulty the child has in learning to produce speech that can be read. Thus even elementary communication yield by speech could result later by speech reading than by the other two methods. Once some competency in speech reading is acquired by the deaf, its efficiency is affected also by visibility—both sender and receiver must be in well-lighted contact—as well as by the idiosyncracies of those communicating orally.

How much speech reading by the deaf is conducive to their effectively commingling with the nondeaf is moot. Unquestionably certain deaf persons have acquired great skill in speech reading and some others have acquired lesser degrees of skill in it. Care must be taken lest some degree of the skill be regarded by others as greater than it actually is. Furth (1973, p. 33) vigorously maintains that "speech reading will always remain a rare skill as little understood as the skill of the creative artist." Research of the nature later to be suggested could indicate the extent to which the merits of speech reading are generalizable.

Speech reading can be conceptually adequate only when both sender and receiver are skilled in it and each comprehends the concepts which are sent and received. This latter is, of course, true in any form of communication, but it is particularly crucial in the case of the deaf, as has been stressed.

The intent here has been to consider aspects of method of communication rather than to evaluate the efficiency of each, which is a matter of research possibly of the nature that will be suggested. In considering the merits of any kind of communication it must be recognized that the demands for the use of verbal symbols in communication vary greatly among situations. There are conditions where, by virtue of the common experiential backgrounds of the communicators, a facial expression, a simple gesture, or even a bodily posture is adequate. There are situations where a single word or phrase suffices. There are situations where fuller though incomplete verbal expressions are adequate. And there are more formal situations in which only symbols (words or signs) communicating complex concepts are required.

Generally preferred among the deaf is the use of a combination of signing and finger spelling, as is seen in the communication on television to the deaf in the audience. Brasel and Quigley (1977) found that the deaf using the Manual English method clearly did better in language performance than did those using oral communication. Attempts to ascertain whether speech reading facility is related to "intelligence" have been psychometrically and psychologically crude, depending predominantly on "IQ" data rather than on the psychologically more relevant test ages on tests which have been chosen properly because of informational yield that would be more relevant to the perception and use of verbal symbols. The findings thus far, for what they are worth, have suggested no positive relationship. "Aptitude and personality tests of lipreaders are inconclusive" (Fusfeld, 1967, p. 308).

Facilitative to the development of rhythm by the deaf, as in marching and dancing, is the input which they receive by feeling, either directly or indirectly, the vibration of music. In learning oral speech, an assist to the visual perception and imitation of the speech of others has been teaching the deaf to associate different sound frequencies with different colors. Vision remains the main channel of input, one reason why some have advocated strongly that the deaf develop and use intensively good reading skills and habits.

Because of the belief that, for all children, verbal symbols are the sine qua non of formal school learning and of much of the communication process both during that learning and later in general social intercourse, the verbal symbol input and output of the deaf have been the focal concern here. Since this problem is greatest among those children with extreme and severe hearing loss, it has been considered in terms of them, the problem being attenuated with increasing hearing. Whatever the loss, the importance of soundly nurtured central processing cannot be ignored since conceptual adequacy is so important in effective communication. That a common communication channel is conducive to the social clustering of the deaf is not unique to them. The one condition that is unique to them is the fact that they must be in visual contact in order to communicate—a very restrictive condition in contrast to that of the visually impaired.

The Visually Impaired

To the extent that visually impaired children have usable vision after proper correction, they can benefit from the usual compensations for limited input that are, or should be, made for them—large-type printed materials and various magnification facilities. Assuming adequate lighting in the learning environs, the learning situation is not markedly different from that of other children. In large school systems and in areas served by centers established for impaired children, the odds are fairly high that they will have access to resource rooms from which the special teachers can provide materials to compensate for limited input and/or which will be a source of help to the regular teacher. Insofar as output needs in the area of written expression are concerned, special writing materials can be provided—large-lined paper, heavy pencils or felt pens, and, if lucky, largetype typewriters. Their central processing of stimuli will vary as in the cases of other children, limited only by the child's basic capacity for such processing and by the teacher's ability to make use of it.

Social problems will arise only to the extent that the presence of limited vision constricts participation in activities making normal visual demands and to the extent that the teachers working with visually impaired neglect or try to overcompensate for the child's impairment. If necessary, teachers may need to work with parents with respect to attitudes toward the child. From the standpoint of conceptual adequacy, only relatively minor limitations as, possibly, in visualizing certain quantitative relationships occasioned by a somewhat restricted range of experience, need exist; in this respect the visually impaired child is better off than is the seriously auditorially impaired child.

Before considering specifics in the case of the functionally blind child, it is well to recognize a different perspective from that employed in regard to the deaf child. Communication was the focus of concern in the case of the deaf because of the basic means of communication had to be established even for formal learning to occur—itself a learning matter. Although deaf children could see, they have to communicate what they see. In contrast, blind children hear and thus learn easily to talk even though they do not see the things about which they hear. They thus have a primary, easily established means of communication, but it needs to be augmented in order that they can also read and write about things. For functionally blind children then, we shall consider learning situations in terms of acquiring input and output compensatory to these ends. We shall proceed in terms of the children who are born functionally blind since the presence of vision for even a few years in early life is inferred to be helpful in learning.

The functionally bli d'; main channels of both input and output of hearing and touching are at times augmented by kinesthesis. Being able to hear and speak facilitates their formal learning of braille by touch. The acquisition of skill in reading and writing braille involves no particularly unique principles of the psychology of learning—the primary channel being touch rather than vision. The central processing of information by the blind is likely to be more productive than in the case of the deaf due to incidental nurturance through hearing, still depending on the basic capacity of the individual and the teacher's nurturance of it.

In contrast with the deaf, there is little in the communication of the blind which leads them to have their own social clusterings. Although their learning braille may involve their doing so in groups apart from the nonblind, their subsequent commingling with the nonblind is limited only by whatever limitations they may have in travel, plus, of course, any attitude of negative self-regard that would be deleterious to their interpersonal relationships. Whereas there is nothing inherent in braille input and output that need negatively affect the conceptual adequacy of any learning/communicating, certain inevitable lacks of experience may and do have a limiting effect, for instance, the lack of comprehension of color and difficulty in spatial conceptualization. Hallahan and Kauffman (1978, pp. 346–347) observe: "While there are studies showing blind people to be inferior to the sighted on spatial concepts (Hartlage, 1967; Juurmaa, 1967; Swallow & Poulsen, 1973), there are a number reviewed by Harley (1973) which show that spatial conceptualization is not impossible for blind individuals." Graphic depiction of, say, three-dimensional representations of phenomena, can be communicated orally to the blind if the phenomena are logically analyzed into their component parts, described in terms within the comprehension of the blind, and then synthesized properly. And it must be recognized that all blind need not "visualize" phenomena or relationships any more than do all sighted individuals.

The Deaf-Blind

If the deaf and the blind have their own difficult problems of input and output, then problems of the deaf-blind are best regarded not as some sum of those problems but as the product of them. The most serious problem is, of course, the impairment of auditory input. As anyone knows who has worked with any child who has a serious learning problem, the crucial moment occurs when the first appropriate response is evoked to an applied stimulus. Until that stage is reached, all attempts at communication are essentially trial and error; once a simple commonality in communication is achieved, subsequent communication can be built on that. Probably it is not the element which is so communicated that is vitally important but the realization that communication is possible. With the deaf-blind, the input channel is cutaneous-kinesthetic; the output channel is essentially manual-motor. A complex of signs and finger spelling constitutes the essence of the communication. As usual, the contribution which central processing can make depends on the capacity of the child and the teacher's nurturance of it. By virtue of the very small number of such children and also by virtue of the nature of their limitations, the social world of the deaf-blind depends essentially on the extent to which their mentors see to it that social contacts are provided. Very few are likely to attain the social involvement of Helen Keller. The conceptual adequacy of the communication of the deaf-blind is more likely to approach that of the deaf than that of the blind.

THE LEARNING LOCALES

The situations in which sensorily impaired children do their formal learning can have overtones with respect not only to academic learning but also to important psychological concomitants of that learning. The psychological specifics of how they do their learning are of fundamental importance wherever these children are. In a gross sense they do their learning in day schools or in residential schools, qualifying this somewhat to recognize that some residential schools have some day pupils. Both types of schools are operated as public schools and as private schools. We shall consider both in terms of the children's learning conditions and of socially and emotionally related factors.

The depiction of the extents to which these children are being educated in day school facilities and in residential school facilities would be of limited value in view of the fact that changes have been and are taking place. Kirk (1972) presents data which indicate that, according to the most recent information available, approximately 50% of the deaf and 40% of the blind are enrolled in residential schools. The trend is toward increasing enrollment in day school facilities.

Whether these children receive any special educational services, receive them in day schools, or receive them in residential schools obviously depends on a number of important factors—the humanitarian and/or economic disposition of society to provide such services, the physical accessibility to appropriate educational units, and the willingness of the parents to have their children so provided for. Many of these children just are not identified. Even though most school personnel are attitudinally disposed to provide special help for these children, the cost of doing so is very threatening. One survey of 18 school systems revealed that the annual per pupil expenditures for the auditorially impaired ranged from $533 to $4671, with a median cost of $2103; in 17 school systems the annual per pupil expenditures for the visually impaired ranged from $856 to $49,105, with a median cost of $2197 (Froelich, 1973). Many parents are reluctant to have their children recognized and provided for as impaired, especially when this involves their going considerable distances for major lengths of time to centers or residential schools.

It will be helpful to note the broader social scene of the "handicapped" in order that the consideration of educating these children can be better understood. Historically such children were regarded generally as social liabilities and/or as stigmas on the family status. Their physical or mental conditions were not medically understood and, of course, not psychologically diagnosed. Some were used by adults for begging but most were dealt with as "closet cases." As understanding of their conditions improved, and most definitely as society moved out of conditions and attitudes of elementary survival, the desire to "do something" for them increased. The provisions that were made for them, largely institutional in nature, represented a mix of humanitarianism on the part of those providing the facilities and of back-room parking on the part of many of the parents and guardians. This mix of attitudes carried over with respect to providing of compensatory facilities in the public schools. Since these facilities were highly specialized, often complex and expensive, and required special competencies which the regular classroom teacher generally lacked, it seemed reasonable to place such children in special classes. Often a single class served several schools or school districts. All too often these special classes were regarded as "back rooms." There were, of course, educational oases—school buildings and school systems in which such special classes were regarded as justifiably helpful special opportunities for those who needed them and as special groups with whom other pupils and groups of pupils could beneficially interact.

With the increase in society's humanitarian thinking and with improving medical and psychological techniques, as well as psychology's increasing concern in the area of social psychology, the possibility and importance of bringing these children more and more into the main social stream became important influencing factors. While evidences of the results of such thinking had been manifest in some situations as early as in the 1930s, it was not until some 30–40 years later that the underlying idea of socially integrating the "handicapped" gave rise to the "mainstreaming" movement—another basically sound idea that developed into emotionally and impetuously overgeneralized expectations. The shift in social attitude from back-room parking to social integration occurred with respect to auditorially and visually impaired children as well as to other impaired children, whether they were being educated in day school or residential settings. A parallel shift has occurred with respect to "handicapped" adolescents and adults, as reflected in vocational rehabilitation efforts and services.

A disturbing element in this movement has been the pervasive disposition to move those involved from one situation where something undesirable was happening to a different locale where something desirable might happen. On the surface such movement constitutes tangible evidence that efforts are being made to improve matters. It usually is simpler to make a shift in locale for learning than to modify educational procedures and intangible, undesirable attitudes which operate in an existing locale.

This admittedly sketchy description of action against the use of separate educational facilities, while pertaining primarily to special education efforts in the interests of the mentally retarded, has considerable relevance to educating sensorially impaired children. The special educational provisions for them were perceived originally in terms of special classes for those who were moderately impaired and separate special schools for those who were more seriously impaired. In large part the psychological factors involved are common to both the auditorially and the visually impaired.

Impaired children whose learning experiences occur wholly or partly in special classes are likely to be confronted with at least some everyday "normal" environmental and interpersonal demands, are reasonably assured of having specially certificated teachers to help them, and operate out of home bases which are assumed to be beneficial to them. Those whose educational provisions are being made in residential settings are, for the most part of their educational terms, in a social group consisting of sensory peers (which some contend contributes to awareness of differentness and which others contend gives them a sense of physical and social security), have teachers at least some of whom are more highly regarded for their devotion and commitment than for their superior professional preparation, and spend most of their school terms away from the presumed solicitude of home. (It must be borne in mind that characterizations such as these, while probably valid from a national viewpoint, very well may depart from reality in one or more respects for certain situations, being more glowing with respect to some and/or unwarrantedly depressing in others.) Each learning locale—the special class and the residential school—has its merits and limitations. Given certain conditions, and even certain children, either can serve its socioeducational purpose superbly. Yet both call for serious examination.

Special Classes

Initially, as tends to be the case when first trying to make special provisions for those who are moderately impaired, the establishment of special classes was regarded as the appropriate first step in meeting their special needs, since the kinds of specialized help and equipment which they need would not be available in the regular classrooms. The special equipment appropriate to the modality would be provided in a central location. A teacher who was specially prepared to work effectively with children having the same impairment thus could work with the children in terms of their common input-output problems. Generally such teachers were required to be certified both as regular and specialty teachers. This manner of meeting such special needs was plausible and seemed inevitable. However, the use of such an approach came to be regarded as contributive to the alienation of the children in these classes from average pupils, thereby depriving the special class children of experiences and activities enjoyed by the non-special class children and also depriving the "normal" children of the opportunity to come to understand the special class pupils as children with differences rather than as different children. Therefore, the special class children were given increasing opportunities to attend regular classes for activities in which their impairments would not be particularly detrimental. This gave rise to the recognition of a need for increased communication between the regular class teacher and the special class teacher directed toward facilitating the special pupil's participating in regular class situations. This psychologically desirable development has led to what seems a much better arrangement.

The special class, as an essentially separately functioning unit, has tended to become a resource class to which impaired children go as educational needs demand. Special class teachers become helpers to special pupils when they have special needs and are regular class teachers when they need help with special pupils, who are now basically in the regular class. When such an operation becomes truly functional we have "mainstreaming" at its best. (It seems likely that this type and quality of functioning is more realizable in the cases of physically impaired children than in the cases of other "handicapped" children whose impairments are less easily observed and understood.)

Whereas many sensorily impaired children—and some parents of these children—took great pride in the fact that special provisions were made for them and in their thereby being able to learn better, others were depressed by their being removed from the regular educational program. Regardless of how such provisions are perceived, whether in the form of rather separate special classes or of a resource usage, it is socially important that the children involved perceive themselves as part of the larger social group, that they come to regard their impairment as an inconvenience rather than as a disability. Of course the school cannot be regarded as the sole determiner of the quality of the child's self-regard; the attitudes held and manifested by all the significant others in the child's environs—especially parents—can play important roles in determining it. In providing for the moderately sensorily impaired child by means of the resource teacher, the school is moving in a psychologically desirable direction. Schools obviously differ greatly in the adequacy with which they accomplish this.

Special Schools

The use of special schools as a means of providing for the serious sensorily impaired is considerably more complicated psychologically. The relatively small number of special schools which are operated by large city school systems may be thought of as rather closely resembling the early special class situation, especially when they are in separate buildings. Counterbalancing special class pupils' feelings of not being able to participate in activities with other children is the fact that the number of sensory peers in the special school is large enough to provide them with a sense of broader social contact. Implementing school activities between the special school and regular schools can be helpful.

The special residential schools which impaired pupils attend involve a still greater degree of psychological complexity. Whereas they were started in order to meet an educational need, often completely outside the formal educational structure, they also served a welfare function by providing better living conditions than some of the children had at home. They differ widely in the quality of educational program and in the psychological climate which they provide. Generally they were much slower than the public schools in requiring their teachers to be specially certified for teaching their kinds of children. From a stance of operating totally apart from the formal educational system, they came gradually to tolerate and accept educational supervision from their respective state departments of education, and a few of them that were appropriately situated started early to arrange to have their pupils attend classes in neighboring public schools. As the public schools progressed in making special provisions for these special pupils, more of the seriously impaired children have attended public rather than residential schools.

Residential school pupils have the psychological problems in learning that already have been considered, tempered positively and negatively according to the professional competence of their teachers. Socially, their underlying problem is essentially similar in kind to that of pupils in special classes but of greater degree and complexity. Being reared with others of like impairment and in an environment developed and maintained just for them for so much of the school year, they become prone to acquire a sense of social reality that can be restrictive in adulthood. Tours, excursions, and even sports competition with the nonimpaired that may be arranged for them are likely to be regarded by them as only brief departures from their reality. Extrainstitutional experiences, provided in some instances for older pupils through the services of vocational rehabilitation and the arrangements for residential pupils to attend public school classes on a part-time or full-time basis, can facilitate their making a psychologically healthy transition to the nonimpaired world in which they later are to live. Just as in the case of the special class pupils attending special classes, the success of such endeavors depends not only upon how well the pupils involved are prepared for the activities they will encounter but also very heavily upon how well the regular class teacher and pupils have been prepared for the functioning of the impaired in their midst.

The "psychology" of residential schools well may be different for the deaf in contrast to the blind. Furth (1973) maintains that the development of self-concepts by the deaf—especially the prelingual deaf—is discernibly different in that they come to see themselves as being in a world considerably apart rather than that they will come ultimately to adjust totally to a nonimpaired world. The deaf maintain a group identity and cohesion to a much greater extent than do the blind. As has been pointed out, their communication situation is strongly contributive to this. The residential school for the deaf would seem to be contributive to a different end for them than that for the blind.

SOCIAL ADJUSTMENT

In a sense a consideration of the social adjustment of sensorially impaired children apart from other facets of their functioning is a psychological artifact, as is true also of their emotional adjustment. As they grow intellectually or acquire educational competence which is highly contributive to their sense of self-realization and to their assuming roles as responsible adults, they do so in social settings involving others and they react emotionally to what happens to and around them. Since it is not possible to say meaningfully a number of things simultaneously about the individual, even though they occur at the same time, one considers one aspect at a time (that which is appropriate to the situation at hand) and then must depend upon a final synthesis to make psychological sense. In such light then we consider the social adjustment of these children as it relates to their communicating with others, as it relates to their mobility, and as it relates to their vocational involvement.

Communication

That communication is inherent in and necessary to the child's learning has been discussed. The fact that the child initially is an active, outgoing organism contributes to a readiness for interacting with others in the environs. By sounds, gestures, signs, and, later, by verbal symbols a communication beachhead is developed by means of which the child's learning progresses. From the early stage in which the child is involved primarily in acquiring the wherewithal of communication (where learning to communicate is basically the end), he advances to that stage in which the act of communicating dominates (where communication is a means to ends). It is this latter aspect of communication with which we are now concerned—essentially that of the postschool world.

When the mildly and moderately hearing impaired have and properly use correct sound amplification, they need not have serious problems in social communication. By strategically placing themselves and by capitalizing upon correlative visual stimuli in the communication act they can function with little or no inefficiency in relation to their hearing peers. Flashing lights and sound amplification on telephones can help some. In the case of the severely and extremely hearing impaired a quite different social condition maintains because of their restricted communication channel. With the exception of those who have acquired considerable competency both in speech reading and in oral speech, their social communication is restricted to interactions only with others who have similar finger spelling and/or signing skills, compensated for, at times, by means of written communication.

The use of "translators" for the deaf by public speakers and the incorporation of closed captions on television are emerging slowly. And the use of specially trained dogs for the purpose of alerting the deaf to sounds in the home and elsewhere is being explored. The hearing person who is unskilled in communicating with the deaf becomes keenly aware, when observing inter-communication by the deaf, of the psychological meaningfulness of their group structure and of his or her and their alienation in the process.

The deaf are also communicated with by what they can read. The adequacy of this form of their input is a function of the effectiveness with which their input has been soundly psychologically programmed to nurture productive central processing. It is quite possible, if not highly probable, that insufficient psychologically sound effort has been directed toward the development of good reading skills in the deaf who must learn so much about their world by means of written/printed verbal input. (Their participation in the solution, and even in the construction, of a graded series of crossword puzzles, for instance, might do much to help them improve their vocabularies.) With the restriction which their manual means of communication imposes upon the number and conceptual adequacy of their verbal symbols, it would seem that they have a unique need for and opportunity in the use of highly efficient reading skills.

The social communication of the visually impaired is greatly different since they have oral speech and can hear the speech of others. Although much of their social communication is aural-vocal in nature, they still have to rely not only upon touch for some input—whether by reading braille or by exploring their environs with their hands—but also upon written braille for some of their output. As in the case of the auditorially impaired, the more seriously impaired have more inconvenience in social communication with each other than do the less seriously impaired. Whereas the deaf make compensatory use of their seeing the facial expressions, gestures, and posturings of those with whom they communicate, the blind learn to enrich their social communication through perceptions of voice quality and inflections plus, occasionally, through the sense of smell. In written social communication with the nonimpaired, from the input point of view, the deaf have recourse to reading and the blind can make use of recorded material; in terms of output, the deaf have recourse to handwriting or typing and the blind to typewriting and the use of recorders and cassettes. Input in printed form constitutes the greatest impediment to the social communication of the blind. As was mentioned, the various kinds of conversion of printed text into sound by means of photoelectric equipment constitutes a major breakthrough. When such facilities are economically feasible and geographically accessible, they can be of great help, but they still are in the innovational stage and sparsely distributed. The national talking book program and the use of readers for the blind are the most common means of providing such input. Obviously the social communication of the blind does not predispose them to the social clustering that is found among the deaf.

Mobility

Apart from the social communication that is inherent in some travel, as in seeking directions and hearing sirens, the mobility of the hearing impaired involves no problems unique to this group. For the visually impaired, particularly those of serious degree, getting around is more troublesome. The complexity of their mobility problems varies with the locales in which they operate—from the classroom as youngsters, to the neighborhood and community as they grow older, to travel at large as adults. Sighted adults frequently are torn between keeping their homes and classrooms rigidly simple if not equipmentally "sterile" and furnishing them fully to sighted standards. Whatever the arrangement, the blind learn their way around the room, building, or immediate grounds with verbal assists by the sighted where necessary. In schools and commercial buildings the use of horizontal bars on major exit doors and of vertical bars on major entrance doors is helpful.

Help for the blind in their more extended travel exists in varied forms. The use of the seeing eye dogs is coming to be accepted widely in the sighted world. However, the psychological bond which exists between the blind person and his or her dog has no equivalent in the blind person's use of the white cane. It has been known for quite some time that at least some blind persons could avoid walls or other obstacles because they reacted to vibrations echoed from the canes (Telford & Sawrey, 1972). Two mechanical aids for the blind that have capitalized upon this phenomenon are the Mowat Senson,[3] a hand-held high-frequency device that vibrates in the hand of the blind to the nearness of objects in front of it, and the Sonicguide,[3] which converts high-frequency sound into audible stereophonic signals which indicate the distance, position, and surface characteristics of objects in the travel path and immediate environment. In some instances embossed maps of areas are used to help the blind become travel oriented. Of at least equal importance to all such developments is the growing realization, on the parts of both the blind and the sighted, that the blind can get around in society more effectively than has long been believed.

Since the deaf can see where they are going, their ability to travel is relatively little impaired. What the hearing person learns to recognize in a barking dog as an auditory sign of threat the deaf have to learn as a gesturing dog. (Even for the hearing, the dog with bared fangs is a visual threatening stimulus.) Other informational cues for the deaf can become conditioned on what are auditory cues for the hearing.

When psychological analyses such as this become projective of the analyzer, the validity of the analysis becomes psychologically clouded, as when the sighted seek to describe and understand behavior of the blind. Such is the case in the use of "visual imagery" in attempting to describe the travel of the blind—all too often in total disregard of the time of onset of blindness in the individual whose behavior is being considered, whether in terms of an assumed isomorphic imagery in the sighted or of more amorphous imagery. It would seem simpler and equally adequate to account for the blinds' learning to travel, within whatever area, in terms of their acquiring motor pattern habits (which is not more psychologically mysterious than or every bit as psychologically mysterious as in the case of a person's acquiring skill in performing an instrumental musical selection), the major difference being the blinds' taking advantage of auditory stimuli that might occur along their routes of travel. That the travel learning of some adventitiously blind may be facilitated by their use of visual imagery could be granted. Travel efficiency depends on the individual, probably with personality overtones, the insecure being less disposed to push out into their environs—or to overcompensate by doing so rashly—and the more secure more likely to do so aggressively.

Vocational Involvement

It is not the intention here to recount specifically the various kinds of vocational involvement which the sensorially impaired experience or can experience. If this were well-done it would properly require a monograph or so. Rather we shall consider certain psychological aspects of such involvement.

Anyone who has even 20 years experience with the vocational involvement of sensorially impaired adults will be aware of the futility of specifically prethinking the vocational future of sensorially impaired youngsters. Just what constitutes a "feasible" vocational activity for any of them depends very much on their own motivation and capability, as in instances in the 1930s of a totally blind college student who intended to teach a foreign language in a public high school (and was so employed) and a totally blind wrestling captain and law student who became a Monday morning Philadelphia commentator on weekend football games. The deaf who plausibly prepared to be linotype operators and the blind who made brooms or prepared to be piano repairers and tuners lived to see societal changes which greatly altered the promise of such means of support. Technological and social changes that used to take a generation before they affected vocational opportunities, not just for the sensorially impaired, now have their impacts in years. The futility of preparing young sensorially impaired while in school for *specific* occupations which may quickly change is becoming recognized; areas of vocational involvement are a more legitimate focus of concern.

Our history of providing for the vocational involvement of the seriously sensorially impaired ranges from the mass welfare solution to a gradually differentiated self-maintenance approach. Early on, such persons were trained (and used) in relatively simple occupations that contributed primarily to the maintenance of the institution in which they were. Gradually thought was given to teaching them to do things which would be of economic value to them as adults after they left their residential schools. An increasing awareness developed that a few pupils would attain high vocational competence, almost in spite of what they were "trained" for; that most of them would need further help, such as through vocational rehabilitation in vocational preparation and in placement in society; and that another small segment of them would need to work in highly protective situations, giving rise to the establishment of sheltered workshops. The public tends to hear more about the few who, by virtue of strong residual motivation and high capability, do surprisingly well in society and, to a much lesser extent, about those needing sheltered work opportunities than it does about the large majority who need level-headed, competent help in finding vocational involvements that are in harmony with their skills, capabilities, and motivations. Since the range of their potential basic intelligence is not different from that of the general population (except as the deaf may have been cognitively stunted), the perception of their vocational placement possibilities need be tempered only by the fact of sensory impairment.

Two conditions contribute to increased vocational placement possibilities for the sensorially impaired. There continues to be considerable promotion of the idea that the "handicapped" are employable and should be employed. When they are well-assessed and well-placed they tend to do well, particularly when they receive proper supervision after placement. The sensorially impaired who work in factories already are known for their low rate of absenteeism and acceptable work performance. For instance, the immediate supervisors of 95% of the employed deaf subjects in one study rated them average or better in job performance (Kronenberg & Blake, 1966; Moores, 1978; Moores, Fisher, & Harlow, 1974). Task analyses and the development of new tools and machinery have resulted in more opportunities for them. And the development of sound amplification and control along with the conversion of printed text into audible content have increased the employment opportunities for the seriously sensorially impaired.

EMOTIONAL ADJUSTMENT

To attempt to present "the" picture of the emotional adjustment of the sensorily impaired in this chapter would be presumptuous. Too often the instruments used to ascertain it have been inappropriate; devices customarily used for this purpose with the nonimpaired have been used without adequate sensitivity to the appropriateness of the vocabularies involved. Too often the populations examined have been ill-defined populations. Although specific findings often must be teased out from dubious generalizations, some possible helpful clinical inferences can be carefully winnowed out.

The findings and implications of three studies are helpful here. The neuropsychiatric evaluations of 92 legally blind children in British Columbia (Jan, Freeman, & Scott, 1977) revealed no cases of depression but found inaccurate diagnoses of mental retardation, autism, and brain damage. But 53% were also cerebral palsied, mentally retarded, and had some central nervous system dysfunction—convulsive disorders, hearing loss, and other "handicaps." The authors observed that blind children are at special risk for problems of dependence and passivity. A study of a clinic outpatient deaf population (Rainer, Altschuler, & Kallmann, 1963), 69% of whom were 13–30 years old, yielded an insight into their "dynamics": "Instead of a retarded depression developing, we get either a paranoid form or the more agitated one. . . . We find that rage is very close to the surface, and the main feeling you derive from it is that they are angry and afraid of their anger, rather than that they are depressed" (p. 73). Bryan and Herjanic (1980) summarize their perception of emotional adjustment problems facing deaf children:

> "(a) Communication of depression by depressed persons who are often filled with resentment, guilt, and ambivalence from the day that they learn their child is deaf; (b) impaired mother-child interaction because of lack of auditory stimulation; (c) the effect of late and limited development of language in both intellectual and emotional development; (d) the long separation from home and family that may be imposed by residential schooling; and (e) the loneliness and isolation felt by the deaf child and adolescent. (p. 62)

Bauman and Yoder (1966), Cooper (1976), and others, have stressed that children with lesser auditory and visual impairments may be more prone to emotional maladjustment than those with more pronounced impairments. This is but part of the more general condition that when children live in two psychological worlds they tend not to adjust well to either of them.

The emphasis in this chapter has been intentionally heavy upon communication—its nature and the role it plays in the child's learning. In the case of the children with whom we are concerned, both their input and output channels have been impaired, limiting both the quantity and conceptual quality of what they receive, which in turns limits the adequacy of what they can express. In both respects the hearing impaired are the more seriously affected and they run the possible added risk of not having their central processing of input effectively nurtured. While these conditions affect the efficiency of their academic learning, it must be recognized that they also affect their emotional adjustment.

The learnings involved in emotional adjustment antedate those involved in formal school learning, and they are much more pervasive even in the school environment. The relative extents to which children's emotional adjustments are genetically predisposed and environmentally influenced are not known. Since we must do the best we can with whatever is inherently provided, we want to facilitate adjustmental learning as best we can. If it be granted that early learnings of this sort are especially important, the part played by the adults in the impaired child's early years must be given serious attention. The impact upon the parents finding out that their offspring is unable to communicate or to travel conventionally greatly affects not only their own emotional adjustment but also the ways in which they relate to their impaired children. One of two possible conditions may result. On the one hand, the parents (and, later, others significant in the child's adjustment) may become overprotective of their child, thus depriving the child of learning opportunities from which he or she could benefit. On the other hand, the parents (and others) may reject the child, thus depriving him or her of the undergirding emotional anchorage which he or she needs much more than does the nonimpaired child. To the sensitive, well-intentioned parent, as well as to significant others in the child's environs, there is always the vitally necessary responsibility of striking a psychologically sound balance between providing adequate but not unduly restrictive protection for the child and studiously allowing him or her to fend alone, without serious bodily risk. The deaf child's problems will be primarily in the communication area; those of the blind child will be in the area of travel.

The impaired child, like all others, grows and develops in a world of significant others. At first these others are the parents, who generally are most favorably disposed toward their child. Later they are the teachers and specialists who by virtue of their occupational bent are predisposed to helping the child as best they can. And then there are the significant others who constitute the child's increasingly "real" world. The others in this real world—both children and adults—vary in their perceptions of, attitudes toward, and expectations of those who are impaired. While our society is slowly becoming more accepting of the impaired, its members are a mixed lot. Some still perceive people with one kind of impairment as generally impaired; others perceive them as persons with impairments rather than as impaired persons. Attitudes toward persons with impairments vary from the studiously avoidant to the stultifyingly solicitous. Some expect persons with impairments to need only care and protection; others expect them to be as productive and self-sustaining as their impairments and capabilities permit. The problem is to achieve a balance between cold rationality and blind emotionality, each extreme often clouded by faulty premises.

The crucial variable in the emotional adjustment of those with impairments is the individual's sense of personal integrity. The manner in which this is cultivated or acquired is fundamentally the same for the impaired as for the nonimpaired. While tomes have been written on this, suffice it here to identify two conditions that contribute importantly to that goal. The impaired person must have a sense of accomplishment. This is acquired by the individual's having more experiences of success than of failure, the magnitude and nature of these depending on the individual's stage of maturity. Added to this, and perhaps of greater importance to the impaired than to the nonimpaired, is the need for a sound emotional anchorage, resulting from experiencing the healthy emotional support and comprehending empathy of his significant others.

A MATTER OF BELIEF AND CURIOSITY

The compilers of this book suggested that each contributor include a statement of personal belief. I choose to include in mine more than the customary admonition that more research is needed. While my beliefs are couched in terms of the seriously sensorially impaired, implications extend beyond this group.

I firmly believe that many more sensorially impaired can do many more things in our society—helping both themselves and contributing to society—than others now believe. While much more can be accomplished even with what we now know and have at hand, new facilitative technological developments will emerge and additional learning conditions will be discovered which will contribute to this end. Granting that there are oases of great devoted and intuitive efforts being made in the interests of this segment of the impaired population, and in the interest of society in general, I have encountered a disappointing excess of desert. I believe that understanding, ingenuity, and sustained effort thus directed are more crucial than funding with sizable grants, helpful though they may be. I believe that the assessments of these individuals must be in terms of both their limitations and their capabilities, with a calm recognition of the respective activities—school learnings, adjustments, vocational preparations—of which these folks are incapable plus a clear delineation of those of which they are believed to be capable, or which they should be helped at least to try realistically. I believe that our impaired must be helped to develop a sustaining sense of personal integrity plus a firm belief that, insofar as capability permits, each is a responsible, contributing member of our society. I believe that each has a right to opportunity plus the responsibility to capitalize upon it. I believe that those who work with the impaired must be not only understandingly sympathetic of them but also as helpful to them as can be, and also firmly expectant that they use effectively whatever residuals they have. I believe that we owe them the benefits of sound research.

As has been indicated, the hearing impaired have a major psychological problem. In its most general sense this problem is in communication. Once it is well described, important implications regarding their learning will emerge. The research to be proposed on this is programmatic in nature; it is not amenable to the single typical doctoral dissertation study, although components in it could be (and have been to a limited extent) so handled. As research projects go, it would not require excessive funding; $300,000 might suffice. It could be accomplished in five years or less—one year to plan and set up the procedures, one year to collect the data, and not more than three years to analyze the data. Only the major aspects of this proposed study will be presented. Refinements and elaborations can be identified easily; they can serve either to convince some that they can't make such a study or to suggest richer possible yields to the truly inquisitive.

Put simply, the program would seek to ascertain how well deaf subjects receive communications meant for them. Figure 15.1 represents the total problem, its dimensions being (1) the content to be transmitted, (2) the transmitters of the content, and (3) the receivers of the content. Each of these is defined illustratively but not exhaustively.

The nature of the content to be transmitted would depend on the ages and degrees of sophistication of those who will be expected to receive it. Its com-

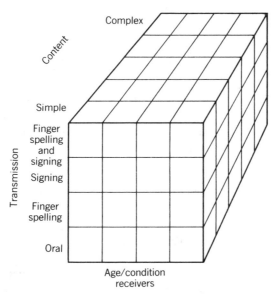

Figure 15.1.   A research domain for deaf-to-deaf communication.

plexity could range from simple, expository material (perhaps appropriate to the comprehension of not more than an average eight-year-old), to somewhat more complex descriptive material, to, possibly, some poetry, or to description or expository material appropriate to the high school or adult level. The material to be transmitted should be selected without regard to the manner of its transmission.

The transmission should be by silent film (not slides). At least four kinds of transmitters—perhaps all of whom are skilled adults—should be employed (probably more than one of each should be considered): one who only finger spells, one who only signs, one who uses a combination of finger spelling and signing, and one whose speech is to be read. The transmitter should be filmed from the waist up. The preparation of the stimuli to be used in the study would be relatively simple.

The population which is to receive these stimuli would need to be most thoughtfully identified. Ideally it should vary systematically in age, with varying degrees of hearing loss at each age level. Within this complex dimension it would be essential that the manners of learning by each subject be known. Additionally contributive to a definitive analysis of the results would be data on each subject regarding his or her learning aptitude—definitely not restricted to performance test data such as those of the Wechslers but including also those like the Hiskey-Nebraska Test of Learning Aptitude, the Columbia Mental Maturity Scale, or of other samples of author's "process" (Newland, 1977). The manner of recording the receptions of the transmissions would be sticky but also the most crucial aspect of the study, and ways of recording could be devised so that the returns could be meaningfully analyzed. Pilot studies performed on older deaf subjects could yield valuable clues to adaptations to/for younger subjects.

As I read studies in this and related fields, I am distressed that so many of them, while probably helpful toward obtaining degrees, tenure, and status, and while yielding bits of information and hunches that admittedly might be helpful, do not present findings that are psychologically integratable because the populations are not representative or are not well defined, the phenomena are so often device-oriented rather than truly function-oriented, and the wheel, or parts of it, is invented again and again.

HOW "BRIGHT" ARE THESE CHILDREN?

The question easily arises "How 'bright,' or 'smart,' are these children in their school learning?" both in comparison with nonimpaired children and in terms of hearing impaired compared with visually impaired. Simplistically, such comparisons tend to be made in terms of their "IQs," but before these questions can be answered meaningfully, it is necessary to examine some of the factors involved.

It should be recognized that we are concerned primarily with children's school-learning aptitude and not with "general intelligence," of which that aptitude is but a part. That the results obtained on tests of general intelligence correlate tolerably with how easily children learn results from the fact that parts of the tests of general intelligence sample behaviors that are involved in school learning.

Even ignoring some of the technical challenges to the soundness of characterizing individuals in terms of IQ, the practice involves dealing with a veritable psychometric iceberg. Consider the following situations. Two hundred and eighty-four twelfth-grade pupils, tested in the same semester, obtained these average IQs on five different tests: 96.4, 103.7, 105.5, 114.2, and 118.2. Taibl (1951) found much more nearly "normal" IQ test performance by cerebral palsied children than had many other testers of them. Pintner and Paterson developed testing materials for the deaf essentially on the assumption that, since deafness did not involve central nervous system pathology, "normal" performance should be expected and reflected in the results of such testing. And Hayes' thinking in adapting the Binet for use with the blind was the same sort.

The wide variation in the average IQs earned by the high school seniors resulted from the use of tests which, although all were called "intelligence" tests, varied in their samplings of behavior from tapping solely or primarily nonverbal behavior, to those tapping a mixture of verbal and nonverbal behavior, to those tapping solely or primarily verbal behavior. Further, the tests used involved varying mixtures of tapping primarily the simple operations by which children learn and of tapping primarily what they already had learned. Hence the resulting IQs reflected different aspects of "intelligent" behavior.

The behavior of Taibl's cerebral palsied children was sampled primarily in terms of nonverbal stimuli involving the basic intellectual operations by which children learn. The Pintner-Paterson work became the basis for the current tendency to do behavior sampling of the deaf by means of the performance portion of the Wechsler tests. (Whereas such behavior samples well may add to the effective measurement of general intelligence, in terms of Wechsler's general adaptability criterion, at no time are the results of such measurement as predictive of children's ease of school learning as are those of the verbal portion, or other comparable verbally loaded samplings.) Even though the Pintner-Paterson assumption of a normal neural potential of the deaf may be tenable regarding them at birth, the strong possibility of lack of nurturance of central processing functioning subsequently can weaken its supportive value.

Especially in the case of children, comparing groups in terms of their average IQs (and many tend to ignore the wide scatters around such averages) can be precarious unless certain precautions are taken. Such comparisons can be psychoeducationally meaningful only to the extent that the following conditions are met:

1.   The populations involved in the comparisons must be adequate in size and composition. Adequacy in size is statistically determinable and may be affected by the number of age levels tested. Unless a large representative age range is involved, any comparison must be made in terms of the level(s) tested. The populations involved must be socioeconomically representative. Clinic populations always are suspect since they tend to be U-shaped—more heavily representative of the lower and upper portions of the socio-economic range. The possibility of even total school populations' being atypical must be considered.

2.   Comparisons must be made in terms of the test(s) used and must be made in terms of the same test(s). Too often reports of the IQs earned by children appear in the literature without specifying the test(s) on which they were obtained, as though IQ were some god-given generality rather than a device-dependent variable.

3.   Comparisons must be made in terms of the kind(s) of intellectual functioning known to be sampled by the test(s) used on the groups being compared. An average IQ earned on, say, the Wechsler performance tests "says" something psychologically quite different from the one earned on the Hiskey or Raven, even though all of them might be called "nonverbal." The content of a test does not well communicate the kind(s) of psychological functioning it taps.

It is only when conditions such as these have been met that one can approximate a psychologically meaningful reply to the question regarding the relative "brightness" of sensorially impaired children. Although it might be placating to couch the answer in terms of average IQs, on the assumption that this condition is reflectible in the IQ, it makes much more sense psychologically to consider the matter in terms of a sounder psychological conceptualization. For this a psychological basis must be established (more fully developed in Newland, 1977, and illustratively dealt with in Newland, 1980). Keeping in mind that we are thinking in terms of children rather than adults and that we are concerned primarily with their ease in school-related learning, their potential for such learning can be perceived and measured in terms of a continuum, one end of which consists of the way(s) in which they accomplish their learning of new, or essentially new, things, and the other end of which consists of the learning which they have accomplished. Much of their learning results from varying mixtures of these two. The one end of this continuum is designated by the term Process (Ps) and incorporates the elementary psychological operations by which children learn—relatable to Guilford's operation of cognition (1967); the other end of the continuum is denoted by the term Product (Pt) and pertains to what the child has learned by means of such psychological operations. Illustrative samplings of Ps are the Columbia Mental Maturity Scale (Blum, Burgemeister, & Lorge, 1972), the Hiskey-Nebraska Test of Learning Aptitude (Hiskey, 1960), the Raven Progressive Matrices (Raven, 1938), and the Blind Learning Aptitude Test (Newland, 1969). The Peabody Picture Vocabulary Test (Dunn, 1965) is a good illustration of Pt sampling. The Wechslers and the Binet sample mixtures of Ps and Pt, the Binet sampling Ps a bit more.

With this psychological background we can make the following observations about the measured learning potential of sensorially impaired children:

1.   Because sensory impairment is not a central nervous system condition, it seems reasonable to assume that the sensorially impaired are, at birth, not typically different from the general child population.

2.   To the extent that children, in the process of growing up, receive a "normal" amount of nurturance of the basic psychological processes by means of which they do their learning, they can be expected to perform "normally" on Ps-dominant measures of learning aptitude. Therefore, (a) hearing impaired children as a group can be expected to perform somewhat below the average for nonimpaired children, the degree of this negative deviation being determined by the severity of hearing loss and by the kind and amount of nurturant limitation they may have experienced, and (b) visually impaired children would, on average, perform no more poorly than would nonimpaired children. (As suggested elsewhere in this chapter, preventive and/or remedial efforts at nurturance could reduce the difference in Ps between the hearing impaired and the nonimpaired.)

3.   When learning potential is measured in terms of what children have learned (Pt), (a) hearing impaired children can be expected to do less well, on average, than nonimpaired children both because of their reduced input and the possible limitation in the nurturance of the central processing of that input, whereas (b) visually impaired children can be expected to do as well, on average, as the nonimpaired. (In the case of both kinds of impaired children,

test content involving sensory-sensitive stimuli would be handicapping—"crooning" for the hearing impaired and "azure" for the visually impaired.)

In sum, although sensorially impaired children are, in terms of school-learning potential, no worse off initially than nonimpaired children, those who have impaired hearing may be less able to capitalize upon it because of diminished central processing nurturance and lowered input which they might have experienced. To couch this possible negative deviation in terms of some numbered IQ points would be fruitless because of the varied measures by means of which any such potential may be sampled. Even though there may be some plausibility in characterizing adult performance on "intelligence" tests in terms of IQ (assuming the test(s) to be specified), the IQ has limited, if any, psychoeducational value in the case of children. At best the IQ has social and educational administrative value; its value in the classroom, necessarily regarded in terms of individual educational planning and instruction, is nil. For instance, at what reading level should a teacher try to work with a child when all that is known about the child is an IQ of 75, 100, or 125? The teacher needs to know the *level* at which the child may be capable of learning, not the rate at which he or she is growing "intellectually." Therefore, the teacher is better informed by means of a designation of a level of learning expectancy for the child. For this, the mental age or, better, test age is the more relevant information. Scaled scores may have certain statistical values, but again they are group-oriented rather than geared to level of individual educational expectation. As a final caveat, all scores on tests of learning aptitude must be regarded as suggesting, within some error of measurement, the least that should be expected of a child rather than as reflecting a ceiling of educational expectation for him or her.

SUMMARY

On the assumption that a consideration of how sensorially impaired children process the information they receive in their learning and thereby are able to communicate, the primary concern of this chapter has been with the nature of the stimuli which they receive, the ensuing central processing of that information, and their use of what they have learned and processed in further learning and communication. To regard formal learning primarily or wholly as a means of getting information into children is to shortchange them; careful thought must be given also to what and how children do to and with the input which is provided them. As a result of the many analyses of cognitive processing, the early general admonition of Dewey that children should be taught to think is coming to receive the specifically analyzed attention it has so badly needed. While this is important in the education of all children, it is particularly important in the cases of the children where the nature of the input is affected by sensory impairment, and it is believed to be particularly crucial in the cases of the seriously auditorially impaired. The results of good central processing of input provide the primary basis for the conceptual adequacy for meaningful communication—whether oral or written—and this in turn is contributive to social, emotional, and vocational adjustment. Electric technical advances in input amplification and conversion are improving conditions for the seriously impaired.

From an era characterized by the use of residential schools for the seriously impaired and by the provision of clearly separate special classes for those of moderate impairment, movement toward full integration of the impaired with the nonimpaired is taking place. Implementation of provisions of PL 94–142 can be conducive to the crucial early education of these children.

The self-concepts and the attitudes of the sensorially impaired are a function of the quality of their interactions with all the others with whom they grow and develop. The emotional tone set by their parents, disconcerted by finding out that their children have impairments, constitutes an early and important factor. That of their classmates and teachers during their schooling is necessarily compensatory. And that of their adult peers with whom they later commingle will do much to help determine whether they perceive themselves, and are perceived by others, as impaired individuals or as individuals with inconveniencing impairments. Increasingly they are becoming self-sufficient and contributing members of society.

NOTES

1. Telesensory Systems, Inc., 3408 Hillview Avenue, Palo Alto, Calif. 94304
2. Kurzweil Computer Products, Inc., 33 Cambridge Parkway, Cambridge, Mass. 02142
3. Wormald International Sensory Aids Corporation, 205 W. Grand Avenue, Bensenville, Ill. 60106

REFERENCES

Barraga, N. *Increased visual behavior in low vision children.* New York: American Foundation for the Blind, 1964.

Bauman, M. K. & Yoder, N. M. *Adjustment to blindness: Re-reviewed.* Springfield, Ill.: Charles C Thomas, 1966.

Benderly, B. L. Dialogue of the deaf. *Psychology Today,* 1980, *14,* 66–67.

Berger, K. W. *Speechreading: Principles and Methods.* Baltimore: National Education Program, 1972.

Birch, J. W. & Stuckless, E. R. *The relationship between early manual communication and later achievement of the deaf* (Cooperative Research Program 1769, Contract OE-3-10-078). Pittsburgh: University of Pittsburgh, 1964.

Blum, L. H., Burgemeister, B. B., & Lorge, I. *The Columbia Mental Maturity Scale (revised).* New York: Harcourt Brace Jovanovich, 1972.

Brasel, K., & Quigley, S. Influence of certain language and communication environments in early childhood on the development of language in deaf individuals. *Journal of Speech and Hearing Research,* 1977, *20,* 95–107.

Bryan, D. P. & Herjanic, B. Depression and suicide among adolescents and young adults with selective handicapping conditions. *Exceptional Education Quarterly,* 1980, *1*(2), 57–65.

Coghill, G. E. *Anatomy and the problem of behavior.* Cambridge: Cambridge University Press, 1929.

Conrad, R. *The deaf school child: Language and cognitive function.* London: Harper & Row, 1979.

Cooper, A. F. Deafness and psychiatric illness. *British Journal of Psychiatry,* 1976, *129,* 216–226.

Dorward, B. *Teaching aids for blind and visually limited children.* New York: American Foundation for the Blind, 1968.

Dunn, L. M. *Peabody Picture Vocabulary Test.* Nashville, Tenn.: American Guidance Service, 1965.

Elliott, L. L., & Ambruster, V. B. Some possible effects of the delay of early treatment of deafness. *Journal of Speech and Hearing Research,* 1967, *10,* 209–224.

Estes, W. K. The state of the field: General problems and issues of theory and methodology. In W. K. Estes (Ed.), *Handbook of learning and cognitive process* (Vol. 1). Hillsdale, N. J.: Erlbaum, 1975.

Frisina, R. (Chairman). *Report of the Committee to Redefine Deaf and Hard of Hearing for Educational Purposes,* 1974 (mimeographed).

Froelich, L. E. Costing programs for exceptional children: Dimensions and indices. *Exceptional Children,* 1973, *39,* 317–324.

Furth, H. G. Linguistic deficiency and thinking: Research with deaf subjects. *Psychological Bulletin,* 1971, *76,* 58–72.

Furth, H. G. *Deafness and learning.* Belmont, Calif.: Wadsworth, 1973.

Fusfeld, I. S. (Ed.). *A handbook of reading in education of the deaf and post-school implications.* Springfield, Ill.: Charles C Thomas, 1967.

Gagné, R. M. Learning hierarchies. *Educational Psychologist.* 1968, *6,* 1–9.

Gentile, A. *Academic achievement test results of a national testing program for hearing impaired students, United States, Spring, 1971* (Series D, No. 9). Annual Survey of Hearing Impaired Children and Youth, Office of Demographic Studies, Gallaudet College, Washington, D.C., 1972.

Gentile, A. *Further studies in achievement testing, hearing impaired students, United States, Spring, 1971* (Series D, No. 13). Office of Demographic Studies, Gallaudet College, Washington, D.C., 1973.

Goldfish, L. H. *Braille in the United States: Its production, distribution, and use.* New York: American Foundation for the Blind, 1967.

Groht, M. A. *National language for deaf children.* Washington, D.C.: Alexander Braham Bell Association for the Deaf, 1958.

Guilford, J. P. *The nature of human intelligence.* New York: McGraw-Hill, 1967.

Gustason, G., Pfetzing, D., & Zawolkow, E. *Signing exact english.* Silver Spring, Md.: National Association for the Deaf, 1975.

Hallahan, D. P., & Kauffman, J. M. *Exceptional children.* Englewood Cliffs, N. J.: Prentice-Hall, 1978.

Hardy, L. H., Rand, G., & Rittker, M. C. *A-O-H-R-R Pseudoisochromatic plates* (2nd ed.). American Optical Corporation, Southhampton, Mass., 1957.

Harley, R. K. Children with visual disabilities. In L. M. Dunn (Ed.), *Exceptional children in the schools.* (2nd ed.). New York: Holt, Rinehart & Winston, 1973.

Hartlage, L. C. *Ability structure and loss of vision.* New York: American Foundation for the Blind, 1967.

Hatfield, E. M. Why are they blind? *Sight Saving Review,* 1975, *45,* 3–22.

Hiskey, M. S. *Hiskey-Nebraska Test of Learning Aptitude.* Lincoln, Nebr.: Union College Press, 1960.

Hurlin, R. G. Estimated prevalence of blindness in the U.S., 1960. *Sight Saving Review,* 1962, *32,* 4–12.

Ishihara, S. *The series of plates designed as a test for color-blindness.* Tokyo: Kanehara Shuppan, 1960.

Jacobs, P. I., & Vandeventer, M. The learning and transfer of double-classification skills in first graders. *Child Development,* 1971, *42,* 149–159.

Jan, J. E., Freeman, R. D., & Scott, E. P. *Visual impairment in children and adolescents.* New York: Grune & Stratton, 1977.

Jarman, R. F. Modality-specific information processing and intellectual ability. *Intelligence,* 1980, *4,* 201–217.

Juurmaa, J. Ability structure and loss of vision. *American Foundation for the Blind Research Series,* 1967, (18).

Kirk, S. A. *Educating exceptional children.* Boston: Houghton Mifflin, 1972.

Kronenberg, H., & Blake, G. *Young deaf adults: An occupational survey.* Hot Springs: Arkansas Rehabilitation Services, 1966.

Levine, E. Psychoeducational determinants in personality development. *Volta Review,* 1971, *73,* 258–267.

Liben, L. S. *Deaf children: Developmental perspectives.* New York: Academic, 1978.

Lowell, E. E. New insights into lipreading. *Rehabilitation Record,* Office of Vocational Rehabilitation, U. S. Department of Health, Education and Welfare, Washington, D.C., July-August 1961, 306–309.

Lowenfeld, B. (Ed.). *The visually handicapped child in school.* New York: John Day, 1973.

Lowenfeld, B. *The changing status of the blind: From separation to integration.* Springfield, Ill.: Charles C Thomas, 1978.

Lowenfeld, B. Psychological problems of children with severely impaired vision. In W. M. Cruickshank (Ed.), *Psychology of exceptional children and youth.* Englewood Cliffs, N. J.: Prentice-Hall, 1980.

Luria, A. R. *The working brain.* London: Penguin, 1973.

Lydon, W. T., & McGraw, M. L. *Concept development for visually handicapped children: A resource guide for teachers and other professionals working in educational settings* (rev. ed.). New York: American Foundation for the Blind, 1973.

Moores, D. F., *Educating the deaf: Psychology, principles, and practices.* Boston: Houghton Mifflin, 1978.

Moores, D. F., Fisher, S., & Harlow, M. *Post-secondary programs for the deaf: Monograph 4, Summary and Guidelines.* (Research Report No. 80). Minneapolis: University of Minnesota Research and Development and Demonstration Center in Education of Handicapped Children, 1974.

Newland, T. E. *The Blind Learning Aptitude Test.* Champaign: University of Illinois Press, 1969.

Newland, T. E. Tested "intelligence" in children. *School Psychology Monograph,* 1977, *3,* 1–44.

Newland, T. E. Psychological assessment of exceptional children and youth. In W. M. Cruickshank (Ed.), *Psychology of exceptional children and youth.* Englewood Cliffs, N.J.: Prentice-Hall, 1980.

Oleron, P. Conceptual thinking of the deaf. *American Annals of the Deaf,* 1953, *98,* 304–310.

Rainer, J. D., Altschuler, K. Z., & Kallmann, F. J. *Family and mental health problems in a deaf population.* New York: Department of Medical Genetics, Psychiatric Institute, Columbia University, 1963.

Raven, J. C. *Raven progressive matrices.* Cambridge: H. K. Lewis, 1938, 1947, 1956, 1962. (Distributed in the United States by The Psychological Corporation, New York and by Western Psychological Services, Beverly Hills, Calif.)

Roberts, J. *Color deficiencies in youths 12–17 years of age, United States* (HRA 74–1616). National Center for Health Statistics, Department of Health, Education and Welfare, National Health Survey, Series II, No. 134, January 1974.

Roberts, J. *Hearing levels of youths 12–17 years, United States* (HRA 75–1627). National Health Survey, Department of Health, Education, and Welfare, Series 11, No. 145, January 1975. (a)

Roberts, J. *Hearing sensitivity and related medical findings among youths 12–17 years, United States.* (HRA 76–1636) National Center for Health Statistics, Department of Health, Education and Welfare, National Health Survey, Series 11, No. 154, November 1975. (b)

Roberts, J. *Eye examination findings among youths 12–17 years, United States* (HRA 76–1637). National Center for Health Statistics, Department of Health, Education and Welfare, National Health Survey, Series 11, No. 155, November 1975. (c)

Roberts, J. *Monocular visual acuity of persons 4–74 years, United States, 1971–1972* (HRA 77–1646). National Center for Health Statistics, Department of Health, Education and Welfare, National Health Survey, Series II, No. 201, March 1977.

Rudio, J. L *Nurturing concept formation with hearing impaired children.* Doctoral dissertation, University of Illinois, 1972.

Snow, R. E. Theory and method for research on aptitude process. *Intelligence,* 1978, *2,* 225–278.

Spearman, C. *The abilities of man.* New York: Macmillan, 1927.

Sternberg, R. *Intelligence, information processing, and analogical reasoning: The componential analysis of human abilities.* Hillsdale, N.J.: Erlbaum, 1977.

Swallow, R. M., & Poulsen, M. K. An exploratory study of Piagetian space concepts in secondary, low-vision girls. *Research Bulletin*. American Foundation for the Blind, 1973 (26) 139–149.

Taibl, T. M. *An investigation of Raven Progressive Matrices as a test for the evaluation of cerebral palsied children*. Doctoral dissertation, University of Nebraska, 1951.

Telford, C. W. & Sawrey J. M. *The exceptional individual* (4th ed.) Englewood Cliffs, N.J.: Prentice-Hall, 1981.

Toth, Z. *Die Vorstellunswelt der Blinden*. Leipzig: Johann Ambrosius Barth, 1930.

U.S. Office of Education *Federal programs administered or monitored by the Bureau of Education of the Handicapped*. Washington, D.C.: Department of Health, Education and Welfare, 1970.

Wallin, J. E. W. *The education of handicapped children*. Boston: Houghton Mifflin, 1924.

CHAPTER 16

Childhood Speech and Language Disorders

PHYLLIS TUREEN AND JACK TUREEN

The most significant unique characteristic that distinguishes humans from other animals is the ability to express thoughts, needs, and wishes through the use of speech and language and to be able to quickly encode and decode in response to the language of others in the speech community. In order to manage successfully within one's speech community this skill must be appropriately acquired by using the criteria established by the community for satisfactory or meaningful communication. If that communication is impaired for any of a number of reasons to be set forth in this chapter, the individual may become isolated, psychologically disturbed, educationally and socially disadvantaged, and/or vocationally and economically affected. The more complex or severe the communication disorder, the greater the handicap and the wider the separation of the individual from his or her community.

It is generally agreed that young children begin to control and manage their environment only with the acquisition of speech and language. Until then their needs and desires are subject to the interpretation of those who nurture them. Their wants can only be guessed at and may or may not be met appropriately. If speech and/or language fails to emerge or emerges defectively, the child's emotional, social, intellectual, and psychological development will be impaired in some way. Certainly the child experiences some form of penalty as a consequence of the inability to perform at an acceptable level. The punishments induced, which are as much internal as external, often include *frustration* because of failure to produce speech that meets the child's needs and those of his or her parents and peers, a condition that often worsens the original disorder. Other penalties include *guilt* because of the failure, *anxiety, fear, anger,* and *rejection*. These emotions may be shared by the parents as well as the child.

This chapter is designed to acquaint the reader with some of the disorders that limit or affect the development of speech and language in children. According to Van Riper (1978), "a difference to be a difference must make a difference." If speech calls attention to itself, interferes with the receiving of the message, or is unpleasant to the speaker or listener, we then have a speech problem.

Estimates of the prevalence of speech and language disorders vary widely from a percentage of the general population to a distribution of disorders by numbers for a particular age grouping. Van Riper (1978) states that there are at least 18 million men, women, and children in this country who cannot speak normally. The ASHA Committee on the White House Midcentury Conference (1952) studied the prevalence of communication disorders in children between the ages of 5 and 21 and estimated that 5% of this population had seriously defective speech. They stressed that these figures were presented as the lowest defensible estimate and could be regarded as serious underestimates by some authorities. They did not include an estimated additional 5% or 2 million children who had minor speech and voice defects, unimportant for the most practical purposes but serious in their side effects or implications for the children themselves. It should be noted that the population investigated consisted of school children and did not include a significant number of other preschool or nonmainstream children.

More recent studies by Milisen (1957), Myklebust (1964), and Wood (1969) estimate larger numbers. Perkins (1971) estimates the number of children with speech and language impairment at more than 12 million, distributed as follows: 8 million with articulatory disorders, 2 million with language disorders, stuttering at 1.4 million and voice disorders affecting 1 million children. Obviously the estimates of the numbers of speech and language handicapped children vary from researcher to researcher because of different definitions of communication disorders, and with the age groups considered. Since most of the research has been concerned with school-aged children, the populations above and below those age criteria would alter those figures dramatically. Many of the severely handicapping conditions manifest themselves before the age of 5. This age group has generally not been included in meaningful statistical studies because of the difficulty in obtaining their data. For example, children with serious organic impairment such as cleft palate, cerebral palsy, hearing deficits, and deafness may first demonstrate speech and language disability at the crucial onset years between ages 1 and 5. Preschool childhood disorders of speech and language resulting from severe psychological problems or problems of psychic deafness have also been omitted from incidence figures because of the difficulty in obtaining data.

The Speech Processes

Speaking quite literally, there are no speech mechanisms or speech organs. The processes of respiration, phonation, resonation, and articulation make use of all structures essential in sustaining life, such as breathing and the chewing and swallowing of food. Since these structures serve more basic biological functions than speech, speech is often designated as an "overlaid" or secondary function.

The first of the four elements of speech production, *respiration*, is the process of inhalation and exhalation. Most speech, with a few unusual foreign dialect exceptions, is produced on the exhalation of air. Normal speech sounds depend on an exhaled stream of voiced or unvoiced air. Differences of pressure between the outside and the air within the respiratory tract produce, upon inhalation, a flow of air into the lungs and, on exhalation, a flow of air out of the lungs.

The major structures involved in the respiratory process are (1) the thoracic cavity, the upper cavity of the torso formed by the walls of the thorax, a bony-cartilaginous cage containing and protecting the heart and lungs and consisting of the ribs, vertebral column, and sternum; (2) the bronchial tubes; (3) the lungs, occupying most of the chest cavity; (4) the trachea or "windpipe," which connects the larynx and the lungs; (5) the diaphragm, a large dome-shaped muscle that serves as a partition between the thorax and abdominal cavity; and (6) the abdominal cavity, the lower cavity of the torso containing the organs of digestion.

On the inhalation of air, there is an upward, forward, and lateral movement of the thorax permitting an enlargement of the thoracic cavity. This increase in volume allows the lungs to expand as air is taken into the body. The diaphragm descends in the torso and displaces the abdominal organs of digestion, thereby contributing to an increase in the volume of the thoracic cavity. On the exhalation of air, the thorax resumes its usual shape. The air passes from the lungs through the trachea and into the larynx, where the next element of speech production takes place.

The second of the four phases of speech production is called *phonation*. It is the process of producing the fundamental sound of voice. This fundamental sound is quite unlike the voice quality we hear. It is a small voice, thin and colorless. The major structure utilized in phonation is the larynx, often referred to as the "voicebox." It is composed of cartilage and muscle tissue and is situated in the neck at the upper end of the trachea. Its cavity is the upward continuation of the cavity of the tubelike trachea. The major parts of the larynx consist of (1) the thyroid cartilage, a shield-shaped cartilage that forms the anterior and lateral walls of the larynx; (2) cricoid cartilage, a ring-shaped cartilage which forms the base of the larynx; (3) arytenoid cartilages, which lie on the posterior rim of the cricoid cartilage; (4) the vocal folds, often referred to as vocal cords, which are composed of muscle tissue extending from the inner surface of the thyroid cartilage to the arytenoid cartilage; and (5) the glottis, the opening or space between the vocal folds.

As an aid to breathing in carrying on the life process, the larynx acts as a closure mechanism in respiration thereby preventing foreign matter from entering the trachea and lungs. In carrying out the speech process the larynx is the source of the original sound for speech. Upon inhalation the glottis is widened by the separation of the vocal folds and air is allowed to pass into the lungs. On exhalation the glottis is narrowed by the vocal folds approximating each other. The pressure of the air rising from the lungs through the trachea sets the vocal folds into vibration as the air passes between them. The vibration of the vocal folds in turn sets the surrounding air into vibration, thereby producing sound.

Pitch changes in the voice are largely the result of the action of the vocal folds. Variations in the thickness, length, and tension of the folds contribute to the pitch differences and changes of voice. The longer, thicker, and looser the vocal folds, the lower the pitch. Conversely, shorter, thinner, and tighter folds result in higher pitch. Loudness depends largely on the amount of air pressure below the glottis. The greater the air pressure, the louder the volume.

The third of the four processes of speech production is called *resonance*, the process of amplifying or building up the sounds produced in phonation. In addition to the build-up of the sound, overtones of sound are introduced that contribute to the quality and richness of the tone produced.

The structures used in the process of resonation are (1) the pharyngeal cavity (throat), a cavity about five inches long and extending from the base of the skull to the esophagus; with openings to the nasal cavity, oral cavity, and laryngeal cavity; (2) the oral cavity (mouth), bounded externally by the lips, teeth, and gums; below by the tongue and floor of the mouth; and above by the palate; (3) the nasal cavity, consisting of two hard-walled passages ending with the nostrils of the nose and divided by a partly bony, partly cartilagenous septum.

As sound passes through these chambers, it builds in intensity or loudness and in timbre or quality. The pharyngeal muscles upon contraction may lengthen or shorten the pharyngeal cavity, making its diameter larger or smaller and altering the tension of the walls. Pitch and quality depend in part on the diameter of the pharyngeal cavity. The larger the diameter of the cavity, the lower the sound and, conversely, the smaller the diameter, the higher the pitch. Excessive tensing of the muscles of the throat may cause a strident, metallic voice quality.

The fourth and last step in the process of speech, *articulation*, involves the momentary approximations of various parts of the mouth to interrupt and modify or change the path of the breath stream. The different ways in which the breath stream is interrupted and modified produces the vowels, diphthongs, and consonants of the language, which join together to produce words and meaningful speech and language. The structures of articulation include (1) the palate, a partition of bone and muscle which separates the oral cavity from the nasal cavity and consists of the soft palate or velum, the movable and muscular posterior part of the palate; the hard palate, the immovable, bony anterior part of the palate; and the alveolar ridge, the upper gum ridge at the forward part of the hard palate, (2) the teeth, (3) the tongue, a mass of muscles covered by a mucous membrane, fastened to the floor of the mouth, (4) the lips, (5) the mandible, or lower jaw, instrumental in shaping the mouth, and (6) the glottis, or space between the vocal folds, used only for one standard sound of English.

The manner in which the articulators are used produce the various vowels, diphthongs, and consonants. For example, the position of the tongue in the mouth and the shaping of the lips, accompanied by the widening or narrowing of the oral cavity by the mandible, is responsible for the articulation of vowels and diphthongs. The position of the tongue in relation to the teeth or palate creates the articulation of most of the consonant sounds. If the wrong structures are used or if the appropriate structures are used incorrectly, misarticulations or serious defects of speech result.

Weiss and Lillywhite (1981) state, and the authors concur, that cerebration is the ultimate process of communication. It provides for thought, symbolic formulation, and comprehension. Without the appropriate function and control of the brain, the four processes of speech production may be limited, seriously impaired, severely deviant, or nonfunctioning.

CLASSIFICATION OF SPEECH AND LANGUAGE DISORDERS

According to the American Speech-Language and Hearing Association, speech disorders may be characterized as disorders of articulation, language, rhythm, voice, and hearing. The categories do not explain etiology but only the effects of a variety of etiologies. The etiologies will be discussed later. In order to understand the problems of the speech and language impaired child the meaning of these categories should be understood.

Articulation disorders involve the incorrect production of the individual sounds or phonemes of the language. Since words are composed of complex combinations of phonemes, a misarticulated phoneme will result in a defectively produced word. The more severe or more numerous the misarticulations, the less intelligible the speech of the child. The child's language ability may be normal but his speech will be impaired and general communication processes affected.

Language disorders involve the inability of the individual to understand or to use the words, phrases, or sentences of his language in a meaningful manner. Language disorders may be receptive or expressive in nature or a combination of both, and may vary greatly in degree of severity. The severity of impairment may range from total absence of language to a linguistic ability slightly below the norm or standard for the age of the child. Language alone may be defective or may be accompanied by defective articulation.

Disorders of rhythm may involve prosody or phrasing but most often involve the fluency of speech and language. The most serious disorder of rhythm is stuttering. Stuttering too may vary in severity ranging from seeming mutism to simple repetition of sounds, syllables, words, or phrases. The more severe the stuttering, the greater the interference with the ability to communicate and the greater the probability of associated emotional difficulty.

Voice disorders represent any deviation in pitch, intensity, quality, or other basic attribute which consistently interferes with communication, draws unfavorable attention, adversely affects the speaker or the listener, or is inappropriate to the age, sex, culture, or class of the individual. It may be organic or functional in nature and may be the result of laryngeal function or resonance disorders (Nickolosi, Harryman, & Krescheck, 1978). Voice disorders may range in severity from total aphonia to relatively minor deviations in quality, such as hoarseness or breathiness. The most severe disorders are those in which the laryngeal mechanism itself is absent or structurally abnormal.

Hearing disorders are those problems which reflect damage in the sensory mechanism that transmits sound from the individual's environment to the appropriate areas of the brain. Damage anywhere along the auditory pathway will manifest itself in the way the individual speaks and/or reacts to his environment. The loss may range from mild to profound and may result in minor speech and language deficits or to the complete absence of the oral communication function. Problems associated with hearing loss and deafness are discussed elsewhere in this book. (See Newland, Chapter 15, this volume, for discussion of hearing loss and deafness.)

Speech and language disorders may also be classified by etiology rather than symptomatology. In this case we look for cause related to broad distinctions between organic, functional, and psychological considerations. In utilizing this method of classification the reader must always be aware of the possible existence of unknown factors and also bear in mind that these etiologies may interact with one another. In general, disorders of organic origin have demonstrable pathologies or structural anomalies. Examples of organic disorders associated with speech or language pathologies include mental retardation, deafness, cerebral palsy, aphasia, cleft palate, endocrinological dysfunction, and many others.

The functional disorders are somewhat more difficult to substantiate since they depend on the absence of demonstrable pathology and may be the result of improper learning or faulty motivation. This classification assumes that no possible organic or psychopathological cause has been overlooked. When correctly classified, the indications are that all structures and functions are intact and that the disorder is caused by their misuse rather than physical pathologies. Some examples of functionally based disorders are infantile perseveration or "baby talk," some lisps, some types of language delay, idioglossia, imitation errors, and others.

If functional disorders are difficult to substantiate, a psychological etiology is even more difficult to diagnose in the young child. In general there is no structural anomaly or easily identifiable organic pathology. Much of this classification depends on determining that the disorder is caused by a mental or emotional reaction of the individual to some factor of his social or physical environment or to some physical condition of his own body that could not of itself directly cause a speech defect. Because of the many grey areas in applying this psychogenic category, it is generally limited to the disorders of autism, schizophrenia, and hysterical or conversion voice, or speech problems, and, by some researchers, to stuttering.

The information derived from knowledge of the aforementioned etiologies is valuable primarily in its importance in planning treatment strategies. It suggests the importance of the interdisciplinary or team approach to diagnosis and treatment. The medical specialist, psychologist, speech pathologist, audiologist, and education specialist can significantly contribute to the knowledge necessary for accurate identification and treatment strategy for children with communication disorders.

ARTICULATION DEVELOPMENT AND DISORDERS

The principal vehicle for conveying meanings, thoughts, ideas, concepts, and attitudes through sounds, words, phrases, and sentences is articulation (Weiss, Lillywhite, & Gordon, 1980). It is dependent upon the mastery of the rules of phonology and contrastive features that govern the perception and production of speech. It is an enormous asset for those children who have mastered it and a serious liability for those who have not.

Articulation disorders are not only the most prevalent of the communication disorders but also the most underestimated with regard to their importance clinically and the ease of remediation. According to Weiss et al. (1980), they also are deceptively variable across etiological modalities. Articulation disorders associated with cleft palate are quite different from articulation disorders associated with cerebral palsy. Similarly, misarticulations associated with verbal apraxia are completely different from those associated with functional infantile perseveration.

Articulation disorders can have a significant influence on the speaker's emotional well-being, achievements, and interpersonal relations (Van Riper, 1978). Since such a large percentage of all communication disorders is associated with disorders of articulation, it is easy to understand why it is viewed as a devastating problem for children and, of course, adults. Because these problems are so apparent to the listener, it often results in value judgments and penalties disproportionate to the disorder itself.

Articulation is a central element in phonology. The speaker with appropriate articulation will not only have the physical and perceptual skills necessary to recognize and produce the distinctive sounds of his or her language but will have mastered the rules underlying their usage (Irwin, 1972). The authors will not reveiw the interrelationships of articulation and language at this point but will approach the problem of articulation disorders from the standpoints of symptom and description.

Articulation defects are traditionally classified as errors of omission, substitution, distortion, and, sometimes, addition.

Omission

As the word implies, omission is the error of leaving a phoneme out of a word in which it should normally appear. The child who says *ook* instead of *look* is obviously omitting the *l* phoneme. The practice of omitting phonemes is fairly typical of the speech of young children. This is the error that is most frequently observed in preschool children and in the first two years of primary school.

Substitution

This is an error in which the individual replaces one standard phoneme of the language with another standard phoneme. The substituted phoneme is correctly articulated but is contextually inaccurate. The child who says "thoap" for soap is producing a perfectly good "th" sound. The problem is that it does not belong in the word soap. The child who says "wing" for ring may be substituting a correctly produced "w" but may indeed be confusing his listener.

Distortion

This involves the replacement of a standard phoneme with a nonstandard sound; a sound that does not appear in the language. In that sense, it is a creative error and indicates that the child is attempting the target sound and failing. The laterally produced production of the "s" sound which is often described as "slushy" is one example of distortion. It is difficult to give additional meaningful examples of this error unless the reader is trained in the use of phonetic transcription. Many phonemes have the potential for distortion. Typical of these misarticulations are distortions of s, z, l, r, ch, j, sh, and others.

Addition

Addition errors refer to the addition of sounds in words where they do not normally appear. These are relatively rare in appearance and may be examples of infantile perseveration or reinforced idioglossia. A simple nonclinical example of an addition error is the intrusive "r" as in "idear" for idea. Hardly catastrophic for a speaker. A more serious illustration of such an error is one in which a young client consistently produced a "t" after every "k" production, resulting in such misarticulated speech as k-topy and k-tat for copy and cat. It was accompanied by many other types of misarticulations and contributed to a nearly unintelligible speech and language pattern. Its origins remain a mystery although it was remediated in the speech clinic. Many researchers, however, disagree about the inclusion of the addition error as a category of misarticulation.

These classifications are not mutually exclusive and children may present one or two or three or all of the errors. There are no absolutes about the consistency, severity, or placement of the errors.

Speech Development

At this point, it is appropriate to indicate that the aforementioned classifications of articulation errors, with the exception of addition, are considered by some speech researchers to also represent stages of normal speech development. According to McDonald (1964), the earliest stages of the normal speech development of all children are characterized by omissions. It is expected that a baby will say "ba" for bottle since he or she is motorically unable to control the finer motor movements needed for the remaining phonemes in the word. As the child matures along both sensory and motor lines, he or she perceives that "ba" is only part of the word and will attempt the missing syllable. The child is still unable to produce the correct phoneme and may then substitute an easier phoneme such as the "t" for the "tl" cluster. The child's "ba" now becomes "bat." With further sensory and motor development the child progresses to a perceptual realization that he or she is still not correct and will ultimately attempt the final phoneme. Early attempts may result in failure with a distorted "l." Continued maturation produces accurate motor movement and sensory perceptions so that finally the correct phoneme appears and the word is articulated accurately.

McDonald's description indicates one aspect of the development of articulation. Prior to the modification of phonemes is the development of speech itself. This development is also in stages and is generally agreed to begin with the birth of the child and his or her birth cry. During the first few weeks of the infant's life the cry remains fairly constant in that it does not reflect differences in needs. The child sounds much the same if he or she is hungry, cold, in need of diaper change, or simply wants attention. This period is the *undifferentiated crying response* stage, also known as the reflexive vocalization stage. The child cries with his or her entire body, legs and arms flailing. The adult is unable to determine what is wanted from the nature of the cry. During this time, the cry is typified by the production of vowel-like sounds. Stages are not discrete but tend to overlap, and one stage continues after the next has begun.

The next stage begins at approximately the fourth week of life and is the *differentiated crying response*. The cries of the baby are still massive, but the parents can begin to distinguish cries of different types. Some authorities believe that conditioning of the parent is taking place rather than substantive changes in the cry of the child. The cry is still primarily composed of vowel and vowel-like sounds with some elements of consonants present.

The next stage begins during the second month of life and continues into the sixth month. This is the stage of *babbling and vocal play*. During this stage an unusually large number of sounds are randomly produced, including sounds that will never be needed or used in the child's language. This period is one in which sounds are produced for the amusement and pleasure of the child. The baby hears himself or herself and is encouraged to continue the vocal play. This production of sounds is a rehearsal for what will occur later. Consonants are produced that require the use of the musculature involved in sucking and swallowing. These are labial and palatal sounds. Earlier vowel productions are reinforced and now vary in length and pitch. Sounds requiring gross motor movements rather than fine muscle coordination appear earliest. It should be noted that all the sounds are meaningless to the child and simply provide pleasurable sensation. If during the babbling period, the child does not receive pleasurable stimulation and sensation both orally and aurally, his or her speech development may terminate at this stage. This is the last stage of normal speech development for the congenitally deaf child.

Sometime during the sixth month of life the child enters the *lalling* stage. He or she produces most of the vowel sounds and additional consonant sounds. Characteristic of this period is the child's ability to repeat the sounds and syllables he or she hears. It should be stressed that he or she repeats productions as a circular response. That is, the child produces a sound, hears it, derives physical satisfaction from it, and finally reproduces it. This is the stage when bisyllabic productions like baba and mama appear. They are accidentally produced and have no meaning for the child but may arouse excitement in the parent who is present when they occur. Critical to this phase is the auditory and kinesthetic pleasures the child obtains from these repetitive vocalizations.

The next stage, *echolalia*, appears during the child's ninth month of life. Jargon and continued imitation of sounds are characteristic. The baby is still motivated by pleasurable sensation, but will now imitate and reproduce sound stimuli supplied by others in his or her immediate environment. Therefore, if the child accidentally produces "mama" in the presence of his mother and she reacts as a positive reinforcer, repeating "mama" for him, he is very likely to respond by reproducing "mama" once again.

Sometime between the tenth and twelfth months of age, the child will begin to associate bisyllables like "mama" with a parent who consistently responds to them and reinforces them. When this association has been made, the child enters the stage of *verbal understanding*, beginning the true use of speech and language, *verbal utterance*, and can now meaningfully use words like mama to achieve an expected result. The correct use of his or her first word precipitates the entire process of learning language which should now proceed at a rapid rate. During the process of language learning he or she continues to learn and improve the articulation of the phonemes of the language.

By the age of 4, the child's speech should be intelligible to others. Phonologically, however, the child continues to master the speech sounds until approximately 7 years of age. Developmental ages have been investigated in terms of group norms or the point at which specific sounds are mastered by children selected from a normal population. Discrepancies between studies exist with respect to the developmental age levels for specific sounds. Later research such as Templin (1957) and Prather, Hedrick and Klein (1975) conclude that children are producing more sounds correctly at earlier ages than was indicated by the pioneeer study of Poole (1934). For example, the last developmental sounds acquired in the Poole study were at age 7 years, 6 months, but, in the Prather et al. study, by age 4. In the authors' experience with both normal and clinical populations, the results of the Templin study tend to conform more closely to their own observations. However, there was agreement for the general sequence of sound development.

These studies serve as sources of normative data to compare children's phonological development and sometimes as clinical guidelines for initiating remediation programs. A misarticulation is not considered a defect until a child is at the age at which the sound should be produced correctly (see Table 16.1 for a comparison of studies of consonant development).

The etiologies of articulation disorders are usually described as functional or organic in origin. Articulation problems resulting from structural abnormalities or neuromuscular pathologies are categorized as organically based disorders. When there is faulty activity of normal structures the disorder is referred to as functional in origin. There may, however, be some overlapping in etiology since it is possible for the original cause to be organic in nature with the persistence of the problem after the organic condition is remediated. An example of this would be an interdental lisp, *th* substitution for *s*, which might originate from the loss of the two deciduous central incisors. When the permanent incisors erupt and the child maintains the lisp the error is considered functional.

Table 16.1. A Comparison of Studies of Chronological Age and Development of Consonant Sounds

Phoneme	Example	Poole	Templin	Prather
p	pie	3.6	3	2
b	boy	3.6	4	2.8
m	may	3.6	3	2
w	will	3.6	3	2.8
h	how	3.6	3	2
t	to	4.6	6	2.8
d	do	4.6	4	2.4
n	no	4.6	3	2
g	get	4.6	4	3
k	can	4.6	4	2.4
ŋ	hang	4.6	3	2
j	you	4.6	3.6	2.4
f	four	5.6	3	2.4
v	vest	6.6	6	4
ð	they	6.6	7	4
ʒ	rouge	6.6	7	4
ʃ	shoe	6.6	4.6	3.8
l	look	6.6	6	3.4
z	zoo	7.6	7	4
s	see	7.6	4.6	3
r	run	7.6	4	3.4
θ	think	7.6	6	4
ʍ	when	7.6	—	4
tʃ	chew	7.6	4.6	3.8
dʒ	jump	7.6	7	4

Note: The sources were drawn from the studies of Poole (1934), Templin (1957), and Prather et al. (1975). The phonemes are taken from the International Phonetic Alphabet. The numbers noted above are years and months.

It has been estimated (Darley & Spriestersbach, 1978) that 81% of school-aged children with clinical speech problems have functional articulation disorders. The functional causes are varied. Since phoneme production is learned through imitation, one of the causes of misarticulation is incorrect learning. This may be the result of the child's imitation of poor models. The poor model may be an adult or another child with a speech problem. Frequently twins or siblings very close in age develop an idioglossia which has both a phonological and linguistic system totally deviant from normal speech and language. The children speak to each other and understand each other while no one else is privy to their conversation. Some children are raised in silent households and never have the opportunity to hear correctly produced phonemes so that their own speech is both slow in emerging and faulty when it does. Other children progress normally until the birth of a new sibling and then regress to earlier speech productions as a means of reobtaining lost attention from their parents. This results in a persistence of babytalk or infantile perseveration. In some instances of functional errors a young child is confused by a bilingual family and cannot separate the phonemes of one language from those of another. Sometimes serious illnesses or hospitalizations traumatize the child and his or her speech productions regress to an earlier stage, perhaps a stage in which life was more secure. The authors have seen numerous cases in which faulty articulation was reinforced. The child is encouraged to retain an infantile misarticulation because the parent enjoys hearing it or wishes to keep the child a baby for as long as possible. The little girl with the lisp is considered cute by some families and is encouraged to retain it. In some households the adult members speak to the child in baby talk and thus delay correct maturation of speech. Sometimes a temporary hearing loss from an ear infection prevents the child from learning appropriate phoneme production and stabilizes an early form of a phoneme. The longer the situation persists the greater the possibilities for the articulation errors to become established. For some children the development of motor control is late and sound errors develop that reflect the child's inability to utilize fine motor movements at the time a phoneme was first learned. This may result in firmly established error patterns. There are also those children who grow up in households where speech has negative connotations and is used for punishment and threat. In those circumstances the child may not wish to talk at all and may abandon speech efforts. These children frequently become speech and language delayed children. The examples and conditions cited are some of the causes of functional articulation disorders; there are innumerable others.

Organic disorders of articulation also have a wide variety of causes. Among the structural causes are problems with dentition such as missing teeth and poor dental formations. Malocclusions which prevent the teeth and jaws from meeting properly may result in an inability to produce some of the phonemes so that substitutions and distortions are common. The tongue tip may be tied to the floor of the mouth, ankyloglossia, so that sounds requiring elevation of the tongue cannot be made. The tongue may be excessively large, macroglossia, so that movement is slow or clumsy with inprecise articulation. The tongue may be congenitally undersized, microglossia, so that it cannot reach the teeth or gum ridge or palate which results in the inability to produce most of the phonemes. The lips may be too short or immobile so that they cannot approximate each other and *p, b, m,* or *w,* sounds are deviant. The palate may be too short or too highly arched and all nonnasal sounds are defective. The palate may also fail to form and result in the anomaly of cleft palate, which will be discussed at length in a later section of this chapter. In addition, any structural malfunction or malformation of the outer, middle, or inner ear which results in diminished hearing acuity or deafness will impact the way in which the child perceives phonemes and consequently misarticulates or omits them.

Another major organic etiology of articulatory disorders is dysarthia. This involves lesions of those portions of the central nervous system which directly innervate and control the organs of articulation. Generally speaking, damage to upper motor neurons cause spastic muscular paralysis while damage to lower motor neurons produce muscle flaccidity. There are several types of dysarthrias. Some of these, such as adventitious or progressive dysarthrias, primarily affect adult populations and are caused by diseases such as Parkinson's syndrome, Alzheimer's disease, Huntington's chorea, or by midlife gliomas and tumors. Dysarthrias in children are usually chronic in nature. Some of them result from pathology within the cranium, prior to the age of speech learning, and result in permanent impairment of motor aspects of speech. Among the causes of chronic dysarthria in childhood are diseases such as encephalitis, congenital syphilis, neoplasms, aneurysms, brain abscesses, subdural hematomas, astrocytomas, hydrocephalus, meningitis, and toxic poisonings from lead, coal tar, or arsenic. Some causes of dysarthria occur prenatally and involve such diseases as maternal rubella, placental disorders causing anoxia, premature birth, Rh incompatibility of the neonate, drugs taken by the mother during pregnancy, iatrogenic anoxias, or agenesis of a motor center or pathway. Whatever the cause of the dysarthria, in many instances it will be manifested in the general form recognized as cerebral palsy or to a lesser degree by a speech disorder in which the child is unable to control the motor movements necessary for speech—verbal apraxia. Language delay may accompany the articulation disorder.

Assessment

Assessment of articulation disorders in terms of which sounds are defective in a specific child, as a prerequisite to providing remedial treatment, may involve several procedures. Generally the articulators are examined to determine whether they are normal in structure and function. Hearing acuity is also examined. Case history data are obtained which provide additional necessary information for determining etiology. Ultimately, however, whether the cause is functional or organic, the specific phoneme errors must be evaluated. Traditional description examines the place and manner in which the misarticulated sound is produced. For example, the phoneme *t* should be produced with the tongue tip placed on the alveolar ridge and pulled off by a short, slightly explosive breath of air. *T* is therefore described as a voiceless lingua alveolar stop-plosive. All phonemes may be similarly described and a misarticulated phoneme analyzed in terms of incorrect placement of articulators or incorrect manner of production. Another means of determining error productions is to examine phonemes in terms of distinctive features (Chomsky & Halle, 1968). Distinctive features are the unique characteristics of each phoneme. No two phonemes are alike. There must be at least one feature difference between the closest of phonemes. The more feature differences the greater the acoustic differences between sounds. The presence of any feature is indicated by a plus sign while the absence of a feature is indicated by a minus sign. Features are judged on a binary basis. Thus in describing the distinctive feature of the *b* sound with regard to use of voice rather than breath, it would be noted as "plus voice." There are 16 features that may be used to describe phonemes. For more information on distinctive features see Darley and Spriestersbach (1978, p. 242–243). Distinctive feature analysis can only be used with errors of substitution and therefore are not applicable if the errors are those of distortion or omission.

There are standardized tests to help determine which phonemes are defective. Among the more commonly used test instruments are Templin-Darley Tests of Articulation (Templin & Darley, 1969); the Fisher-Logemann Test of Articulation Competence (Fisher & Logemann, 1971), and the Goldman-Fristoe Test of Articulation (Goldman & Fristoe, 1970). Other tests of articulation measure the consistency of articulation error, such as A Deep Test of Articulation (McDonald, 1964), while the Arizona Articulation Proficiency Scale (Fudala, 1970) yields a percentage of improvement through serial testing.

The problem of articulation disorders is magnified when the child displays multiple misarticulations. No articulation disorder is slight nor should its treatment be slighted. Remediation requires patience, skill, and perseverance regardless of the intervention strategy that is utilized. Articulation therapy should be appropriate for the age of the child in terms of frequency and length of each session as well as in the selection of the phoneme sequence for remediation.

Cleft Lip and Palate

Among the many organic anomalies which produce speech and language problems in children, cleft lip and/or palate is probably the most traumatic. The expectant parents have anticipated a normal, healthy baby, but are greeted by a facially disfigured newborn whom they are ashamed to have family and friends see. The parents of the cleft palate child often react with shock, disappointment, guilt, anger, and confusion. In spite of their initial condition, the prognosis for cleft palate children today is very positive. They are usually able to be restored to leading a fully normal life.

Cleft palate is not a new phenomenon. Palatal and lip clefts have been reported throughout history. Egyptian mummies and ancient Peruvian skulls have been found with palatal clefts. Celsus, in the first century A.D., reported cleft palate and its treatment as did a Chinese text from the fourth century A.D. (Wells, 1971). There is not much evidence of surgical repair for cleft lip prior to the sixteenth century and then only for acquired cleft rather than congenital cleft. Two Frenchmen, Franco and Paré, were known to have attempted lip repair for battle wounds during the late 1500s. These two men were barber-surgeons since surgery was not yet a respectable area of medicine. Nothing was done for congenital lip and palate clefts since they were regarded as the mark of sin by the clergy and because the unfortunate infants rarely survived. Those children who did survive were frequently kept hidden for as long as they lived and became "attic children."

Prior to the eighteenth century, very little was attempted in the nature of surgical repair of the palate since it was less accessible than the lip and more difficult to repair. The first known palatal surgery was performed in 1764 by LeMonnier, a French dentist. Most of the early repairs were not done by physicians but by barbers, barber-surgeons, or dentists, and involved the use of filler materials to fill the gaps in the palate. It was not until the nineteenth century that two independent events made surgical repair a more realistic possibility. There was the discovery of anesthesia in 1846, which could control the pain of palatal surgery, and the development of antiseptic surgery by Lister in the 1860s to prevent infection. Another factor furthering palatal repair was the advent of antibiotics to control infections when they did occur. The major need for palatal repair, however, arose as a result of acquired battlefield injuries sustained by soldiers in World War I and World War II.

The incidence of cleft lip and palate in the United States is estimated at 1 in every 750 live births. These figures vary slightly with racial factors, blacks having somewhat fewer clefts than whites, and racially mixed populations showing higher incidence of cleft. Geography also seems to have an influence, with cold climates reporting a higher incidence of clefting than warmer climates. The incidence figures also change if a close family member, parents, grandparents, aunts, or uncles have a history of clefting. The odds then increase to a 1 in 20 possibility of cleft occurring. If a sibling is born with a cleft, the odds once again increase to 1 in 5 that the next child will be born a cleft.

It is also interesting to note the distributions of clefting between the sexes. For cleft lip alone there seems to be a 2:1 male to female ratio. For clefts of lip and palate, the most severe form, there is also a 2:1 male to female ratio. For isolated cleft palate the ratio changes to a 2:1 female to male figure. Generally speaking, more male children are born with a cleft and the clefts they have are likely to be more serious in terms of extent.

Congenital clefts are caused by a failure of fusion of one or more embryonic processes of the face during the first trimester of pregnancy. The lip fusions are completed by the end of the sixth week of embryonic life and the palatal fusions completed by the tenth week (Morley, 1970). The fusions always take place in an anterior to posterior direction. If palatal fusion is interrupted anywhere along the line, no further fusion will occur beyond the point of the first fusion failure. The fusions are along the midline of the palate with the right and left halves of the perpendicular processes of the maxillary bones fusing, followed by the fusion of the right and left palatine bones, and completed with the fusion of the soft palate and formation of the uvula. Because the upper lip and alveolus arise from a different embryonic structure than the hard and soft palate, the former are referred to as the prepalate or primary palate while the latter is called the secondary palate. Fusion failure may be caused by the failure of the embryonic palatal structures to move toward the midline or by a tissue proliferation failure resulting in an insufficient amount of tissue to reach the midline for fusion. Nothing that happens after the first three months of pregnancy will have any further effect on the lip and palate of the embryo.

There are many ways in which to describe the extent or location of clefts in children. The most commonly used classification of clefts was developed by Veau in 1931 and was based on the establishment of four distinct types. Type I cleft represents a cleft of the soft palate only. Type II is a cleft of the soft and hard palate. Type III clefts go through the soft palate, hard palate, the alveolus on one side, and may go through one side of the lip (this is often referred to as a unilateral complete cleft). Type IV cleft is a bilateral complete cleft. Veau did not include the submuccosal or occult clefts in his classifications. This last descriptor refers to clefts below the visible surface of the palate or to congenitally insufficient palates (a palate that is too short). In general the more extensive the cleft, the greater the problem for the child.

Most of our information about the etiology of cleft lip and palate comes from three sources: laboratory experiments with rats, the examination of spontaneously aborted fetuses, and after the fact reports about the pregnancies of women who have given birth to infants with clefts. Although the etiology for all instances of clefting is not known, some of the most widely accepted causes are known. Among these are interruption of the oxygen supply to the developing embryo; interruption of the nutritional supply to the embryo, which may be the result of placental abnormality in the mother; nutritional imbalance or malnutrition of the mother; and vitamin deficiency, especially vitamin A or conversely excessive vitamin A, in the mother. Endocrine disorders in the mother, especially those involving pituitary gland and thyroid gland hormones, are also among the causes. Maternal anoxia and parental age factors including the ages of both father and mother are of major concern. Older parents are more likely to produce cleft lip and cleft palate offspring. Maternal hypothermia resulting from overexposure to extreme cold is a factor, as is generally poor maternal health involving chronic conditions of anemia, kidney disease, heart disease, or alcoholism. Other factors of a more acute nature involve rubella during early pregnancy; maternal exposure to x-ray irradiation; drugs taken during pregnancy, especially hydrochloride related drugs; and childhood diseases during pregnancy such as chicken pox. Additional etiological factors include accidental fetal movement which places a fetal finger or fist in the oral cavity and blocks palatal fusion or failure of the fetal tongue to drop in time for palatal fusion. Uterine tumors may also produce clefts. Of all the possible etiologies, the most common factor seems to be heredity.

The birth of a child with a cleft presents many problems, both immediate and long term. At first the pediatrician is concerned with the survival of the baby, who must be fed with special nipples while held in an upright position to prevent choking or drowning. The lip will have to be closed surgically before the infant can be taken home. At about the time the lip is repaired, temporary prosthetic appliances to close the palate and realign the dental arches are provided for the child. The young child is prone to frequent upper respiratory infections, which often lead to middle ear infections and surgical drainage of the ear. The child's hearing must be closely monitored during early years.

The speech problems of the child are primarily those of articulation and resonance disorders. The only phonemes he or she can produce correctly are the nasal sounds *m, n,* and *ng.* All vowels and diphthongs are produced with excessive nasal resonance while all consonants are emitted through the nose instead of the mouth. The result is the substitution of nasal consonants for non-nasal ones and speech that is unintelligible. By the age of 3 or 4 the child will undergo numerous surgical procedures in order to close the cleft, lengthen the palate, and make the palate functional for speech. The child will need extensive training to produce and habituate normal speech production after the palate is repaired. He or she will need early speech and language stimulation if he or she is to acquire normal language. The child and parents will also need psychological support services to overcome the trauma of both the cleft and the extensive treatment necessary for habilitation.

The most effective management of the many problems of the cleft palate child is through the combined efforts of a team of specialists from a variety of disciplines. The end result of this team approach is usually a child who looks, sounds, and functions normally.

STUTTERING

As was pointed out in the section concerned with articulation disorders, there are appropriate and inappropriate variations in articulation and there are appropriate and inappropriate variations in the rhythm or fluency with which speech is uttered. Since all speakers are dysfluent to some degree in that we all may hesitate, interject, stumble over sounds or words, have word retrieval problems, or use circumlocutions in our normal speaking lives, there is a reasonable tendency to be tolerant of deviations in fluency. When, however, those deviations become so marked because of their frequency and severity, or when accompanied by extraneous motor movements, they become particularly noticeable or troublesome to the speaker or his or her listener and may be described as stuttering. Although there are other disorders of fluency, such as cluttering (which most specialists view as primarily a disorder of articulation and timing), or those that are found in cerebral palsy, Parkinsonism, or other neurological syndromes, this section is concerned with the most frequently encountered fluency disorder, stuttering.

As a communication disorder, stuttering has been viewed with fascination by researchers and writers from many disciplines. It has elicited remediation efforts from well-intentioned parents, friends, teachers, and others, sometimes successfully but more often than not these have met with failure and frustration.

Stuttering has probably received more attention than any other speech disorder because of the way it dramatically exposes many of the unpleasant sides of social living (Van Riper, 1982). More has been researched and written about this disorder than any other and, undoubtedly, this has generated more theories of causation and ideas for treatment than any other. The literature on stuttering dates back thousands of years. Writings from the Bible and the Koran indicate, for example, that Moses was afflicted with stuttering. Whether Moses really was a stutterer is not certain, but there are other references to "stammering" in the Bible.

The early Greeks knew of stuttering and wrote of their treatment of the disorder. Herodotus, a Greek historian, recorded the treatment of stuttering more than 2000 years ago. The therapy recommendation was "emigration south to Libya," presumably for the more salubrious climate. Aristotle described a number of speech defects and attributed the cause of stuttering to the tongue. Demosthenes is said to have been cured of this stuttering by Satyrys, a Greek actor, who prescribed talking with pebbles in his mouth while watching himself in a mirror or walking uphill.

Hippocrates, the father of medicine, recommended a surgical treatment for the disorder, as did many other medical researchers. Diefenbach, a German surgeon in the 1800s, began a surgical treatment that became fashionable in Europe for several years. His treatment consisted of excising a small portion of the root of the tongue. An English physician of the same period, Dr. Braid, attempted to cure stuttering by removing the tonsils or uvula. Two thousand years earlier, Galen attributed the cause of stuttering to various abnormalities of the tongue and suggested cauterization and the cutting of the nerves to the "afflicted part."

Avicenna, an Arabian philosopher and physician who lived from A.D. 930 to 1037, described the disorder as due largely to the tongue, brain lesions, and sometimes to the epiglottis, which he advised should be treated by taking a deep breath before speaking. A remarkable theory for stuttering was advanced by Sir Francis Bacon, who attributed stuttering to a coldness and dryness of the tongue and recommended large draughts of hot wine as an invariably successful cure.

Undoubtedly many of their patients experienced some relief from the stuttering for varying amounts of time since even to this day research indicates that almost every method of treatment has worked or been effective for some stutterers. Conversely, no single method of treatment has been effective for all stutterers. This phenomenon has added to the enigma of stuttering.

Stuttering is difficult both to define and to describe. For example, there is no clear-cut point that separates normal dysfluencies from abnormal dysfluencies. Definitions of the disorder tend to be either descriptive in a general way or slanted with a specific theoretical viewpoint. "The variability among them makes clear that this complex and variable disorder is hard to delimit" (Van Riper, 1982).

To cite some examples, stuttering has been described as an "anticipatory, apprehensive, hypertonic, avoidance reaction" (Johnson, 1959). "Stuttering is an evaluational disorder. It is what results when normal non-fluency is evaluated as something to be feared and avoided; it is outwardly what the stutterer does in an attempt to avoid nonfluency" (Johnson, 1946). In brief, it is what a stutterer does to avoid stuttering. Coriat (1943) described stuttering as a psychoneurosis caused by the persistence into later life of early pregenital oral nursing, oral sadistic, and anal sadistic components. Glauber (1958) described stuttering as a "symptom in a psychopathological condition classified as a pregenital conversion neurosis." Brutten and Shoemaker (1967) describe stuttering as a form of fluency failure that results from conditioned negative emotion. A simply stated definition given by Van Riper (1978) is "a word improperly patterned in time and the speaker's reactions thereto." Luper and Ford (1980) define stuttering as "an involuntary aperiodic disruption of speech-production processes, resulting in repetitions and/or prolongations of individual speech sounds or syllables, frequently accompanied by excess tension in the speech musculature." Bloodstein (1979) described stuttering as consisting of "brief periods of interruption in speech that have abnormal duration or frequency. The interruptions may be accompanied by facial, vocal, or other mannerisms, often known as associated or secondary symptoms." He goes on to say that "the essential feature of stuttering is an identifiable moment of interruption, generally known as a blockage or block."

Since stuttering afflicts nearly 1% of the population, it is viewed as a disorder of considerable concern. It has its onset in early childhood and, for many, persists into adult life, although for some children it may disappear with age. Some researchers claim its onset as early as 18 months of age (Johnson, 1959, Dickson, 1971). The peak periods of stuttering onset appear to be between the ages of 2 and 7 with the disorder rarely beginning after the mid-teens.

Research in stuttering over the last 40 years (Van Riper, 1982; Bloodstein,

1975) has presented well-documented, although sometimes controversial, phenomena about the disorder and those afflicted with it. Among the more significant phenomena are the following:

1. There is a tendency for stuttering to occur primarily in male children. There is a sex ratio of approximately 4:1.

2. As a group, the intellectual abilities of stutterers fall within the range of average intelligence.

3. Stutterers generally are unable to move their paired muscles as rapidly as normal speakers and general motor skill is inferior to that of normal speakers.

4. There appears to be a tendency for left-handedness to be more common among stutterers than nonstutterers.

5. There appears to be a history of shifted-handedness among stutterers. Bryngelson (1939) reported that almost 80% of the stutterers in the speech clinic at the University of Minnesota had been forced to change from preferred left handedness to right-handedness as young children.

6. Most stutterers speak fluently when they participate in acting, singing, or choral speaking and choral reading activities.

7. There appears to be a grammatical factor in stuttering with more severe and more frequent dysfluency on nouns and verbs in the adult stutterer. Young children tend to have more difficulty with prepositions and conjunctions.

8. As a group, stutterers are slower in learning to speak. Speech onset is somewhat later than normal.

9. There seems to be a familial tendency toward stuttering. Stutterers often report a history among other family members and in past generations of the family.

10. Stuttering is more frequent on propositional or self-revealing material.

11. There is a tendency for stuttering to be more common among twins than single-birth children.

12. Stutterers have a tendency toward articulatory disorders either accompanying or preceding the onset of the stuttering.

13. Stutterers rarely stutter when they are alone, speaking to animals, speaking to younger children, or when communicative responsibility is minimal.

14. Stutterers have specific phoneme fears and often can predict the words or sounds they will have difficulty with.

15. Stuttering is an intermittent disorder. Stutterers often report that they are fluent for periods of time of varying lengths.

16. Some stutterers recover spontaneously.

The speech of the stutterer is characterized by the manner in which he or she reacts to the stuttering block. For some stutterers the block is a *clonic* one; that is, he or she fixates on the blocked sound by pressing his or her articulators together and prolonging the production of a phoneme or by almost "freezing" in a fixed position and not producing meaningful sound at all. For other stutterers the *tonic* block is more common. In this case the individual experiences repeated uncontrolled contraction and relaxation of the speech musculature and the repetition of sounds result in something like a "b-b-b-but." Another stuttering block is one in which there is a long hesitation or pause and there is no visible movement of the articulators. This sometimes gives the impression that the stutterer is deep in thought and, indeed, he may be going through a mental rehearsal of what he wants to say. In others, a facial tremor or tic or unrelated physical body movement may be observed.

The block, or moment of stuttering, is all that is required for an individual to be a stutterer. All other extraneous actions such as the facial tics, eye blinks, head and jaw tremors, hand, arm or leg movements, tongue clicks, lip smacking, and so on, are learned reinforced behaviors commonly referred at as secondary symptoms. Most of those secondary symptoms originally served to break the block, were voluntary in nature, and may have produced fluency. When these distractions became habituated, they ceased to break the block and remained to complicate the stuttering picture. They then frequently added to the stutterer's emotional difficulties and embarrassment.

In addition to the *overt* secondary symptoms there are *covert* behaviors. These behaviors are not heard or seen by the listener but are frequently described by the stutterer. They include word substitutions, circumlocutions, situational avoidances, feelings of anxiety, fear or panic, tension, silent rehearsal, and deep introspection. These symptoms and behaviors more typically apply to the older stutterer. The stutterer with secondary symptoms is considered a *secondary stutterer*.

An earlier form of stuttering found among young children or beginning stutterers is typified by easy, effortless repetitions, hesitations, or prolongations without any awareness of speech difficulty on the part of the child. This is referred to as *primary stuttering*. Since there is a lack of awareness of the problem, the child exhibits no tension, struggle, or anxiety. The terms primary and secondary stuttering were first used by Bluemel (1932). At one time the goal of therapy was to return the secondary stutterer to the stage of primary stuttering, a stage in which the speech difficulty was minimal. Obviously it is impossible to erase the awareness or the memory of the speech difficulty. In addition, most children do not progress from primary to secondary stuttering suddenly but experience a period of transition with gradually developing awareness and struggle. For these reasons in 1954 Van Riper added the term *transitional stuttering* to indicate the intermediate stages of progression. Later, Bloodstein (1960, 1961) further refined the progression of severity by using a four-phase classification system: incipient, transitional, confirmed, and advanced. Each phase was carefully described in terms of awareness, severity of the dysfluency, types of blocks, emotional reactions to the stuttering, and secondary symptoms. The major difficulty with any classification of stuttering stages is that no two stutterers progress in exactly the same way and the stages are not discrete or mutually exclusive.

The etiology of stuttering is still unknown despite all of the research devoted to the disorder. There are numerous theories of causation. Traditionally the theories of causation have been classified into three major categories: (1) those that consider stuttering to be primarily a learned behavior, (2) those that stress the underlying emotional problems, and (3) those that emphasize organic factors. Although these classifications of etiology enable us to make some distinctions among the theories, there is a good deal of overlapping. Even theorists who stress organic etiology acknowledge that the problem may be intensified by learning or emotional factors. In addition, many theorists consider the factors that maintain the stuttering to be different from those that originally caused the problem.

During the late 1920s and early 1930s, organic theories were primarily concerned with cerebral or hemispheric dominance. These theories stressed either a failure of one hemisphere to establish dominance over the other or to improperly timed impulses coming from the hemispheres to the peripheral speech mechanism (Orton & Travis, 1929, Travis, 1934). Somewhat later the cerebral dominance viewpoint changed so that emphasis shifted to a failure of the higher cortical centers of the brain to control lower centers. The theorists of this period stressed the establishment of a dominant side in treating the stutterer. During the next decades, theorists cited metabolic or biochemical imbalances as a cause of fluency failure, and brain dominance theories were largely abandoned. Treatment was attempted through the use of various drugs. By the 1970s, temporal lobe dysfunction was cited as a cause of stuttering. This led to studies involving tests of hemispheric functioning through the use of dichotic listening experiments and influenced current theories involving language processing irregularities. These involve reaction time differences between the two hemispheres of the brain and differences in hemispheric preferences for language processing between stutterers and nonstutterers (Hand & Haynes, 1983). Among the many other organic theories are those concerned with laryngeal spasms, delayed myelinization, delayed auditory feedback, constitutional predisposition, and seizure disorders. It is interesting to note that much of the current research is once again investigating organic etiology.

Emotional or psychological theories run the gamut from mild maladaptive behavior to deeply rooted psychoneurosis. Some of the theories treat stuttering as a symptom of a basic personality problem in which the hesitations and anxieties are considered symptoms of the stutterer's attitude toward life. Other theorists regarded stuttering as the result of a fixation at the oral or anal stage of psychosexual development and claimed that stuttering is a symbolic form of sucking. Travis (1957) viewed stuttering as a way in which the child inhibited himself or herself from speaking his or her most unspeakable thoughts;

thus stuttering became a kind of martyrdom. One theorist viewed stuttering as a repression disorder. Sheehan (1958) wrote extensively about stuttering as an approach-avoidance conflict in which there are opposing urges to speak and to hold back from speaking. The need to hold back may be to inhibit the expression of unacceptable feelings or to prevent difficulty in interpersonal relations. Other investigators such as Bluemel (1932) stated that stuttering represented a psychoneurotic disorganization. Still others saw stuttering arising from states of fear, dread, worry, and from feelings of inferiority. Freud, who wrote very little about stuttering, viewed it as a classic psychoanalytic problem. Many psychologists feel that any speech therapy program for stuttering should be accompanied by a psychotherapeutic program since stutterers who become fluent too quickly as a result of therapy are often unable to cope with their new speech fluency.

Learning theories of stuttering etiology also vary widely in nature. The earlier theorists of this century viewed stuttering as a bad habit learned through imitation. They frequently cited a close family member or playmate of the child who might be serving as a speech model. During the 1940s and 1950s the focus of learning theory shifted to a diagnosogenic or semantogenic one. The work of Johnson (1959) pointed to misdiagnosis and the effects of mislabeling as the cause of the child's problem. In effect the diagnosogenic theorists claimed that the normal hesitations and repetitions in the speech of the young child were erroneously diagnosed as stuttering by a perfectionistic parent who then reacted negatively to the semantic label *stuttering*. The child who either sensed the parental concern for his or her speech or was forcefully made aware of his or her speech "failure" began to try harder to speak more fluently in an attempt to please parents. The harder he or she tried for fluency, the less automatic his or her speech became, and the more dysfluent he or she became. As this happened the parents became more sure of their diagnosis and even more reactive to the child's speech. This became a vicious cycle in which the fluency of the child's speech was ultimately destroyed. Later researchers in diagnosogenic theory found that stutterers would stutter less with repeated utterances of the same material. This led to the formulation of the *adaptation effect* principle, that consecutive, repeated readings of the same passage produced a significant decrease in the number of stuttered words. Wischner (1950) noticed that the adaptation curves obtained by graphing the speech dysfluencies in the repeated readings of stutterers resembled normal learning curves. This was followed by another generation of learning theorists who now tried to explain how stuttering was learned.

Brutten and Shoemaker (1967) viewed stuttering as being learned through both operant and classical conditioning. Their work was the impetus for a still larger group of conditioning theories and theorists. Perhaps the most significant outcome of current learning theory in stuttering is the development of new therapeutic techniques. Researchers such as Webster (1972), Mowrer (1979), Shames (1980), Ryan (1971), and others have developed programmed approaches to therapy based on principles of learning.

Another major area of consideration involves the assessment of stuttering. There are three fundamental determinations which must be made: (1) Is the individual actually a stutterer? (2) How severe is the stuttering? (3) What is the nature of the stutterer's symptoms? The first determination is particularly important in the case of the young child. Since all children exhibit some dysfluency in the normal process of learning speech and language, it is imperative that these normal developmental hesitations and repetitions not be misinterpreted, penalized, or misdiagnosed. Very often the child with normal developmental dysfluency is doing much the same thing as the primary stutterer. The difference is often one of degree and interpretation of the behavior.

The severity of the stuttering should be assessed in order to obtain baseline data. This provides necessary information for determining progress and the success of any therapy technique for a given individual.

The assessment of the stutterer's symptoms is essential for planning an appropriate intervention program. If a stutterer shows strong evidence of learned, reinforced stuttering behaviors, a remedial program utilizing behavior modification techniques might be most effective. If assessment reveals a randomness of stuttering behavior, a more traditional therapeutic approach may be indicated.

It is possible that no single etiology for stuttering will ever be found, and that all three etiologies (organic, psychological, and learning) will be found to be valid as stuttering precipitators. It is possible that we may have to maintain an eclectic outlook about the origins of stuttering behavior. Nonetheless, the authors are optimistic regarding the future of the stutterer as it relates to therapy.

Counseling for the primary or incipient stutterer's parents has become increasingly sensitive to their feelings and attitudes as well as to their reactions to the stuttering child. It no longer merely involves a series of do's and don'ts to help the child ease communicative difficulty but also actively engages the parents in understanding their own feelings and behaviors. Many children with primary stuttering have been helped considerably and often have no further need for treatment.

Recently developed and promising treatment programs for children and adults which prompt a positive outlook for large numbers of stutterers who are more severely impaired include the Precision Fluency Shaping Program, the Stocker Probes Technique, biofeedback, delayed auditory feedback, and a variety of other techniques.

LANGUAGE DEVELOPMENT AND DISORDERS

The historic basis of interest in disorders of language development resulted from the early work done by educators of deaf children and from the medical research done with adult aphasia and other medical disorders having as a common factor diminished linguistic ability.

Language Development

It is arbitrary to separate normal articulation development from normal language development since both proceed along a parallel time frame. Language development without the ability to articulate speech is almost as handicapping as the ability to articulate sound without the language needed to provide meaning. There are thus two aspects of language, use and comprehension. Comprehension always precedes use. On the average, children say their first word by age 1 and their first sentence by 18–24 months of age. The child's ability to use language presupposes a receptive vocabulary of about 50 words and exposure to spoken language (Piaget, 1962). The child must first understand the spoken word. (For a discussion of the beginning of verbal understanding see the section on articulation development.)

The child's skill in using language is strongly dependent on the development of cognitive skills. These cognitive skills develop in four stages over a period of 15 years. They start at birth with the earliest stage, *sensorimotor intelligence*, in which behavior is primarily motor. There is no conceptual thinking, and reflexive behavior grows into intellectual behavior. This period lasts for the first two years of life.

Stage two of cognitive development, *preoperational thought* occurs between age 2 and 7. This period of language development is characterized by the rapid development of concepts and intellectual development on a conceptual level. The child's thought processes are still prelogical.

Stage three, *concrete operations*, from 7 to 11 years of age, sees the child develop the ability to apply logical thought to concrete problems but not to hypothetical problems.

Stage four, *formal operations*, from 11 to 15 years of age, produces a refinement level of development in which logic may be utilized for all classes of problems. The adolescent tries to examine human behavior in terms of what is logical rather than what is real (Nicholosi et al., 1978).

Along with the development of cognitive skills, the child develops the ability to process information from verbal symbols; that is, he receives the stimulus through auditory pathways and transmits it to association areas of the brain for interpretation and then to other motor areas for further processing of an expressive nature which leads to the spoken response. Any breakdown along the pathways will produce processing difficulties. Language has been mastered when the child can adequately utilize appropriate lexicon, phonology, semantics, syntax, morphology, and pragmatics, the major dimensions of language.

Language Disorder

Language disorders may be broadly defined as the inability to understand or to express meaning through the use of verbal symbols. Language disorders are closely related to disorders of auditory processing as well as to specific learning disabilities and to articulation disorders of speech. They involve cognitive factors as well as expressive factors. Defective processing of verbal symbols, in terms of both encoding and decoding, are part of the language disorder. Thus the language disabled child may have problems in several modalities of language processing: the auditory reception segment, the central language segment, and the speech production segment.

A simple classification of language disability includes the following major categories:

1. Failure to acquire language—children who by 2 years of age have shown no sign of acquiring the language of their speech community. Included in this group are failure to use speech sounds, absence of or very limited vocabulary, failure to form concepts, and/or failure to use sentence formations by 3 1/2 years of age.

2. Delayed language acquisition—children whose use of language is below their age level in articulation, vocabulary or concept formation, and sentence formation.

3. Deviant language acquisition—children who use language in a way so different from that of their community that they cannot be understood even when the utterances are quantitatively numerous.

4. Acquired language disability—children who acquired language and later suffered a partial or complete loss of their ability to use language (Marge, 1972).

Factors that influence language development include intelligence, gender, language environment, and heredity. Intelligence is highly related to language skill and to the manner and speed with which language is acquired. There are numerous exceptions to the principle, and one would not ordinarily assume that language delay is automatically the result of low intelligence. It would, however, be an important factor for diagnosis. Nonetheless, for children as a group, the relationship is high and significant.

Another important factor in language development is gender. Although the most recent research data indicate that sex differences in early language acquisition are not as great as once thought, it still appears to be true that girls develop language skills earlier and more rapidly than boys for several years. The explanations offered for this earlier acquisition are most often speculative, based on family relationships and role identification.

The language environment of the child has long been accepted as an important factor in language development. Children who have been reared in relatively silent environments, or whose playmates are younger children, or who have been relegated to television sets for company may be missing the stimulation essential for acquisition and development. As a consequence they may be slower in development or the development may be inappropriate. Conversely, children who have experienced environments in which parents provide a great deal of language stimulation or whose associates are older or good speakers often acquire language earlier and better than expected for their age.

There is relatively little evidence to support the relationship of heredity to language development. There is considerable clinical evidence that children whose language is delayed often have case histories in which other members of the family reported similar problems. Although it may be a generational continuation of a behavioral factor, the biological factor of heredity should not be ruled out and warrants further investigation.

These are some of the major factors that are known to influence language development. Further study of this area is continuing at a relatively rapid pace with new information emerging with each research study.

The etiologies of disordered language are numerous. Many of the etiologies also produce articulation and other speech and language problems and have been discussed previously. At the same time, for some of the cases of delayed language seen in clinical settings, no cause is immediately apparent. Among the causes of disordered language, perhaps the most significant and frequent is mental retardation. Mental retardation may be hereditary or familial or may be a concomitant of severe cerebral palsy, hydrocephalus, brain injury, childhood schizophrenia or other psychosis, or Down's syndrome. Other causes include congenital deafness, childhood aphasia, autism, prolonged childhood illness, social deprivation or isolation, parental overprotection, or a confused system of reward and punishment for language behavior in which the child is encouraged to be silent.

Language Assessment

Over the years language assessment involved evaluating the child's receptive vocabulary through the use of standardized tests such as the Peabody Picture Vocabulary Test (Dunn, 1965) or through the use of standardized elicited language tests such as the Carrow Elicited Language Inventory (1974). More recently language assessment has come to involve obtaining a spontaneous speech sample from the child and analyzing this sample in terms of sentence structures based on norms for articulation, lexicon, expressive syntax, grammatical forms, mean length of utterances, comprehension, associative ability, and morphology. Numerous test materials have been developed for these purposes (Weiss & Lillywhite, 1981).

The approach to remediation is dependent on the cause, nature, extent, and severity of the language handicap. For some language problems, especially those associated with profound mental retardation or with severe psychoses, the prognosis is poor. For many of the language disordered children, remediation involves language therapy of intensive nature over a long period of time. Each language impaired child is an individual for whom the remedial strategy must be specifically designed to meet individual needs based on individual language deficit and potential.

Childhood Aphasia

Aphasia refers to a loss of speech and language ability resulting from damage to the language or language association areas of the brain. Another term is dysphasia, which indicates diminished function or partial loss of language and speech with similar etiology. Since aphasia is the more commonly used descriptor for both aspects of this severe disorder, we will use only the term aphasia.

Almost all that we have learned about aphasia is the result of observation and data from adult populations who have experienced brain trauma. Indeed the primary impetus to the treatment of aphasic patients was an outgrowth of head injuries sustained by soldiers in the two world wars. Prior to World War II there was relatively little interest in providing rehabilitative programs for adults who suffered this devastating loss of the communicative functions. There was even less interest and research for the problem when it occurred in children.

In contrast to adults, young children have not lost their language abilities; rather, these abilities have failed to be acquired through normal development. This difference has led some researchers to reject the term childhood aphasia in describing this language deficit and substitute such terms as congenital aphasia, developmental aphasia (Aram & Nation, 1982), or minimal brain dysfunction (Bloodstein, 1979). Other researchers and aphasiologists view the disorder in children as unrelated to aphasia, since you cannot lose what you have never acquired, and consider the problem to be a severe form of delayed language with unknown etiology.

The diagnosis of childhood aphasia depends on ruling out deafness, mental deficiency, psychotic disorders, severe paralysis of the speech musculatures, and a history of severe social deprivation as possible etiologies for the lack of language development. Only then is the assumption made that there is organic damage to the immature brain. In most instances the damage is related to some prenatal condition, often verifiable, or to trauma during the birth process or to injury, toxicity, or oxygen deprivation of the neonate. Neurologists performing autopsies on brain damaged children have sometimes found that the damage was so situated and so extensive that these children would certainly have had severe aphasia if they had been adults (Bloodstein, 1979). In other cases there is no demonstrable brain injury or pathology to account for the failure of language to emerge.

In addition to the language failure, other symptoms seem to be common to children with congenital aphasia. Many of these children go through the early stages of speech development like cooing, babbling, and vocal play, but obtain no pleasure from them and therefore the stages do not further language growth and development in appropriate fashion (Weiss & Lillywhite, 1981). In many instances the child develops echolalia, a parrot-like repetition of words he hears with no understanding of them. The echolalia tends to raise false expectations of language use and development among family members and professionals working with the child. Eisenson (1972) describes other typical behaviors manifested by these children as tendencies toward hyperactivity, short attention spans, high levels of distractibility, compulsive traits, and catastrophic responses if routines are altered or possessions are moved. Other researchers (Aram & Nation, 1982) indicate that some of the young aphasics show normal or better than normal levels of intelligence on nonverbal tests.

The children described here are children who were born without the normal ability to learn speech and language. In contrast, another group of children with serious language problems includes those who suffer serious head injuries or illnesses after they have mastered speech and language and lose their communication skills as a result of the trauma. These children acquire aphasia and are similar to the adult aphasics in their behavior. It is more accurate to think of these children as aphasic children rather than childhood aphasics or congenitally aphasic children (McCormick & Schiefelbusch, 1984), a seemingly minor distinction but one that is meaningful in terms of treatment and prognosis. Recent research (Hecaen, 1976) has revealed the plasticity of the immature cerebral hemispheres in terms of recovery of function. This plasticity decreases with age, however, and a younger child will probably make a better recovery than an older one, all other things being equal. Evidence seems to indicate that brain reorganization lasts until puberty and operates on a continuum. Significant factors in the recovery of function based on cerebral reorganization involve the extensiveness of the brain damaged area and the location of the damaged area. For as yet unknown reasons, the child with the congenital disorder does not experience the same recovery of function. Language recovery occurs in children who acquire cerebral damage, with factors such as age of trauma occurrence and degree and location of damage determining the extent of the recovery. These same factors apply to the recovery of linguistic functions in the teenage and adult populations of aphasic individuals.

Treatment for the childhood aphasic involves intensive and extensive language therapy often accompanied by articulation therapy. In some cases training in the use of manual language may be useful either to stimulate language interest generally or to supplement oral language training. When language therapy has been successful enough to allow these children to enter school and be mainstreamed, they usually present other learning deficits, the most serious being reading disability. More recently the belief has emerged that development aphasia may, in some cases, be the earliest indication of learning disabilities to come, and is the result of injury or abnormal development of brain centers responsible for interpreting the meaning of visual and verbal symbols.

PERSONAL PERSPECTIVE

Since speech and language deficits vary in degrees of severity from child to child, even for those with the same disorder, the impact on the child and his family reflects this variability. In general, the more severe the handicap the more upsetting and disruptive to the family unit. Families cope with their speech and language disordered children in different ways. In the extreme, some parents deny the existence of a problem while others respond in an exaggerated, overprotective manner and drive the child and his therapists for unrealistic progress.

Among the more frustrating experiences of the authors has been the appearance for speech and language evaluation and therapy of a child who should have been evaluated years earlier. In some instances well-intentioned friends or someone from a different discipline told the parents that the child would outgrow the problem. In other cases children have been dragged from one therapy setting to another by overanxious or perfectionist parents for a minor or nonexistent problem that did not need remediation, producing unnecessary anguish for everyone concerned. With regard to the examples cited, in each instance the child becomes a disadvantaged victim who has been put at risk unnecessarily.

The question therefore is when should intervention be sought to provide the best possible opportunity for success with speech and language handicaps in children? There is no single answer to that question. Most speech pathologists consider both the severity of the problem and the etiology before deciding if intervention is appropriate at a particular time. For those children with organic problems which would interfere with the ability to learn to produce normal speech and language (cerebral palsy, deafness, cleft palate, etc.), intervention is appropriate as early as possible. With the very young child the early intervention may take the form of language stimulation through play therapy until the child is old enough for more structured remediation procedures. Children with severe organic problems are not likely to outgrow speech and language problems spontaneously and usually require long periods of intensive therapy.

Children who manifest articulation problems which are not related to organic or structural anomalies should be allowed time to mature and self-correct their misarticulations. For these children remediation should not begin until the upper age limit for the defective sound has been reached (see Table 16.1). Bear in mind that the speech pathologist may sometimes make different clinical judgments for intervention based on other input factors that take priority over any set of tables. Similarly, children with minor language lags whose scores differ as a result of which assessment tool is used should be given time to mature while the parents are encouraged and instructed to provide optimal language stimulation for them at home.

A major reason for withholding remedial procedures from young children with minor speech and language problems is to avoid creating anxiety and negative reactions toward speech and speaking situations. Most young children pass through a stage of developmental hesitation while they are learning to master the mechanics of speech and language. If they become anxious about speech during this period because of the attention called to inaccurate production or misarticulation, this may exacerbate the normal hesitations and result in more dysfluent speech, which can lead to primary stuttering. It would be tragic to eliminate a minor speech problem and in so doing create a more serious one.

The authors feel strongly that children with oral communication disorders should be referred to speech pathologists and audiologists for evaluation and determination of the nature, time, and type of intervention. It may be their judgment that the child will outgrow the problem through maturation alone. It may be their judgment that immediate intervention is required. It may be their judgment to delay treatment or to seek additional information from specialists in other disciplines before the onset of therapy. The best interests of the child and the family are served by having the child seen and evaluated by those professionals most qualified and experienced in the rehabilitation of speech and language disorders.

REFERENCES

Aram, D. M., & Nation, J. E. *Child language disorders.* St. Louis: Mosby, 1982.

ASHA Committee on the Midcentury White House Conference. Speech disorders and speech correction. *Journal of Speech and Hearing Disorders* 1952, *17,* 129–137.

Bloodstein, O. The Development of Stuttering. 2. Developmental phases. *Journal of Speech and Hearing Disorders, 25,* 1960, 366–376.

Bloodstein, O. The development of stuttering. 3. Theoretical and clinical implications. *Journal of Speech and Hearing Disorders,* 1961, *26,* 67–82.

Bloodstein, O. *A handbook of stuttering* (rev. ed.). Chicago: Easter Seal Society, 1975.

Bloodstein, O. *Speech pathology: An introduction.* Boston: Houghton Mifflin, 1979.

Bloom, L. *Readings in language development.* New York: Wiley, 1978.

Bloom, L. & Lahey, M. *Language development and language disorders.* New York: Wiley, 1978.

Bluemel, C. S. Primary and secondary stammering. *Quarterly Journal of Speech,* 1932, *18,* 187–200.

Brutten, G.J. & Shoemaker, D. J. *The Modification of Stuttering.* Englewood Cliffs, N.J. Prentice-Hall, 1967.

Bryngelson, B. A study of laterality of stutterers and normal speakers. *Journal of Speech Disorders,* 1939, *4,* 231–234.

Carrow, E. *Carrow elicited language inventory.* Boston: Teaching Resources, 1974.

Chomsky, N. & Halle, M. *The sound pattern of English.* New York: Harper & Row, 1968.

Coriat, I. H. Psychoanalytic concept of stammering. *Nervous Child,* 1943, *2,* 167–171.

Darley, F. L. & Spriestersbach, D. C. *Diagnostic methods in speech pathology* (2nd ed.). New York: Harper & Row, 1978.

Dickson, S. Incipient stuttering and spontaneous remission of stuttered speech. *Journal of Communication Disorders,* 1971, *4,* 99–110.

Dunn, L., *Peabody Picture Vocabulary Test.* Circle Pines, Minn: American Guidance Services, 1965.

Eisenson, J. *Aphasia in children.* New York: Harper & Row, 1972.

Fisher, H. B. & Logemann, J. A. *Fisher-Logemann Test of Articulation Competence.* Boston: Houghton Mifflin, 1971.

Fudala, J. B. *Arizona Articulation Proficiency Scale.* Los Angeles: Western Psychological Services, 1970.

Glauber, I. P. The psycho-analysis of stuttering. In J. Eisenson (Ed.), *Stuttering: A symposium.* New York: Harper & Row, 1958.

Goldman, R. & Fristoe, M. W. *Goldman-Fristoe Test of Articulation.* Circle Pines, Minn. American Guidance Services, 1970.

Hand, C. R. & Haynes, W. O. Linguistic processing and reaction time differences in stutterers and nonstutterers. *Journal of Speech and Hearing Research,* 1983, *26,* 181–185.

Hecaen, H. Acquired aphasia in children and the ontogenesis of hemispheric functional specialization. *Brain and Language,* 1976, *3,* 114–134.

Irwin, J. V. *Disorders of articulation.* Indianapolis: Bobbs-Merrill, 1972.

Johnson, W. *People in quandaries.* New York: Harper & Row, 1946.

Johnson, W. *The onset of stuttering.* Minneapolis: University of Minnesota Press, 1959.

Luper, H. L. & Ford, S. C. Disorders of fluency. In R. J. Van Hattum (Ed.), *Communicatioin disorders: An introduction.* New York: Macmillan, 1980.

Marge, M. The general problem of language disabilities in children. In J. V. Irwin & M. Marge (Eds.), *Principles of childhood language disabilities,* Englewood Cliffs, N.J.: Prentice-Hall, 1972.

McCormick, L., & Schiefelbusch, R. L. *Early language intervention,* Columbus, Ohio: Charles E. Merrill, 1984.

McDonald, E. T. *A deep test of articulation.* Pittsburg: Stanwix House, 1964.

McDonald, E. T. *Articulation testing and treatment: A sensory-motor approach.* Pittsburg: Stanwix House, 1964.

Milisen, R. The incidence of speech disorders. In L. E. Travis (Ed.), *Handbook of speech pathology,* New York: Appleton-Century-Crofts, 1957.

Morley, M. *Cleft palate and speech* (7th ed.). Baltimore: Williams and Wilkins, 1970.

Mowrer, D. E. *A program to establish fluent speech.* Columbus, Ohio: Charles E. Merrill, 1979.

Myklebust, H. Learning disorders: psycho-neurological disturbances in childhood. *Rehabilitation Literature,* December, 1964, 354–360.

Nicholosi, L., Harryman, E. & Krescheck, J. *Terminology of communication disorders.* Baltimore: Williams and Wilkins, 1978.

Orton, S. & Travis, L. E. Studies in stuttering 4. Studies of action currents in stutterers. *Archives of Neurological Psychiatry,* 1929, *21,* 61–68.

Perkins, W. H. *Speech Pathology: An applied behavioral science.* St. Louis: Mosby, 1971.

Piaget, J. *Play, dreams, and imitation in childhood.* New York: Norton, 1962.

Poole, I. Genetic development of articulation of consonant sounds in speech. *Elementary English Review,* 1934, *11,* 159–161.

Prather, E., Hedrick, D, & Klein, C. Articulation development in children aged two to four years. *Journal of Speech and Hearing Disorders,* 1975, *40,* 179–191.

Ryan, B. P. Operant procedures applied to stuttering therapy for children. *Journal of Speech and Hearing Disorders,* 1971, *36,* 264–280.

Shames, G. H. & Cheri, L. F. *Stutter-free speech.* Columbus, Ohio: Charles E. Merrill, 1980.

Sheehan, J. Conflict theory of stuttering. In J. Eisenson, (Ed.), *Stuttering: A symposium*. New York: Harper & Row, 1958.

Templin, M. *Certain language skills in children*. Minneapolis: University of Minnesota Press, 1957.

Templin, M. & Darley, F. L. *Templin-Darley Tests of Articulation* (2nd ed.). Iowa City: University of Iowa, 1969.

Travis, L. E. Disassociation of homologous muscle function in stuttering. *Archives of Neurological Psychiatry*, 1934, *31*, 129–133.

Travis, L. E. *Handbook of speech pathology*. New York: Appleton-Century-Crofts, 1957.

Van Riper, C. *Speech correction: Principles and methods* (6th ed.) Englewood Cliffs, N.J.: Prentice-Hall, 1978.

Van Riper, C. *The nature of stuttering* (2nd ed.). Englewood Cliffs, N.J.: Prentice-Hall, 1982.

Webster, R. L. *An operant response shaping program for the establishment of fluency in stutterers: Final report*. Hollins College, Va.: Hollins College, 1972.

Weiss, C. E., Lillywhite, H. S., & Gordon, M. E. *Clinical management of articulation disorders*. St. Louis: Mosby, 1980.

Weiss, C. E. & Lillywhite, H. S. *Communication disorders—Prevention and early intervention* (2nd ed.). St. Louis: Mosby, 1981.

Wells, C. G. *Cleft palate and its associated speech disorders*. New York: McGraw-Hill, 1971.

West, R. W. & Ansberry, M. *The rehabilitation of speech* (4th ed.). New York: Harper & Row, 1957.

Wischner, G. J. Stuttering behavior and learning: A preliminary theoretical formulation. *Journal of Speech and Hearing Disorders*, 1950, *15*, 324–335.

Wood, N. *Verbal learning. Dimensions in early learning series*. San Rafael, Calif.: Dimensions, 1969.

CHAPTER 17

Epilepsy and Other Neurological and Neuromuscular Handicaps

PATRICIA L. HARTLAGE AND LAWRENCE C. HARTLAGE

The purpose of this chapter is to introduce a diverse population of children called the neurologically handicapped, to define what is meant by some of the various diagnoses, and to explore the impact of the specific disability on the child's psychological development and especially on his formal education. Some neurological handicaps like spastic cerebral palsy are easily recognized. For these physically disabled children most of the challenges to the schools are as obvious as the disabilities, including minimizing physical barriers to participation in school activities, adapting the curriculum to what the child can do, and maintaining the child's self-worth and identity as an individual, not as a disability. Other neurological handicaps are not so easily recognized, nor is their significance to the child's development. Epilepsy, like other hidden handicaps such as diabetes, cystic fibrosis, or a specific learning disability, may have a profound, but often unappreciated, impact on a child's psychological development. This chapter deals separately with the hidden and the obvious neurological disabilities because the needs of children are different and not because a hidden handicap is necessarily less disabling.

EPILEPSY: AN EXAMPLE OF A HIDDEN HANDICAP

Epilepsy has been a matter of concern since recorded history. It is a fairly common problem with many famous persons among its victims including Julius Caesar, Alexander the Great, and Napoleon. Humans have always sought to understand and explain epilepsy in the light of current knowledge. Hippocrates was among the first to dispute the belief that epilepsy was a divine origin and to attribute epilepsy to natural causes arising in the brain.

Seizures are not rare. Approximately 1 in 20 persons has a seizure sometime in his or her life. During a seizure the normal electrical activity of the brain is interrupted by abnormal discharges which cause a temporary loss of control of body functions. Some seizures are very dramatic, with loss of consciousness and violent jerking of the limbs, whereas others are so subtle as to be overlooked by all but the most careful observer because they are manifested only by a momentary state of confusion.

Only about one in eight persons experiencing a seizure will develop epilepsy or recurrent seizures. The incidence of epilepsy is low, only about 1%, in the regular classroom but is much higher in the special education programs. These classes serve more children with central nervous system disorders, and most special education teachers have personal experience with children with epilepsy. As many as 20% of children in classes for the trainable mentally retarded have a history of seizures. Epilepsy is not, however, a sign of retardation and is found in children in gifted classes as well. Epilepsy affects approximately 2 million Americans, three-quarters of them having the onset in childhood or adolescence.

Assessment

Most important in the correct identification of seizures is an accurate description of the event by a good observer. A severe convulsion is hard to overlook, but there are mild as well as severe seizures and these milder attacks may go unrecognized. The possibility of epilepsy should be considered in any child with periodic changes in consciousness or behavior, and if epilepsy is suspected a medical referral should be made.

The medical history begins with detailed review of the seizure or seizures and what events may have preceded and followed. Since seizures arise in the brain, whether other symptoms of brain problems are present is also questioned. A systematic review is made of the child's health history beginning with a history of the pregnancy and birth. Significant illnesses and injuries are reviewed. Any allergies or drug reactions are sought, immunization record is reviewed, and the family history is reviewed for neurological problems. Inquiry is made as to the function of all major organ systems, and the child's developmental and academic history is reviewed. A thorough physical and neurological examination is performed, and the physician formulates an initial diagnosis as to whether the episodes represent seizures, what type, and probable causes. Special diagnostic studies are used to confirm or amend this initial impression. Typically these include a series of blood and urine tests which survey general health, and spinal fluid is examined if infection is suspected. A variety of other radiographical techniques are available to study the anatomy and blood supply to the brain. Electroencephalograms (EEGs) are also performed routinely. Although this recording of the electrical activity of the brain from electrodes attached to the scalp is only truly diagnostic of seizures when one is recorded during the session, abnormalities in brain rhythms often are detectable between seizures. During the EEG recording a variety of maneuvers are employed to try to trigger these abnormal rhythms, including hyperventilation, photic stimulation with a strobe light, and trying to record a period of drowsiness and light sleep during the session. Plain skull films are often performed, but they are increasingly being replaced by computerized tomography which, although much more costly, can visualize radiologically the brain as well as the surrounding bones when there is concern about structural brain lesions causing the seizures.

Other highly specialized diagnostic techniques used to study persons with epilepsy in research centers include long-term monitoring of EEG with simultaneous recordings of other biological parameters and video recordings of patient behavior; studies of the changes in blood flow to different parts of the brain after inhalation of radioactive gases; and quantitative analyses of spontaneous EEG rhythms and evoked responses to visual, auditory, or other stimuli (Baird, John, Ahn, & Maisel, 1980).

The initial assessment concludes with reviewing and explaining the results of all the data available with the child and parents and formulating a plan of management. The primary treatment may consist of treating an underlying disorder either medically or surgically or may consist of symptomatic treatment with appropriate anticonvulsant drugs which can control or nearly control the majority of seizures. In one special instance of childhood seizures, treatment is usually withheld. This is in the case of brief generalized seizures associated with fever in otherwise healthy preschoolers. These usually hereditary fever fits or febrile convulsions seem to have little correlation with the development of epilepsy or any neurological or psychological handicaps later in life, and most physicians consider the risks of drug treatment to outweigh the potential benefit of reducing the chance of recurrence.

Etiology

Although epilepsy may have an identifiable cause, such as damage to the brain around the time of birth, head injury, infection, or brain tumor, often no cause is found. The terms symptomatic and idiopathic epilepsy, respectively, are used to designate whether or not a cause is known.

Types

There are three major types of epileptic seizures.

1. *Generalized tonic-clonic seizures.* Formerly called grand mal, these are characterized by falling, stiffening, and jerking of the limbs, loss of consciousness, and irregular breathing. These seizures usually last from one to several minutes and may occur once a day or only once every few years.

2. *Generalized non-convulsive or absence seizures.* Formerly called petit mal, these are seen only as a lapse in awareness lasting a few seconds. Sometimes staring, eye blinking, or slight twitching accompany them. This type of

seizure most commonly occurs in children of grammar school age and may occur 100 or more times a day.

3. *Partial complex or psychomotor seizures.* These are manifest as periods of confusion or purposeless activity lasting up to 20 minutes.

There are a number of less common types of seizures classified as generalized if the abnormal electrical discharge is present throughout the brain or partial if only in part of the brain. A seizure may begin as a partial seizure and become generalized. A partial seizure is often an expression in crude form of the function subserved by the area of the cerebral cortex where it arises. For example, a localized epileptic discharge in the motor cortex may cause movement of one limb, and a discharge in the visual cortex may cause a visual hallucination or distortion.

Seizures must be differentiated from other conditions which can cause a loss of consciousness. Fainting and cardiac problems can usually be distinguished by a careful history. Most difficult to distinguish from seizures are the various behavioral episodes resembling them. Hyperventilation attacks, triggered by anxiety and beginning with deep and rigid breathing, may be mistaken for seizures. Hysterical seizures or "pseudo-seizures" with no abnormal electrical activity in the brain are seen in children who also have true epilepsy as well as in nonepileptic children. The term "episodic dyscontrol syndrome" has been applied to periodic rages, and some are said to be benefited with anticonvulsants. In these behavioral episodes, which occur with varying degrees of conscious control, the person almost invariably avoids personal injury even though he may fall, often demonstrates some emotion by yelling or swearing, does not loose control of his bladder or bowels as may occur in a true seizure, and rapidly recovers his prior mental state after an episode. Purposeful aggressive acts are extremely rare in epileptic seizures, although the person may flail out to avoid restraint during or just after a seizure.

The Academic Impact of Epilepsy

Even very brief seizures interfere with attention and learning. Absence attacks usually occur frequently during the day, and occasionally children referred for medical evaluation of attentional deficit disorders are found to be having absence seizures. When a child has a more prolonged or severe seizure the period of disability extends beyond the few minutes of seizure because of the recovery period or postictal phase. After a generalized tonic-clonic convulsion the person may need a brief nap or rest period before recovering alertness. For the child in school this usually means missing at least one class period. Occasionally there is a personal injury from a sudden loss of control. Although some children only have their seizures at night, their teachers may be aware that their school performance is noticeably poorer the following day.

Among epileptic children attending regular schools, almost half have been rated as markedly inattentive by their teachers (Holdsworth & Whitmore, 1974). In one recent study only boys with epilepsy were found to be significantly more inattentive and overactive by parent and teacher assessment and by various tests of sustained attention in comparison to nonepileptic peers (Stores, Hart, & Piran, 1978). Neither seizure type nor drug treatment could account for the differences. A novel observation in the latter study was that in both boys and girls with epilepsy there was a paradoxical effect of distracting stimuli slightly improving performance.

Children with epilepsy tend to be underachievers in the classroom, falling behind expectancies based on their age, class placement, and intellectual ability. Underachievement in arithmetic is more striking than in reading (Bagley, 1970; Green & Hartlage, 1971). There are probably multiple reasons for this underachievement, including the underlying neurological disorder which gives rise to the seizure, the effects of the seizure on attention, the potential of the seizure itself to cause harm to the developing brain, medication effects, social rejection, higher absenteeism, the lowered expectations of overprotective parents (Hartlage & Green, 1972), and teachers who equate current performance with intelligence (Bagley, 1970).

In one survey of over 200 adolescents with epilepsy (Goldin, Perry, Margolin, Stotsky, & Foster, 1971) the presence of an additional handicap markedly increased the school dropouts (20% versus 2%) and the chances of being academically behind peers (95% versus 16%). The adolescents with epilepsy alone were making fairly adequate adjustments and only one medical variable, age of onset, appeared to influence academic, social, and emotional adjustment. The authors suggest that the observed increased school dropout rate, difficulty in social interaction, and inability to handle everyday problems seen in children with epilepsy of early onset may result from the altered psychodynamic interaction between parent and child in a crucial phase of psychological development.

The academic underachievement of epileptic children is often a presentment of their later vocational underachievement. All surveys have shown a high rate of unemployment among epileptics which is out of proportion to the severity of their handicap; again social adjustment may be an important factor.

Cognitive Abilities

Although the individual child with epilepsy may be severely retarded or be a genius, persons with epilepsy as a group have a higher incidence of mental retardation (6%) than the general population (3%). This is to be expected since epilepsy is a symptom of brain dysfunction. The IQ of noninstitutionalized epileptics approximates that of the normal population, but epileptic children seem to have lower IQs than epileptic adults, and the earlier the onset of epilepsy the greater the depression of intelligence (Epilepsy Foundation of America, 1975). The frequency of seizures is related to depressed intelligence but less so than early onset of seizures or etiology of seizures (Ounsted, Lindsay,

& Norman, 1966; O'Leary, Seidenberg, Berent, & Boll, 1981). Specific areas of cognitive disability may correlate with the laterality in localization of an epileptogenic focus (Dennerll, 1964; McIntyre, Pritchard, & Lombroso, 1976).

Psychosocial Aspects of Epilepsy

Is there an "epileptic personality"? Tizard (1962) reviewed the literature on the question and distinquished among previous reports, changing ideas about epileptics, and their behavior. In the first three decades of the twentieth century there was an accepted concept of a universal epileptic personality: concrete, perseverative, emotionally explosive, selfish, excessively religious, and suspicious. No positive personality traits were mentioned. In the 1930s and 1940s the popular position became that epileptics are no different from anyone else regarding personality disturbances. More recently epileptics have been thought to have no stereotype but were believed to more frequently suffer neuroses; to resemble in personality persons with organic brain damage; and to have different personality disturbances associated with different types of seizures, especially those arising from the temporal lobes. Tizard points out shortcomings of earlier studies and warns against generalizations from atypical populations.

Although evidence for (Bennett, 1962; Gibbs & Gibbs, 1964; Glaser, 1964; Waxman & Geschwind, 1975) and against (Guerrant, Anderson, Weinstein, Jaros, & Desking, 1962; Stevens, 1966; Small, Small, & Hayden, 1966) abounds, most neurologists note a relatively greater frequency of behavioral problems in their admittedly preselected epilepsy patients when the seizures are of partial complex type and of temporal lobe origin. Because the temporal lobe is related to the limbic system, an association between seizures arising in these areas and behavioral changes seems a logical and expected one. There may be a higher incidence of psychopathology when the focus is in the left temporal lobe (Pritchard, Lombroso, & McIntyre, 1980).

In 100 children with temporal lobe epilepsy followed for an average of five years by Ounsted et al. (1966), 26 of the children developed a hyperkinetic syndrome in early childhood. Most were boys who had suffered definite cerebral insults early in life, and mental retardation was common. Thirty-six had outbursts of catastrophic rage not associated with seizures, but resembling the reaction to frustrating situations in brain damaged persons. Unlike the hyperkinetic syndrome, rage reaction occurred as frequently in girls as boys and could begin at any age. The authors felt this 36% figure probably was an underestimate of the frequency of rage reactions in children with temporal lobe epilepsy since many had not reached the age when others had their first symptoms of rage. Some nonepileptic children with severe behavioral disturbances and EEG abnormalities have been reported to improve with anticonvulsant therapy (Zimmerman, 1956), and aggressive behavior has improved by removal of tissue from the temporal lobes for treatment of epilepsy (Mark & Ervin, 1970).

Treatment

Seizures in most cases can be controlled or greatly reduced in frequency with medication. Surgery or special diets are employed on rare occasions. A medication which results in markedly reduced frequency of seizures may appear to have an enhancing effect on mental function because mental efficiency is not impaired by the seizures or during the postseizure recovery periods. However, there is growing concern that long-term treatment with these drugs may itself impair cognitive function. Reviews of the literature on the psychological effects of anticonvulsant drugs in children and adults (Stores, 1975; Trimble & Reynolds, 1976) mention repeated observations of mental or behavioral regression as the only sign of intoxication or overmedication with the common anticonvulsants. They also mention idiosyncratic behavioral reactions to these drugs, the most common of which appears to be hyperkinetic reactions and disturbances of sleep in certain children with barbiturates. Studies have raised concern about impairment of cognition with phenobarbital, the most widely prescribed seizure drug for children, even when the levels of the drug are in the range termed "therapeutic" and nontoxic. Different types of seizure drugs, such as phenytoin and phenobarbital, may affect different cognitive and psychomotor abilities (Hartlage, Stovall, & Kovach, 1979: Camfield, Chaplin, Doyle, Shapero, Cummings, & Camfield, 1979). It is to be expected that medications which work on the brain to lessen the chance of seizures would exert some influence on brain functions. An awareness of the possible intellectual effects is important in selecting the most appropriate medication. For example, the child who was previously hyperactive is probably at risk to have this worsened by barbiturate drugs.

The *Physicians' Desk Reference* (PDR), an annual volume subsidized by the pharmaceutical manufacturers and often available in school nurse's offices, gives a good deal of information about the use and physical side effects and toxic effects of anticonvulsants and other drugs. Color pictures of many preparations are given to help identify medications, but it contains little about the more subtle behavioral effects of these drugs. Nor does it mention the costs of therapy, which may range from less than 5 to more than 100 dollars per month.

Seizures are less likely when the child is active mentally and physically, and the academic and extracurricular activities of school become important parts of the treatment program for the child with epilepsy. Physical activity is an important part of staying healthy for any child, especially the one with seizures. But should the youngster be encouraged to play football with the school team? There has been fear among many professionals (Committee on the Medical Aspects of Sports, 1968; McLaurin, 1973), as well as among many parents, that the risk of recurrent head trauma may lead to worsening of the epilepsy. Regardless of advice, nearly all teens with epilepsy who are involved in sports choose some potentially hazardous ones (Goldin et al. 1971). When their seizures are only an occasional problem, the risk of acquiring attitudes of inferiority and "differentness" often outweigh the risk of some injury in athletic contests. Livingston and Berman (1973), proponents of allowing young people with suitably controlled seizures to participate in athletics, recall experience with at least 15,000 children with epilepsy over a 36-year period. They state that while hundreds of these patients played tackle football and similar sports, they recalled not a single instance of recurrence of seizures related to sports-acquired head injuries.

In one survey of over 700 teachers (Force, 1965) more than half had no experience with or information about seizures, and of those who had received instruction on how to handle a seizure, only 44% felt they could actually handle the situation. What should be done when someone has a major seizure? There is a higher likelihood that a person unfamiliar with the situation will do too much rather than too little. It is helpful to see that the person's head is protected and that he can breathe freely. This can be done by having the person lie on his side, leaving him there until he begins to wake up. In this position the person can be observed, will not hurt himself, and if he is unable to swallow, will not become choked. Restraining the person, putting hard objects in his mouth, stimulation by touching and calling, and administration of cardiopulmonary resuscitation are not desirable. A period of confusion often follows a seizure, and the person may be very sleepy for a while. Only when a series of seizures occurs without the patient awakening between should medical attention be urgently sought.

The public information program of the Epilepsy Foundation of America (1838 L Street, N.W., Washington, D.C. 20036) provides pamphlets on various aspects of epilepsy addressed to specific target groups such as children, parents, and teachers. Usually these publications are made available at no charge.

MOTOR DISABILITIES IN CHILDHOOD: EXAMPLES OF OBVIOUS HANDICAPS

The diversity of the population of some children termed physically or orthopedically handicapped presents a unique dilemma in programming. If we consider, for example, a group of wheelchair-bound children: most have fairly static disabilities like cerebral palsy but some have progressive disorders like muscular dystrophy; others are recovering from recent accidents or illness and may improve with time. Intelligence may range from retarded to gifted. Some will have difficulty using their arms as well as their legs. Speech impairments, vision and hearing impairments, and emotional handicaps may coexist. The board of education will be aware of the needs of the wheelchair: ramps, accessible classrooms, lunch rooms, restrooms, and buses equipped with lifts and locks. In addition, school psychologists should be aware of the psychosocial as well as physical needs of the kids in the chairs.

Cerebral Palsy

Actually a lay term and not a medical diagnosis, cerebral palsy refers to the motor handicaps resulting from brain damage occurring around the time of birth. Complications of pregnancy and delivery, pre- and postnatal infections, and prematurity are among the leading causes. The motor impairments range from mild to severe and are classified descriptively by which limbs are involved and by which motor centers in the brain are affected. The incidence of the major types of cerebral palsy and the frequency of mental impairment in each type are described in Table 17.1. These figures are based on Hagberg's (1978) description of 692 children by predominant type of motor disability. Many have combinations of motor impairments. Cerebral palsy in the population studied involved approximately 1.5% of children, an incidence one-half that of severe mental retardation and one-seventh that of epilepsy. The prevalence of cerebral palsy in school-age children in other studies varies from 1.4 to 6.0 per 1000 depending on age and screening methods (Nelson & Ellenberg, 1978). Advances in perinatal medicine have been reflected in a decreasing incidence of cerebral palsy, especially those cases due to the complications of prematurity and the Rh incompatibilities.

Drugs used to reduce spasticity such as diazepam, dantrolene, and baclofen are of limited benefit to the cerebral palsied child because of their side effects (Young & Delwaide, 1981). Chronic stimulation of the cerebellum by implantation of a battery powered "brain pacemaker" may decrease spasticity without the troublesome side effects of the drugs, but it does not improve strength or decrease involuntary movements (Cooper, Riklan, Amin, Waltz & Cullenam, 1976; Davis, Cullen, Flitter, Duenas, Engle, & Ennis, 1977) and results have not been uniformly impressive (Gahm, Russman, Cerciello, Fiorentino, & McGrath, 1981). The mainstay of treatment of cerebral palsy remains early

Table 17.1.   Syndromes of Cerebral Palsy

Type	Percent of total	IQ over 70
Diplegia		
(weakness of legs » arms)		
Spastic (with stiffness) or		
Ataxic (with loss of balance)	40%	70%
Hemiplegia		
(weakness of one side; arm » leg)	35%	85%
Dyskinetic		
(having involuntary movements)		
Athetotic (with writhing movements of limbs) or	3.5%	70%
Dystonic (with strong primitive reflexes involv-		
ing trunk)	10.5%	40%
Ataxic		
(having poor balance)	7%	40%
Tetraplegia		
(or quadriplegia; weakness of all four limbs)	4%	0%

and vigorous rehabilitation therapy by physical, occupational, and speech therapists skilled in the treatment of children. A variety of techniques to stimulate normal and inhibit abnormal movement patterns have been developed (Levitt, 1975). New technologies such as electromyographic biofeedback can be useful adjuncts to movement training (Ball, Combs, Rugh, & Neptune, 1977). Ingenious adaptive devices have been devised for the physically impaired child; some can be homemade (Nathan, Slominski, & Griswold, 1970). Corrective orthopedic surgery and bracing are used adjunctively in the therapy program. Current research in adaptive equipment aims to apply space age technology to rehabilitation (NASA, 1974).

Prior to entering school, the cerebral palsied child may have had a severely limited number and frequency of the motor experiences considered necessary for normal cognitive development. The child may have been or may still be dependent on others for basic needs like feeding, dressing, and toileting, that others the same age have mastered. These immaturities and the child's physical appearance may lead people to underestimate the child's intellectual abilities and to treat him appropriate to his motor rather than his chronological age. Despite their handicaps and often in the face of little preparation by the schools, there has usually been good acceptance of physically disabled children in the classroom (Anderson, 1973). Often the most frustrating problem for the child with cerebral palsy, as well as for others in his environment, is the involvement of the muscles of speech which are commonly involved in the dyskinetic and mixed forms of the disorder. Language boards with symbols, words, and letters are valuable aides to the child unable to express himself verbally. More recently electronic communicators with visual displays or voice synthesizers have been developed for these patients, and with increased interest in application of biomedical engineering to patient aides it is likely that such efforts will accelerate.

There are some characteristics uniquely common in families with children who have cerebral palsy which make the parents invaluable resources to the special education personnel. Their child's problem was recognized in infancy, the probable cause of the disability and a descriptive diagnosis was made, and a program of therapy was started very early that closely involved the parents. These circumstances have enabled the parents to develop considerable expertise about the child's disability and about working with a variety of professionals. They have developed skills in handling and helping their child and children with similar disabilities because most cerebral palsy centers have physical and occupation therapy sessions with groups of children of similar age together with their parents. These are skills which can be and should be used especially in the kindergarten and primary-grade classrooms. Since cerebral palsy of mild or moderate severity does not affect the child's general health or longevity the parents of these children are extremely motivated to see that the society in which they will grow up will incorporate them. They can be a very potent political force in identifying and obtaining necessary services and opportunities.

A most useful book for anyone working with cerebral palsied children that is endorsed by many of our patient's parents is Nancy Finnie's *Handling the Young Cerebral Palsied Child at Home* (1968). Information about various aspects of cerebral palsy in a form appropriate for explaining the disorder to the lay public is provided on request by the United Cerebral Palsy chapters located in most large communities.

Muscular Dystrophy

Muscular dystrophies are inherited diseases causing progressive weakness. There is considerable variation among the different types of muscle disease, with some causing death in childhood and others resulting in only mild chronic disability.

Most children with muscular dystrophy do not have any trouble speaking and can express themselves very well orally. They may enter school with minimal disability and appear no different from their peers but show increasing physical limitations each year.

The emotional burden upon the family with a chronic and progressive disease in their child, especially when it is inherited, is often more heavy than that of the child's considerable physical care needs. Although there are exceptions, the energies of the families of school children with muscular dystrophy are fairly well used up in coping with the child's needs during the time he is at home, and school time is viewed as a welcome period of independence by both child and parents.

Pseudohypertrophic or Duchenne Type Muscular Dystrophy

This is inherited as a sex-linked recessive. This disease affects only male children but is transmitted through unaffected female carriers. The disease is remarkably similar in all affected persons. The weakness is apparent in early childhood, often manifested by toe-walking and trouble rising from the floor and climbing stairs. Sometimes the calf muscles appear large, but most muscles are soft and small to the touch. By about age 10 most children cannot ambulate and must use a wheelchair. This is followed by progressive joint deformities as well as progression of the the weakness. The dystrophic patient finally becomes too weak to tolerate sitting, and death usually occurs in the late teens or early twenties from pneumonia due to involvement of the respiratory muscles. There is no cure for Duchenne type dystrophy, although physical therapy, bracing, and surgery may delay loss of function. Emphasis is placed on prevention by identification of the carrier state in female relatives. While deterioration occurs only in voluntary muscles, and to a lesser extent in the heart muscle, for some curious reason intelligence is usually slightly below that of parents and siblings, following a bell-shaped curve approximately 20 points below that of other children (Dubowitz, 1978). The intellectual impairment, if present, is nonprogressive and intelligence is not impaired in female carriers. The social aspects of attending school are viewed positively by patients and families and acceptance by classmates is surprisingly good. Education for these students is not geared to vocational achievement since the severity of the physical disability precludes employment, but no one would dispute the value of education for the dystrophic as well as for the normal child in enhancing the present and future quality of life.

Limb-Girdle Muscular Dystrophy

This follows an autosomal recessive pattern of inheritance and may be transmitted to male or female children when both parents carry the defective gene. The disorder is less predictable in its course than pseudohypertrophic muscular dystrophy and may begin anytime from childhood to young adult life. Loss of strength in the proximal muscles of the shoulder and hip girdles is noted. The progression of the disease may be rapid but more often is relatively slow and compatible with a fairly normal life expectancy. Despite progressive disability most persons can be successfully employed for many years and many are parents of normal children. Educational credentials are one of the most important predictors of self-sufficiency and vocational success in adult life, and educational programs appropriate to their needs are extremely important for children with this disorder. Intellectual impairment is rare in this disorder.

Facioscapulohumeral Dystrophy

This is the mildest of the three classic muscular dystrophies. Weakness is usually limited to the face, shoulders, and upper arms, and the progression of the disease is very slow. Inheritance is by autosomal dominant transmission from affected parent to children of either sex. It has been observed that although patients with this disorder have intelligence levels comparable to nondystrophic relatives, verbal IQ tends to be lower than performance IQ, a phenomenon also observed in Duchenne type dystrophy (Karagan & Sorensen, 1981).

Progressive Spinal Muscular Atrophy

This is one of the most common of the neuromuscular diseases which can mimic muscular dystrophy. Although the problem arises in the motor nerve cells in the spinal cord rather than in the muscle itself, the effects in the child are very similar, mainly involving progressive weakness of the proximal muscles. Inheritance is autosomal recessive. Several varieties of the disease are known. The infantile form of the disease, called Werdnig-Hoffmann disease, is apparent in the early months of life, and some children live only a short time. Others follow a course not unlike pseudohypertrophic muscular dystrophy, and few will live an average life span despite considerable disability. The juvenile onset form, called Kugelberg-Welander disease, is much more slowly progressive and most patients live to old age. Intelligence is spared, and, anecdotally, children with this disease are often described as more intelligent than unaffected siblings.

Myotonic Muscular Dystrophy

This is described separately from the classical muscular dystrophies because it is a disorder which commonly involves many body tissues besides the muscle. Endocrine disturbances and cataracts are frequently present. It is an autosomal dominant disease which causes weakness in the face, giving a characteristic lax expression and weakness in, and an inability to relax, distal muscles after a voluntary contraction called myotonia. The disorder is extremely variable in its severity. Many adults are diagnosed only incidentally when seeking medical attention for an unrelated problem. Some children are born with signs of the disease already recognizable. They often have congenital joint contractures. When the muscle symptoms are manifest early in life severe physical handicaps, mental retardation, and speech impairment are common.

Polymyositis

This means, literally, "multiple muscle inflammation." It is not a hereditary disease and may affect persons at any age. It appears to be one of many autoimmune diseases where the body's defense mechanisms go awry and begin to misdirect their attacks upon a particular body tissue. In this disorder the target tissues are the muscles and the blood vessels supplying them, and, as in rheumatoid arthritis, the major target is the joints of the body. Since it is an inflammatory disease there may be fevers, aches, and pains as well as weakness. The signs and symptoms are different from one patient to another, but the pattern of weakness is very similar to muscular dystrophy, with the muscles closest to the body weakened more than those of the hands and feet. Polymyositis in years past had a high fatality rate in children, but now with improved medical treatment most children do recover. It is usually a long and difficult battle with many setbacks and complications both of the disease and of the potent drugs needed to control it. In approximately half of these children the inflammation also involves the skin and its blood vessels, causing breakdown of skin as well as muscle; this form is called *dermatomyositis*. The inflammation may also involve other body parts. Even when the condition remits, there may be residual disabilities.

Myasthenia Gravis

This means literally, "serious muscle fatigue or weakness." Like polymyositis this is an acquired, nonhereditary, autoimmune muscle problem. In recent years it has become perhaps the best understood of all the neuromuscular diseases. Normally voluntary movement results when the chemical signal or transmitter, acetylcholine, is released from the nerve ending to join or synapse at a specific receptor site on the muscle. For years it was known that the problem in myasthenia gravis was at this neuromuscular junction. Recently it has been shown that myasthenia gravis patients form antibodies which circulate in their blood and specifically attack proteins in the muscle receptor sites for acetylcholine.

In children, myasthenia gravis usually is first noted by rapid tiring of the muscles of the face. The eyelids droop progressively during the day, speech slows after they talk for a while, and chewing food tires their jaws. The other muscles of the body may also become fatigued easily. The youngster with myasthenia gravis usually looks healthy and strong, and the unusually rapid tiring of the muscles, the "pathologic fatigability" which is the hallmark of the disease, is often misinterpreted as laziness. The stress of any physical illness may precipitate a dreaded "myasthenic crisis" with severe weakness and sometimes a need for assisting breathing with a respirator. Medical treatment has advanced remarkably since the nature of the disease has been clarified. Medications which gave brief temporary relief when taken every few hours have been supplanted by specific treatment to halt the body's production of the antiacetylcholine receptor antibodies. In addition to medical treatments similar to those used in polymyositis to suppress the body's immune reactions and to remove antibodies by removing and replacing the patient's plasma, surgical removal of the thymus gland, an immune system related organ in the neck, has been effective in most cases in halting the progress of the disease and sometimes leading to a permanent cure. Although the child with poly-or dermatomyostis may vary in his strength from week to week, the myasthenic child's changes in strength sometimes occur in hours. Of all the neuromuscular diseases, it is probably most prototypical of the need for anyone establishing educational goals to know the condition, how it now affects and in the future may affect function, what (if any) limits should be set in physical demands, and whether specific precautions should be taken. This information should be in writing from the parents and from the child's doctor. An example of a physician's reply to some well-phrased questions by a teacher about a third grader with myasthenia gravis follows:

Q.   What is Frederick's diagnosis and what has he been told about it?

A.   It is myasthenia gravis, a condition causing muscles to tire extremely easily. It is not inherited, nor is it contagious. He has been told if anyone asks, he has "a muscle problem" (He can't pronounce its name). He knows medication helps him stay healthy.

Q.   What are the signs of the disease in him?

A.   The disease shows itself by the drooping of his eyelids, which becomes very noticeable in the afternoon. It shows too in the fact that his left eye can no longer look outwards or upwards, and sometimes looks "crossed." He also has to stop for brief rest periods in vigorous play.

Q.   Will the disease be expected to change during this school year?

A.   He has not recently had much change and we do not expect any big changes in this condition. However, if you notice any changes please send a note home to his parents describing what you have observed.

Q.   Does the regular school curriculum need to be modified in any way because he has this problem?

A. Yes.

1. Please do not sit him in the front row. Tipping his head backwards to see the teacher and the board when his eyelids droop is not very comfortable.

2. Please tell the gym teacher to allow Frederick to rest a few minutes if he needs it. The gym teacher might want to call the parents or write to me about this if there are any questions. With this modification physical education will be helpful not harmful to him.

3. Get a doctor's permission in writing for any team sports.

4. Walking, stair climbing, writing, carrying books, and expressing himself orally are not problems. No modifications are needed for transportation, restrooms, or lunch. Learning is not affected by his muscle problem.

Q. Does he need to take medicine at school?

A. He can take all his medicine at home.

Q. Are there any side effects?

A. He occasionally has had stomachaches as a side effect in the past and gets weaker when he forgets his medicine.

Q. Are there any special precautions?

A. Please have in his folder, the school office, and his classroom the telephone numbers of his home, his parents' place of business, and my office. It is extremely unlikely that his condition will suddenly worsen, but it would be reassuring to have those numbers handy.

Q. Are there any special observations we should make?

A. If you notice any changes in Fred's strength please send a note home. Your observations of his eyes drooping in the afternoons were the reason his parents sought medical advice and had his problem identified. Thank you.

The information exchanged above is an example of how carefully phrased individually pertinent questions can yield information useful in formulating individual educational plans without the confusing technical jargon often elicited by requesting copies of medical records or sending a standard medical form to be completed.

Over 40 different neuromuscular diseases are listed by the Muscular Dystrophy Association, and the disorders mentioned here represent just a few of the diseases. With so many different conditions commonly lumped under the term muscular dystrophy, it is imperative in the educational and vocational planning for affected children to have an accurate diagnosis and an understanding of how the disability is expected to influence function in the future. Most children with neuromuscular diseases will have slowly progressive loss of strength, although a few will improve with age.

For some mysterious reason there seems to be a mental block in many education systems when it comes to considering the dynamics of a disability. This peculiar rigidity in the system manifests itself very clearly in many of the neurological problems of childhood. Following a stroke or head injury learning capacities may be obviously altered. If a psychoeducational assessment of the brain-injured student can be obtained before or shortly after return to school, decisions to alter the educational program in the face of the new limitations seem to ignore any expectations of changes or at what rate they might occur. Legally mandated reassessments at three-year intervals cannot be expected to be adequate for the child with a changing mental disability. Similar and much less excusable frustrations are experienced by the families of children with changing motor capabilities like the children with muscular dystrophy. In most of these children changes occur gradually and special needs can be anticipated well in advance. Unfortunately some school systems tend to reject such anticipation, and assignment of a ride on an adapted bus and construction of a ramp at the school door does not occur until the first day the child appears in his or her wheelchair, and inadequate restroom facilities are not addressed until an embarrassing accident in the classroom. The child with recurring ups and downs presents a bigger dilemma when curricula are inflexible. Children with polymyositis or myasthenia gravis may experience recurrent unpredictable crises between periods where they are relatively symptom-free. A gradual return to full school attendance after a setback is often medically and psychologically desirable yet impossible when a forced choice exists between classroom or homebound instruction.

Muscular dystrophy is not as common as cerebral palsy, and many people are ignorant about it and consequently are initially ill at ease with the child and his family.

In an indepth study of the home life of six families with one or more children afflicted with severe neuromuscular disease, Duchenne type dystrophy, or Werdnig-Hoffmann, some similar patterns were noted in all the families which offer some insights into family dynamics. Parents changed their focus from the future to the present, strove to keep family life as normal as possible, sought to maximize their personal strengths and to cultivate support networks (Bregman, 1980). These patterns of adaptation would be admirable ones for the teachers of these children to emulate.

For more information about muscular dystrophy and the other neuromuscular diseases you can write to The Muscular Dystrophy Association, In., 810 Seventh Ave., New York, N.Y., 10019.

OTHER NEUROLOGICAL DISABILITIES

For school psychologists or other advanced degree school professionals whose work is primarily or heavily involved in serving students with chronic health problems or disabilities, the families, physicians, and paramedical specialists actively involved in the child's care would be the major and best resource of information about the specific disability, its effects, and its treatment. Each "exceptional" child is as unique in his health care needs as he is in his learning style and in his personality. A few additional neurological disorders which occur with sufficient frequency in the school-aged population to merit mention are briefly described next.

Congenital Abnormalities of the Nervous System

Among the most serious birth defects of the nervous system are the *neural tube defects*. The central nervous system develops embryologically as a long flat plate which rolls up into a tube. Failure of the neural tube to close completely at its posterior end causes incomplete development of the covering bones and skin, as well as the arrested development of the lower spinal cord. The extent of disability depends on the size and location of the defect. A small low defect might cause no loss of function or only slightly impaired bladder and bowel control; slightly larger defects cause incontinence and impair strength and sensation below the knees; and more extensive defects render the child paraplegic.

Myelomeningocele, the technical name for an open spine defect involving the spinal cord and its coverings, is often compounded by hydrocephalus, an abnormal accumulation of spinal fluid within the head, because of associated abnormalities of the lower part of the brain. The variety of rehabilitation needs of these children dwarf those of all other handicapped groups. Their care typically involves neurosurgeons, orthopedic surgeons, urologists, pediatricians, neurologists, physical, occupational, and speech therapists, and programs of personal and financial support for the child and his family. Intelligence is relatively spared even when hydrocephalus is present.

A large closure defect in the upper or cranial portion of the neural tube, called anencephaly, is incompatible with life, but children with less severe cranial defects may survive. The most common site of these "encephalocoeles" is at the back of the head, and if brain tissue is involved in the malformation it is the occipital or visual cortex. Because this defect involves the brain, intellectual and visual impairments are common but not inevitable.

Hydrocephalus may occur as an isolated problem, either resulting from a congenital defect in the pathways of fluid flow or occurring secondary to bleeding or infection in the brain in the neonatal period. All of the conditions which cause hyrocephalus result in uneven growth of intelligence in childhood, with nonverbal intelligence developing less well than verbal intelligence (Dennis, Fitz, Netley, Sugar, Harwood-Nash, Hendrick, Hoffman, & Humphreys, 1981).

Dementia

A gradual decline in mental function is often first noted in school performance, just as in adults impaired job performance may be the initial sign of problems. All psychologists are aware of characteristic psychological test profiles of individuals with declining abilities, but they may be unaware that children as well as adults can be affected by dementias. Mass lesions, drugs and other toxins, smoldering infections, endocrine disturbances, and a number of degenerative diseases can cause the picturre of dementia in children. Some of these diseases are medically or surgically treatable, and suspicion of dementia mandates medical referral.

Encephalitis

Encephalitis, meningitis, and Reye's syndrome (a severe brain illness triggered by a viral disease) are common neurological illnesses in school-age children. Transient or permanent intellectual sequelae are common complications. These are life threatening, dramatic illnesses which trigger an outpouring of concern, and survivors are briefly raised to celebrity status. Any child returning to class after even a short absence who appears to have good return of health following an illness or injury which involves the brain may have subtle alterations in cognitive function. It is important to realize that hazards of illnesses which affect the brain are unique and different from those affecting other organs. One should exercise extreme caution in attributing any observed changes to the accompanying social phenomena.

Inborn Errors of Metabolism

Phenylketonuria (PKU) is the best known of several hundred identified inborn metabolic errors. Since mental retardation can be modified or even prevented by careful dietary management or other therapies in some of these disorders, and since most states have mandatory screening programs of all newborns for treatable metabolic diseases, these conditions, while relatively uncommon, are important. In view of the expanding evidence of biochemical bases of psychiatric conditions like schizophrenia and manic depressive illness, biochemistry may well become a required course for all psychologists because of its importance in understanding the function of the nervous system and the disorders which affect it.

Involuntary Movements

Signs of dysfunction in brain motor structures remote in location and function from the centers of higher cortical function deserve mention because they are almost invariably mistaken for hysterical or emotional disorders.

Gilles de la Tourette's Syndrome

This is by far the most frequent of these conditions. It is caused by a familial imbalance in the chemical neurotransmitters that regulate and inhibit movement. Sufferers usually begin to display "nervous mannerisms" like eye blinking, grimacing, or head tossing between the ages of 2 and 10. These mannerisms, or tics, as they are called, vary in intensity, frequency, and character. Approximately half of the sufferers will have verbal as well as motor tics. These vary from soft grunts to loud barks and may include swear words or obscenities. Although distressingly embarrassing for teens and young adults, most younger children are less bothered by the sumptoms than are those around them. Most patients can get at least partial relief with use of tranquilizing drugs like haloperidol in low dosage, and the symptoms often improve spontaneously in adult life. Intellectual function is not affected, although emotional health may suffer from misdiagnosis and from the negative reactions of others. The Tourette Syndrome Association Inc. (41–02 Bell Blvd, Bayside, N.Y., 11361) has been a model of service through public information programs, research efforts, support groups, and publication and distribution of medical and nonmedical information about the disorder.

Dystonia Musculorum Deformans

This is a progressive movement disorder which, as its name implies, leads not only to impairment of motor function but also to twisting of limbs. In early stages, dystonia can be mistaken for hysteria since well-learned, automatic movements become extemely awkward. For example, the child may no longer be able to write legibly with his or her preferred hand although he or she can do a good job with the other hand. Forward walking may be severely impaired yet a child can run well and walk backards with seeming ease. There is a resemblance in these apparent paradoxes to stutterers who can sing in normal fashion. These movement disorders illustrate well the common mistake of calling neurological disease "emotional."

Migraine Headaches

These are among the most common neurological problems in the school-age population. Migraines are severe, throbbing, usually one-sided headaches often accompanied by nausea and vomiting. They are unrelieved by aspirin but relieved by sleep. If frequent and severe, migraines can incapacitate a student. Migraine headaches are usually a hereditary problem, and medical treatments can help most migraine sufferers. Academic problems arise occasionally because of absences due to the headaches—unless the teacher or a school official also happens to be a migraine victim! Persons unfamiliar with the problem underestimate the degree of pain and incapacitation that accompanies the attacks. Neurologists have often noted a link between personality and migraines. Most sufferers tend to be orderly and hardworking, both as young people and as adults. Accordingly, the school psychologist will seldom be involved with these children.

Multiple Sclerosis

This is primarily a disease of young adults and a rare occurrence in school-aged children. It is confused in some people's minds with muscular dystrophy since both are medical tongue twisters beginning with "M." It is an unpredictable and still mysterious disease usually resulting in a series of neurological signs and symptoms involving any part of the nervous system. Visual loss, bladder dysfunction, balance problems, and paralysis may result. Intellectual decline is not usually present, although personality changes are common.

Neurocutaneous Disease

These are relatively common neurological disorders in children. Since the story of John Merrick, the "Elephant Man" (Treves, 1923), a victim of an unusually severe form of neurofibromatosis, was told in a popular play and movie public awareness of these conditions has expanded. Neurofibromatosis and tuberous sclerosis are the most common neurocutaneous disorders. Both are inherited as autosomal dominant traits and are developmental defects of the embryologic ectoderm, the tissue from which both skin and nervous system are derived. Both are manifested by birthmarks on the skin, light brown spots in neurofibromatosis and white spots in tuberous sclerosis. The diagnoses are not necessarily predictive of any disability. There are many normal looking and normally functioning individuals with these disorders, but the disorders carry markedly increased risks of developing certain health problems. In tuberous sclerosis mental retardation and epilepsy are markedly increased in frequency. Small growths of abnormal tissue may develop in the brain and in the skin, usually in the central part of the face, resembling acne. In neurofibromatosis tumors of central and peripheral nervous system are frequent, and in advanced age numerous small tumors arising from small nerves in the skin may be seen. Birth defects of various sorts and mental retardation are increased in frequency. Large and disfiguring tumors as seen in the famous case of John Merrick are very rarely encountered.

Strokes

Cerebral vascular accidents are seen in children as well as adults, but the underlying causes differ. The most frequent causes of stroke in children are congenital heart and vascular disease and blood diseases like sickle cell anemia, rather than high blood pressure. The physical and cognitive impairments associated with left or right hemisphere strokes in adults are also observed in children. In contrast to the older patient, recovery of function may occur over a much longer time in the young stroke victim.

PERSONAL PERSPECTIVES

Evolutionary Trends in Conceptualization and Treatment of Epilepsy (Lawrence C. Hartlage)

Although epilepsy has been recorded in medical literature as early as 2080 B.C. (Schmidt & Wilder, 1968), and the subject of scientific study since 400 B.C.

(Livingston, 1963), it was Hippocrates who developed a conceptualization of the disorder as a disease exclusively involving the brain (Tempkin, 1971). Through subsequent centuries there were a number of other conceptualizations, mainly related to spiritualistic explanations of etiology (e.g. Coleman, 1964). Thomas Willis (1622–1675), often called the founder of modern neurology (Scott, 1973), essentially reestablished the Hippocratic conceptualization as the official scientific explanation, so it is not surprising that the vast majority of research and treatment emphasis with epilepsy followed this model for many years (e.g., Lennox & Lennox, 1960; Livingston, 1963). In the nineteenth century Dr. John Hughlings Jackson conceptualized the epileptic seizure as a state provided by a sudden, violent discharge of brain cells (Schmidt & Wilder, 1968), and subsequent research on epilepsy has in general tended to focus on either the characteristics of the discharges or the effects of various medications on epilepsy (e.g., Brain & Walton, 1969; Merritt, 1973).

This historic tendency of epilepsy research to focus on physiological and biochemical aspects of the disorder is to some extent reflected in the more than 17,000 publications on epilepsy during the 25-year period of 1950–1975 (Penry, 1976). During the decade of the 1970s, however, there began to emerge a new focus of epilepsy research which became more concerned with social aspects of the problem. Bagley's (1971) work on the social psychology of epileptic children was closely followed by a number of studies involving dependency (Green & Hartlage, 1971; Hartlage, Green, & Offutt, 1972) and underachievement (Hartlage & Green, 1972; Green & Hartlage, 1971) in epileptic children. Parallel to the work with children's social development, concern with social problems of epileptic adults also increased with special emphasis on vocational matters. Thus while the 17,000 papers from 1950 to 1975 contained only seven references to vocational aspects of epilepsy, during the 1970s this aspect of epilepsy gained in stature as an important area. In the most recent Plan for Nationwide Action on Epilepsy (1978), for example, it is noted that "since the Federal Vocational Rehabilitation program was initiated in 1944, those with epilepsy have consistently proven to be one of the most difficult groups to rehabilitate" (p. 90).

Historically part of the difficulty with vocational rehabilitation of patients with epilepsy has been employer resistance to such workers (Hartlage & Roland, 1971; Hartlage, 1971). However, there has been progressive improvement in ameliorating employer resistance to hiring workers who may have epilepsy (Hartlage & Taraba, 1971; Hartlage, 1973, 1974) to the point where employer attitudes no longer appear to be a major obstacle to vocational rehabilitation of the worker with epilepsy. Another problem which has begun to be recognized as an important correlate of both academic performance in children and vocational performance in adults involves the effects of anticonvulsant medication on the adaptive capacities of those treated with specific antiepileptic drugs (Reynolds, 1978). Recent research in this area has suggested fairly specific relationships between common anticonvulsant medication and the development of adaptive (Hartlage & Stovall, 1980) or vocationally relevant abilities (Hartlage & Mains, 1981) with striking correlations between serum levels of certain anticonvulsant medications and performance on these measures (Hartlage, 1981).

Dodrill (1980) reported the relevance of psychosocial problems in epilepsy to employment and developed and validated an objective score for the assessment of social problems among epileptics (Dodrill, Batzel, Queisser, & Temkin, 1980), and subsequently with his co-workers related these measures to a number of factors related to employment success in epilepsy (Batzel, Dodrill, & Fraser, 1980). Where does this appear to be leading? In keeping with the current *Zeitgeist* of behavioral medicine, emphasizing the well-being of the whole patient rather than focusing on specific aspects of the disease, the trend appears to be toward blending biochemical with social research and treatment emphasis. Thus phenomena such as seizure control are approached with increasing attention given to the total milieu of the context in which the child or adolescent with epilepsy must function. As increased attention is directed toward the effects of treatment on the life of the child, it may be possible to develop seizure control medications which do not have behaviorally toxic side effects. A treatment approach oriented toward this sort of goal is reflected in the renewed interest in resection of cortical areas of seizure foci, with the goal of enabling the child to be seizure controlled on much lower medication levels (Hartlage & Flanigan, 1981). This approach, based on careful preoperative and intraoperative assessment of adaptive functions mediated by given cortical areas, which in turn have been electrophysiologically correlated with seizure foci, appears to offer considerable promise for helping bring seizures under control at medication levels low enough to cause minimal impairments to social academic functioning without sacrificing cortical tissue of measurable consequence for such functioning.

Changing Attitudes Toward the Neurologically Handicapped (Patricia L. Hartlage)

In the nineteenth and early twentieth century there was a progressive growth of residential schools for the blind, deaf, and mentally retarded usually under state auspices, and epilepsy was often grouped with mental retardation. For years epilepsy remained linked with idiocy in the beliefs of many, and this was reflected in eugenic and other restrictive legislation. For example, in 1956 17 states had laws prohibiting the marriage of persons with epilepsy and an equal number had statutes providing for involuntary sterilization of epileptics (Barrow & Fabing, 1956). Until 1968 immigration of persons with epilepsy to the United States was not allowed. As late as in 1959, 22% of public schools excluded children with epilepsy (Wallace, 1960).

In 1900 the first public school class in the United States for crippled children opened in Chicago, and day schools in the communities to serve exceptional children began to evolve. The impact of this country's involvement in two world wars on public attitudes toward the handicapped was a considerable one (Cruickshank, 1967). Returning disabled veterans were a visible part of every community, and the positive attitudes of people toward these men were transferred in part to all handicapped people, children and adults. Not only was acceptance of handicapped persons enhanced by the war veterans, but they pointed out many unmet needs of handicapped persons including transportation, physical access, educational, vocational, and recreational, as well as physical rehabilitation needs. A second major impetus to improved services and more intense educational interest in the exceptional child was the establishment and growth in the 1900s of parent groups whose persistence in demanding better educational services for their children was gradually rewarded on a local, state, and national level as evidenced by subsequent legislation. In the 1960s a Division of Handicapped Children and Youth was established in the government which was later replaced with the Bureau of Education for the Handicapped. Also, the Education of the Handicapped Act (PL 91–230) was passed. In 1971 the Development Disabilities Services and Facilities Construction Act (PL 91–517) marked the passage of the first legislation which specifically identified and offered aide to, instead of restrictions upon, children with epilepsy. This law also specifically outlined services to those with cerebral palsy, mental retardation, and other neurological handicaps originating in childhood.

The American public is increasingly aware of specific disabilities. Knowledge is dispelling the ignorant fears which people have held of epilepsy and other neurological handicaps, but social stigmata still exist. Every 5 years for the last 30 years public attitudes toward epilepsy have been surveyed. These surveys show a gradual increase in familiarity with the nature of the disorder and a concomitant decrease in negative attitudes. In 1949, 24% of persons said they would object to their children being associated in school or at play with someone with epilepsy; in 1979, 6% would object (Caveness & Gallup, 1980). Within the past decade, passage of the Education for All Handicapped Children Act (PL 94–142) accomplished the transition from exclusion of handicapped children to actively seeking them out, even at preschool ages, so that their multiple educational, psychological, and related needs can be better be met. At least one effect of this legislation has been to bring many children with both hidden and obvious neurological disorders into the realm of public education programs, placing educators, neurologists, occupational, physical, and speech therapists, and parents into interrelated and interactive roles in implementing steps to meet these multiple needs. It is hoped that this brief outline of such diverse neurological disorders as epilepsy, cerebral palsy, and muscular dystrophy will help to bridge the communication gap among these groups and to facilitate the provision of appropriate services to those with these types of childhood exceptionality.

REFERENCES

Anderson, E. M. *The disabled schoolchild: A study of integration in primary schools.* London: Methuen, 1973.

Bagley, C. R. The educational performance of children with epilepsy. *British Journal of Educational Psychology*, 1970, *40*, 82–83.

Bagley, C. *The social psychology of the epileptic child.* Coral Gables, Fl.: University of Miami Press, 1971.

Baird, H. W., John, E. R. , Ahn, H., & Maisel, E. Neurometric evaluation of epileptic children who do well or poorly in school. *Electroencephalography and Clinical Neurophysiology*, 1980, *48*, 683–693.

Ball, T. S., Combs, T., Rugh, J., & Neptune, R. Automated range of motion training with two cerebral palsied retarded young men. *Mental Retardation*, 1977, *15*, 47–50.

Barrow, R. L. & Fabing, H. D. *Epilepsy and the law.* New York: Hoeber, 1956,

Batzel, L. W., Dodrill, C. B., & Fraser, R. J. Further validation of the WPSI Vocational Scale: Comparisons with other correlates of employment in epilepsy. *Epilepsia*, 1980, *21*, 235–242.

Bennett, A. E. Psychiatric aspects of psychomotor epilepsy. *California Medicine*, 1962, *97*, 346–349.

Brain, L. & Walton, J. N. *Brain's disease of the nervous system* (7th ed.). London: Oxford University Press, 1969.

Bregman, A. M. Living with progressive childhood illness: Parental management of neuromuscular disease. *Social Work in Health Care*, 1980, *5*, 378–408.

Camfield, C. S., Chaplin, S., Doyle, A. B., Shapiro, S. H., Cummings, C., & Camfield, P. R. Side effects of phenobarbital in toddlers: Behavioral and cognitive aspects. *Journal of Pediatrics,* 1979, *95,* 361–365.

Caveness, W. F., & Gallup, G. H., Jr. A survey of public attitudes toward epilepsy in 1979 with an indication of trends over the past thirty years. *Epilepsia*, 1980, *21*, 509–518.

Coleman, J. C. Abnormal behavior associated with epilepsy. In *Abnormal psychology and modern life*, Glenview, Ill.: Scott Foresman, 1964.

Committee on the Medical Aspects of Sports and Committee on Exercise and Physical Fitness. Convulsive disorders and participation in sports and physical education. *Journal of the American Medical Association*, 1968, *206*, 1291.

Cooper, I. S., Riklan, M. Amin, I., Waltz, J. M., & Cullenan, T., Chronic cerebellar stimulation in cerebral palsy. *Neurology*, 1976, *26*, 744–753.

Cruickshank, W. M. & Johnson, G. O. *Education of exceptional children and youth.* Englewood Cliffs, N.J.: Prentice-Hall, 1967.

Davis, R. M., Cullen, R. F., Jr., Flitter, M., Duenas, D., Engle, H. & Ennis, B. Control of spasticity and involuntary movements. *Neurosurgery*, 1977, *1*, 205–207.

Dennerll, R. D. Cognitive deficits and lateral brain dysfunction in temporal lobe epilepsy. *Epilepsia*, 1964, *5*, 177–191.

Dennis, M., Fitz, C. R., Netley, C. T., Sugar, J., Harwood-Nash, D. C. F., Hendrick, E. B., Hoffman, H. J., Humphreys, R. P. The intelligence of hydrocephalic children. *Archives of Neurology*, 1981, *38*, 607–615.

Dodrill, C. B. Objective assessment of psychosocial problems in epilepsy and its relevance to employment. In B. H. Kulig, Meinardi, & G. Stores (Eds.), *Epilepsy and behavior 1979.* Lisse, The Netherlands. Swets & Zeitlinger, 1980.

Dodrill, C. B., Batzel, L. W., Queisser, H. R., & Temkin, N. R. An objective method for the assessment of psychological and social problems among epileptics. *Epilepsia*, 1980, *21*, 123–135.

Dubowitz, V. *Muscle disorders in childhood*. Philadelphia: W. B. Sanders, 1978.

Epilepsy Foundation of America. *Basic statistics in the epilepsies*. Philadelphia: F. A. Davis, 1975.

Finnie, N. R. *Handling the young cerebral palsied child at home*. London: Heineman, 1968.

Force, D. A. *Descriptive studies of the incidence of seizures and teachers' attitudes toward children with epilepsy in the Minneapolis, Minnesota public schools.* Minneapolis: Minnesota Epilepsy League, 1965.

Gahm, N. H., Russman, B. S., Cerciello, R. L., Fiorentino, M. R., & McGrath, D. M. Chronic cerebellar stimulation for cerebral palsy. A double blind study. *Neurology*, 1981, *31*, 87–90.

Gibbs, F. A. , & Gibbs, E. L. *Atlas of electroencephalography* (Vol. 3). Reading, Mass.: Addison-Wesley, 1964.

Glaser, G. H. The problem of psychosis in psychomotor temporal lobe epileptics. *Epilepsia*, 1964, *5*, 271–278.

Goldin, G. J., Perry, L., Margolin, R. J., Stotsky, B. D., & Foster, J. C. *The rehabilitation of the young epileptic*. Lexington, Mass.: D. C. Heath, 1971.

Green, J. B., & Hartlage, L. C. Social and academic achievement in epileptic children: The role of parental attitudes. *Fourth European Symposium on Epilepsy*, Amsterdam, 1971.

Green, J. B., & Hartlage, L. C. Comparative performance of epileptic and nonepileptic children and adolescents. *Disorders of the Nervous System*, 1971, *32*, 418–421.

Guerrant, J., Anderson, W. N. Weinstein, M. R., Jaros, J., & Desking, A. *Personality in Epilepsy*, Springfield, Ill.: Charles C. Thomas, 1962.

Hagberg, B. The epidemiological panorama of major neuropaediatrics handicaps in Sweden. In J. Apley (Ed.) *Care of the handicapped child.* Lavenham, England: Lavenham Press, 1978.

Hartlage, L. C. *Changes in attitudes toward different types of handicaps.* Paper presented at National Rehabilitation Association, Atlantic City, N.J., 1973.

Hartlage, L. C. *A decade of change in employer attitudes toward epilepsy.* Paper presented at American Psychological Association, New Orleans, La., 1974.

Hartlage, L. C. Neuropsychological assessment of anticonvulsant drug toxicity. *Clinical Neuropsychology*, 1981, *3*, 20–22.

Hartlage, L. C., & Flanigan, H. F. *Neuropsychological aspects of temporal lobe resection in epilepsy.* Paper presented at National Academy of Neuropsychologists, Orlando, Fla., 1981.

Hartlage, L. C., & Green, J. B. The relation of parental attitudes to academic and social achievement in epileptic children. *Epilepsia*, 1972, *13*, 21-6.

Hartlage, L. C., Green, J. B., & Offutt, L. Dependency in epileptic children. *Epilepsia*, 1972, *13*, 27-30.

Hartlage, L. C., Green, J. B.,& Offutt, L. Dependency in epileptic children. *Epilepsia*, 1972, *13*, 27-30.

Hartlage, L. C., & Mains, M. R., *Intellectual educational, neuropsychological and vocational test correlates of serum*. Paper presented at ABL Southwestern Psychological Association, Houston, 1981.

Hartlage, L. C., & Roland, P. E. Attitudes of employers toward different types of handicapped workers. *Journal of Applied Rehabilitation Counseling*, 1971, *2*, 115-120.

Hartlage, L. C., & Stovall, K. W. *Serum anticonvulsant levels and adaptive capacity in humans*. Paper presented at American Association for the Advancement of Science, Toronto, Canada, 1980.

Hartlage, L. C., Stovall, K. W. & Kovach, B. *Behavioral correlates of anticonvulsant blood levels*. Paper presented to the American Epilepsy Society, New York, 1979.

Hartlage, L. C., & Taraba, D. Implications of different employer acceptance of individuals with physical, mental and social handicaps. *Rehabilitation Research and Practice Review*, 1971, *2,* 45-48.

Holdsworth, L., & Whitmore, K. A study of children with epilepsy attending ordinary schools. 1. Their seizure patterns, progress, and behavior at school. *Developmental Medicine and Child Neurology*, 1974, *16*, 746-758.

Karagan, N. J., & Sorensen, J. P. Intellectual functioning in non-Duchenne muscular dystrophy. *Neurology*, 1981, *31*, 448-452.

Lennox, W. G., & Lennox, M. A. *Epilepsy and related disorders*. Boston: Little, Brown, 1960.

Levitt, S. Stimulation of movement: A review of therapeutic techniques. In Kenneth Holt (ed.), *Movement and child development*. Philadelphia: Lippincott, 1975.

Livingston, S. *Living with epileptic seizures*. Springfield, Ill.: Charles C. Thomas, 1963.

Livingston, S., & Berman, W. Participation of epileptic patients in sports. *Journal of the American Medical Association*, 1973, 236-238.

McIntyre, M., Pritchard, P. B., III, & Lombroso, C. T. Left and right temporal lobe epileptics: A controlled investigation of some psychological differences. *Epilepsia*, 1976, *17*, 377-386.

McLaurin, R. L. Epilepsy and contact sports. *Journal of the American Medical Association*, 1973, *225*, 285-287.

Mark, V. H., & Ervin, F. R. *Violence and the brain*. New York: Harper & Row, 1970.

Merritt, H. H. *A textbook of neurology*. Philadelphia: Lea & Febiger, 1973.

Nathan, C., Slominski, A., & Griswold, P. *Please help us help ourselves: Inexpensive adapted equipment for the handicapped*. Indianapolis: United Cerebral Palsy of Central Indiana, 1970.

National Aeronautics and Space Administration. *Technology and the Neurologically Handicapped*. Washington, D.C.: NASA, 1974.

Nelson, K., & Ellenberg, J. Epidemiology of cerebral palsy. *Advances in Neurology,* 1978, *19*, 421–435.

O'Leary, D. S., Seidenberg, M., Berent, S., & Boll, T. J. Effects of age of onset of tonic-clonic seizures on neuropsychological performance in children. *Epilepsia,* 1981, *22*, 197–204.

Ounsted, C. Aggression and epilepsy-rage in children with temporal lobe epilepsy. *Journal of Psychiatric Research,* 1969, *13*, 237–242.

Ounsted, C., Lindsay, J., & Norman, R. *Biological features in temporal lobe epilepsy.* Lavenham, England: Lavenham Press, 1966.

Penry, J. K. (Ed.). *Epilepsy Bibliography 1950–1975* (NIH 76-1186). U.S. Department of Health, Education, and Welfare, 1976.

Pritchard, P. B., III, Lombroso, C. T., & McIntyre, M. Psychological complications of temporal lobe epilepsy. *Neurology* 1980, *30*, 227–232.

Reynolds, E. H. Report of the commission on antiepileptic drugs of the international league against epilepsy. *Epilepsia,* 1978, *19*, 115–117.

Schmidt, R. P., & Wilder, J. P. *Epilepsy.* Philadelphia: F. A. Davis, 1968.

Scott, D. *About epilepsy.* London: Duckworth, 1973.

Small, J. G., Small, I. F., & Hayden, M. P. Further psychiatric investigations of patients with temporal and non-temporal epilepsy. *American Journal of Psychiatry,* 1966, *123*, 303–310.

Stevens, J. R. Psychiatric implications of psychomotor epilepsy. *Archives of General Psychiatry,* 1966, *14*, 461–471.

Stores, G. Behavioral effects of anti-epileptic drugs. *Developmental Medicine and Child Neurology,* 1975, *17*, 647–658.

Stores, G., Hart, J., & Piran, N. Inattentiveness in school children with epilepsy. *Epilepsia,* 1978, *19*, 169–175.

Temkin, O. *The falling sickness; A history of epilepsy from the Greeks to the beginning of modern neurology.* Baltimore: Johns Hopkins Press, 1971.

Tizard, B. The personality of epileptics: A discussion of the evidence. *Psychology Bulletin,* 1962, *59*, 196–210.

Treves, F. *The elephant man and other-reminiscences.* London: Cassell, 1923.

Trimble, M. R., & Reynolds, E. M. Anticonvulsant drugs and mental symptoms: A review. *Psychological Medicine,* 1976, *6*, 169–178.

U.S. Department of Health, Education and Welfare. *Plan for nationwide action on epilepsy* (NIH 78-276), 1978.

Wallace, H. M. School services for children with epilepsy in urban areas. *Journal of Chronic Disease,* 1960, *12*, 754–663.

Waxman, S. G., & Geschwind, N. The interiotal behavior syndrome of temporal lobe epilepsy. *Archives of General Psychiatry,* 1975, *32*, 1580–1586.

Young, R. R., & Delwaide, P. J. Drug therapy: Spasticity. *New England Journal of Medicine,* 1981, *304*, 28–33, 96–99.

Zimmerman, F. Explosive behavior abnormalities in children on a epileptic basis. *New York State Journal of Medicine,* 1956, *56*, 2537–2543.

Author Index

Subject Index